Science in Marketing

The Wiley Marketing Series

WILLIAM LAZER, Advisory Editor
Michigan State University

MARTIN ZOBER, *Marketing Management*

ROBERT J. HOLLOWAY AND ROBERT S. HANCOCK
The Environment of Marketing Behavior—
Selections from the Literature

GEORGE SCHWARTZ, Editor
Science in Marketing

SCIENCE IN MARKETING

George Schwartz, *Editor*

College of Business Administration, University of Rochester

John Wiley & Sons, Inc.

NEW YORK · LONDON · SYDNEY

Contributors

JULES BACKMAN is Research Professor of Economics at New York University, where he has been a member of the faculty for more than 25 years. He is a long-time student of business pricing and has written extensively on this subject. Among his writings are *Price Practices and Price Policies* (Ronald Press, 1953) and *Pricing: Policies and Practices* (National Industrial Conference Board, 1961).

Dr. Backman has testified before a number of congressional committees on pricing problems and has been a member of, or advisor to, several government committees dealing with price questions. In addition, Dr. Backman has served as a consultant on pricing problems to corporations and industries.

ROBERT BARTELS is Professor of Business Organization at The Ohio State University, from which he received a Ph.D. degree in 1941. He has also been on the faculties of a number of other universities including the Universities of Washington, California, Iowa, and Colorado. He has lectured on American marketing in India and Ceylon as well as in Moscow, where in the Spring of 1963 he addressed groups of the faculty and graduate students of Moscow University and the Plekhanov Institute.

He is the author of several books: *The Development of Marketing Thought* (Irwin, 1962), *Comparative Marketing: Wholesaling in Fifteen Countries* (ed.), (Irwin, 1963), and *Ethics in Business* (ed.), (Ohio State University Bureau of Business Research, 1963). Many of his articles dealing with theoretical aspects of marketing have appeared in the *Journal of Marketing*.

WARREN J. BILKEY is Associate Professor of Economics at the University of Notre Dame. He studied at the University of Wisconsin and at Harvard, from which he received a Ph.D. degree. He was formerly on the faculty of the University of Connecticut and has served as Economic Advisor to the President of the Dominican Republic.

NEIL H. BORDEN is Professor of Marketing Emeritus, Harvard University. He is a recipient of a number of awards including the Paul D. Converse award and election to the Hall of Fame in Distribution. He

v

was President of the American Marketing Association in 1953 and 1954. Professor Borden is a long-time student of advertising and has written numerous books and articles on this aspect of marketing.

JOHN U. FARLEY is Assistant Professor of Industrial Administration, Carnegie Institute of Technology. A graduate of Dartmouth College and The Amos Tuck School, he received his doctorate from the Graduate School of Business, The University of Chicago in 1963. His thesis, " 'Brand Loyalty' and Consumer Preferences for Branded Goods," dealt with a number of issues discussed in this paper. He has contributed to *The Journal of Marketing Research* and *The Journal of Business,* and has also spoken to professional groups. He was co-leader of marketing groups in Faculty Workshops for Quantitative Research in Business sponsored by The Ford Foundation in 1963 and 1964.

JAC L. GOLDSTUCKER is Associate Professor of Marketing at De Paul University. He has studied at the University of Oklahoma, Southern Methodist University, and the University of Minnesota, from which he obtained a Ph.D. degree.

He has written articles on retailing for the *Journal of Marketing* and the *Journal of Retailing* and is a member of the Committee for the Teaching of Retailing of the American Marketing Association. Dr. Goldstucker spent a number of years in retailing just prior to, and subsequent to, World War II.

DAVID HAMILTON is Professor of Economics at the University of New Mexico. He attended the University of Pittsburgh and the University of Texas, from which he received a Ph.D. degree. He is a long-time student of the consumer in our society and has published several studies on this subject.

JAMES G. HAUK is Associate Professor of Marketing at Syracuse University. He received B.S. and M.B.A. degrees from Indiana University and a Ph.D. from the University of Michigan. Dr. Hauk has previously been on the faculty at the University of Missouri, the University of Michigan, and The Ohio State University. He is a past vice-president of the Central Ohio Chapter of the American Marketing Association.

He is the author of *Technical Service in the American Economy,* Graduate School of Business Administration, University of Michigan, Ann Arbor, Michigan, 1962.

EUGENE J. KELLEY is Professor of Marketing at Pennsylvania State University. He has studied at the University of Connecticut, Boston University, and New York University, from which he received a Ph.D. degree. He has taught at the Babson Institute, Clark University, Harvard Business School, Michigan State University, and New York University. He has published in the areas of marketing management, regional shopping centers, and the usefulness of information from various sciences to marketing.

ROBERT LEROY KING is Associate Professor of Marketing at the University of South Carolina. He was educated at the University of Georgia and Michigan State University, from which he received a Ph.D. degree. Dr. King has written extensively on various marketing subjects, (and is a member of Sigma Epsilon).

ALFRED A. KUEHN is Associate Professor of Industrial Administration, Carnegie Institute of Technology. Also a graduate of Carnegie Tech, he received his Ph.D. in Industrial Administration in 1958. He has contributed articles to several marketing books, co-edited *Quantitative Techniques in Marketing Analysis,* co-authored *The Carnegie Tech Management Game: An Experiment in Business Education,* and published in a variety of professional journals including *Management Science, Journal of Marketing, Journal of Advertising Research, Journal of Business,* and the *Harvard Business Review.*

WILLIAM LAZER is Professor of Marketing at Michigan State University. He attended the University of Manitoba, the University of Chicago, and Ohio State University, from which he received a Ph.D. degree. Before coming to Michigan State University, he was on the faculty of the University of Manitoba. He has been a recipient of a Ford Foundation Fellowship to study mathematics and its applicability to business affairs. He has had a number of books and articles published on various aspects of marketing.

ROBERT W. LITTLE is Associate Professor of Marketing at the University of Washington. He was educated at Indiana University, from which he received a D.B.A. degree. Before coming to his present teaching position, he was on the faculty at the University of Omaha. Dr. Little has published in the area of marketing theory and packaging.

BERT C. McCAMMON, JR. is Associate Professor of Marketing at Indiana University. He holds B.S., M.B.A., and D.B.A. degrees from

Indiana University. Dr. McCammon has been a visiting faculty member at the University of Southern California, Ohio State University, and the University of Washington. He has written many publications on various aspects of marketing.

JOSEPH W. NEWMAN is Associate Professor at the Graduate School of Business of Stanford University. He attended Kansas State University and Harvard University, from which he received a D.C.S. degree. Dr. Newman has previously taught at the University of Michigan and the Harvard Business School. For many years he has had a keen interest in the behavioral sciences in relation to marketing and in the use of research to provide a useful flow of information for organizational decision making. Among his publications are *Motivation Research and Marketing Management* (Harvard University Press, 1957) and "Put Research Into Marketing Decisions," *Harvard Business Review* (March–April, 1962).

ROBERT W. PRATT, JR. is an economist with the Consumer and Public Relations Research Program, General Electric Company. Mr. Pratt completed his undergraduate work at the University of Texas and did graduate work at the University of Michigan, where he received his M.B.A. with high distinction. For four years he served on the staff of the Economic Behavior Program, Survey Research Center, and for one year as an Instructor in Marketing, Graduate School of Business Administration, both at the University of Michigan. Mr. Pratt is co-author of a book, *Automobile Accident Costs and Payments: Studies in the Economics of Injury Reparations* (University of Michigan Press, 1964).

GEORGE SCHWARTZ is Assistant Professor of Marketing at the University of Rochester. He holds an A.B. degree from Brooklyn College and a Ph.D. degree from the University of Pennsylvania, where he served as an Instructor in the Marketing Department. Dr. Schwartz is author of *Development of Marketing Theory* (Southwestern, 1963) and has written a number of articles in the area of marketing theory and marketing science.

STANLEY J. SHAPIRO is Director of Marketing Planning, Canadian Advertising Agency, Ltd. in Montreal. He received an A.B. degree from Harvard College and earned his M.B.A. and Ph.D. at the University of Pennsylvania, where he was an Assistant Professor of Marketing in the Wharton School. Dr. Shapiro was co-editor with Reavis Cox and Wroe Alderson of the second edition of *Theory in Marketing*. He has done research in the areas of marketing history, metropolitan information systems, and livestock marketing.

JOHN B. STEWART is a Professor at the School of Business Administration of the University of Richmond. Professor Stewart attended the University of Colorado and Harvard University, from which he received a D.B.A. degree. He has also been on the faculty at M.I.T. and Harvard.

Dr. Stewart is a long-time student of new product development. He has written articles for the *Journal of Marketing* and the *Harvard Business Review*, and in 1964 the Harvard Business School published his monograph entitled *Repetitive Advertising in Newspapers—A Study of Two New Products*.

Dedicated to the development of a realistic
and useful body of knowledge about marketing
which meets the requirements of science.

Preface

Whether marketing is or will ever be a science is a subject that has been loudly debated from time to time by students of marketing. Although the substance of this book is pertinent to this debate, it is not intended as a polemic supporting either side in this controversy.

Rather, this cooperative effort, involving nineteen authors, stems from the belief that a science of marketing has utility for those in society concerned with marketing and seeks to contribute to and facilitate the continued development of such a science. This book does not present new knowledge about marketing; its aim is to contribute to the development of marketing science through an appraisal of the current state of marketing knowledge and to suggest areas of marketing that require further study by marketing scholars.

In the early part of the book, the nature and goals of marketing science are discussed, along with the usefulness of such a science to various segments of society involved in the marketing process. Moreover, a chapter is devoted to a brief description of the development of marketing thought.

Much of the remainder of the book divides the various aspects of marketing into conventional segments, for example, pricing, personal selling, and so on. With respect to each such aspect of marketing, an author was asked to write a chapter that essentially answered two questions: (1) what empirically ascertained descriptive, and empirically validated predictive and control, knowledge is now available concerning the specific aspect of marketing—product development for instance—about which you are writing, and (2) what research studies ought to be undertaken in order that new knowledge can be uncovered about the aspect of marketing which is the topic of your chapter.

In addition to these substantive chapters, a chapter is devoted to an evaluation of the utility and limitations of operations research to marketers, and, another discusses the strengths and weaknesses of stochastic brand switching models. A discussion of the relationship of ethics to marketing science is presented because the belief is held that marketers, just as is the case with other segments of our population, need to be concerned with the impact of their activities on the society in which we live. A final chapter presents an overview of the state of marketing knowledge based on the work done for this book and contains suggestions for future research aimed at acquiring new knowledge about marketing.

It is recognized that the objectives undertaken in this book are extensive, and that owing to the circumstances under which this book was written these objectives could be fulfilled only imperfectly. Moreover, the book does not treat certain aspects of marketing, such as advertising and the usefulness of marketing science to businessmen, which obviously belong in a book of this type. In a cooperative effort such as this, however, unforeseen events occur that prevent authors who have agreed to contribute from fulfilling their commitment. Despite these imperfections, however, it is hoped that this work proves useful to those concerned with marketing and that it contributes to the further development of a science of marketing.

As a book moves along the difficult path leading to ultimate publication, debts of assistance are incurred that deserve grateful acknowledgement. When this book was not much more than idea, Dr. William Lazer (Michigan State University), consulting editor to John Wiley and Sons, and John P. Young, editor of the Wiley Business Book Series, saw merit in the idea and did much to encourage completion of the project. Each of the contributing authors deserves to be complimented for his willingness to add to his responsibilities the research and writing that yielded a contribution to this book.

Acting Dean Henry C. Mills and Assistant Dean Richard W. Fortner, of the University of Rochester's College of Business Administration, were generous in making available needed facilities. Gene Hoff, a graduate student at the University of Rochester, performed certain editorial duties and compiled the index. Mrs. Betty Lou Woodland and Mrs. Jacqueline Frankel merit a vote of thanks for their effective secretarial performance.

And last, gratitude is expressed to those publishers who granted permission to quote certain materials.

GEORGE SCHWARTZ

Rochester, N. Y.
December, 1964

Contents

1

Nature and Goals of Marketing Science

GEORGE SCHWARTZ

During the more than sixty years in which marketing has been studied seriously in universities, business enterprises, and government agencies, researchers have gradually chipped away at our ignorance of the people, activities, and institutions involved in the marketing of goods and services. These efforts have made much, but incomplete, headway in yielding knowledge about marketing in the United States and are spreading out to encompass study of marketing elsewhere in the world.

Along with these assaults on our marketing ignorance there have appeared various articles relating to the desirability and feasibility of developing a science of marketing.[1] While the various expressions of opinion have not revealed anyone who is opposed to the development of a science of marketing, there are those who argue that it is impossible to develop such a science, and there are others who just as strongly assert the contrary.

Since acceptable proof of the possibility or impossibility of developing a science of marketing has not yet been forthcoming, one might suggest that we will know whether such a feat is possible only when success is attained in obtaining the knowledge which meets the requirements of a science. In this connection it is perhaps appropriate to reflect that in 1950 few people believed that man would ever land on the moon. Today

Note: This chapter was written during the author's participation in the 1963 Ford Foundation Workshop in Marketing at the University of California at Berkeley. The contents of the chapter are, of course, the sole responsibility of the author.

[1] See, for example, Robert Bartels, "Can Marketing Be a Science?" *Journal of Marketing*, Vol. XV, No. 3 (January 1951); Robert D. Buzzell, "Is Marketing a Science?" *Harvard Business Review*, Vol. XLI, No. 1 (January–February 1963). A recent development reflecting interest in the development of marketing science was the formation of the Marketing Science Institute in June 1962 with the financial support of 29 corporations.

it is no doubt safe to say that these few have been joined by many others who now hold this belief.

WHAT IS A SCIENCE?

A science consists of a body of knowledge about the phenomena in a particular aspect of our environment and of the research tools available for obtaining accurate and reliable knowledge about these phenomena. Those who are working to contribute to the development of marketing science are studying the various phenomena grouped under the category known as marketing.

These phenomena consist of people—consumers, salesmen, retailers, wholesalers, advertising people, marketing vice presidents and others; business enterprises—retail and wholesale establishments, brokers, selling agents, manufacturers agents, warehouses, transportation facilities, advertising agencies, and others; marketing activities—buying and selling, credit extension, product development, storage, transportation, advertising, pricing, and other activities.

The kind of knowledge that comprises a science is of three types— descriptive, predictive, and control. The knowledge sought is knowledge which would be useful not only in one specific situation but also for a number of similar purposes.

The descriptive aspect of a science includes facts about the phenomena which comprise the aspect of the environment being studied. For example: How many retailers are there? What are the characteristics of the different types of retailers? What changes take place in the activities and structure of retailing institutions over time? How did consumers behave in the past; how do they behave now? How do marketers set prices? Such are descriptive facts which tell us what exists in the marketing environment in the same sense that some maps tell us about the geography of an area, the location of cities, and of roads.

These descriptive facts are usefully informative in and of themselves and constitute the raw material of marketing science. When these exist, the marketing scientist next seeks to relate facts in an attempt to predict the variation of some marketing phenomenon. Thus a marketing scientist might attempt to predict the value of all retail sales in the United States during some coming year by reference to estimates of disposable income and total number of retail establishments operating in that year.

When the marketing scientist seeks to predict he does not attempt, initially, to demonstrate a cause and effect relationship between the phenomenon whose variation is being predicted and the reference phenomena. That is, in the example cited, he does not seek to establish the existence of such a relationship between retail sales, on the one hand, and disposable income and number of retail establishments on the other. If he is able to predict accurately, this is a substantially useful achievement in and of itself.

If the marketing scientist is able to predict accurately by reference to any of the descriptive facts of marketing, he next becomes interested in whether, to continue the example used above, changes in disposable income and/or number of retail outlets *cause* changes in the magnitude of retail sales. If he can predict accurately by reference to these data and can demonstrate cause and effect between retail sales and these data, then the marketing scientist has unearthed control knowledge. That is, by effecting changes in disposable income and/or number of retail outlets, it would then become possible to attain specific magnitudes of retail sales.

Since many of the basic facts of marketing change over time, the inventory of these basic descriptive facts must be kept up to date, and predictive and control knowledge must be periodically tested to determine whether previously ascertained relationships have not been upset.

The descriptive, predictive, and control knowledge of a science of marketing can be valid with respect to geographic areas of any size. They can apply to a town, a city, a state, region, country, or all countries. A complete marketing science would include descriptive, predictive, and control knowledge which is valid in all areas of the world and would point up the similarities and differences between marketing phenomena existent in different geographic areas.[2]

MARKETING SCIENCE AND OTHER SCIENCES

The facts which are pertinent to marketing science are more inclusive than those which are investigated by researchers in other sciences. When the marketing scientist studies the behavior of people involved in marketing—consumers, salesmen, decisions makers—he does not restrict himself to any one component of behavior. Rather, he focuses on the way economic, psychological, sociological, and any other relevant factors determine the marketing behavior of people.[3] And to the extent that the facts

[2] Such knowledge would be particularly useful to businessmen who market products and services outside their native countries. It would enable them to avoid the mistake of using marketing practices of their own country which are inconsistent with the marketing milieu of the foreign country.

[3] The relevance of the behavioral sciences to marketing science is illustrated in William Lazer and Eugene J. Kelley, *Interdisciplinary Contributions to Marketing Management*, Michigan State University Press, East Lansing, Michigan, 1959; and Perry Bliss (ed.), *Marketing and the Behavioral Sciences*, Allyn and Bacon, Boston, 1963.

of history, anthropology, and politics are pertinent to changes which occur in marketing activities and institutions, marketing science needs to include such knowledge also.[4]

Additionally, when certain marketing phenomena behave in a manner similar to phenomena in some natural science, the marketing scientist attempts to adapt the knowledge of that natural science in an attempt to predict and control changes in the marketing phenomena being studied. This can be illustrated by the work of John Q. Stewart, an astrophysicist, who is now studying social phenomena with a view to developing a science called social physics. He believes that there are natural laws governing social phenomena just as there are such laws in the area of natural phenomena. Social physics, according to Stewart, ". . . analyses demographic, economic, political, and sociological situations in terms of the purely physical factors of time, distance, mass of material, and number of people with recourse also to social factors which can be shown to operate in a similar way to two other physical agents, namely temperature and electrical charge." [5]

TOOLS OF KNOWLEDGE ACQUISITION AND ANALYSIS

Knowledge about marketing phenomena can be stated verbally or can appear in the form of numbers. That is, one can say that there are more retailers in the United States than wholesalers, or the statement can be that in 1964 there were 1,500,000 retailers and 500,000 wholesalers. Similarly, one can state that if the Status Automobile Company increases its advertising expenditures, its sales will increase. Or, if true, the statement might read as follows: If the Status Automobile Company increases its advertising expenditures by 10 per cent, its sales will increase by 12 per cent.

While verbal statements and numerical statements can be equally valid, the quantification of knowledge may be more precise and informative than verbal knowledge. The quantification of knowledge is, more-

[4] See Charles Winick, "Anthropology's Contributions to Marketing," *Journal of Marketing*, Vol. XXV, No. 5 (July 1961). The pertinence of history to marketing science is illustrated in Chapter 14 of this book by Stanley Shapiro, "Comparative Marketing and Economic Development"; see also Edward A. Duddy and David A. Revzan, *Marketing: An Institutional Approach*, McGraw-Hill, New York, 1953. That knowledge of politics is relevant to the development of marketing science is well demonstrated in Joseph C. Palamountain, Jr., *The Politics of Distribution*, Harvard University Press, Cambridge, 1955.

[5] John Q. Stewart, "A Basis for Social Physics," *Impact of Science on Society*, Vol. III, No. 2 (Summer 1952), p. 110.

over, useful because knowledge in this form can more readily be analyzed through the use of statistical and mathematical tools.[6]

Such tools of knowledge acquisition and analysis are pertinent to marketing science because these are devices which facilitate the marketing scientist's efforts to describe, predict, and control marketing phenomena. The statistical method known as frequency distribution analysis, for example, is a useful tool for describing marketing phenomena. Similarly, regression analysis is a tool which may be useful in enabling prediction of changes in some marketing phenomena by reference to changes in one or more other marketing phenomena. And mathematics may supply devices which might enable the marketing scientist to control marketing phenomena with a view to attaining some optimum level of another marketing phenomenon.

Psychometric and sociometric techniques are also pertinent to marketing science. These aim to elicit and measure the psychological and sociological determinants of marketing behavior. If, for example, attitudes are a factor in the determination of behavior, then such devices as scaling techniques may enable the investigator more precisely to describe and analyze knowledge about the attitudes held by such marketing participants as consumers, middlemen, and salesmen.[7]

Sociometric techniques can be used to describe and analyze the networks of interrelationships and interactions which occur among groups of people involved in and affected by marketing. Such techniques may be a useful aid in enabling the marketing scientist to analyze the influence that groups have on the marketing behavior of their members.[8]

In other sciences the invention of mechanical devices such as the microscope and the telescope has facilitated substantial advances in the acquisition of knowledge. Similarly, for marketing the invention of a device such as the electronic computer has had an important impact on the analysis of marketing facts.

---

[6] William F. Massey, "Statistical Analysis of Relations between Variables," published in R. F. Frank, A. A. Kuehn, and William F. Massey, *Quantitative Techniques in Marketing Analysis*, Richard D. Irwin, Homewood, Ill., 1962, pp. 56–105; Alfred A. Kuehn, "Complex Interactive Models," *ibid.*, pp. 106–123. See also, Frank M. Bass et al., *Mathematical Models and Methods in Marketing*, Richard D. Irwin, Homewood, Ill., 1961.

[7] See, for example, G. David Hughes, "A Controlled Field Experiment to Measure the Effects of Sales Promotion," unpublished Ph.D. dissertation, University of Pennsylvania, 1963.

[8] The utility of such techniques to the development of marketing science is well illustrated in James Coleman, Herbert Menzel, and Elihu Katz, "Social Processes in Physician's Adoption of a New Drug," *Journal of Chronic Diseases*, Vol. IX, No. 1 (January 1959), pp. 1–19.

Not only does the computer enable the marketing scientist to analyze larger amounts of facts at a more rapid speed than could heretofore be accomplished, but it may also be possible to simulate all or a segment of what goes on in marketing on the computer.[9] If this possibility materializes, then experiments could be accomplished on the computer which might be too expensive or impractical to perform in the real world. That is, control acts could be performed on the computer simulation and the result would be that which would occur if the act were actually carried out in a real world marketing situation. These potential benefits will not become available, however, until analysts succeed in actually simulating the salient features of the real marketing world on the computer.[10]

The relevance of the discovery of knowledge acquisition and analytical devices to the development of marketing science can be additionally illustrated by the recent development of an eye camera for marketing research purposes. This camera is used by Marplan, a research organization, to photograph changes in the dilation of a respondent's eye pupils when the respondent views an advertisement or package.

Marplan asserts that there is a correlation between variation in eye pupil size and the interest and pleasure value of visual stimuli.[11] If the latter statement is true, then this technique will enable researchers to obtain accurate information from respondents as to the degree to which they find some visual marketing stimulus pleasant or interesting. Such a device is needed by marketing researchers because some respondents do not give accurate answers when interviewed.

COMPONENTS OF SCIENCE

In the development of a science the basic facts describing the phenomena of an aspect of our environment are usually put together and analyzed to make up what are termed concepts, theories, and laws.

Concepts consist of elements of marketing phenomena which are brought together in a larger whole which has descriptive and analytical utility. Thus the concept of elasticity of demand, for example, joins price

[9] Wroe Alderson and Stanley J. Shapiro (eds.), *Marketing and the Computer*, Prentice-Hall, Englewood Cliffs, N.J., 1963; Frederick E. Balderston and Austin C. Hoggatt, *Simulation of Market Processes*, Institute of Business and Economic Research, University of California, Berkeley, 1962.

[10] Computerized business situations are in the category of business games, rather than simulation, if the analyst has not succeeded in actually duplicating the salient features of the real world on the computer.

[11] E. H. Hess and J. M. Polt, "Pupil Size as Related to Interest Value of Visual Stimuli," *Science*, Vol. 132, No. 3423 (August 5, 1960), pp. 349–350.

and sales in an effort to provide a measure of the response of sales to changes in price, and the consequent effect on profit. Additionally, the concept of the channel of distribution is used to describe the various sequences of marketing and facilitating enterprises, if any, which are involved in the marketing of products as they move closer to points of use or consumption.

A theory can consist of a few or many verbal statements and/or numerical statements which describe the behavior of some marketing phenomenon by reference to other marketing phenomena. The purpose of a theory is to enable one to predict the behavior of this dependent phenomenon.

Thus E. T. Grether sought to formulate a theory which aimed to predict the marketing of goods and services among regions by reference primarily to the marketing phenomena of costs and prices.[12] While Grether sought to formulate a theory about only one aspect of marketing, another theorist, William C. McInnes, attempted to develop a holistic or general theory which aimed to explain the operation of all of marketing.[13]

A recently published piece, "A Normative Theory of Marketing Systems," formulated by Wroe Alderson [14] is both piecemeal and holistic. It relies on functionalism, cultural ecology, and economics in its discussion of how individual "systems," for example, business enterprises, and larger "systems," for example, industries, communities, national marketing mechanisms, operate. Alderson asserts that each of the many small and large "systems" in the environment has survival as its goal.[15] The control (normative) aspect of his discussion specifies how decision makers ought to behave if they wish to attain their goal, that is, the survival of the small and large "systems" in which they are interested.

[12] See George Schwartz, *Development of Marketing Theory*, South-Western Publishing Company, Cincinnati, 1963, pp. 68–84.

[13] W. C. McInnes, "A General Theory of Marketing," unpublished Ph.D. dissertation, New York University, 1954. E. A. Duddy and D. A. Revzan also appear to favor the holistic approach to marketing theory formulation. See Duddy and Revzan, *op. cit.*, pp. 621–628, and D. A. Revzan, "Review of *Theory in Marketing*, edited by Cox and Alderson (1950)," *Journal of Marketing*, Vol. XV, No. 1 (July 1950), pp. 101–109.

[14] Wroe Alderson, "A Normative Theory of Marketing Systems," published in Reavis Cox, Wroe Alderson, and Stanley Shapiro (eds.), *Theory in Marketing: Second Series*, Richard D. Irwin, Homewood, Ill., 1964.

[15] Alderson does not present the empirical evidence on which this statement is based. It is thus not known whether the statement is entirely true, partly true, or entirely false. It might be noted in this connection that the microeconomic theorist asserts that the goal of business enterprises is profit maximization. Unfortunately, the latter also fails to substantiate his assertion with the necessary empirical evidence.

There does not appear to be any *a priori* basis for stating that either the piecemeal or the holistic approach to theory formulation is likely to be more fruitful in yielding formulations which will permit prediction of the change of some marketing phenomenon or marketing phenomena. However, the existence of gaps in our descriptive and predictive knowledge of marketing would appear to suggest that the piecemeal approach to the development of marketing theory is likely to be more practicable.[16]

In the formulation of a marketing theory it is not uncommon for theorists to begin with a hypothesis. A hypothesis differs from a theory in that the accuracy of its predictive power has not yet been tested. For a hypothesis to be termed a theory in marketing science, it must yield predictions with an accuracy greater than would be the case if the predictions were made using some random device, such as taking the prediction from a well-mixed set of possible predictions. Thus a so-called "bad" theory is a hypothesis which is never accepted as a theory, using the above criterion.

In the event that marketing science included several theories which aimed to predict changes in the same marketing phenomenon, how would one determine which of the several theories was the best theory? Here the accuracy of prediction criterion would apply. That is, that theory which yielded the most accurate predictions when the several theories are used simultaneously could be regarded as the best theory.

A law is a former theory which over time, and for the geographic area to which it is supposed to apply, has been demonstrated to yield perfectly accurate predictions each time it is used. William J. Reilly, for example, has formulated a mathematical equation which he terms the "law" of retail gravitation.[17] This equation sought to predict how two competing retail trading centers would divide the shopping goods purchases made by residents of intermediate towns outside of their home towns. This formula cannot, however, be termed a law, for it has not been demonstrated that it meets the prediction criterion stated above.[18]

CAUSE AND EFFECT

Demonstration of a cause and effect relationship between a marketing phenomenon whose behavior one seeks to change in some desired way

---

[16] The piecemeal approach to the development of marketing theory has been espoused by, among others, Reavis Cox. Cox is of the opinion that the development of valid theories about component parts of marketing may some day enable the formulation of a general theory of marketing.

[17] Schwartz, *op. cit.*, pp. 9–34.

[18] *Ibid*, pp. 29–34.

by reference to other marketing phenomena is pertinent to the problem of obtaining control information for marketing science. Advertising can be used for the purpose of presenting a simple illustration bearing on this matter.

More than 12 billion dollars a year is spent by United States marketers in the use of advertising as a promotional tool. Those who believe in the sales-producing ability of advertising are explicitly or implicitly acting as if advertising is one factor which causes people to buy their products. If this is true, then the marketer is acting wisely; but if the belief is not true, then he is, of course, not using his promotional funds effectively.

But how can one demonstrate that advertising, or anything for that matter, causes sales? The most reliable method is the use of appropriate controlled experiments in real life.[19] In such experiments, experimental and control groups are used. In the conduct of such an experiment, everything affecting sales needs, strictly speaking, to be the same in each experimental and control group (in this instance the experimental and control groups are markets). The marketing phenomenon, for example, advertising, whose causative effect on sales is being tested, is introduced into the experimental market but not into the control market. The effect on the phenomenon whose variation it is desired to control, for example, sales, is then measured. If the change in this latter phenomenon in the experimental market relative to the control market is determined to be statistically significant, then the hypothesized causative factor, in this instance, advertising, can be regarded as being the factor which caused the observed change in the phenomenon whose variation it is desired to control, in this instance, sales.

If such an experiment were carried out to test the causative effectiveness of advertising, and the results were determined to be positive and could be measured, then a marketer, using advertising in a situation similar to the experimental situation, could change his sales in a predictable way through the use of this promotional tool.

THE EMPIRICAL PHILOSOPHY OF KNOWLEDGE

The empirical philosophy of knowledge, which many believe should be the basis of marketing science, holds that what is to be known is derived from experience. That is, the descriptive facts of marketing science are those which can be in some sense observed. As regards pre-

[19] See Seymour Banks, *Experimentation in Marketing*, McGraw-Hill, New York, 1964.

dictive knowledge contained in theories and laws, the empiricist knows that he has unearthed such knowledge only when he has been able to use such knowledge in real life and observed that he has predicted accurately.

The empiricist who is attempting to simulate on a computer some segment or all of marketing knows that he has in fact simulated reality only when some action taken on the computer simulation yields a change which is the same as that which results in real life when the same action is taken.

The empiricist as a normative analyst wishing to prescribe a course of action which yields, in some sense, an optimum result, or a specifically desired result, knows that he has in fact come up with such a solution only when the recommendation is put into practice in real life and the result observed. If the normative analyst has neglected to take into account all of the relevant factors in the situation, then implementation of his recommendation may disrupt a situation to such an extent that costs or losses are incurred which substantially vitiate any gains resulting from the recommended course of action.

Although the empirical philosophy of knowledge emphasizes observable knowledge, the meaning of "observable" knowledge in marketing needs to be elucidated. The most obvious meaning of "observable" refers to things that we can see—the purchase of a specific brand, the characteristics of different types of marketing institutions, the expenditure of family income on different products, and so forth. But it would be a mistake to restrict the basic facts of marketing science to that which is observable in this sense. Psychological feelings and motives as well as sociological considerations provide knowledge which is also fundamental to marketing science.

While it can be seen that a consumer does not patronize a discount store, the reason for his action cannot be seen with one's eye. It may be, for example, that this consumer refuses to patronize a discount store because he feels that customers of such a store are in a lower social class. Or, a young lady may purchase a particular brand of shampoo, not because of its washing effectiveness but because she believes that the shampoo makes her hair look lovely and will aid her in obtaining a husband.

Although such determinants of behavior cannot be seen, and must be ascertained using some appropriate interview technique, the knowledge which is sought is of obvious relevance to a science of marketing whose users need to adjust to and/or influence the behavior of people.[20] Motiva-

---

[20] See Joseph W. Newman, *Motivation Research and Marketing Management*, Harvard University Press, Boston, 1957.

tion, for example, is a concept which, in a narrow sense, is used to refer to the psychological components of behavior. This concept is derived from the knowledge that human beings—consumers, salesmen, decision makers —are affected in their behavior, in part, by such factors as fear, the desire to dominate, the desire to be loved, the desire to be in a higher status than others, and so forth. Although these factors cannot be seen, knowledge about their presence and the influence they have on the behavior of people involved in marketing is important to marketing science if the knowledge goals of such a science are to be achieved.

Among the various knowledge acquisition tools available to the marketing empiricist, random sampling and inference making techniques, as well as significance testing, are particularly valuable because they enable him to obtain knowledge about large numbers of marketing elements, for example, all consumers in the United States, from representative fractions of the large groups being studied.

VALUE JUDGMENTS, ETHICS, AND MARKETING SCIENCE

All of us have several roles in society. The marketing scientist in his role as a scientist seeks knowledge about the aspect of society with which he is concerned. But he is also a citizen and a consumer. In these roles he is affected by what marketers do and may develop opinions about the social desirability of what marketers do.

For example, he may develop the opinion that the immaturity displayed in many advertisements is undesirable because it does not contribute to raising the intellectual and esthetic level of our people. Or, he might consider it unethical for marketers to use a product policy of planned obsolescence. While all of us are free to have and express opinions about the desirability or ethics of what marketers do, the marketing scientist has no special competence when it comes to evaluating the social value or ethics of what marketers do.

As is the case with each of us in various occupations, the marketing scientist has his particular function to fulfill in society. Like the others, he is a specialist, specializing in seeking accurate descriptive, predictive, and control knowledge about marketing. As a citizen and a consumer he is, of course, free to have opinions about the value and ethics of what goes on in marketing. But in this realm his opinions are no more than opinions, and they have no greater or less authoritative significance than do the opinions of other citizens.

As a scientist his competence consists, if he has the necessary knowledge, of an ability

1. to state what is going on in marketing.

2. to predict the consequences of actions and events insofar as they pertain to marketing.

3. to advise marketing practitioners or society how best to attain goals specified by either.

MARKETING SCIENCE AND MANAGEMENT SCIENCE

Since the end of World War II a number of analysts have focused their efforts on matters which are classified under the title of management science. And while unanimity of opinion does not exist as to what management science is, one can say that this field of study focuses, in part, on the discovery of optimum decisions for problems faced by business executives.

Judging from the activities of management scientists, one of their major concerns appears to be the identification and development of analytical techniques which will yield optimum solutions.[21] This concern would seem to be a basis for distinguishing between the management scientist and the marketing scientist. Unlike the former, the latter focuses primarily on the unearthing of substantive knowledge about marketing.

Although the focus of their respective activities appears to differ in the manner suggested above, the activities of the two groups can be regarded as complementary. That is, the management scientist who seeks, for example, an optimum allocation of a company's advertising budget among available media, needs information on the sales that are likely to be generated by spending different amounts of money in specified media. That is precisely the kind of predictive and control information that the marketing scientist seeks to obtain.[22]

---

[21] See, for example, C. West Churchman, Russell L. Ackoff, and E. Leonard Arnoff, *Introduction to Operations Research*, Wiley, New York, 1957.

[22] Marketers must make decisions even though pertinent predictive and control knowledge may not be available to them. Robert Schlaifer's book, *Probability and Statistics for Business Decisions*, McGraw-Hill, New York, 1959, puts forth a method for making decisions in the absence of such knowledge. This method is usually referred to as Bayesian Decision Theory because it is substantially based on a theorem originally formulated by Reverend Bayes. One student of Bayesian Decision Theory has characterized this decision making method as follows: "In highly oversimplified terms, the Bayesian approach to decision making under uncertainty provides a framework for explicitly working with the economic costs of alternative courses of action, the prior knowledge or judgment of the decision maker, and formal modification of these judgments as additional data are introduced into the problem." This quotation is from Paul E. Green, "Bayesian Decision Theory in Pricing Strategy," *Journal of Marketing*, Vol. XXVI, No. 1 (January 1963), p. 5.

SOME RANDOM OBSERVATIONS

1. The reader should not develop the mistaken notion that the development of a science of marketing is a straightforward, frictionless task. The facts of the matter are that efforts in this direction are beset with all sorts of problems which make difficult the acquisition of accurate geographically general and temporally stable knowledge.

Because of the dynamic nature of marketing phenomena, it is exceedingly difficult to obtain predictive knowledge which will remain true over time. And because it is difficult and expensive to conduct experiments in the real world, it is frequently not feasible to obtain control knowledge in this way. And even when such an experiment is conducted, the results are usually not precise because often it is not possible to obtain experimental and control groups which are exactly comparable and which represent the relevant population of phenomena under study. Moreover, the results of a study conducted in one locality may not be valid in other geographic areas.

But there are substantial barriers to the acquisition of even accurate descriptive knowledge at any point in time and with respect to one locality. If the marketing scientist wished to describe the buying motivations of consumers of just one consumer product, he would need to conduct an appropriate survey among a representative sample of households. If the study pertained to the United States, then several thousand households would have to be studied, which would involve a substantial cost. Such funds are frequently not available to the marketing scientist.

Even if the marketing scientist is able to clear the financial hurdle, he must cope adequately with other problems if he is to obtain accurate knowledge. He must have the information which enables him to select a random sample; write a questionnaire, if this technique is used, which will be understood by all respondents as he intended it to be understood; obtain the cooperation of all who are included in the sample; obtain interviewers who will perform their task correctly and honestly; code the questionnaires meaningfully and accurately; transfer the information from the questionnaires on to computer cards without mistake; take

See also R. D. Buzzell and C. C. Slater, "Decision Theory and Marketing Management," *Journal of Marketing*, Vol. XXVI, No. 3 (July 1962), pp. 7–16.
Marketing research is pertinent to the decision making process in that the marketer can use these techniques to obtain knowledge which is useful in (1) suggesting alternative courses of action and (2) in evaluating the probable consequences of alternative courses of action which are being considered.

steps to ensure that the computer does not err in processing the data; and then see to it that the typist reproducing the data for the final report does not make any mistakes.

It is, of course, easy to write that these operations need to be performed. But, carrying them out so that they are performed without error requires careful planning and meticulous execution of the plan.

2. Like other persons in society, scientists are human beings with psychological, sociological, and economic drives. The satisfaction of such drives has been observed on occasion to take the form of a researcher's persisting in maintaining the truth of a hypothesis even though adequate empirical evidence is lacking or even though evidence does not support the hypothesis. Hopefully, persons who seek to contribute to the development of marketing science will guard against the operation of such drives as possible interferences in the quest for accurate knowledge.

3. The usefulness of quantifying knowledge about marketing was referred to earlier in this chapter. However, the quantification of knowledge is of dubious value if such a process renders the qualitative information less meaningful or meaningless.

On one occasion the writer was exposed to a talk describing a sophisticated quantitative analytical procedure aimed at discovering the interaction of several variables believed to influence buying behavior. The results of this analysis "revealed" that advertising, one of the variables, had a zero effect on buying behavior and that buying behavior had a large effect on consumer awareness of product advertising. On querying the analyst, this writer learned that the measure of advertising awareness used was a poor one—an evaluation shared by the analyst— and that this probably accounted for his arriving at the conclusion that advertising had a zero effect on buying behavior in the situation which was studied.

4. The normative solution component of marketing science is potentially useful for those marketers who wish to optimize. But it should be noted that the optimum nature of such a solution is dubious if the normative analyst plugs numbers into a mathematical equation which are meaningless and/or inaccurate.

In dealing with the acceptance or rejection of normative statements it is important for marketing scientists to determine whether what is being optimized is what is desired to be optimized. For example, some economists assert that a perfectly competitive society would produce maximum social welfare. However, if one regards psychological and sociological well being as well as material possessions as the factors to be optimized in an affluent society, then one can seriously question whether a perfectly competitive society would, in fact, optimize social welfare.

5. While it is customary for researchers to begin a research study with a hypothesis, it may perhaps be useful to point up a pitfall which may be associated with such a research procedure. Such a research plan may blind the researcher to all the actual facts of the study situation, for he may look only for facts relating to his hypothesis.

Some investigators use a study procedure which permits the facts to determine the direction and content of a study. This latter procedure, although involving much fumbling and stumbling, may be just as or more fruitful in yielding knowledge than is the case when an investigation begins with a hypothesis. But if a study is conducted starting with a hypothesis, the investigator should not delude himself into thinking that he is obtaining knowledge when, during the course of the study, he manipulates his data so that they conform to a major or subhypothesis.[23]

6. It is not uncommon for some investigators to begin a non-normative research study about business behavior with the assumption that the businessman's behavior flows from a desire to maximize profits. It is apparently unimportant to such assumers that a businessman, even if he had this goal, frequently cannot pursue it because the necessary information is not available to him. But enough evidence is available, prosaic as it may be, such as the experience of daily life, that many businessmen do not seek to maximize profits. True, businessmen need to earn profits if they are to remain in business long, but how many of them seek to optimize? In this connection it is worth noting that an empirical study of the pricing practices of certain large companies revealed that this sample of companies sought to attain a number of different pricing goals.[24]

If marketing is to become a science, we must avoid making assumptions about behavior, for example, the goals of businessmen or the determinants of consumer actions. Rather, from a representative sample of the relevant human beings, we need to attempt to secure a frequency distribution of motives and then seek to determine how these motives are reflected in the marketing behavior of the people being studied.

While students of marketing do not yet fully know and understand the specific components and composition of the motives which determine the behavior of businessmen and consumers, it is obvious to all who

---

[23] On one occasion the writer heard an analyst report on his attempt to study a complicated aspect of marketing. In his report the analyst stated that at one point in the study some of the collected data did not conform to a subhypothesis of the over-all study. Because he believed so strongly in his prior expectation, the analyst adjusted the data so that they conformed with this expectation. The analyst referred to this adjustment as being based on a "visceral source of knowledge."

[24] A. D. H. Kaplan, J. B. Dirlam, and R. F. Lanzillotti, *Pricing in Big Business: A Case Approach*, The Brookings Institution, Washington, D. C., 1958.

observe the world around them that businessmen and consumers are people. For this reason the marketing scientist is not surprised when his research yields knowledge that businessman and consumer behavior reflect psychological and sociological as well as economic motives. People, regardless of their function in society, are human beings, not computers, and for this reason are likely to, in various degrees, reflect these motives in their behavior.[25]

A case in point is the Xerox Corporation. This corporation contributes at least one and one half per cent of its gross profits before taxes in support of education, health, and welfare activities. Moreover, Xerox, in April 1964, announced that it would spend 4 million dollars to sponsor six 90-minute film dramas about the United Nations on the ABC and NBC television networks in prime evening time. Under the arrangement, Xerox's sponsorship would be *noted* at the beginning and at the end of each program.

In connection with the Xerox sponsorship of the United Nations television programs, Joseph C. Wilson, President of the Company, made the following address at a luncheon at the United Nations on April 10, 1964:

> Emerson, in a little piece about "Beauty" once wrote, "From a great heart secret magnetisms flow incessantly to draw great events."
>
> Here in this shrine dedicated to the highest passion of them all, Man's yearning for peace, you must feel, as I do, the urgent tugs to do better by our fellows. There can be no greater event in this century than the very fact that there is this building, there is this organization, there is this company of "great hearts" who resolutely fill their days with effort to make a future for men.
>
> For me, therefore, perhaps even for you, the ones whose reputation for reaching people has no equal, it is a very great privilege indeed to be associated in this task to help the world better understand what the United Nations means to it. It is not for me to try to articulate it; rather it is for you to capture that transient spirit, to portray it in all its weakness which so heavily underlines its innate strength, to depict it with realism, but, at the same time, to project its promise, to say, as you must, that it is human and

[25] Examine, for example, John Howard, *Marketing: Executive and Buyer Behavior,* Columbia University Press, New York, 1963, Chs. 4 and 5; also Alfred Oxenfeldt, David Miller, Abraham Shuchman, and Charles Winick, *Insights Into Pricing From Operations Research and Behavioral Science,* Wadsworth Publishing Company, Belmont, California, 1961, Chs. 4–6.

fallible, but also to cry that its impact will inexorably shape the time to come, shape it in a way which will make man's role a nobler one. What greater privilege than to work together toward this goal! This is *our* motive, as it must be yours.

But we of Xerox are in a different position from the rest of you because, after all, we do have over 50,000 people of whose treasure we are custodians. We must answer them when they ask, "What value for Xerox is there in this $4,000,000 expenditure?" As a matter of justice to them, no matter what ideals you and we may have, we must be able persuasively to assert that there is value for Xerox in this idealism. For me to pretend otherwise would be hypocritical and false.

After all, for a business to take this action is, I gather, unprecedented; it is bound to bring criticism, at the least, and possibly to bring much more aggressive attack than that. Our eyes are wide open about it. But it is a part of our philosophy that the highest interests of a corporation are involved in the health of the earth's society. How ridiculous it is to build a showroom in New York without simultaneously trying to help build a peaceful world!

Our objectives, like yours, but ours are much less glamorous, are to help men better communicate with each other, and, therefore, it is all important for Xerox to be favorably known throughout the world as an institution which is willing to risk in order to improve understanding, which will innovate boldly, but not recklessly, which will accept challenge of its short range position in order to buttress the long years ahead. It is our deeply considered judgment, cold and calculated, that this company will benefit by its association with the U. N. and with you. We are proud to be a part of this enterprise, which, as all know, is making history.

There are a few favorite lines of mine in Christopher Fry's *A Sleep for Prisoners* which go about like this:

> Thank God our time is now
> When wrong comes up to face
> us everywhere
> Never to leave us 'til we take
> The longest strides of soul
> men ever took.
> Affairs are now soul-size.

These men of the U.N., of all the earth's people, are living soul-size lives. It is a joy and a value—however briefly, however humbly—to join with them.

Not all companies behave in the manner that Xerox does, but if we are to understand the business world as it is, we need to be aware of those that behave as Xerox does, as well as those companies whose business behavior falls into different categories.

7. A frequently used basis for the evaluation of a textbook is the kind of approach it uses, such as the management, functional, institutional, commodity, or some other approach. Although the approach used in a textbook is an important appraisal criterion because it determines the kind of information included and the point of view from which the information is treated, textbook evaluation ought to go beyond the pertinence and relevance of the approach.

In addition to a textbook's approach, another important basis for its appraisal should be whether its assertive remarks are based on acceptable evidence and whether it raises considerations and questions which are pertinent. Unfortunately, gaps in our knowledge about marketing results in a situation wherein those studying marketing spend effort in the learning of information which does not always reflect the real marketing world.

8. The attitude displayed by some normative analysts toward marketing practitioners, and by some of the latter toward normative analysts, does not facilitate the development of marketing science or the application of such knowledge in the solution of real business problems. To some normative analysts, a number of marketing practitioners are incompetent because they do not use certain optimum procedures which are clearly optimum and desirable to these analysts. And the antiscience type of marketing practitioner has little faith in what marketing scientists do because they are alleged to be too "theoretical," that is, they are not familiar with and do not understand the facts of marketing life.

Hopefully, the development of marketing science will, *inter alia,* aid the businessman better to attain his desirable goals. But this is likely to come about only if the marketing scientist becomes aware of and understands the forces which have produced what is in marketing, and how these forces determine what is feasible in the way of marketing plans and actions. On the other hand, marketing practitioners who may not understand the research and analytical techniques of the marketing scientist will have to be patient with the normative analyst as he explores a problem situation in an effort to determine the most important variables in the situation.

9. Science in any field of investigation is the direct antithesis of dogmatism. In marketing, the scientist is sensitive to both the reliability of research methodology and the validity of evidence yielded by any research technique. As a scientist the marketing analyst is careful to

make statements based only on knowledge. If knowledge about an aspect of marketing with which the marketing scientist is concerned is lacking, the scientist devises a research plan and method which is likely to yield the desired knowledge.

For the marketing scientist who is an empiricist, the facts of the real marketing world are the source of basic knowledge about marketing. Normative solutions, if desired, are accepted as normative only after they have been tried in the real marketing world and their consequences evaluated to determine whether the results are, in fact, optimum in the sense desired.

POTENTIAL USEFULNESS OF MARKETING SCIENCE

At the beginning of this chapter marketing science was characterized as a body of accurate descriptive, predictive, and control knowledge about marketing. The accumulation of such a body of knowledge will require the expenditure of much time, effort, and money. To justify these expenditures, a science of marketing should make a desirable contribution to society. That is, a science of marketing should provide knowledge which will be useful in the attainment of the desirable goals of those individuals in society who are concerned with marketing.

Who are these persons? They are students of marketing, teachers of marketing, businessmen, consumers, and government officials concerned with the regulation of marketing in the public interest.

2

Marketing Science:
Significance to the Professor of Marketing

JOSEPH W. NEWMAN

The move to more scientific marketing has ushered in a period of rapid and significant change for the professor of marketing. If he adjusts to it successfully, he eventually will enjoy greater satisfaction from working with a richer discipline which will bring him higher professional status and better students. If he does not, he will suffer the pains of hastened obsolesence.

In either event, his life will be more complicated and frequently upsetting in the next several years. He will discover much of what he has taught in the past to be outmoded or, at least, no longer sufficient. He will face the necessity of supplementing his background if he is to contribute to knowledge through research or if he is to become able to participate in the implementation and, hopefully, the design of major changes in what is to be taught and how.

The adjustment problem will tend to be greatest for those who have been out of school the longest but it will not be confined to them. Important advances have been made in recent years in what have come to be recognized as relevant disciplines. As a result, up-to-date formal training which includes a sound grounding in at least one of these fields is advantageous. While more depth is desirable, so is more breadth. Recent graduates as well as others, therefore, will need to become more familiar with subjects other than those of their major area of concentration in order to cope with the broad demands of the applied discipline of marketing.

SCIENTIFIC MARKETING: A RADICAL CHANGE

The implications are sweeping because the actual implementation of the idea of developing more scientific marketing represents a radical change. In business, it means moving from personal, seat-of-the-pants decision making to a new era of professional management based on information regularly sought and expertly interpreted. Intuition will remain important, but it will have much more to go on. In academic institutions, the move must be to provide training appropriate for the management of the future and to encourage research which will contribute needed substance. The changes involve new attitudes, new ways of thinking, and new ways of approaching problems.

In the past, the business executive responsible for product and distribution decisions has had little choice but to rely heavily on his intuitive judgment, making what he could out of his experience. Marketing has had little research of a basic character. As a result, it has had little in the way of theory, principles, and knowledge useful for purposes of predicting what would happen in response to a given action taken in a given situation.

Naturally enough, the business executive has proceeded more or less unsystematically, using available sources of help which were limited. He has looked to sales results, for example, as a primary source of information. Unfortunately, they often are difficult to interpret because of the large number of variables which influence the final result. In particular, the executive has been handicapped by a lack of adequate means of ordering and analyzing sales and other performance data for purposes of gaining the understanding of people's wants and behavior which is basic to marketing planning.

In attempts to think more specifically about buyer behavior, the marketer has relied to a large extent on his own informal studies of himself and other people. While they have produced ideas, they have been of mixed quality. The business executive typically is unable to examine his own feelings and behavior very fully, particularly in their nonlogical aspects. He usually is not trained as an observer of human behavior. His procedure may be faulty, and he is likely to be unable to see important meanings in people's words and actions because of limitations of his own background. In addition, the people he chooses to observe may not be representative of the market for the product in question.

In addition to the informal, personal kinds of inquiries, the executive increasingly has turned to research. The use of research by marketing management, however, has been on a relatively small scale. In addition, the capacity of research to be of help has suffered from technical handicaps of the means of gathering and analyzing data and from the limited backgrounds and ways of thinking of the researchers who have employed them. Research in marketing typically has been descriptive rather than analytical. Tests of various kinds have come into greater use, but they often have not been well designed. Surprisingly little use has been made of research to provide full explanations of test results or to aid in the creative process of bringing into being product and marketing ideas.

In summary, there has been a dearth of knowledge about people's wants and the influences on their buying behavior although admittedly it is fundamental to marketing. At the same time, research activity addressed to correcting the deficiency has been limited as has the ability of research to be of help. Marketing management, therefore, has been left with many major unanswered questions.

RELEVANCE OF BEHAVIORAL SCIENCES AND QUANTITATIVE ANALYSIS

For a variety of reasons, things have changed in recent years. Although marketing has not suddenly come into possession of answers to its important problems, there is new hope based on important new resources. Fundamental to the improved outlook is the progress made in the past fifteen years in a number of fields which increasingly have been helping themselves by joining forces. In psychology, sociology, and cultural and social anthropology, more has been learned about human behavior and how to identify and measure influences on it. Work of special interest to marketing has been done on perception, memory, attitudes, learning, personality, motivation, communication flow, opinion leadership, and social classes and mobility.

The analytical tools of mathematics have been improved, and work is under way on developing mathematical models to describe the functioning of economic units and to predict the outcome of given inputs into the economic system. A major new advance has been made in the field of statistics which earlier developed probability sampling and experimental design. It is called statistical decision theory. It specifies how both judgment and statistical evidence should be combined in the making of decisions and offers a new way of deciding how much evidence should be obtained before a decision is made.

By drawing on other fields, marketing now is acquiring a vastly improved potential for tackling its problems and improving the quality of business decisions. Its stock of research resources is at a significant all-time high, and even faster growth lies ahead as the interdisciplinary movement gains momentum in a new age which features the combined use of the intellect of man and the intellect of the computer.

Both business and academic institutions have begun to put the new resources to work. The development is young, but it is far enough along in certain circles to be indicative of what will come on a much larger scale in the future.

In firms known for advanced thinking and practice, marketing management now is calling on research to play a much fuller role. Marketing research is becoming notably more interdisciplinary in character. The trend in research staffs is toward requiring advanced formal training in such fields as psychology, social anthropology, sociology, economics, mathematics, and statistics. Research now reflects thinking in terms of theories and systems.

TREND TOWARD SCIENTIFIC MANAGEMENT

The trend to a more scientific approach is seen in marketing management as well. Firms are becoming more systematic about determining objectives and formulating strategies and programs on the basis of information especially ordered for the purpose. The marketing manager typical of the past increasingly is coming in for criticism as top business management is becoming more insistent on more rational decision making in marketing. The reference is to the manager who has depended largely on intuition, or, if he used research, he has mistakenly assumed that he knew exactly what he should ask for. While he was schooled to make intuitive decisions under conditions of uncertainty, he was not well trained to think in terms of whether he should seek more information to reduce the uncertainty before making a decision. Frequently he has been criticized for a lack of creative ability.

In keeping with the trend of the times, a new kind of marketing manager who is more systematic and analytical is appearing. He employs a staff of specialists to help define problems, produce relevant information, and assess it before deciding what to do. He is skilled as an administrator of information as well as of people.

The trend is evident elsewhere, too. A number of companies recently contributed substantial funds to establish the Marketing Science Institute for the purpose of producing knowledge for marketing. Professional groups such as the American Marketing Association are active in the same direction. An encouraging amount of research in marketing now is appearing in educational institutions, backed by funds from business and foundations.

In view of the young but substantial efforts under way, we now can say that a science of marketing is emerging if science is viewed as activity

directed to lowering the degree of empiricism involved in solving problems. No over-all conceptual scheme for reliably guiding future development now exists but there are encouraging starts. Although marketing's
conceptual framework remains to be developed, this is to be expected.
Important conceptual schemes are the goals of scientific endeavor. It is
necessary to start on a smaller scale with a variety of projects which
eventually will have a beneficial cumulative effect.

SCIENTIFIC MARKETING AND MARKETING EDUCATION

Marketing education now faces the challenge of gearing up to play a
central role in the development of marketing science through programs
of research and instruction. A major effort is required if the programs are
to be able to serve well the demands of the future which will differ
markedly from those of the past. While promising changes have begun
to appear, programs of instruction in marketing have undergone surprisingly little fundamental change for 20 to 30 years.

The programs have been of two main types, which often have been
employed together. One has emphasized the handling of individual business problems presented in the form of written cases. The other has
concentrated on describing marketing institutions and practices and
related public policies and regulations. The descriptive approach has
offered useful background information but little training in making
decisions in a specific context. The case approach has focused on making
decisions but on a seat-of-the-pants basis. Both approaches have value,
but neither as customarily practiced is adequate for meeting future requirements. The situation, then, is that marketing courses generally have
not been well equipped to prepare students for decision making fed by
research which employs new concepts, methods, and computers.

Marketing courses have contained little material on human needs and
ways of life and their relevance to demand for goods and services. The
textbooks usually have done little more than note the primacy of information on buying motivation. Their brief treatments of the topic have
consisted of presenting one of several lists of "buying motives." The
latter have not been of much help because the so-called "motives" have
been classifications of observed behavior rather than explanations of it.
The lists provide no guidance for determining what "motives" were responsible for what behavior. Modern psychologists have pointed to the
futility of classifying behavior according to a universal set of "motives,"
but this thinking has been very slow to penetrate marketing texts, which

tend to neglect the question of how human wants can be met by products and services and concentrate instead on describing the mechanism for moving goods to the market place. A similar statement can be made about economics. Economists traditionally have not concerned themselves with identifying people's wants. Instead they have specified how people should go about spending their money, assuming that their wants and the relative want-satisfying abilities of all goods available for purchase were known. The unavailability of such information, of course, has left the marketer in a predicament.

Marketing instruction generally has failed to provide exposure to the various methods of scientific investigation. Marketing research courses typically have proceeded on the mistakenly narrow premise that research consists of conducting direct question surveys.

Marketing education naturally has reflected the state of business practice and the inevitably limited backgrounds of its teachers. Most of them were trained before many of the important recent developments and the interdisciplinary movement could have had much effect on what was taught. While understandable for the past, the educational programs we have known nevertheless are inappropriate for the future. What, then, should be done so that academic institutions can speed the development and the effective practice of more scientific marketing?

A review of the past provides some guidance. It shows that progress has been impeded by failure to regard marketing explicitly in terms of a field of knowledge or potential knowledge; failure to think enough in terms of the process by which development takes place; and restricted ways of thinking and approaching problems by those engaged in marketing as teachers, researchers, and managers. Changes are needed to eliminate the deficiencies.

Attention could be focused on the concept of marketing as a discipline if educators assumed a greater responsibility for carefully identifying what is known and what is not known in the field. The heavy emphasis in academic circles on research and publication by the faculty has encouraged specialization by techniques and rather narrow topical areas within marketing. An unfortunate by-product seems to be a neglect of the need for scholars whose primary concern is with the development of the discipline as a whole. They are necessary to help direct attention to the needs for basic research and to foster a healthy sense of what is important and what is trivial in the over-all scheme of things.

The concept of marketing as a discipline also could be furthered by encouraging more study of the historical development of marketing thought. A review of the backgrounds as well as the contributions of leading scholars and practitioners in the field would provide a basis for understanding the nature of marketing's development, how it has come about and how further progress might be achieved.

In this connection, we need to help our students acquire a sound understanding of science in general. We should help them see that science is not basically a matter of techniques but instead is a process of getting ideas and testing them in order to achieve greater understanding. Emphasis should be given to the fact that it is a continuing activity so the student gains a sense of movement and a perspective for viewing new developments. The process of science employs whatever concepts, skills, and techniques can be useful. The expectation is that today's "knowledge" will be obsoleted. The objective, however, remains the same: the development of better concepts.

These ideas also are relevant to what should go on in the classroom. Learning must start from what is in the mind of each student. A logical first step in teaching is that of causing the student to identify his own concepts and thinking about how they came into being. The stage then would be set for examining and testing his mental images and the assumptions they represent and for exposing him to the concepts of others. Remaining is the important creative step by which one carries his thinking forward to arrive at fresh ideas or images which hopefully are improvements over those with which he started.

Our courses of instruction, then, might well be more directly designed and taught to guide the student through a process of conceptual development summarized by such questions as these: What are my concepts? How good are they? How do others conceive of the same thing? How else could it be conceived? The process also is relevant to what should go on in a business organization if it is to improve its performance over time.

Thinking in terms of a process of decision making and how it might be improved is vital to more scientific marketing. We must offer training which will enable the student to develop skill in identifying the issues in a given situation, assessing the adequacy of the informational base for the making of a decision, and considering whether the base should be supplemented. This represents a marked change. Case materials typically have been used either for illustrative purposes or to train the student to reach intuitively bright recommendations for action based on whatever information happened to be immediately available.

In focusing on decision making, we become better able to cultivate an understanding of research as an integral part of the process. Research then can be more effectively pictured as a variety of kinds of inquiries which can be made in a systematic approach to the essential tasks of getting ideas and testing them. Research, of course, should bring to these tasks whatever concepts and methods promise to be of help. They will change over time. Remaining constant, however, will be the idea of a careful search to generate a flow of ideas and information to help executives make better decisions.

The value of research is directly dependent on the power of the ideas and methods it can employ. The blinders which have handicapped marketing in the past and the notable advances made in the past decade or two in other disciplines highlight the importance of bringing relevant concepts and methods from other fields into the marketing curriculum. The resources of related fields are needed to enhance both the science and the art of marketing. The theories, knowledge, and skills of others are essential to the development of marketing's conceptual framework. Broader backgrounds not only make for better applied scientists but they also presumably make for better intuitive artists.

While we may agree that educational programs should become more interdisciplinary, implementation is difficult. There is the necessity of learning more about which other fields can be of help and what concepts and methods in them are relevant to marketing. Finding out is not easy. We also face the question of how business school students can best be exposed to these disciplines. Should they take courses in other departments of the university or should special courses be tailored to the needs of business students? Available offerings of other departments often do not constitute a satisfactory answer because they are designed for other purposes. The development of special courses for business school needs, however, is a substantial undertaking. Only partial answers to questions such as these are available now. More systematic reviews of other disciplines are needed by qualified people who have a marketing orientation.

A few business schools have added courses in mathematics, statistics, economics, and the behavioral sciences. The introduction of such courses is important but it is only a first step. Our main interest is not in these subjects for their own sake but in the use of their knowledge, ideas, and techniques for solving business problems. The next step is that of providing training in the making of such applications. Accomplishing this in courses for marketing management entails major redevelopment which probably can best be done by a faculty team whose members represent different outside disciplines but have a common interest in education for marketing management. Faculty recruitment can be guided by criteria which will ensure an appropriate mix of backgrounds. The success of such an effort depends not only on the team being able to draw effectively from appropriate disciplines but on its maintaining a marketing problem orientation. Familiarity with the kinds of decisions and variables important to marketing management is essential.

New educational materials and pedagogy must be developed which can be effective in meeting the future training needs. Marketing management simulations which make use of the computer represent on approach that is receiving greater attention as a means of providing training in the analysis of data and the making of various kinds of decisions under conditions which emphasize their interrelationships. A few simulations now incorporate a sufficient number of marketing variables to make them attractive for use in the marketing curriculum.

Another promising approach is that of the sequential use of new cases based on especially selected business situations. A brief description of one of several two-case sequences I have been developing will indicate the nature of the approach and its objectives. In the initial case the student is placed in the role of a product manager responsible for the development and marketing of a given product line. A comprehensive picture is presented of the background, including the results of research undertaken, the marketing programs employed, and the company's competitive position. The product manager is concerned with the question of how to innovate to achieve product differentiation which will improve sales and profits. The student's assignment is that of outlining the procedure he would follow in an attempt to achieve the successful product innovation sought.

The first case in the sequence is intended to provide training in analyzing a specific situation and in thinking about steps which should be taken to get into a position to decide, in this instance, what kinds of innovations should be attempted and to whom they should be directed. It provides an opportunity for the student to bring to bear his entire background in reviewing the adequacy of the available information and considering whether attempts should be made to gather more. The student is not given anyone else's procedure to criticize. Instead, he is asked to come up with his own. An important educational objective is the development of his individual creative potential. Another is the cultivation of an appreciation of new concepts and methods by first allowing him to experience frustration while wrestling with a problem completely on his own.

The subject business situation was chosen so that the second case in the sequence could describe an approach actually taken which involves advanced research drawing on other disciplines. In this example, the second case describes in detail research which employs important concepts in psychology and social anthropology. Among other things, it is concerned with market segmentation on the basis of personality categories. The case, then, serves as a means of introducing new ideas and techniques in an applied setting. In handling the second case, the student is expected to weigh the advantages and limitations of the research and then decide what, if anything, he would do on the basis of the findings if he were the product manager.

EDUCATION OF MARKETING PRACTITIONERS AND MARKETING PROFESSORS

My comments thus far have been directed largely to training for marketing management. Much of what has been said, however, also is applicable to instructional programs for future researchers and teachers of marketing. An important question remains, however. Should students seeking careers as researchers or teachers receive the same training as those preparing to become managers? If not, specifically how should the training differ and why? These are important questions which are not easy to answer. The trend is toward greater requirements across the board.

One can take the position, as I do, that the roles, and, therefore, the training needs, of the manager and the researcher differ both in kind and in degree. Marketing management at a high level is the work of a generalist. The successful manager of the future will be one who knows how to employ a variety of specialists, who has a broad enough background to be able to weigh many different kinds of considerations, and who is able to view the making of a particular decision in the context of the whole situation. At the same time, however, he will be more scientific than his predecessor. He must know a great deal about available research resources so that he can call them into use when needed and intelligently evaluate research results. Required will be a technical background substantially greater than marketing managers, or even most marketing researchers, have had in the past. Yet it will not be the same as that needed by the researcher of the future.

The trend within research is toward greater specialization. Future staffs will consist of a larger number of different kinds of more highly trained specialists. Hence training for marketing research must provide for more concentration in one or more fields than it has in the past.

Limitations of human capacity and time make it impossible for any one individual to become expert in all disciplines relevant to marketing. It is neither desirable nor feasible for the future manager to get substantially the same education as the specialists who may serve him in a staff capacity. As for the student interested in an academic career, he faces a dilemma. It arises from the conflicting demands of breadth for purposes of course development and classroom instruction and of specialization for engaging in research which will enable him to maintain the flow of scholarly publications typically required of him for promotion.

The doctoral dissertations being written today reflect the difficulty of achieving a balanced educational program under current conditions. The best of them typically demonstrate high technical competency in the quantitative subjects but reveal less than a desirable understanding of the nature of marketing problems and human behavior. The deficiency often severely limits the researcher's capacity to make a helpful contribution. As we provide opportunity for the greater specialization which is essential for certain purposes, we inadvertently contribute to a problem which plagues business. It consists of the fact that the people best qualified to develop quantitative techniques tend to have the least understanding of the variables and people they must deal with.

In this connection, I am reminded that James B. Conant, former President of Harvard University, warned us some years ago that ". . . this is an age of experts of all types; one of the vital problems of education is to start a trend of mind among our young people that will lead to a better understanding by one group of experts of what other groups of experts are doing." [1]

A more interdisciplinary approach is necessary not only in our programs of instruction but in our research in marketing as well. The need is reflected, for example, in what has happened in the field of consumer behavior, which has received much research attention in the past ten years. More than anything else, experience to date has served to highlight the complexity of the subject. While the work done has produced useful information, it has contributed little in the way of theory. Some of the researchers now admit that they were more optimistic about developing useful theory of consumer behavior several years ago than they are now. In retrospect, they were expecting too much from the limited resources and the particular points of view of their respective disciplines. While the disciplines are relevant, each is concerned mainly with some, but by no means all, of the influences at work. And all important influences are of concern in marketing.

We might observe, too, that to a large extent quantitative specialists have been contributing immediately to marketing by applying their techniques to existing kinds of data. The day is approaching, however, when this ore will be mined to reveal more clearly the need for more and different kinds of data. Attention then can be expected to move more to social scientists and others with backgrounds suited to the creative re-

[1] James B. Conant, *Modern Science and Modern Man*, Doubleday, Garden City, New York, 1955, p. 114.

search tasks that lie ahead. I am convinced that interdisciplinary team efforts are essential to substantial progress on many of marketing's most important problems. Unfortunately, there are barriers to such efforts in both educational institutions and business which we must work to remove.

RAPID FUTURE ADVANCES LIKELY

Looking ahead, the future can be expected to bring greater changes at a faster rate than we have known thus far. The number of other disciplines recognized for being of potential importance to marketing will grow, and the rate of advance in each of them will increase as it will in marketing itself. The trend has a number of important implications. There will be a mounting outpouring of literature fed by growing research activity. It will become increasingly burdensome for one in an applied field like marketing to keep up to date on all the developments important to him. Not only is limited time a problem, but the further development of various specialties will make it more difficult, if not impossible, for any one person to read and understand all that is written. Summaries and translations of the published materials will be needed to enable those in marketing to keep themselves reasonably up to date.

As the trend to more intensive specialization continues, it will become more necessary to consider employing more than one instructor in the teaching of a given marketing course. The instructors would be selected for the appropriateness of their backgrounds and each would handle the parts of the course most in line with his training and experience.

It is apparent that developing programs of instruction for the future and keeping them up to date is a task growing rapidly in size and complexity. A much greater portion of faculty time must be made available for the performance of this function, which deserves to be valued along with teaching and research as essential in a school of business administration.

Accelerating change will force development of continuing programs of education to provide the opportunity for "students" to return to school periodically after they have graduated from the customary programs of instruction to take courses especially designed to help them keep up to date and avoid premature obsolescence.

In the planning of future research, there is a need for more clearly defining what kinds of projects can best be done by educational institutions, business firms, and special professional organizations and what kinds of contacts should be maintained between these parties. As each becomes more active in research, it would appear that much closer working relationships than have existed in the past offer substantial mutual advantage.

Whether one's main interest is in research, program development, or teaching, an exciting future lies ahead for those engaged in marketing education. They have the opportunity to contribute to the greatest period of advance yet experienced in the ability of our economy to perform the functions of innovating, developing, and distributing goods and services to satisfy human wants.

3

Marketing Science:
Usefulness to the Consumer

DAVID HAMILTON

ECONOMIC DEVELOPMENT—MARKETING—THE CONSUMER

The usefulness of marketing science to the consumer becomes clear when we examine the relationship of the marketing process to production and consumption processes. Marketing as a process exists in those societies in which, by virtue of tool-skill development, some degree of specialization has developed. The social processes which link production and consumption are marketing. These may be very rudimentary ones in societies with a rather elementary tool development. But they become much more extensive as tools develop and may cover vast distances, both socially and geographically, in economies possessing an elaborated technology. Their significance in the modern industrial economy is compounded. In the industrial economy the severance of production and consumption has been carried to an extremely high degree.

Of course, in paleolithic cultures, such as those of the Australian aborigine or the Eskimo of North America, one can hardly note a distinction between production and consumption. Here it is most certainly true that one eats in order to produce. Consumption and production are not acts which have been severed in time and place. Even in these simple societies, however, some degree of specialization does exist. But it is not developed to the point at which one can readily distinguish between consumptive and productive processes. The absence of marketing under such primitive conditions of production was made very clear by Daryll Forde in an essay on "primitive" economics:

> In an economy for which these general conditions hold true, economic exchange is necessarily limited. Markets remain undeveloped because the advantages of internal exchange are slight.

The household provides for its daily needs from its own production. Surpluses cannot speedily be sent to areas of scarcity because of the difficulties of transport. On the other hand, if the surplus is to be used at all, it must somehow be distributed at once, because of the technical difficulty of storage. As everyone produces much the same range of articles as everyone else, there will be little demand locally for any excess production. Often the only way an individual can dispose of a surplus is by holding a lavish feast or simply by giving it to kinsmen and neighbors who will feel bound to repay one day.[1]

This situation is, however, superseded, especially after the neolithic revolution, by the advance of tools and technology which bring about a higher degree of specialization.[2] Marketing as a social and economic process becomes significant as one which intervenes between and synchronizes the processes of production and consumption. This does not infer that production and consumption are never directly related even under the highest degree of specialization. But it does state that marketing is an absolutely essential process existing between these two. It performs an integrative function.

Perhaps the point may be drawn even more clearly by referring to life in early rural America. This has been described very well by Henry Adams in the first volume of his monumental *History of The United States*.[3] In the first chapter he describes the life on a semi-subsistence level which characterized the farmer 50 miles from the Atlantic seaboard in 1800. Houses were constructed of materials found on the land and a glass window was a mark of affluence. Cloth was almost wholly homespun and was fashioned into clothing at home. The diet was composed of foodstuffs homegrown and stored for the long winter periods. Certainly some items were secured through rather crude marketing processes. But by and large it could be argued that the vast majority of consumption was linked directly to the productive process without the interposition of a marketing process. This simple condition characterized American life on the moving and shifting agrarian frontier throughout much of the nineteenth century. And although one could hardly argue

[1] Daryll Forde, "Primitive Economics" in Harry L. Shapiro (ed.), *Man Culture, and Society*, Oxford University Press, New York, Galaxy edition, 1960, p. 334.

[2] See for example, Karl Polanyi, Conrad M. Arensberg, and Harry W. Pearson (eds.), *Trade and Market in the Early Empires*, The Free Press, Glencoe, Ill., 1957; Paul Bohannan and George Dalton (eds.), *Markets in Africa*, Northwestern University Press, Evanston, Ill., 1962.

[3] Henry Adams, *The United States in 1800*, Cornell University Press, Ithaca, Great Seal Books, 1955, Ch. 1.

that the marketing process was not significant to those within urban centers or within close proximity to these urban centers, it could not be argued that even here the marketing process possessed the same dire necessity to the consumer that it does in the industrial economy today.

This latter statement is based on the restricted standard of living characteristic of the American consumer even one hundred years ago. This is supported by data from the expenditure budgets of three families in the decade of the 1850's. The limited variety of expenditure reported and the high proportion for food in two of them are testimony to the limited significance of the marketing process. Even that of the third family, obviously then in the upper income brackets, is indicative of the limited variety of consumer expenditure. Although a significantly small percentage of consumer expenditure was for food, this did not mean a large variety of other items. Over half was spent for housing. This lack of variety at all income levels is illustrated in Table 3.1.

The transformation of consumption and the life of the consumer from the post Civil War period to the present may be traced in budget and expenditure studies which have been made throughout this period. In 1874–75 the Massachusetts Bureau of Labor Statistics made one of the

Table 3.1 Consumer Expenditures of Three Families in the 1850's

Expenditure for:	A (1851)	B (1853)	C (1857)
Income	$538.44	$600.00	$1,500.00
	%	%	%
Food	41.1	45.5	27.7
Shelter	38.4	24.7	58.2
Housing	(29.0)	(16.7)	(36.7)
Household operation	(5.1)	(4.7)	(21.5)
Furnishings	(4.3)	(3.3)	–
Clothing	19.3	22.0	–
Transportation	–	2.0	–
Medical care	–	1.7	–
Reading	1.2	1.6	–
Other		.8	–
Savings	–	–	14.1
Gifts and personal taxes		1.7	
	100.0	100.0	100.0

Source: Drawn from Edgar W. Martin, The Standard of Living in 1860, University of Chicago Press, Chicago, 1942.

most complete expenditure studies in the United States up until that time. It is interesting to compare the items listed in these studies with the items listed in the 1960 Bureau of Labor Statistics expenditure study. Such a comparison sharply defines the changes which have taken place in the role of the consumer as a result of vast technological advance. The Massachusetts studies of almost ninety years ago included only five major categories—subsistence, clothing, rent, fuel, and sundry expenses.[4] In all the budgets reported, regardless of income size, the proportion spent for subsistence exceeded 50 per cent. Sundry expenses, which included everything not listed in the major categories, was for all income classes only 5.7 per cent of the total expenditure. For the highest income classes, $1200 and over, it was 10 per cent.

These facts are significant, for they indicate the lack of variety in consumption and the absence of consumer affluence when compared with very recent consumer data. In the survey of consumer expenditures in 1960 fifteen major categories of expenditure were listed, and at no income level did the expenditure for food or subsistence amount to 50 per cent of the expenditure. In the latter study the proportion spent for food by wage and salaried clerical worker families was 27.1 per cent. This very marked reduction in the proportion of expenditure for food between the 1874–1875 study and that of 1960 alone is testimony to the vast increase in the variety of items which now compose the consumer way of life.

The Bureau of Labor Statistics traced these changes in more detail and decade by decade in a volume entitled *How American Buying Habits Change*.[5] In a much less technical fashion the same course of events has been traced by some popular writers.[6] Listings of items common to the consumer today in comparison to some earlier period also emphasize the point. Even a small percentage of items not found in average budgets in 1900, but which are common today, would make quite a sizable list. One item, electrical household appliances, not available in 1900 but common today, alone would make an impressive list.

Not only have American levels of living been in transformation for at least one hundred years, but the rate of transformation has been an accelerating one. Perhaps the increasingly rapid pace at which consumption patterns are being altered is revealed most clearly by examining the

[4] See U.S. Bureau of the Census, *Historical Statistics of the United States, Colonial Times to 1957*, Washington, D.C., 1960, p. 181.
[5] U.S. Department of Labor, *How American Buying Habits Change*, U.S. Government Printing Office, Washington, D.C., 1959.
[6] Frederick Lewis Allen, *The Big Change*, Harper, New York, 1952; Lloyd Morris, *Postscript to Yesterday*, Random House, New York, 1947 and *Not So Long Ago*, Random House, New York, 1949.

expenditures of the people of Muncie, Indiana in the 1920's as revealed in the Lynd's famous social study of that town.[7] The patterns of expenditure were already considerably changed and enlarged from what budget studies as late as 1900 revealed about consumer behavior. But even so the expenditure studies made by the Lynds of 100 Muncie families for the year October 1923 through September 1924 possess a much closer affinity to those of 1900 than to those of today. For example, less than half these families indicated any expenditure for automobile purchase and upkeep. The expenditure for household appliances on the scale common today was unthinkable, for this was the decade in which such implements were just beginning to make their presence known.

The relationship between this growth in the amount and variety in consumption and its impact on marketing is revealed by the changes in the proportion of the work force engaged in wholesale and retail trade between 1919 and 1957. Within that time the proportion of employees in nonagricultural establishments who were employed in wholesale and retail trade increased from approximately 17 to 21 per cent. This figure undoubtedly underestimates the significance of marketing as an economic process. It does so because it is restrictive to wholesaling and retailing establishments and fails to consider all those engaged in marketing activities for manufacturers, finance, insurance, real estate, and service and miscellaneous trades. Most of these would have to be included in any estimate of the proportion of nonagricultural employees engaged in the marketing process. When included, the case for the growth in significance of marketing is even greater. In 1919 the percentage was approximately 29. By 1957 this proportion had increased to more than 38 per cent.[8]

The increase in the amount of consumer expenditure, the increase in the variety of that expenditure, and the increase in the technological complexity of consumer purchases have indeed made the marketing process a crucial one for the consumer. In traditional economic theory, however, the process was stated to be quite a simple one. The consumer was alleged to be a seeker of satisfaction who knew what he wanted and how to secure it. He made his wants known through bids in the marketplace. The producer, guided always by calculations of profit maximization, responded to the desires of the consumer as manifested in price and profit margins. He thus, as though guided by an "invisible hand," produced goods in just the quantity and quality in which the consumer desired them. If the producer failed to respond in such a simple and

---

[7] Robert S. and Helen Merrill Lynd, *Middletown*, Harcourt Brace, New York, 1929, especially Section II, "Making a Home," and Table VI in the Appendix.
[8] *Historical Statistics of The United States, op. cit.*, p. 73.

direct fashion, he would fail financially. Producers who refused to respond and those who were incapable of recognizing their own best interests were eliminated from the marketplace. Thus the consumer was portrayed as being sovereign.

The theory defined a simple set of almost direct relationships between the producer and the consumer which may have been near the mark in an era when producers combined manufacture with shopkeeping and industry was on the order of handicraft. But this has not been the case for most of this century and for most commodities in the United States. Marketing as an integrative process, one which integrates the wants of consumers with the productive capabilities of producers, has developed to the point where it is an absolute essential process.

Perhaps this necessity is what has led to the development of the formal study of marketing. At least the development of the systematic study and teaching of marketing as an economic and social process dates to the early decades of this century in the United States.[9] The parallel development of the complexity of the marketing process, of the complexity of the items which compose almost any level of living, and of the study of marketing suggests such an origin.

MARKETING SCIENCE AND THE CONSUMER

During the past half century the unearthing of marketing knowledge has been closely associated with the interests of the producer. It was the producer who, at least initially, footed the bill for marketing. Both this close producer association and the theory which implied that the consumer was sovereign in a very direct and simple way have obscured the very close association which does exist between the consumer and marketing science. Since this is the case, we are apt to overlook the usefulness of marketing science to the consumer.

Today's consumer is in a position much more complicated than that in which the corporate purchasing agent finds himself. Most consumers are called on to procure a range of items which exceeds in variety that which the corporate purchasing agent is called on to purchase. But the consumer is not a specialist in purchasing. Purchasing is but one of many functions he or she is called on to perform. Consumers are mothers and fathers, husbands and wives, maintainers of houses, chauffeurs of automobiles, child psychologists, educators of offspring, earners of money income, and

[9] Theodore N. Beckman and William R. Davidson, *Marketing*, Ronald Press, New York, 1962, p. 16.

what have you. Among those many duties they are also household purchasing agents.

The consumer in his role as a purchasing agent suffers another disadvantage when compared to the corporate purchasing agent. The consumer may buy in greater variety than his corporate counterpart, but very often the individual purchase is of far greater significance than are the purchases of the corporate purchasing agent. To the consumer the purchase of an automobile may actually be a commitment of a large part of the family income. On the other hand, the corporate purchaser may buy cars for a whole fleet, replacement of which may allow for some informal corporate testing to ascertain the best buy. Certainly there does exist the possibility of error. But error may not be as disastrous as it is for the consumer who has sufficient income for only one car.

Marketing science, or the systematic study of the whole marketing process, is of value to the consumer in a very general way because he is, after all, one half the process. That is, the consumer is caught up in the marketing process in the industrial economy. He cannot avoid it. Thus it is almost essential that he know his way around.

The consumer faced with the same kinds of problems that confront the corporate purchasing agent benefits both directly and indirectly from marketing science. As a consumer purchasing agent he needs information. Part of the information he needs concerns the structure of the market itself. We have always conceded that the market process works most effectively when consumers are informed and know their way around. Part of being informed is to know the market structure, prices, and alternative sources of supply.

The market process, however, developed long before there was such a thing as marketing science. No one could argue that the entire structure of today's market is a reflection of an ideal marketing mechanism which was the product of something called marketing science. In fact, it was the prior existence of the marketing process which suggested its systematic study. To many consumers the marketing process probably presents a "blooming, buzzing, confusion," to borrow a phrase from William James. It is a part of a larger "buzzing confusion" which makes up the world in which he exists. But intelligent behavior on the part of the consumer requires that what order does exist be made known to him. This is one of the indirect benefits of marketing science to the consumer. The student of marketing science, by his studies of the marketing process, in effect provides a map by which the consumer may more effectively find his way around. This type of plodding research and fact finding may be looked on as less glamorous than other areas of study in marketing science, but its great value to the consumer should not be overlooked.

But the study of the marketing structure is of greater value to the consumer than just as a road map. The systematic study of the marketing process should result in its more effective organization. We mentioned earlier that the marketing process is one which is almost totally non-existent in a paleolithic community. Marketing is a product of technological specialization, the extent of which increases as science and technology are elaborated. Thus the marketing process becomes more extensive as technology and specialization are elaborated. Today we recognize this fact in the relative decline of manufacturing employments and the relative increase in employment in marketing and intervening processes.[10] To the extent that the systematic study of marketing leads to rationalization of an ever-growing marketing system it is of benefit to the consumer directly. It is so in two ways.

By systematic study of the marketing process needless waste may be eliminated. Systematic study is essential to this. For it is only by such study that duplication, cross haulage, and other economic wastes may be identified. This identification is preliminary to their elimination. The consumer benefits to the extent that the savings are passed on. The advantages of rationalization of the manufacturing process to the consumer have long been recognized. We have welcomed the work of industrial engineering and scientific management to the field of production. We have today, however, a problem of mass marketing, and scientific management is likely to be useful in enabling marketing to be more effective. Just as the consumer benefitted from scientific management in production, he also benefits from the introduction of scientific management to the mass marketing process.

Secondly, the consumer benefits from such rationalization of the market process through a meshing of the efforts of the producer with the wants and needs of the consumer in a way which trial and error marketing can accomplish only in a rough and ready manner. By studying the market process in detail, marketing science makes it possible to eliminate some miscalculation which leads to goods where there are no consumers and consumers without goods. Producers as well as consumers benefit from a full appreciation of the market structure. But the benefits which accrue to knowledgable producers and marketers benefit consumers as well. Devices and techniques for gauging production to a realistic assessment of genuine consumer demand are obviously of benefit to consumers as well as to the producer.

This latter argument can be carried one step further. Correct assessment of consumer expenditure is very helpful in estimating the per-

---

[10] George J. Stigler, *Trends in Employment In The Service Industries,* Princeton University Press, Princeton, for National Bureau of Economic Research, 1956.

formance of the economy in general. Consumer expenditure is much more volatile than once was conceded.[11] Because consumer expenditures, in the aggregate, are so large, minor fluctuations in this total produce significant effects on other sectors of the economy. Perhaps it would be an exaggeration to claim that when the consumer sneezes the producer catches pneumonia, as it was once claimed happened to Europe when the American economy sneezed. Nevertheless, fairly accurate assessment of consumer expectations is of help in bringing about a closer coordination of the aggregate production and consumption processes.

In recent years marketing science has been placing much emphasis on the systematic study of consumer motivation and consumer behavior. One does not need to endorse all of the ends to which this knowledge may be put by the marketer to conclude that this may be of value to the consumer. Some criticisms of motivational research from the consumer standpoint have concentrated on the potential exploitation of the consumer to which this new knowledge might lead.[12] This misses the point that this new knowledge has also been available to the consumer. Many consumers today are probably aware of the deliberative and nondeliberative elements in their behavior to a far greater extent than has been true of consumers in the past. Today consumers are conscious of the symbolic as well as the instrumental use of goods, partly because of the studies of consumer behavior made by those engaged in marketing science.[13] Certainly it cannot be argued that the present state of our knowledge of consumer behavior is wholly attributable to marketing science. But the student of marketing science has participated in a general inquiry concerning human behavior and has made very useful discoveries concerning how this is related to a specific area of behavior, that of the consumer in the marketplace.

If consumers do use goods as a means of expressing certain unconscious urges, and apparently they do, being aware of these "hidden persuaders" would seem to make them much more effective consumers. In other words, "the hidden persuaders" have been operative in consumer motivation long before the student of marketing science discovered them. It is, therefore, of help to consumers, as well as to marketers, to make these facts known. Consumers as well as marketers benefit from a clearer understanding of what "makes them tick."

So far we have been discussing general benefits which fall to the consumer from marketing science. But more direct benefits are also

[11] George Katona, *The Powerful Consumer*, McGraw-Hill, New York, 1960, Part IV.
[12] Vance Packard, *The Hidden Persuaders*, David McKay, New York, 1957.
[13] See, for example, Jane Wolff, *What Makes Women Buy?*, McGraw-Hill, New York, 1958.

realized. Product research is an area of marketing science which directly benefits the consumer. This covers research into the more effective design of established products as well as the development of new products. This assumes that such efforts are genuine and also that the results represent a genuine advance. The improvement is one which matters. The product improvement or new product meets a genuine need by the consumer and does so by solving more effectively a real problem now faced by consumers. This type of research, however, must not be of the armchair variety in which improvements are conjured in a product for a hypothetical consumer with a hypothetical need. It must be based on the needs of real consumers in the process of actual consumption.

Market surveys, an older type of market research, benefit the consumer. They do so by enabling producers to secure information concerning genuine consumer needs. As we have stressed throughout this chapter, the relationship between consumption and production is one of continuity. This has often been overlooked because of the erroneous notion that all production has a final end in consumption. Actually both production and consumption are parts of the total life process. The integrated nature of production and consumption is still apparent in those economies whose industrial arts are on a paleolithic or neolithic basis. This is also apparent in peasant agrarian cultures where the rural family is essentially both a producing and consuming unit. Anyone observing a Philippine family caught up in the rice culture complex cannot avoid wondering, as he observes the husband working in the rice fields while the wife winnows the grain for the noontime meal, just whether consumption is not for production. Actually the activities of production are conditioned by those of consumption and vice versa. The notion that a hard and fast line can be drawn between production and consumption, or that the former is for the latter which is a final and discontinuous process, is plausible only because of specialization which technological advance has caused in the industrial economy. The locus of production activity has in most cases been severed from that in which consumption takes place. Nevertheless, these are two interdependent processes which are linked in the industrial economy by the marketing process. The market survey makes possible a better integration of these two processes. The market survey which enables a more effective matching of production and consumption maintains a continuity between these two processes which would otherwise be made on a hit or miss basis.

Test marketing is also of direct benefit to the consumer. It is so in precisely the same fashion that testing of commodities before placing them in full production is of benefit to producers. No one could argue that test marketing was not of chief benefit to the producer, but the benefits are mutually shared with consumers. It is possible by test marketing to eliminate features in a good which do not clearly contribute to the effective employment of that good by the consumer. This, of course, assumes that the producer is concerned with the design of a product which does sell on its consumer merits and is not concerned with just how to get around legitimate consumer objections. In other words, test marketing may be used as a device to ascertain how effective a good is in achieving some consumer end-in-view. Weaknesses in the commodity which could not have been foreseen may be detected once goods have been placed in service. Failures in design may be tested in actual consumer use which were not in evidence in prior testing under even the best laboratory simulated consumer usage. In this way test marketing does serve the purpose of more effectively integrating production and consumption. In doing so it is of benefit to the consumer.

There is one other advantage of test marketing to the consumer. Even very useful and legitimate improvements in products may run into institutionally centered resistance. New products also run into this type of cultural resistance. Gas street lamps were originally opposed because they lacked the soft glow (less foot candle power) of the oil lamps they were replacing even though they did give more effective street lighting. In turn, gas lamps were defended against electric street lighting on the same basis. The electric lamps were alleged to possess a harshness (more foot candle power) which was offensive compared to the soft gentle glow of the gas lamp. In more recent times plastics, which have very legitimate consumer uses, ran into similar resistance. Among some individuals "plastic" is used almost as an epithet. Most technological innovation does run into some resistance and just plain cultural inertia. Test marketing may uncover this type of resistance and enable the producer to devise means for overcoming such resistance.

Consumer test panels, a common feaure of market research, are also of help to the consumer by enabling producers to design products which are satisfactory to consumer needs. In other words, test panels are one more technique by virtue of which the linkage between production and consumption may be maintained.

We have been emphasizing the usefulness of marketing science to the consumer in what is often referred to today as the "affluent society." We have emphasized throughout this chapter that the marketing process becomes increasingly important as the general level of living rises. It is both the complexity of our levels of living and the complexity of marketing which have led to the systematic study of the marketing process.

Galbraith, who is most frequently associated with the affluent society concept, maintains that in the very act of production we create the wants essential to the consumption of the output. This reverses the traditional view of the relationship between consumption and production. It leads to the notion that wants have a dependent relationship to production. To the student of marketing science this notion should not be as startling as it has been to some economists. Marketing science has always argued that one of the functions of advertising is to inform the consumer of the existence of new products and of the possibilities of new uses for old products. This is want creation in the same sense in which Galbraith argues that it takes place. Galbraith, of course, argued that advertising would not be particularly appropriate in a culture close to the subsistence level, one in which most of consumption was taken up with traditional essentials of life, food, shelter, and clothing.[14] In other words, in the first half of the last century advertising would have a very limited function compared to that it now serves.

Today, with the vast amount of commodities in the consumer's budget, one could hardly quibble with this argument for advertising. It is a means of communication from the producer by way of the marketer to the consumer. Marketing science, by its systematic study of such a form of communication, helps in the clarification of its aims, objectives, and techniques. Again, as in the case of consumer motivation, one need not endorse all the present practices in advertising to appreciate fully its usefulness to the consumer as an informative device.

As a matter of fact, we might carry Professor Galbraith's observation several steps further than he might be willing to carry it. If we separate marketing processes from production, it is wholly incorrect to state that in the act of production we create the wants which in turn justify the production. And if we assume that consumer well-being is enhanced by a general advance in the level of living, whether by goods and services privately or publicly produced, then advertising is an essential part of the process to the consumer. Certainly information does circulate informally concerning the availability of new goods to achieve some consumer end-in-view. But informative advertising is essential as a formally organized process to disseminate such information.

MARKETING SCIENCE: FUTURE USEFULNESS TO THE CONSUMER

If all these aspects of marketing science are already useful to the consumer, we may now ask what remains to be done from the consumer

---

[14] J. K. Galbraith, *The Affluent Society*, Houghton Mifflin, Boston, 1958, Ch. XI.

standpoint. Although it may sound like a contradiction of what was said earlier, much more could be done in the study of consumer behavior. If we regard marketing as a connecting link between producer and consumer, then it is in fact the handmaiden of neither. In outlook, marketing science, in contradistinction to marketing, should also be wholly unbiased in its approach. So far very much of the emphasis on the study of consumer behavior has seemingly centered on the consumer in the act of purchase. Perhaps this is only natural in view of the fact that purchasing is in a certain sense a dramatic culmination of all that has preceded and an anticipation of all which is to follow. But this emphasis is also perhaps unconsciously one which follows from the overwhelming producer interest in the act of purchase. Producers are apt to be biased by the short-run, and in the short-run it is the purchase which pays off.

But the act of purchase has the same significance to the understanding of consumer behavior that the act of balloting has to the understanding of voter behavior. To understand consumer behavior fully involves a rather intricate study of all of the relevant experience prior to the act of purchase itself and the subsequent behavior after the act of purchase when the good or service purchased fulfills the expectations, fails to do so, or has consequences not originally anticipated. In other words, we need to study consumer expectations, hopes, and aspirations and the derivation of these in the behavior and experience of consumers before the actual act of purchase. And we need studies of how, in fact, consumers use goods after the act of purchase and whether their judgments of these goods at the time of purchase were fulfilled.

To return to our reference to politics for illustration, it should be pointed out that an actual vote does not represent a permanent sentiment or attitude. Certainly some people would not be affected by the subsequent governmental performance of their choice. They have very fixed political habits. But as the periodic polls indicate, the assessment of the worth of an elected official changes almost day to day with his performance. And in the long haul, it is this performance on the job which determines our assessment of his true worth. The same thing can be said for consumer goods. Thus it would seem to be of value to study all factors which have affected an initial choice and all factors which affect the subsequent and continuing judgment of the choice. The act of consumption is not over when the pecuniary transaction has been completed.

Another area in which marketing science might increase its usefulness to the consumer is in the reduction of the process itself. We have already indicated that the proportion of the work force engaged in marketing has been on the increase. Are all of these jobs essential to the effective synchronization of production and consumption? We are prone to ignore such questions because we all too readily make the assumption that in the realm of business, in contrast with government, waste is eliminated automatically. Failure to do so would diminish profits, and businessmen are forever on the outlook for cost reducing methods. But with the large corporate organization of today, in which management and ownership have been severed, this is not of necessity a valid assumption. Marketing science could certainly do more in the way of what might be called market engineering. How can the number of individuals engaged in taking care of one consumer be reduced? The question and approach would not be dissimilar to that asked by the military on how to reduce the number of individuals essential to keeping one man on the firing line.

SUMMARY COMMENTS

In summary, we may state that marketing science in an "affluent society" is as essential to consumer well-being as it is to that of the producer. As the general level of living rises, this dependency increases. Sometimes the relationship between marketing science and the consumer is obscured by the fact that much of the immediate cost is borne by the producer. This lends credence to the notion that the end product is of primary usefulness to the producer. However, the usefulness is a shared one, and, especially in a culture with a high level of living, one which can be expected to change and increase in the future. The American level of living is highly volatile so that the consumer, who might be able to establish satisfying habitual responses to some stable level of living, is unable to do so without outside help. One of the primary sources of help is marketing science.

4

Development of Marketing Thought:
A Brief History

ROBERT BARTELS

Two theories of art appreciation are relevant to the appraisal of marketing science. One is that a work of art is complete only when every detail of it has been finished. The other is that the completeness of a work lies in its basic conception, composition, and structure, independent of the details which embellish its fundamental outline, and that completeness is a quality inherent in every stage of its development.

By what might be called a terminal appraisal, interest is centered on the *extent* of the development of thought. Its character at different stages is compared, and a continuum is conceived ranging from incomplete to more complete and, ultimately, to complete development. Marketing thought is thus seen beginning as simple inquiry and findings, progressing to the status of a discipline, and emerging as a science. Critics differ as to the stage attained, and some doubt that marketing can be a science. Thus the picture is judged in terms of preconceptions as to what the finished product should be.

The other point of view is relative rather than absolute in its appraisal of marketing thought. A stage of thought is appraised not in relation to its past or future character but in *relation* to the concurrent circumstances which bring forth that stage of thought. Completeness is defined in terms of adequacy. Thought is appraised not as an independent variable evolving of itself but as a variable dependent on other factors for its emergence, form, and character. Thus marketing thought is depicted as relative to the world of market problems and practice. Comparability of thought at different times is a function of its inherence in a changing setting.

Actually both views are important and inseparable in understanding the evolution of marketing thought. Until recently the former was predominant. This evoked consideration of such questions as whether marketing is a science, whether there are principles of marketing, and whether there are marketing theories or "schools" of marketing thought. Increasingly, the other viewpoint is being adopted. This is leading to consideration of marketing as a social phenomenon, to market behavior as social behavior, and to comparative marketing studies.

Throughout this chapter both viewpoints are explored. The evolution of marketing thought through six successive periods is described. In each, the content of thought is related to the socio-economic circumstances which impelled and formed it. On the other hand, major threads of thought are traced through several periods to facilitate interpretation of the present status of marketing thought.

THE PERIOD OF DISCOVERY

The beginnings of marketing thought might be dated at the beginning of the twentieth century, for it was between 1900 and 1910 that "marketing" was conceived or discovered and initial expression was given to ideas which became incorporated in the body of marketing thought.

Prior to 1900, market behavior and trade practice were explained mainly from the macro viewpoint, in economic theory. As the scientific study of management practice developed, attention turned from public to private economic problems, but management theory was unconcerned with distributive activity. There remained, therefore, a gap in theoretical explanation as social and economic conditions departed increasingly from the assumptions concerning the market on which existing trade theory was built. Competition no longer characterized some markets; demanders and suppliers were farther removed from each other; customary relations of demand and supply were becoming reversed; and new patterns of living were evolving. New interpretations of economic activity were needed, as were new applications of management science to distributive business. These needs nurtured the discovery of "marketing."

Marketing was a discovery only as "marketing" is recognized as an *idea* and not simply as an *activity*. Every conception is a discovery to the person who first perceives the concept. Until the *idea* was conceived to which the term "marketing" was applied, the simple *activity* had been called only "trade," "distribution," or "exchange." Thus early studies of market practice were titled "Distributive and Regulative Industries of the United States" or "The Distribution of Products." Use of the term "marketing" evidently began sometime soon after the turn of the century. It was found in university course titles in 1905 at the University of Pennsylvania, in 1909 at the University of Pittsburgh, and in 1910 at the University of Wisconsin. Among the men who taught such courses prior to 1906 were E. D. Jones, Simon Litman, George M. Fisk, W. E. Kreusi, H. S. Person, and James E. Hagerty.

Growing interest in trades and conception of a new meaning in economic distributive activity were not confined to any one locality or person, for the impelling circumstances were widespread. However, Ralph Starr Butler was probably among the first to articulate a concept of marketing. He has explained [1] that by "marketing" he meant to designate "everything that the promoter of a product has to do prior to his actual use of salesmen or of advertising." Thus from its inception "marketing" was conceptually different from mere selling and advertising, as well as from any other functions considered singly. Marketing originally—and continually—has meant a collective, integrative, or aggregative phenomenon. In more recent years this idea has been expressed anew in the concepts of "managerial marketing" and "management of the marketing mix."

With one exception, there seem to have been no notable general writings on marketing during the decade ending in 1910. Some economists [2] had been dealing with certain phases of trade in the new market circumstances, but none wrote as fully of it as did John Franklin Crowell in the *Report of the Industrial Commission on the Distribution of Farm Products*.[3] Drawn mainly from agricultural markets, his generalizations were not typical of all marketing practice. This publication, nevertheless, served as a general marketing reading until more integrative studies began to appear in the early 1920's.

Before general works on marketing began to appear, however, specialized studies were made prior to 1910 concerning advertising, credit, and selling, and a few writings appeared before then in each of these fields. By contrast, no writings before 1910 were concerned with sales management, retailing, wholesaling, or marketing research.

Interest in advertising increased around 1900 as a natural consequence of two circumstances—the need for promotional stimulus as buyers' markets began to replace sellers' markets and the application of new psychological findings to the motivation of consumers in this evolving

[1] Robert Bartels, *The Development of Marketing Thought*, Richard D. Irwin, Homewood, Ill., 1962, p. 225.
[2] See Frank G. Coolsen, *Marketing Thought in the United States in the Late Nineteenth Century*, Texas Tech Press, Lubbock, Texas, 1961.
[3] U.S. Government Printing Office, Washington, D.C., 1901.

marketing situation. Both psychologists and businessmen contributed to the advertising literature of that period, and prominent among the writers were W. D. Scott, E. E. Calkins, R. Holden, G. H. Powell, and T. A. DeWeese. Believing psychology to be the only stable foundation for a theory of advertising, Scott introduced into advertising such concepts as attention, association of ideas, suggestion, fusion, perception, apperception, illusions, and mental imagery.

The same circumstances which nurtured advertising also stimulated the development of personal selling—new products, new markets, and new forms of competition. Although both the "art" and "science" of selling were discussed, the subject was dealt with subjectively and, to a considerable extent, psychologically. Early writers who gained some lasting place among contributors to this field were P. L. Estabrook, H. E. Read, T. H. Russell, and L. D. H. Weld.

That the subject of credit should have been one developed during the earliest years of marketing thought was due less to market demands on credit than to financial demands. Marketing implications of the subject were slow to develop despite the fact that the financing of market and marketing activities through the use of credit had been increasing throughout the nineteenth century. Earliest writers on credit, therefore, such as W. A. Prendergast and T. J. Zimmerman, dealt with the economic and financial aspects of the subject, describing the effects of credit on social and economic institutions, the implications of distinctions between mercantile and bank credit, and the instruments then in common use in credit practice.

While roots of marketing thought were unmistakably planted in economic and conceptual developments prior to 1910, one could with imaginative hindsight easily attribute too much rather than too little to the intellectual achievements of writers of that period. It would be more accurate and just to say that between 1900 and 1910 thought began to be focused on market problems from the standpoints of agriculturists, psychologists, and financiers. New problems were arising in old fields of business practice, and some new concepts were introduced to illuminate thought in those fields. A general reaching out to know more of the facts of trade and markets was occurring. Out of all of this emerged one new term symbolizing a discovery of paramount importance—marketing.

THE PERIOD OF CONCEPTUALIZATION

In the second decade of this century, 1910–20, basic concepts on which the structure of marketing thought was built for the next forty or fifty years emerged and were crystalized. Advances were made both in specialized areas of marketing and in the general statement of the subject. Contributors to marketing thought during this period were some of the estimable pioneers in this realm of applied economics of business science.

This decade was one in which the economy and the society of the United States grew in many respects. It was a period of increasing urbanization and industrialization. New industries spawned new products which called for both more sales effort and for sales effort of improved quality. Industrial practices quickened social consciousness of business and provoked establishment of the Federal Trade Commission and amendment of the Sherman Act in the Clayton Act. Labor unions pressed new claims on management. Agricultural production was increasing, as were exports. Eminence was gained by both wholesale and retail establishments.

Several of these developments had direct bearing on the study of marketing and advanced it substantially. Three lines of approach to the analysis of marketing were identified—the institutional, the functional, and the commodity approaches.

Very early, interest focused on the functional character of marketing, for it was recognized that certain activities repeatedly occurred in different marketing situations. These elemental activities became known as the "elements" of marketing, which during that decade were primarily identified as selling, buying, transporting, and storing. Various authors identified additional elements, supplementing these, which were generally acknowledged. Before 1915 Arch W. Shaw associated the "motion" of distribution with the "motion" of administration, in which he included financing, credits and collections, purchasing, employment, and accounting. At the same time L. D. H. Weld listed the functions of middlemen as assembling, storing, risk bearing, financing, rearranging, selling, and transporting. By 1920 Paul T. Cherington elaborated the functional concept in a book entitled *The Elements of Marketing*.[4]

The institutional approach to marketing during this decade is identified with Weld and with Paul H. Nystrom. Weld, writing of wholesale middlemen engaged in distribution of agricultural products, saw merchants as specialists in handling commodities at successive stages in their distribution, economic specialists whose contribution was the reduction of distribution costs. Nystrom laid the foundations of the field of retailing thought in his *Retail Selling and Store Management*[5] and in *The Economics of Retailing*.[6] The former was essentially an operating

[4] Macmillan, New York, 1920.
[5] D. Appleton–Century, New York, 1913.
[6] Vols. 1 and 2, Ronald Press, New York, 1915.

manual, but it contained the structural elements on which the body of retailing thought was hung by subsequent writers. In the latter, he not only dealt with operating principles but also recounted the history of retailing and made comparisons between American and foreign retail establishments.

The commodity approach to marketing was, prior to 1920, confined largely to the marketing of agricultural products. Subsequently, more detailed attention was given both to this class of products and to manufactured goods.

Another concept which is found expressed in the marketing literature between 1910 and 1920 was that of the types of utilities supposedly created by marketing. Marketing was under fire during those years, for practical questions as to the economic contribution of marketing had not yet been answered logically. A concept of economic utility creation, common in economics treatises, was adopted by students of marketing. Time and place utilities had long been recognized as types of economic value, in contrast to form utility, and they were promptly claimed as part of marketing. To these were added another—possession utility—as a kind of general embodiment of all of the marketing activity which resulted in exchange, or the consummation of the market. These three utilities, later supplemented by some others, were key concepts in the economic rationalization of marketing at that time.

In the specialized fields of marketing, notable progress was made in the development of thought concerning advertising, credit, and selling. Psychologists continued to interpret new discoveries in terms of advertising applications. So specialized were the writings of some psychologists that the measurement of advertising appeals, memory, etc. were principal considerations, and no mention was made of marketing, economics, salesmanship, journalism, or advertising agencies.[7] On the other hand, divergent points of view were being focused on the subject, and by 1915 the subject was being interpreted not only from the psychological standpoint but also from that of the writer, the artist, and the advertising manager.[8] This transition of advertising practice from the application of mere psychological principles to the application of an integrated group of principles was a major development and even at that time was regarded as a "great change" taking place in business practice.

Advertising thought then found expression in such periodical media as *Printer's Ink, System,* and *Advertising and Selling.* Articles published

[7] H. L. Hollingworth, *Advertising and Selling*, D. Appleton–Century, New York, 1913.

[8] Harry Tipper, H. L. Hollingworth, G. B. Hotchkiss and F. A. Parsons, *Advertising: Its Principles and Practices*, Ronald Press, New York, 1915.

in such media became the basis of Paul T. Cherington's *Advertising as a Business Force*,[9] which was one of the early integrative works on the subject.

The new use which was made of advertising following 1910 proved that it was a significant force in business. As a force, however, it was one which was directed mainly toward ultimate consumers, and relatively little attention was given the use of this medium of communication in selling to industrial or business customers. Psychologists acquainted themselves with the mental processes of individuals mainly as personal buyers.

By contrast, theory concerning the force which lay in personal selling developed along two lines, retail selling and nonretail selling. Throughout ensuing years the former unfolded along lines emphasizing storekeeping, merchandising, and techniques of informing and convincing the retail customer. The latter developed along lines of application of psychological principles to personal selling and was concerned with the enlarging responsibilities of the salesman, particularly the traveling salesman.

While psychologists were uncovering new ways of tapping the mental processes of individuals which lead to purchasing, a new philosophic note was found in some writings which represented the emerging concept of marketing. Both personal and impersonal manifestations of the selling "force" were found increasingly in business, but it remained to be seen whether this force was constructive or destructive, unifying or divisive. Tradition generally held selling to be successful which resulted in a sale. The fact that the buyer had to beware of sellers' taking advantage of him for centuries was not questioned in earliest treatises on selling— either advertising or personal selling. However, between 1910 and 1920 the coincidence of interests of buyers and sellers began to be recognized and expressed. Norris A. Brisco was one who pointed out in several books [10] that the notion which long associated "trader" with "falsifier" was not necessarily descriptive of modern retailing. John Wanamaker in 1876, for example, had established a policy that his salesmen were not to importune customers to buy, thus rejecting the haggling and pressure selling which had long characterized retailing.

That attitude, however, was not universally held then. Much of the literature on selling during that period emphasized the subjectivity of selling. It was regarded as an art that did not lend itself to analysis or interpretation. Difference, rather than similarity, of interest and point

[9] Doubleday, Page, Garden City, New York, 1913.
[10] *Fundamentals of Salesmanship*, D. Appleton–Century, New York, 1916; *Retail Salesmanship*, Ronald Press, New York, 1920.

of view was emphasized, and selling was explained as the process whereby customers are induced to accept the seller's point of view. When it was recognized that selling could be taught and learned, it was also recognized that the best selling required the development in the salesman of the better human qualities, such as genuine interest in others, courtesy, intelligence, etc.

The increase of selling during the post-World War I years represented a demand for proficiency in a marketing activity and the progressive emergence of a harmony of economic interests which came to characterize marketing. It also called for a new type of management talent—the management of the selling function. Nothing that had been written of marketing up to that time really dealt with the managerial aspects of this process. Market considerations of which businessmen should be aware had been discussed, and techniques of advertising and credit administration had been presented, but the line of thought which was to develop into marketing management theory had its origin in what was written concerning the management of selling.

Several significant concepts of sales management came forth at that time. Popularity of Frederick W. Taylor's theories of management and work analysis led some businessmen to see sales management as supervisory behavior, as systematization and organization of salesmen's activities. Others regarded it as a more penetrating type of analysis and planning of selling. Opinions differed as to whether sales management was simply an advanced stage of selling talent or talent basically different from selling. Whichever it seemed to be, it was generally recognized to be a function indigenous to the evolving market circumstances of the time. Some individuals with broad perspective saw sales management in relation to the total marketing activity, even in relation to the entire business enterprise. J. George Frederick, for example, beheld the sales manager in an executive capacity, in a top-level position, contributing to the shaping of policies and responsible for carrying them out, concerned with qualities of the production and conditions in the factory.[11]

The force attributed to both selling and advertising was not during early years equally associated with credit. Credit was a phenomenon of finance, rather than of marketing, although it was employed in attaining marketing objectives. Moreover, credit as employed prior to 1920 pertained almost wholly to mercantile transactions involving credit; consumer credit was found in retail stores, but installment credit and cash lending to consumers were minimal. Consequently, credit thought of

[11] *Modern Sales Management*, D. Appleton–Century, New York, 1919.

this decade related mainly to business uses of credit. In 1913 James E. Hagerty wrote *Mercantile Credit*,[12] which typified the practical approach to the subject taken also by most other writers of the period. The concept of the "C's" of credit—Character, Capacity, and Capital—was generally accepted, and the analysis of creditworthiness in terms of them was the principal responsibility of "credit men," as credit managers were then called.

THE PERIOD OF INTEGRATION

The years between 1920 and 1930 marked the coming of age of the discipline of marketing. During that decade not only did all the branches of the subject attain a general or integrated statement, but two additional areas of specialization appeared—wholesaling and marketing research.

The integration and generalization of the subject of marketing were proclaimed as the "principles" of marketing. This term appeared in the general marketing writings of Paul W. Ivey, of Fred E. Clark, and of H. H. Maynard, Walter C. Weidler, and Theodore N. Beckman. It appeared also in writings on selling and on advertising. By "principles" was meant several things—that economic deductions concerning the market had in some measure been confirmed by empirical experience, that logical statements of cause and effect had been generalized among the concepts and classifications of marketing thought, and that marketing experience had become so definitized that rules of thumb could be postulated as guides to action. The principles of marketing set forth during that period were of all these types. They inspired a confidence in the knowledge and mastery of marketing which was to continue for many years.

The elements, the approaches, the concepts which emerged during previous years were blended during the 1920's in a macroanalysis of marketing which had some managerial implications. The operations of the marketing system or institutional structure were described, with increasing attention given to identification and definition of classes of phenomena, whether they be customers, products, channels, or establishments. Judging from the writings of Clark, Maynard, Weidler, Beckman, and Paul D. Converse, which became the "classical" statement of marketing, marketing was an economic activity. It was affected by the economic and social conditions of the market; it involved the performance of basic functions, mainly by marketing establishments, in the

[12] Henry Holt, New York, 1913.

distribution of products; it was a performance in which business managers operated in a framework of social control in the form of governmental regulation and assistance. The essence of this concept was the oft-quoted definition of marketing as "all of those activities involved in the distribution of goods from producers to consumers and in the transfer of title thereto."

Among the concepts which gained a place in marketing thought at that time were the following:

Convenience, shopping, and specialty classes of consumer products, attributed to Melvin C. Copeland but based on a classification of products as "convenience, emergency, and shopping goods" presented about 1912 by C. C. Parlin.

Buying, selling, transporting, storing, standardizing, financing, risk-bearing, and providing market information—as the "marketing functions." There were some minor variations of this list among several authorities.

Wholesaling and retailing, differentiated on the basis of purchase motive of the buyer.

Marketing channel—the course taken in transfer of title.

The inherence, pervasiveness, and universality of the marketing functions.

Such were some of the indicators of the level of thought reached in the general statement of marketing during the 1920's.

Apart from the general development of marketing thought at that time, one of the most impressive single advancements was in retailing thought, in the form of what has been called "The Retailing Series." Imbued with confidence in the potentialities of research for improving retail management, a number of New York merchants and professors at New York University produced a series of books explaining the application of the scientific method to the solution of retailing problems. Progress in both scientific management and in statistical analysis of distribution practices contributed to this development in marketing thought. Beginning in 1925 with James L. Fri's *Retail Merchandising, Planning, and Control*,[13] the series included throughout ensuing years works on such retailing subjects as buying, credit, accounting, store organization and management, merchandising, personal relations, and salesmanship. It included also a number of works on general aspects of retailing. This series was unequaled in the marketing literature for its contribution to institutional operation and management.

[13] Prentice-Hall, New York, 1925.

It was during the 1920's also that the subject of wholesaling received its first scientific analysis and description. Perceptive of both practical and theoretical differences between retailing and wholesaling, Theodore N. Beckman undertook a study of the latter which threw new light on activity which bore much of the criticism of marketing in general. Although distinctions were commonly made between wholesalers and retailers, between wholesaling and retailing, and between wholesaling and wholesalers, more precise definition of these concepts was necessary before this branch of marketing thought could be much developed. Not only these contributions were made by Beckman throughout the successive revisions of his works on wholesaling, but wholesaling itself was depicted as an institution. Its economic service was presented, and comparisons were made with the role which wholesaling played in other nations.

Many influences wrought changes in credit during the 1920's and allied the treatment of this subject more closely to marketing. Noteworthy trends occurred both in mercantile and in consumer credit. The former was affected by the use of new terms of sale, new credit instruments, and new agencies involved in the role of credit—the Federal Reserve System, credit bureaus, and new forms of credit management assistance provided by established agencies. Economic instability and economic growth of the period evoked thought concerning better collections and the use of credit in industrial distribution.

Retail credit and consumer loan credit also experienced changes which were reflected in the body of marketing thought. With the introduction of consumer durable goods and the greater use of automobiles, impetus was given to the use of installment credit, which in fact became a promotional tool. Management rules for administration of this credit were developed by credit specialists, and economic appraisal of this credit was made, mainly by E. R. A. Seligman, whose *The Economics of Installment Selling* [14] established the critical framework by which not only consumer credit but also more general aspects of marketing were judged for some years.

The true marketing character of credit, however, was not universally appreciated, and the attitude still found expression that "the merchant gives credit and gets nothing for it." Such a dark view preceded the enlightenment which was to come with a more promotional, a more marketing-oriented view of credit.

In the area of sales thought, during the 1920's perhaps the most significant trend was the reconception of salesmanship which, because

[14] Harper, New York, 1926.

of the increasing breadth given the term, led to new measures of integration of salesmen's work. The highly subjective and personal concept of selling having been superseded by objective consideration of it as a learnable technique, selling became more than the mere exchange between seller and buyer. Selling became regarded as a whole occupation requiring preparation, as for a business career. Selling included the salesman's responsibility to know pricing policies, advertising programs, distribution channels, and, above all, customer needs. Some writers saw the salesman as part of the selling team of his employer, who was responsible for coordinating his individual activity with the broader promotional program disclosed to him by the sales manager. H. K. Nixon, showing in still another manner the broadening concept of selling, spoke of it [15] as combining inspirational, psychological, economic, personal, and sociological types of activity.

With the integrative trends manifest in all other phases of marketing thought, it is understandable that those who wrote of sales management should have shared this perspective. Management of salesmen became viewed as a key role in business, for it was thought that on the success of this function depended in large measure the volume of sales of a business firm. Most important, however, was the beginning tendency to link the selling effort with the broader marketing objectives and activities of the selling organization. Excessive emphasis of specialization obscured this view, but the persistent integrative tendency of the inquiring mentality inevitably found the broader relations of selling.

Leverett S. Lyon introduced in postwar years some military concepts into sales management theory [16] and employed the term "marketing manager" to designate a type of management talent not then generally found. The term "marketing strategy" was in accord with the developments in general management theory which placed determination of business objective or end ahead of the means by which it was to be obtained. Strategy was equated with means or "instruments"; within the over-all strategy were programs or campaigns of lesser scope. The "instruments" included salesmen, advertising, credit terms, price, etc. The "ammunition" of the marketing manager consisted of the talking points that he presents through the various instruments. Perhaps even more important than these concepts, were those of Lyon's which regarded the marketing manager as operating in "the economic-social order of our time." He saw him concerned with diverse internal aspects of the business, including production and finance. He saw him in an organizational

[15] *Principles of Selling*, McGraw-Hill, New York, 1931.
[16] *Salesmen in Marketing Strategy*, Macmillan, New York, 1926.

position above sales management, consumer-oriented, and having a sense of social responsibility.

Advertising thought, too, moved to a higher sense of integration during that period, and a variety of books marked "principles" were turned out. A useful link between advertising and marketing practice was formed by Otto Kleppner in his conception of three stages in advertising a product—pioneering, competitive, retentive. Known as the "advertising spiral," this concept gave a unity to the presentation of advertising thought, a practical rallying point around which other marketing actions and decisions could be organized. Elsewhere, George B. Hotchkiss, Hugh E. Agnew, and others were refining and enlarging the technical aspects of advertising.

New to marketing thought in the 1920's was the interest which became expressed in market and marketing research. Prior to that time, scientific inquiry had been conducted with interest in findings rather than in methodology; now attention turned more to the methods and procedures of research. Urgency characterized the development of this field of knowledge at that time, not only because of the expansion of markets but because of the cyclical economic fluctuations and business postwar adjustments as well. A. W. Shaw, Paul H. Nystrom, Paul T. Cherington, and C. S. Duncan had already linked marketing with systematic and scientific research, and C. C. Parlin in the years following 1912 instituted the practice of marketing research. It was not until the 1920's, however, that more formal writings on the subject began to appear under the authorship of George J. Frederick, Percival White, J. Eigelberner, W. J. Reilly, and Virgil D. Reed.

The content of marketing research during any period has depended, mainly, on the prevailing concept of marketing and the prevailing sense of marketing problems. Prior to 1910, for example, as has already been pointed out, the predominant problems of marketing were psychological or so it seemed at that time. During the following decade, because of the growing size of distributive establishments, attention turned to internal data, and research consisted largely of analysis of operating figures such as were supplied concerning department stores by university bureaus of business research. Between 1920 and 1930 attention shifted to markets, and discoveries in the use of questionnaires supplied a new technique for analyzing markets and marketing.

From the writings which have been mentioned, one might justifiably conclude that there was a growing unity in marketing thought and literature throughout the first quarter of this century. The institutional, the functional, and the commodity studies, complemented by research techniques suited to the concept of problems inherent in each, constituted

the main body of marketing thought. So broad was the accepted understanding of marketing at that time that among the individual differences
it would have been difficult to detect dissidences, especially any which
were to have long-run significance. However, among the points of view
published then were a few which in retrospect deserve some attention.
They are found in the writings of W. D. Moriarity,[17] Percival White,[18]
Floyd L. Vaughan,[19] and Roland S. Vaile, and Peter L. Slagsvold.[20]

In general, these authors differed from the traditional or popular
statements of marketing in one or more respects. Moriarity attempted to
analyze marketing in terms of classical economic theory. Inasmuch as
the disappearance of many conditions underlying such theory had
brought forth this new body of thought, his work did not make much of
an impression. Its significance lay, however, in the fact that not everyone
saw the distributive practices or the predominant marketing problem in
the same light. Vaughan criticized the increasing cost of marketing.
White exposed some of the "abuses" of marketing as wastes of the
distributive system and proposed a system for the guidance of individual
companies. Vaile and Slagsvold were concerned with certain aspects of
price making and contrasted the forces at work in competitive agricultural markets with those in the manipulatable markets for manufactured
goods.

THE PERIOD OF DEVELOPMENT

By 1930 marketing thought had attained a substantial character, but
the changing social and economic conditions of the next decade molded
it further. Among the prominent environmental influences on marketing
thought and practice between 1930 and 1940 were the following: the
economic depression, expansion of urban population into suburban areas,
emphasis throughout the economy on savings and low price, the vocaliza-
tion of consumer attitudes known as the Consumer Movement, the trend
toward government participation in as well as regulation of business
activity, and severe forms of competition in distribution as a result of
adoption of new marketing concepts and techniques. Among the effects
of these changes during the 1930's on the distributive system were the
development of large-scale retailing, the rise of countervailing institu-

---

[17] *The Economics of Marketing and Advertising,* Harper, New York, 1923.
[18] *Scientific Marketing Management: Its Principles and Methods,* Harper, New York,
1927.
[19] *Marketing and Advertising,* Princeton University Press, Princeton, N.J., 1928.
[20] *Marketing,* Ronald Press, New York, preliminary ed., 1929.

tional powers in voluntary and cooperative associations, the alteration of traditional distribution channels, the conformation of distributive activity to new social values and controls, recognition of consumer interests as the primary objective of marketing effort, and the evolution of marketing in the solution of new types of market problems.

All these circumstances had little actual effect on the structure of marketing thought which was then beginning to gain wide acceptance. Marketing continued to be viewed as a functional management area and as a form of economic production. The Clark-Converse-Maynard type of analysis which employed the commodity-functional-institutional basis for postulating marketing principles was predominant. A measure of greater attention was given to pricing theory by Charles F. Phillips in his general work *Marketing*,[21] but few other changes were made in the manner in which marketing was conceived and explained. Maturity in this line of thought was further indicated by simplifications which began to appear in its statement. Whereas elaboration and detailing of thought characterized one line of its development, reduction of the general statement of marketing to a concise, even elementary, form also occurred. The writings of H. E. Agnew, R. B. Jenkins, and J. D. Drury,[22] and of C. W. Barker and N. Anshen [23] were of this type.

Notwithstanding the satisfaction and benefits derived from this particular concept of marketing, desire to express other views of it, to formulate new views of the problems and solutions with which marketing was concerned, continued to challenge students of this subject. Thus there continued to evolve ideas which differed from the usual exposition of marketing. As in the previous decade the contributions of Moriarity and others constituted an uncommon part of marketing thought, so in the 1930's some ideas presented by Ralph F. Breyer [24] and by H. B. Killough [25] also displayed concepts of marketing to which little heed was given at that time.

The objective of those who espoused these more or less unorthodox concepts was to portray the functioning of the marketing system "as a whole." Traditionally it had been dealt with as a separate functional area in which decisions had to have an expected consistency but which was not highly integrated either with other functional areas within a business or with other aspects of the distributive system outside the business. In this emerging concept marketing was becoming viewed as

[21] Houghton Mifflin, Boston, 1938.
[22] *Outlines of Marketing*, McGraw-Hill, New York, 1936.
[23] *Modern Marketing*, McGraw-Hill, New York, 1939.
[24] *The Marketing Institution*, McGraw-Hill, New York, 1934.
[25] *Economics of Marketing*, Harper, New York, 1933.

a process broader than mere internal programming or even than a type of economic behavior. The full import of these new ideas, however, was not then clearly apparent.

Breyer broke with the conventional concepts of marketing, functions, channels, and system. He viewed marketing as the activity involved in fulfilling certain tasks rather than as any set list of activities or functions themselves. The tasks he identified as contactual, negotiatory, storage, measurement, quality determination, packing, transportation, payment, financing, and risk-bearing. Channels were regarded not as series of stages in which distinct and separate operations occurred but as circuits through which "flows" of events take place in opposite directions—flows of merchandise, payments, information, obligations, etc. In developing his concepts Breyer drew on theory in such fields as physics, sociology, psychology, and other social sciences.

Killough's writing was less original although it, too, was atypical. Its chief merit was in its depicting in some detail the relationship between American business and its economic and geographic setting. This was not truly a conception of business in its social setting, but compared with many other expositions it was a step in that direction.

Marketing thought became considerably more quantitative during the 1930's. That is, many of the qualitative judgments which had been formed without much factual support during preceding years were validated by evidence collected in the increasing numbers of censuses and surveys. Simple opinion surveys were superseded by complex questionnaire investigations which were concerned not only with market studies but also with research of different kinds of marketing problems. Lyndon O. Brown [26] was one who during the 1930's made significant contributions both to the adaptation of scientific research methodology to market problems and to the body of knowledge to which such methods contributed.

The increased knowledge of markets had direct application to sales management, and it influenced thought in that field in several ways. It particularly produced studies of sales quotas and distribution cost analysis. Both internal and external statistics were employed in arriving at more scientific statement of management of this portion of the marketing function.

In most of the other specialized fields of marketing thought, the developmental stage of the 1930's was evidenced in their embracing the changing business practices and in their extending the dimensions of organized thought to both new depths and new breadths. In credit, changes were occurring in uses of consumer credit. Installment plans

[26] *Market Research*, Ronald Press, New York, 1937.

increased with the improvement of economic conditions. Personal loan credit was stimulated by the increased number and types of agencies providing this service, especially by the entry of commercial banks into this market. However, not only were the technical aspects of credit management explored, so also were the economic aspects, inasmuch as there were several theories relating consumer credit to economic cycles, and the social aspects, considering that ethical obligations of both creditors and debtors are involved. This represented the growing concern for customer interests which was appearing in different areas of marketing.

In advertising, new dimensions were gained in technical thought through psychological discoveries, media studies, and technological advancement. Economic analyses were made in response to interest in the relation of advertising to the depression. And social studies of advertising reflected the justifiable criticism which was made of advertising uses and abuses.

THE PERIOD OF REAPPRAISAL

The period of 1940–1950 was not a particularly fertile one for the development and expression of marketing thought. For the span of World War II, both industrial and academic activities were disrupted, and an opportunity was provided for new technologies and new lines of thought to develop. In the marketing literature, the lines of thought which were already manifest continued to find expression.

The traditional forms of marketing thought that emphasized functional and institutional concepts were projected in revisions which updated content and reinforced the type of generalizations which had come to be regarded as inherent and universal in the knowledge of marketing. Status consciousness of students of marketing was extended beyond satisfaction found in marketing principles, however, and increasing concern was felt for whether the body of marketing thought had, or could, attain the proportions and attributes of a science. Papers dealing with aspects of this question were presented as early as 1946 at meetings of the American Marketing Association.

However, concurrent with this maturation of marketing thought along one line, divergence therefrom continued to appear, both before and after the war. In 1940 a shift toward a managerial approach to the explanation of marketing was made by Ralph S. Alexander, F. M. Surface, R. F. Elder, and Wroe Alderson in their book, *Marketing*.[27] In

[27] Ginn, Boston, 1940.

neither its broad nor detailed character was the book revolutionary, but it was significant in that it extended lines of difference from the usual interpretation of marketing which were begun some years before, and it contained viewpoints which were to find fuller expression in the following decade. More attention was given by those authors to managerial marketing functions rather than merely to marketing functions. The planning of marketing, research, and budgetary control received more attention, and mere description was subordinated to a management viewpoint.

Following the war, amidst ascendent popularity of more traditional concepts, another somewhat unorthodox mold of thought was cast, entitled *Marketing, An Institutional Approach*,[28] by E. A. Duddy and D. A. Revzan. It represented not so much a managerial approach as a holistic interpretation of marketing in our economy. They undertook to explain the marketing structure as "an organic whole made up of inter-related parts, subject to growth and change and functioning in a process of distribution that is coordinated by economic and social forces." They interpreted functions as giving rise to structural organization, which is coordinated through instrumentalities of price, management, and government. Such an analysis of marketing differed from the traditional in several respects. It visualized the operation of the *whole* marketing mechanism rather than the operation of any one particular segment or establishment. It employed a conceptual framework unlike the functional-institutional-commodity analysis which had typically been made. It introduced the agency of government more as a social participant in business rather than merely as a regulator of business.

Few significant conceptual developments were made in the specialized areas of marketing thought during the 1940's, but in periodical literature and in manuscripts in preparation a number of provocative issues were being raised. Complacency with the accomplishments in marketing thought was being affronted; satisfaction with the structure, as well as with the details, of marketing thought was being shaken.

Wroe Alderson and Reavis Cox wrote in 1948:

> Students of marketing thus far have reaped from their efforts remarkably small harvests of accurate, comprehensive, and significant generalizations. Marketing literature offers its readers very few true and important "principles" or "theories". . . . Existing theories fail to satisfy students because they do not account for or

---

[28] McGraw-Hill, New York, 1947.

take into consideration all of the relevant observed facts. In essence, this is today's situation in the study of marketing.[29]

At the same time E. T. Grether was saying:

> We are surfeited with knowledge in the sense of isolated facts and narrow bands of factual interpretation. . . . In marketing, at present, there is no need for "pure" theory—that is, theory ranging so widely as to take the form of a logical framework with little or no relevance to reality. In marketing, rather we need various types of "applied theory," developed out of varied interests. . . .[30]

Other evidences of the reappraisal of marketing thought were found at that time in the writings of several people:

Jones, F. M., "A New Interpretation of Marketing Functions," *Journal of Marketing,* Vol. VII, No. 1 (January 1943), p. 256.
Bartels, Robert, "Marketing Principles," *ibid.,* Vol. IX, No. 4 (October 1944), p. 151.
Converse, P. D., "The Development of the Science of Marketing: An Exploratory Survey," *ibid.,* Vol. X, No. 3 (July 1945), pp. 14–32.
Bartels, Robert, "Marketing Theory: Its Essential Nature," *Proceedings of the Christmas Meetings of the American Marketing Association,* 1946.
Brown, Lyndon O. "Toward a Profession of Marketing," *Journal of Marketing,* Vol. XIII, No. 3 (July 1948), p. 27.
Vaile, R. S., "Towards a Theory of Marketing: A Comment," *ibid.,* Vol. XIII, No. 2 (April 1949), p. 520.
Bartels, Robert, "Can Marketing Be A Science?" *ibid.,* Vol. XV, No. 1 (January 1951), p. 319.
Bartels, Robert, "Influences on the Development of Marketing Thought," *ibid.,* Vol. XVI, No. 3 (July 1951), p. 1.
McGarry, E. D., "The Contractual Function in Marketing," *ibid.,* Vol. XIV, No. 2 (April 1951), p. 96.
Wales, Hugh G. (ed.), *Changing Perspectives in Marketing,* University of Illinois Press, Urbana, 1951.

Still another development in thought at that time was a growing historical perspective of marketing. Evidence of this is found in the following publications:

Hagerty, James E., "Experiences of Our Early Marketing Teachers," *Journal of Marketing,* Vol. I, No. 3 (July 1936), p. 20.
Maynard, H. H., "Training Teachers of Marketing and Research Workers," *ibid.,* Vol. II, No. 2 (April 1938), p. 282.

[29] "Towards a Theory of Marketing," *Journal of Marketing,* Vol. XIII, No. 4 (October 1948), p. 139.
[30] "A Theoretical Approach to the Analysis of Marketing," in *Theory in Marketing,* Reavis Cox and Wroe Alderson (eds.), Richard D. Irwin, Chicago, 1949, pp. 113, 114.

Agnew, H. E., "The History of the American Marketing Association," *ibid.*, Vol. V, No. 2 (April 1941), p. 374.

Maynard, H. H., "Marketing Courses Prior to 1910," *ibid.*, Vol. V, No. 2 (April 1941), p. 382.

Weld, L. D. H., "Early Teachers of Marketing," *ibid.*, Vol. VII, No. 4 (October 1942), p. 158.

Converse, P. D., "Fred Clark's Bibliography as of the Early 1920's," *ibid.*, Vol. X, No. 3 (July 1945), p. 54.

Litman, Simon, "The Beginnings of Teaching Marketing in American Universities," *ibid.*, Vol. XV, No. 4 (October 1950), p. 220.

Bartels, Robert, "Influences on the Development of Marketing Thought," *ibid.*, Vol. XVI, No. 3 (July 1951), p. 1.

THE PERIOD OF RECONCEPTUALIZATION

Prior to 1950 there was little to support any claim that there were different "schools" of marketing thought. Marketing thought was essentially monolithic. No one would have contended that there was a theory of marketing; neither were there identifiable *theories* of marketing, nor large groups with widely differing opinions about marketing education. Yet cleavages growing out of differing concepts of marketing and of the need for marketing thought became more pronounced. Throughout the ensuing years they grew, to produce in the study of marketing the kind of period of original conceptualizing which had characterized it fifty years earlier. It was as though marketing itself were being reconceived and new meaning assigned to an old term, and new terms were being employed to convey new ideas. In this stage of development it was difficult for a number of years to determine which direction the further development of marketing thought would take. Clues to dispel this uncertainty, however, might have been found in the trends of thought during the preceding years.

In general, a clear line of distinction was drawn between the traditional concept of marketing, with the form of thought which was based on it, and the conception of marketing in broader terms. The reconception of marketing, however, took several forms, most of which were embryonically present in earlier criticisms or presentations of marketing.

One development was the increased emphasis of managerial marketing. Whereas heretofore operational aspects of marketing had been stressed, sometimes from a functional standpoint, marketing management came to be seen not only as an area of decision making but also as a point of view in general management and as a coordinative management task above and beyond mere sales management. The concept of "marketing mix" was employed to express the fact that this was management through conscious manipulation of variables for the achievement of predetermined objectives. Leverett S. Lyon in 1926 had not only used the term "marketing management," but he had glimpsed the idea of "strategy" and "instruments" being employed for the achievement of a marketing plan. In the 1950's John A. Howard [31] interpreted marketing management as the making of decisions concerning products, channels, price, promotion, and locations. Concepts of cost allocation, marginal analysis, and recent developments from the behavioral sciences were woven into his fabric of marketing management. Others also explored and amplified the new role of marketing manager, mainly as an evolution of the sales manager position. William J. Stanton and Richard H. Buskirk [32] typified the increased emphasis given to the planning function (in contrast to the selection, training, and compensation of salesmen) and to the social responsibility of marketing managers. D. Maynard Phelps and J. Howard Westing [33] showed the increased authority given to marketing executives in manufacturing concerns for product planning, market investigation, pricing, inventory control, and production scheduling.

Still another element in marketing management was the adoption of the consumer viewpoint as the starting point of all marketing planning and administration. Something of this concept, which again employed concepts that had recurred in marketing thought in earlier years, was incorporated in the writings of Hector Lazo and Arnold Corbin.[34] Thus from the time of Arch W. Shaw's writing and teaching around 1912 until the 1960's, a greater or lesser emphasis was placed on management as a principal modification of marketing thought. After 1950 this form of marketing thought was held to be increasingly important.

Traditional marketing thought was not essentially managerial in character, although it was technical and, in the specialized literatures, inclined to the level of describing "how to do it." Yet neither was it wholly firm-oriented, for it included much description of the marketing structure and of how the market mechanism and the marketing establishments function in a general way. Notwithstanding this macroaspect of marketing thought, its generalizations were not universally regarded as a truly broad, inclusive analysis of the marketing process.

A second development in marketing thought, therefore, has been the interpretation of marketing as a broad, pervasive, interrelating process. Some people visualize it as a system of "flows," somewhat after the manner that Breyer conceived it in the 1930's. Thus emphasis is given

---

[31] *Marketing Management: Analysis and Decision*, Richard D. Irwin, Homewood, Ill., 1957.

[32] *Management of the Sales Force*, Richard D. Irwin, Homewood, Ill., 1959.

[33] *Marketing Management*, Richard D. Irwin, Homewood, Ill., 1960.

[34] *Management in Marketing*, McGraw-Hill, New York, 1961.

to the business policies and relationships that link all units in the channel, that make prices at all levels the concern of the manufacturer, or that make ultimate market conditions important to primary producers. Holism, or the viewing of marketing as a whole rather than as separately managed units in a complex process, has been the interest of several writers, particularly of David Revzan and of Wroe Alderson.

So long as the "whole" of marketing is a total *mechanism,* this viewpoint is still distinguishable from yet another that has found expression in this period of reexamination of the structure and concepts of marketing thought, namely, the social approach to marketing. The social interpretation of marketing, however, has itself been subject to varying interpretation as a result of the newness of this concept. To some, social approach to marketing means the adoption into marketing analysis of research methods devised and developed in other social sciences. To others, it represents recognition that the consumer market reflects not only economic and psychological factors but also social or cultural environmental factors. In addition to this, the social concept of marketing regards the whole marketing process not as a means by which *business* meets the needs of consumers but as a means by which *society* meets its own consumption needs. Thus from this standpoint sociological concepts of positional roles and theories of group behavior and interaction are brought to bear on the explanation of market and marketing behavior. This is one of the lesser developed new concepts, but it is introduced into marketing thought through some of the writings of Wroe Alderson.[35]

Akin to the social concept of marketing is another which in recent years has been gaining expression—comparative marketing. When marketing is seen to be a social phenomenon, rather than merely a mechanistic performance, it follows that cultural orientation accounts for differences in the marketing institution and process in different places and is the basis of interpreting it in any one place. This point of view is illustrated and interpreted in the book *Comparative Marketing: Wholesaling in Fifteen Countries.*[36]

CONCLUSIONS

The history of the development of marketing thought in the United States is, in broad perspective, an account of the thinking of men in a succession of periods to solve the market problems of their day.

Both marketing and marketing thought were altered in the change of

[35] *Marketing Behavior and Executive Action,* Richard D. Irwin, Homewood, Ill., 1957.
[36] Robert Bartels (ed.), Richard D. Irwin, Homewood, Ill., 1963.

market conditions at the beginning of the twentieth century, a change which found the economic facts of life departing farther and farther from the theories which had been devised to explain economic activity and to guide entrepreneurs and government authorities in behavior concerning the market.

The principal stimulant and determinant of evolution in marketing thought was the prevailing concept of marketing itself. From its initial conception out of earliest impressions to its more recent definition, marketing has been regarded as a simple activity, as the coordination of a group of activities, as a business process undertaken from the consumers' point of view, as an economic function of production, and as a social phenomenon. It is natural that the structure of thought evolved from such differing concepts would themselves differ.

The predominant concept of marketing throughout this period was mechanistic, whereby management of the marketing process consisted of manipulation of variables within the framework of commodity, function, and institution concepts or classifications. So widely accepted and so long-standing was this concept that it became for more than a quarter of a century the usual or traditional marketing analysis.

Such a concept, however, was not all-embracing, and unsatisfied needs gave rise to other lines of thought, identifiable as early as the 1920's. These lines reflected several important ideas: that the whole of marketing is greater than the sum of its parts, that the marketing system is the product of the society which it in turn influences, and that marketing is basically what *people* do rather than preconceived business processes.

A final observation returns to the proposition with which this discussion began, namely, that marketing thought may be viewed either as a continuum evolving toward a full exposition replete with details and implications or it may be viewed as a framework of thought, structured and complete at any time, to express the logic of the prevailing concept of marketing and to solve the problems of marketing as then conceived. The former is the view which leads to the expectation that marketing thought has or will attain the proportions of a science. The latter is the view which embraces the diversity of concepts of marketing which together constitute the unity of this body of knowledge and which express the role of marketing as an ever-changing function that is indigenous to its environment.

In the evolution of marketing thought since 1950, both the traditional and the unorthodox forms of marketing thought are melded into an inseparable whole which must at this time, and for years to come, be understood both as separate and as allied for a proper appreciation of what marketing means as a whole.

5

The Marketing Concept

ROBERT L. KING

A basic function of business management is the continuing search for, and development of, balance between the firm and its market offering and the environment in which it exists. Just as the twentieth century American economy has been dynamic, business management has adapted to changing conditions through re-evaluation of managerial orientations and actions.

The 1950's witnessed the development of such an orientation, which is popularly called "the marketing concept." Adherents readily associated themselves with the "philosophy" in impressive numbers and intensity. The concept was viewed by some critics as a panacea for corporate ills; others saw it as nothing more than a restatement of historical business truths hardly deserving the substantial attention given to it in business and trade papers.

The significance of the concept's development at this time, however, is not necessarily related to its recency or to its "all-curing powers." Rather, the concept is important because it offers evidence of business management's sensitivity to market conditions and its continuing search for better ways of approaching its market opportunities. The marketing concept should be viewed as the most recent of a series of managerial orientations which have evolved during the present century as a result of changing environmental conditions. This chapter discusses the nature and environmental bases of these orientations and concludes with a definition and model conceptualization of the marketing concept.

EVOLUTIONARY BASES OF THE MARKETING CONCEPT

Basic Managerial Orientations

Although definition and evaluation of managerial orientations are complicated by the insufficiency of a substantial tangible evidence and the basically intangible nature of such orientations, it is possible to develop such emphases for purposes of study. Addresses and papers read by businessmen before business and academic conferences, the content of articles appearing in business and trade publications, trends in corporate promotion of persons identified with specific functional areas of business to top management positions, and other related evidences provide an indication of the areas of primary managerial concern. Based on a review of selected business and academic periodicals, books and addresses, three directions of managerial orientation in twentieth century American business may be observed:

1. A production orientation, 1900–1930.
2. A sales management orientation, 1930–1950.
3. A marketing concept orientation, 1950–present.

Each of these orientations is described below.

Production Orientation in Business, 1900–1930

The period of production orientation may be summarized as an era of managerial concern with problems of capacity creation, work methods, and volume production. Names of men associated with "scientific management," such as Taylor, Emerson, and Gilbreth, are closely identified with this period. Although it is not suggested that corporate management gave no consideration during this period to the markets for which they produced, it appears that, generally, problems related to manufacturing assumed greater significance than did those related to identification and development of markets.

An example of business orientation during this period is provided by Robert J. Keith, a vice president of Pillsbury Company, who notes that during the period 1896 to 1930 the managerial philosophy of his company could have been stated as follows:

> As professional flour millers, blessed with a supply of the finest North American wheat and with excellent milling machinery, we turn out flour of the highest quality. We know our product is good because it meets our professional standards of quality. Our function is to mill high quality flour and of course, we must hire salesmen to sell it. . . .[1]

[1] Robert J. Keith, "An Interpretation of the Marketing Concept," *Advancing Marketing Efficiency*, Proceedings of the Forty-First National Conference (Chicago: American Marketing Association, 1959), pp. 105–106.

In describing the historical development of the Pillsbury Company, Keith describes this first period as "the era of manufacturing." He notes:

> It is significant that the idea for the formation of our company came from the availability of high-quality wheat and the proximity of water power—not from the availability and proximity of growing major market areas, or the demand for better, cheaper, more convenient flour products.[2]

The first new product offered by Pillsbury Company, middlings, the bran remaining after milling, was developed as a result of attempts at finding ways of disposing of this by-product, not as a result of market analysis concerned with determination of nutritional needs of cattle. According to Keith, the new product decision was production oriented, not marketing oriented.

Similarly, Anshen has described the orientation of the Bell Telephone System, until recently, as a traditional engineering-manufacturing orientation. He notes:

> Only a few years ago—certainly up to 1950—the Bell System was largely ignorant of, and insensitive to, the marketing philosophy. . . . In spite of its unparalleled construction program in the years following the end of the Second World War, the System was still unable to serve the natural demand for communication facilities. As far as most System managers were concerned, the prime problem was finding the money, . . . products, and materials necessary to furnish telephone service to those whose desire for service was realized without marketing stimulation.[3]

When attempts were made recently to implement the marketing concept into the system's operation, Anshen reports that one of the greatest difficulties to overcome was a "deeply rooted engineering orientation that appraised even the quality of customer service by engineering standards rather than user standards." [4]

Another example of continuance of a production orientation into recent years is reported by Hughes. Former President Doughty of Burroughs Adding Machine Company, who retired in 1946, served as factory

[2] *Ibid.,* p. 105.
[3] Melvin Anshen, "Introducing the Marketing Concept Through Management Development," *Advancing Marketing Efficiency,* Proceedings of the Forty-First National Conference (Chicago: American Marketing Association, 1959), p. 254.
[4] *Ibid.*

manager before assuming the presidency. His business philosophy is summarized by Hughes, as follows:

> Until he retired he was primarily interested in production. Doughty's reactions and career seemed to have been stamped in large degree by a friend and fellow mechanic named Henry Ford. If Burroughs built well enough, and sold at a low-enough price, the customers would have to buy. The building was what mattered.[5]

A few scholars of the period identified marketing problems as the area of most pressing concern, however, even when the major focus of attention was on manufacturing aspects of "scientific management." Noting that the "chaotic condition" of distribution would serve as a check on further development of production, as well as create increasing social waste, Shaw wrote:

> The most pressing problem of the businessman today . . . is systematically to study distribution, as production is being studied. . . . He must apply to his problems the methods of investigation that have proven of use in the more highly developed fields of knowledge. He must introduce the laboratory point of view.[6]

Shaw further emphasized the discrepancy which existed between the studies of the fields of production and distribution, noting that the way to company success lay in exploration and development of the latter:

> While we are only upon the threshold of the possibilities of efficiency in production, the progress thus far made has outstripped the existing system of distribution. If our producing possibilities are to be fully utilized, the problems of distribution must be solved. A market must be found for the goods potentially made available.[7]

However, most writings of the period suggest primary concern with problems of production and lend credence to Drucker's position that "fifty years ago the typical attitude of the American businessman toward marketing was still: 'The sales department will sell whatever the plant produces.' "[8]

---

[5] Lawrence M. Hughes, "Total Sales Takes Over at Burroughs," *Sales Management*, Vol. LXVII (February 15, 1952), p. 26.
[6] Arch W. Shaw, *Some Problems in Market Distribution*, Harvard University Press, Cambridge, Mass., 1915, p. 44.
[7] *Ibid.*, p. 43.
[8] Peter F. Drucker, *The Practice of Management*, Harper, New York, 1954, p. 38.

The Sales Management Emphasis, 1930–1950

Shaw described the period of production orientation as an era during which the manufacturer was in no sense a merchant; rather he deplored the distribution system of the day which failed to acknowledge and appreciate the relationship of the consumer to continued success of the firm. As early as 1912 he proclaimed the systematic study of distribution to be the most pressing problem of the businessman. A review of the literature of the following decades indicates that the point of view expressed by Shaw gained widespread acceptance. The change in direction and emphasis of managerial thinking was summarized by Borsodi, as follows:

> The day is gone when the recipe for fabulous profit was simply "production; more production; still more production!"
> The golden age of production is past.
> The age of distribution is upon us.[9]

Similarly, Reed wrote of the shifting of emphasis to the marketing area:

> Only a few years ago industry was necessarily production-minded. Today it has to become market-minded. Production has so far outdistanced marketing that there is no longer a problem of increasing production but one of profitably disposing of the capacity available.[10]

Interesting summaries of company operation during the period of sales management orientation are provided in the literature in statements by company officials regarding their own firms. Two such statements are presented below. The operating philosophy of Pillsbury Company during the sales management era has been described by Keith, as follows:

> As a flour milling company, manufacturing a number of products for the consumer market, we must have a first-rate sales organization which can dispose of all the products we can make at a favorable price. To accomplish this objective, our sales force must be backed up by consumer advertising and market intelligence. Our salesmen should have all the tools they need for moving the output of our plants to the consumer.[11]

Conflict and lack of coordinated effort existing among the operating divisions of Chain Belt Company is emphasized by President Lynn B. McKnight, as follows:

[9] Ralph Borsodi, *The Distribution Age*, D. Appleton, New York, 1929, p. 3.
[10] Vergil D. Reed, *Planned Marketing*, Ronald Press, New York, 1929, p. 3.
[11] Keith, *op. cit.*, p. 106.

Time was . . . when inventory was the worry of the Production Department. And since Production seemed to know better than Sales what could be sold, there was usually some maneuvering behind the scenes. Why? Because the Production Department had to take the blame if inventories went too high, knowing, at the same time, that the finger would undoubtedly be pointed at the Sales Department if business were adversely affected because of low inventory. In other words, why not play it a little safe? There always seemed to be a tendency to shy away from sizable inventories when —in the opinion of the Production Department—we were accumulating more items than our Sales Department could sell.[12]

The period of sales management emphasis may be summarized as an era during which problems of distribution assumed special significance in American industry. The position of the sales manager was strengthened, although during this period the definition of his task was subject to considerable revision, generally resulting in the assignment of broader responsibilities. The measure of the sales manager's effectiveness, and the basis of his own remuneration, most frequently appears to have been the level of sales volume which his actions generated. Although profit was not ignored, the sales manager had little, if any, direct profit responsibility. The assumption that higher sales volumes lead to higher profits was widely accepted. Also, there is evidence that conflict and lack of coordination existed among the several operating divisions, and also among the marketing areas. The former may be explained in part on the basis of the supposed threat presented by the sales department to the traditionally superior position of the production department. The latter is due in part to the emphasis placed on the sales force's role in the absence of an appreciation of the other areas' contributions to over-all marketing effort. The most significant developments of the period probably were recognition of the importance of marketing problems and the initiation of widespread use of marketing research to aid the sales department in its efforts.

Emphasis on the Marketing Concept, 1950–present

The period of marketing concept orientation was ushered in amidst considerable publicity in business publications in the early 1950's. Most of these articles, however, appeared in publications which had readership primarily among marketing management, and the concept generally was

[12] Lynn B. McKnight, "Keeping Production Lines Open," *Broadening the Sales Department's Role*, Marketing Series No. 94, American Management Association, New York, 1955, p. 5.

described in terms of its implications for marketing personnel. Typically, authors differentiated the concept from the production and sales management orientations in terms of marketing management's concern with profits and return on investment, not sales volume alone. Also, customer awareness and concern, referred to as "consumer orientation," were discussed frequently. By the mid-1950's, management members of numerous firms made public statements, in articles and in addresses, regarding their firms' "acceptance" and "implementation" of the marketing concept. It appears that implementation, in the majority of cases, referred to reorganization of the several marketing activities resulting in the establishment of formal marketing departments, consisting of centralized marketing staffs, and headed by a vice-president in charge of marketing, or a marketing director. Consequently, the chief marketing officer became a "planner," and the sales manager became a "doer."

The shift in managerial thinking from a sales management to a marketing concept orientation, described by Phelps as a shift from a *caveat emptor* to a *caveat vendor* system, has been acknowledged by numerous businessmen. Distinction between the two approaches to business problems has been described by Fred J. Borch, Vice-President of Marketing Services, General Electric Company, as follows:

> . . . the sales concept alone concerns itself primarily with volume. Marketing means customer orientation—a true alliance with the fellow at the other end of the pipeline, but it insists upon a course of action of mutual benefit.[13]

In comparing the two emphases, McKay stresses the role of marketing in over-all company planning under the marketing concept:

> Under the traditional "sales" concept, engineering designed a product, manufacturing produced it—and then the sales people were expected to sell it. Under the modern "marketing" concept, the whole business process starts with marketing research and sales forecasting to provide a sound, factual, customer-oriented basis for planning all business operations, and the business function which has sales responsibility now participates in all the stages of the business planning process.[14]

[13] Fred J. Borch, *The Marketing Philosophy As a Way of Business Life,* General Electric, New York, 1957.
[14] Edward S. McKay, "The Marketing Concept in General Electric," an unpublished paper dated September 30, 1958.

Of the several companies reporting interest in the marketing concept in the early 1950's, most attention in the literature has been given to the impact of the concept's acceptance by General Electric Company management. By 1950 its management had recognized the need for strengthening marketing procedures and pooling marketing experience, and marketing management positions were established throughout units of the decentralized organization. Further, a Marketing Services facility was established and a Vice-President of Marketing Policy was appointed. McKay has noted:

> The marketing concept was developed as an integral part of a broad Company organization and management program. Top management recognized, more than ten years ago, that the tremendous growth opportunities—in the American economy over-all and specifically in the electrical industry—called for an entirely new approach to long-range planning, organization structure, managerial competence, and personnel development. This program included: decentralization of product businesses into autonomous Operations; provision of technically competent functional services (including one in marketing) to do advanced research, teaching, and counseling; development of a more professional approach to managing; and a marketing concept which would orient each Operation and the Company to the consumer.[15]

In the Annual Report for 1952, President Cordiner, referring to the Company's new emphasis on marketing, noted that the marketing concept:

> . . . introduces the marketing man at the beginning rather than the end of the production cycle and would integrate marketing into each phase of the business. Thus marketing, through its studies and research, will establish for the engineer, the designer and the manufacturing man what the customer wants in a given product, what price he is willing to pay, and where and when it will be wanted. Marketing would have authority in product planning, production scheduling and inventory control, as well as in the sales, distribution and servicing of the product.[16]

Each of the more than 100 product departments of General Electric Company had a marketing section headed by a marketing manager.

---

[15] *Ibid.*
[16] General Electric Company Annual Report, 1952.

The impact of the decision by General Electric Company's management to accept and implement the marketing concept, and of the publicity given to that decision, extended rapidly far beyond the limits of the company. Almost immediately executives of other leading companies acknowledged acceptance of this business orientation. Wide publicity has been given to the resulting programs of General Foods Corporation, Kraft Foods Company, Campbell Soup Company, Motorola, Inc., Westinghouse Electric Corporation, Bulldog Electric Products Company, American Telephone and Telegraph Company, and others. The names of several hundred firms have been associated in the literature with the marketing concept, for the most part since 1954.

The operating philosophies of the Pillsbury Company during the eras of production and sales orientation have been described previously. Keith has described the Company's present view of marketing's role as follows:

> Marketing is viewed in our company today as the function which plans and executes the sale—all the way from the inception of the idea, through its development and execution, to the sale to the customer. Marketing begins and ends with the consumer. The idea for a new product is conceived after careful study of her wants and needs, her likes and dislikes. With the idea in hand, the marketing department functions as a universal joint in the corporation, marshalling all the forces of the corporation to translate the idea into product and the product into sales.[17]

In summary Keith notes that Pillsbury Company emphasis has shifted from production to marketing problems, from the product that could be made to the product that consumers wanted made, and from the company itself to the marketplace.

Perhaps the expanded definition of marketing which had developed by the 1950's is best summarized by McKay, who suggests that marketing is

1. a philosophy of consumer orientation
2. a method of managing by objectives
3. a system of commercial intelligence
4. a road to dynamic business strategy
5. an orderly process of business planning
6. an emphasis on innovation
7. a modern form of organization
8. an approaching profession

[17] Keith, *op. cit.*, p. 107.

9. an essential for performance evaluation
10. a focus on future opportunities [18]

SOME FACTORS AFFECTING EVOLUTION OF THE MARKETING CONCEPT

In the preceding pages it is noted that during the present century managerial orientation in American business has undergone significant revision, resulting in emphasis on different aspects of business at different times. It is proposed by this writer, first, that shifting business emphases and orientations are a natural phenomenon in a dynamic economy; second, that development of the marketing concept and the timing of that development are reasonable, given the dynamic nature of the economy; and third, that factors in the contemporary economy which were instrumental in development of the marketing concept still direct managerial attention to the area of marketing activity and probably shall continue to do so in the years immediately ahead.

Half a century ago Shaw recognized that economic conditions prevalent in eighteenth century England were directly responsible for the emphasis which was placed on mass production and which was responsible in part for the development of the factory system. Noting that the explanations for the changes which occurred, as well as the reasons why distribution was not regarded as a problem area worthy of study, are to be found in the study of economic history, Shaw wrote:

> Chief among the causes for the industrial changes leading to the establishment of the factory system in England in the Eighteenth Century was the constant widening of the market. It was a rapidly increasing pressure on the producer for greater quantities of staple articles for mass consumption that gave incentive to revolution in the method of production. For a century thereafter the necessity of supply a continually widening market, as means of transportation steadily improved and the population increased with unprecedented rapidity, made production the dominant problem.[19]

Similarly, Marshall recognized that knowledge of marketing was far less advanced than knowledge of production in 1921. Again the difference is

[18] Edward S. McKay, "The New Responsibilities of Marketing," lecture at Graduate School of Business Administration, New York University (January 9, 1958).
[19] Shaw, *op. cit.*, p. 42.

explained in terms of the economic situation of the time. Regarding this disparity he wrote:

> The reason is simple and plain. We have behind us more than one hundred years of study of production problems during a time when the market was ever yawning for more output. . . . Marketing problems, on the contrary, have become pressing only in the last generation or two. . . .[20]

It is reasonable that as factories were established and the more basic needs of the population were filled, emphasis should shift from the original problems of engineering and production to those of selling, that is, "moving the goods out of the factories." Several advocates of the marketing concept have suggested that the sales manager of the selling era was "a pusher" or "a good drummer" who worked for volume sales. Viewed within the historical framework, such comments need not be interpreted as disparagements. Indeed, for a number of years, it is probable that profits of firms were maximized through such efforts rather than through concern with the various physical manifestations associated with the marketing concept. That is, given the nature of prevailing competition and consumer demand, it is possible that during an intermediate period profits and return on investment would not have been enhanced by managerial emphasis on certain specialized marketing functions.

However, the economic system is dynamic. Actions of competitors, such as changes in product lines, and price structures, and changes in consumers' situations, including the stock of goods already accumulated and their desire and ability to consume more, require adjustments within the firm. Such changes have occurred in recent years, and they have been vast changes of considerable consequence to the firm. It is becoming increasingly evident to business management that the sales orientation is no longer acceptable, for the conditions within which it yielded reasonably satisfactory results are no longer present. It is for this reason that Doscher wrote:

> Today's emphasis on the total marketing concept is simply another step in the evolution of American industry under our competitive system in which, to survive, we must continually look to improved organization, the adoption of new techniques and principles, and the more effective orientation of brainpower to the ever growing complexities of modern industry.[21]

[20] Leon Carroll Marshall, *Business Administration*, The University of Chicago Press, Chicago, 1921, p. 308.
[21] Fen K. Doscher, "The Vice-President for Marketing: What Kind of Man Must

Prerequisite to full appreciation of the marketing concept is recognition of various forces which constitute the environment within which the firm must operate. Although the impracticability of enumerating and discussing all components of such a system of forces is recognized, a brief description of several of the most significant environmental bases of the marketing concept is presented below so as to provide a framework for interpretation of the concept. The areas discussed are, respectively, general economic, competitive, firm, and consumer factors.

General Economic Factors

Although discussions of the marketing concept are generally concerned with firm, competitive, and market forces, it should be recognized that several general trends in the economy have had a direct bearing on evolution of the concept. The following are among the most significant of these forces.

First, a gap has developed between the ability of firms to produce quantities of goods and their ability to dispose of such quantities profitably. This situation may be explained in terms of historical deference shown to production problems, of expansion of production capacity in certain industries for war production, or of the shifting of consumer demand from one industry to another, for example. Some critics interpret this development to be indicative of business' need for "educating" people to consume more goods and services; others suggest that basic changes in managerial thinking are required.

Second, since the end of World War II the shift from a sellers' market to a buyers' market has occurred. The traditional production orientation and even the aggressiveness of the hard-sell orientation have proved to be insufficient for operation in the contemporary business climate.

Third, management generally is tending toward professionalism. The trend toward a more professional approach to the study and practice of business administration is emphasized by growing memberships of "professional" business associations, the nature of the content of these associations' publications, managerial concern with corporate philosophies, the curricula content of professional schools of business, and so on.

Fourth, there is an evident trend toward systematic management, based on analysis of corporate goals and procedures, and even of the bases of corporate existence. Emphasis is placed on rational action based on facts, thereby reducing risks which arise from lack of information.

He Be?," *The Marketing Concept: Its Meaning To Management*, American Management Association, New York, 1957, p. 23.

Substantial corporate research expenditure levels and concern with planning and internal communication are partial evidence of this trend.

Fifth, widespread attention currently is given to the role of marketing in supporting a high level of employment, economic growth and stability, and optimum utilization of national resources generally. It is to be expected that, as marketing's share of the total labor force continues to increase, this sentiment will gain even wider acceptance.

Sixth, it is occasionally suggested that in this age of ideological conflict, to a considerable degree, preservation of the capitalistic system is dependent on marketing's effectiveness in providing for fulfillment of wants and needs of the people and on its contribution to higher levels of employment.

Competitive Factors

Probably of more immediate concern to most company managements, however, are problems related to competition with other firms in the marketplace. The following are among the most significant competitive forces leading to development of the marketing concept.

First, the marketer today faces consumers who have attained a relatively high level of living. For the most part, the necessities of life have been met; yet discretionary spending power continues to rise. As a result, the marketer is faced with competition not only from other firms in his industry but from firms in other industries as well. For example, the marketer of boating equipment competes with the marketer of tours through Europe, as well as with other boating manufacturers.

Second, narrowed profit margins have stressed the significance of maximum return on all company investments. As a result, more effective methods and better controls are required in marketing management.

Third, during this period of narrow profit margins, the contributions to companies' profits made by new products become most evident. Frequently marketing managers describe new products as the basis of company survival, growth, and stability.

Fourth, the practice of planned obsolescence, common in many industries, is conducive to rapidity of new product appearance and, consequently, to the destruction of existing markets. Thus additional emphasis is placed on new product development.

Fifth, problems such as the extensive period of time required in development of new products, as well as the consequent failure in the market of many of these products, indicate the need for more effective product planning and research.

Firm Factors

Of the several areas of factors related to development of the marketing concept, the one most frequently mentioned by business management is "firm" factors. Similarly, management's reports of implementation of the concept typically indicate concern with organizational structures, titles and positions, and job descriptions. The following are among the most significant firm factors related to development of the concept.

First, during recent years many firms have undergone periods of rapid growth, based in part on natural growth in an expanding economy and further on extensive programs of company mergers. The current merger movement appears to be directed primarily toward enhancement of market position and creation of a broad business base, providing for greater profit stability. Earlier merger movements are typically described in terms of managements' efforts toward capital accumulation and financial strength.

Second, as firms have grown larger, managements have discovered that their traditional organization structures frequently impede, rather than facilitate, effective operation. Many managements have developed highly decentralized organizations in their efforts toward equating organization structure and company needs.

Third, nevertheless, it appears that the problems of ineffective internal communications and lack of coordinated effort and unified direction have not yet been resolved in many company situations. The tendency toward uncoordinated operation reported among traditional sales and production managements as well as among the several marketing forces, support this statement.

Fourth, the merger trend previously mentioned, with its resulting widening of firms' product lines, tends to complicate problems of coordination and direction further. However, growth and stability resulting from such broader bases of operation support the desirability of the merger trend.

Fifth, increased automation of firms' production and marketing operations has generated new problems also. Usually accompanying automation is the ability to manufacture a larger quantity of goods; yet the firms' selling efforts meet greater consumer resistance in the marketplace.

Sixth, narrowing of profit margins and increased ability to produce goods in large volumes emphasize firms' need for "guaranteed annual customers." Typically the capital investment involved in automation requires a high rate of utilization if profit potentials are to be realized.

Seventh, increased company investment in costly fixed equipment determines at least the general nature of firms' outputs for a considerable future period. Such investments tend to restrict the freedom of management to react to changing competitive and market conditions.

Eighth, for these reasons and others, business management is becoming increasingly aware of the need for planning for future profitability. Also they are aware of their increased ability to do such planning, given more accurate and more complete information from broader bases, more highly developed, marketing research activities.

Consumer Factors

Attention given by business management to the role of the consumer appears to have expanded in accordance with the latter's ability and desire to expand beyond his traditional consumption patterns. Certainly the development of a buyers' market at a time when firms actively seek stability of operation emphasizes the consumer's crucial role. Some consumer factors which have been instrumental in development of the marketing concept are presented below.

First, in general, consumers have satisfied the basic necessities of life and are able to maintain a high level of consumption. One result of such consumption has been the accumulation of vast stocks of goods by households.

Second, although such stocks have been accumulated, households today are financially able to expand their consumption significantly, due to their rising discretionary spending power.

Third, however, as most households have satisfied their more basic needs, they are now able to postpone or cancel specific purchase decisions and actions at their discretion. The significance of the stock of goods already owned and the probable diminishing utility of other goods which might be added to this stock are being recognized by business management.

Fourth, consumers are acquainted with a greater number and variety of goods, due in part to higher levels of educational attainment and improved transportation and communication facilities. As a result, increased travel and greater exposure to national advertising media and international markets increase consumer sophistication and further frustrate the businessman's search for profitable growth and stability.

Fifth, business management indicates growing concern regarding its problem of communication with the marketplace. Historical concern appears to have been with the flow of information from manufacturer to consumer. Today the situation frequently described as ideal by businessmen is a consumer-market-designer-manufacturer system of communication which stresses the multidirectional flow of information at each of these unit levels.

DEFINITION OF "THE MARKETING CONCEPT"

Discussions of "the marketing concept" by businessmen and business academicians generally have centered on two of its elements, consumer orientation and organizational structuring. Relatively little attention has been given to its other elements, such as the role of marketing intelligence, formal long-range planning, and the significance of the new-product function. This emphasis, combined with the absence of a generally accepted definition of the concept, has led to frequent semantic arguments and misunderstanding of the broader nature of the concept.

As employed in this chapter, "the marketing concept" is defined as a managerial philosophy concerned with the mobilization, utilization, and control of total corporate effort for the purpose of helping consumers solve selected problems in ways compatible with planned enhancement of the profit position of the firm. More specifically, the marketing concept involves:

1. companywide managerial awareness and appreciation of the consumer's role as it is related to the firm's existence, growth, and stability. As Drucker has noted, business enterprise is an organ of society; thus its basic purpose lies outside the business itself. And the valid definition of business purpose is the creation of customers.

2. active companywide managerial awareness of and concern with interdepartmental implications of decisions and actions of an individual department. That is, the firm is viewed as a network of forces focused on meeting defined consumer needs and comprising a system within which actions taken in one department or area frequently result in significant repercussions in other areas of the firm. Also, it is recognized that such actions may affect the company's equilibrium with its external environment, for example, its consumers, its competitors, etc.

3. active companywide managerial concern with innovation of products and services designed to solve selected consumer problems.

4. general managerial concern with the effect of new-product and service introduction of the firm's profit position, both present and future, and recognition of the potential rewards which may accrue from new product planning, including profits and profit stability.

5. general managerial appreciation of the role of marketing intelligence and other fact finding and reporting units within, and adjacent to,

the firm in translating the general statements presented above into detailed statements of profitable market potentials, targets, and action. Implicit in this statement is not only an expansion of the traditional function and scope of formal marketing research but also assimilation of other sources of marketing data, such as the firm's distribution system and its advertising agency counsel, into a potent marketing intelligence service.

6. companywide managerial effort, based on participation and interaction of company officers, in establishing corporate and departmental objectives, which are understood by, and acceptable to, these officers, and which are consistent with enhancement of the firm's profit position.

7. formal short- and long-range planning of corporate goals, strategies, and tactics, resulting in defined and coordinated effort of the firm's functional areas.

8. creation, expansion, termination, or restructuring of any corporate functions as deemed necessary in mobilizing, utilizing, and controlling total corporate effort toward the solution of selected consumer problems in ways compatible with enhancement of the firm's profit position.

A MODEL OF THE MARKETING CONCEPT

Introduction

Based on the preceding definition of the marketing concept, it is possible to demonstrate schematically the significance and relationship of the concept to business management. In relating the concept to managerial action and behavior, three hypothetical situations are discussed in terms of the model presented in Figure 5.1. These situations are, respectively,

1. The firm which operates under conditions of market-product offering balance.
2. The firm which discovers that modification of the market offering, within the bounds of existing corporate policy, appears desirable.
3. The firm which discovers that market conditions necessitate major modification of corporate policy and market offerings.

The model illustrates the relationship of the firm in the marketplace, the conscious sensitivity of corporate management to imbalance between market offering and market demand, and the mechanism through which balance is regained by management. Essential features of the model are the "sensitivity monitor" and the bases of "managerial action," to which reference shall be made in the following pages. The "sensitivity monitor"

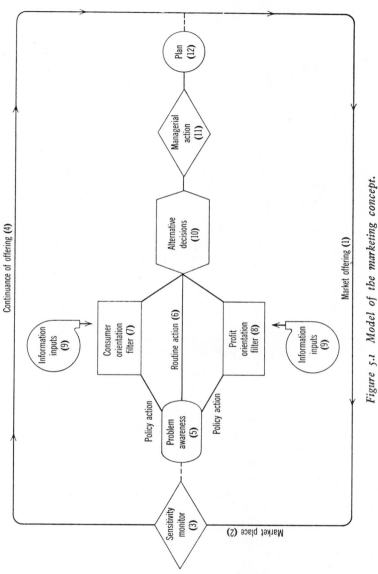

Figure 5.1 Model of the marketing concept.

represents the firm's total, integrated marketing intelligence force, including company units and external agencies. Included, for example, are
marketing and logistics research, which are engaged in the collection of
market information and the interpretation of this data into market
intelligence. A broader area than traditional marketing research is im-

plied, with its focus directed toward the market offering-market demand balance. "Managerial action" refers to corporate management's selection from a number of alternative decisions a course of action consistent with the firm's dual objectives implicit in the definition of "the marketing concept." For convenience of the reader, each component of the model has been numbered, and in the following discussion, mention of components is accompanied by the appropriate identifying number.

Operation Under Conditions of Balance—Situation 1

In the first situation, it is assumed that the firm's market offering (1) is found to be in balance with demands of the marketplace (2) that is, the market offering is found to be compatible with the dual objectives of the firm: satisfaction of selected consumer problems in ways profitable to the firm. This determination is based on comparison of company plans and estimates (12), on which this market offering was predicted, with acceptance of the market offering in the marketplace, as observed by the market sensitivity monitor (3). Further, it is assumed that conditions in the marketplace, that is, consumer, competitive, industry, and economic factors, do not indicate the desirability of changes in the market offering. That is, the sensitivity monitor detects no present or approaching imbalance of market offering and marketplace demand which would make adjustment necessary.

While this balance between market offering and market demand exists, the firm continues "normal" operations (4). Plans have been constructed by management, and these plans are carried out. The sensitivity monitor confirms the validity of these plans and remains as a sentinel, watchful for the appearance of any element in the marketplace which threatens the situation of balance. Accordingly, the course of action is described in the model by the outer ring circuit: market offering—marketplace—sensitivity monitor—continuance of offering, etc. (1-2-3-4, etc.).

This situation, which illustrates an equilibrium position, is of value primarily in that it affords a framework within which change may be studied. The element of change, or recognition of and reaction to imbalance, is injected into the model in the two following situations. However, the equilibrium situation also serves to illustrate the basic nature of the marketing concept, involving

1. companywide managerial involvement in creating a market offering which solves consumers' problems in ways compatible with consumers' desires and enhancement of the firm's profit position.
2. continuing sensitivity, involving recognition and reaction, to changes

in marketplace conditions which indicate existing or approaching imbalance in the market offering-marketplace demand relationship.

Recognized Need for Minor Adjustment—Situation 2

In the situation just described it was assumed that balance existed between market offering and marketplace demand and that such balance was continually monitored by the sensitivity monitor. As long as no discord was detected by the monitor, the firm continued its market offering.

In the present situation, however, it is assumed that discord is detected by the sensitivity monitor (3). Automatically, the monitor feeds back this information to company management, resulting in problem awareness (5). It is further assumed that the problem, so reported, is of such nature that it can be resolved within the structure of existing corporate policy. That is, the problem indicates the need for "routine" managerial action (6). Examples of such problems are the need for minor changes in production requirements, marginal increases in promotional efforts in certain markets, and minor adjustments in discount structures. Because none of these problems involves major policy action by management, alternative decisions (10) are formulated. Consistent with conditions of the marketing concept, action (11) is taken, resulting in a revised plan (12) of market action. Thus a modified market offering (1) is made in the marketplace (2). Assuming that the modified offering is consistent with marketplace demand, as observed by the sensitivity monitor (3), this offering is continued (4). However, should the modified offering (1) be found by the monitor (3) to be inconsistent with marketplace demand (2), the monitor feeds back this information to management in the form of problem awareness (5), and additional managerial attempts at adjustment are made.

Again, the sensitivity monitor and managerial action indicate the crucial points in implementing the marketing concept. That is, management immediately is made aware of problem areas, and based on the marketing concept philosophy, management attempts to regain balance, leading to consumer satisfaction and corporate profit.

Recognized Need for Major Adjustment—Situation 3

In situation 2 the sensitivity monitor detected a market offering-marketplace demand imbalance, leading to problem awareness and ultimately to corrective action in the form of a modified market offering. The problem was resolved within the framework of existing corporate policy. The present situation describes corrective action involving a problem which necessitates major policy action by management.

It is assumed that the sensitivity monitor (3) discovers that the firm's market offering (1) is out of balance with marketplace demand. The automatic feedback informs management of the imbalance (5). Unlike situation 2, however, it is discovered that corrective action involves reconsideration of basic corporate policy. For example, it may be discovered that major additions to the firm's product line appear desirable; however, such action involves expansion of production capacity and substantial money outlay. Such a problem is resolved not by "routine action" but through managerial evaluation of corporate policy, based on recognition of the dual objectives of the firm. Therefore consideration of such problem areas follows a pattern different from that described in situation 2.

Accordingly, due to management's keen awareness of the seriousness of the existing imbalance, policy decision considerations are subjected to a consumer orientation filter (7) and a profit orientation filter (8), each of which is supported by information inputs (9). Basically, the filtering process involves the conscious and exhaustive consideration of policy decisions in terms of the firm's dual objectives, which previously were summarized in terms of consumer and profit orientations. Such deliberation involves companywide managerial participation, for it is recognized that although there is a tendency to associate problems with specific functional areas of the firm, "marketing problems" often have significant and direct implications for financial and production management and vice versa. Further, it is probable that major policy decisions, once established, tend to commit the firm's resources to a rather specific course of action for a considerable period of time. Hence management places special emphasis on such decisions and relies heavily on the information inputs which supply necessary specific data related to conditions in such areas as the consumer and financial markets. These information inputs are derived from specialized internal data-collecting agencies, such as marketing research, from knowledge which accrues to individual managers and their staffs in the normal course of business activity, and from information accruing to external sources on which the firm draws, such as advertising agencies and financial institutions.

Based on managerial concern with the firm's dual objectives, and supported by facts, alternative decisions (10) are defined. Managerial action (11), consistent with attainment of these objectives, leads to selection of a course of action and the construction of plans (12) which will facilitate implementation of the selected course of action. Consequently, a revised market offering (1) is made in the marketplace (2), and the sensitivity monitor continues its search for evidence of present or impending imbalance. Assuming that the revised market offering is compatible with marketplace demand, and that the monitor evidences correction of the imbalance, the revised market offering is compatible with marketplace demand, and that the monitor evidences correction of the imbalance, the revised offering is continued (4). Should the monitor discover continuing imbalance, such information is relayed to management, and reconsideration of the problem results (5).

Summary Comments Concerning the Model

The following comments are presented as applicable to the three situations just discussed and as vital to understanding of the marketing concept model.

1. The distinguishing and crucial features of the model are the sensitivity monitor and the bases of managerial action. The functioning of the former is of relatively little consequence if companywide management lacks comprehension of the marketing concept. Fulfillment of the dual objectives of the firm requires general management involvement, based on such comprehension, in mobilizing, utilizing, and controlling total corporate effort. Therefore close coordination of purpose between these two features is necessary for effective functioning of either.

2. The sensitivity monitor represents activity basically different from that of "traditional" marketing research, that is, feeding back sales, profit, and inventory data. Rather, it implies a continuing acute awareness of developments in consumer, competitive, industry, and general economic areas, in so far as such developments are related to the firm's market offering-marketplace demand balance.

3. As the sensitivity monitor is involved in over-all corporate intelligence services, its functions extend beyond reporting "trouble" areas. That is, the monitor is sensitive to existing and potential opportunity as well as to existing or potential difficulty. Therefore it is concerned also with such areas as development of new markets and product innovation.

IMPLEMENTATION OF THE MARKETING CONCEPT

As the preceding pages indicated, businessmen have given the marketing concept numerous and widely divergent interpretations. Consequently, it is improbable that one could compile a list of firms which have implemented the concept in each of its details as provided in the definition in this chapter. Many firms, however, have apparently accepted a number of its elements, which include the following: consumer orientation, organizational aspects, marketing planning, product planning, profit planning and control, and the role of marketing research. A number of relevant managerial pronouncements originating in firms in which the marketing concept allegedly has been implemented are presented below as evidence of thought and action as affected by adoption of the concept.

Consumer Orientation

Pillsbury Company:

> . . . I see my company, and American business in general, in the midst of a . . . Revolution—a complete reorientation of thought and point of view. No longer is the company at the center of the business universe; today the customer is at the center. . . . Today our attention has moved from problems of production to problems of sales; from the product we can make to the product the customer wants us to make; from the company itself to the marketplace it serves.[22]

Westinghouse Electric Corporation:

> For too long we have regarded the customer primarily in terms of our needs to influence him favorably toward our products. Our marketing concept requires that we recognize him as an important source of information on needs and desires—with this information serving as the basis of planning and controlling our entire business operation.[23]

Bulldog Electric Company:

> The customer and his requirements provide the dynamic force that dictates how we will market our goods. . . . The marketer is the logical one to provide all the essential data concerning the marketability of a product to all segments of a company at the beginning —not the end—of the production cycle. The marketer—through studies and research and through his particular sensitivity to customer and market conditions—should familiarize the engineer, the designer, and the production department with the customers' re-

[22] Robert J. Keith, *op. cit.*, pp. 104–105.
[23] "New Marketing Concept at Westinghouse: Decentralize and Study the Consumer," *Printers' Ink*, Vol. CCLXII (January 24, 1958), p. 33.

quirements to assure compliance as to the form an end product shall take.[24]

Organizational Aspects

Bulldog Electric Company:

It is the marketing department's job to do the over-all marketing planning: to establish marketing policies and programs, to guide the development of products which will be acceptable after they are produced and selling begins. Consequently, marketing should include in its scope market research and analysis, market forecasting, market policy formulation, market planning—including the determination of product design, pricing, delivery, and distribution sources—and the direction and control of advertising and sales promotion and sales solicitation. The marketing executive must include on his staff specialists who are adept in advertising, sales promotion, market research, sales forecasting, sales training, and customer service, as well as sales management.[25]

General Electric Company:

It is our conviction that successful business operation today requires that those who provide the facts and figures for the business through research, those who plan our products and service them, those who schedule production to meet sales requirements, and so on—all these members of the team form an essential organic, unified segment of the total business organization. In other words, the marketing function is more than a convenient organization marriage of diverse activities.[26]

Marketing Planning

General Electric Company:

. . . Marketing has a key role as a participant in over-all planning for the business in addition to its more obvious marketing planning responsibility. We believe that an orderly business planning process

[24] A. A. Togesen, "The Switch From Sales to a Marketing Concept," *Broadening Horizons in Marketing*, American Management Association, New York, 1956, p. 29.
[25] *Ibid.*
[26] Edward S. McKay, "The New Responsibilities of Marketing," Lecture at Graduate School of Business Administration, New York University (January 9, 1958).

is essential for survival and growth; that such planning is a continuing process, with many interrelated steps; and that there is a logical sequence . . . of such work which is greatly facilitated where the business is organized with a strong, full-functioning marketing component.[27]

Cryovac Division, W. R. Grace and Company:

We found that in the ever-changing pattern of distribution it became increasingly important to emphasize long-range planning if we were to organize ourselves . . . to meet the demands that would be placed on our organization with the expanding economy. Since we were embarking on a program of diversification and expansion of our basic product lines, long-range planning was our only salvation.[28]

General Foods Corporation:

Long-range, i.e., five year, plans are prepared by each operating division . . . and each Corporate department and updated each year. These plans do not seek merely to forecast the natural course of events for the business; they seek, rather to develop challenging objectives for existing and new products, new processes, new methods, new everything.[29]

Product Planning

General Electric Company:

First, one of the most clearly defined differences lies in the area of new product development . . . in oversimplification, the process starts with design, and moves successively through engineering, manufacturing and sales toward the customer. Now, if we study this process from the standpoint of how it occurs under the marketing concept, we find a change right at the beginning—the process now starts with the customer. . . .[30]

[27] Ibid.

[28] A. R. Hahn, "The Marketing Concept: A Major Change in Management Thinking?," *Sales Management*, Vol. LXXIX (November 10, 1957), p. 73.

[29] Wayne C. Marks, "How to Secure Management Effectiveness in the 1960's," paper read before Mid-Year Executive Conference, National Association of Wholesale Grocers of America, Bermuda (October 28, 1959).

[30] Charles E. St. Thomas, "Marketing and the Small Business," paper read before meeting of the National Fluid Power Association, Chicago (November 4, 1958).

American Telephone and Telegraph Company:

> We had to recapture the aggressive spirit and accelerate the development process. New products became the vehicle for "showing." In the past, new-product introduction had been a rather informal procedure.[31]

Bissell, Incorporated:

> We not only restyled the line, but we set up a program of continuing product development and restyling to make sure that our line is always up to date and that we are regularly introducing product innovations to stimulate our market.[32]

Profit Planning and Control

General Foods Corporation:

> Annual profit plans, which are reviewed and revised quarterly, establish the specific volume and profit targets by products and divisions and are the principal basis for the day-to-day operation of the business. Significant variations from the profit plan are reported to and discussed with corporate management promptly. The annual profit plan forms the basis for individual objectives established through agreement between a manager and his superior on what needs to be done and what will constitute satisfactory performance.[33]

Philco Corporation:

> Operations must set prices on the goods it "sells" to marketing that will allow it to make a "reasonable" return on investment; marketing, which in effect operates as a super distributor, is expected to order the right number of the right models so that it can earn a maximum profit. Marketing estimates its volume a year in advance, and operations makes its plans accordingly. Once these prices are established, they are seldom changed. This makes it easy to tell which division is turning a good profit showing, which is not. If marketing decides a model change is necessary during

---

[31] "New Products Help A.T. & T. Sell Phone Calls," *Printers' Ink*, Vol. CCLX (July 31, 1959), p. 53.
[32] "Upsweep in Bissell Advertising—Budget Triples in One Year," *Printers' Ink*, Vol. CCLIII (December 2, 1955), p. 24.
[33] Marks, *loc. cit.*

the year, or has to cancel part of its order, the extra costs involved are charged to marketing only. If marketing achieves higher-than-expected sales, it gets credit for any lowered unit production costs. Conversely, if operations can produce at lower cost than originally anticipated, it gets credit for the extra profit.[34]

Westinghouse Electric Corporation:

The lamp division marketing department aids each of the five profit centers in evolving its individual production, sales, and profit procedures, and quotas. Consumer Products group headquarters in Pittsburgh oversees the division's work. But the basic responsibility and planning rests in the profit center.

In effect, the sixty-six profit centers are separate businesses, guided and supported by the corporate high command, which functions as a sort of holding company. In that corporate setup, the marketing department has served more and more as the medium for coordinating efficiently the operations that produce profits.[35]

Marketing Research

Mead Johnson and Company:

First, we take a good look at the general prospects for the product. . . . During the developmental stages, when the product has been undergoing lengthy investigation and testing in our laboratories and in clinical studies, the Market Research Department has been checking various data on potential, market trend, our probable sales volume, the share of market we can shoot for and the best price range. Research work and market evaluation go side by side to assure that we end up with the right kind of new product at the right time. When the research and clinical scientists release the product as technically sound, market research places its findings before the marketing committee for our guidance in developing the promotion program.[36]

[34] Edward T. Thompson, "The Upheaval at Philco," *Fortune*, Vol. LIX (February 1959), p. 113. (Quotation reproduced courtesy of *Fortune* magazine.)
[35] "New Marketing Concept at Westinghouse: Decentralize and Study the Consumer," *Printers' Ink*, Vol. CCLXII (January 24, 1958), p. 34.
[36] Bernard Tolk, "New Team Paces Market Expansion at Mead Johnson and Company," *Printers' Ink*, Vol. CCLI (June 17, 1955), p. 23.

General Electric Company:

> An effective commercial intelligence program requires an orderly system for acquiring, ethically and continuously, preselected types of information we need about our own customers and our competitors in order to predict their marketing actions and the success of ours.[37]

SUGGESTIONS FOR FURTHER RESEARCH

A review of academic and business trade literature and public pronouncements provides ample evidence that academicians and businessmen have evidenced substantial concern with the marketing concept. Regretably, however, they have been less concerned with exercising precision and thoroughness in their discussions. As a consequence, no substantive studies have been conducted to determine (1) whether individual firms have undertaken programs of marketing concept implementation, (2) the degree to which they have succeeded in doing so, where attempted, and (3) whether implementation, where it has occurred, has enabled the firm better to achieve specified goals.

Further research, concerned with development of a scale or measure of implementation, should prove most helpful in seeking answers to these questions. As much of the implementation process is directly identified with companywide managerial perceptions and comprehension of the concept, the use of attitude scales should prove useful. Regarding study of managerial participation, direct observation of the decision making process probably would yield more valid results than would a review of corporate policy statements and organization charts.

Finally, the relevance of the marketing concept as a managerial action guide should be tested through the conduct of a series of intensive company case histories. Numerous companies, including General Foods Corporation, Kraft Foods Company, Campbell Soup Company, Motorola, Inc., Pillsbury Company, American Telephone and Telegraph Company, Westinghouse Electric Company, Bulldog Electric Products Corporation, and F. and M. Schaefer Brewing Company, have been associated with the marketing concept in literature. However, these materials generally leave the reader with substantial doubt regarding the status of the concept within the individual firm. In the absence of such inquiries, desirability of implementing the marketing concept rests more on plausibility than sound evidence.

---

[37] McKay, *loc. cit.*

6

Consumer Behavior:
Some Psychological Aspects

ROBERT W. PRATT, JR.

INTRODUCTION

The essence of the marketing concept is that the needs and wants of consumers should be served, rather than shaped, by the goods and services offered by a seller in the marketplace.[1] As a prescription for business success, the basic concept has been warmly embraced by scholar and practitioner alike. However, practical application requires that a business somehow bring the customer into the decision structure; the business must be able to view the world through the collective eyes of its customers. The task is a formidable one. In seeking to achieve the consumer point of view, marketing executives have increasingly sought counsel from social scientists—including economists, psychologists, sociologists, social psychologists, and cultural anthropologists—each of whom brings to the area of consumer marketing his professional tool kit of theories, concepts, hypotheses, and empirical evidence.

There can be no doubt that the trend toward effective application of social science theory and technique to marketing problems will continue; indeed, the pace can be expected to accelerate. To understand the impetus behind these interdisciplinary efforts, one might start by asking why market analysts sought assistance from social scientists in the first place? What useful knowledge has been gained from the association? And, in view of past successes and failures, what general direction can be foreseen for future efforts? The present chapter provides some insight into these questions.

[1] For a discussion of the marketing concept, see Chapter 5 of this book and, J. B. McKitterick, "What is the Marketing Management Concept," *The Frontiers of Marketing Thought and Science*, American Marketing Association, Chicago, 1957.

Before proceeding, however, the reader should be aware that, from a marketing point of view, recent changes in the economic environment have had two important consequences. First, the present economic position of the consumer is such that contemporary research in the area of buying decisions must draw heavily on principles of behavior developed by social scientists. Second, as a basis for prediction, the traditional explanation for buying behavior has become increasingly obsolete. With this in mind, the present chapter begins with a description of the traditional theory of buying behavior, followed by a discussion of the relatively recent economic changes that make the validity of this explanation suspect. The reader is then provided with a broad overview of what is now known about selected psychological characteristics of the American consumer and the relevance of this knowledge to an understanding of buying behavior. And, finally, the chapter briefly speculates on areas of inquiry that might usefully supplement and expand current knowledge.

The breadth of the topic dictates that the coverage be in no sense exhaustive. Although many of the social disciplines have made important contributions to marketing, only psychological concepts are discussed in this chapter. Even the introductory material presented reflects certain modes of thinking to which the writer subscribes; unanimous endorsement of any one set of behavioral concepts among students of consumer behavior is far from achieved. Notwithstanding these qualifications, however, this chapter will have more than fulfilled its purpose if the marketing oriented reader who heretofore has avoided contact with such topics as "behavioral theory" and "motivation research" concludes the chapter with both an awareness of the importance of psychology to marketing and a realization that the barriers to an understanding of the basic principles involved are not insurmountable. The chapter is addressed primarily to those who have had no formal training in psychology.

References are provided. In most instances, recourse to these references will, in turn, provide extensive additional references for the topic being discussed. Wherever appropriate, the text emphasizes marketing implications of the information presented.

CONSUMER BEHAVIOR: THE ECONOMIC SETTING

Background: The Traditional View of Consumption

Neoclassical "economic man" was characterized by economists as an individual whose wants exceeded his ability to buy. Buying decisions were thought to be made by a rational process involving the assignment of a specific "value" to each product wanted. Value was determined by a subjective assessment of the ability of a product to satisfy the wants of the individual or household. The want-satisfying ability or "utility" of a product was quantified in "utils," a util being defined as a fixed unit of satisfaction. Rational behavior then dictated the purchase of as many utils as possible with the income available.[2]

There are a number of important parallels between the foregoing explanation for household behavior and the economist's traditional explanation for the behavior of business firms. Households were considered to maximize utility; firms maximized profits. Households and firms came together and conducted business in a marketplace crowded with buyers and sellers, all of whom possessed a full knowledge of existing market conditions. Products offered by different sellers were similar in all important respects, and there was no discrimination. Thus, sellers would sell to any buyer at the market price and buyers would buy from any seller. In short, "perfect competition" held sway.

Given the postulated goals for both households and firms, and the assumptions explicit in the theory, the behavior to be expected from an individual household or an individual firm under specified circumstances could be deduced, and the resulting aggregate behavior for all households and/or firms could be estimated. Individual deviations from the postulated pattern of behavior were considered to be offsetting; hence it was assumed that they would not influence aggregate forecasts.

This same basic approach to estimating aggregate buying behavior is reflected in the Keynesian consumption function. In a now famous paragraph, Lord Keynes stated that:

> The fundamental psychological law, upon which we are entitled to depend with great confidence both *a priori* from our knowledge of human nature and from the detailed facts of experience, is that men are disposed, as a rule and on the average, to increase their consumption as their income increases, but not by as much as the increase in their income.[3]

Hence Keynes proposed that, on an aggregate basis at least, economists could be assured that consumption would be a stable function of income.

Keynes also recognized that the expectation of future events could influence the behavior of both individuals and households at the micro-

---

[2] For more detail regarding neoclassical "economic man," see J. W. Newman, *Motivation Research and Marketing Management*, The Plimpton Press, Boston, 1958, Ch. 2. For a discussion of utility theory, see G. J. Stigler, *The Theory of Price*, revised ed., MacMillan, New York, 1952, Ch. 5.

[3] J. M. Keynes, *The General Theory of Employment, Interest and Money*, Harcourt, Brace, New York, 1935, p. 96.

level; for example, the expectation of a reduction in income in the near future could cause either a single person or a family to decrease spending and increase savings. But Keynes felt that "whilst it (expectations regarding changes in the future level of income) may affect considerably a particular individual's propensity to consume, it is likely to average out for the community as a whole." [4] Algebraically, Keynes expressed *the propensity to consume* as

$$C = f(Y)$$

where $Y =$ a given level of income
$C =$ the expenditure on consumption out of that level of income.

Keynes' theory that consumer spending is a function of personal income finds wide acceptance and application in today's business forecasting techniques.[5] It has proved to be the single largest catalyst for economic research and debate in the area of consumer buying behavior. More important for the present chapter, Keynes offered an explanation of buying behavior which, if correct, would constitute a valuable forecasting device. But there is substantial evidence, much of it contributed by social scientists, that Keynes' hypothesis is not entirely correct.

To view this evidence in proper perspective, the reader should first be aware of the enormous economic changes that have propelled the United States, in three decades, from the depths of the Great Depression to what Galbraith has described as *The Affluent Society*.[6] These changes underlie the need for greater understanding of the dynamics of consumption; hence they underlie the application of behavioral theory to marketing.

Before reviewing recent economic changes in the United States, the reader might benefit from a recapitulation of the major similarities present in the two theoretical approaches outlined above. Neoclassical "economic man" was considered to behave in a predictable way. Theory, based on the deductive reasoning of the theorist, specified how a consumer must behave in order to maximize utility; any other behavior was not acknowledged as being rational. Since deviations from the theoretical pattern of behavior canceled each other, aggregate estimates could be compiled. Keynes' propensity to consume simply states a fixed relationship between consumer spending and personal income. If one value is known, the other can be accurately estimated. Thus, for forecasting aggregate consumer spending, the "economic man" approach relies

[4] *Ibid.*, p. 95.
[5] For example, see J. K. Galbraith, *The Affluent Society*, Houghton Mifflin, Boston, 1958, p. 237. See also R. A. Gordon, *Business Fluctuations*, Harper, New York, 1952, p. 471.
[6] J. K. Galbraith, *loc. cit.*

on a theoretically deduced pattern of human behavior based on fixed assumptions. Assumptions about human behavior are implicit in the Keynesian formulation also. It should be noted, however, that neither approach explicitly recognizes the possibility that an individual's motives, attitudes, emotions, expectations, etc., will influence how he reacts to a given situation, nor do these theories allow for the possibility that an individual will react to a similar situation differently at two points in time. The human element is absent. Processes internal to the individual are not considered.

One of the principal themes of this chapter is that the more *economic choice* an individual has, the greater will be the influence of these internal processes on his overt economic behavior. Hence, as real income has advanced in the United States, empirical data concerning individual psychological processes have become increasingly important to both the evaluation and the formulation of theories about consumer behavior; conversely, deductive theory has become correspondingly less useful as a basis for accurate business forecasts, particularly for forecasting sales of a given product or brand.

Perhaps a marketing example will highlight the importance of the difference between the empirical approach and the deductive approach to understanding and predicting behavior. Among the most difficult decisions that must be faced by a consumer-goods marketing manager are those associated with the introduction of new products. Not only must a decision be reached as to whether or not a particular type of product should be manufactured, but, if that decision is yes, additional decisions must then be made regarding product specifications, production schedules, packaging, pricing, channels of distribution, promotion, and so on. Also, the actions of competitors must be anticipated.

Consider, for example, the introduction of television into the American home in the late 1940's. For the marketing manager, would either the "economic man" or the Keynesian approach have provided answers to the critical marketing questions posed in the preceding paragraph? They would not! Not only were many of the assumptions underlying the "economic man" approach not present in the late 1940's (e.g., "perfect competition"), but from a practical standpoint how was one to estimate the number of utils to associate with each model of each brand? Not knowing the strategy of competitors, how were such hypothetical figures to be translated into production schedules? In the 1940's, personal income was rising, as were consumption expenditures. Keynes was correct. But what did this tell the marketing manager about the number of television sets to produce? Only that his production schedule should be higher than it would have been had personal income been declining. This is not to deny that these theories are correct when the assumptions on which they are predicated are present; but even when the assumptions hold, the theories—formulated by economists to gain insight into *economic problems*—do not provide a practical basis for answering many *marketing* questions. Marketing managers must know *why* income is allocated to one product category rather than another, and, within a category, how preference for a particular brand and model is established.

Nevertheless, few researchers would question the value of a theoretical structure in formulating research designed to forecast behavior; such a structure determines what facts must be collected in order to test the assumptions or the implications of the theory. However, to aid in the solution of consumer marketing problems in a society where consumers enjoy a high level of choice, subjective aspects of human behavior must be introduced into the existing theory. It is unrealistic to consider that present-day Americans behave like mechanical robots; they need not, and they do not. The "how" and the "why" of human behavior must play a role in any theory of consumer behavior that is to be applied to marketing problems. Indeed, isn't this what the marketing concept is all about?

Personal Income in the United States

There are numerous people alive today who were born into a world in which virtually all families were required by necessity to spend their cash income for subsistence—food, clothing, and shelter. A large proportion of all income was received by a few individuals; the vast majority received very little. These conditions still prevail throughout much of the world. In contrast, although poverty has not been eliminated in the United States, most American consumers currently enjoy a level of real income unparalleled in world history. Table 6.1 summarizes the income position of family units for the years 1948 and 1954 to 1961. Note that in 1961, 30 per cent of all American family units had an annual income of $7500 or more; up from 8 per cent in 1948. As indicated in the bottom row of Table 6.1, price increases have somewhat mitigated the real increase in purchasing power for the average family (between 1948 and 1961, 18 cents of every dollar of income was lost to inflation); nevertheless, it is evident that American families have experienced a substantial gain in economic well-being over the fourteen-year period. There is no reason, short of the possibility of nuclear war, to suspect that this trend will not continue.

The *income levels* shown in the table represent the single most important condition that enables a family to purchase goods. A second important "enabling" condition is represented by a family's accumulation of *liquid assets*—usually defined to include savings deposits in banks,

Table 6.1   Income of Family Units before Taxes
1948 and 1954 to 1961
(Percentage distribution of families) *

Family Income	1948	1954	1955	1956	1957	1958	1959	1960	1961
Under $1000	11%	9%	11%	8%	7%	6%	6%	5%	6%
$1000 to $2999	35	23	22	21	21	22	19	18	19
$3000 to $4999	32	29	26	24	23	23	21	20	19
$5000 to $7499	14	24	24	25	26	25	27	28	26
$7500 to $9999	4	8	9	11	12	13	13	15	14
$10,000 and up	4	7	8	11	11	11	14	14	16
	100	100	100	100	100	100	100	100	100
Mean family income (not adjusted for price changes)	$4020	$4900	$5060	$5640	$5650	$5580	$6080	$6230	$6480
Mean family income (in 1948 dollars)	$4020	$4490	$4650	$5100	$4950	$4760	$5140	$5190	$5340

* *Source:* G. Katona, C. Lininger, and R. Kosobud, *1962 Survey of Consumer Finances,* Monograph No. 32, Survey Research Center, The University of Michigan, 1963, p. 11. For data for 1948 and for 1954 to 1956, see Table 1-2, *1960 Survey of Consumer Finances.*

In this table a *family unit* is defined as (1) two or more people living in the same dwelling unit and related to each other by blood, marriage, or adoption, or (2) a single person either living alone or unrelated to the other occupants in the dwelling unit.

savings and loan associations, and credit unions, as well as checking accounts and U.S. Government savings bonds.[7] The median liquid asset holdings of families in 1960 was almost $500, although 12 per cent of all family units reported liquid assets of over $5000.[8] A third factor which contributes significantly to the ability of an American family to fulfill its needs in the marketplace is the availability of *installment credit.* The *income security* afforded most families as a result of medical insurance,

[7] For a definition of "liquid assets," see *1960 Survey of Consumer Finances,* Survey Research Center, The University of Michigan, 1960, p. 268.
[8] *Ibid.,* p. 77.

workmen's compensation, unemployment compensation, social security, company and union emergency plans, etc. is still another factor which influences a family's general propensity to spend rather than save.

In considering the relationship between income levels and the fulfillment of needs, an arbitrary, but nonetheless useful, approach classifies the amount of money necessary to purchase *absolute necessities* during a specified period as a *subsistence income level* and all income over the subsistence level as *discretionary income*. Thus discretionary income may be thought of as income over and above that required to meet fixed expenses and outlays necessary to provide a family with its minimum subsistence requirements. The problem of conceptualizing discretionary income through time and between cultures is extremely complex and will not be discussed here. For the purpose of this chapter, it is sufficient to re-emphasize that in most countries today the vast majority of consumers are required to spend a large portion of their earnings on food, clothing, and shelter in order to survive. Under these conditions, discretionary buying power is absent.

In contrast, the majority of today's American consumers, primarily as a result of the enabling conditions discussed above, enjoy the prerogative of deciding whether to spend or save a sizable portion of their earnings. In fact, in the short-run at least, installment credit permits most consumers to spend substantially more than their earnings if family requirements so dictate.

How much discretionary income does the American consumer have? Obviously, determination of the exact number of discretionary dollars available to a family depends on where the line is drawn between "necessary" and "discretionary" expenditures.[9] But some benchmarks are available. Per capita disposable income (i.e., income after taxes) averaged over $2000 in 1963.[10] Of this amount, the National Industrial Conference Board estimates that about $750 (over 37 per cent) can be classified as "discretionary."[11] *Fortune* magazine, in a series of articles entitled "America in the Sixties," defined a subsistence income as $4000 per family per year. On this basis, it was pointed out that:

[9] For a discussion of the concept of discretionary income, see "Discretionary Income: A New Measure of Consumer Markets," *The Business Record*, National Industrial Conference Board, May, 1958. Also *Discretionary Income*, Technical Paper No. 6, NICB, 1958.

Discretionary income statistics are published regularly in *The Business Record*. See also G. Katona, *The Powerful Consumer*, McGraw-Hill, New York, 1960, pp. 16–18.

[10] Department of Commerce, 1963.

[11] *A Graphic Guide to Consumer Markets*, National Industrial Conference Board, 1963, p. 24.

In 1959, there was some $140 billion of discretionary income in the U.S. . . . and 60 per cent of U.S. family units had at least some of this after-$4000 money. By 1970, these discretionary dollars will just about double, *to around $255 billion. More than half of all disposable personal income will be discretionary by 1970. And the overwhelming bulk of this discretionary income, perhaps 85 per cent of it, will belong to the 25 million families with more than $7000.*[12]

By any standard, a high level of discretionary income exists in the United States at the present time, and the level can be expected to increase substantially in coming years. In an economy without discretionary income, buying behavior can be predicted with a high degree of accuracy—consumers must spend their disposable income on subsistence items; their range of choice among categories and within categories is relatively narrow. As the level of discretionary income increases, it becomes incumbent on those who compete for the consumer dollar (including sellers of *both* goods and services) to seek an understanding of the decision-making processes by which an individual determines both the amount of income he wishes to strive for and the manner in which he will allocate available income among alternatives. In a society in which it is not difficult for most individuals to earn more than a subsistence wage, a decision regarding the amount of income one wishes to strive for is closely related to the problem of how one wishes to allocate the *time* available to him. Thus, within limits, the amount of income a person earns is itself discretionary.

Are there aspects of consumer decision processes that are susceptible to quantification for predictive purposes? It is in the search for answers to questions such as this that social scientists and market analysts have most notably combined efforts. Much of the empirical data resulting from such collaboration are referenced in the next chapter; however, to understand the present state of knowledge in this area, it will be useful to examine a number of the theoretical concepts on which present explanations of consumer buying behavior are based.

CONSUMER BEHAVIOR: SOME PSYCHOLOGICAL ASPECTS

The Concept of Intervening Variables

As described above, traditional economics explained buying behavior by means of an elegant, yet simple, theory which stated that at all times

[12] Reprinted in: *America in the Sixties*, Harper, New York, 1960, pp. 96–97. The quote is from Chapter 5, "The Decade of the 'Discretionary' Dollar." Originally published under the title *Markets of the Sixties*.

a rational consumer would work toward one goal—the maximization of utility. Further, many economists considered behavior to be caused entirely by environmental stimuli, in much the same way that a billiard ball responds to the impact of a cue. For example, unit sales were considered to respond to changes in price, and borrowing was considered to respond to changes in the rate of interest. In discussing these kinds of relationships, the consumer was implicitly considered to be passive, that is, he was assumed to react in a known way to a given stimulus—his behavior was predictable. Of the "schools" of psychology, John Watson's "Behaviorism" is one of those that most nearly adheres to this stimulus-response explanation of human behavior.

In contrast, another mode of thinking, most nearly represented by adherents of the "Gestalt" school of psychology, maintains that rational behavior is a function of how an individual perceives a given stimulus or external event and, further, that such behavior can be explained in terms of certain "intervening variables" which are postulated to function within an individual; these variables are considered to be a part of the inward, psychic experience of the consumer. Intervening variables provide the psychological framework within which environmental stimuli are interpreted. The interpretation, in turn, leads to overt behavior.[13] Schematically, the causal process appears as shown in Figure 6.1.

To give a brief example of how this process might work in a school

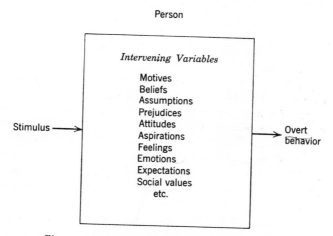

Figure 6.1 *Intervening variables and behavior.*

[13] For a discussion of the basic theory, see W. Kohler, *Gestalt Psychology*, 2nd ed., Liveright, New York, 1947. For examples that demonstrate the Gestalt theory of perception and learning, see M. Wertheimer, *Productive Thinking*, Harper, New York, 1959.

situation, it would *not* be expected that failing an examination would elicit identical behavior from all students. Some would work harder to make up the lost ground. Others would rationalize the failure and continue as before, and still others would psychologically quit. The stimulus is the same, but the overt behavior varies as a result of the intervening variables that are brought into play within each individual's internal psychological frame.

Comparing traditional theory (stimulus-response) with Gestalt theory (stimulus-intervening variable-response), consider the anticipated effect of a price reduction for a consumer product that is assumed to exhibit positive price elasticity. Application of traditional economic theory would result in a statement that for a given price reduction the total number of units sold would increase by some predictable number, regardless of other factors. When intervening variables are postulated, however, consumers would be expected to respond in accordance with their perceptions of the price change. For example, some consumers might perceive the price reduction as offering a real "bargain" and purchase when they would not have otherwise done so. Other consumers might view the price reduction as the first of a number of price reductions (e.g., if they thought inventories were excessive or that the store was in financial difficulty) and postpone their purchases in anticipation of further reductions. Still others might not perceive that a price reduction had taken place at all. Thus the Gestalt approach holds that a price reduction cannot *directly* affect sales in any simple, uniform manner. The price reduction influences individuals and the behavior of these individuals influences sales. The final effect of a change in price will depend on how the change is perceived and acted on by potential customers.

Gestalt psychologists further point out that the above theory is dynamic, in the sense that the structure of the intervening variables within a psychological frame is constantly changing through time as a result of new learning and experience.[14] Thus, as a result of experiencing the consequences of flunking one course, the "quitter" mentioned earlier may respond quite differently when confronted with the same stimulus a second time. Or, to cite a second example, an investor who follows the advice of a broker and loses heavily may not respond in the identical fashion when offered similar advice in the future. For any one individual, the dynamics of the basic process may be visualized as shown in Figure 6.2.

To consider a specific (and very much simplified) example, assume that the "STIMULUS" shown in the diagram is a one-page advertise-

---

[14] The technical term for this phenomenon is "plasticity."

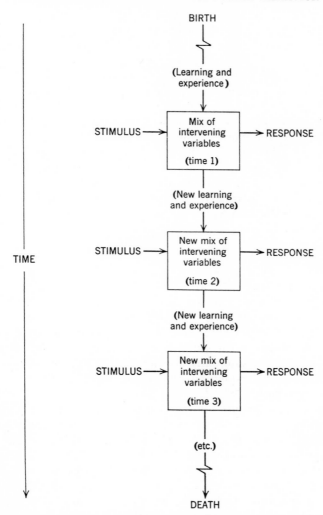

Figure 6.2 Intervening variables: a dynamic concept.

ment for a soft drink run at two-week intervals on the inside front cover of *The Saturday Evening Post*; further, assume that the advertisements themselves are identical in format. If a particular housewife reads all three ads, the following might be observed: Her overt behavior is not altered in any preceptible way at time 1; at time 2 she adds the product to her shopping list; and at time 3 she purchases the product. The stimuli are identical, but the responses are not. The differences in overt behavior occur because the mix of intervening variables is, in some unspecified way, different at the three times of exposure.

In a more general context, it can be assumed that any given promotional effort (stimulus) will cause varying responses among potential customers. The differences in overt behavior are caused by differences in the way in which the stimulus is perceived, organized and interpreted by each individual, that is, the *cognitive processes* internal to the individual. In recent years a great deal of theoretical knowledge has been published concerning these cognitive processes. But much remains to be learned, especially regarding the application of principles derived from controlled laboratory experiments to the understanding of observed buying behavior.[15] This chapter now turns to a discussion of two areas of psychology that are particularly relevant to an understanding of the way in which an individual organizes and interprets perceived stimuli—motivation and learning.

Motivation

Observation of the behavior of shoppers in a retail outlet—for example, in a department store—evokes a number of interesting questions. Why does one shopper decide to purchase while another decides to go home empty-handed? Why does a shopper purchase one product rather than another? Why does he select a particular brand rather than one of the alternatives? In sum, why do individuals behave as they do? A partial answer to these questions can be found in an understanding of the concept of motivation.

Most buying behavior is rational in the sense that the reasons underlying a purchase are "self-approved" by the buyer, that is, the buyer has reasons (often conscious) for his actions, even if these reasons are not readily apparent to an observer. Such rational buying behavior is generally considered to be motivated.[16] The concept of motivation can be thought of as "behavior that is instigated by needs within the individual and is directed toward goals that can satisfy these needs." [17] Graphically, the process appears as shown in Figure 6.3.

---

[15] See J. F. Engel, "The Influence of Needs and Attitudes on the Perception of Persuasion," *Toward Scientific Marketing*, American Marketing Association, Chicago, 1963.

[16] A discussion of the difference between rational and irrational behavior will be found in E. C. Bursk, "Opportunities for Persuasion," *Harvard Business Review* (September–October 1958), pp. 114–115; see also G. Katona, "Rational Behavior and Economic Behavior," *Psychological Review*, Vol. LX, No. 5 (September 1953), pp. 307–318. Katona's article outlines a theoretical framework for the study of rational buying behavior.

[17] C. T. Morgan, *Introduction to Psychology*, McGraw-Hill, New York, 1956, p. 56.

Figure 6.3   The motivational process.

The term "need" in the psychological sense refers to the initiating factor in a motivational sequence; needs may be thought of as underlying all behavior.[18] Although numerous lists and classifications of "needs" or motives have beeen published and widely discussed,[19] two general categories of needs go undisputed. The first category consists of *physiological needs,* such as those associated with hunger, thirst, sleep, sex, warmth, cold, and pain. The human body maintains an internal physiological balance or equilibrium, which is referred to as "homeostasis." When the body enters a disequilibrium state, tension is created within the physiological system and a need arises. Behavior must then be instigated by either the individual or by the physiological system itself to correct the imbalance. The underlying need results in a drive directed toward a specific goal which the individual anticipates will relieve the need. The specific behavior that is instrumental in satisfying a physiological need may be a reflex action, it may be behavior that is instinctive, or it may be some kind of specific activity, such as eating, drinking, or going to sleep.

The second broad category of needs, often referred to as *learned needs,* includes needs that, in one way or another, are precipitated by tension that develops as a result of an individual's association with other people. When studying the decision process by which discretionary income is allocated among alternatives, this second category is much more important than the first—it is assumed that physiological needs will generally be met. Unfortunately, as compared with physiological needs, there is much less agreement among behavioral scientists as to the specific

[18] The term "motive" is technically defined to include both a need and a direction of behavior (drive); however, the terms "need," "want" and "motive" are frequently used synonymously, and they are so used in this chapter.
[19] For example, see E. L. Brink and W. T. Kelley, *The Management of Promotion,* Prentice-Hall, Englewood Cliffs, N.J., 1963, pp. 86–88. See also, J. W. Newman, *op. cit.,* pp. 16–26 and pp. 53–58.

conceptualization and labeling of learned needs. One widely accepted way of classifying these needs is to group them into the following three basic categories.

1. *Need for affiliation.* In the highly organized society that exists in the United States today, people are very much interdependent; they are required to interact a great deal with one another. However, over and above required associations, most people have a strong desire for companionship. There is a natural desire to give and receive affection. Relationships with other people are necessary to satisfy basic emotional needs.

2. *Need for achievement.* Many people are motivated to achieve, through their own efforts, high levels of performance, or to work hard to overcome adversity. Underlying this drive to excel is a high need for achievement.

3. *Need for power.* The basic goal here is to be able to control or dominate the behavior of others, often by striving for recognition or status in a group.

Techniques have been developed for measuring these basic needs empirically; the resulting empirical research has demonstrated that a relationship does exist between these needs and human behavior.[20] Nevertheless, as with the deductive economic models described earlier, one should question the applicability of these basic categories to the solution of marketing problems. Actually, these categories have proven useful in a number of ways. First, they have been successfully applied to the understanding of broad economic questions such as an individual's dedication to, and striving for, the acquisition of wealth, or the general manner in which an individual chooses to allocate both his time and his income. Because the allocation of time and income has direct relevance to marketing, these categories provide a structure within which the market analyst can work toward the solution of certain problems, particularly those associated with decisions regarding alternative expenditures of large sums of money, such as whether to invest in a college education or a summer home. For purchase decisions that do not engage

[20] See J. Atkinson (ed.), *Motives in Fantasy, Action, and Society*, D. Van Nostrand, Princeton, N.J., 1958; J. N. Morgan, "The Achievement Motive and Economic Behavior," *Economic Development and Cultural Change*, Vol. XII (April 1964); D. C. McClelland et al., *The Achievement Motive*, Appleton-Century-Crofts, New York, 1953; D. C. McClelland, *The Achieving Society*, D. Van Nostrand, Princeton, N.J., 1961. *The Achieving Society* presents evidence to support McClelland's hypothesis that "a particular psychological factor—a need for achievement—is responsible for economic growth and decline."

strong motivations—frequently the case for purchases of nondurable goods—the preceding categories are often not salient. Of equal importance with their direct application to marketing problems, however, is the fact that these relatively concise categories will provide the reader with a useful frame of reference for the consideration of more extensive need classifications encountered both in this chapter and elsewhere.

Indeed, there are numerous classifications of needs, drives, and motives available to the market analyst that are likely to prove more useful in the solution of specific marketing problems than are the categories just described (for examples, see reference 19). In general, however, these more extensive classifications do not conflict with the basic classification presented; they merely provide a more extensive framework for empirical research. Although the majority of these classifications were developed by psychologists and psychiatrists, a few resulted from the efforts of marketing men—such as Copeland and Starch—who tailored their proposals to the solution of marketing problems. Copeland's work first appeared in the early 1920's.

An extensive discussion of the various need classifications currently available to the market analyst would require a chapter by itself. But the need structure proposed by Maslow as part of his theory of motivation is widely quoted and will serve here as an example of a second categorization that provides an appropriate frame of reference for the solution of certain marketing problems. Maslow proposes seven categories of needs —physiological needs, safety needs, the need for love and affection, the need for esteem, the need for self-actualization, the need to know and understand, and aesthetic needs.[21] Maslow further suggests that these needs have priority in the order listed; hence, when physiological needs have been gratified, safety needs can then be expected to receive attention. The theory also recognizes that no one category of needs will achieve a level of complete gratification before lower-priority needs are attended to. At any one time, needs at all levels may be partially met, but the higher-priority needs will have achieved a relatively greater degree of gratification.

For the purposes of market analysts, as opposed to those of economists, Maslow's theory can be applied in a number of ways. For example, the relative strength of the need, or combination of needs, underlying purchase of a particular product can be determined by positioning the product on a need continuum (high-priority to low-priority). A product positioned at the low-priority end of the continuum would be expected to

[21] See A. H. Maslow, *Motivation and Personality*, Harper, New York, 1954, Chapter 5.

experience a rapid drop in sales if aggregate disposable personal income declined. Therefore, if a low-priority need position were recognized, the marketing manager would be wise to make an effort to change the position of his product on the continuum; this could be achieved by means of advertising and other promotional efforts designed to appeal to selected higher-priority needs. Also, various models of a brand can be positioned on a need continuum in order to determine the most appropriate promotional appeals for "trading up" a potential customer.

As a framework for researching consumer behavior, Maslow's work can also be used to demonstrate the relationship between the type of behavioral theories put forward by psychologists—who, as a group, tend to emphasize characteristics inherent to the individual—and the theories stemming from the sociological tradition—which tends to emphasize cultural variables, such as the role of "social class" and "reference groups." To cite a brief example, using the need classification shown on page 112, an individual's selection of reference groups and his attitudes regarding "social class" will primarily reflect his need for affiliation, although his need for achievement and need for power could play secondary roles. Using Maslow's classifications, social group and reference group attitudes and activities would be a function of an individual's need for love and affection and his need for esteem. Need classifications overlap at many points; the researcher's job is to find the particular classification that is most appropriate for the problem at hand.

Both the psychological and the sociological approach to motivation have obvious importance to the understanding of purchasing behavior. Each individual has his own configuration of needs and wants, but these must operate in an environment which requires interaction with members of a person's immediate family, as well as with members of the community at large. In varying degrees, people adapt to the culture of the community in which they live. A detailed discussion of the relevant sociological concepts is beyond the scope of this chapter.

To recapitulate, needs arise from two principal sources. The first is a result of physiological deprivation or disequilibrium within an individual; the second results from the way in which an individual perceives or relates to his environment. Both types of needs result in behavior directed toward goals that the individual believes will satisfy these needs. The basic task of a business that markets to private households is to offer a product and/or brand that will serve as a goal toward which need-oriented behavior can be directed. Further, by means of its promotional mix, the business must ensure that the consumer is aware of both the offering and its attributes. Of course, no amount of promotion can bring about repeat purchases if, in fact, the need satisfaction anticipated by the consumer does not materialize as a result of the initial purchase.

As an indication of the importance that the concept of motivation has achieved in the area of marketing in the postwar period, one need only turn to the truly monumental volume of literature concerned with "motivation research." [22] In reality, these research efforts are manifestations of the desire to implement the marketing concept. The goal is to understand the "why" of behavior, to become "customer oriented," to view the world as the customer views it.

There are two other aspects of motivation, not yet discussed in this chapter, that can be useful to the market analyst. The first is that when an individual exhibits overt behavior, he is almost always driven by a *combination* of needs or motives.[23] At any one point in time, the needs that are operative are likely to be functioning at various levels and in various strengths. Some needs are mutually reinforcing or complementary, in the sense that they encourage similar behavior. Other needs are partially or completely offset or neutralized because they are functioning concurrently with needs that tend to drive the individual in an opposite direction, that is, toward dissimilar behavior. The presence of a multiplicity of both motives and goals accounts for the fact that well-conceived selling efforts—including advertisements, point-of-purchase materials, sales talks, and so on—are designed to appeal to a variety of needs, not just one. For example, the need for affiliation in one of its many forms (e.g., affection, companionship, tenderness, love, etc.) is an appeal frequently used in advertising copy; but if the primary focus of an ad is an appeal directed toward the need for affiliation, a number of other "secondary" appeals will almost always be found in the same ad.[24]

---

[22] The following represent only a few of the many publications in this area. W. Alderson, *Marketing Behavior and Executive Action*, Richard D. Irwin, Homewood, Ill., 1957, especially Chapter 6, "The Motivation of Consumer Buying"; C. J. Clawson, "Family Composition, Motivation, and Buying Decisions," in N. Foote (ed.), *Household Decision-Making*, New York University Press, New York, 1961; T. Levitt, "M–R Snake Dance," *Harvard Business Review* (November–December 1960); *Use of Motivation Research in Marketing*, Studies in Business Policy, No. 97, National Industrial Conference Board, 1960; J. W. Newman, *loc. cit.*; A. W. Rose, "Motivation Research and Subliminal Advertising," *Social Research*, Vol. XXV, No. 3 (Autumn 1958), pp. 271–84; G. H. Smith, *Motivation Research in Advertising and Marketing*, McGraw-Hill, New York, 1954; *Projective Techniques in Consumer Motivation Research*, The Foundation for Research on Human Behavior, Ann Arbor, Michigan, 1955.

[23] See G. Katona, *Psychological Analysis of Economic Behavior*, McGraw-Hill, New York, 1951, pp. 70–81; G. Katona, "The Relationship between Psychology and Economics," in S. Koch (ed.), *Psychology: A Study of Science*, McGraw-Hill, New York, 1963, pp. 663–666.

[24] See J. D. Scott, *Advertising Principles and Problems*, Prentice-Hall, Englewood Cliffs, N.J., 1953, Chs. 4 and 5.

The combination of needs that are active within an individual is constantly changing through time. Each time behavior is instigated, a need or combination of needs is met; consequently, the remaining set of operative needs must seek a new equilibrium. As the most urgent needs are gratified, other needs that had been suppressed will increase in intensity and take their place. Thus, for purposes of illustration, consider the following (much simplified) example. A man may return home from work hungry (physiological need) and is motivated to eat. After eating, he may be required to choose from among a number of alternative evening activities. Should he remain at home with his family (need for affiliation), go bowling (need for affiliation), attend his local lodge meeting to further his campaign for office (need for power), or attend a training lecture at his place of employment (need for achievement)? Whatever his decision, some needs will be met, others will be partially met, and still others will not be met at all; and, of course, it can be predicted that the hunger motive will soon return and again take its place among the combination of active motives.

For those interested in the analysis of spending and saving decisions, an understanding of the relative influence of immediate needs versus future needs is also important. Katona points out that "satisfaction of present needs is usually achieved by what is called spending and satisfaction of future needs by what is called savings." [25] This "principle of immediacy," as discussed by psychologists, has quite diverse influences on the behavior of different individuals and different families.[26] The principle will not be examined in detail here. However, it might be noted in connection with future needs that Maslow would consider saving as a response to the need for "safety"; other need classifications would equate saving with a need for "security."

There is another aspect of motivation that cannot be overlooked by market analysts—aspiration theory. This chapter has pointed out that gratification of a physiological need results in reduction or elimination of the need, at least temporarily. But since a large proportion of all promotional appeals is aimed at the so-called learned needs, it is important to know whether these needs respond to gratification in the same manner as their physiological counterparts. If a learned need leads to the purchase of a home, or an automobile, or a television set, how long will the service provided by the item purchased continue to satisfy the need? Will the need remain dormant until the product is no longer serviceable and must be replaced? If newlyweds describe their goals as including "a

[25] G. Katona, op. cit., Psychological Analysis of Economic Behavior, p. 71.
[26] Ibid.

small house in the suburbs, a station wagon and a color television set," how do they behave when these goals are achieved? Does fulfillment automatically lead to contentment, or do they find themselves saddled with a new set of learned needs urging them toward behavior directed at a new set of goals? Market saturation for many household durables in the United States is at, or approaching, 90 per cent. At these levels, is the market limited to replacement demand and initial purchases resulting from new family formation? Answers to these questions are essential to the formulation of effective marketing policy.

One theoretical framework for seeking some of the necessary answers can be found in the work of Kurt Lewin and his associates.[27] In general, Lewin found that most individuals aspire to goals that are just beyond their immediate grasp. If these goals are achieved, the normal response is to reformulate the initial goals and aspire to still higher accomplishments. If the initial goals are not achieved, aspirations are adjusted downward. The initial goals are such that failure to achieve them is usually not catastrophic; the downward adjustment is taken in stride without serious psychological damage. Note the resemblance here to Maslow's basic approach. Both are essentially analogous to the situation of moving up or down a long flight of stairs one step at a time.

There is an abundance of empirical evidence to support Lewin's theory; only a few examples will be reported here. First, in the area of upward adjustment of aspirations, it is well documented that a large proportion of those purchasing consumer durables are replacing products with which they have had little or no mechanical difficulty. Their dissatisfaction with the product is psychological. One important reason for their decision to replace is that they perceive and are attracted by innovations in product design.[28] For example, at this writing the so-called "free-standing, high-oven" ranges have been on the market for only a few years. When compared with traditional models, they represent a radical innovation in design. But can design innovation, by itself, attract buyers who would not have otherwise replaced their ranges? The evidence indicates that it can. In 1963, the average age of ranges *replaced* by new units of a traditional design was almost two years greater than the average age of ranges replaced by new high-oven units. A large part of this difference can be accounted for by the design appeal of the high-oven units; for one segment of consumers, the length of the replacement

[27] K. Lewin et al., "Level of Aspiration," in J. Hunt (ed.), *Personality and the Behavior Disorders*, Ronald Press, New York, 1944.

[28] For example, see E. Mueller, "The Desire for Innovation in Household Goods," in L. Clark (ed.), *Consumer Behavior*, New York University Press, New York, 1958.

cycle has been shortened. Also, although this writer has no specific data, design appeal is most certainly an important factor in many new automobile purchase decisions.

Turning to an example in a different area: Many young men who entered the labor force in the late 1940's and early 1950's had, by 1960, achieved income levels that surpassed their initial expectations. Were these individuals satisfied? In most cases, emphatically not! More often, they were surprised by the degree of their own dissatisfaction. In most instances new learned needs developed that required an upward adjustment in goals. These upward adjustments were manifested in a continued striving toward still higher income and, of course, the goods and services that such income would provide.

On the other hand, when goals are not achieved, sights are lowered. Most people will lower their aspirations in response to major unexpected events, such as a war or a serious depression. Since such reactions are widespread, the effect on aggregate consumer demand (in an economy with high discretionary income) could be staggering; as is implicit in the definition, discretionary purchases can be *postponed*. And further, the short-run consequences to the economy of a major switch from spending to saving would be worsened if financial institutions were unable to find borrowers for the dollars saved. Since a *single dollar* is used to purchase goods or services by a number of different individuals or firms during the course of a year, when a dollar is removed from circulation, the effect on the gross national product is multiple; indeed, the end result of an increase or a decrease in the total amount of money being spent in the economy is generally referred to as the "multiplier" effect.

Katona's notion that the proportion of aggregate disposable personal income spent at a given time is a function of the relative degree of optimism or pessimism felt by consumers collectively is, essentially, an application of aspiration theory to the explanation of economic behavior. This work has culminated in the *Index of Consumer Attitudes and Inclinations to Buy,* published quarterly by the Survey Research Center, University of Michigan.[29] Katona has summarized the influence of aspirations on economic behavior as follows:

> Gratification of needs does not mean saturation; instead it results in the raising of sights, provided people are optimistic and confident about the future. New wants arise when more pressing

[29] For an evaluation of the effectiveness of this index for forecasting discretionary spending by consumers, see E. Mueller, "Ten Years of Consumer Attitude Surveys: Their Forecasting Record," *Journal of the American Statistical Association,* Vol. LVIII, No. 304 (December 1963), pp. 899–917.

wants have been satisfied. Frustration, disappointment, or a pessimistic outlook make for feelings of saturation.[30]

Learning

Earlier in this chapter the statement was made that intervening variables are altered through time as a result of new learning and experience (page 108). Almost all overt behavior is "learned," the exceptions being behavior brought about by normal physical maturation processes, injury or disease, imbalance in the body's physiological system, and so on. The intervening variables listed earlier in this chapter—for example, motives, beliefs, prejudices, attitudes, feelings, emotions, expectations, and social values—are shaped by the entire complex of environmental influences to which a person is exposed throughout his lifetime, including other persons with whom he comes in contact (however brief the contact), all visual and auditory stimuli to which he is exposed (e.g., books, motion pictures, music, advertising), and much more.

Basically, learning may be accomplished in two ways, by memorizing or by insight.[31] The procedure for *memorizing* dictates repeated exposure to the information to be learned; for example, most people have "memorized" their addresses, telephone numbers, the instructions for operating both their automobiles and other durables, the local laws and ordinances, and so on, by simply being exposed to these bits of information over and over again through time. This information is "stamped" into their memories; it has been learned, and often it is not readily forgotten. Thus, much to their chagrin, many veterans of World War II can still recite their service serial numbers. Learning by *insight* occurs when a person perceives the combination of elements comprising a problem in a different manner than he had perceived them or thought about them before the insightful learning takes place; thus it requires a reorganization of the perceptual field.

To compare briefly the two types of learning, consider the process by which an individual works toward the understanding of a mathe-

[30] G. Katona, "Long-Range Changes in Consumer Attitudes," in C. Lininger (ed.), *Dynamic Aspects of Consumer Behavior*, Foundation for Research on Human Behavior, Ann Arbor, Michigan, 1963, p. 100. For additional information regarding the relationship between levels of aspiration and buying behavior, see G. Katona, *op. cit.*, "The Relationship Between Psychology and Economics," pp. 666–670; G. Katona, *op. cit.*, *The Powerful Consumer*, especially Chapter 8; G. Katona, *op. cit.*, *Psychological Analysis of Economic Behavior*, especially pp. 91–98.

[31] See M. Wertheimer, *loc. cit.* Wertheimer provides examples that demonstrate clearly the differences between these two forms of learning.

matical or statistical formula. Usually the first step toward understanding involves memorizing the formula, using it to solve problems, and perhaps studying its derivation. The second step, which is often not achieved, takes place when the true meaning and purpose of the formula become clear to the user. Once this insight or integration of the perceptual field has taken place, the formula has real meaning. It will be remembered longer than it would have been if the insight had not been achieved, and it can be applied to the solution of a variety of related problems.

Learning requires reinforcement or reward if it is to continue. In the motivational framework already described, goal-oriented behavior must gratify a need if it is to be repeated. The behavior must be reinforced; gratification of a need provides the incentive for repeat behavior when the same need reoccurs in the future. Continuous reinforcement of a particular mode of behavior underlies the formulation of habits. Habits, then, are response patterns that have become automatic to given stimuli. They can be broken in two ways. The automatic response pattern may cease to gratify the need (this usually comes about because the basic need is altered in some way), or the individual may find an alternative response that is more gratifying. Getting consumers to accept product innovations or to switch brands is essentially a problem of introducing an alternative response (goal) that will be perceived by the individual and cause him to reconsider a previous decision. The automatic response pattern is thus arrested. A new decision is reached (which may be identical to the previous decision), and reinforcement must again be forthcoming if the development of a new habit is to be encouraged.[32]

Most behavior is habitual; hence, when confronted with the same stimulus at a number of different times, an individual will tend to behave in about the same way each time. For overt behavior to change, the structure of the intervening variables must be altered—usually as the result of the impact of a *perceived* change in the environment.[33]

In marketing, habitual behavior is most often evidenced in purchase patterns for *nondurable goods,* such as grocery products, where a particular item is frequently bought, hence the repurchase cycle is short.

[32] For a discussion of theory and empirical evidence concerning post-purchase reinforcement, see L. Festinger, *A Theory of Cognitive Dissonance,* Stanford University Press, Stanford, Calif., 1957.

[33] An individual does not perceive all the stimuli to which he is exposed. Psychologists refer to the smallest amount of stimulus that can be perceived by an individual as a "threshold." The threshold for a given message will vary among individuals, as well as for any one individual at different times. Repetition is a device often used in marketing to ensure that the impact of a message exceeds the threshold level of perception.

Once a housewife has considered alternatives and arrived at a decision that a particular brand will best satisfy the needs and wants of her family, it is not necessary for her to reconsider this decision each time the product is purchased. Indeed, it would be next to impossible to make a decision about each product purchased on every visit to a grocery store. For competitive products with a short repurchase cycle, a principal task of promotional efforts is to encourage a housewife to reconsider her original decision by introducing stimuli that will cause her to recognize that an alternative brand may better serve her family's needs. In contrast, habit rarely plays a part in the purchase of *durable goods*. Few appliances or automobiles are acquired without consideration of alternatives, followed by a genuine decision. Thus the problems associated with brand "loyalty," and its marketing antonym brand "switching," are quite different for those who market durable goods as opposed to nondurable goods. Most "loyalty" and "switching" studies published to date, particularly those using sophisticated statistical techniques, are concentrated in the nondurables area, where, for reasons suggested above, the probability of an individual purchasing a particular brand is often a function of his recent buying behavior.

Perceived environmental changes play an important role in spending and saving decisions, also. For example, a worker who is unexpectedly fired will generally experience a dramatic change in his attitudes and expectations toward the future. Is it not reasonable to expect that these changes would be reflected in his spending and saving behavior? Similarly, considering all consumers as a group, the sudden prospect of a prolonged steel strike or higher (or lower) taxes might be expected to cause many individuals within the group to experience changes in expectations at the same time, and consequently to alter their buying behavior at the same time *and in the same direction*. Katona states that "expectations tend to change infrequently, radically, and simultaneously." [34] The reasoning underlying this statement is sociological. Individuals are a part of a larger social or cultural system. Such a system provides a frame of reference which introduces a common element of meaning to

[34] G. Katona, *op. cit.*, *Psychological Analysis of Economic Behavior*, p. 55. These conclusions conflict with the Keynesian view regarding the influence of changes in expectations about future income levels on the propensity to consume.

Katona and his associates have published considerable evidence to support the theory that attitudes and expectations play an important role in decisions regarding the allocation of discretionary income (for example, see reference 29 and G. Katona *loc. cit.*, *The Powerful Consumer*). However, it should be pointed out that strong disagreement still exists regarding the usefulness of attitudinal and expectational data (see Chapter 7).

events that are perceived by members of the system. In this sense, the system itself becomes a source of information; it also serves as a vehicle for the dissemination of information. With the advent of *mass communication* techniques, it has become possible for members of a cultural group to be exposed to information almost simultaneously; therefore their reactions can also occur simultaneously. Mass communication of information is a relatively new phenomenon. When Lee surrendered to Grant on April 9, 1865, it was months before the news was generally known in all parts of the United States. When President Kennedy was assassinated on November 22, 1963, the news spread throughout the world in a matter of hours. Thus, to the extent that a "common element of meaning" is transmitted to a group, individual members of the group tend to behave *in the same way;* to the extent that the information is received simultaneously, members of the group tend to behave *at the same time.*

One final psychological consideration of importance to market analysts is found in the fact that consumers, like businessmen, do plan their purchases. The planning period may vary from seconds (e.g., for so-called "impulse" items) to years (e.g., for a college education for the children or for a new home), and it may vary radically between different families for the same item. But the fact of planning makes it meaningful to ask people about future plans, and to check subsequently to see if these plans were carried through. Note that an "impulse" purchase, in the context used here, is considered to be both rational (i.e., "self-approved" by the buyer, see page 110 and planned. This approach to rationality restricts the use of the word "irrational" to either excessively neurotic or psychotic behavior.

To summarize the preceding sections of this chapter, American consumers enjoy a high level of discretionary income; an explanation of the decision making process by which this income is allocated requires an understanding of certain psychological concepts, including those of intervening variables, motivation and learning. The introduction of these concepts into the search for a better understanding of consumer behavior has brought about an erosion or breakdown of traditional thinking in this area.

PSYCHOLOGICAL ASPECTS OF BUYING BEHAVIOR: IMPLICATIONS FOR MARKETING

Without exception, the topics that have been discussed in this chapter are in a state of ferment. There is disagreement, even among psychologists, regarding the definition and classification of such basic concepts as needs; economists argue about the relative importance of buying intentions and general expectations for business forecasting; market analysts debate the usefulness of "motivation research." And, interestingly, each adversary is able to buttress his position with an impressive array of theoretical concepts and empirical data. It seems probable that these disagreements will not be resolved in the immediate future, nor perhaps should they be; progress is aided by intelligent debate. As in the past, the struggle toward agreement on the conceptualization and labeling of concepts will continue hand in hand with, and partially aided by, the efforts of many individuals to validate their positions empirically.

Within this environment of uncertainty, the fact remains that social scientists have made many useful contributions to marketing. Much remains to be done. To suggest the direction that future empirical efforts should take is presumptuous; to predict the direction they will take entails obvious risk. Nonetheless, this writer believes that indications can be found in past research and research now in progress that point toward certain tasks that must be accomplished in the future. These tasks are outlined below.

Communication of Existing Social Science Concepts to Market Analysts

The existing theoretical body of knowledge relevant to the behavior of consumers has been developed primarily by social scientists. As published, much of this knowledge is at a level that is not appropriate for application to specific marketing problems. For example, economists are interested in how a family allocates its income; question areas here often include spending as opposed to saving and the allocation of spending among such broad categories of goods as durables, nondurables, and services. To do their jobs effectively, however, market analysts often require more detail. They are interested in forecasting the sales of particular products and of particular brands. Psychologists may be interested in studying the interaction among members of a household in order to determine the effects of such interaction on mental health. Market analysts are interested in how the interaction within a household influences buying decisions. Many such examples could be listed. The essential point is that the applicable research techniques are frequently similar; often the differences are only in the specific purposes for which the research is designed.

Unfortunately, a large number of the concepts and techniques made available by social scientists to market analysts are not used. And the reason is a very simple one: They are not understood, or, worse, they are misunderstood. The offering of each social discipline tends to be couched in a precise language, useful to members of that discipline, but often unintelligible to others. There are few multilingual market analysts. Therefore, in order to make maximum use of *current* knowledge, an effort must be made to improve interdisciplinary communication. The trend toward research involving "teams" of specialists lends increased urgency to this need. Benefits from improved communication would accrue to all concerned. The effectiveness of contributions made by marketing research to management decisions would be greatly enhanced; hence the support that social scientists require to continue their efforts would be more readily forthcoming.

The problem of improving communications among disciplines will not be solved swiftly, nor is there any single solution. Initiatory factors are in evidence. They must gain impetus from a recognition of mutual interests by the individuals and groups concerned. Under the auspices of the Ford Foundation, Dahl, Haire, and Lazarsfeld have highlighted presently neglected aspects of existing business institutions that would be appropriate for study by political scientists, psychologists, and sociologists.[35] To the marketing group, Newman has made one specific recommendation that warrants attention—the training of what he ably describes as "research generalists." [36] Although Newman describes the functions of a research generalist in some detail, the essential aspects of the job are two. First, the man must have a basic understanding of the strengths and limitations of research techniques, and second, and most important, he must be able to serve effectively as a middleman between the research specialists (both from marketing and from the social disciplines) and marketing management. This is a difficult job. It calls not only for an ability to communicate effectively with specialists from a variety of disciplines and to know when the services of technical specialists should be employed, but also for an ability to interpret and present research results in a manner which makes them useful in arriving at marketing decisions.

The complexities associated with successfully translating a theoretical finding into forms that can be applied to practical problems has received a great deal more attention in the physical sciences than in the social sciences. Research and development groups of various kinds are frequently used to bridge the gap. The problems faced by those who wish to apply theoretical advances in the social sciences are basically anal-

[35] R. Dahl, M. Haire, and P. Lazarsfeld, *Social Science Research on Business: Product and Potential*, Columbia University Press, New York, 1959.
[36] J. W. Newman, "Putting Research Into Marketing Decisions," *Harvard Business Review* (March–April 1962).

ogous to those faced by physical scientists; perhaps the organization necessary to accomplish the transition should be analogous too. Certainly the general approach deserves investigation.

Direction of Future Empirical Research

Not only must present knowledge be diffused more widely, but, at the same time, new knowledge must be developed. A number of areas of inquiry can be expected to supplement and expand current knowledge usefully. These range from (1) the application of social science concepts to the understanding of relatively specific marketing phenomena to (2) the development of integrated behavioral models of the United States economy. A number of these frontier areas are discussed below.

a. Application of Social Science Concepts to Specific Marketing Problems

By definition, research in this area is addressed to relatively narrow problems. However, empirical results from these studies become the building blocks for conceptual development and empirical testing of the broader theories and models described below. Literally hundreds of studies might be mentioned here. To cite a few recent examples, Yankelovich has proposed a method for segmenting markets based on the scaling of psychological and sociological characteristics of consumers (values, needs, attitudes, etc.).[37] Also addressing himself to the segmentation of markets, Benson has developed a technique for determining the market franchise for individual products and brands by combining concepts and techniques from psychology and mathematics.[38] These same techniques can also be used to determine a potential franchise by defining a segment of consumers whose needs are not being met by products presently on the market. Kuehn and Day have described a similar approach applied to the measurement and evaluation of consumer preferences.[39]

[37] D. Yankelovich, "New Criteria for Market Segmentation," *Harvard Business Review* (March–April 1964). This article challenges the assumption that demography is always the best way to segment markets.

[38] P. H. Benson, "Psychometric Procedures in the Analysis of Market Segmentation," *Innovation: Key to Marketing Progress,* American Marketing Association, Chicago, 1963; P. H. Benson, "Consumer Preference Distributions in the Analysis of Market Segmentation," *Emerging Concepts in Marketing,* American Marketing Association, Chicago, 1962.

[39] A. Kuehn and R. Day, "Strategy of Product Quality," *Harvard Business Review* (November–December 1962).

In the communications area (radio, television, magazines, etc.) Frankel has developed an experimental technique that offers promise of making a substantial contribution to the development of a "theory of mass communication" capable of increasing the efficiency of media advertising schedules.[40] This work uses concepts from both psychology and mathematics.

b. Development of New Techniques for Empirical Research

Many research procedures have traditionally been employed by market analysts to determine attitudes or behavioral characteristics of consumers, both in the aggregate and for subgroups. These procedures —including cross-section "polls," the analysis of sales records, and so on —have had a long and well documented history of both success and failure. The failures have tended to cluster most notably in areas where the techniques applied were not appropriate to the questions being researched; for example, traditional methods have not proven effective when the objective has been to quantify basic aspects of the "why" of human behavior in a manner such that the resulting variables could be applied to the prediction of future behavior. This section discusses three areas of research in which new procedures are being developed that should usefully supplement traditional research technology.

Measurement of Psychological Variables. For those who have attempted to use survey research techniques to gain an understanding of behavior, a major limitation has been the difficulty of measuring psychological variables under field conditions. Clinical psychologists have developed and validated tests that purport to measure such characteristics as ability, aptitude, interests, and various personality dimensions. However, as a rule these tests take from 45 minutes to many hours to administer and are given under controlled conditions, often to individuals who have requested guidance and therefore are motivated to follow instructions and complete the test. In addition, many of these instruments must be administered by a technically competent person. It is apparent that standard psychological tests cannot be successfully administered as part of the typical marketing research questionnaire. Even if respondents were willing to cooperate—and few would be—the time required to measure any one psychological variable would be prohibitive; there would be too little time remaining for other questions.

Hence researchers have been confronted with the problem of develop-

---

[40] L. R. Frankel, "Mass Media: The Process of Communication," paper presented to the International Marketing Federation Conference, Hamburg, Germany (October 1963).

ing valid measures of psychological variables that can be incorporated into questionnaires. Although much of the experimental evidence in this area has not been published, some recent results can be cited. In a study of the behavior of injured workers, Morgan used an adaptation of the Thematic Apperception Test (TAT) to measure each respondent's need for achievement, need for affiliation, and need for power.[41] One finding of this research was that the injured male workers interviewed, most of whom had incurred serious injuries, attained much lower "need achievement" scores than those generally found in the population as a whole. In terms of rehabilitating the seriously injured, one of the implications drawn from this finding by the authors is that these individuals should not be encouraged to become independent businessmen, since, in general, successful independent businessmen score relatively high on a "need achievement" test. Contrary to this conclusion, advocates of lump sum redemption settlements for injured workers often argue that a single large payment would enable an injured individual to go into business for himself and thus ensure his financial independence.

Another recent study demonstrates a high correlation between education, a "need achievement" score, and an index of the amount of planning done by a family. The authors conclude that planning "may be a mechanism by which motivation to achieve success is translated into high levels of income."[42] Any variable that is both measurable and reflected in a high level of income should not be overlooked by the market analyst.

In still another study, broad questions designed to elicit general attitudes of hostility and suspicion were asked of respondents who had been involved in automobile accidents.[43] The hostility scores were found to be highly associated with the respondents' more specific attitudes toward the accident and reparation experience, such as the respondents' attitudes toward the outcome of the case. Of the respondents with a high hostility score, 57 per cent expressed dissatisfaction with the outcome of their case. The figure is 38 per cent for the remaining respondents.

One need only talk with his neighbor to recognize that there are basic personality differences among individuals; these differences do influence behavior. Although the preceding examples are not directly concerned with marketing problems, they serve to indicate the potential

[41] J. Morgan, M. Snider, and M. Sobel, *Lump Sum Redemption Settlements and Rehabilitation*, Survey Research Center, University of Michigan, 1959, pp. 113–116.
[42] J. N. Morgan et al., *Income and Welfare in the United States*, McGraw-Hill, 1962. The quote is from p. 436.
[43] A. Conard et al., *Automobile Accident Costs and Payments: Studies in the Economics of Injury Reparation*, The University of Michigan Press, Ann Arbor, Michigan, 1964.

value of applying measures of personality differences to the analysis of behavioral questions. The implication is clear: Market analysts who are charged with a responsibility for gaining knowledge about the rationale underlying consumer behavior must continue to seek reliable methods for adapting the measuring instruments developed by psychologists to formats that are appropriate for marketing research questionnaires.

Development of Models. The research discussed thus far in this section provides, as an end product, bits of new knowledge that will be useful in solving many specific marketing problems. To make a maximum contribution, however, much of this new knowledge (along with knowledge presently available) must also be integrated into more general behavioral models of systems and processes. Such models take into account the relationships and interactions among the *configuration* of variables that influence a particular action, such as a decision to purchase.

A number of theoretical models have been proposed that deserve attention. For example, Morgan has formulated a general theory of household decision making that allows for two major sets of forces that influence behavior—those associated with *each* individual involved in the decision (e.g., each individual's physiological and learner needs) and those associated with the interaction of individuals within a family or group.[44] Howard has written a cogent statement of the potential use of normative decision models by marketing executives to optimize business decisions in terms of some specified criteria.[45] And Orcutt and his associates at the University of Wisconsin's Social Systems Research Institute have suggested the framework for a large-scale integrated microanalytic model of the United States.[46]

The advent of large-scale computers has made it feasible to test empirically relatively complex theoretical models. There are two criteria for such tests. First, the variables used to develop the theoretical constructs must be researchable, that is, they must be measurable within the practical constraints imposed by the research design. Second, adequate financing must be forthcoming. To generate the empirical data necessary to develop and test complex models can be extremely expen-

---

[44] J. N. Morgan, "Household Decision Making," in N. Foote (ed.), *Household Decision-Making*, New York University Press, New York, 1961.
[45] J. A. Howard, *Marketing: Executive and Buyer Behavior*, Columbia University Press, New York, 1963.
[46] G. H. Orcutt et al., *Microanalysis of Socioeconomic Systems: A Simulation Study*, Harper, New York, 1961.

sive. In 1961 Orcutt estimated the cost of constructing a "highly useful model of the United States economy" at about one hundred million dollars, spread over a ten-year period.[47] Obviously, many efforts are less ambitious and correspondingly less costly; however, the construction and testing of models frequently require large expenditures of money.

The empirical testing of models represents one important area where, in the writer's opinion, business and academic researchers may be able to find a mutually advantageous basis for collaboration. Many of the *theoretical* models currently available in the area of consumer behavior have been developed by academicians, many of whom do not have sufficient resources for empirically testing their theories; in the archives of commercial firms can often be found the basic data necessary for testing these same models, either in whole or in part.

Applications of Longitudinal Analysis. Turning again to research methodology, empirical studies of the behavior of a defined universe of individuals or households through time can be approached in two ways. First, data obtained from independent cross-section samples drawn at different points in time can be used to make inferences both about the behavior of all members of the defined universe and about the behavior of selected subgroups. Second, one sample of individuals or households from a defined universe can be selected and interviewed at two or more *different* points in time. The second approach is referred to as the "panel" or reinterview technique, and the analysis of information elicited from or about the same sampling unit at two or more points in time is referred to as "longitudinal" analysis. Any discussion of research techniques appropriate for the study of psychological variables would not be complete without mention of the increasing use being made of panel studies by market analysts.

In the broadest sense, the purpose of a panel is to provide information that will permit the analysis of selected aspects of the dynamics of changes in behavior through time. "Change" may be thought of as referring to the relative growth and development of such variables as ideas, attitudes, intentions, expectations, patterns of behavior (e.g., habits), and decision processes, as well as to additions or deletions from the inventory of material assets owned by an individual or family. Although inferences about such changes are often made on an aggregate basis from cross-section studies, much of the microanalysis that is possible with panel data cannot be duplicated using the cross-section approach. Marketing areas in which the panel technique has been used as

[47] G. H. Orcutt, "Microanalytic Models of the United States Economy: Need and Development," *American Economic Review*, Vol. LII, No. 2 (May 1962), p. 240.

a research device include audience measurement, media selection, and the acceptance of new products.[48] The panel technique has also been used successfully in a number of other substantive areas, most notably to study political behavior.

When compared with the traditional cross-section study, what are some of the major advantages exhibited by a panel design? First, because panels provide a factual record of the behavior of the *same household* through time, changes in behavior within the household can be studied in relation to changes associated with the household itself, such as changes in demographic characteristics, psychological characteristics, opinions and attitudes, activities pursued by the household, and intended behavior as recorded on a previous questionnaire. An individual's behavior can be examined in relation to events that take place in his environment, a number of which he may not have anticipated at the time of the previous interview—for example, changes in the international political climate (such as those brought about by changes in the "Cold War"), or changes in one of the major statistical indicators of national economic well-being (such as an increase or decrease in unemployment), or changes in a local situation (such as the influx or exodus of industry). Unexpected events might also occur within the individual's own household that will alter intended behavior, for example, a serious illness.

Second, reinterviewing the same individuals or families holds forth promise of providing an extremely useful approach to achieving refinements in the formulation and application of buying intentions data to both the prediction of the behavior of microunits and the forecasting of aggregate behavior.[49] Reinterview data can be used to explore questions such as these: What are the psychological, sociological, and demographic characteristics of those who fulfill their buying intentions as opposed to those who do not? What are the characteristics of individuals who tend to plan their purchases well in advance as opposed to those whose purchasing takes on the appearance of impulse behavior? What kinds of events or other stimuli tend to cause people to alter their plans?

[48] For a discussion of these applications, and a number of others, see H. W. Boyd, Jr. and R. L. Westfall, *An Evaluation of Continuous Consumer Panels as a Source of Marketing Information*, Monograph, Marketing Research Techniques, Series "A," American Marketing Association, 1960; R. Ferber, *Collecting Financial Data by Consumer Panel Techniques*, Bureau of Economic and Business Research, University of Illinois, Urbana, 1959.

[49] For a demonstration of the analysis of reinterview data, as well as a discussion of the usefulness of buying intentions data for forecasting, see F. Thomas Juster, *Anticipations and Purchases: An Analysis of Consumer Behavior*, Princeton University Press, Princeton, N.J., 1964. See also E. Mueller, *loc. cit.*, "Ten Years of Consumer Attitude Surveys: Their Forecasting Record."

Which of these stimuli, if any, can be incorporated into a company's promotional mix? To consider a specific example, longitudinal analysis can be used to examine the relationship between changes in behavior and the information media to which an individual or a household has been exposed, with the objective of isolating the most effective advertising appeals.

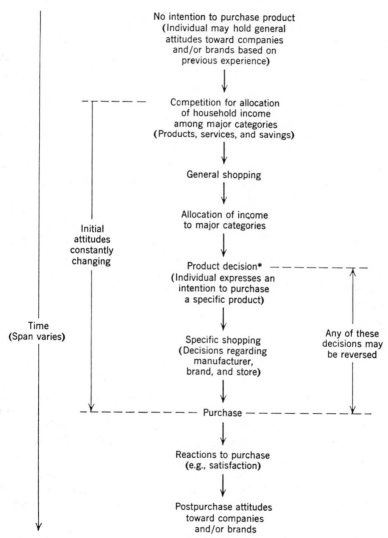

Figure 6.4 Paradigm of the purchase process. (*Details of decisions regarding saving and expenditures for services are omitted.)

Another application of panel research can be found in the problem of researching the *process* by which a consumer is led to make a purchase. A decision to purchase a particular item is a multistage process, though there may often be a series of subprocesses that change in simultaneous sequences. In its most basic form, a paradigm of the purchase process might look as shown in Figure 6.4. To begin to gain any real understanding of the process (or processes) involved, it is important to study both the prepurchase stage and the postpurchase stage. Because the sequence of stages may often involve learning (a critical aspect of the willingness of an individual to accept product innovation), changes in attitudes (which may, for example, result in switching brands or switching stores), the allocation of decision roles within a family, and rationalization after purchase, it is usually impossible for an individual accurately to reconstruct attitudes, emotions, and intentions as they existed at various points prior to purchase. Panels improve the quality of data by vastly reducing reliance on memory.

In summary, the increasing use of longitudinal studies has been dictated by a desire to understand better the major factors underlying consumer behavior and to apply the knowledge gained not only to aggregate economic forecasting but also to product planning, increasing the effectiveness of all forms of promotion, and so on. Indeed, it would not be inappropriate to conclude that here is still another research technique that can make a major contribution to the effective implementation of the marketing concept. Panel research is currently being conducted by agencies of the federal government, by academic organizations, and by commercial firms, including the General Motors Corporation and the General Electric Company.

SUMMARY

The discipline of psychology attempts to answer questions dealing with the behavior of individuals; the discipline of economics is concerned with the allocation of scarce resources. When the two are combined, the focus becomes one of understanding the behavior of individuals in their capacities as the allocators of scarce resources, that is, to understand why individuals elect to earn, invest, spend, and transfer wealth as they do. To demonstrate that this latter area, economic psychology, is a vital part of any "science of marketing" has been a primary aim of this chapter.

In addition, the chapter has also attempted to fulfill a number of secondary aims. To the extent that the material can be summarized, the foregoing paragraphs add up to this: High levels of discretionary purchasing power in the American economy tend to negate the traditional "utility" theory of buying behavior. In order to understand how consumers allocate their discretionary buying power, one must first understand certain concepts and theories applicable to the broad area of *human* behavior—concepts and theories that are equally relevant to the narrower problems of *buying* behavior; these include the concept of intervening variables, and the theories of motivation and learning. These concepts and theories, in combination with others from psychology and sociology not discussed here, represent the vehicle by which the marketing concept can be implemented.

Properly applied, principles and techniques that have been developed by psychologists hold forth the promise of placing needs and wants of consumers in much closer proximity to the corporate decision structure than has thus far been possible. Before this potential can be realized, however, a number of tasks must be accomplished. First, so that market analysts can make effective use of principles and techniques that are now available, communication among market analysts and social scientists must be improved. Second, both substantive and methodological research must be vigorously pushed forward in a number of basic areas. In the realm of substantive research, more evidence is needed regarding the application and relevance of individual psychological concepts and theories to specific marketing problems. This evidence can, in turn, be applied to the development of integrated behavioral models of systems and processes; such models represent one of the important long-term goals toward which all the efforts described in this chapter should be pointed, whether directly or indirectly. In the area of methodological research, new techniques must be developed that will permit measures of psychological variables to be incorporated into marketing research questionnaires. And, to prognosticate, the writer is convinced that longitudinal analysis, as a method for gaining insight into behavioral patterns that change through time, will gain rapidly increasing acceptance in the future.

A postscript: Present evidence indicates that the major task confronting market analysts is one of *learning how to apply* the theoretical knowledge that has already been developed by psychologists in order to gain a better understanding of specific aspects of consumer behavior. Most of the theories and concepts relevant to consumer behavior have been tested in a controlled laboratory environment, but a great deal of the testing has been done either with animals or with human beings who exhibit abnormal behavior. Clearly, the immediate challenge is to adapt present theoretical knowledge to existing marketing problems; in the near future, at least, the state of theoretical knowledge can be expected to remain well in advance of the state of applied knowledge.

BIBLIOGRAPHY

Alderson, W., *Marketing Behavior and Executive Action*, Richard D. Irwin, Homewood, Ill., 1957.

Atkinson, J. (ed.), *Motives in Fantasy, Action, and Society*, D. Van Nostrand, Princeton, N.J., 1958.

Benson, P. H., "Consumer Preference Distributions in the Analysis of Market Segmentation," *Emerging Concepts in Marketing*, American Marketing Association, 1962.

_____, "Psychometric Procedures in the Analysis of Market Segmentation," *Innovation: Key to Marketing Progress*, American Marketing Association, Chicago, 1963.

Boyd, H. W., Jr. and R. L. Westfall, *An Evaluation of Continuous Consumer Panels as a Source of Marketing Information*, Monograph, American Marketing Association, 1960.

Brink, E. L. and W. L. Kelley, *The Management of Promotion*, Prentice-Hall, Englewood Cliffs, N.J., 1963.

Bursk, E. C., "Opportunities for Persuasion," *Harvard Business Review* (September–October 1958).

Clawson, C. J., "Family Composition, Motivation, and Buying Decisions," in N. Foote (ed.), *Household Decision-Making*, New York University Press, New York, 1961.

Conard, A., et al., *Automobile Accident Costs and Payments: Studies in the Economics of Injury Reparation*, The University of Michigan Press, Ann Arbor, Michigan, 1964.

Dahl, R., M. Haire, and P. Lazarsfeld, *Social Science Research on Business: Product and Potential*, Columbia University Press, New York, 1959.

Engel, J. F., "The Influence of Needs and Attitudes on the Perception of Persuasion," *Toward Scientific Marketing*, American Marketing Association, Chicago, 1963.

Ferber, R., *Collecting Financial Data by Consumer Panel Techniques*, Bureau of Economic and Business Research, University of Illinois, Urbana, 1959.

Festinger, L., *A Theory of Cognitive Dissonance*, Stanford University Press, Stanford, Calif., 1957.

Fortune (editors of), *Markets of the Sixties*, Harper, New York, 1960.

Foundation for Research on Human Behavior, *Projective Techniques in Consumer Motivation Research*, Ann Arbor, Michigan, 1955.

Frankel, L. R., "Mass Media: The Process of Communication," paper presented to the International Marketing Federation Conference, Hamburg, Germany (October 1963).

Galbraith, J. K., *The Affluent Society*, Houghton Mifflin, Boston, 1958.

Gordon, R. A., *Business Fluctuations*, Harper, New York, 1952.

Howard, J. A., *Marketing: Executive and Buyer Behavior*, Columbia University Press, New York, 1963.

Juster, F. Thomas, *Anticipations and Purchases: An Analysis of Consumer Behavior*, Princeton University Press, Princeton, N.J., 1964.

Katona, G., "Long-Range Changes in Consumer Attitudes," in C. Lininger (ed.), *Dynamic Aspects of Consumer Behavior*, Foundation for Research on Human Behavior, Ann Arbor, Michigan, 1963.

————, *The Powerful Consumer*, McGraw-Hill, New York, 1960.

————, *Psychological Analysis of Economic Behavior*, McGraw-Hill, New York, 1951.

————, "Rational Behavior and Economic Behavior," *Psychological Review*, Vol. LX, No. 5 (September 1953).

————, "The Relationship between Psychology and Economics," in S. Koch (ed.), *Psychology: A Study of Science*, McGraw-Hill, New York, 1963.

Katona, G., C. Lininger, and R. Kosobud, *1962 Survey of Consumer Finances*, Monograph Number 32, Survey Research Center, University of Michigan, 1963.

Keynes, J. M., *The General Theory of Employment, Interest and Money*, Harcourt, Brace, New York, 1935.

Kohler, W., *Gestalt Psychology*, Liveright Company, New York, 1947.

Kuehn, A., and R. Day, "Strategy of Product Quality," *Harvard Business Review* (November–December 1962).

Levitt, T., "M–R Snake Dance," *Harvard Business Review* (November–December 1960).

Lewin, K., *et al.*, "Level of Aspiration," in J. Hunt (ed.), *Personality and the Behavior Disorders*, Ronald Press, New York, 1944.

Maslow, A. H., *Motivation and Personality*, Harper, New York, 1954.

McClelland, D. C., et al., *The Achievement Motive*, Appleton-Century-Crofts, New York, 1953.

————, *The Achieving Society*, D. Van Nostrand, Princeton, N.J., 1961.

McKitterick, J. B., "What is the Marketing Management Concept," *The Frontiers of Marketing Thought and Science*, American Marketing Association, 1957.

Morgan, C. T., *Introduction to Psychology*, McGraw-Hill, New York, 1956.

Morgan, J. N., "The Achievement Motive and Economic Behavior," *Economic Behavior and Cultural Change*, Vol. XII (April 1964).

————, "Household Decision-Making," in N. Foote (ed.), *Household Decision Making*, New York University Press, New York, 1961.

Morgan, J. N. et al., *Income and Welfare in the United States*, McGraw-Hill, New York, 1962.

Morgan, J., M. Snider, and M. Sobol, *Lump Sum Redemption Settlements and Rehabilitation*, Survey Research Center, University of Michigan, 1959.

Mueller, E., "The Desire for Innovation in Household Goods," in L. Clark (ed.), *Consumer Behavior*, New York University Press, New York, 1958.

————, "Ten Years of Consumer Attitude Surveys: Their Forecasting Record," *Journal of the American Statistical Association*, Vol. LVIII, No. 304 (December 1963).

National Industrial Conference Board, "Discretionary Income: A New Measure of Consumer Markets," *The Business Record* (May 1958).

————, *A Graphic Guide to Consumer Markets*, 1963.

————, *Discretionary Income*, Technical Paper No. 6, 1958.

————, *Use of Motivation Research in Marketing*, Studies in Business Policy, No. 97, 1960.

Newman, J. W., *Motivation Research and Marketing Management*, The Plimpton Press, Boston, 1958.

_____, "Putting Research into Marketing Decisions," *Harvard Business Review* (March–April 1962).

Orcutt, G. H. et al., *Microanalysis of Socioeconomic Systems: A Simulation Study,* Harper, New York, 1961.

Orcutt, G. H., "Microanalytic Models of the United States Economy: Need and Development," *American Economic Review,* Vol. LII, No. 2 (May 1962).

Rose, A. W., "Motivation Research and Subliminal Advertising," *Social Research,* Vol. XXV, No. 3 (Autumn 1958).

Scott, J. D., *Advertising Principles and Problems,* Prentice-Hall, New York, 1953.

Smith, G. H., *Motivation Research in Advertising and Marketing,* McGraw-Hill, New York, 1954.

Stigler, G. J., *The Theory of Price,* Macmillan, New York, 1952.

Survey of Consumer Finances (1960), Survey Research Center, University of Michigan, 1960.

Wertheimer, M., *Productive Thinking,* Harper, New York, 1959.

Yankelovich, D., "New Criteria for Market Segmentation," *Harvard Business Review* (March–April, 1964).

7

Consumer Behavior:
Disbursements and Welfare

WARREN J. BILKEY

This chapter presents an overview of the current state of consumer behavior analysis but focuses on those aspects which seem most relevant for market analysts. It does not catalogue all the various consumer studies to date, for such bibliographical listings are already available.[1]

Consumer behavior analysis is concerned essentially with two considerations, consumer disbursements and consumer welfare. The former is analyzable by the scientific method and has absorbed the lion's share of analytical attention. The latter is largely a philosophical problem, and the basic methodology for its analysis has not been worked out. Both are discussed below, with inferences drawn for market research.

CONSUMER DISBURSEMENT ANALYSIS

Rationale Involved

Consumer disbursements can be analyzed either in terms of a successive delimitation approach or a general equilibrium approach. Both come essentially to the same thing; the difference lies in the manner of analysis.

---

[1] Robert Ferber, "Research on Household Behavior," *American Economic Review,* Vol. LII, No. 1 (March 1962), pp. 19–63; James N. Morgan, "A Review of Recent Research on Consumer Behavior," in L. H. Clark (ed.), *Consumer Behavior,* New York University Press, New York, 1954, pp. 93–219; and G. Orcutt and A. D. Roy, "A Bibliography of the Consumption Function" (mimeographed), Cambridge University, Department of Applied Economics, 1949.

Successive Delimitation Approach

This approach is an intellectual descendent of monopolistic competition theory. According to the successive delimitation concept, consumer disbursement predictions are to be made in the following sequence. *First,* estimate the probable national income for the year in question. *Second,* estimate what per cent of the national income will go to personal income. *Third,* estimate what per cent of the personal income will be spent. *Fourth,* estimate what per cent of the personal expenditures will go to each disbursement category (food, clothing, transportation, etc.). *Fifth,* estimate what per cent of the disbursements for each category will go to the various subcategories (e.g., what per cent of transportation expenditures will go for the purchase of new automobiles). *Sixth,* estimate what per cent of the subcategory expenditures will go for a particular brand of that item (e.g., what per cent of the new car purchases will be Fords).[2] The first two of the analytical stages (the size of the national income and the proportion of this income going to households) are economic problems. The remaining four analytical stages are the direct concern of consumer behavior analysts.

General Equilibrium Approach

General equilibrium analysis dates back explicitly to Walras but has become practicable only with the advent of computers. Logically, it involves the construction of a complex of simultaneous equations that have been developed from interview and other data, and from all this ascertaining the general equilibrium relationships. In broad outline these equations would be of the following types, although hundreds or possibly even thousands would be required for given problems.

1. Equations for the relation between the level of national income and the level and composition of personal income.
2. Equations for the relation between the level of personal income and the consumers' various disbursements (including savings).
3. Equations for the relation between varying consumer disbursements and national income. (Some of these equations would be concerned with the direct effects of consumption expenditures on national income, and others with the indirect effects, for example,

[2] Earlier consumer analysts had hoped that all six of the analytical stages listed above would be reflected in consumer buying anticipations, so that the purchases of specific items could be predicted solely by means of consumer interviews. Experience has not borne out this hope. (See James Tobin, "On the Predictive Value of Consumer Intentions and Attitudes," *Review of Economic Statistics,* Vol. XLI, No. 1 (February 1959), pp. 1–11.

on investment, foreign trade balances, etc., which in turn affect national income.

4. Equations for the "other" determinants (investment, foreign trade balances, etc.) of national income.

The types of equations suggested above imply *not* that income is the only influence on consumer disbursements but rather that variations in consumer disbursements set into motion various economic changes which further influence consumer disbursements—and that these interrelations are significant. To be adequate, the equations may have to be sufficiently specific to account for the particular brands of items purchased. The reason is that each firm has its own unique amount of excess capacity and its own particular location and labor force. The former consideration affects the accelerator, and the latter influences the multiplier. Major shifts between brands, therefore, can set into motion considerable economic repercussions.

In practice, the successive delimitation approach and the general equilibrium approach come to the same thing. If the changes in consumer disbursements have no perceptible effect on national income, the corresponding general equilibrium equations will have no more than a negligible value. If, on the other hand, the changing consumer disbursements have an impact on national income, analysts using the successive delimitation approach must revise their national income estimates accordingly and recompute the probable consumer disbursements. This in turn may necessitate a further recomputation of national income, etc. Thus the successive delimitation approach involves a first approximation, a second approximation, and so on. Successive approximations will more and more approach the results yielded by the general equilibrium approach.

Analysis

This is a description of what seems to be the relevant consumer relationships involved. The format is in terms of the successive delimitation approach.

Aggregate Spending

This involves the determination of the consumption function. A considerable literature has been developed on this subject because of the emphasis given it by Keynes and the observed differences between the short-run and the long-run consumption functions. As textbooks [3] ex-

[3] Gardner Ackley, *Microeconomic Theory*, Macmillan, New York, 1961, pp. 236–246.

plain, the short-run function (in terms of a Hansen-type diagram) tends to be less steep than the long-run consumption function. It is as though the former shifts upward over time along a path which outlines the latter.

Four hypotheses have been offered to explain this phenomenon. First, there is the absolute income hypothesis,[4] which holds that consumption is a function of absolute income but that this functional relationship shifts upward over time because of exogenous forces, such as growing population, improving tastes, and the increasing complexity of life. Second, the relative income hypothesis,[5] which holds that the per cent of income consumed is a function of the person's income relative to that of all other persons in that community, that is, of his decile position in the community's income distribution hierarchy. Third, there is the previous peak income hypothesis,[6] which holds that the per cent of income consumed is a function of the family's present income relative to their previous peak income. This has been refined into the proposition that the per cent of income consumed is a function of the family's present income relative to their previous peak consumption.[7] Fourth, there is the "permanent" income hypothesis,[8] which holds that consumption is primarily a function of the more-or-less constant component of family income and only slightly a function of the transitory component of family income.[9] Note that each of the foregoing hypotheses regards consumption as being in some sense a function of income; they disagree only as to the particular nature of this relationship.

Thus far no consensus has been reached as to which of these hypotheses is most nearly correct, or of the relation between them.

[4] Robert Ferber, op. cit., pp. 21–23; James Tobin, "Relative Income, Absolute Income, and Saving," in Money, Trade and Economic Growth, Essays in Honor of John Henry Williams, Macmillan, New York, 1951, pp. 135–156.
[5] D. S. Brady and Rose Friedman, "Savings and the Income Distribution," National Bureau of Economic Research, Studies in Income and Wealth, Vol. X, New York, 1947, pp. 247–265; J. S. Duesenberry, Income, Saving and the Theory of Consumer Behavior, Harvard University Press, Cambridge, 1949, pp. 25–46; and Robert Ferber, op. cit., pp. 23–25.
[6] J. S. Duesenberry, op. cit., pp. 69–92.
[7] T. E. Davis, "The Consumption Function as a Tool for Prediction," Review of Economic Statistics, Vol. XXXIV, No. 3 (August 1952), pp. 270–277.
[8] Robert Ferber, op. cit., pp. 26–28; Milton Friedman, A Theory of the Consumption Function, National Bureau of Economic Research, Princeton, 1957; and F. Modigliani and A. Ando, "The 'Permanent' Income and the 'Life Cycle' Hypotheses of Saving Behavior: Comparison and Tests," in I. Friend and R. Jones (eds.), Proceedings of the Conference on Consumption and Saving, Vol. II, University of Pennsylvania Press, Philadelphia, 1960, pp. 49–174.
[9] To illustrate, a salesman's income may vary greatly from month to month. Yet his family's spending each month is determined more by the average income that he counts on receiving over time than by the income that he actually receives each month. Transitory income presumably affects special purchases.

Empirical studies of aggregate spending behavior indicate that roughly 90 per cent of the change in per capita total spending is accounted for by changes in per capita income over that same period. The remainder presumably is accounted for by errors in the particular relationship used and by other considerations. A wide variety of studies have been concerned with obtaining empirical insight on this matter. Some of the more suggestive are outlined below.

Studies by Klein [10] indicate that households experiencing income decreases, and who expect further decreases to occur, tend to spend a smaller fraction of their current income than do households experiencing income decreases and who expect an income increase in the near future. Furthermore,[11] households with a given amount of liquid assets who experience a decline in income tend to spend a larger fraction of their income than do households with the same decline but with less liquid assets. However, the influence of liquid asset holdings tends to be smaller for households with higher incomes than with lower incomes.[12] The influence of liquid asset holdings seems not to be constant over time. During the late 1940's the relation between liquid asset holdings and durable goods purchases seemed to be much stronger than during the early 1950's.[13]

Occupation, too, has been found to be an influence. Bureau of Labor Statistics data [14] have shown that families owning small businesses tend to spend a smaller fraction of their personal incomes than do families

[10] L. R. Klein, "Estimating Patterns of Savings Behavior from Sample Survey Data," *Econometrica*, Vol. XIX, No. 4 (October 1951), pp. 438–454.

[11] George Katona, "Effect of Income Changes on the Rate of Saving," *Review of Economic Statistics*, Vol. XXXI, No. 2 (May 1949), pp. 95–103; L. R. Klein, *loc. cit.*; L. R. Klein, "Patterns of Savings," *Bulletin of Oxford University Institute of Statistics*, Vol. XVII, No. 2 (May 1955), pp. 173–214; and L. R. Klein, "Statistical Estimates of Economic Relations from Survey Data," in G. Katona, L. R. Klein, J. B. Lansing, and J. N. Morgan, *Contributions of Survey Methods to Economics*, Columbia University Press, New York, 1954, pp. 189–240.

[12] L. R. Klein, "Assets, Debts, and Economic Behavior," in Conference on Research; in Income and Wealth, *Studies in Income and Wealth*, Vol. XIV, National Bureau of Economic Research, New York, 1951, pp. 210–217 L. R. Klein, "Estimating Patterns of Savings Behavior from Sample Survey Data," *Econometrica*, Vol. XIX, No. 4 (October 1951) pp. 438–454.

[13] L. R. Klein, "Statistical Estimates of Economic Relations from Survey Data," in G. Katona, L. R. Klein, J. B. Lansing and J. N. Morgan, *Contributions of Survey Methods to Economics*, New York, 1954, pp. 189–240.

[14] I. Friend and I. B. Kravis, "Entrepreneurial Income, Saving and Investment," *American Economic Review*, Vol. XLVII, No. 3 (June 1957), pp. 269–301; L. R. Klein, "Patterns of Savings," *Bulletin of Oxford University Institute of Statistics*, Vol. XVII, No. 2 (May 1955), pp. 173–214; and L. R. Klein and J. Margolis, "Statistical Studies of Unincorporated Business," *Review of Economic Statistics*, Vol. XXXVI, No. 1 (February 1954), pp. 33–46.

at the same income levels whose entire income is from wages or salaries. The decreasing relative importance of small business (particularly when agriculture is taken into account) makes this a significant long-run influence for our country as a whole. The family life cycle [15] also has been found to influence aggregate household spending. Families at the household formation stage (immediately after marriage when housekeeping is started) tend to spend more than they earn; at the family formation stage (when adding to the size of their family) they tend to spend all that they earn; at the child-rearing stage (when no more children are being added but children are growing) they tend to spend less than they earn; at the higher education stage (when children are being sent to college) they tend to spend more than they earn; at the "empty nest" stage (when the children all have left home) they spend less than they earn; at the retirement stage they spend more than they earn. Changes in rates of population growth change the proportion of households in these various stages of the family cycle, which in turn alters the proportion of aggregate personal income saved.[16] Other influences are expectation and general attitude. This has been widely studied by the Survey Research Center. The major expectations involve general economic conditions, the general price level, personal well-being, etc. Favorable expectations tend to increase the per cent of income spent and vice versa. Katona holds that general expectations and attitudes are more significant than buying intentions for explaining purchases. A considerable body of data [17] tends to support the opposite position, however.

[15] See S. G. Barton, "The Life Cycle and Buying Patterns," in L. H. Clark (ed.), *The Life Cycle and Consumer Behavior*, New York University Press, New York, 1955, pp. 53–57; D. S. Brady, "Family Saving, 1880–1950," in R. W. Goldsmith, D. S. Brady, and H. Mendershausen, *A Study of Savings in the United States*, Vol. III, Princeton University Press, Princeton, N.J., 1956, pp. 139–276; L. H. Clark (ed.), 1955; Janet Fisher, "Income, Spending, and the Saving Patterns of Consumer Units in Different Age Groups," in National Bureau of Economic Research, *Studies in Income and Wealth*, Vol. XV, New York, 1962, pp. 75–102; Janet Fisher, "Postwar Changes in Income and Savings Among Consumers in Different Age Groups," *Econometrica*, Vol. XX, No. 1 (January 1952), pp. 47–70; Janet Fisher, "Family Life Cycle Analysis on Research on Consumer Behavior," in L. H. Clark (ed.), *The Life Cycle and Consumer Behavior*, New York University Press, New York, 1955, pp. 28–35; Harold Lydall, "The Life Cycle in Income, Saving, and Asset Ownership," *Econometrica*, Vol. XXIII, No. 2, (April 1955), pp. 131–150; U. S. Government, Bureau of Labor Statistics, Family Income and Expenditures in (selected areas), U. S. Department of Labor Bulletins 642–649, 1938–1941; and U. S. Government, Department of Agriculture, "Family Income and Expenditures" (titles vary), miscellaneous publications between No. 339 and No. 489, 1939–1941.

[16] T. E. Davis, *loc. cit.*

[17] See L. R. Klein and J. B. Lansing, "Decisions to Purchase Consumer Durable

Disbursements Between Categories

For this, three explanations have been offered, utility theory, preference (or indifference) theory, and the vector hypothesis of consumer behavior. The first two are so commonly described in elementary economics texts that they need not be presented here. We need only note that both utility and preference theories have been well developed conceptually but not operationally. Suggestive breakthroughs have been made for the measurement of both utils and indifference functions,[18] but thus far neither has been measured in a way that permits testing against subsequent purchasing behavior. As generally formulated, both utility and preference theories are rigidly rationalistic, but this is not inherent in the theories themselves. Preference theory, for example, may be formulated as a purely behavioristic relationship; [19] ultimately this view underlies the concept of revealed preferences.

Vector theory is much newer than either utility or preference theory, and it is not widely known. For this reason it will be outlined briefly. Its strongest point is that the critical relationships involved are easily measurable, and it can be compared with actual consumer behavior. This permits the vector hypothesis to develop continually as new data become available.

In its barest fundamentals, vector analysis posits that the purchasing act involves psychic conflict—represented by force vectors—between the person's desire for the item in question and his self-imposed resistance against spending the money that the item costs. If the person's desire for that item exceeds his resistance regarding it, he will tend to purchase it and vice versa. The greater the excess of desire over resistance, the greater the probability that the item will be purchased. The greater the

Goods," *Journal of Marketing*, Vol. XX, No. 2 (October 1955), pp. 109–132; A. M. Okun, "The Value of Anticipations Data in Forecasting National Product," in *The Quality and Economic Significance of Anticipations Data*, National Bureau of Economic Research, Princeton, 1960, pp. 411–428; James Tobin, *loc. cit.*; U. S. Government, Federal Reserve Board, "Report of Consultant Committee on Consumer Survey Statistics," July 1955; and Universities—National Bureau of Economic Research, *The Quality and Economic Significance of Anticipations Data*, Princeton University Press, Princeton, N.J., 1960.

[18] R. Frisch, "New Methods for Measuring Marginal Utility," *Beiträge zur Okonomischen Theorie*, No. 3, Tübingen, 1932; L. L. Thurstone, "The Indifference Function," *Journal of Social Psychology*, Vol. II (May 1931), pp. 139–167.

[19] According to the behavioristic view, consumers' indifference maps merely show the combinations of goods they will tend to purchase under various income and price relationships. This view emphasizes consistency of behavior; the question of rationality is irrelevant.

excess of resistance over desire, the greater the probability that the item will not be purchased. A person's desires for various items seemingly are interrelated in accordance with his conception of what constitutes balanced consumption, but how this conception arises or how it changes is not yet known. For this reason, the composition of the person's or family's standard of living is merely taken as given.

The magnitude of a person's desire for any item or disbursement category appears, then, to be the difference between the dollar value of what constitutes his standard of living regarding that item or category and the dollar value of that item or category that he already has.[20] The general level of a person's resistances against spending appears to vary directly with the difference between the dollar value of his standard of living [21] for all items and his income, but then fluctuates around that general level because of changes in his uncommitted balances and his psychological reaction to income change, price change, changing expectations, etc. Thus the purchase of a major household appliance would reduce one's uncommitted balances, which in turn would tend to increase his resistances regarding other expenditures—making him less likely to purchase other items than he otherwise would have been.

Desire-resistance relationships apply to all household disbursement categories in a manner such as that illustrated in Figure 7.1. The distance along each ray out from the circle represents dollar amounts disbursed for that category per unit of time. Distances in from the circle represent negative disbursements, for example, dissaving. A change in either desire or resistance (beyond the reaction threshold limit) regarding any disbursement category would lead to a disbursement change, which would alter the person's level of uncommitted balances and therefore the resistances regarding each of the other disbursement categories. This in turn could lead to further disbursement changes, which would alter both his desires and resistances, etc., until a new equilibrium is reached.

Thus far four techniques have been developed for measuring desires and resistances. Only one will be discussed here, the "self-rating" method. For it, the subject evaluates the magnitudes of his desires and resistances on a 0 to 100 scale—a picture of a centigrade thermometer is commonly used for this purpose. (The writer has discovered that about 2 per cent of the persons he has contacted seem unable to scale their

---

[20] Analysis in dollar value rather than in physical units permits an equating between quantity and quality for the item or category in question.
[21] The standard of living refers here to the value of the goods and services to which the person actively aspires during the year in question.

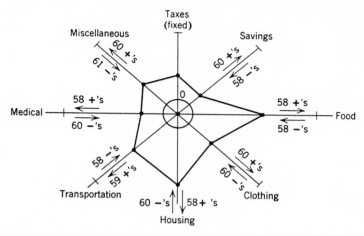

Figure 7.1   A vector relationship in equilibrium. The existence of a reaction threshold requires a certain amount of divergence between desire and resistance before a disbursement change occurs.

desires and resistances, but for the rest there has been no difficulty.) The behavioral reliability of the responses from any one individual are quite low because of a seemingly random error in self-analysis. For a group, however, the random error element tends to cancel out, so that the average of a group's desires and resistances regarding a given item tend to correlate highly with the subsequent average of their purchases of that item—either cross sectionally or sequentially.

To illustrate, in May 1956 a major automobile manufacturer mailed out questionnaires to a nationwide sample of 1000 families. As part of the information requested, they were asked to rate on a "centigrade thermometer" scale, which was pictured on the questionnaire, the magnitude of their desire to buy an automobile, and on another such scale the magnitude of their resistance against incurring the financial cost which such a purchase would entail. Altogether 859 responses were obtained. In June 1957 the respondents again were contacted by mailed questionnaire to ascertain whether they had purchased an automobile during the intervening twelve months, how many they had purchased, etc. There were 779 responses from the second questionnaire. Both questionnaires yielded 695 usable responses. Analysis was in terms of net valences, which is the magnitude of desire minus the magnitude of resistance. The possible range of net valences (−100 to +100) was divided into five groups as shown in column a of Table 7.1, with midpoints given in column b. The per cent of respondents in each net valence group who subsequently purchased one automobile is shown in column d; the per cent that purchased two or more automobiles is shown in column e. The correlations are given at the bottom of Table 8.1. Note that they are very high.

Table 7.1   Relation between the Average Net Valences of 695 Respondents and Their Purchases of New or Used Automobiles during the Subsequent Twelve Months

Net Valences		Number of Respondents in Group (c)	Per Cent of Respondents Who Bought at Least One Car* (d)	Per Cent of Respondents Who Bought Two or More Cars † (e)
Range (a)	Midpoint (b)			
+60 to +100	+80	25	64.0%	20.0%
+20 to +59	+40	86	60.0	8.1
−19 to +19	0	196	40.3	3.5
−59 to −20	−40	206	32.5	2.9
−100 to −60	−80	182	19.2	2.2

* Correlation between columns b and d: $r = +.985 \pm .023$.
† Correlation between columns b and e: $r = +.867 \pm .144$.

Subsequent studies, which will not be described here, have shown that the type of cross-sectional relationship in Table 8.1 is not stable over time. That is, the percentages listed in columns d and e may all rise or all decline. This will occur for several reasons—because incomes change after the desire and resistance data were obtained, because expectations change after the data were obtained, and because of changes in the sequence of purchases. The last may be explained as follows. Suppose that in one year the average net valences regarding an automobile were +65 and regarding a house were +45. In this case experience has shown that the automobile would tend to be purchased first. This would reduce the net valences regarding a house (because of the reduction in uncommitted balances) and reduce the probability of house purchases from what the net valences at the time of interview would suggest. Another year might find the net valences regarding an automobile unchanged at +65 but regarding a house increased to +75. In this situation the house would tend to be purchased first. When that happens, uncommitted balances would decrease, which would reduce the net valences regarding the automobile—thereby causing automobile purchases to be substantially less than what they would have been the first year even though the net valences regarding an automobile were the same both times. Purchases of any particular item cannot be predicted accurately by gathering information regarding only that one item, whether this involves desire-resistance data, consumer buying intention data, or other data.

Buying anticipation studies are concerned with predicting consumer disbursements between categories. Essentially it is a purely empirical approach which by a stretch of logic might be rationalized in terms of utility theory. It involves asking a sample of consumers whether they plan to purchase particular items, and the definiteness of those plans. Cross sectionally (e.g., in the sense of Table 7.1), the buying intentions have been found to correlate highly with purchases; dynamically (sequentially), however, the results have been disappointing. In this writer's opinion, the poor predictive ability of buying anticipations has resulted from a failure to take into account the considerations found to be important for vector analysis—subsequent changes in income and in income anticipations and changes in purchasing sequence.

Studies have shown that buying intentions and net valences correlate roughly. In the automobile purchase study referred to, 752 persons were asked to indicate their intentions to buy a new automobile, and their desires and resistance regarding a new automobile. Their answers to these questions are recorded in Table 7.2 (desire-resistance answers are recorded there in terms of net valences). Considerably more analysis on this relationship still remains to be done, however.

The foregoing summary is sufficient to indicate that the relationships involved in consumer disbursements are very complex. Only a beginning has been made in ascertaining them.

Disbursements Between Brands

A deliberative theory of brand choice has been developed by Norris.[22] She conceives that a person considering the purchase of an automobile might exhibit the following preferences.

Brand	Cost	Preference
A	$2400	prefers car
B	2350	prefers money
C	2300	prefers money
D	2500	prefers money
E	2450	prefers car
F	2350	prefers car

[22] R. T. Norris, *The Theory of Consumers' Demand*, Yale University Press, New Haven, 1941.

Table 7.2   Relationship between 752 Respondents' Stated Buying Intentions Regarding a New Automobile and Their Corresponding Net Valences

Stated Buying Intention	Average Net Valence Rating
Very definitely plan to buy	+31.2
Fairly definitely plan to buy	+ 2.8
Not yet sure about buying	− 2.5
Do *not* plan to buy *	−41.9

* Degree of definiteness about *not* buying was not asked.

On the basis of these preferences an elimination occurs. Any car that the person values less highly than the money necessary to purchase it is dropped from consideration. The remaining brands then are ranked according to preference, perhaps as shown below.

Brand	Cost	Preference Rank
E	$2450	first
F	2350	second
A	2400	third

The most preferred brand (automobile E in the above case) will tend to be purchased. Although not stated explicitly, the preferences determining the choices made presumably are indigenous to the consumer.

The preceding "preference rank theory" is complemented by the "theory of item attributes," which seeks to explain *why* consumers tend to prefer certain brands of a particular item to other brands of that item. The "theory of item attributes" involves the following propositions. First, from the consumers' standpoint any given item is essentially a bundle of attributes, some of which are liked and some of which are disliked. This includes the circumstances accompanying its sale as well as the physical characteristics of the item as such. For a suit, for instance, this would include such matters as its cost, the buying time involved, the store where sold, its brand name, style, color, fit, and material. Second, the brand selected tends to be the one which the buyer believes to have the greatest excess of favorable over unfavorable attributes.[23] This comparison is not necessarily made consciously; it may be entirely subconscious. Third, the magnitude of a person's like or dislike regarding any particular attribute is not necessarily constant over time. The reason is that his desire for a particular attribute is affected by the extent to which his potential want for that attribute has

---

[23] If for each brand considered the unfavorable attributes outweigh the favorable attributes, no purchase logically would be made.

been satisfied from other sources. Fourth, at any given time different people are likely to have different reactions to the attributes that an item might possess.[24] Because of this difference between persons, the producer faces a dilemma: (1) the greater the number of favorable attributes that his product contains relative to that of his competitors, the relatively more attractive a buy is his product likely to be; yet (2) the greater the number of attributes his product contains the greater is the possibility that some of them will be disliked by certain consumers.

Several techniques are available for measuring the magnitude of consumers' likes and dislikes of particular attributes.[25] The "frequency of mention" method is based on the proposition that the importance to a person of a particular attribute in an item is directly proportional to the frequency with which that attribute is mentioned. This measuring technique may be illustrated by Kurt Lewin's [26] study of the relative significance which particular consumer groups attached to certain attributes of food. He selected 107 persons and engaged them in general conversation regarding food. Note was taken of the frequency with which four selected frames of reference, or attributes, were mentioned by each interviewee. Following are typical comments regarding each of the attributes considered.

Money—"Our family loves oranges, but we have stopped buying them. They are too expensive."

Health—"My children have to have a quart of milk a day for their teeth."

Taste—"I don't serve desserts at lunch time. We're not very fond of desserts."

Status—"We have our meat sent from Chicago."

Table 7.3 shows the average number of times per person that each of the four listed attributes was mentioned. These tabulations were taken by Lewin as an indication of the relative significance of each of these attributes for the various groups interviewed.

The "rank-order" measure technique involves having the analyst select the attributes of an item to be studied and then having a group of interviewees each rank these attributes—from those most liked to those most disliked. The interviewees also must indicate where their indifference

[24] For example, some people may like nuts in candy, while others may not; some may like candy to be chewy, while others may not; etc.

[25] Many technical considerations underlie the reliability of each measuring technique. Because of space limitations, they cannot be discussed here.

[26] Kurt Lewin, "Forces Behind Food Habits and Methods of Change" (bulletin), *National Research Council Bulletin*, No. 108, 1943.

Table 7.3   Average Frequency of Mention of Various Attributes in Food, by Groups, as Found by Lewin *

Attributes	Total $N = 107$	High Income Group $N = 23$	Middle Income Group $N = 19$	Low Income Group $N = 21$	Czek. $N = 23$	Negro $N = 21$
Money	2.80	1.30	3.57	3.81	2.21	3.42
Health	2.08	2.61	2.57	1.34	2.61	1.19
Taste	0.90	1.34	0.63	0.76	0.78	0.95
Status	0.04	0.08	0.00	0.00	0.00	0.14

* Numbers indicate the average frequency per person that each of the listed attributes regarding food was mentioned by the interviewees.

Source: Kurt Lewin, "Forces Behind Food Habits and Methods of Change," *National Research Council Bulletin*, No. 108, 1943, Table 7.

point falls in the rank continuum, that is, which of the attributes are liked and which are disliked. The analyst then applies a given weight to each rank-order position: either the sigma-deviate weighting method [27] or the deductive weighting method [28] may be used for obtaining these weights. The score weights given to each attribute then would be averaged for all of the persons being interviewed, and the net rating would be regarded as a measure of the significance of these specified attributes for the group of consumers in question.

The "self-rating" technique for measuring item attributes involves having the analyst select the attributes to be studied. Interviewees then rate their values and attitudes regarding these attributes on a "centigrade thermometer" scale. To illustrate, a group of interviewees might be asked: "Suppose that you were to reduce your food consumption (either in quantity or in quality) by 10 per cent from your current rate, how great an effect do you believe that that would have on your health, happiness, convenience, social prestige?" The numerical answers given would be regarded as the interviewee's "attitudes" regarding food—see column b of Table 7.4.

Next, the interviewee would be asked: How important are each of these considerations (health, happiness, convenience, social prestige) to you? These ratings also would be in terms of the "centigrade thermometer" scale. The latter presumably indicate the importance of each of

[27] L. W. Ferguson, *Personality Measurement*, McGraw-Hill, New York, 1952, pp. 128–134; Rensis Likert, "A Technique for the Measurement of Attitude," *Archives of Psychology*, No. 140, 1932.
[28] Kurt Lewin, *loc. cit.*

Table 7.4   Illustration of the "Self-rating" Technique for Measuring the Importance to a Consumer of Certain Attributes in Her Family's Food *

Attribute (a)	"Attitude" Rating (b)	"Value" Rating (c)	Weighted Attitude (Column b × Column c) (d)
Health	0	100	0
Happiness	75	100	7500
Convenience	50	69	3450
Social prestige	25	27	675
			11625

* Data are the actual responses obtained from an interview.

these considerations to the person being interviewed, that is, they represent his or her "values"—see column c of Table 7.4. Multiplying the "attitude" answers by the corresponding "value" answers, as illustrated in column d of the table, the importance to the interviewee of the item's various attributes are obtained. This writer has found a high correlation between people's weighted-attitudes regarding food and their desire answers regarding food. In turn, their desire answers relative to their resistance answers regarding food correlated with their subsequent food expenditures.

From the above rational theories of consumer behavior (the "preference rank theory" and the "theory of item attributes") it follows that the essence of brand choice is deliberation, whether at the conscious or the subconscious level of behavior. Purely passive reaction is not allowed for.

Nondeliberative theories of consumer behavior are implicit in the works of analysts, such as Galbraith,[29] who argue that consumption is determined more nearly by the sales efforts of producers than by indigenous consumer preferences. This seems to involve the following stimulus-response conception of consumer behavior: (1) consumers are mere response mechanisms who react passively to competing stimuli emanating from producers, and (2) once channeled, consumers' actions will tend to be repeated more or less blindly (or habitually) until altered by changed stimuli. Involved in these stimuli are matters such as advertising, product design, display, and salesmanship. "Motivation research," image analysis, etc.[30] have been developed for conceptualizing these

[29] J. K. Galbraith, *The Affluent Society*, Houghton Mifflin, Boston, 1958.
[30] Gardner Ackley, *op. cit.*, Ch. 6; R. Ferber and H. G. Wales, *Motivation and Market Behavior*, Richard D. Irwin, Homewood, Ill., 1958.

stimuli. Word association tests, Rorschach tests, TAT tests (where subjects make up stories regarding pictorial situations), feeling tests, identification tests, etc. are used for measuring reactions to these stimuli. Such analyses draw heavily from psychiatry and psychology.

From the nonrational theory of consumer behavior it follows that the essence of brand choice is passive reaction; deliberation is not involved.

General observation suggests that consumer behavior is neither completely rational nor completely nonrational. A more comprehensive theory that can harmonize both explanations seems called for, but such an effort is dependent on more empirical data than is currently available.

The most useful research on this subject was a study on consumer deliberation conducted by Mueller and Katona [31] in 1953. It involved 1000 persons drawn randomly from all parts of the United States who were interviewed regarding their purchases of household durables and men's sport shirts. The method used for determining the amount of deliberation these families exercised in their purchase of these items was to question them regarding (1) the extent of circumspectness—length of planning before buying, amount of family discussion before buying and consideration of alternatives prior to a purchase, (2) the extent of information seeking regarding the item to be purchased, (3) the extent of price comparison before buying, (4) number of brands considered before buying, and (5) the number of item attributes looked for in the items when shopping.

The results indicated that consumers chose much more deliberately when they bought a major household appliance than when they bought a sport shirt. Spur-of-the-moment decisions were not uncommon in the buying of sport shirts but were very rare in the purchase of a major household durable. Approximately one fourth of the durable goods purchases analyzed exhibited the essential features of deliberate decision making; another fourth exhibited almost a complete lack of deliberation. Approximately half the durable goods purchased exhibited partial deliberation, that is, the deliberations were short or casual or the buyer concentrated on only a very few features of the product, neglecting others. Mueller and Katona [32] also reported the following.

Highly deliberate decision making in connection with durable goods purchases occurred most among the following groups of buyers: those with a college education, those with incomes between

[31] E. Mueller and G. Katona, "A Study of Purchase Decisions," in L. H. Clark (ed.), *Consumer Behavior*, New York University Press, New York, 1954, pp. 30–87.
[32] *Ibid.*, p. 80.

$5000 and $7500, those under 35 years old, white collar workers, and people who expressed a liking for "shopping around." Furthermore, there was a tendency toward deliberate behavior among people who felt no urgent or immediate need for the product and those who either had no previous experience with the product or had an unsatisfactory experience. . . . absence of deliberation occurred most among durable goods buyers with education limited to grammar school, earning incomes below $2000, working in unskilled or service jobs, aged 65 or over, and also among those expressing a dislike for shopping. Deliberation further tended to be lacking when the product was inexpensive relative to the buyer's income. Also when the need for the product was urgent or when a special deal was available through relatives or acquaintances, there was often no time for weighing of alternatives. Finally, we found that a previous satisfactory experience with the same household good made for a low level of deliberation.

The foregoing findings confirm the "common sense" position that brand choice is neither completely deliberate nor completely haphazard. One possible means for harmonizing rational and nonrational consumer behavior concepts is the introduction of the reaction threshold.[33] That is, within the range of the brand choices which consumers feel would make negligible difference to their well-being, little deliberation is attempted. The particular brand purchased within that range would tend to be selected nonrationally, perhaps determined entirely by producers' influences. Outside that range of brand choices, deliberation would tend to occur. For any particular person this reaction threshold range (the range of indifference regarding brands) would vary between items, and for any given item would differ between persons. Consistencies in these ranges can be expected among persons in similar situations, however. This writer has found evidence of reaction threshold behavior in the relation between consumers' vectors regarding item categories (food, clothing, etc.) and their purchases of these items, and this range has tended to be wider for moderate income than for low income households. Presumably, therefore, this would apply also to brand choice, although no study has been made on the matter.

At the beginning of this chapter it was pointed out that consumer behavior is of concern to market analysts for several purposes. The area in which most of the consumer research has been conducted (sales pre-

[33] C. L. Hull, *Principles of Behavior*, Appleton-Century-Crofts, New York, 1943, pp. 322–330.

diction) has been outlined above; space limitation has prevented a survey in depth of the relevant materials on this subject. We turn now to a survey of the research done in other matters of interest to market analysts. Unfortunately, only sporadic research has been done in these other areas; even basic departure points are not agreed on.

WELFARE

Although books have been written on the subject of economic welfare, no concensus has been reached on it. Freedom of individual choice is the usual point of departure; yet no attention has been given to *which* choices are most relevant for welfare. Thus a person's budget plan presumably reflects his best judgment as to what he should do with his income during the ensuing year; his expenditures presumably reflect his most preferred use of income during the course of the year; at the end of the year that person may review his expense records and reflect on how he wishes that he would have used his income; ten years later he may again reflect on how he should have used that year's income. Only by chance will all these judgments coincide.

Furthermore, a decision by ballot as to how people wish to use their income (e.g., a democratic decision as to how much they are willing to tax themselves for politically supported education) undoubtedly would be quite different from the amounts they would spend for the same purposes if the decisions were made by market transactions. These differences have considerable practical significance. Should consumers decide that in their best judgment actual purchases do not correspond with their best interests, they might elect through the democratic process to enact legislation regulating the appeals and the marketing techniques that sellers may make on them. (This, of course, is already done regarding the sale of habit-forming drugs, pornographic literature, etc.) This whole issue warrants considerable research.

The welfare issue is clouded further by uncertainty as to the social losses and gains which result from an individual's consumption. Question: Does an individual's possession of a noisy motorcycle affect the well-being of his neighbors? How about his possessing a revolver, his drinking hard liquor, his reading pornographic literature, his obtaining a college education, etc.? How *great* is the social effect in each case?

Unfortunately, even the most rudimentary data on this whole problem have not yet been gathered. Even if they were, there still would be the problem of equating (1) the welfare loss that an individual would experience if his freedom of choice is restricted by society with (2) the welfare loss that society would experience if the individual is completely unrestricted in his choices; also (3) the welfare gain that a person would experience from certain subsidized consumption plus (4) the welfare gain that other people would experience from specified groups having subsidized consumption with (5) the welfare loss that the rest of society would experience through paying for that subsidized consumption.

In addition to the foregoing, analysis must be made of the relation between various consumption alternatives and national income (via the multiplier and the accelerator) which in turn affects the personal incomes of various groups in different ways. Until these basic considerations have been ascertained, fundamental analysis regarding the welfare aspects of marketing is greatly restricted.

A limited amount of welfare analysis perhaps can be made from the concept of basic and derived desires. This concept, which follows from a substantial body of psychological thought,[34] holds that consumers have certain more or less vague basic desires that are satisfied only indirectly. Those things that people want as a *means* for satisfying their basic desires are referred to as derived desires. The latter tend to exist in a sequence chain, and there may be considerable confusion and error between its links.

To illustrate, a person's basic desire may be for personal fulfillment; he may feel that this desire can be achieved through obtaining social status, and that status can be achieved through the purchase of a Cadillac. (Both social status and the Cadillac would be derived desires; the Cadillac would be the manifested desire because that is what is manifested in the market.) If through experience the person discovers that the possession of a Cadillac fails to add to his sense of personal fulfillment, he is likely to alter his derived desires—which the market would interpret as a change in preference.

The concept of basic and derived desires just outlined suggests that consumer welfare at the individual level should be measured in terms of contributions to and detractions from peoples' basic desires rather than in terms of the extent to which their manifested desires are satisfied. From this several corollaries follow. First, merely increasing consumption (satisfying manifested desires) does not necessarily increase welfare. Second, sales activity which promotes a fallacious chain of derived

[34] Sigmund Freud, *A General Introduction to Psychoanalysis* (translated by Joan Rivere), Garden Publishing Co., Garden City, New York, 1943; William McDougall, *Outline of Psychology*, Scribners, New York, 1926; G. Murphy, L. B. Murphy, and T. M. Newcomb, *Experimental Social Psychology*, Harper, New York, 1937, pp. 92–93; and O. Oppenheimer, "The Nature of Motivation," *Journal of Social Psychology*, Vol. XXVI (Second half), (November 1947), pp. 213–214.

desires is detrimental to consumer welfare. For example, advertising that uses snob appeal may stimulate sales, but if the item does not actually increase consumers' social prestige or if increased social prestige does not contribute to their basic desires, that advertising is misleading and therefore harmful to the consumers' welfare. Third, products that fail to contribute to consumers' basic desires fail to promote the consumers' welfare; products that detract from the consumers' basic desires are harmful to the consumers' welfare.

Psychiatric techniques are needed for determining what desires are really basic, and these techniques are far from perfect. This, however, is a complex subject that cannot be discussed here.

IMPLICATIONS FOR MARKETING

Sales Prediction

The preceding material is most applicable to sales prediction. It suggests that account must be taken of probable personal income changes, of probable disbursement pattern changes, and of probable brand shifts. Once these are ascertained, intensive sales analysis can be made of the particular item with which the analyst is concerned. All this is such a comprehensive task, however, that it appears feasible only for very large market research organizations.

Product Design

Unfortunately, consumer behavior analysis has not been sufficiently well developed to explain the complexities of consumer tastes as it relates to product design. Because of this deficiency, there is an unfortunate tendency for analysts to reason as if the aspect of consumer behavior with which they are concerned is somehow an independent entity rather than merely a dependent part of a broader set of behavioral relationships. Until a comprehensive theory of consumer behavior has been developed, all our consumption findings must be regarded as provisional. That is, firm conclusions from a limited study cannot safely be drawn.

To illustrate, in the early 1950's Chrysler Corporation's consumer surveys indicated that for themselves people preferred "sensible" cars—moderately compact, economical, functional, easy to operate, etc. Those surveys indicated also that most people believed that their neighbors preferred "exotic" cars—flamboyant, high powered, large, etc. At that time Chrysler's version of the "sensible" car was losing sales to competitors' "exotic" cars. The conclusion drawn was that people do not know what they really do want, so Chrysler shifted to the manufacture of "exotic" cars. Their automobile sales remained disappointing, however. Within a few years compact cars were introduced to the public, and they were purchased in tremendous quantities. Question: Were the consumers' stated preferences fairly accurate despite what they were actually purchasing at that time? The conclusions drawn from those surveys now appear to have been insufficiently provisional.

Buick provides us with a different type of illustration. During the early 1950's *Consumer Reports* were continually criticizing Buick for its relatively poor performance and durability (the latter was determined from Consumers Union surveys of their readers). During that same period Buicks were selling well, holding fourth and sometimes third sales position in the market. The conclusion then apparent was that consumers were not concerned with performance and durability. In the later 1950's Buick sales slipped badly. Now it appears that performance and durability were perhaps important to consumers after all, but that they responded to those considerations with a lag. (We are not yet able to explain why and how this presumed lag operates.)

Contemporary market analysts must remain provisional in their research on consumer motivation, buying images, etc., or they too may draw erroneous conclusions. This problem is accentuated by the relative ease of designing research in ways that will measure consumers' immediate reactions to particular items (the counterpart of an initial purchase), and the difficulty of designing research in ways that measure consumers' net reactions after they have had experience with those items (the counterpart of repeat purchases). The analyst must keep in mind that an adequately comprehensive theory of consumer behavior is not yet available and that conclusions from a particular study might be misleading.

Selling Methods

Marketing analysts concerned with advertising, personal selling, and product design problems have studied consumer behavior via a general motivation analysis, which draws heavily from psychology and psychiatry.[35] Consumer behavior analysts do not seem very much concerned with sales promotion, however, and bibliographies of the latters' works [36]

[35] Wroe Alderson, *Marketing Behavior and Executive Action: A Functionalist Approach to Marketing Theory*, Richard D. Irwin, Homewood, Ill., 1957, Ch. 6.
[36] M. J. Farrell, "The New Theories of the Consumption Function," *The Economic Journal*, Vol. LXIX, No. 276 (December 1959), pp. 684–687; J. N. Morgan, "A Review of Recent Research on Consumer Behavior," in L. H. Clark (ed.), *Consumer Behavior*, New York University Press, New York, 1954, pp. 93–219.

show that they have given practically no consideration to motivation research.

There is an obviously fundamental difference in viewpoint regarding the significance of motivation research, buying images, etc., for understanding consumer behavior. In this writer's opinion, the difference revolves around the relative importance of repeat purchases versus initial purchases. Initial purchases seemingly would be based on what satisfactions the consumer *anticipates* that the item in question will yield. For this his image of the item, his motivations, his impulses, the manner and extent to which his attention is drawn to that item, etc. are matters of obvious importance. On the other hand, repeat purchases seemingly are based largely on the consumer's *experiences* with the item in question; for this, *preferences* rather than buying images, motivations, etc. presumably are of dominant importance.

The differing emphases of marketing analysts and consumer behavior analysts are not inherently incompatible. Certainly repeat purchases are fundamental to both consumers and to the marketer. This is evidenced by the high degree of consistency in consumer disbursements that occur from one year to another. Yet rapid product changes reduce the relevance of past experiences for decision making and result in each repeat purchase being to some degree a new purchase. In short, the marketing analyst appears to have overemphasized the significance of such matters as buying images, buying motives, and symbolism, relative to consumer preferences as being a matter of experience. The consumer behavior analyst, on the other hand, appears to have made the opposite malemphasis. This interpretation suggests that a greater cross fertilization of effort between marketing and consumer behavior analysts is called for. Thus far such efforts have not been made effectively. In this writer's view, appeals to psychology and to psychoanalysis will not solve the problem until the relative significance of initial purchases versus repeat purchases has been ascertained and their interrelationship understood.

A note of caution seems warranted for marketing analysts concerned with consumer behavior. Either they must make their analyses sufficiently broad to consider consumer welfare, or they must be prepared for adverse reactions. That is, if they are going to be concerned with matters that increase sales without regard for what that does to consumer welfare, marketers should not be surprised at being criticized.

SUMMARY AND SUGGESTIONS FOR FURTHER RESEARCH

The state of knowledge regarding consumer behavior is at such a fragmentary state that *nobody* can attempt to construct a more or less comprehensive hypothesis regarding it and indicate the accuracy of the predictions that it yields. On the other hand, partial analyses are valid only so long as everything else remains constant—and only a comprehensive theory can suggest the likelihood of that accuracy in any particular case.

Most of the consumer behavior analysis made to date has been concerned with predicting consumer purchases. Even in this area, research has been uneven. In recent years considerable attention has been given to the analysis of aggregate consumption expenditures (the consumption function), and relatively little has been given to the question of expenditure allocation between disbursement categories or between brands. Nevertheless, some promising starts have been made in this direction. Welfare analysis and sales potential analysis are almost virgin areas for research at the present time. Sales promotion analysis has tended to give a rather lopsided emphasis to matters important for initial purchases and has failed to relate these considerations to the consumers' previous experiences.

Research is so highly personal that one may question the usefulness of anyone suggesting projects for others. Nevertheless, three different types of consumption research projects will be suggested in the hope that the effort may facilitate the unearthing of new knowledge about the behavior of consumers.

Living Pattern Studies

On the basis of his consumer interviews this writer is convinced that many insights can be obtained by analyzing living patterns and then determining what goods or services would more perfectly complete these living patterns. People living nomadically in tents seemingly would have many different specific desires than if they lived in seaside cottages, or than if they lived in a downtown apartment. For such studies, living patterns probably would have to be examined according to the methodology of sociologists. The analyst probably would discover that certain new items (historically, the automobile, television, etc.) alter consumer living patterns, which in turn tend to alter their specific desires. This type of analysis might enable researchers to anticipate many potential desires regarding which consumers themselves are unaware.

Buying Decision Games

Another type of research that might yield useful insights would be the development of consumer buying decision games. This is envisioned as a counterpart of management decision games. They could be structured in many different ways according to the problem involved. One objective might be to ascertain the effects of income uncertainty, another to ascertain the effects of changing inequality of income distribution as between players, another to ascertain the effects of changing prices, another to ascertain the effects of changing fixed commitments (the counterpart of taxes), etc. It might be discovered that responses are as much a function of *how* the variable is changed as of the *amount* by which it is changed. Studies then could be designed to ascertain the correlation between the results of consumer buying decision games and actual consumer behavior.

Questionnaire Studies

Payroll data might be obtained from firms; this would give evidence regarding the employees' incomes, ages, length of employment with the firm, sex, etc. Questionnaires then could be sent to a sample of those employees to get various useful information to correlate with the payroll data. One possibility would be to get reasons for saving, place of saving, reasons for borrowing, place of borrowing, etc. This would permit an analyst to ascertain by income bracket whether various savings and credit institutions are complementary or competitive, whether firms are adjusting their services to the desires of the various income groups, etc. In this writer's experience some firms always can be persuaded to divulge payroll data. Questionnaire responses are relatively easily obtainable when properly made out.

BIBLIOGRAPHY

Ackley, Gardner, *Macroeconomic Theory*, Macmillan, New York, 1961, pp. 236–246.

Alderson, Wroe, *Marketing Behavior and Executive Action: A Functionalist Approach to Marketing Theory*, Richard D. Irwin, Homewood, Ill., 1957.

Barton, S. G., "The Life Cycle and Buying Patterns," in L. H. Clark (ed.), *The Life Cycle and Consumer Behavior*, New York University Press, New York, 1955, pp. 53–57.

Brady, D. S., "Family Saving, 1880–1950," in R. W. Goldsmith, D. S. Brady and H. Mendershausen, *A Study of Saving in the United States*, Vol. III, Princeton University Press, Princeton, N.J., 1956, pp. 139–276.

————— and Rose Friedman, "Savings and the Income Distribution," Conference on Research in Income and Wealth, *Studies in Income and Wealth*, Vol. X, National Bureau of Economic Research, New York, 1947, pp. 247–265.

Clark, L. H. (ed.), *The Life Cycle and Consumer Behavior*, New York University Press, New York, 1955.

Davis, T. E., "The Consumption Function as a Tool for Prediction," *Review of Economic Statistics*, Vol. XXXIV, No. 3 (August 1952), pp. 270–277.

Duesenberry, J. S., *Income, Saving and the Theory of Consumer Behavior*, Harvard University Press, Cambridge, 1949.

Farrell, M. J., "The New Theories of the Consumption Function," *The Economic Journal,* Vol. LXIX, No. 276 (December 1959), pp. 684–687.

Ferber, Robert, "Research on Household Behavior," *American Economic Review,* Vol. LII, No. 1 (March 1962), pp. 19–63.

——————— and H. G. Wales, *Motivation and Market Behavior,* Richard D. Irwin, Homewood, Ill., 1958.

Ferguson, L. W., *Personality Measurement,* McGraw-Hill, New York, 1952.

Fisher, Janet, "Income, Spending, and the Saving Patterns of Consumer Units in Different Age Groups," in National Bureau of Economic Research, *Studies in Income and Wealth,* Vol. XV, New York, 1962, pp. 75–102.

———————, "Postwar Changes in Income and Savings Among Consumers in Different Age Groups," *Econometrica,* Vol. XX, No. 1 (January 1952), pp. 47–70.

———————, "Family Life Cycle Analysis on Research on Consumer Behavior," in L. H. Clark (ed.), *The Life Cycle and Consumer Behavior,* New York University Press, New York, 1955, pp. 28–35.

Freud, Sigmund, *A General Introduction to Psychoanalysis* (translated by Joan Rivere), Garden Publishing Co., Garden City, New York, 1943.

Friedman, Milton, *A Theory of the Consumption Function,* National Bureau of Economic Research, Princeton University Press, Princeton, N.J., 1957.

Friend, I., and I. B. Kravis, "Entrepreneural Income, Saving and Investment," *American Economic Review,* Vol. XLVII, No. 3 (June 1957), pp. 269–301.

Frisch, R., "New Methods for Measuring Marginal Utility," *Beiträge zur Okonomischen Theorie,* No. 3, Tubingen, 1932.

Galbraith, J. K., *The Affluent Society,* Houghton Mifflin, Boston, 1958.

Hull, C. L., *Principles of Behavior,* Appleton-Century-Crofts, New York, 1943, pp. 322–330.

Katona, George, "Effect of Income Changes on the Rate of Saving," *Review of Economic Statistics,* Vol. XXXI, No. 2 (May 1949), pp. 95–103.

Klein, L. R., "Assets, Debts, and Economic Behavior," in Conference on Research in Income and Wealth, *Studies in Income and Wealth,* Vol. XIV, National Bureau of Economic Research, New York, 1951, pp. 195–227.

———————, "Estimating Patterns of Savings Behavior from Sample Survey Data, *Econometrica,* Vol. XIX, No. 4 (October 1951), pp. 438–454.

———————, "Patterns of Savings," *Bulletin of Oxford University Institute of Statistics,* Vol. XVII, No. 2 (May 1955), pp. 173–214.

———————, "Statistical Estimates of Economic Relations from Survey Data," in G. Katona, L. R. Klein, J. B. Lansing and J. N. Morgan, *Contributions of Survey Methods to Economics,* Columbia University Press, New York, 1954, pp. 189–240.

——————— and J. B. Lansing, "Decisions to Purchase Consumer Durable Goods," *Journal of Marketing,* Vol. XX, No. 2 (October 1955), pp. 109–132.

——————— and J. Margolis, "Statistical Studies of Unincorporated Business," *Review of Economic Statistics,* Vol. XXXVI, No. 1 (February 1954), pp. 33–46.

Lewin, Kurt, "Forces Behind Food Habits and Methods of Change," (bulletin), *National Research Council Bulletin,* No. 108, 1943.

Likert, Rensis, "A Technique for the Measurement of Attitude," *Archives of Psychology,* No. 140, 1932.

Lydall, Harold, "The Life Cycle in Income, Savings, and Asset Ownership," *Econometrica,* Vol. XXIII, No. 2 (April 1955), pp. 131–150.

McDougall, William, *Outline of Psychology,* Scribners, New York, 1926.

Modigliani, F. and A. Ando, "The 'Permanent' Income and the 'Life Cycle' Hypotheses of Saving Behavior: Comparison and Tests," in I. Friend and R.

Jones (eds.), *Proceedings of the Conference on Consumption and Saving*, Vol. II, University of Pennsylvania Press, Philadelphia, 1960, pp. 49–174.

Morgan, James N., "A Review of Recent Research on Consumer Behavior," in L. H. Clark (ed.), *Consumer Behavior*, New York University Press, New York, 1954, pp. 93–219.

Mueller, E. and George Katona, "A Study of Purchase Decisions," in L. H. Clark (ed.), *Consumer Behavior*, New York University Press, New York, 1954, pp. 30–87.

Murphy, G., L. B. Murphy, and T. M. Newcomb, *Experimental Social Psychology*, Harper, New York, 1937, pp. 92–93.

Norris, R. T., *The Theory of Consumers' Demand*, Yale University Press, New Haven, 1941.

Okun, A. M., "The Value of Anticipation Data in Forecasting National Product," in *The Quality and Economic Significance of Anticipations Data*, National Bureau of Economic Research, Princeton University Press, Princeton, N.J., 1960, pp. 411–428.

Oppenheimer, O., "The Nature of Motivation," *Journal of Social Psychology*, Vol. XXVI (Second half), (November 1947), pp. 213–214.

Orcutt, G. and A. D. Roy, "A Bibliography of the Consumption Function" (mimeographed), Cambridge University, Department of Applied Economics, 1949.

Thurstone, L. L., "The Indifference Function," *Journal of Social Psychology*, Vol. II (May 1931), pp. 139-167.

Tobin, James, "On the Predictive Value of Consumer Intentions and Attitudes," *Review of Economic Statistics*, Vol. XLI, No. 1 (February 1959), pp. 1–11.

Tobin, James, "Relative Income, Absolute Income, and Saving," in *Money, Trade and Economic Growth, Essays in Honor of John Henry Williams*, Macmillan, New York, 1951, pp. 135–156.

U.S. Government, Bureau of Labor Statistics, Family Income and Expenditures in (selected areas), U.S. Department of Labor Bulletins 642–649, 1938–1941.

————, Department of Agriculture, "Family Income and Expenditures," (titles vary), miscellaneous publications between No. 339 and No. 489, 1939–1941.

————, Federal Reserve Board, "Report of Consultant Committee on Consumer Survey Statistics" (July 1955).

Universities—National Bureau of Economic Research, *The Quality and Economic Significance of Anticipations Data*, Princeton University Press, Princeton, N.J., 1960.

8

Product Development

JOHN B. STEWART

After reviewing last year's performance, the executives of Company X usually decide to do better next year and, more often than not, "doing better" requires increased sales volume. Should the new volume be obtained by securing additional retail outlets, by increasing the efficiency of promotional expenditures, by price changes, or through new products? If through new products, can the existing knowledge of product development "principles" provide substantial help to management? Most practitioners would agree that the existing state of knowledge leaves much to be desired.

The intent of this chapter is to review the current state of product development activity, to explore areas in need of future improvement, and to suggest means of accomplishing the improvements. As used in this chapter, the term "product development" will refer to the creation of either new or improved products and services and will include the functions from formulating product line policy through the establishment of an initial marketing program. While the first section of the chapter is primarily devoted to describing current practices, the last section focuses more on conceptionalizing the process and problems of product development. Throughout, the observations are made from a marketing point of view.

THE PURPOSE OF PRODUCT DEVELOPMENT

The "common sense" purpose of product development is to provide a company with increased profits. But, while this is frequently true, a more general statement of purpose would be "to help a firm maintain or improve its current position, that is, to more nearly approach its objectives." This more general statement emphasizes that the purpose of any particular product development program will vary according to the firm's particular position and particular objectives. Similarly, the product being developed must help consumers maintain or improve their present position, that is, to more nearly approach their individual objectives. As shown in Figure 8.1, the product serves as a *mutual vehicle* for the firm and consumers to reach their respective objectives. Evaluating the worth of a product idea, therefore, should begin with a clear understanding of the current position and objectives of both the firm and consumers. Unfortunately, this is more easily said than done.

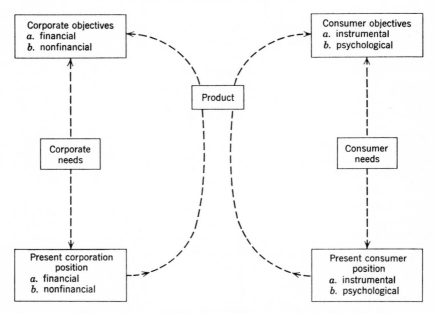

Figure 8.1   The product—a vehicle for attaining corporate and consumer objectives.

Many facets of company objectives may provide the motivation behind product development. Some examples:

Financial Growth (greater net profit/year). Probably the most commonly stated benefit sought through new or improved product development can be achieved if product modification reduces cost of production or selling, if it enables higher unit selling price at the same volume, or if it results in more units sold (to same customers more frequently or to additional numbers of customers).

Financial Efficiency (greater return on assets or equity). Of increasing interest to many managers and owners who were formerly preoccupied with being "bigger" is the improvement of financial efficiency through product modifications. They are interested in product changes which reduce required plant investment (by enabling use of more completely processed materials, more standardized components, or more subcontracted assembly), make possible expanded production without increased investment (such as making fuller use of designs, skills, waste materials, etc.), or for higher return on equity, encourage greater use of debt funds by increasing stability of earnings.

Financial Stability (small range of earnings fluctuation over time). Of special concern to firms which are (1) small, (2) in seasonal or cyclical industries, (3) dependent on just a few suppliers or customers, or (4) selling style goods, is the improvement of financial stability through product modifications which provide diversification.

Financial Certainty (probability of actual earnings equaling predicted earnings) is similar to financial stability but differs in that some firms (e.g., suppliers of building materials) can predict with fairly high certainty that future earnings will be *unstable* and how they will fluctuate by looking at the determinants of demand (e.g., family formations as projected from birth rates, etc.). Just as with financial stability, financial certainty can be improved through product development that gives diversification, or it can be improved within the firm's existing sphere of operation by increasing the firm's technological lead over competitors. Whenever the lead can be increased, it not only raises the certainty of desired profits next year but also increases the probable number of years over which future earnings will flow.

Financial Durability (years of earnings flow), or "long-run profits," is a frequent goal of product development and with good reason. Numerous surveys have shown that the turnover of products on the market is too high for firms to escape the need for development work. For an example of how management has come to expect constant change, see Figure 8.2.

All the above represent various aspects of *financial* objectives, but some product development programs have little or nothing to do with finance; they have to do with the *personal* goals of the owners or operating management. Although frequently playing an important role in development programs, these nonfinancial goals (such as desire for recognition as an innovator, as an industry leader, as an international executive, etc.) are rarely volunteered as objectives. Somehow it seems improper to many businessmen to get pleasure *directly* from a business operation—it seems more proper to make money first and then use the money to buy someone else's products, which in turn will give pleasure. An exception to this tendency is found among the growing number of scientists and engineers who have formed their own companies and retained operating control. Here it is common to hear nonfinancial objec-

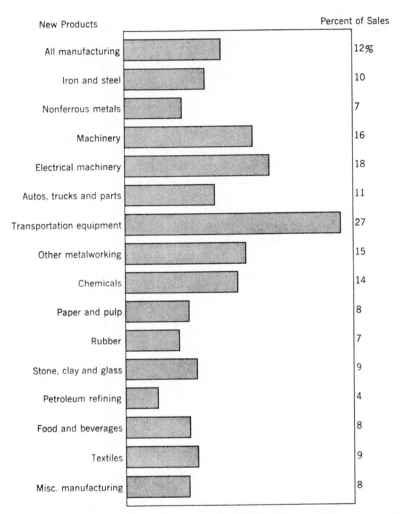

Figure 8.2 Expected impact of new products. The hopes manufacturers have for new products are illustrated by this chart. Bars indicate percentages of sales that will be accounted for in 1963 by products that didn't exist four years ago, according to manufacturer estimates. New products are defined as products "not produced in 1959 or products sufficiently changed as to be reasonably considered as new products." Source: McGraw-Hill.

tives placed foremost in priority. Such objectives as "the creation and maintenance of a work environment conducive to 'creative productivity,' or 'self-fulfillment,'" is frequently stated *and* really used in an operational way. In these cases, product development becomes an end instead of a means. The challenge of the process itself provides the motivation and, potentially, the satisfaction.

Since these nonfinancial facets of corporate objectives are usually not admitted, and never described explicitly, the success of virtually all development programs is judged on the basis of the relatively measurable financial objectives. On this basis, many of the programs result in failure; a failure that comes from lack of predictive ability. During the development process, someone either predicted demand incorrectly or predicted the firm's relative ability to fulfill that demand incorrectly.

In making these predictions, product developers go through a spiral-like process: on first exposure to an idea, they quickly project an expected outcome on the basis of first impressions and intuitive judgments; for those ideas which appear to have promise, the possible outcomes are examined with much more care. The process of examining, affirming, and reaffirming goes on and on, with each succeeding round costing more money, taking more time, and producing increasingly good, new product gambles.

CURRENT PRACTICES AND PROBLEMS

Although every company has its own somewhat unique product development procedures, a common set of stages used to describe the process is given below.[1]

Exploration—the search for areas of corporate needs, opportunities, and product ideas to meet company objectives.

Screening—a quick analysis to determine which ideas are pertinent and should be given careful investigation.

Specifications—the expansion of an idea into a concrete recommendation for the product design specifications.

---

[1] This set of stages is essentially the same as that given by Ralph W. Jones, "Management of New Products," *The Journal of Industrial Engineering*, Vol. IX, No. 5 (September–October 1958). For a variety of different stage breakdowns and problems related thereto, see Delmar W. Karger, *The New Product*, The Industrial Press, New York, 1960. Peter Hilton, *Handbook of New Product Development*, Prentice-Hall, Englewood Cliffs, N.J., 1961. Philip Marvin, *Planning New Products*, American Management Association, New York, 1958.

Development—turning the idea-on-paper into a product-in-hand, producible and demonstrable.

Testing—the commercial experiments necessary to verification of earlier business judgments.

Commercialization—launching the product in full-scale production and sale, committing the company's reputation and resources.

Table 8.1   Probability of Commercial Success of New Product Ideas

| | Success Percentages | | |
	New Product Ideas	Product Development Projects	New Products Introduced
All Industry Groups	2.4% [a]	12.5% [b]	49.0% [c]
Chemical	2%	10%	47%
Consumer packaged goods	1	6	40
Electrical machinery	3	17	57
Metal fabricators	2	14	38
Nonelectrical machinery	2	20	52
Raw material processors	4	13	60

Note: The manner in which this table should be read is illustrated as follows:
[a] Of the new product ideas considered by management, 2.4% eventually became successful.
[b] Of the new product ideas which survive as far as the "product development project stage," 12.5% eventually became successful.
[c] Of the new product ideas which were carried through to market introduction, 49.0% were successful.

Source: Management Research Department, Booz, Allen and Hamilton "Management of New Products," Chicago, 1960, p. 14.

Rate of Success

Management's job is to select the best ideas in the least time, the least cost, with the lowest risk of going amiss when the product is marketed. But, despite all of the screening, reconsidering, testing, etc., many of the new products put on the market are unsuccessful. This failure rate has been estimated to be as high as 80 per cent for consumer products and as low as 40 per cent for industrial products.[2] A more recent survey which covered 922 new products (produced by 65 "prominent companies") in a variety of industries showed: successful new products, 49 per cent; future doubtful, 34 per cent; failure, 17 per cent. The success percentages as they varied by industry and by development stage are shown in Table 8.1. Why such frequent failure? As a basis for speculation, some of the practices and problems are described in the following pages.

Exploratory Phase

In addition to starting product development work with objectives (the financial ones) defined, the more sophisticated firms also have an inventory of their corporate strengths and weaknesses. This amounts to an appraisal of the company's resources, such as research, production, or management skills; financial resources; distribution capabilities; and reputation among consumers—all of which must be appraised *relative to the same resources of competitors.* Knowing corporate objectives, strengths and weaknesses, and with best guesses about future changes in economic and competitive conditions, these firms develop a corporate strategy. Within the strategy, general product plans and product policies are laid out. Once established, these serve as a basis for guiding the exploration and evaluation of new product ideas.

Ideas for new products originate from hundreds of different sources. Many companies prefer to rely on internal sources—the company's engineering or design department, the research department, management, salesmen, or from general employees in the form of "suggestion box" ideas. These internal sources have the virtue of little or no legal liability.[3] Other firms make a point of cultivating retailers and wholesalers, independent inventors, consumers, outside consultants, the research departments of other companies, government research projects, and companies that are in the business of finding potential producers of new product ideas. As yet there appears to be little evidence concerning which sources are likely to produce the most profitable ideas. Most literature on idea sources simply list the possibilities and present methods of making greater use of the sources. Some specific observations on the various sources are given below.

[2] Ross Federal Research Corporation, "A Survey of 200 Leading Package Goods Manufacturers on Experiences and Problems Prevalent in the Introduction of a New Product," Ross Federal Research Corp., New York, 1945, p. 4; Department of Commerce.

[3] For an outline of these legal pitfalls, see J. W. Bohlen, "A Basic Guide to Legal Problems in New Products," *Industrial Marketing* (November 1958), pp. 69–73.

Engineering Department

While it is logical to expect that a company's own engineering department would be a good source of new product ideas, it frequently does not work out that way in practice. In the course of interviews with several dozen manufacturers of consumer durables, the writer noted that these departments supplied many "little" ideas but few major ones. A large portion of their time was allocated to eliminating operational defects rather than developing new products or product features. For instance, the product manager at Admiral Corporation cited an example of the kind of problem which, in the experience of many companies, has fully occupied the engineering group—to the exclusion of the development of new products. One summer Admiral's district sales offices complained that the company's refrigerators were "sweating." It was hot and humid over many parts of the country, and many other manufacturers were having similar problems. The sweating was caused by cold being conducted out of the box, chilling an outer surface, and condensing moisture from the air. The problem was to find the cause of the outer surface chilling and correct it. Investigation by the engineering group found that cold was conducted through a bracket used to support the door hinges. To cure the problem the engineers redesigned the bracket to reduce its conductivity.

When "product correction" problems do not absorb all their time, engineering departments frequently develop minor product improvements. For instance, at the Jacobsen Manufacturing Company the engineering department developed the first recoil starter on a power lawnmower (the same feature had been on outboard motors before). But, while such minor improvements are commonplace from engineering departments, big ideas are scarce. The biggest innovation in the lawnmower industry, for instance, the development of the rotary mower, did *not* come from an engineering department. In fact, it did not even come from a mower manufacturer—it came from two men in Florida in the early 1930's who had trouble cutting their own lawns.

Industrial Designers

While engineering groups are busy correcting minor product defects in operation or internal construction, industrial designers are usually concerned with minor changes in external shape or appearance. Only occasionally do they produce major product ideas. One instance in which they did illustrates an interesting point—that creativity and willingness to take risks may be greatly increased by relaxing the normal job requirement of being realistic. At Elgin National Watch Company, designers were primarily concerned with watch styling, but it was the head of the design department who suggested that the company make a direct reading watch, that is, a watch in which the hands are eliminated by having the dial rotate and the time is shown through a small window in the watch case. This idea was not totally new; the same kind of watch had been made by another company thirty years before and had turned out to be a flop. The reason management was willing to go ahead and develop the idea again was that it was not intended to be for "real"; only a nonworking model was to be made for a "watch of the future" show. As it turned out, trade reaction at the show was enthusiastic enough to nearly force production. To produce working models required that the watch movement be modified so that the hour indicator jumped from one number to the next. The costs of engineering changes, however, were more than worth it. When marketed, it quickly became Elgin's best selling model.

Not all managements are so tolerant of designers' futuristic ideas. Said the president of another company, "We've been using individual designers for over 20 years, but they have not always been productive. Their value seems to be in stimulating our own thinking as much as giving us specific and usable ideas. Their designs often cannot be produced inexpensively, and often their ideas are not mechanically sound. Many designers are primarily artists and are not always aware of production or functional problems."

Customers' Ideas

Both satisfied and dissatisfied customers can prove to be valuable sources of ideas. The Armstrong Cork Company embarked on a wandering series of product developments that all started as a result of a customer complaint. Their original business was the production of various cork products, including the cork gaskets for the inside of bottle caps. This cork seal worked well only so long as both the caps and the bottles met certain specifications. Customer complaints about leakages led Armstrong first into the production of caps and later into the production of glass bottles—all to ensure that their original product, the cork gasket, would provide a good seal. Once in the glass bottle business, it seemed logical to start production of electrical insulators made of glass. And so their product line developed into a fascinating and bewildering array of products which, on the surface, bore little relationship to one another. Fortunately, most customer suggestions have less drastic consequences.

While customers should not be expected to do actual product invent-ing, their expressions of needs and dissatisfaction may be among the best sources of ideas. Such was the finding of one study made of the problem of finding and screening new product ideas.[4] In this study, several hundred manufacturers of electronic equipment were contacted to determine the initial source of the idea for their new products during the preceding two years. Significant differences did exist in the success achieved with ideas from the different sources. The ideas which proved most likely to be successful were those which came from customers and salesmen; those least likely to be successful came from the company's own top management. The conclusion drawn to explain this phenomenon was that the ideas originating with top management never had to under-go an objective preliminary screening. Who was going to refuse further consideration of an idea suggested by a vice-president? On the other hand, ideas from customers and the trade were evaluated objectively, and although many good ideas may have been accidentally rejected, at least fewer poor ideas did get serious consideration.

Perhaps the most recent innovation in the generation of new product ideas is the practice, being started by at least two firms, of anticipating consumer needs (and, therefore, products needed) five to ten years in the future. One study of this nature was started by first identifying those individuals in a community whose way of living seemed to be characteristic of how the great bulk of consumers would be living in another five to ten years. Having identified a group of such individuals to their satisfaction, they then studied various details of their behavior patterns (as revealed through detailed diary records) and attempted to deduce needs which were currently unsatisfied and, in some cases, as yet unrecognized. From this set of futuristic needs, they attempted to generate new product ideas far enough in advance to enable several years of laboratory development work plus several more years of field testing.

Although an expensive way to get ideas, this sequence of "consumer observation-need identification-product idea generation," is an excellent way to focus creative efforts.[5] The clear and factual problem definitions which result can be used to guide creative talents to the most fertile fields, and perhaps because of the restraints of realism imposed, a small

[4] Paul Champlain, "How Manufacturers of Electronic Equipment Determine Po-tential Markets for New Products," unpublished thesis, Bachelors Degree, School of Industrial Management, M.I.T., 1953.
[5] Although expensive for any single firm to undertake on its own, it could be quite economical if a service were started to monitor consumer behavior and the results sold to many firms.

number of high quality ideas are likely to result rather than a large number of poor ideas.

Preliminary Screening of Ideas

Among companies which have a conducive attitude toward the expression of new ideas, distinguishing the "good" from the "poor" is usually a greater problem than the original idea creation. Here again there are numerous books and articles which present "Check lists" which help a screener sort ideas.[6] The weakness of the lists is that the ideas rejected depend largely on the individual screener. Unfortunately, there is no way of really knowing how many good ideas are screened out along with those that would in fact have turned out to be poor ideas.

It has been pointed out that each corporation tends to have a single individual who acts as a "gatekeeper" regulating the flow of new ideas.[7]

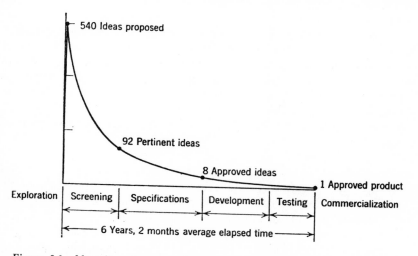

Figure 8.3 Mortality of new product ideas, from twenty chemical companies, during 1955. Source: Commercial Chemical Development Association. This chart is reproduced from Printer's Ink, *February 1, 1963, p. 27.*

[6] Richard C. Christian, "A Checklist for New Industrial Products," *Journal of Marketing*, Vol. XXIV, No. 3 (July 1959), pp. 70–73. R. H. Moulton, "Before Introducing New Products Check This List," *Printers' Ink*, Vol. CCLI (May 20, 1955), p. 34; "What to Look for Before Leaping at New Products," *Dun's Review and Modern Industry*, Vol. XXII, No. 8 (August 1951), pp. 113–114.

[7] Ernest J. Enright, Jr., *Planning and Administering Test Marketing Campaigns For New Products*, an unpublished doctoral thesis, Graduate School of Business Administration, Harvard University, 1957.

These individuals, who assert a powerful, even if perhaps informal, influence on the fate of new product ideas, may hold the future destiny of the corporation in their hands. As such, one would expect them to be unusually well informed about the market, corporate objectives, strengths, weaknesses, strategies, and competitors. In fact, the function of screening product ideas is too often given to individuals because they have a tactful way of saying "no."

The ease with which potentially valuable new ideas can be rejected is a serious problem. Nothing is more indefensible than a new product idea in the vague, undefined stage in which it is described only in terms of words or rough sketches. An idea expressed in terms of hardware—even if not a working model—seems a hundred times more defensible than an idea in verbal, written, or sketch form.

But it takes time and money to get from ideas to hardware; only the better ideas are worth the effort. Figure 8.3 gives one indication of how many ideas get through this screening stage and the average time taken in the chemical industry.

To provide maximum screening with minimum "erroneous rejection," some companies use committees. These groups include a diversity of interests and knowledge with representatives from engineering, production, marketing, and a senior generalist who can remember when the same idea was tried thirty years ago. Together these individuals try to spot quickly the ideas that have low chance of success.

Rather than try to say "yea" or "nay" to ideas, some firms use rating systems.

A few companies have experimented with numerical formulas or equations to secure a quantitative indication of an idea's worth. They include the Quaker Oats Company, Monsanto Chemical Company, Olin Industries, Inc., and American Alcolac. In most of these schemes, the rater assigns a point score from a specified range to each of a series of product criteria. In some of them, plus and minus values are used. Others require simple mathematical calculations. But they all provide a total point score or an index number. Their purpose is to establish priorities for developmental consideration. A few firms using new product rating systems have scored past projects, successful and unsuccessful as bench marks for comparison. These schemes have been controversial. Opponents argue that they are arbitrary and lack flexibility. Supporters rebut with the contention that they force consideration on an organized basis of all of the key variables influencing product success. And their users point out that the factors and weights can be modified to meet changing conditions. They also point out that the ratings can be supported or refuted by other data.[8]

Establishing Feasibility and Specifications

Although the vast majority of product ideas will be rejected in the preliminary screening, the ones passed through will be accompanied by many unknowns. Someone must now start serious data collection to determine if the product can be made and sold profitably. Simultaneously, someone must determine just what is really meant by "the product"—in what form will it be made, with what capacity, with what features, etc. The basic questions to be answered at this stage are still the same as before:

1. What would be (or could be) the size and nature of demand for this product?
2. What would be the production problems and costs?
3. How closely would the endeavor fit our firm's capacities and objectives?

The difference is that now some money can be spent for more accurate answers. Just how much should be spent at this "preworking model" stage depends largely on the cost of producing a working model. Although the accuracy of evaluations at this early stage is less than in later stages, the attempt is worthwhile if a working model requires substantial time and money to develop. In the biscuit industry, for instance, development of a "new" cooky may be so inexpensive to try out that the idea can go directly to a taste panel or small-scale market test. In contrast, producing the first week's issue of a new news magazine may cost hundreds of thousands of dollars.

Estimating Consumer Demand

Accurate estimates of demand for a new product are difficult to develop. Some ideas, of course, concern the fulfillment of needs which are established beyond any doubt, and there is no need to spend time confirming demand. A pharmaceutical company has no reason to confirm

[8] Taylor W. Meloan, "New Products—Keys to Corporate Growth." Presented at the Winter Conference of the American Marketing Association, December 28–30, 1960, St. Louis, and reprinted in William Lazer and Eugene J. Kelley, *Managerial Marketing: Perspectives and Viewpoints*, Richard D. Irwin, Homewood, Ill., 1962.

the magnitude of need for anticancergenic drugs. The only problem is to develop the product. On the other hand, the same firm will have a difficult problem in determining the merits of marketing a special line of cosmetics designed for people allergic to the regular brands. Are there enough women allergic to regular cosmetics to make a special formulation worthwhile? If so, is a pharmaceutical firm really the one to capitalize on the opportunity?

Simply by using secondary sources of information, the merit of some ideas can be established. This is especially apt to be true when the market is shown to be either extremely small or extremely large. More often, secondary sources only provide the barest outlines of market potential, and some field work is, therefore, desirable to get consumer reactions.

Assuming that no working model is yet available, the question arises of just how the idea should be presented to consumers: a verbal description, an artist's conception, or a mock-up. This choice among symbolic forms will depend mostly on the particular product, but whatever choice is made will influence the nature and amount of marketing research work that is profitable.

Whatever form of presentation is chosen, most companies find that the greatest barrier to accurate appraisals from consumers comes from the unnatural test conditions. It has long been recognized that there is a strong tendency for respondents to give favorable reactions to an idea as a means of being polite. One way of combating this tendency is to present several product ideas together. These supplementary product ideas need not be really new inventions, but they should be generally comparable in expense, frequency of use, area of application, etc. These extra product ideas do two things: they enable the respondent to say nice things to the interviewer without involving the real test product and they provide a basis for *relative* evaluations of the test products in contrast to *absolute* evaluations.

Another barrier to accurate consumer evaluations of a product idea may come from consumers' inability to perceive what a really new product would mean to them. How can a person know how useful they would find some new product they have never used? Few consumers can accurately forecast their potential satisfaction, and yet researchers frequently are guilty of asking them to do so. Unfortunately, consumers will almost invariably give some answer to the question asked to avoid looking incompetent in the eyes of the tester.

The simple truth seems to be that there is no sure-fire method of predicting demand without an actual prolonged test sale. What appears to be a highly enthusiastic consumer response may simply reflect the respondent's conviction that the new product would be good for "other people." If the response were unenthusiastic, it may reflect only a lack of understanding by consumers of the real merits of the product, especially when the test products are quite different from any with which the consumers have had previous experience. Since accurate estimates of demand are so difficult to obtain at this stage, and yet so necessary to save large development expenses, it represents an area in great need of improvement.

Identification of Prospect Types

In addition to estimating the magnitude of demand through consumer contact, the interviews are often used to get indications of the particular type of consumers who show most interest in the product. Are men more interested than women? Does interest vary by age, by education, by home ownership, by geographical area? This prospect identification is critically important is assessing the feasibility of *efficiently* marketing the new product. Companies which have an established product line are anxious to know if the new product appeals to its existing set of customers; if not, are the deviations desirable? Will it be necessary to establish new channels of distribution to reach those interested in the new product?

Stimulating Ideas from Respondents

The initial presentation of the new product idea to consumers is sometimes used as a means of refining the basic idea or the expression of that idea. There are two conditions under which this consumer feedback is especially helpful:

1. when the product must operate in conjunction with the consumer's existing set of goods, potential conflicts may be disclosed;
2. when the product can take any one of many potential forms.

Although direct contact with consumers is highly desirable even at these early, preworking model stages, the research can become expensive. As an interim measure—between reliance on estimates from secondary data on the one hand and direct consumer contact on the other—some researchers find it best to confine their field work at this stage to reaction from the trade. Interviews with a dozen purchasing agents of retail stores, for example, can give invaluable information in little time and at little cost. Because of their intimate knowledge of consumer tastes, buyers frequently provide excellent judgments on what the product's speci-

fications should be. Should the product design include features x, y, or z?
Would the packaging form be critical? How sensitive would volume be
to various price levels? What would be the closest form of competition?
How much consumer education would be required?

It is neither possible nor necessary to answer all the preceding questions with complete certainty at this stage. What is desired by the end
of the feasibility and specification stage is a general appraisal of the
product idea which is sufficiently inclusive and accurate to justify the
gamble of entering the next phase—the considerably more costly product
development and refinement stage. This is the time at which working
and testable units of the product are made.

As numerous people have pointed out, the process of product development is analogous to a game of poker in many respects. In poker,
the cost of staying in the game increases over time and the question is
when one should drop out rather than pay the price of more cards (or
more strategic information). The same is true in product development.
Whereas the initial idea screening phase is quite inexpensive, and the
feasibility stage need not be extravagant, the product development and
refinement stage is likely to require substantial time and budgets. Only
the most promising ideas can be developed to the point of working
models.

Once working models have been produced, it becomes possible to
begin a new round of testing. These tests may be through the placement
of test units with consumers or through actual sales test.

Reaffirming Demand with Product Samples

Especially when products are quite new to consumers, it is advantageous to leave a working model of the product with prospects for a
trial period, the length varying according to the product itself. Actual
consumer use of the product in a natural setting begins to provide the
kind of testing that produces highly significant reactions. This period of
use may also turn up unexpected product difficulties that were overlooked in the laboratory tests. Usual practice is to conduct one interview
at the time the product is placed with the prospect and to conduct a final
interview after the trial period. It may, however, be even more advantageous to schedule several intervening interviews in order to learn the
rate at which various reactions toward the product unfold as experience
with it is gained.

With some products it is relatively easy to conduct short and yet
meaningful product use tests. Food and flavor developers, for instance,
have an unusually easy time in getting their product ideas tested eco-

nomically, either through individuals in their own homes or through groups at meetings. It is easy for a soup manufacturer to prepare several variations from his regular product and to perform many tests among church social groups, women's club meetings, consumer panels, etc., and therefore to compare many alternatives. It is strange to note in view of this ease of testing that as recently as the mid-1950's, a large producer of margarine completed elaborate plans for production and sale of a different formulation of margarine, including the acquisition of expensive new production equipment, before making a systematic taste test among consumers. When a blind test was made between the old and the new formulation in 500 households over a two-week testing period, it was learned that 40 per cent preferred the new, 40 per cent preferred the old, and 20 per cent had no preference. Because all plans were completed before the test result was in, the new product was introduced (at considerable expense), but it was certainly not clear that the company was better off by dropping the old and adopting the new product.

Where preference testing is relatively easy, there have been helpful improvements in technique. Predicting the popularity of patterns for wallpaper, dishware, and silverware, for instance, was improved through a clever technique. This method consists of asking respondents to specify the pattern they would like if they were to win some of the product in a lottery at the end of the testing session. By comparing that pattern choice to the one previously specified as "being best," large differences often appear. Using the pattern selected for their own use (if they won the lottery) proves considerably more accurate in predicting demand than using the patterns they selected as being "best."

A great virtue of these easily arranged testing situations is that a wide range of product modifications can be tested easily—thus more accurately determining an optimum product formulation or configuration. The value of such variations was well illustrated in the case of making pork and gravy.[9] The problem was to determine the optimum time-temperature integral at which pork and gravy should be processed during canning for maximum palatability to the consumer. By testing values substantially removed from the suspected optimum, the chances of learning the true optimum accurately are increased.

More accurate appraisals of trade reaction can also be obtained after working models are in hand. It is interesting to note in this regard that when the first Polaroid Land Cameras were taken to photographic retailers they flatly refused to handle the camera. They were certain that consumers would not pay the price for any camera which did not have

[9] Purnell H. Benson and Francis J. Pilgrim, "Testing Less Desirable Product Possibilities," *Journal of Marketing*, Vol. XXVI, No. 3 (July 1961), p. 65.

a fast lens, a wide range of shutter speeds, and the other similar features that had been offered on similarly priced cameras. Thus Polaroid was forced to get initial distribution through department stores. In retrospect, this turned out well because the department stores did large amounts of cooperative advertising, thus greatly increasing Polaroid's advertising budget and making the funds go further through the low local newspaper space charges granted to department stores.

Common sense would suggest that industrial market demand appraisals would be more easily established. While this is sometimes true (because potential buyers are often more easily found and more articulate) there have been many instances in which the "rational" purchasing habits of the industrial buyer are not so rational—at least not rational from the seller's point of view. When the innovator leaves trial samples with a prospective company, for example, it may be more difficult to get a fair trial than it would be with a housewife. One producer of a new type of paint additive learned that almost none of the samples it had left with paint manufacturers had been tried. Investigation by the writer showed the person who would be making a decision on using the new product was often the same person responsible for maintaining consistent quality control of all production. Although admitting the new paint additive would cost less and would probably offer advantages, the prospects refused trial simply to avoid having to make any changes in their smoothly operating production process. (Is this the often- spoken-of "resistance to change," or just common sense from the user's point of view?)

The reluctance of industrial purchasers to disrupt smoothly operating production processes presents many problems to the innovator.[10] Numerous small companies have gone bankrupt because of the unexpectedly long time lag between an industrial prospect agreement to try the new product and the actual placement of a quantity order. Because of this time lag it often pays the producer to start marketing efforts considerably before it has a saleable product which it could deliver in quantity. Time lags may also result from gaining approval from regulatory agencies. Producers of new building materials often find, to their dismay, that outmoded building codes must be changed before trial of their new material is possible. One small company producing high pressure fluid valves encountered serious financial trouble while city engineering departments did extended testing. Pharmaceutical manufacturers are experiencing increasingly serious delays in getting approval of new drugs, even for purposes of restricted testing.

[10] For several excellent and detailed examples of this reluctance, see E. Raymond Corey, *The Development of Markets For New Materials*, Division of Research, Graduate School of Business Administration, Harvard University, Boston, 1956.

Commercial Test Sales

The foregoing types of testing are done as soon as working models become available. To engage in the still more informative test sales, many additional decisions must first be made. The product name, packaging, pricing, legal clearance, channels of distribution, advertising program, guarantee policy, and perhaps a servicing facility must be established. At the same time, the test sale itself is often used to evaluate variations in these factors; sales results at one price versus another, for example.

By far the most valuable piece of information learned from the actual test sale is the volume sold under "real" conditions. Regardless of what consumers have previously said they "would do if . . . ," nothing can be believed until they have actually elected to exchange their money for the new product under normal market conditions. Even then, adequate time must be allowed to get consumer reaction after the initial novelty phase wears off. If repurchase is necessary for success, the time of the test must be extended accordingly. Indeed, measures of repurchase may provide the most valuable clues to long-range success.[11]

Trying to get market test results too soon is probably the most serious and frequent mistake made by management at this stage. In 14 case studies of test campaigns, Enright observed mistakes made by

1. testing before production could manufacture an adequate stock for testing needs;
2. testing during the off-season for the product;
3. testing before the company had notified its wholesalers of the role that the company wanted them to play;
4. testing before the shelf life of the product could be checked;
5. concluding the testing phase before the research work designed to provide wanted information could be finished or, in one case, before the research work ever began.[12]

Management's tendency to cut corners on testing is understandable because of the many pressures to get on the market quickly. Alberto-Culver, for instance, was reportedly so eager to beat Procter and Gamble's Head and Shoulders shampoo to market that it filmed the TV

[11] For illustrative examples, see Benjamin Lipstein, "Tests for Test Marketing," *Harvard Business Review*, Vol. XXXIX, No. 2 (March–April 1961), pp. 74–77; and William D. Barclay, "A Probability Model for Early Prediction of New Product Market Success," *Journal of Marketing*, Vol. XXVII, No. 1 (January 1963), pp. 63–69.

[12] Ernest J. Enright, "Market Testing," *Harvard Business Review*, Vol. XXXVI, No. 5 (September–October 1958), p. 75.

commercials for its Subdue shampoo even before it had developed the product!

Most experienced companies now, however, are adopting a more patient attitude. The huge errors made by inadequate testing—such as Lever Brothers' loss of 24 million dollars on Surf, which had to be withdrawn from the market—are just too high a price to pay. Even with patience it is hard enough to conduct reliable tests. Despite well-laid plans, competitors may "muddy the test waters."

> A classic demonstration of water-muddying was staged some years ago by the Toni Corp., then the leading producer of home-permanent preparations. When Colgate began to market test a product called Lustre Creme Home Permanent, Toni launched a counteroffensive referred to, in intracompany memoranda, as Operation Snafu. Toni already had three home permanents on the market, Toni, Prom, and Bobbi; in addition to stepping up greatly its local advertising of all three of these brands, the company introduced a fourth brand, called Epic, in the cities Colgate had chosen for its test. The object was to scare Colgate off entirely, or failing that, to make Colgate underestimate the potential sales of its new product, and therefore to launch it with a relatively small advertising and promotion budget —which would, of course, make life easier for Toni. Whether or not Operation Snafu was the deciding factor, Colgate did in fact drop its plans to market Lustre Creme Permanent nationally.[13]

In looking for the appropriate balance between extensive testing versus fast action, one can find successful examples of both extremes. The development of Ban, for instance, was a painfully slow, careful, arduous, and eventually successful illustration of the slow and safe route.[14] The development of Ban started in 1948 when the product planning group of Bristol-Myers Co. "saw the need for a new kind of deodorant." In brief, the first version of the new lotion was tested in 1949, after finding and curing settling problems, it was introduced in 1950, returned to the laboratories in 1951 for development of a roll-on bottle, tested in the new bottle in six cities in 1952, returned to the laboratory for package performance improvement in 1953, test marketed in four cities in early 1954, tested in two more cities in September, then "rushed" to full

---

[13] Spencer Klaw, "The Soap Wars: A Strategic Analysis," *Fortune*, Vol. LXVII, No. 6 (June 1963), p. 186.

[14] Both of the following examples are abstracted from detailed cases reported in Neil H. Borden and Martin V. Marshall, *Advertising Management, Text and Cases*, Richard D. Irwin, Homewood, Ill., 1959, pp. 498–533.

national distribution in February, 1955. Estimated development expenditures were $750,000 over the seven-year period.

In contrast, at about the same time, in the same industry, Jules Montenier, Inc., was developing Stopette Spray deodorant. Starting in 1947, the newly organized firm put a newly developed liquid deodorant in a newly developed spray bottle and began selling through major department stores in Chicago with no previous tests of liquid, package, or marketing methods. By 1950 they were estimated to hold second sales position with 10 per cent of the United States market. Does the success of both methods suggest testing is a matter of indifference? Obviously not. Jules Montenier, Inc. was willingly exposing itself to an extremely *high* risk of losing very *little*. Bristol-Myers Co., with a valuable reputation among consumers and the trade, had good reason to seek low risk in gambling its reputation and funds.

Some helpful factors to examine in deciding what extent of testing is desirable have been suggested by Robert Weigand.

1. The degree of newness in the product—the newer, the more testing.
2. The speed of feedback from the market—the slower, the more testing.
3. The capacity to correct mistakes—the less, the more testing.
4. The time length of commitment—the longer, the more testing.
5. The interaction with existing product line—the more, the more testing.
6. The desire or need for secrecy—the less, the more testing.
7. The relative position of competitors—the farther behind they are, the more testing.[15]

The market test stage can be used as a marketing mix testing laboratory. By trying various combinations of personal selling, margins, advertising budgets, prices, trade deals, etc., information is collected to make the full-scale launch more effective than it would be otherwise. Not only the best mix of marketing tools but also the best absolute amount of marketing pressure may be estimated from well-designed tests, that is, given a good mix of selling tools, what scale of expenditure this month, next month, etc., will provide greatest returns.

The Launching Stage

The high expense of launching new products has surprised many inexperienced marketers. The old cliche, "Make a better mousetrap and

[15] Robert E. Weigand, "How Extensive the Planning and Development Program?", *Journal of Marketing*, Vol. XXVI, No. 3 (July 1962), pp. 56–57.

the world will beat a path to your door," is rarely true even with basically new and obviously better products and is never true with the slightly or moderately new products that constitute 99 per cent of the "new" products marketed today.

Because of the high expense (and the many questions yet to be answered) nearly all small companies and many large ones introduce new products in one area at a time. When done in this way, the funds generated from sales in one area can be used to finance expenditures in the next. Equally important, mistakes are made on a local basis rather than a national basis, and knowledge gained in one area can be used to improve operations in the next.

Of all the high-risk decisions made at the launch stage, those concerning the advertising program probably represent the greatest risk. Large sums are often spent, and, *if not well spent, there is no salvage value.* What appeals should be used? What media? What schedule? Over what time period?

One controlled experiment in the advertising of two new products showed that the advertising was most efficient if continued for a substantial time. This test, conducted by the writer, used 6000 personal interviews to trace changes in consumer brand name awareness, product information, attitudes, purchase intents, claimed purchases, and brand preference as they changed during the introductory period. The test was done in Fort Wayne, Indiana, with Lestare, a new dry bleach packaged in a dissolvable unit of use; and Chicken Sara Lee, a prepared, frozen chicken dish of high quality packaged in a plastic, boilable bag. The test city was divided into four quadrants, and the distribution of newspapers carrying the advertisements was controlled in such a way that subscribers in each area received varying amounts of exposure. At no time during the twenty weeks of the test did the ads appear in papers delivered to the no-exposure area. Subscribers in another area were exposed once a week for four consecutive weeks and then no more. Similarly, subscribers in another area received eight exposures, and in another area twenty exposures. In all instances, the same 1000-line, black and white newspaper advertisement was run weekly, and arrangements were made to preclude any other form of advertising reaching the city.

By tracing changes in the level of brand awareness over time, it was found that advertising caused a rapid initial rise in awareness which tended to drop as soon as advertising was stopped. In fact, there were strong indications that some "negative awareness" existed after three months in the areas where there had been only four or eight exposures. Meanwhile, in the twenty-exposure area, the levels of awareness continued to hold or rise slightly. Thus the value of extended repetition, in

terms of brand awareness, came in the form of maintaining a given level
of awareness rather than in the form of continually increasing levels of
awareness. See Figure 8.4.

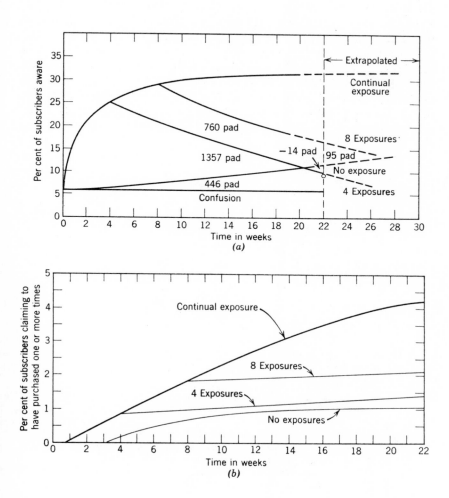

*Figure 8.4 Changes in brand recall and number of purchasers over time. Note:
Data standardized via cell-by-cell method for respondent age and education. (a)
Aided brand recall for Chicken Sara Lee. PAD = Percent Aware Days, that is, one
PAD is one percent of subscribers aware of the brand name for one day. (b) Cu-
mulative purchasers of Chicken Sara Lee with varying amounts of advertising.
Source: John B. Stewart,* Repetitive Advertising in Newspapers, *Division of Re-
search, Harvard Business School, Boston, 1964, p. 123.*

Perhaps the most important finding from the study was that it did require substantial repetition to achieve efficient purchase results. In contrast to the rapid rise in brand awareness, there was a time lag before the awareness was transformed into purchase behavior, and the transformation only occurred where repeated exposures reminded prospects to buy. For instance, the lowest advertising costs per "extra" purchaser did not occur until the fifteenth consecutive weekly advertisement had appeared. Thus, under the conditions of this particular test, a short campaign of only three or four insertions was quite inefficient, while sustained repetition increased the efficiency of the expenditures. The relationships among brand awareness, purchasers, and dollar efficiency in the case of Chicken Sara Lee are presented in Figure 8.5.

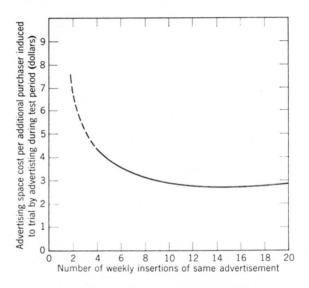

Figure 8.5 Relative efficiency of continued advertising versus discontinued advertising for Chicken Sara Lee. Source: John B. Stewart, Repetitive Advertising in Newspapers, *Division of Research, Harvard Business School, Boston, 1964, p. 254.*

Despite the limited effectiveness of just a few advertisements, some firms knowingly use such a program anyway. Although they know consumers will not be appreciably influenced, they run a few ads to make an impression on the trade. Getting shelf space may make or break a launching program, and the amount of space gotten is often disproportionately determined by the proposed advertising schedule. For some reason, retailers seem overly reluctant to pass up either the benefits of a few advertisements or a special introductory price deal.

When the launching plans do succeed in creating sales, that very success can cause problems. More than one company has been caught short when sales exceeded expectations and demand could not be met. Those firms that frequently add new products to the line become proficient at estimating the volume required to "fill the pipelines" and can plan accordingly. But even firms that should know better can get caught short—especially when national distribution is attempted all at one time. Polaroid's inability to provide adequate supplies of film when introducing its new Model 100 will undoubtedly become a classic case in point. Even six months after purchasing the camera, some customers were still unable to find a store that had the film in stock.

Determining Success

As the turmoil and excitement of the launching phase die down, an appraisal must be made of how well the new product has really done. Has it moved the firm closer to its goals? How much closer? For how long will the benefits continue? Although one would expect most firms to have a good system for measuring the value of a new product, this is actually an area where much improvement is needed.

Part of the evaluation problem arises from internal accounting figures. Are costs accurately allocated to the new product? Are the depreciation rates based on valid assumptions? If a million dollars were spent on the introductory advertising campaign, was the whole amount charged against the product this year even though everybody agrees it was really a capital investment? Did the validity of the per unit cost figures depend on assumptions about levels of plant activity? For many such reasons a firm may not know the "true" costs of its new product. If costs are not known accurately, can success be appraised?

The rate of sales to consumers may also be hard to determine. Usually a company knows only its own shipments and must set up special retail store audits to measure purchases by the ultimate consumer. Even when this is done, it is often hard to tell if initial sales reflect the real continuing demand or merely reflect a pent-up demand that will quickly evaporate. Thus, even for the simplest and most measurable kind of objective—net profit—it is not easy to tell whether a new product has helped the company's cause, or just how much help it has been.

Determining success on the more meaningful measure of return on investment is still more uncertain. In addition to determining the true net profit, the investment utilized by the new product must be decided on.

This in turn raises a host of questions: Should fixed assets be taken at gross or net value? At historical cost or replacement cost? Should intangibles, not usually shown on the balance sheet (such as the company's reputation among consumers and the trade), be included for purposes of computing the return figures? These are the questions for which accountants have no pat answers, and each management group must choose its own procedure to fit its needs.[16] The point to be made here is that these are not simple nor clear-cut decisions, yet how they are made influences whether the new product is "successful." Success to one firm under its rules may not be success to the next.

How about the objectives of financial stability, certainty, or durability? Most businessmen would agree with the general principle that a new product could be highly "successful" even if it did not add new profits so long as it did stabilize operations, increase the certainty of the profit flow, or prolong it. But, underneath the general principle, just how much certainty must a new product bring the firm to be counted successful? And even if someone could say, who could predict how much certainty the new product would in fact bring the firm. To make such predictions would require foretelling future consumer demand, technological developments, and competitive action.

Product Protection

Inevitably, evaluting the success of a development requires guesses about protection of the idea. Small firms are often swamped so quickly by the imitations of large firms that they are unable to recoup research expenses, and even the largest firms may not be able to stop infringements in time to be effective. Westinghouse recently found a company copying its new hair dryer so exactly that even the instruction book was the same! Thus it was with a heroic sense of humor that one small company recently answered the question about the success of its new product, "Yes, it will be a success if present sales continue for 14.3 years."

The more successful a firm's new product, the more effort competitors will make to copy it. In the case of new product features such as power steering, self-winding watches, automatic defrosting refrigerators, one study showed that among 5000 new product features advertised one or more times, the innovating company's new feature was copied by an average of one competitor within two years after its introduction. The following rate was higher than this, however, among the "successful" new

[16] Clarence B. Nickerson, *Managerial Cost Accounting and Analysis*, McGraw-Hill, New York, 1955, p. 524.

features. Among the features that the innovator advertised for at least two years (thus indicating that it was considered good enough to warrant continued emphasis and, therefore, judged successful) there were, on the average, nearly twice as many copying competitors. As might be expected, these following rates varied considerably from one industry to another. New features were copied very quickly in the television set industry and relatively slowly in the automobile industry. See Figure 8.6.[17] The speed with which competitors will copy the best developments means that the innovator must be prepared to capitalize on his innovation very quickly.

When a company's new development is quickly followed, there are still indirect benefits that accrue. Having been first to market, the innovator can get extensive free publicity, get increased enthusiasm from its salesmen, get a more progressive image among consumers (and potential investors), and can get a morale boost for the company's management. Any one or all of these benefits may provide a way to rationalize the new product as a success for the firm, regardless of the direct financial returns.

The Degree of Innovation

Thus, despite the uncertainty of producing a successful new product or fears of having that success copied, the balance of pressures are in favor of product change and development. But, judging by the type of "new products" that flow onto the market, these innovative pressures are not of a sort to produce radically different products; rather, they seem to produce a large volume of modified products.

By scanning the products announced in their newsletter during the first six months of 1960, *Printers' Ink* made the following observations about the 106 new product announcements: [18]

1. The great majority of new products are, in fact, new in the sense of being improvements upon existing products.
2. Me-tooism is a compelling force, probably the most dominant force in new product development and follow-the-leader is a popular game.
3. . . . it was a packaging change that made a product "new" in four out of ten cases.

[17] John B. Stewart, "Functional Features in Product Strategy," *Harvard Business Review*, Vol. XXXVII, No. 2 (March–April 1959), p. 65.
[18] "New Products: Their Purpose, Pattern—and Profits—for 1960," *Printers' Ink* (January 15, 1960), p. 23.

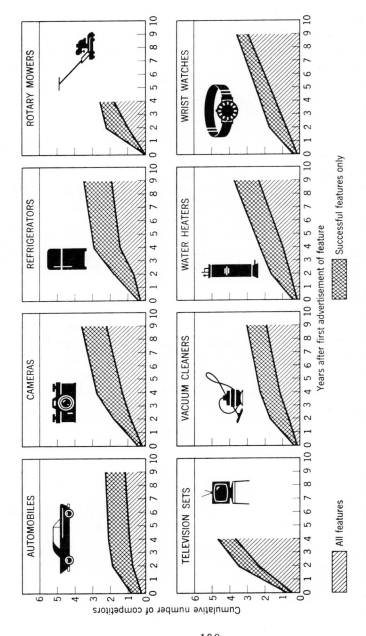

Figure 8.6 Competitive follow rates in the various industri es. Source: John B. Stewart, "Functional Features in Product Strategy," Harvard Business Review (March–April, 1959), p. 65.

4. The attempt to build greater convenience into products is the strongest motivating force in product planning.
5. Research-and-development work, now estimated to be running nationally at an annual rate of betweeen $8 and $10 billion may produce some more radical innovations. Meanwhile, the emphasis is likely to be on evolutionary "rather than revolutionary" items in which the product plus—the special feature—sets it apart and makes it more than just a me-too.

A follow-up three years later by *Printers' Ink* suggested that the large national research expenditures, which had reached $16 billion in 1963, were still not resulting in a flood of basically new innovations. They raised the question: [19] "Who's to blame for the dearth of new products which are new in the way the first TV sets were new?" and suggest the following answers: R & D lethargy on the part of consumer manufacturers; ignorance about free reference sources; self-delusion as to what constitutes a new product; misguided drive for profit.

And so, with rather gentle exploratory probing, manufacturers are producing an increasingly wide variety of only slightly different products. This product proliferation raises numerous problems and questions. Particularly among economists, there is concern that the hundreds of superficial product modifications are causing a gross waste of national resources. The typical marketers' answer to this concern is that product proliferation is a natural and vital part of a country's economic development—that without the frequent changes of models and styles, consumption would decrease and thereby lead to a declining economy. Actually, of course, no one knows what the effects would be of reducing the superficial product changes, but it is interesting to note that many business executives express concern about the abundance of superficial product obsolescence. In response to the question, "Do *you* feel that, for the long-run benefit of the United States, too large a part of our present economy is based on superficial product obsolescence, inducing people to buy new models before their old models are worn out?", the majority (64%) said "yes," that they believed there should be less superficial product obsolescence. Surprisingly, this concern was voiced quite consistently by the 2300 responding executives, regardless of the industry in which they themselves worked. This response is shown in Table 8.2.

Surely this widespread concern on the part of business managers suggests that research efforts should be directed toward helping firms learn how to do real innovation. As Theodore Levitt and others have pointed out on numerous occasions, major innovations rarely come from the

[19] "Why So Few Really New Products?", *Printers' Ink* (February 1, 1963), p. 25.

industries which they affect.[20] Why was the electronic organ not developed by the conventional organ or piano manufacturers? Why was
the Diesel locomotive not developed by the manufacturers of steam
locomotives? Why was the Polaroid type film not developed by the
photographic film industry? If this lack of innovation by those closest

*Table 8.2   The Extent to which Executives See a Problem, that is, Feel that
Too Large A Part of Our Present Economy Is Based on Superficial Product
Obsolescence*

Industry	Percentage of Respondents Who Are In This Industry	Percentage of Respondents In This Industry Who See A Problem
Manufacturing, consumer goods	16.7%	57.8%
Manufacturing, industrial goods	23.9	60.0
Retail or wholesale trade	7.5	61.4
Transportation	2.6	64.2
Communication	4.3	68.8
Banking, investment, insurance	9.0	70.0
Business services, consulting	7.5	72.5
Engineering	7.0	75.0
Construction	2.4	77.1
Other (education, labor union, government, etc.)	19.1	72.5
	100.0	

Source: John B. Stewart, "Problems in Review: Planned Obsolescence,"
Harvard Business Review, Vol. XXXVII, No. 5 (September-October 1959).

to the problem is caused by too great an ego identity with the old way of
doing things (as has been suggested by some students of the history of
innovation), surely it must be possible to make managers aware of their
myopia and thereby help them toward substantial innovations.

[20] Theodore Levitt, *Innovation in Marketing*, McGraw-Hill, New York, 1962.

LESSONS LEARNED

In looking back over the current practices in new product development, several major points seem to stand out.

1. On the one hand, there is much talk about the importance of new products to the American way of living—importance to the future economic growth of the nation, importance to the survival of the individual firm, and importance to consumers striving for a higher standard of living.
2. The actual response on the part of industry in recent years seems to have been a great deal of "slightly new" product development with very little genuine innovation.
3. When major innovation occurs it is frequently (perhaps even usually) done by someone other than the industry concerned.
4. In executing the "slightly new" product development plans, the chances of success are rather low and the cost of failure rather high.

What lessons can be learned by observing current product development efforts on a case by case basis? Although generalizations are difficult, Chester R. Wasson has suggested 13 characteristics of a product which seem to have a bearing on the extent of difficulties which may be encountered from the market. By evaluating the product on each characteristic, management can better predict expected marketing costs. These characteristics are as follows: [21]

A. Six novel attributes are positive, in the sense that they ease the job of introduction:
   1. New cost—or, better yet, price—if lower.
   2. New convenience in use—if greater.
   3. New performance—if better, more dependable and in the range of experience of the prospect—if believable.
   4. New availability, in place, or time, or both (including antiseasonality).
   5. Conspicuous-consumption (status symbol) possibilities.
   6. Easy credibility of benefits.
B. At least four characteristics make the job more difficult, slow up market development, and usually make it costlier:
   7. New methods of use (unless obviously simpler).

[21] Chester R. Wasson, "What Is New About a New Product?", *Journal of Marketing*, Vol. XXV, No. 3 (July 1960), p. 54.

8. Unfamiliar patterns of use (any necessity for learning new habits in connection with performance of a task associated with the new product).
9. Unfamiliar benefit (in terms of the prospect's understanding).
10. Costliness, fancied or real, of a possible error in use.

C. Three others are ambivalent in their effect—that is, the effect on market development probably depends not only on their exact nature, but also on the cultural climate at the moment. However, extreme unfamiliarity would probably be negative in effect:

11. New appearance, or other sensed difference (style or texture, for example).
12. Different accompanying or implied services.
13. New market (including different channels of sale).

And, as rather general guide lines for achieving smoothly operating product development programs, Ralph W. Jones has suggested the following basic principles for successful new product development.[22]

1. *Business strategy is expressed in products; product programs are the foundation of forward company planning.* A company can be no more successful than its products will allow it to be; without definitive new product programs, advance planning is indefinite and incomplete.

2. *The new product program is a top management responsibility.* This is a responsibility that cannot be delegated without abandoning a primary responsibility for leadership of a business.

3. *The new product function should be organized as a top executive staff function, headed by a manager of stature adequate for coordination of vice presidents.* There are many ways to tailor this principle to fit each company's situation, by department or committee. An example of new product organization appears in the May issue of the *Harvard Business Review,* a case history of S. C. Johnson & Sons, Inc.—The Johnson Wax Company.

4. *Organization and control should be established in conformance with the stages of new product evolution.* This concept of planning and control, as adapted to industry characteristics, has been highly valued in programs we have developed and installed for our clients.

5. *Coordinated new product effort is best achieved through interdepartmental product teams, representing all function areas of the business, tailored to fit the characteristics of each product.* There seems to be no effective substitute for this approach. We know about a dozen ways to do it, each of which may work or not work in other cases.

6. *A definitive program, carefully planned and closely managed, signif-*

---

[22] Ralph W. Jones, *op. cit.,* p. 434.

icantly improves new product results. Wherever a company has undertaken a *sound plan* to achieve better management leadership and control of this vital activity, they have been generally pleased with better results.

7. *New idea creation can be directed and cotrolled to achieve improved pertinence and quality of product ideas.* Quantity of ideas is more a problem than a solution. The requirement is for better quality and increased pertinency.

8. *New product selection is accomplished by a continuing series of evaluation in all stages; no single screening is adequate.* One magic screening will not do the job properly, despite popular literature to the contrary.

9. *Selection standards for products to be developed should be upgraded persistently to achieve an ever-increasing yield from available manpower and resources.* It is no trick at all to fill a lab with "pretty good" ideas. But, most companies have just so much in the way of resources, and the trick is to capitalize these at a minimum return, by recognizing and exploiting real bellringers.

10. *Product planning requires development of specifications and a program for each product prior to laboratory project.* Without preproject authorization management does not have control of the new product program; each product idea should be framed as a business proposition and so evaluated, as a basis of such authorization.

11. *Market requirements and opportunities are the primary consideration in product planning.* It is pretty conclusively demonstrated by experience that it is much harder to sell (at a profit) than it is to make a product in the first place; most products benefit if planned and programmed from the starting point of market needs and opportunities.

12. *Company acquisition should be integrated with internal development to achieve a balanced new product program.* These two programs are complementary and should be keyed to each other as mutually supporting activities.

In addition to the foregoing suggestions, I believe it is safe to make the following generalizations about new product activity:

1. The more concisely corporate objectives are stated, the more chance there will be retaining the best ideas and only rejecting the poor ideas.

2. Ideas which come into the company from the "outside sources" (customers, salesmen, and distributors) are more likely to reflect a genuine market need than ideas originating with top management. At a minimum, ideas from top management should be submitted to the same objective evaluations that are given to ideas from less prominent sources.

3. A major limitation on the accuracy of predictions made from survey

data stems from the unnaturalness of the questioning procedures. Consumers frequently do not know how they would react to, benefit from, or rate a new product. As a result, their answers to such questions as "Would you buy this if . . ." must only be taken as the grossest approximation of true demand.

4. The newer the product, the less accurate market predictions will be. Newness as used here has nothing to do with technological newness, but rather concerns only the extent to which this product differs from existing products *as perceived by the buyer*. A transistorized radio may be radically new to the technician, yet present few marketing problems.

5. Acceptance will probably be slow when the new product must be used in close conjunction with the buyer's existing set of goods. Buyers can find many reasons for maintaining the status quo if adoption of a new product requires altering other parts of their existing operations and the result may be extremely slow adoption.

6. Inventors and their sponsors invariably tend to over-rate the importance to others of the improvement their product offers. Thermoelectric modules offer a more reliable, quieter, and more readily controllable method of refrigeration, but because of higher costs it is amazing how many people can continue to get by with the conventional mechanical refrigeration systems.

7. Inventors and their sponsors invariably tend to over-rate the virtue of maintaining secrecy. Secrecy does, of course, have value, but where it precludes market testing the price (in terms of risk) can be exorbitantly high.

8. Because of an ego identity which often develops between the inventor and his invention, there is a strong tendency for him to want to try "just one more" way of improving performance. To prevent this from leading to exorbitantly high development costs, the manager must have the capacity to wean products away from the researcher on the one hand and, on the other, still maintain a work environment which is conducive to creative and productive work. The latter usually means freedom from daily, weekly, or monthly pressure to produce tangible results.

9. Too little time allowed for test marketing may be worse than no test marketing at all. Initial market reactions *are* different from what will become normal, and major capital outlays should be based only on the norm.

10. There is a tendency for management to underestimate both the time and costs of product development. If initial estimates are doubled, budgets will still be overshot, but less often.

11. The marketing costs of special interest products are particularly susceptible to underestimation. By the nature of established channels of distribution and promotion media, some highly specialized products can

be marketed reasonably efficiently (hobby products such as model rail-roads, boating supplies, hunting equipment, etc.) because there are special retail outlets and publications which reach the interested buyers. Much higher marketing costs may be encountered for special products developed to appeal to harder to reach market segments—left-handed consumers, eyeglass-wearing consumers, unusually tall consumers, etc., even though a larger potential market may exist.

12. An extremely high degree of coordination among corporate functions is required to achieve a smooth new product launching. This coordination (between engineering research, marketing research, corporate planning, production sales, and advertising) cannot be suddenly legislated—it must be a natural outgrowth of interdepartmental participation throughout an entire development program.

13. New product success is not easy to determine. It is only in the rarest instances that new products achieve dramatic and clear-cut success for the innovator. In the vast majority of cases new products are judged to have been successful on a rather intuitive basis as they take their place as just one part of a product line—perhaps adding some to sales volume, perhaps adding some to the stabilization of operations, or perhaps just forestalling a loss that would have occurred without the new product.

These, and undoubtedly other, generalizations can be extracted from past experience. Each has a grain of truth, and each has an exception to its validity. In the normal course of development work, the observations, trials, and retrials will undoubtedly render many more useful generalizations. These can and should be collected, re-examined, and refined until a much larger and more accurate body of knowledge is assembled. Surely great strides in current practice could be made by simply applying existing knowledge. Even more progress could be made through applying similar future generalizations. But, while this process of extracting generalizations from current practices proceeds, it would seem that there should also be an additional effort underway—the development of a conceptual framework to make possible major, even if only long-term,

TOWARD A SCIENCE OF PRODUCT DEVELOPMENT

Backing away now from current practices and generalizations derived therefrom, the question arises, "How might work proceed toward the development of a science of product development?" Is such a thing possible? How useful would it be? The following sections present some exploratory ideas addressed to those questions.

First, is it likely that continued observations of a large number of new product case studies will lead to a basic understanding of product development work? I will argue that they would not. The problem is that our observations—at least so far—are not of a basic enough sort. Each instance of a new product development appears to be largely a unique example. To the extent that this continues, the generalizations drawn from them will have severe limitations. Only when basic common denominators have been identified will substantial progress be possible. Marketers, in general, and new product developers in particular, need the equivalent of a periodic table of elements. They need some basic building blocks with which to make more effective observations and to

This raises a second question: Can there be a science of developing and marketing new products before there is a science of marketing in general? Again, I think not. The handling of new products is but a special case of the more general problem, and although there are certainly unique problems created by virtue of a product's newness, it is likely that the general problem must be solved before the special problem is solved. Despite the formidable obstacles this poses, the following ideas are offered.

Restating the Problem

About the most basic statement that can be made about product development work is that it is the process of creating instruments of need fulfillment. As depicted in Figure 8.1, to be successful the product must serve as a mutually beneficial vehicle to meet the needs of consumers and the needs of the company. Since most failures result from not meeting consumer needs, primary attention will be directed to that half of the problem.

When product development is thought of as a means of need fulfillment, it shifts attention from the product itself and to consumer needs. It emphasizes the importance of gaining a thorough understanding of consumer needs, how they arise, why they exist, and how they are satisfied. Unfortunately, marketers have done so little in the study of needs that there is no solid basis on which to build a science of need fulfillment. *If product development were referred to as "fill development," it would serve as a constant reminder that products only have usefulness to the extent that they do fill needs.* Is it reasonable to hope that it will be possible to develop a science of need fulfillment without having first developed a science of needs?

What is required, therefore, in this writers' opinion is

1. a sophisticated means of describing the needs (or wants) of indi-

viduals (including the establishment of new units of measure) and techniques for measuring these needs;

2. a sophisticated means for describing the manner in which products (or services) fulfill the needs of individuals;

3. a sophisticated means of describing large collections of individual needs, i.e., the needs of "the market," or segments thereof;

4. the development of strategies which will help guide management to act profitably in the fulfillment of the market needs.

Although it is far beyond the intent of this chapter to present refined solutions to the above problems, it does seem possible to make a start.

Individual Needs

In attempting to describe individual needs, it seems desirable to divide the discussion into two separate parts: one part concerns the *subjects* of needs and the other concerns the more general *characteristics* of needs, regardless of the subject. By need subject is meant the topic which the need concerns—thirst, hunger, pain, affection, etc. It has been evident for many years that such lists of need subjects are virtually useless for marketing purposes, and there have been numerous controversies about which need subjects should be included on the list and which were more basic subjects than others. While there is widespread discontent with such behavioristic views of motivation, it is not at all clear what should replace it. Because this topic is so controversial and nebulous, the simpler half of the problem will be approached first: the characteristics of needs which could be profitably explored and formally recognized by marketers.

A variety of need characteristics are listed below. While many of these characteristics are intuitively recognized by marketers in their daily practice, it seems highly desirable that standardized terminology be developed as a means of achieving more sophisticated descriptions and measurements of consumer needs.

Characteristics of Individual Needs

Need Intensity: the strength with which a need is felt.

Need Quantity: the amount of change that must occur to satisfy the need.

Need Clearness: the preciseness and definiteness with which the individual perceives his need.

Need Complexity: the number of facets or aspects which are perceived by the individual as a part of the need.

Need Acceptability: the social acceptability of the subject of the need.

Need Frequency: the typical number of times per unit of time that the individual becomes aware of the need.

Need Duration: the length of the time period during which the individual remains aware of the need.

Need Excitation: the manner in which the individual's awareness of the need may be triggered.

Need Proximity: the need closeness in time (a present need or a future need) or closeness in psychological space (closeness to the individual's main stream of consciousness).

Need Urgency: the extent to which fulfillment of a need today in a given way gives greater satisfaction than filling the same need in the same way at a future time.

Need Certainty: the subjective probability which the individual associates with the need arising.

Need Reducibility: the ease with which a need may be satisfied through some behavior, whether it be through rationalization or through carrying out physical behavior such as purchasing.

Each of the foregoing need characteristics is pertinent to understanding the process of need fulfillment. Major efforts should be made to extend the list, clarify the definitions, establish units of measure, and devise means of measurement, even if the means must be imprecise initially. All of this can be done even before there is agreement on the most useful way of conceptualizing the subjects of the needs. This activity would represent a first fundamental step toward building a "census" of market needs.

As previously mentioned, marketers have been highly unproductive in clarifying the subjects of consumer needs. While most marketing textbooks continue to list apologetically a variety of human motivations which are not very useful, a few individuals have broken away from the behavioristic notions of motivation. Such writing practitioners as Burleigh Gardner, Pierre Martineau et al., have been highly successful in their efforts to utilize the phenomenological approach to behavior in understanding and solving marketing problems. In this approach, which has been well expounded by psychologists such as Prescott Lecky, Carl Rogers, and Snygg and Combs, the emphasis is on identifying needs as the individual sees his needs in contrast to how an objective observer may see that individual's needs. Emphasis is also on the phenomenal self—that is, the self-concept which the individual holds of himself.

From birth to death the defense of the phenomenal self is the most pressing, most crucial, if not the only task of existence. Moreover, since human beings are conscious of the future, their needs extend into the future as well, and they strive to preserve not only the self as it exists but to build it up and to strengthen it against the future of which they are aware. We might combine these two aspects into a formal definition of the basic human need as: *the preservation and enhancement of the phenomenal self.*[23]

Adopting this view, the term "individual need" is here defined as the existence of any difference, of which the person is aware, between his present self-concept and his desired self-concept. Under this definition, it becomes necessary to begin understanding the multitude of roles which individuals play and then to understand the way in which products and/or services help them in these roles.

Under this view, the subjects of individual needs become one and the same as the subjects of one's self-concept. The basic drives of hunger, thirst, pain, etc., are encompassed just as under the behaviorist's approach, but they are encompassed in a different way—if a person says he's hungry, he's hungry. The need is taken to be real whether he has just eaten or not. The question of rationality becomes irrelevant. Reality and the realness of needs are determined only by how the subject sees himself in relation to how he would like to be. In addition to encompassing all the physiological subjects of needs, the phenomenological view opens up a host of new subjects of needs. Each respect in which the individual judges himself—honesty, smartness, youngness, kindness, etc.—becomes a potential need subject. Thus it is unnecessary to compile a complete list of need subjects. Under this view, the only time when a person has no needs would be when the person was aware of no difference between his present self-concept and his desired self-concept.[24]

This latter situation raises an intriguing question: Why do needs exist at all? If a person wants to think of himself as a good father and a good fisherman, why must he go out and buy the children a set of encyclopedias and himself a new fishing pole in order to see himself as he would like to be? Whatever this characteristic of the mind that enables a need to exist—be it touch with reality or otherwise—it is vital to the subject of marketing and product development. If it were not for this mental form of impedance, there would be no individual needs, there would be no reason for purchase behavior.

[23] Snygg and A. W. Combs, *Individual Behavior*, Harper, New York, 1949, p. 58.
[24] For an interesting investigation of how differences between an individual's present self-concept and ideal self-concept can be measured, see Gene Marshall Smith, "Six Measures of Self-Concept Discrepancy and Instability: Their Interrelations, Reliability, and Relations to Other Personality Measures," *Journal of Consulting Psychology*, Vol. XXII, No. 2 (April 1958).

In the study of other sciences, as much attention is devoted to system impedances as is given to system forces or system flows. In mechanics it is friction and inertia. In electronics it is resistance and inductive or capacitive reactance. Why then have marketers not explored the fundamentals of need existence—the characteristics that enable motives to build up force?

Under the definition adopted for a need, the task of need fulfillment consists of helping the consumer think of himself more nearly like he wants to think of himself. Presumably this can be done in any of three ways:

1. Render inoperative that mental quality which ordinarily prevents a consumer from thinking of himself as he would like to be, that is, put him to sleep or tranquilize him.
2. Help the consumer modify his desired self-concept to correspond to his present self-concept.
3. Help the consumer modify his present self-concept to correspond to his desired self-concept.

The third approach is, of course, the conventional way, but any science of need fulfillment should recognize and explore all three. They are not too absurd to contemplate.

In searching for more definitive terms with which to describe need fulfillment, many of the same terms previously used to describe need characteristics are helpful. For instance, the counterpart of need quantity is fulfillment quantity. Fulfillment quantity simply means the amount or volume of need-satisfying capacity possessed by a product. Other useful counterparts of the need characteristics are suggested below.

Fulfillment Clearness: the preciseness and definiteness with which the product fills the individual's need.

Fulfillment Complexity: the number of facets or aspects of the product which are capable of fulfilling various needs.

Fulfillment Acceptability: the social acceptability of a particular product as a means of fulfilling a need.

Fulfillment Frequency: the typical number of times per unit of time that the individual is aware that a product has fulfilled the need.

Fulfillment Duration: the length of the time period during which the product remains capable of fulfilling the need.

Fulfillment Certainty: the subjective probability of the product being able to fulfill the intended need.

In addition to these fulfillment characteristics, which are counterparts of need characteristics, there is another important fulfillment characteristic. This is the directness of the manner in which a product fulfills a need. Some products fill needs in a relatively straightforward and simple manner, for example, purchase and consumption of a hamburger. Other products are only capable of filling needs through a complex, indirect series of situations, for example, purchase of a screwdriver which must act in an instrumental manner, such as facilitating a repair which in turn improves the appearance of an object which in turn gives a sense of pride to the user. This characteristic has been referred to as products which fulfill *basic desires* (the hamburger) versus those which fill *derived desires* (for a fuller description, see Chapter 6), but such a dichotomy seems unnecessary and somewhat unrealistic in comparison to thinking of a continuous spectrum from highly direct need fulfillment to highly indirect need fulfillment.

Another aspect of fulfillment directness concerns the importance of symbolization in the fulfillment process. The benefits derived from some products are 100 per cent symbolic, whereas others have no symbolic value. Among those products which are largely symbolic in value, some may operate in symbols which provide highly direct satisfactions, whereas other types of symbolism are quite indirect. Knowledge about this topic is so vague at present that it is not possible to suggest usable definitions until psychologists (or psychiatrists) learn more about the thinking process, how symbols become associated with objects, and how meanings of various symbols develop and decay.

Just as with need characteristics, major efforts by marketers (and psychologists) should continue to be made to add to the list of fulfillment characteristics, to clarify the definitions, to standardize the terms, to develop units of measure, and to develop techniques of measurement. Once done, it will become possible to make much more effective observations of product development practices. New products can then be classified according to basic types from a marketing point of view. With products grouped according to such basic characteristics, order can be derived from chaos and general principles derived therefrom.

Acquiring a basic understanding of needs and need fulfillment will lay the groundwork for effective product development, but the task will yet remain of helping the individual firm to profit from its endeavor to create need fulfillment. In order to profit, the firm must not only fill consumer needs effectively, it must fill the needs *more* effectively than its competitors. It must develop and maintain preference. This necessity to develop preference raises a host of new problems and opportunities.

At the present time there seem to be virtually no established strategies concerning preference—either in regard to the optimum amount of preference for a firm to achieve or in selecting the best means of achieving that preference. In thinking about these possibilities, one is again confronted with lack of existing nomenclature by which to describe amounts of preference, types of preference, or means of achieving preference. The work that has been done in this area does not seem to have been readily assimilated by marketing practitioners. The work that has been done on the theory of choice by such individuals as Arrow, Churchman, Bilkey, and others has not received widespread use. Although there remain numerous technical problems in working out a theory of choice and in the measurement of individual preference, such as lack of transitivity and instability over time, it nonetheless seems possible to evolve some elementary strategies for the firm which would serve as some guidance in their product development activity. Simply by using two dimensions of market preference, *preference intensity* and *breadth of preference,* for example, some beginnings toward strategy can be developed.

If it is granted that it is usually impossible for a firm to develop a product which has both a broad appeal (appealing to 50 per cent or more of the market) and an intense preference (sufficient to make consumers pay an extra 10 per cent in money or the equivalent in shopping effort expenditure), then a strategic decision must be made between developing a bland product capable of achieving a mild preference among many consumers versus developing one or more products capable of achieving intense preference among a small market segment.

The strategy of producing a bland product with broad preference of low intensity is the simplest strategy to execute: it carries with it all the virtues of mass production and the sale of a single product, but it is also the most unstable strategy. Since the bland type product configuration creates preference of only low intensity, even slight improvements made on competitors' products may have a large effect in changing market shares. In contrast, the strategy of producing a specialized product, or a series of specialized products, offers greater immunity from competitive activity once established but may be more costly to establish initially. Higher initial cost is especially likely to result when the product image accounts for a major part of the preference. A firm producing toothpaste, for instance, will experience high initial marketing expenses in trying to establish two brands under different names, each with a different image because none of the advertising for one brand (such as Crest with an appeal to the health conscious) will aid establishment of the other brand (such as Gleem with an appeal to those who want help rationalizing once-a-day brushing). Also, if a strategy is chosen which requires intense preference among a few, great care is necessary to avoid accidental overspecialization.

Combining Specializing Product Characteristics

In this regard, it is helpful to distinguish between those means of achieving brand preference which have general appeal and are not controversial versus those means which are considered preferable by only part of the market and are disliked by part of the market. Such differentiating means as lower operating expenses, greater durability, and greater operating safety are almost always of general interest and, therefore, will not be dangerous to incorporate in a product design, regardless of the market segment being sought. On the other hand, such differentiating means as the product image, the product styling, and the initial product cost may be severely limiting in the preference they engender.

Combining a variety of product characteristics with general appeal is not dangerous. It may not be an efficient way to obtain preference either because of high development costs or because almost all competitors can advantageously follow them. In contrast, combining the specializing means of differentiation may be dangerous, depending on their specific effects. If the product characteristic is such that some prefer it and others are indifferent, no harm will be done. An example would be adding an electronic flash synchronization on a 35 mm. camera. While this might appeal strongly to a special segment of the market, it is not apt to bother those who do not need it. Some other types of specialized product characteristics, however, may gain the preference of one group of consumers while being disliked by others.

For example, a reflex-type view finder is preferred by some camera purchasers, while others insist on having an eye-level view finder. The latter type—potentially market limiting—may in some cases be made optional in order to add value for some consumers, yet not detract value for any consumers. Other market limiting types cannot be made optional at reasonable costs and hence are inherently market limiting.

Despite the danger of using inherently limiting means of differentiation, it is sometimes necessary and desirable to do so. They are sometimes the least expensive method of achieving an intense preference within a small part of the market. Because of their market limiting effect, they may be less attractive for large competitors to follow. It may also be necessary for management to accept an existing market limiting characteristic of their product (or its brand image) and build additional differentiation around this existing characteristic.

For purposes of discussing the problem of combining two or more market limiting means of differentiation, two terms are suggested and defined as follows:

Parallel means of differentiation refers to any and all distinguishing characteristics of the product which appeal to the *same* market segment.

Divergent means of differentiation refers to any and all distinguishing characteristics of the product which appeal to segments of the market that bear no clear relationship to one another, that is, it is a matter of random chance whether the members of one segment are also members of another segment.

To illustrate, take a hypothetical (but not unrealistic) manufacturer of automobiles. Suppose that this manufacturer were one of the smaller producers and decides it would be advantageous to specialize its brand to avoid direct competition from the larger firms. To do this, the manufacturer may develop a small, light-weight automobile with an engine of small displacement. These characteristics are limiting, but they *parallel* one another in building an appeal to the economy-minded segment of the market. But, then, suppose the brand were also given a divergent "distinctive" styling. If only 10 per cent of potential automobile purchasers were interested in economy enough to prefer this type of automobile over larger, more powerful, and softer riding makes, and if also only 10 per cent of the total market were willing to accept the "distinctive" styling, the result is apt to be an over-all preference by only 1 per cent (.10 x .10) of the market.

When there is no reason to believe that the market segment preferring one type of differentiation also tends to prefer a second type of differentiation, the two characteristics may be cross dimensional or completely divergent. In the foregoing example, the 10 per cent of the market preferring an economy-type automobile are no more likely to prefer the brand's styling than any other segment of the market taken at random. If a styling cannot be developed which will appeal to economy-minded consumers, then care should be taken to ensure that the style is not market limiting.

If additional means of differentiation are used, which are also market limiting in nature, the size of the remaining group which prefers the brand continues to drop at a geometric rate.

In practice, most differentiating devices are neither exactly parallel nor completely divergent. There is usually some degree of overlap between the segments being appealed to. However, it is not safe to assume that the segments will overlap enough to eliminate the dangers of overspecialization. To ensure that a product is not overspecialized, management must know *who* the consumers are that prefer certain characteristics of their brand—not just how many consumers prefer each of the individual characteristics when rated separately.

The rapid rate at which a product may become overspecialized places particular value on those means of differentiation which are either not inherently market limiting or which can be made optional. In either case they cannot limit the market for a brand. It also places particular emphasis on those means which—if they are limiting by nature—can be focused to parallel existing dimensions of the product's specialization. Finally, the geometric rate at which a product can become overspecialized places particular emphasis on those means of differentiation which can be changed rapidly if the need arises.

There are numerous other interesting facets of selecting the best means for a firm to use in achieving product differentiation and, hence, market preference. Certainly gains could be made by greater study of the advantages and disadvantages of obtaining preference primarily through such characteristics as styling, low price, functional features, and product image. Each such means, for example, could be rated according to the following factors:

Speed of Effect: the speed with which market preference could be achieved after the differentiating characteristic had been adopted. Preference on the basis of low price or styling would seem to be much faster in achieving their effect than would the product image.

Communicability: the ease of communicating the differentiating characteristics to consumers. Again, low cost and styling would seem to be much more economically conveyed to consumers than functional features or the product image.

Focusability: the extent to which a differentiating characteristic may be used to obtain the preference of a specific preselected market segment. Here functional features probably rate better than image or styling.

Credibility: the ease with which consumers can be made to believe the benefits claimed. Certainly product durability is a more difficult characteristic on which to achieve credibility than would be price or styling.

Flexibility: the ease with which management can alter the basis of preference in accordance with changes in market tastes or competitive actions. A product image, for instance, is far less changeable and hence a much less flexible basis of preference than is styling.

Protectability: the probability of preventing competitors from following the differentiated characteristic. While functional features should be good in this respect, because of patents, actually they rarely provide much protection. Styling and price are usually no better, whereas an image may in fact provide superior protection over a substantial time period despite the lack of any legal restraints.

The foregoing generalizations are intended as suggestive rather than definitive. They represent areas in which future observations could be made profitably and thereby work toward more sophisticated thinking by management in the process of creating more profitable product preference.

Before leaving the subject of preference development, it is worthwhile noting the additional need for untangling the relationship between brand preference and information. It is obvious to all that a consumer's preference for a brand depends on the amount and type of information he possesses concerning the brand. The preference ranking of various brands by consumers with "perfect" knowledge is a useful reference point in studying consumer preference; however, it would seem equally desirable to establish some methods by which preference rankings changed as a function of lesser amounts of information. While it is commonly recognized that the perceived value of some products benefits greatly by giving consumers large amounts of information, and that in fact this product characteristic plays a basic role in determining the best marketing mix, it remains true that there is no standardized procedure for expressing this relationship.

The Value of Brand Preference as a Function of Company Size

Although it is extremely complex to predict the value of a unique product innovation, it is possible to make an approach to the problem if some simplifying assumptions are made. For purposes of illustrating what may be done, the following section presents some theoretical conclusions on the effect which a single variable—a company's market share—has on the value to a company of a differentiating characteristic.

Let S represent the value of a particular differentiating characteristic (of general interest to consumers) at any point in time. S is defined as the number of consumers who would be willing to *switch* their purchase to whatever brand adopts the improvement. Now, if a particular brand already has 100 per cent of the market for this product and then adopted an improvement with S value, it would get none of the potential switching power. By definition, there would be no remaining market to "switch" from other brands. Thus the efficiency (the ratio of customers who *actually* switch brands to those *willing* to switch brands) with which an innovating company can use the potential value of an improvement depends in part on the market share initially held. To explore this relationship further, assume.

1. The size of the total market for a product remains constant.
2. The improvement is of general interest to consumers.
3. Whatever brands adopt the improvement will divide their new customers between them in proportion to their market shares before adopting the feature.

Under the above conditions the following relations exist:

1. The efficiency (S_i) with which an innovating company can use a product improvement decreases at a linear rate as the company's initial market share (i) increases.

$$S_i = 1 - i$$

Thus the smallest firms can make the most efficient use of an innovation.

2. But the efficiency with which a small innovating company can use an improvement decreases very rapidly as competing firms duplicate the innovation. When the initial market share held by the follower is represented by f,

$$S_i = \left(\frac{i}{i+f}\right)(1 - i - f)$$

If an innovating company has an initial market share of 1 per cent, it will be able to use the improvement with the very high efficiency of $1 - .01$ or $.99$ if no competitors follow. However, if a competing firm with an initial market share of 10 per cent follows, then the innovator's efficiency of use drops to $\left(\frac{.01}{.01 + 10}\right)(1 - .01 - .10)$, or $.081$. At the same time, the efficiency with which the follower (S_f) in this case can use the improvement is quite high, $.81$.

3. Out of the preceding relationship comes the rather surprising fact that there is an optimum-sized innovator in that a company of a particular size can make more efficient use of a given improvement than companies of different sizes. The optimum size for an innovating company varies from one having about 10 per cent of the market to one having about 25 per cent of the market, the exact size depending on the number of competitive followers. The optimum-sized innovator may be found by differentiating the expression given in (2) with respect to i, while holding f constant, and setting the result equal to 0.

$$S_i = \left(\frac{i}{i+f}\right)(1 - i - f)$$

$$\frac{\partial S_i}{\partial i} = \frac{f}{(1+f)} 2 - 1 = 0$$

$$\text{Optimum } i = f^{\frac{1}{2}} - f$$

4. But for purposes of predicting, this expression requires knowledge of the size of competitive companies who will follow an innovation. Since this is in fact rarely known, it is more useful to convert the expression

to give the optimum-sized follower. This may be done by simply interchanging the two terms:

$$\text{Optimum } f = i^{1/2} - i$$

Using this expression it is possible for a company to compute the best sized innovator for it to follow.

5. The efficiency with which an optimum-sized follower can use another company's innovation may be derived as follows:

$$Sf = \left(\frac{f}{i+f}\right)(1 - i - f)$$

$$\frac{\partial Sf}{\partial f} = \frac{i}{(i+f)^2} - 1 = 0$$

$$\text{Optimum } S_f = (1 - i^{1/2})^2$$

While the preceding relations only express the value of innovations under simplified conditions, they do illustrate some interesting approaches that might be pursued in future research. To the extent that they hold true, they suggest the following conclusions:

1. A small company (with a market share of 1 or 2 per cent) should not spend much money developing means of differentiation which have a wide and general appeal to consumers unless it has strong protection. While the small company can use the drawing power of such differentiation more efficiently than larger companies, the value to them of-the differentiation drops *extremely* quickly as competitors follow. The value to the small company drops much more quickly, for example, than for an innovator which has 15 to 25 per cent of the market initially.

2. Since companies with a market share of 15 to 25 per cent can initiate and follow advantageous product differentiation relatively more efficiently than companies of other size, it would appear desirable (from this standpoint) for a very large company to sell two brands each with 20 per cent or so of the market rather than one brand with 40 per cent of the market.

Summary of Product Development as a Science

In exploring the possibilities and problems in developing a science of product development, it was argued that success will only be achieved in conjunction with the broader development of a science of marketing. The development of either science should start by achieving a basic understanding and cataloguing of consumer needs. While some aspects of such an understanding will have to await further work by psychologists, there are many need characteristics which can be better described with our existing understanding. As more precise terms are developed for describing consumer needs, it will automatically become possible to observe and describe need fulfillment more accurately. While many would argue that marketers should await the development of better theories of consumer behavior by professional psychologists, it seems to this writer that marketers should do their own conceptualizing of need creation and need fulfillment. At a minimum, marketers should exert increased pressure on the behavioral scientists to develop conceptual schemes of greater use in predicting consumer choice.

In the meantime, before the reasons underlying consumer choice are understood, there appear to be a variety of ways in which the individual firm might do a more systematic job of selecting the most profitable type of market preference to acquire and the most effective means of attaining that preference. In particular, the following were suggested:

1. Most firms cannot develop a product that is preferred by all consumers over similar competing products.

2. Since only a fraction of the market will prefer a given product, it might be well to recognize this fact and take advantage of it through offering a specialized product or group of products which can achieve a more intense consumer preference.

3. When possible, it is desirable to specialize the product so that it will appeal to an easily "reachable" segment of the market.

4. When strategies of market segmentation are adopted, the particular means of achieving differentiation should be studied carefully because each means has its own strengths and weaknesses.

5. Great care must be taken to avoid useless overspecialization of a brand. All market-limiting characteristics of the product should parallel one another so as to appeal to the same segment. Divergent differentiation adds little appeal to the brand, and it seriously limits the size of the potential market.

6. Some exploratory thinking on the relationship between the size of a company (in terms of market share held) and efficient use of innovations suggest that there is an optimum-sized innovator and follower. A follower who initially holds 15 to 25 per cent of the market can generally make more efficient use of a general interest product improvement than either larger or smaller companies.

BIBLIOGRAPHY

Barclay, William D., "A Probability Model for Early Prediction of New Product Market Success," *Journal of Marketing*, Vol. XXVII, No. 1 (January 1963), pp. 63–69.

Benson, Purnell H. and Francis J. Pilgrim, "Testing Less Desirable Product Possibilities," *Journal of Marketing*, Vol. XXVI, No. 3 (July 1961), p. 65.

Bohlen, J. W., "A Basic Guide to Legal Problems in New Products," *Industrial Marketing* (November 1958), pp. 69–73.

Borden, Neil H. and Martin V. Marshall, *Advertising Management, Text and Cases*, Richard D. Irwin, Homewood, Ill., 1959.

Champlain, Paul, "How Manufacturers of Electronic Equipment Determine Potential Markets for New Products," unpublished thesis, Bachelor's Degree, School of Industrial Management, MIT, 1954.

Christian, Richard C., "A Checklist for New Industrial Products," *Journal of Marketing*, Vol. XXIV, No. 3 (July 1959), pp. 70–73.

Corey, E. Raymond, *The Development of Markets for New Materials*, Division of Research, Graduate School of Business Administration, Harvard University, 1956.

Enright, Ernest J. Jr., "Market Testing," *Harvard Business Review*, Vol. XXXVI, No. 5 (September–October 1958), p. 75.

_____, *Planning and Administering Test Marketing Campaigns for New Products*, unpublished doctoral thesis, Graduate School of Business Administration, Harvard University, 1957.

Hilton, Peter, *Handbook of New Product Development*, Prentice-Hall, Englewood Cliffs, N.J., 1961.

Jones, Ralph W., "Management of New Products," *The Journal of Industrial Engineering*, Vol. IX, No. 5 (September–October 1958).

Karger, Delmar W., *The New Product*, The Industrial Press, New York, 1960.

Klaw, Spencer, "The Soap Wars: A Strategic Analysis," *Fortune*, Vol. LXVII, No. 6 (June 1963), p. 186.

Levitt, Theodore, *Innovation in Marketing*, McGraw-Hill, New York, 1962.

Lipstein, Benjamin, "Tests for Test Marketing," *Harvard Business Review*, Vol. XXXIX, No. 2 (March–April 1961), pp. 74–77.

Marvin, Philip, *Planning New Products*, American Management Association, 1958.

Meloan, Taylor W., "New Products—Keys to Corporate Growth," in Lazer, William J. and Eugene J. Kelley (eds.), *Managerial Marketing: Perspectives and Viewpoints*, Richard D. Irwin, Homewood, Ill., 1962.

Moulton, R. H., "Before Introducing New Products Check This List," *Printers' Ink*, Vol. CCLI (May 20, 1955), p. 34.

Nickerson, Clarence B., *Managerial Cost Accounting and Analysis*, McGraw-Hill, New York, 1955.

Ross Federal Research Corporation, "A Survey of 200 Leading Package Goods Manufacturers on Experiences and Problems Prevalent in the Introduction of a New Product," Ross Federal Research Corporation, New York, 1945.

Smith, Gene Marshall, "Six Measures of Self-Concept Discrepancy and Instability: Their Interrelations, Reliability, and Relations to Other Personality Measures," *Journal of Consulting Psychology*, Vol. XXII, No. 2, 1958.

Snygg, Donald and Arthur W. Combs, *Individual Behavior*, Harper, New York, 1949.

Stewart, John B., "Functional Features in Product Strategy," *Harvard Business Review*, Vol. XXXVII, No. 2 (March–April 1959), p. 65.

_____, *Repetitive Advertising in Newspapers*, Division of Research, Harvard Business School, Boston, 1964.

_____, "Problems in Review: Planned Obsolescence," *Harvard Business Review*, Vol. XXXVII, No. 5 (September, October 1959).

Wasson, Chester, "What is New About a New Product?", *Journal of Marketing*, Vol. XXV, No. 3 (July 1960), p. 52.

Weigand, Robert E., "How Extensive Is the Planning and Development Program?", *Journal of Marketing*, Vol. XXVI, No. 3 (July 1962), pp. 56–57.

9

Research in Personal Selling

JAMES G. HAUK

If one were to ask one hundred authorities what we now know about
personal selling of a predictive and descriptive nature, and what we need
to know in order to further science in marketing, one hundred different
answers would be secured. The answer to this question depends on the
individual's knowledge of the area, the extent to which he is familiar
with past research, and the criteria he uses in deciding on the existence
of knowledge. There is also the question of whether one is of the opinion
that science in marketing is most efficiently advanced by investigating
selling from the standpoint of the salesman, the marketing manager, or
the economy as a whole.

One can reasonably assert that the function should be researched from
all points of view. Consequently, some attempt is made in the following
pages to give attention to each, with emphasis on those areas where there
is a particular need for additional study. The purpose is to present what
has been done, primarily by the more recent work, and to suggest the
kind of research which is needed in the future. Because of the breadth
of the field it is not feasible to cover it completely in one chapter.

Here the assumption is made that the salesman will be an element in
our economy for some time, even though mechanization is changing the
significance and the character of his job. The telephone, automobiles and
airplanes, television, and vending machines have all had many effects,
some of which are apparent, others still unrecognized. There will probably be more mechanization in the future, but it surely will not involve
the use of mechanical robots to travel sales territories. Instead, machines

Note. The author expresses appreciation to Professor Richard R. Still, Chairman
of the Marketing Department, Syracuse University, for helpful comments during
the preparation of this chapter.

will be used to perform certain functions presently performed by salesmen, which may either make travel unnecessary or perhaps free the salesman from other tasks. Thus it will tend to change the *way* personal selling is performed by the human being.

We might imagine a marketing system where most of it was conducted similarly to the demonstrations appearing on household television. Each salesman would have television receivers stationed at the customer's place of business. Sales calls could then be conducted by turning a switch at the office and conversing with, advising, and demonstrating for customers located thousands of miles away. A major selling task under such circumstances might be to get television receivers in the customer's place of business.

Further research into the possibilities of mechanizing the salesman's job should have high priority in any attempt to advance science in marketing. Knowledge in the area is necessary as a way of determining the future character of selling, and its future characteristics are important in delineating research needs today. Here it will be assumed that mechanization will not eliminate the salesman. It may change the proportion of the total population engaged in personal selling (perhaps increase it), and it will change its character otherwise. But if research is framed with a recognition of these possibilities, it can have a payoff.

NEGLECT OF PERSONAL SELLING

Past research has been concerned largely with managing salesmen and with salesmanship. The problems of selecting, training, motivating, evaluating, and compensating salesmen are covered in many textbooks. Similarly, a large number of research articles, particularly in the personnel and psychology journals, have been published on personnel subjects such as selecting salesmen. In combination with the practicing sales manager's interest, this emphasis is presumably responsible for the statement that "there is little question but what the salesman is one of the most extensively studied men in the business world." [1] Another author notes that nearly a million copies of books on selling are marketed in the United States each year.

Even if such contentions are correct one can argue that the function has been greatly neglected by academic *marketing* people. One is struck by the shortage of current, published research and by the extent to which advertising is emphasized. This has been true despite the greater volume of resources devoted to selling, as well as its relative importance in the

---

[1] J. B. Miner, "Personality and Ability Factors in Sales Performance," *Journal of Applied Psychology*, Vol. XLVI, No. 1 (February 1962), p. 6.

marketing program. One authority feels that personal selling is in danger of becoming a "dark corner" as the mathematical research specialists devote their energies to advertising and other marketing problems.[2]

There are many reasons for this apparent neglect. One justification often cited is that mass distribution, the routinization of transactions, and "self-service" retailing have reduced the magnitude and importance of personal selling. At times these contentions imply that the salesman is disappearing in marketing. In most cases, however, such implications are not based on thorough empirical research. Moreover, they probably reflect a consideration of the marketing of consumer goods primarily.

NEED FOR EXPENDITURE DATA

The hypothesis that the function is declining in magnitude and importance suggests the need for accurate expenditure data to aid in testing the hypothesis. One estimate indicates that sales worker compensation increased from 8.7 billion in 1948 to 15.8 billion in 1958. The changes in expenditures relative to other demand stimulation activities are approximated in Table 9.1.

"Sales worker compensation" is defined by the Department of Commerce as the "algebraic sum of money wages and salaries, net income from self-employment, and income other than earnings." Consequently, it tends to overstate the compensation arising from sales work, for it evidently includes interest, rental annuity, and other such sources of income. On the other hand, it excludes many expenditures for selecting, training, and managing salesmen, as well as the large amounts spent on travel and customer entertainment. Moreover, many service specialists, engineering personnel, and television performers are engaged in personal selling even though they may not be called salesmen. On balance the estimates probably understate the total expenditures in the American economy. If Tosdal's estimates of the amount spent on travel and supervision are taken into account ($5.7 billion for earlier years)[3] total personal selling expenditures probably exceeded $20 billion for the year 1958. Note also that the money paid for salesmen increased $7.1 billion between 1948 and 1958, while advertising expenditures increased only $5.4 billion.

It is not at all clear that the function has become less significant in marketing, either in an absolute sense or relative to advertising and other activities. It is even less clear as to what will happen in the future.

[2] Wendell R. Smith, "The Role of Selling in Modern Marketing," *Emerging Concepts in Marketing*, William S. Decker (ed.), AMA, Chicago, 1963, p. 174.
[3] Harry H. Tosdal, *Selling in the American Economy*, Richard D. Irwin, Homewood, Ill., 1957, pp. 30–31.

Supermarket and discount house retailing has reduced the importance of the salesman in some lines at the retail level, and this self-service approach will be carried further. In addition, some wholesalers are now relying on the telephone to secure orders from retailers. But these segments are only part of the aggregate marketing channel.

Table 9.1   Estimated Expenditures for Three Kinds of Demand Stimulation Activities, 1948–1958

| | Expenditure by Year | | | |
| | 1948 | | 1958 | |
Demand Stimulation Activity	Billions of Dollars	% of Total	Billions of Dollars	% of Total
Sales promotion	1.4	9.1	2.6	9.1
Advertising	4.9	32.5	10.3	35.9
Sales worker compensation	8.7	58.4	15.8	55.0
Total	15.0	100.0	28.7	100.0

Source: Thadeus Spratlen, "An Appraisal of Theory and Practice in the Analysis of Sales Activities," unpublished doctoral dissertation, The Ohio State University, 1962, as indicated in Beckman and Davidson, *Marketing*, The Ronald Press Co., New York, 1962, p. 446.

Automation over the long run might even cause an *increase* in the number of salesmen relative to other occupational classes, not only because it increases our ability to produce (which calls for aggressive demand stimulation) but also because it seems much less adaptable to replacing the salesman than many other individuals in society. We can imagine a system where push button mechanization produced and distributed all goods. Most individuals here would be employed in systems management, repairing machines, and selling products and services.

In addition to further research on total expenditures, and on the influence of automation, we need research on the functions and activities of the salesman in various industries. Most of the information available to date has been arrived at by observation of a few companies. To my knowledge no thorough study has been made for the economy as a whole. We know that individuals such as those employed as a clerk in some retail stores perform a distribution function primarily—they take orders, wrap packages, and hand the product to the customer. Others, for example those representing chemical companies, may have Ph.D.'s in chemistry and spend much of their time working with customers in the solution of complex technical problems. We need enough information on the salesman's functions in various industries to be able to group industries according to similarity in selling problems. Present grouping is likely to be based on whether the salesmen represent a retail store, a wholesale house, or a manufacturing establishment. Study on the basis of activities performed, problems encountered, and significance in the general marketing program is lacking.

With respect to the marketing program in particular we would like to know the character and importance of personal selling relative to other activities in various industries. An examination of its cost as a percentage of total sales provides some evidence in this regard. It does not answer the question "why," however, nor does it enable a classification of industries according to the types of activities engaged in by the salesman.

AN EXCHANGE ORIENTATION

Emphasis should also be placed on a broad approach to the study of personal selling, the purpose of which is to integrate it with exchange theory. Exchange is the central concept in marketing, and to best advance knowledge about marketing any particular piece of the total job should, in this writer's opinion, be integrated with its central concept. Here I am partly arguing that we should do far more than study personal selling from an occupation viewpoint.

Certainly a kind of understanding would be possible which is not likely to be secured by studying the AIDA theory of salesmanship. Thus more extensive analysis of the history of selling in exchange is needed similar to Kelley's "Development of Early Thought in Marketing and Promotion." [4] Or, an alternative is to research it from an intersociety point of view, either over time or at one point in time. The developing countries should receive attention, although it is sometimes stated that marketing, and personal selling, are relatively unimportant in such economies. A group of business executives from foreign countries which I taught recently took this position initially. It became evident in the course of the discussion that they were regarding marketing, selling, and demand stimulation synonymously.

This is unfortunate. The central feature of marketing is exchange, not demand stimulation. Moreover, wherever exchange takes place personal selling exists unless trade is completely impersonalized as in "silent" trade. Even if selling is regarded only as a kind of demand stimulation

[4] William T. Kelley, "Development of Early Thought in Marketing and Promotion," *Journal of Marketing*, Vol. XXI, No. 1 (January 1957), pp. 62–67.

one can argue that it is important in the developing economies in the sense that it is one prerequisite to economic growth. Some historians, and many marketing people, have noted that economic growth and mass production are dependent on the size of the market. Many factors influence market size, and selling is one factor. It is integral to the development of a commercial revolution, and the latter is a forerunner to the industrial revolution.

It is said that for Latin America as a whole only about 9 per cent of total marketing is inter-country trade. Poor transport facilities, inadequate market information, and lack of distribution intermediaries are some of the things responsible.[5] In other world areas, where standards of living are low, marketing is not elaborate or complex, but the same can be said for "production" (manufacturing), finance, and most other elements of business. Thus marketing and selling are peculiar in this sense only when exchange is minor as compared with total manufacturing and consumption activities. Moreover, their importance should be judged not only by present complexity and magnitude but also by the extent to which their expansion can contribute to economic growth.

Examining exchange in primitive economies can also help. One author describes a barter system where an Eskimo might trade a blue fox skin for a lantern and 5 gallons of kerosene. Selling is identified by reference to the individual who takes the initiative. An anxious individual might go from house to house asking for bids. After a trade was consummated either party might later demand a re-exchange even though a considerable time had elapsed. "An 'honest' seller, it is said, would realize that he had taken too much, and set some of the purchase price aside for return to the buyer should he request it." [6] At other times the seller might repent and demand the return of the goods which he had released. This case provides a clear contrast with conditions in our own society where salesmen are ordinarily employees of business organizations and where a readily accepted standard of value exists. Both conditions tend to make it unnecessary for the salesman to "repent and demand the return of the goods which he has released."

In some primitive societies, and elsewhere, the salesman is, in effect, a traveling wholesale-retail house. Beals and Hoijer discuss the Aztecs of the Valley of Mexico, where specialization and exchange were highly developed. Here salesmen were linked together in a closed guild with hereditary membership and with their own insignias, gods, and system of

[5] Bela Balassa, *The Theory of Economic Integration*, Richard D. Irwin, Homewood, Ill., 1961, pp. 54–55.
[6] Robert F. Spencer, *The North Alaskan Eskimo: A Study of Ecology and Society*, U.S. Government Printing Office, Washington, D.C., 1959, p. 195.

justice. They traveled together in groups which were strongly guarded, their goods being carried by a retinue of porters. Not only did they sell goods to distant markets, but they also returned with goods to sell in their home market, a function which most salesmen obviously do not perform today. The salesman in the Aztec empire also acted as a spy, and he was protected by the government. Any injury to him was a cause for war.[7]

In contemporary Jamaica the women do most of the personal selling work. The relatively large number of saleswomen in this economy may be caused by a desperate attempt to earn a living, but in any event the fact suggests higher selling costs, as a percentage of total costs, than is sometimes associated with underdeveloped economies. We should know more about its function in other societies, not only to interpret it correctly in our own country, but because science in marketing necessitates principles and generalizations which have applicability to all types of countries.

Another approach, particularly applicable to a highly specialized economy, is to regard the salesman as a link tying together firms in the marketing channel. He was essential for the development of specialization. His economic significance also increased as the trend toward specialization continued and the number of necessary exchange transactions rose. Advertising also assumed a greater task, but there were certain communication and contactual functions which had to be performed on a personal and individual basis. McGarry has presented his notion of the broad character of the contactual function.[8] His view can be oriented more directly toward personal selling by examining the salesman's role in building an organized system.

PERSONAL SELLING THEORY

Personal selling today is regarded largely as a process of personalized persuasion, communication, and service. From the firm's viewpoint it is carried out by individuals who are given titles such as company representative, sales engineer, communications consultant, account executive, detail man, and other titles which partly describe the nature of the job. Because persuasion, communication, and service pervade nearly all selling positions, however, each is elaborated on below. They represent

[7] Ralph L. Beals and Harry Hoijer, *An Introduction to Anthropology,* Macmillan, New York, 1959, p. 431. The authors call the salesman a "traveling merchant."
[8] Edmund D. McGarry, "The Contactual Function in Marketing," *Journal of Business,* Vol. XXIV, No. 2 (April 1951), pp. 96–113.

alternative points of view which can be emphasized in developing theory in personal selling and in conducting empirical research on it.

Psychology of Persuasion

One of the major purposes of the salesman is to persuade present and prospective customers to buy. In order to persuade effectively he must communicate and serve the customer so that needs are satisfied. Some would argue that emphasis should be placed on discovering the motives responsible for purchase, measuring their relative importance, and manipulating the most important motives. Salesmanship books have presented various theories oriented in this general direction. Professor Bursk has offered an additional hypothesis.

> I claim that persuasion is more a matter of strategy than of manipulation; that it is a process of arraying logical forces so that people themselves decide to do what you want them to do, rather than actually changing people's minds; and that any effort to get action by tampering with people's emotions not only runs up against the psychological limitations of resistance, but also can be prohibitively time consuming and expensive.[9]

His hypothesis also emphasizes the importance of discovering the self-approved motives which will give the customer a rationalization for buying. Appeals to these motives are often more effective than appeals to the real motives for purchase.

Many practicing salesmen emphasize the significance of the individual situation. They maintain that no single approach holds the key unless the approach is to adjust to each customer situation according to the circumstances. One of the frequently stated advantages of personal selling over advertising is flexibility in adapting messages to individual customer motives and needs.

In placing selling theory on a sound foundation there is need for utilizing the basic research conducted in psychology and sociology. For example, Festinger's theory of cognitive dissonance could provide a basis either for formulating theory in selling or for empirical testing as applied to the selling process. Dissonance often exists before the purchase decision is made as well as subsequent to it. It has been maintained that the

---

[9] Edward C. Bursk, "Opportunities for Persuasion," *Harvard Business Review*, Vol. XXXVI, No. 5 (September–October 1958), p. 111.

buyer may go into a state of "virtual panic" as he reaches the point of decision in buying an automobile for example. He may rush into the purchase as an escape from the problem or he may simply put off the purchase because of the difficulty of deciding on the car which is best for him. The salesman's role at this point in the purchase cycle would differ from that during the early stages of the consumer's search process.

Salesmanship could also be approached with the hypothesis suggested in an early paper that the relationship between the salesman's characteristics and the customer's characteristics is pertinent in explaining the salesman's persuasive power. This appears to be the one used in a study of life insurance agents. The attempt is to determine the characteristics of both the salesman and his prospects, half of whom purchased from him and half of whom did not purchase from him. The research covers the salesman's opinion of the prospects, the prospect's opinion of the salesman, personality, social and sociometric characteristics of both salesman and prospect, as well as a number of other phenomena.[10]

Ethics of Persuasion

Some would argue that the study of ethics has no place in the development of science in marketing, but for a number of reasons, which I will not discuss here, my opinion differs. Certainly if the empirical and philosophical study of ethics in selling is excluded we will never attain completely the kind of knowledge about marketing which is desirable and necessary in a free society.

It has been noted that the significant ethical problem is not *whether* persuasion should be exercised but *how* it should be exercised. There may be a number of unanswered questions in both areas, however. They are particularly pertinent in a highly specialized economy where the salesman usually knows more about the product at the time of negotiation than does the buyer. Many of the problems are ignored or, in some cases, examined in a biased way.

First, I am referring to the question of whether or not it is acceptable for a knowledgeable person to persuade a less knowledgeable one to buy his product when the competitor's product would do a better job. Certainly there is often uncertainty as to which product would work in the customer's best interests. In addition, one might argue that if all competing salesmen persuade on behalf of their own products the outcome of the rivalry will be desirable for the customer. In this sense the com-

[10] Franklin B. Evans, "A Sociological Analysis of the Selling Situation: Some Preliminary Findings," *Emerging Concepts in Marketing, op. cit.,* pp. 476–482.

petitive persuading is analogous to the court of law where prosecutor and defense each present a one-sided case.

It may be that the question of relative knowledge between the seller and the buyer is not significant. However, if the knowledge and maturity discrepancy is taken to the extreme, cases arise which cause one to wonder. Advertising frequently is directed at children, but is it acceptable for a mature salesman to persuade children to buy products?

No attempt will be made to evaluate such issues. Instead, the point is that there are many questions which could be dealt with more intensively. In addition to those already cited, the following continue to be relevant to the selling field: Does the salesman have any obligation to present the "truth" about his product or service to the customer? Should he withhold facts from the customer which will damage his chances for securing the sale, even though the customer requests them? How far can selling justifiably go in invading the privacy of the individual? Is subliminal selling acceptable?

A study of 129 executives attending the 1963 Graduate School of Sales Management and Marketing at Syracuse University yielded an interesting result. The executives were independently asked whether or not they thought sales management had an ethical responsibility to the customer beyond the requirements of the law. Nearly all the executives felt that such responsibilities did exist, and the vast majority were very strong in their feelings. While one can interpret such findings in a number of ways, they are symptomatic of some basic issues.

Studying the ethical question from a historical point of view is also revealing: ". . . and there shall be no praising goods, or oath taken about them. If a person disobey this command, any citizen who is present, not being less than thirty years of age, may with impunity chastize and beat the swearer." [11] Of course, as Kelley points out, there were merchants in ancient Athens (who undoubtedly praised their goods), and they were probably not beaten. Plato's laws were proposals for an "ideal" state.

The later views of Thomas Acquinas suggest a tolerance for persuasion but insistence on high standards, particularly with regard to the sale of defective goods. Such a philosophy is markedly different from that implied in the Law Merchant during the Middle Ages: Every bargain, once consummated was to remain closed, "and if the purchaser repents of his purchase, and wished to recede from the contract, let him lose what he has given." [12]

[11] William T. Kelley, op. cit., pp. 62–63.
[12] W. Mitchell, An Essay on the Early History of the Law Merchant, University Press, Cambridge, 1904, p. 3.

Selling as a Communications Process

Personal selling can also be researched from the communications point of view. Some would argue that all communication has persuasion as its intent or result. Others simply define selling as a communication process with emphasis on the outflow of information from the salesman to the buyer. It is designed to cause the buyer to perceive the product as an aid in achieving his goals. It can be accurate or untruthful, and while persuasion may be the purpose, it accomplished this purpose by the provision of information. A variation of this view is to regard personal selling as *two-way* communication, while advertising is one-way communication. Salesmanship cannot only individualize and personalize outflow messages, it can also facilitate the informational feedback which is necessary to the development of a system.

In integrating personal selling with communications theory, it should be recognized that the communications process is basically a medium of social interaction. With selling, it is a medium between the salesman and the customer. Consequently, any integration attempt should recognize basic knowledge about human interaction as well as about communications. With respect to the latter, the major elements are the source, encoding, the message, the channel, decoding, and the receiver. Selling could be studied with these elements as the general structure. This requires an understanding of the psychology and sociology of each element, if the study is to be effective.

The informational role of the salesman justifies a communications emphasis. Not only must specialized firms be coordinated, but, in an economy where the rate of product innovation is high, sound buying depends on sound information. For example, buyers need information on the existence of the innovation, on whether to try it out, and on how to put it into effect, including instructions on use and perhaps repair. Where and how does the salesman fit in the process of providing the needed information?

One early study of the introduction and acceptance of hybrid seed corn among farmers indicated that salesmen were the most important source of information regarding the *existence* of the product.[13] His importance declined, however, as the product was diffused through the market. Several years subsequent to product introduction the new purchaser was most likely to hear about it from neighbors.

The sources of information most influential in actually inducing the

[13] Bryce Ryan and Neal C. Cross, "The Diffusion of Hybrid Seed Corn in Two Iowa Communities," *Rural Sociology*, Vol. VIII, No. 1 (May 1943), p. 19.

farmer to buy also varied over time: salesmen were most influential during early years and neighbors most influential in later years. A more recent study indicates that mass media, agricultural agencies, and other farmers were the most important sources of first knowledge, while commercial sources ranked high in providing information on how much material to use, where to use it, and other problems of application.[14] As the studies suggest, the salesman's communication function relative to that of other information sources will vary over time and between products.

In introducing new technical products to the market, the salesman may be crucial, for potential users may have to be located and the benefits of the product explained. And in marketing established products, new users enter the market, often as ignorant of the facts pertinent to selection as the consumer who purchased the product during the innovation stage of the product cycle. Personal communication is particularly significant in marketing high priced products where careful deliberation characterizes customer buying behavior.

Such questions as the following should be answered: What proportion of the total communication task should be allocated to the salesman? What kinds of informational outflow should be assigned to them? What kinds of information are best collected by the salesman? In what industry situations is the sales representative primarily a disseminator of information and in what situations is he primarily a collector of information? These are only a few of the questions on the communication role of the salesman which deserve attention.

Service for Need Satisfaction

Another view to take is to regard selling as a process of providing individualized service to satisfy the customer's needs. The sales representative may go far in surveying the customer's operations as a basis for designing the product or for recommending the product best able to solve his problems. He may also help in installing it, in demonstrating it, in training the customer's employees to use it, and in repairing it subsequent to sale. In this respect the selling function may be one of supplying individualized service to the customer rather than attempting to deal with his emotions.

One sales manager in the industrial paint industry argues that technical service is the essence of selling in his company. Another sales

---

[14] Eugene A. Wilkening, "Roles of Communicating Agents in Technological Change in Agriculture," *Social Forces* (May 1956), pp. 361–367.

manager in handling orthopedic products does not employ salesmen. Service to the customer is so important in selling his product that he employs only "service representatives." Others find that selling is a highly complex job which may call for a group approach where several company specialists combine their specialized skills to solve customer problems. In some cases technical representatives from competing concerns cooperate in designing and installing a system which requires the use of the products produced by each of the competing firms.

In this general area the lack of knowledge is embarrassing. Not much is known, for example, about the conditions under which selling and technical service should be assigned to the same company representatives and, conversely, the conditions under which it should be specialized. In part, the lack of attention springs from the fact that until recently service itself had been largely ignored in marketing literature. This has helped to hide the very existence of specialization possibilities. A thorough examination could be made of business practice to identify the factors conducive to specializing the two.

There is also the question of how far the salesman should go in specifying the product needed by the customer and in specifying the need itself. One manager in the roller bearing industry maintains that product specifications is the prerogative of the salesman, at least in his own company. Here several thousand varieties of roller bearings are available for customer purchase, and the salesman knows far more about their correct application than does the customer. In view of the problems created by incorrect application, refusal to sell is in order unless the company retains the specification task.

In other industries it is precarious for the salesman to assume much responsibility in this respect. Where needs are emotional, for example, the customer is usually most qualified to determine whether the product will satisfy him. In other cases product specification is not the crucial issue. Services which help the customer manage or operate his business are more useful as a sales tool. But the product specification question is not only basic to marketing in general but is also basic to sound personal selling in most industries. For both reasons additional analysis in this area can contribute to marketing thought in a fundamental way.

Section 15 (1) of the Uniform Sales Act indicates the minimum amount of specification advisable and the circumstances under which it should be performed:

> Where the buyer expressly or by implication makes known to the seller the particular purposes for which the goods are required,

and it appears that the buyer relies on the seller's skill and judgment (whether he be the grower or the manufacturer or not) there is an implied warranty that the goods shall be fit for such purposes.[15]

This provision may necessitate the supply of survey work, installation, and demonstration as a way of seeing to it that the product is adapted to buyer needs and that it satisfies the particular purpose designated by him.

The revised Uniform Commercial Code, which has gone into effect in a few states, appears to shift some additional responsibility to the seller.[16] It recognizes, implicitly at least, that the salesman may designate the purpose or function to be fulfilled by the product rather than rely on the buyer for this task. The buyer may indicate only that he has problems in inventory control for example (or leave it up to the salesman to point out the problem). The salesman may define the problem, recommend a system or process which will alleviate it, and specify the kind of products necessary to enable the system to function correctly.

Strategy of Need Satisfaction

Cash and Crisy have elaborated on the need satisfaction theory of selling, where the ratio between the time the salesman talks during the interview and the time the customer talks is supposed to change over the interview. However, when technical service is involved in selling the talking time may be minor compared with the time devoted to surveying the customer's business, demonstrating the product, and other services prior to securing the order. The question here is how far the salesman should go in assisting the prospective customer when there is no guarantee that he will purchase the product. If the service is charged for separately, the problem is minimized, but separate pricing is the exception when the primary purposes of the business is to sell tangible products.

One salesman representing an office equipment firm draws up sketches showing how the customer might best arrange the office operation. The purpose is to sell their own office equipment, but prospective customers sometimes use the proposals as a basis for buying the products of discount firms. The same thing happens in other firms and industries, and at the retail level.

[15] 1 U.S.A. Section 15 (1).
[16] Lawrence Vold, *Cases and Materials on the Law of Sales*, 2nd ed., West Publishing Company, St. Paul, 1949, p. 805.

In another case, a plumbing and heating contractor refuses to run surveys or to submit proposals in selling to industrial concerns unless the prospective customer assures him beforehand that he will buy. In selling to home owners, however, no commitment is required, for residential surveys are more standardized, less complex, and less expensive. There is some justification for both policies although one might question the wisdom of the first one. An inexpensive preliminary study can be conducted to estimate the expense of a more elaborate survey and to keep the negotiations alive. During the process the salesman can also estimate the probability of securing an order from the customer and can use the preliminary survey, along with the promise of a more elaborate one, to promote sales.

More formalized methods are being developed for handling such uncertainties. In some cases where negotiated bidding is used, the salesman may have to take into account the competitor's service expenditures as well as his price strategy, for the probability of securing an order will depend on what the competitor does in both areas. Suppose an analysis of the competitor's past behavior, customer motivation, and the relative characteristics of the products offered by the two firms leads to some judgment on the probability of securing the order with various combinations of service and price. The probabilities are estimated and placed in matrix form as in Table 10.2. Assume also that other incremental expenses associated with the order amount to 20 per cent of sales.

With this information, an expected contribution to profit can be computed for each combination of price and service by applying the equation: $Cij = (pij) (Pi - Sj - .20Pi)$, where Cij is the expected contribution to profit associated with the ith price and the jth service expenditure, pij is the probability of securing the order with a price of i and a service expenditure of j, Pi is the i selling price, and Sj is the j service expenditure.

Table 9.2 *Probability of Securing the Customer's Order with Varying Combinations of Price and Sales-Service Expenditures*

Sales-Service Expenditure (j)		Price (i)		
		P_1	P_2	P_3
		$10,000	$12,000	$15,000
S_1	$1000	0.50	0.40	0.30
S_2	3000	0.70	0.55	0.45
S_3	5000	0.90	0.65	0.50

Table 9.3 Expected Contribution to Profit of Varying Combinations of Price and Sales-Service Expenditure

Sales-Service Expenditure (j)		Price (i)		
		P_1 $10,000	P_2 $12,000	P_3 $15,000
S_1	$1000	$ 3500	$ 3840	$ 3300
S_2	3000	3500	4180	4050
S_3	5000	2700	3640	3500

Given the probability coefficients presented in Table 9.2, a contribution to profit matrix can be constructed (Table 9.3). The price-service combination which maximizes expected profit contribution is $S_2 - P_2$, or a price of $12,000 and a sales service expenditure of $3000. Here expected contribution to profit is $4180.

This analysis for decision making obviously assumes that probabilities can be estimated with some accuracy. It is also clear that if the salesman does secure the order at a price of $12,000 and a service expenditure of $3000, he will not actually contribute $4180 to profits. Instead, faced with a very large number of sales situations, identical to the one under consideration, he will contribute an *average* amount of $4180 over the long run if he follows the $P_2 - S_2$ strategy on every occasion. He will lose the order 45 per cent of the time using this strategy, which means that he will contribute nothing to profits on these occasions.

If he follows strategy $P_1 - S_3$ in contrast, he will lose the order only 10 per cent of the time. Stated differently, he is almost certain of making a sale if he quotes a $1,000 price and supplies $5000 worth of service. For this reason, and because identical sales situations are rarely encountered over time, one might reason that the $P_1 - S_3$ strategy is preferable. That is, expected profits are maximized by simply selecting the strategy which has the highest probability of resulting in an order, assuming that incremental revenues exceed incremental costs. The effect on future profits should also be considered.

ECONOMICS OF PERSONAL SELLING

In any attempt to develop science in marketing, we should be prepared to justify economically those things which we research. The selling area is particularly popular for attack by critics. The economics of advertising has received treatment in many journal articles and in the pioneering book written by Professor Neil Borden, but the economics of personal selling has not been afforded much attention.

Much of the analysis of advertising has application to personal selling, but some of it does not. Certainly the persuasive, service, and communications aspects of each differ, which suggests that the economic implications are also likely to differ, both in degree and in kind. By concentrating on personal selling, its unique economic implications could be uncovered more readily.

Specifically, the notion that selling causes excess capacity in industry by tilting the demand curve down and to the right should be examined. According to the theory of monopolistic competition, a downward sloping demand curve inevitably results in an equilibrium at an output level below the minimum point on the average unit cost curve. Thus, by affecting the demand curve, selling is said to cause excess capacity in industry. This contention should be explored on the grounds of the economist as well as on the grounds of the businessman.

Another area where published research is needed is on the relationship between personal selling and economic growth. A rise in productivity will enable an expansion in the size of the market and thereby cause an increased need for personal representation over the market. Similarly, selling can expand market size, thereby enabling increased productivity. In many less developed economies, however, it is said that the first need is to be able to produce effectively, suggesting that selling should follow an emphasis on production. This is consistent with the proposition that an affluent society can afford, and needs, large expenditures on persuasion, but it is not entirely consistent with the proposition that the industrial revolution followed the commercial revolution.

As an economy increases in affluence, the question arises as to whether there is a limit on the capacity to consume all the goods that can be produced. Over the long run the propensity to consume has remained relatively stable. It has fluctuated in the short run but seems to return to a 93 per cent equilibrium point. Can this phenomenon continue in view of the limits on the capacity of individuals to use and enjoy goods?[17] If there is a tendency for the propensity to consume to fall over the long run, what are the implications to the selling field?

In part, the answer to this question depends on whether selling can actually affect the propensity to consume. Intuitively, we are inclined to reason that it can because of its influence on attitudes and desires. On

[17] Wroe Alderson has referred to this problem, noting the need for theory in the study of consumption *per se*. He has coined the word "hedonomics" to cover such a field of study. *Marketing Behavior and Executive Action*, Richard D. Irwin, Homewood, Ill., 1957, pp. 284–289.

the other hand, it may simply switch demand between companies and industries. According to Keynes, consumption is dependent on income, not on selling! However, we know that consumers need persuasion, information, and service help if they are to appreciate and actively to desire many products.

Moreover, personal selling, by affecting desires, can move the labor supply curve. It can also affect the marginal efficiency of capital by altering the expectations of the innovator. Both results will have a tendency to increase production, employment, and income. Even so, the the question remains as to whether consumption can be maintained at a level consistent with increased production; that is, can the ratio between consumption and income be maintained?

MANAGEMENT OF SALESMEN

There is an unlimited amount to be said on the economic effects of selling, but in order to get breadth of coverage attention will be focused on the problems involved in managing salesmen. These fall into two categories, those of a personnel variety and those having to do with planning and strategy. The latter will receive major attention because, in my opinion, this is where more research emphasis is needed.

How Much to Spend on Selling

The first major strategy question is how much to spend on personal selling in the marketing program. In attempting to answer this question it is well to examine the broader one first, which is how much should be spent on promotion in general. According to Chamberlain all the functions of business can be divided into production and promotion (he called the latter selling). Production activities create a bundle of utility, while promotion affects buyer attitudes about the utility offered. This distinction has limitations as indicated in the previous discussion of communications and service. Nonetheless, it is useful as long as we understand that reference is made primarily to those promotional activities that affect buyer attitudes by means other than offer change.

As suggested in the discussion of sales-service, part of the problem is to determine the combination of price and promotion cost which will maximize profits. Here, however, the concern is with general market reaction, rather than the reaction of any individual customer. Boulding has treated the problem in a unique way by presenting data similar to that shown in Table 9.4.[18] The top number in each box represents the

[18] Kenneth E. Boulding, *Economic Analysis*, Harper, New York, 1948, pp. 719–723.

Table 9.4   *Unit Sales, Total Revenues, and Net Production Revenues Resulting from Various Price-Promotions Cost Combinations*

Total Promotion Cost					
140	92	90	78	70	50
	0	90	156	210	200
	−140	−50	16	70	70
120	90	88	75	65	49
	0	88	150	195	196
	−120	−32	30	75	76
100	88	85	70	60	48
	0	85	140	80	192
	−100	−15	40	80	92
80	85	80	65	50	45
	0	80	130	150	180
	−80	0	50	70	100
	0	1	2	3	4

Price of output
dollars/ton

quantity which can be sold at a price equal to that at the bottom of the column and with a promotional expenditure equal to that at the left of the row. For example, at a price of $3 per ton and a promotional expenditure of $100, 60 tons will be sold. The second figure in each box is the total revenue secured at the price-promotional cost combination, while the third figure is the production revenue, or the difference between total revenue and promotional cost. Units sold decline as price is increased at any given promotional expenditure, and they increase as promotional expenditures are increased at any given price. The highest production revenue among the alternatives presented is secured at a price of $4 and a promotional expenditure of $80. As an alternative, sales contour and production revenue contours can be presented graphically as in Figure 9.1.

Each sales contour shows the combination of price and promotional cost which will sell a given output. (S_{25}, for example, gives the various combinations for selling 25 tons.) Each production revenue contour, the solid rings, shows the combinations which will yield a given production revenue.

This means that every point on a given production revenue contour represents a combination of price and promotion yielding identical production revenues. Production revenue contours closest to point M yield higher production revenues than do those far away from M.

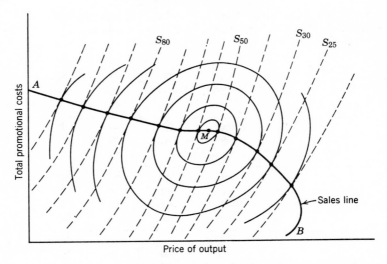

Figure 9.1   Sales contours and production revenue contours.

The best way to sell any given quantity in order to maximize production revenues is to find the point at which the sales contour representing that particular quantity is tangent to a production revenue contour. At this point production revenues are maximized because the point of tangency will be associated with the production revenue contour closest to M. By connecting these points of tangency for all sales contours, a "sales line" is secured (AB). This line shows the combination of price and promotion which will maximize production revenues for each of various possible sales volumes. As combinations move along AB toward M (from either direction), total production revenues increase.

The final solution to the problem of how much to spend on promotion is obtained by comparing the production revenue along the sales line with the cost of producing each quantity. The combination of promotional expenditure and price which is associated with the most profitable output is selected for use.

Obviously the practical usefulness of this approach depends greatly on the ability to predict the effect on sales of various price-promotion combinations. This, however, does not negate the value of the theory, for the response of sales volume to expenditure combinations must be predicted regardless of the theory used if the expenditure decision is to be sound. The so-called "objective-task" method often advocated as a basis for deciding on the magnitude of promotional expenditures is also a guide for such purposes, but it is conceptually inferior to the one mentioned here.

Moreover, in deciding on the kind of empirical research needed to understand normative marketing behavior, *sound* theory is essential. That is, recommendations for empirical research should be based not only on the facts about marketing practice which are presently known but also on a basic understanding of the way business *should* operate in order to attain its stated objectives.

Determining the Best Number of Salesmen

After the total amount to be allocated for promotion has been determined, the next problem is to divide this sum between personalized selling, advertising, and other forms of promotion. This problem is interrelated with the one above, and a similar approach is useful in establishing a theoretical framework for empirical research. However, it is discussed separately here with emphasis placed on the applied aspects of the problem and on the question of how many salesmen should be employed.

The "push-pull" concept suggested that some products could be "pulled" through the marketing channel with advertising, while other products required a "push" type of promotion with personal selling being emphasized. Criteria were developed to explain the conditions under which each might be possible. But the allocation of funds between personal selling and advertising cannot be accurately explained or determined by the push-pull criteria.

Ideally funds should be allocated between promotional functions until the marginal productivity of each expenditure is equal between functions, and since the productivity of selling depends on the level of expenditures on each of the other functions, the number of combinations to be evaluated is immense. Studies of this nature can keep experimental researchers busy for some time.

Expenditures on personal selling include the costs of selection, training, motivation, compensation, as well as travel costs. In determining the resources to devote to these items, the initial step might be to find the best number of salesmen to employ, first holding constant expenditures on other functions. In this part of the analysis Semlow's suggestions can be useful.[19] His approach has the advantage of practicality in that it uses data from sales experience. Existing territories are examined for the purpose of establishing a relationship between the share of the total potential contained in various territories and the sales actually secured by territory. The investigation might show that the high potential terri-

[19] Walter J. Semlow, "How Many Salesmen Do You Need," *Harvard Business Review*, Vol. XXXVII, No. 3 (May–June, 1959), pp. 126–132.

tories typically yield lower sales per "1% of potential" than do those with a low share of the total potential. Suppose, for example, that a correlation study revealed a relationship of $Y = \$20,000 - \$2000\ (X)$, where Y is the sales per 1 per cent of potential and X is the share of total potential falling in the territory. This equation could then be used to estimate the total sales likely with a varying number of salesmen. For example, if 20 salesmen were employed and territories were assigned with equal potential, then

$$Y = 20,000 - 2000\left(\frac{100}{20}\right) = \$10,000$$

With 20 salesmen the most probable sales volume per 1 per cent of potential is $10,000, and the total sales estimate is $1,000,000 ($10,000 × 100). Computing the most probable sales for each of several sales force sizes and determining the expenses and investment associated with each sales estimate yields an estimate of the rate of return on investment for each number of salesmen.

The method has a number of weaknesses, however. It assumes an accurate determination of potential, an existing sales force, a sales force of substantial size, a relationship between share of total potential in each territory and sales per 1 per cent of potential, and salesmen of equal ability. Moreover, it assumes that territories of equal potential should be established and that they should be established through an analysis of territories of unequal potential. None of these assumptions or procedures is necessarily sound for an individual company. At the same time, the method might yield better results than pure qualitative methods.

Sales Effort Approach

An alternative to the Semlow approach is the one implied in marketing and sales management textbooks. This starts with the number of customers in the market and raises the question: How many salesmen are needed in order to call on, and service, these customers? Both present and prospective customers in each group are determined. The series of steps, expressed symbolically, is as follows:

$$S = \frac{E_1 + E_2 \ldots + En}{e} + \frac{Ep_1 \ldots + Epn}{ep}$$

where S is the number of salesmen needed, E_1 is the sales effort which should be directed toward established customer class number one, En is the sales effort which should be directed toward the nth established customer class, Ep is the sales effort which should be directed toward *prospective* customers, e is the time available per salesman per year to call on established customers, and ep is the time available per salesman per year to call on prospective customers. The numerator of the model can be presented in terms of hours per year which should be devoted to existing accounts and to the development of new accounts. Similarly, the denominator can be expressed in hours per year.

Each E is a function of the number of customers in each potential class, the travel time between customers, the best call frequency, and the time which should be spent in selling and service within the customer's establishment in view of the potential volume available. The major problem is to determine how sales are likely to respond to call rate variation for each customer, as well as the relationship between sales and the time spent with the customer in selling and service work on each call.

This necessitates either an analysis of present methods being used by salesmen, perhaps with a time and duty study, or specially designed experiments to uncover the desired relationships. One paper describes an experiment where each salesman in the force was assigned 36 customers divided into three groups.[20] The salesmen were instructed to allot 16 hours of sales effort per month to those in group I, 4 hours per month to those in group II, and 1 hour per month to those in group III. The sales secured by each approach were used as a basis for determining the best effort level. This study did not recognize the distinction between call frequency as an effort factor and time spent with the customer on each call. Also, it is apparent that *what* the salesman does during the interview is often more important than the amount of time which he spends with the customer.

Once relationships between effort factors and sales results have been estimated for various customer groups, the number of salesmen needed to attain each possible combination of call frequency and time spent in the interview can be computed. Then total sales and expenses associated with various number of salesmen are estimated. This provides the basis for estimating the profits and rate of return on investment associated with alternative number of salesmen.

To some extent the call frequency, and particularly the time spent with each customer, is not entirely under the control of the salesman, but some control is usually possible. Few customers will refuse service from sales representatives, assuming that the service is really helpful.

[20] Arthur A. Brown, Frank T. Hulswit, and John D. KeHelle, "A Study of Sales Operations," *Operations Research*, Vol. IV, No. 4 (July–August 1956), pp. 296–308.

One salesman who sells vacuum cleaners to retail appliance dealers has gone so far as to wash the retailer's windows and dust off display cases each time he visits the store. One might question the wisdom of the approach, but at least it illustrates the possibilities of using service to control the time spent with each customer. Moreover, service of certain kinds will certainly have an influence on sales volume.

Thus the broad problem in establishing the best expenditure level is to predict the effect on sales volume of sales force size and each qualitative approach to personal selling. Thus whether we have 50 salesmen or 100 salesmen, there is still the question of whether the men should spend their time in demonstrating the product or in entertaining customers, for example. The selection, training, and compensation of salesmen will also affect the results secured, which means that the sales budget problem necessitates predictions with regard to the relationship between sales volume and the allocation of the budget between the various activities in developing a sales force. In view of the breadth and significance of such problems to marketing management, extensive research on them is justified.

Experimental Methods

Experimentation is the most promising approach for predicting results from alternative selling methods and levels. No longer can marketing people justifiably argue that experimentation is impractical or not applicable in the area. We now recognize that experiments do not necessitate holding all variables constant except the one under observation. All that is necessary is that the effects of the other variables be taken into account. This can be accomplished by careful design of an experimental group and a control group.

Suppose, for example, that two random samples of customers are selected within the market. One of the sample groups is used for control purposes, which might require that the customary selling procedures be used in calling on these customers. The second group is used for experimental purposes. Here the call frequency, or perhaps the service time per call, is increased beyond the customary level. Thus, to simplify, let E_2 equal the sales rate in the experimental group during and immediately subsequent to the experiment and let C_2 equal the sales rate of the control group during and immediately subsequent to the experiment. When compared with sales rates prior to experimentation (E_1 and C_1), some judgment is possible regarding the effect of the variable change on sales volume. More precisely, the sales effect is measured by the quantity $(E_2 - E_1) - (C_2 - C_1)$. If both the experimental group and the control group are selected by probability sampling methods, then $(E_2 - E_1) - (C_2 - C_1)$ will reflect two factors: random sampling errors and the difference in sales effort to which the two groups were exposed. Although experimentation is more complex than suggested by this statement, even elementary application of it would be preferable to pure guess or qualitative judgment only.

THE SALES TERRITORY PROBLEM

This problem has at least three dimensions where further research is needed. The first has to do with establishing territories for the individual salesman, the second is concerned with territories for branch offices and other field sales facilities, and the third with sales territories for the company as a whole. Studies of business practice should be conducted with a view to describing practice and of interpreting it to explain the difference between companies within an industry and the differences between industries. The practices should also be integrated with the problems involved in managing salesmen.

The territories covered by field service and distribution facilities and by individual service representatives should be included. The best number and location of field sales offices are connected with decisions on service territories and physical distribution methods. Should the field sales office serve as a housing and control point for selling, service and physical distribution, or should the control points be separated? If service personnel use sales offices as points of departure for service work, how should sales and service territories be designed in order to best coordinate the two functions?

Allocating Salesmen over the Market

Designing the salesman's territory is frequently discussed, but we need to get further below the surface on the subject. First, a distinction should be made between two kinds of assignment problems. One is indicated by the question of whether a man born and raised in New York City should be assigned to an Alabama territory in view of the possible difficulties of establishing rapport with the people in that area. A second is quantitative in that it has to do with the *number* of salesmen to be assigned to the various geographic parts of the over-all market. Should one salesman be assigned to the state of Alabama or should the territory be split among several salesmen? The latter question is similar to the one discussed previously concerning the number of salesmen to employ for developing the over-all market. But assuming that the selling budget is fixed, the problem is to allocate the given sales force over the company sales area.

A common method is to divide this sales area into territories of equal potential and to assign one salesman to each territory. Several marketing textbooks recommend this procedure, and in the study of 129 marketing and sales executives mentioned previously, almost 40 per cent agreed that it was sound. It is so common that science in marketing is furthered by exposing the fallacy and developing methods which are superior.

Equal potential territories almost inevitably result in different size territories for each salesman, for geographic areas differ with respect to the number of customers per square mile and the volume distribution of customers in each geographic area. And varying territorial size results in varying opportunity for sales. Consequently, some salesmen may be discriminated against when evaluation is conducted by comparing actual sales with potential sales, or when salesmen are compensated by a commission plan with uniform rates between salesmen. Also, salesmen differ in ability, which suggests that equal potential territories will not make the most profitable use of the good salesman's ability.

The optimum is achieved by establishing territories so that the incremental sales revenues per dollar of selling expenditure are equated between territories.[21] In order to follow this rule, territorial establishment must reflect coverage difficulty and salesmen's ability as well as potential volume. No satisfactory approach has been developed which reflects all three elements. Certainly, it is only coincidental if equal potential territories achieve the optimum.

Take a simple case of three salesmen assigned to equal potential territories where coverage difficulty is uniform and where territorial potential is $300,000. The best salesman will realize this territorial potential, while each of the other two will secure a part of the potential, the amount depending on his ability relative to the other salesmen. The situation is as shown in Table 9.5.

If the salesmen are paid a commission rate of 5 per cent and other

Table 9.5   *Assignment of Salesmen to Territories of Equal Potential*

Territory	$ Potential	Salesmen Assigned	Ability Index
A	$300,000	1	1.0
B	300,000	2	0.8
C	300,000	3	0.5

[21] H. R. Wellman, "The Distribution of Selling Effort Among Geographic Areas," *Journal of Marketing*, Vol. III, No. 3 (January 1939), pp. 225–241.

variable expenses amount to 25 per cent of sales, salesman 1 will contribute $210,000 to profits, salesman 2 will contribute $168,000, and salesman 3 will contribute $105,000. These estimates are secured by applying the equation $C = (P)(I) - (V)(P)(I)$, where P is the dollar sales potential, I is the index of sales ability, and V is variable expenses expressed as a percentage of sales. The total profit contribution secured by assigning equal potential territories is $483,000. The accuracy of this estimate depends greatly on whether salesmen can be ranked according to selling ability in some meaningful way. Assuming that the above ranking is reasonably accurate, can territories be redesigned so that the total profit contribution will exceed $483,000?

Suppose boundaries are established with potentials that differ in proportion to the difference in salesmen's ability. Assignments are made so that the best salesman is assigned to the high potential territory and the poorest salesman is assigned to the low potential territory. With a total area potential of $900,000, this distribution would result in the arrangement shown in Table 9.6.

Table 9.6 Design of Territorial Potentials in Accord with Salesmen's Productive Ability

Territory	Potential	Salesmen Assigned	Index of Ability
A	$391,000	1	1.0
B	313,000	2	0.8
C	196,000	3	0.5

The profit contribution here would amount to $518,000 which is $35,000 greater than that resulting from equal potential territories. Moreover, only one of the many possible divisions of total potential between salesmen has been considered. For example, the market could be divided so that the best salesman is assigned a $450,000 territorial potential as opposed to $391,000. In addition, for each division of potential there are six different sets of territorial assignments ($n!$ different possibilities, where n is the number of salesmen). Consider Table 9.7.

Table 9.7 Profit Contribution Resulting from Various Territorial Assignments

Territory	Salesman		
	1	2	3
A	$274,000	$219,000	$137,000
B	219,000	175,000	110,000
C	137,000	110,000	69,000

Here is the case where territories have been designed so that their potentials are proportionate to the salesmen's ability. Profit contributions are computed for each possible assignment. Each cell in Table 9.7 represents the profit contribution associated with the assignment of a salesman to a territory. Thus, if salesman 1 is assigned to territory A, he will contribute $274,000 to profit, while if he is assigned to B, he will contribute $219,000. The total contribution for each of the six possible sets of assignments then can be computed and the assignment which maximizes contribution to profit selected. As indicated in Table 9.8, the optimum allocation is secured by the assignment set 1 A, 2 B, 3 C, which consists of assigning the best salesman to the high potential territory, the second best salesman to the territory which has the next highest potential, and the poorest salesman to the low potential territory.

Table 9.8   Profit Contribution Resulting from Alternative Territorial Assignment Sets

Assignment Set	Contribution to Profit
1 A, 2 B, 3 C	$518,000
2 A, 1 B, 3 C	507,000
3 A, 1 B, 2 C	466,000
1 A, 3 B, 2 C	494,000
2 A, 3 B, 1 C	466,000
3 A, 2 B, 1 C	449,000

Three of the assignments yield a contribution to profit greater than that yielded by establishing territories of equal potential. Moreover, as indicated above, territories can be established so that total potential is distributed between territories in many ways other than the one selected. Assigning to the best salesman a territory with a greater potential than $391,000 would be profitable, assuming that coverage difficulty was not affected. When coverage difficulty changes as larger potential territories are established, it must be taken into account in order to attain the optimum arrangement.

It should be emphasized that the results secured in the above analysis were dependent on the assumption that the indices of salesmen's performance were constant among territories. In reality, a salesman may perform well in one territory and poorly in another even though territorial potential and coverage difficulty are similar between territories. Customer characteristics and other such intangible factors may well cause a variance.

This point should be emphasized. The outstanding salesman is not necessarily outstanding in all sales situations, nor is a poor salesman always poor in all situations. Not only do variances in sales productivity occur over time but they also occur in space. Performance is conditioned by environmental forces, the way in which an individual reacts to these forces, and by changes in the rate of individual growth over time. It is questionable to assume, therefore, that the indices of sales ability will maintain their relative magnitudes as salesmen are switched between territories.

To illustrate its possible effect on an optimum allocation of salesmen over the market, take a situation where salesmen maintain their *general* performance ranking as they are switched between territories, but the degree to which they perform relative to one another is altered. Suppose that with the assignment 1 A, 2 B, 3 C the performance ranking is 1, .5, .4. When the assignment 1 B, 2 A, 3 C is used, however, the performance ranking changes to 1, .8, .5, as assumed above. In other words, salesman 1 performs better than salesman 2 regardless of which assignment is used. (He will secure a larger part of territorial potential.) However, when 1 A, 2 B, 3 C is used he performs 100 per cent better, whereas with the assignment 1 B, 2 A, 3 C he performs only 25 per cent better.

Also assume that the territorial potentials have been set as follows: A—$490,000, B—$240,000, and C—$180,000. Using the cost figures of the previous example (variable expenses = 30% of sales), a contribution to profit for each of the two assignment sets can be computed.

Table 9.9   Profit Contribution with Change in Sales Productivity and Territorial Assignment

Assignment Set	Territorial Contribution			Total Contribution
	A	B	C	
1 A, 2 B, 3 C	$343,000	$ 84,000	$50,400	$477,400
1 B, 2 A, 3 C	274,400	168,000	63,000	505,400

Here $477,400 is contributed to profit by assigning the best salesman to the best territory, while $505,400 is contributed by assigning the best salesman to the territory with the second largest potential. This case makes it clear that the *better salesmen should not necessarily be assigned to high potential territories.* Nor should a salesman necessarily be assigned to the territory where he is able to contribute more to profits than any other salesman.

The proof is a demonstration of the principle of comparative advantage in the assignment of salesmen. This principle states that a salesman should be assigned to that territory where his *relative* contribution to profit is the highest. In Table 9.9 salesman 1 can contribute more to profits in territory A than can salesman 2, but he can contribute more relative to 2 when assigned to territory B. Similarly, salesman 2 has a *relative disadvantage* which is smaller when he is assigned to territory A than when assigned to territory B.

Since relative performance can change as assignment sets change, a forecast of performance ranking for each set is necessary. When 10 salesmen are to be assigned, for example, there are 10! (3,628,800) assignment sets to be analyzed. This makes the sales territory problem complex. Certainly it is not solved by simply establishing territories of equal potential.

Once again, however, the question arises as to the practical value of the approach proposed here. For one thing, some doubt that an ability index can be constructed which will have much accuracy and usefulness. This objection is of doubtful validity on two counts. First, serious study can surely result in indexes which are more accurate than those which the sales manager presently constructs in his own mind with intuitive methods. Even if perfect indexes cannot be constructed, they might be accurate enough to enable an allocation of salesmen which is superior to the equal potential method.

The method does suggest the need for more research aimed at evaluating and predicting the salesman's performance within a given territory, and between territories. In addition, further empirical research is needed on the relationship between territorial size and the ability of salesmen to achieve potential volume.

Other Territorial Problems

There are two other territorial problems which will be mentioned. One has to do with deciding on the base to use for dividing sales territories. There is the frequently discussed alternatives of county versus state and county versus trading area boundaries, but there is also the question of whether a geographic base should be used at all. There is nothing sacred about dividing territories by geographic area. Instead, customers might be grouped by potential volume, by buying motives, by products purchased, or even by the intelligence quotients of the purchasing agents employed. Salesmen then could be hired and assigned according to customer characteristics.

In some instances there is great difference in the ability of salesmen to open up new accounts and to sell existing accounts. To recognize this ability variance, two salesmen could be placed in each geographic territory, one to spend a large percentage of his time calling on prospective customers and the other to service existing accounts. Geographic territories would overlap for the two salesmen, but an optimum allocation of sales time might still be more closely achieved.

The second problem has received some attention by the mathematicians, but it is my impression that it has not been satisfactorily solved, certainly from a more practical sales management standpoint. This is the question of how best to route salesmen within a territory. Suppose there are 10 customers and the salesman is to be routed so the total distance traveled is minimized. There are $\frac{1}{2}n!$ (1,809,400) possible routes if reverse order routes are eliminated. One could compute the distance for each route and select the shortest one, but this process is somewhat arduous to say the least. A number of approaches to the solution of this "traveling salesman problem" are covered in the literature. But even if the problem is solved as stated, the ideal route would still remain unknown. Distance traveled and cost of travel are not the only criteria for routing. In fact, in many cases they are the least important. Customer availability in time, personal desires of the salesman, customer needs from a service standpoint, and many other determinants of sales volume are often of equal or greater significance.

ORGANIZATION AND SALES PERSONNEL RESEARCH

Personnel will not be discussed extensively here, although the matter of selecting salesmen and some recent approaches to the study of personnel should be mentioned. Selecting salesmen probably has been treated more than any other topic in the area, which is understandable because of high sales force turnover, the importance of correct selection to company success, the interest in judging human qualities, and the ease associated with researching this topic as opposed to many others. Some salesmen's characteristics are easily measured and secured, which facilitates the use of correlation, factor analysis, and other methods. Moreover, pertinent data are available in company records.

Despite the extensive research, not much is known about correct selection, in this writer's opinion. The idea that the characteristics needed for exceptional selling in one industry are the same as those needed for a different kind of selling job has been discarded gradually. It is now common to state that the selection process should start with a job analysis, but there are weaknesses in this theory also. It assumes that a job analysis will be revealing with respect to the qualities needed in an individual. Second, it assumes that even if the job analysis is useful in this respect, it is more useful than other alternatives. Moreover, carried to the extreme it would require that an analysis be conducted for every sales situation.

One study attempted to develop specific selection instruments for car salesmen.[22] The used car salesman has a different job than a new car salesman, and an individual selling Brand X car has a different job than one selling Brand Y. It was concluded that the more elaborate procedure did not result in any significant improvement in validity as compared with developing a single key for car salesmen in general. It might also be true that a single key to represent car salesmen, door-to-door salesmen of aluminum ware, and other industry types would yield as much validity as selection oriented around car salesmen in particular. Thus we return to the point made previously that studies of the activities of salesmen in various industries are needed as a way of grouping salesmen according to similarity of functions performed.

Starting with a job analysis also assumes that the duties uncovered will be revealing with respect to the kind of individual needed. Certainly, opinions on what characteristics are indicated will differ between selectors. Thus, under certain conditions, it may be more enlightening to start with the individuals already in the salesforce with the purpose of determining the characteristics of the high and low sales producers. These characteristics can form the basis for future selection.

It is not surprising that a great deal of research has been devoted to the second approach in recent years, particularly as applied to life insurance selling, and where the salesforce is of substantial size. Merenda and Clark studied 522 agents three years after they were hired with the purpose of determining the relationship between performance and temperament characteristics as well as personal history. They conclude that men were not likely to be successful if they perceived themselves as passive and submissive individuals as opposed to aggressive and socially confident individuals.[23] One wonders whether self-perception is a *cause* of success or a *result* of success, however.

The authors also concluded that certain personal history variables were good predictors, although few were of this nature. Age was useful in predicting failure for those individuals above and below certain age limits. This finding is similar to that in an earlier study published about

[22] James E. Kennedy, "A General Device versus More Specific Devices for Selecting Car Salesmen," *Journal of Applied Psychology*, Vol. XLII, No. 3 (June 1958), pp. 206–209.

[23] Peter F. Merenda and Walter V. Clark, "The Predictive Efficiency of Temperament Characteristics and Personal History Variables in Determining Success of Life Insurance Agents," *Journal of Applied Psychology*, Vol. XLIII, No. 6 (December 1959), pp. 360–366.

salesmen in The Minnesota Mining and Manufacturing Company. Here 539 salesmen employed by the company were given tests used for selection purposes. Salesmen around age 40 scored the highest, and these men were also ranked best by management.[24] Such studies face the difficulty of measuring performance and also in arriving at the underlying cause of performance. Age is often symptomatic of more basic variables, such as experience, motivation, marital status, desire for security, and financial ambitions. It would be precarious, as a result of the latter study, to look only for men who are 40 years old for future selection purposes.

Without first reviewing all the literature on selection it is difficult to recommend sensible research. But certain questions arise from an examination of textbooks and more recent journal articles. (1) Is the job analysis the appropriate starting point for selecting salesmen or should the selector start with an analysis of the characteristics of outstanding and poor salesmen already on the salesforce? (2) How specific should the job analysis be? Is it revealing to conduct it for each selling position in a company? (3) Are the methods of selecting salesmen basically different from selecting other kinds of employees? (4) How does the sales manager reconcile the dilemma of selecting a few high quality and high paid salesmen versus selecting a large number of medium quality, lower paid salesmen? These are, of course, only a small part of the unanswered questions in the selection area.

The Selling Group

Insight might be secured on salesman's performance by orienting study around the selling group. French reports the results of research conducted in a large retail furniture store over a period of four years.[25] The purposes included an attempt to determine the relationships between off-the-job attitudes and productivity, between informal group structure and productivity, and between group norms and productivity. The primary methods employed were observation and formal and informal interviewing. Written records were maintained of habitual interaction between individuals as well as "patterns of hostility." Allegedly, the salesmen were unaware that they were being observed.

The author concludes that the salesmen who were still "moving

[24] Wayne K. Kirchner, Carolyn S. McElwain, and Marvin D. Dunnette, "A Note on the Relationship Between Age and Sales Effectiveness," *Journal of Applied Psychology*, Vol. XLIV, No. 2 (April 1960), pp. 92–93.
[25] Cecil L. French, "Correlates of Success in Retail Selling," *American Journal of Sociology*, Vol. LXVI, No. 2 (September 1960), pp. 128–134 as reprinted in *Marketing and the Behavioral Sciences*, edited by Perry Bliss, Allyn and Bacon, Boston, 1963, pp. 235–246.

toward their goals" tended to be high sales producers, whereas those who had attained their goals were the low producers. The latter group were also in a better occupational position than were their fathers, and they felt relatively satisfied with the prestige and earnings in their job.

In addition, medium and low producing salesmen tended to be more popular than the high producers. Those expressing their sociometric choices said these salesmen were "fair and honest," while the high producers were "gonophs." (This being an expression used for the salesman who allegedly rewrote orders by taking advantage of, and even encouraging, customer discontent with the original items purchased. It is a Yiddish word meaning crook.) The high producing salesmen who were disliked partly because of a violation of group norms tended to name as their friends individuals in occupations more highly placed than their own, while the high producing salesmen who happened to be liked tended to name friends on their own occupational level.

The general approach of this study is feasible in cases such as retail selling where salesmen are grouped in a central location, but for the salesforce that is spread out over a national market, it has little usefulness. In the first case, it might shed light on the forces conducive to high and low output for the salesforce as a whole as well as for the output of any single member. It also may be useful in uncovering factors pertinent to selecting, training, motivating, and evaluating salesmen. Whether it is the most efficient method for achieving such goals is debatable.

Simulation and Laboratory Research

Simulation also might be used to research the organizational and the personnel aspects of selling. Various sales compensation and motivation plans might be designed and tested by using individuals to act as salesmen under each plan and observing behavior as market conditions change or other variables under the control of the experimenter are altered.

Simulation necessitates simplification of reality, but this is an advantage in that many variables can be held constant during the experiment in order to observe the influence of the one(s) under consideration. Cause and effect can be tested, and the method is obviously less costly than is research which involves widespread travel. In addition, wide experimental variation, which is not usually feasible in a going sales organization, can be used.

In one project experimental organizations consisted of two subgroups, each with three individuals.[26] One group acted as producers and the other

[26] Harold Guetzkow and Anne E. Bowes, "The Development of Organizations in a Laboratory," *Management Science*, Vol. III, No. 4 (July 1957), pp. 380–402.

group acted as sellers. External market information was fed to one group for use in planning rational behavior. Their decisions were output variables, but they also were inputs of information to the second group. Written communication was allowed among producers, among sellers, and between sellers and producers. Records were kept of the number of messages, their direction, and their content.

CONCLUDING COMMENTS AND SUGGESTIONS FOR FURTHER RESEARCH

No attempt has been made to cover all of the research which has been done in the area of personal selling. Some problems have not even been mentioned because of time and space limitations. Instead, emphasis has been placed on the areas which have been neglected, and where future research could be most productive. In general, and in my opinion, too much emphasis has been placed on the occupational aspects of salesmanship and on the personnel problems in managing a salesforce. While both areas deserve attention, it is desirable to provide greater balance by researching selling as an aspect of marketing strategy. Additional emphasis is needed in the analysis of salesmen utilizing the newer methodological approaches that have been developed in recent years as well as the research and perspective provided by the behavioral sciences.

From a functional marketing viewpoint, research is needed in many areas, and it is somewhat arbitrary to single out a few which should have priority. However, the influence of automation, the communications and service aspects of selling, and the salesman assignment problem are three where knowledge is extremely limited. In addition, it seems to me that a great deal of basic knowledge could be secured by investigating personal selling historically, particularly as it is related to the theory of exchange.

We also know too little about the economics of the function. Is our economy devoting too much to selling in view of the need for faster economic growth, or should an even greater proportion of total resources be devoted to it? How much is spent on the function and what is the trend in this regard? How do expenditures compare with other countries in the world, both in an absolute sense and relative to gross national product? In view of automation and other economic developments, how is the personal selling job likely to change in the future? Will a larger, or a smaller, proportion of the total population be employed as salesmen? These are only a few of the many unanswered questions which need attention.

BIBLIOGRAPHY

Benton, A. L. and G. I. Kornhauser, "A Study of 'Score Faking' on a Mechanical Interest Test," *Journal of the Association of the American Medical Colleges*, Vol. XXIII (1948), pp. 57–60.

Bolanovich, Daniel J. and Forrest H. Kirkpatrick, "Measurement and Selection of Salesmen," *Educational and Psychological Measurement*, Vol. III (1943), pp. 333–339.

Brown, Arthur A., Frank T. Hulswit, and John D. Katelle, "A Study of Sales Operations," *Operations Research*, Vol. IV, No. 4 (July–August 1956), pp. 296–308.

Bursk, Edward C., "Opportunities for Persuasion," *Harvard Business Review*, Vol. XXXVI, No. 5 (September–October 1958), pp. 111–119.

Clark, W. V., "The Personality Profiles of Life Insurance Agents," *Journal of Psychology*, Vol. XLII (1st half), (July–October 1956), pp. 295–302.

Dantzig, R., R. Fulkerson, and J. Johnson, "Solutions of a Large Traveling Salesman Problem," *Journal of the Operations Research Society of America*, Vol. II (1954), pp. 393–410.

Davis, James H., *Increasing Wholesale Drug Salesman's Effectiveness*, Bureau of Business Research, College of Commerce and Administration, The Ohio State University, Columbus, Ohio, 1948.

Day, Ralph L. and Peter D. Bennett, "Should Salemen's Compensation be Geared to Profits?" *Journal of Marketing*, Vol. XXVI, No. 4 (October 1962), pp. 6–9.

Evans, Franklin B., "A Sociological Analysis of the Selling Situation: Some Preliminary Findings," *Emerging Concepts in Marketing*, William S. Decker (ed.), American Marketing Association, Chicago, 1963, pp. 476–482.

Flood, Merril M., "The Traveling Salesman Problem," *Journal of the Operations Society of America*, Vol. IV (1955), pp. 61–75.

French, Cecil C., "Correlates of Success in Retail Selling," *American Journal of Sociology*, Vol. LXVI, No. 2 (September 1960), pp. 128–134.

Gehman, W. S., "A Study of Ability to Fake Scores on the Strong Vocational Interest Blank for Men," *Educational and Psychological Measurement*, Vol. XVII (1957), pp. 65–70.

Groes, G. A., "A Method for Solving Traveling Salesmen Problems," *Journal of the Operations Research Society of America*, Vol. VI (1958), pp. 791–812.

Kelley, William T., "The Development of Early Thought in Marketing and Promotion," *Journal of Marketing*, Vol. XXI, No. 1 (January 1957), pp. 62–67.

Kennedy, James E., "A General Device Versus More Specific Devices for Selecting Car Salesmen," *Journal of Applied Psychology*, Vol. XLII, No. 3 (June 1958), pp. 206–209.

Kirchner, Wayne K., Carolyn S. McElwain, and Marvin D. Dunnette, "A Note on the Relationship Between Age and Sales Effectiveness," *Journal of Applied Psychology*, Vol. XLIV, No. 2 (April 1960), pp. 92–93.

Kirchner, Wayne K., "Predicting Ratings of Sales Success with Objective Performance Information," *Journal of Applied Psychology*, Vol. XLIV, No. 6 (December 1960), pp. 398–403.

————, " 'Real Life' Faking on the Strong Vocational Interest Blank by Sales Applicants," *Journal of Applied Psychology*, Vol. XLV, No. 4 (August 1961), pp. 273–280.

Magee, V. F., "The Effect of Promotional Effort on Sales," *Journal of Operations Research Society of America*, Vol. I (1952–1953), pp. 64–74.

McMurry, Robert N., "How to Win or Lose Sales at the Point of Purchase," *Journal of Marketing*, Vol. XXIV, No. 4 (April 1957), pp. 41–49.

Merenda, Peter F., and Walter V. Clark, "The Predictive Efficiency of Temperament Characteristics and Personal History Variables in Determining Success of Life Insurance Agents," *Journal of Applied Psychology*, Vol. XLIII, No. 6 (December 1959), pp. 376–380.

Merenda, Peter F., Walter V. Clark and Charles E. Hall, "Cross Validity of Procedures for Selecting Life Insurance Salesmen," *Journal of Applied Psychology*, Vol. XLV, No. 6 (December 1961), pp. 376–380.

Merenda, Peter F., Walter V. Clark, "Activity Vector Analysis Validity for Life Insurance Salesmen," *Engineering Industrial Psychology*, Vol. I (1959), pp. 1–11.

Miner, J. B., "Personality and Ability Factors in Sales Performance," *Journal of Applied Psychology*, Vol. XLVI, No. 1 (February 1962).

Murray, Lester E. and Martin M. Bruce, "A Study of the Validity of the Sales Motivation Inventory in Differentiating High and Low Production in Life Insurance Selling," *Journal of Applied Psychology*, Vol. XLIII, No. 4 (August 1959), pp. 246–248.

Robbins, George W., "Is Selling Good for Society," *Frontiers in Marketing Thought*, Stewart Rewoldt (ed.), Indiana University Press, Bloomington, Ind., 1954.

Rodgers, David A., "Personality of the Route Salesman in a Basic Food Industry," *Journal of Applied Psychology*, Vol. XLIII, No. 4 (August 1959), pp. 235–239.

Schiff, Michael, "The Sales Territory as a Fixed Asset," *Journal of Marketing*, Vol. XXV, No. 2 (October 1960), pp. 51–53.

Seelye, Alfred L. and Frank M. Bass, "Sales Compensation Policies of Grocery, Drug, and Hardware Wholesalers," *Journal of Marketing*, Vol. XXI, No. 4 (April 1957), pp. 443–445.

Semlow, Walter J., "How Many Salesmen Do You Need," *Harvard Business Review*, Vol. XXXVII, No. 3 (May–June 1959), pp. 126–132.

Spratlin, Thadeus, "An Appraisal of Theory and Practice in the Analysis of Sales Activities," unpublished doctoral dissertation, the Ohio State University, 1962.

Tolley, Walter J., Jr., "How to Design Sales Territories," *Journal of Marketing*, Vol. XXV, No. 3 (January 1961), pp. 7–13.

Tosdal, Harry H., *Selling in the American Economy*, Richard D. Irwin, Homewood, Ill., 1957.

Tosdal, Harry H. and Walter Carson, Jr., *Salesman's Compensation*, Vols. I and II, Division of Research, Graduate School of Business Administration, Harvard University, 1953.

Tosdal, Harry H., "The Advertising and Selling Process," *Annals of The American Academy of Political and Social Science* (May 1940), pp. 62–70.

Wallace, S. Rains, Jr. and Constance M. Twichill, "Evolution of a Training Course for Life Insurance Agents," *Personnel Psychology*, Vol. VI (1953), pp. 25–43.

Wallace, S. R., W. V. Clark, and R. J. Day, "The Activity Vector Analysis as a Selector of Life Insurance Salesmen," *Personnel Psychology*, Vol. IX (1956), pp. 337–345.

Wellman, H. R., "The Distribution of Selling Effort Among Geographic Areas," *Journal of Marketing*, Vol. III, No. 3 (January 1939), pp. 225–241.

10

Pricing

JULES BACKMAN

Prices are the heart of the economic system. Essentially, price is a convenient way of comparing the value of one good or service with another. Complexity rather than simplicity is the essence of the price system.

Prices and price relationships influence what and how much shall be produced (*stimulating function*) and who will get the available supply of goods (*rationing function*). Both the stimulating and rationing functions are important. Although the price system may not be the sensitive regulator portrayed in theory, it does operate within broad limits which producers cannot afford to ignore.

Sellers may compete either in terms of price or of nonprice factors. There has been increased emphasis on nonprice considerations over the years. The increasing complexity of many products and the difficulty of comparing them directly because of differences in quality have meant that price competition plays a less significant role than formerly. The inadequacy of our knowledge as buyers stimulates businessmen to differentiate their products—often with no effect on functional usefulness —and then to seek to expand their sales by accentuating these differences. Businessmen also seek to obtain a larger share of the market by developing trademarks and brand names. If these can be promoted successfully, consumer confidence is created in a particular product and the resulting brand loyalty leads to larger sales. Under these circumstances, product differences, alleged or real, frequently play a more important role in the decision by a consumer than do price differences.

Note: Some of the materials in this chapter have been adapted from my *Pricing: Policies and Practices,* National Industrial Conference Board, New York, 1961, 143 pp.

Businessmen prefer nonprice competition to price competition in many instances because

1. They generally believe that the good will derived from nonprice factors will be more lasting than that based on price appeal.
2. Competitors may find it more difficult to match nonprice factors than to meet price changes.

Nonprice competition may take many forms, such as packaging, availability of credit, advertising, quality differences, service, and performance. The widespread development of nonprice competition has complicated the task of the ultimate consumer. The simple problem of choice among identical goods has been replaced by the need to select from a wide variety of goods with differences in quality and performance that are not easily determined and, in many instances, with differences in price.

Although nonprice competition undoubtedly has brought significant benefits to the consumer, price competition often would be preferred by part of the consuming public. For example, some consumers might be better off with lower prices than with an array of services or gadgets that do not add significantly to the performance of the product but do add to the price they must pay. Under these circumstances, the alternatives available to the consumer are limited. The seller has made the choice for the consumer when he decides to emphasize nonprice factors with the accompanying higher prices.

In this chapter the main concern is with price practices and price policies. However, nonprice factors, as noted above, play an important role in marketing policy. First, the assumptions of competitive price theory are reviewed. This is followed by a brief consideration of the nature of administered prices and pricing objectives. Attention is then turned to the main factors to be considered in setting prices. The special factors involved in new product pricing and retail pricing are then reviewed.

PRICES IN THEORY AND IN PRACTICE

Economists have developed an elaborate body of theory to explain how prices are determined. Supply and demand schedules, average and marginal costs, indifference curves, elasticity of demand and of supply— these are among the tools used to describe pricing. Theory describes the tendencies at work rather than the method of price determination. Even if businessmen were willing to follow such theoretical procedures in setting prices, they could not do so because the required data are not available.

It must also be kept in mind that under the theory of perfect competition, price determination is based on several assumptions which are found in practice to only a limited extent for most products. These assumptions are summarized briefly below.

1. *A large number of buyers and sellers so that no buyer or seller can exercise any influence over price.* Very few products meet this test. For some items, such as steel rails, there are a few buyers and a few sellers. For products like appliances there are a few sellers and many buyers.

2. *Capital and/or labor can enter an industry or withdraw from an industry readily so that required adjustments can be made.* However, ease of entry into, and exit from, an industry often is very difficult to achieve. Thus, for example, fixed capital investments in machinery cannot easily be withdrawn or disinvested. On the other hand, it is relatively easy to enter many service industries.

3. *Products are homogeneous or identical.* Although many products are standardized, most consumer goods would not meet this test. To attract buyers, products often are differentiated. Trademarks, brand names, promotion, packaging, and actual product changes are important in this connection.

4. *Buyers and sellers have complete information about terms and conditions of sale as well as the opportunity to take advantage of such knowledge.* However, this condition is rarely found. Consumers do not have the technical knowledge to compare different makes of television sets, automobiles, and many other products. Moreover, they often know little or nothing about alternative opportunities to buy a product at a lower price. Industrial buyers, on the other hand, tend to have more complete knowledge about products, about competitors' prices, and about the prices of substitute products because of the information they receive from potential customers and from their own salesmen.

5. *The economy is operating at capacity, that is, there is full utilization of resources.* However, the economy as well as most industries operate below capacity for considerable periods of time. Thus production and sales can be expanded without a significant change in price. The seller establishes a price to be charged and is prepared to provide a considerable range of quantities at that price.

6. *A standard assumption in economics is ceteris paribus, that is, all things remain equal.* In real life, of course, population, income, tastes, prices of substitutes, and so on do not remain constant. As they change, the demand for and supply and costs of the product also change.

In brief, the assumptions which underlie competitive price theory usually are found to only a limited extent in practice, and hence it does not provide a precise mechanism for determining prices. However, this theory does describe the broad forces that affect pricing. We have imperfect rather than perfect markets. Some are characterized by relatively few sellers (oligopoly) and/or buyers (oligopsony). Even where there is a larger number of sellers, each may strive to pre-empt a share of the market through product differentiation and other types of nonprice competition. Under these conditions, individual sellers do have some influence over price and often take into consideration the probable reactions of their competitors and of their large customers (and sometimes of government officials) when they consider changes in prices or in products. Competition remains a very active force but it tends to take forms other than price.

ADMINISTERED PRICES

The activities of the Kefauver Committee starting in 1957 gave considerable publicity to business pricing under the general heading of administered prices.[1] Some of the ensuing public discussion implied that administered prices are peculiar to big business or to large concentrated industries. Administered prices, however, are found throughout the economy. Any price set by a company official is an administered price in contrast to the competitive market prices described in theory. Every retail price is set by administrative action and close to 90 per cent of the wholesale price index is in the administered price category. It is evident, therefore, that the term does not describe the pricing process in big business alone. The term administered prices has no special connotation, for it merely describes the process of price making. It does not indicate per se whether the price is too high or too low, whether it is fair or unfair.

The price administrator must consider all the factors discussed in this chapter. He is limited in his freedom of action by the broad forces of supply and demand that affect his products. Usually an accumulation of pressures must develop before an administered price is changed. There is, moreover, no choice as between administered prices and competitive market prices for the overwhelming majority of products, for the prerequisites for competitive market price determination generally are not present in our economy.

[1] See "Administered Prices," *Hearings before the Subcommittee on Antitrust and Monopoly of the Committee on the Judiciary*, United States Senate, pursuant to S. Res. 57 and S. Res. 231, Washington, D. C., 1957–1963, and Jules Backman, "Do Administered Prices Create a Problem," in *Administered Prices: A Compendium on Public Policy*, Subcommittee on Antitrust and Monopoly of the Committee on the Judiciary, United States Senate, 88th Cong., 1st Sess., Washington, D. C., 1963, pp. 25–43.

PRICING OBJECTIVES [2]

We may seek to achieve a variety of goals by pricing. Some of the most frequently stated objectives are

1. Attainment of *a target rate of return.* Prices are set so that they will yield some designated return on investment. (See pages 265 to 267.) This pricing objective has been emphasized by General Motors, International Harvester, and Alcoa.

2. *To maintain or improve the company's share of the market.* This approach has been pursued by A & P, Swift, and Sears Roebuck.

3. *Stabilization of price and margin.* This goal in pricing has been emphasized by Kennecott Copper.

4. *Pricing to meet or follow competition.* Price leadership as a technique is discussed elsewhere in this chapter. Price followership develops when a concern finds out what its competitor is charging and then endeavors to meet those prices. Firms that have pursued this policy include National Steel, Gulf Oil, and Kroger.

5. *Product differentiation given greater emphasis as a selling tool than pricing.* This approach has been followed by General Electric and General Foods.

SETTING INDUSTRIAL PRICES

Pricing is closely related to other business policies including those dealing with sales promotion, wages, finance, and expansion. The pricing process has several aspects—setting the price and the discount structure (cash, quantity, and functional), the goals that pricing may help to attain (e.g., target rates of return, share of the market sought, stability of price), the frequency of price review, price relationships among similar products of different quality and size, and market targets (e.g., geographic market and type of customer).

Nonprice factors such as service, convenience, styling, or special sales efforts may be as effective or more effective in attracting sales than reductions in price in many instances. Thus price decisions are part of the broad marketing strategy.

It must be emphasized that prices cannot be determined by mathe-

[2] For a comprehensive discussion of these objectives in 20 leading industrial firms, see A. D. H. Kaplan, Joel B. Dirlam, and Robert F. Lanzillotti, *Pricing in Big Business,* The Brookings Institution, Washington, D. C., 1958.

matical formulas. In fact, most of the ingredients of a price decision cannot be reduced to numbers. This will be quickly recognized when the main factors in pricing are noted: economic characteristics of the product, level of demand, extent of surplus capacity, domestic and foreign competition, costs, federal and state legislation, political pressures, and public relations. Each of these factors will be discussed below.

Economic Characteristics of the Product

Proper pricing is closely related to the type of product involved and its economic characteristics. The more important economic characteristics may be grouped under two headings, (1) the type of product and (2) the kind and size of firm.

Type of Product

Is it a capital good or a consumer's good? Is it differentiated or standardized? Is it perishable or nonperishable? Is style important? Is it original equipment or a replacement? Is it a durable or nondurable good? These varying economic characteristics will play a primary role in determining the proper pricing policy and tactics. The significance of these characteristics in terms of pricing may be indicated briefly. Thus, in connection with capital goods, the purchaser is motivated primarily by the profit he can make from their use. When large profits can be realized, price plays a subordinate role in the decision to buy. On the other hand, low prices in periods of recession do not induce large demand for capital goods. As a result, sellers have little inducement to reduce prices at such times.

Durable goods provide repeated uses of a product. When incomes decline, consumers tend to postpone the purchase of such products as automobiles and furniture and to utilize those they already own for longer periods. Under such conditions, price reductions tend to have little stimulating effect on demand for consumer durable goods. Nondurable goods, on the other hand, tend to be consumed in one operation —for example, foods and gasoline—and hence are subject to frequent replacement. Price changes can be more effective in steering demand for such products.

A company has more freedom in its pricing when a product is differentiated markedly from competitive substitutes than when it sells a standardized product. This is true even when the products are completely substitutable as in the case of dentifrices or detergents. When products are standardized (e.g., copper and many steel products), producers must charge the same price.

Similarly, the pricing of perishable products involves different problems than the pricing of nonperishable products. The need to dispose of unsold supplies before they spoil and become unsalable often is an important factor for perishables. Style may be important for some products, such as women's clothing. When new styles are introduced, higher prices may be obtained. But new styles are quickly pirated and made available in lower cost models.

When the relative cost of raw materials and/or labor is very high, this factor may play a key role in pricing. A can company, for example, has indicated that its pricing is largely determined by the cost of steel at its factories and by labor costs. For meat and shoes, the relatively high cost of raw materials also is a primary factor in pricing.

Kind and Size of Firm

The size of the firm influences its freedom in pricing. Is the company a multiproduct or single product firm? Is it a price leader or a price follower? Is it a large company or a small one? The answers to these questions influence the pricing policy adopted.

Most companies are multiproduct firms. In such companies it is necessary to delegate responsibility to determine many prices, although broad policy decisions may be made by top management. Multiproduct firms may offer a full line to build up good will for the entire line even though the volume for some products is too small to be profitable. Problems also arise in connection with the determination or allocation of costs.

Different characteristics of products play a key role in determining the appropriate price policy. Hence multiproduct companies must follow varying pricing practices and procedures, depending on the nature of the product and the competitive pressures affecting each product. These different practices, however, are followed within the framework of an over-all policy designed to achieve company objectives.

The Role of Competition

Competitive factors play a key role in price determination by most companies. There may be price competition from other companies making the same product here or abroad or from substitute products produced by other industries. Foreign competition has played an increasingly important role in many industries in the 1950's and 1960's.

The extent of the pressure from competition will depend in large measure on the economic characteristics of the product. For standardized products or those completely substitutable (for example, different brands of toothpaste), competition from other producers in the industry will be a potent factor in pricing. On the other hand, for unique products, highly differentiated products, or those for which style is important, there are varying degrees of insulation from this type of competitive pressure.

The structure of an industry in terms of the number and the size of competitors is important. Some industries are dominated by Big Threes and Big Fours (cigarettes and automobiles), while others have a large number of smaller firms with relatively small volume concentrated in the largest companies (textiles and apparel). Some products are affected significantly by competition from substitute products (butter and flexible packaging materials); for others this is a factor of considerably less importance (bread and milk). Some products are affected by foreign competition to a significant degree (transistor radios and cameras), while for others (dishwashers and furniture) this factor is not very important.

The significance of competitive pressure has been well illustrated by John T. Connor, President of Merck & Company, who has reported that ". . . our files contain multitudes of reports of competitive offerings [of steroids] at lower prices and in the form of free goods and other concessions, many of which we felt it necessary to meet." [3]

Generally, a company must sell the same or similar products at about the same price as its competitors. But it may be difficult to determine exactly what competitors are charging. An interesting illustration of the unsatisfactory state of intelligence concerning competitors' prices developed in 1961 for capacitors. Federal Pacific Electric raised the price to $117 per 50-kvar unit and was followed by Sangamo Electric Co. and Allis Chalmers Co. About the same time, General Electric cut the price to $97.33. As *Electrical World*, a trade publication, reported: "Part of the reason for the two-way stretch is of course lack of communications." [4]

The information concerning competitive prices is not always readily available. However, it can be obtained from a variety of sources including salesmen, customers, competitors' advertising, trade press, public bidding (where that plays a role), and dealers who handle the products of several competitors. Sometimes one division of a multiproduct company buys from a competitor of another division and hence can provide the necessary information concerning prices, discount structures, and, on occasion, probing of the market by competitors.

By relating these data to its own sales and to the reports by salesmen of customer reactions, a company may obtain very useful information. What price will induce customers to shift to substitute products? Do customers favor or oppose foreign sources of supply? How promptly do competitors follow a price change? The answers to such questions can be

[3] "Hearings on Administered Prices," *op. cit.*, Part 14, p. 8030.
[4] *Electrical World* (March 13, 1961), p. 21.

invaluable in reaching decisions concerning competitors' pricing and the timing of changes.

Price Leadership

Many companies, large and small, exercise little or no initiative in the determination of many prices. They compete by following the leadership of other companies which assume the initiative in making changes in prices. To some economists, price leadership reflects "tacit collusion." [5] Tacit collusion is a possibility under these conditions, and price leadership has been practiced in collusive agreements. But price leadership is not necessarily evidence of collusive actions, nor is it usually contrary to the public interest.

Price leadership is particularly important for products which are standardized or which are considered to be completely substitutable for each other. The initiative for price changes usually falls on one or a few of the leading companies in an industry. The price leader determines the timing and magnitude of the price change. Some company must raise or lower price in response to changing conditions, and it is usually one of the leading companies that does so. Such firms often have more adequate staffs to evaluate these developments.

A price leader generally will be reluctant to raise or lower prices in the absence of a major change in the economic conditions affecting the product. The initiating factor may be a significant rise in labor costs, changes in raw material costs, large increases or decreases in demand, changes in the prices of substitute products, a general condition of inflation, or some other development. As a rule, all or most companies in an industry are affected by such developments. This is why price leaders often are followed when they raise prices as well as when they reduce prices.

However, if economic conditions are not favorable for higher prices, price leaders may not be followed. In 1962–1964, price increases were not followed for plywood, polyethylene, tool steel, urea, aluminum siding sheets, refrigerators, and grocery bags, among other products. In 1963, for example, Union Carbide increased the price of acrylonitrile. When American Cyanamid, another large producer, did not change its price, Union Carbide withdrew the increase "in order to remain competitive." [6]

[5] George J. Stigler, *The Theory of Price*, Macmillan, New York, 1952, p. 234.
[6] For brief discussion of other chemicals for which price leaders were not followed see Jules Backman, *Competition in the Chemical Industry*, Manufacturing Chemists' Association, Inc., Washington, D. C., 1964, pp. 37–38, 88–90.

The unwillingness of many companies to follow the leader in the early 1960's suggested that competitive influences as well as economic pressures were of great significance. The general willingness to follow price increases in the earlier postwar years probably reflected the inflationary environment in which those patterns emerged. Prices rise during a period of general inflation. That a large company makes the first move is less important than the fact that competitors are anxious to raise prices, too, and feel that they must wait until the largest companies have done so.

Consistent matching of the prices of one firm by all other sellers over long periods may develop without any agreement and without any coercion by one firm over others. Each firm acting independently in its own interest may compete by following the leadership of another firm and all the firms acting in this manner produce the phenomenon known as price leadership. Competitive conditions rather than changes in costs clearly provide the motivation for price "followership" for most of the companies involved.

The Role of Demand

Public explanations by companies of price changes usually give major emphasis to costs. Nevertheless, demand is of equal, and in some instances of greater, importance than costs. Ralph Cassady has concluded that "Increased demand justifies an increase in price just as much as, and perhaps more than, an increase in cost. . . . Moreover, an increased cost may appear to justify an increased price, but the demand situation may not permit it."[7]

Harlow Curtice, formerly President of General Motors, included "market demand" as one leg in a tripod of pricing factors. "The first leg that any manufacturer must consider is the market in which he sells. . . . Our studies over many years prove conclusively that the size of the new-car market is importantly influenced by the general level of consumer income after taxes."[8]

The number of units of a product sold often is determined by the price charged. For some products, sales can be increased by a relatively larger percentage than the decline in price (an *elastic demand*). The larger volume in units (and revenues), in turn, tends to reduce unit costs by permitting the distribution of overhead costs over more units

[7] Ralph Cassady, Jr., *Price Making and Price Behavior in the Petroleum Industry*, Petroleum Monograph Series, Volume I, Yale University Press, New Haven, Connecticut, 1954, p. 72.

[8] "Hearings on Administered Prices," *op. cit.*, Part 6, p. 2474.

and sometimes by permitting the economies of larger scale production. Thus, price can be a dynamic force which adds to profits where large increases in demand can be tapped at lower price levels. Conversely, this approach is of little value if the potential increase in demand for a product is relatively smaller than the reduction in price (an *inelastic demand*).

Although there is a reluctance to make public statements which indicate that pricing may be based on *what the traffic will bear,* a company on occasion does admit that it has increased its price because of improved demand. Thus, for example, in September 1957 Amerotron Corporation announced it was raising the prices for woolen fabrics to "reflect slightly improved market conditions." [9] When companies price at levels which reflect what the traffic will bear, it is evident that pricing is influenced significantly by demand.

Companies producing new items give considerable emphasis to demand and to the opportunities available to broaden the market by reducing price. These companies recognize that effective demand may increase as the price is lowered. The question that a company must answer is whether the increase in volume of sales at the lower price will be sufficient to compensate for the lower revenues per unit and bring about a rise in total profits. DuPont frequently has announced price reductions to broaden the market for its products (methanol, dacron, silicon).

Henry Ford, Sr. was an outstanding practitioner of price cuts to stimulate demand and profits. In his words:

> My policy is to reduce the price, extend the operations, and improve the article. You will notice that the reduction of price comes first. . . . I first reduce the price to a point where I believe more sales will result. Then we go ahead and try to make the price. . . . One of the ways of discovering what a cost ought to be is to name a price so low as to force everybody in the plant to the highest point of efficiency.[10]

To determine whether price reductions will stimulate demand sufficiently to make the change profitable, a company may experiment with a new price in one or more localities. Care must be taken to ensure that such experimentation does not violate the Robinson-Patman Act. If the results in the test area are successful, it can then extend the lower price

[9] *The Wall Street Journal* (September 24, 1957).
[10] Edward A. Filene, *The Way Out,* Doubleday, Page, Garden City, New York, 1925, pp. 100–101.

to other areas. In other instances, the decision as to the price set may be based on comprehensive market studies.

Consumer survey research often is undertaken in connection with new products. For example, General Electric followed this approach in connection with a cordless automatic toothbrush that it was planning to market at $19.95 as compared with the average price of about 50 cents for an advertised brand of a conventional toothbrush. A survey in the Boston area revealed that two-thirds of those interviewed were willing to purchase the item. Tests also were made in Chicago and New York. The company concluded that people would be interested in the electric toothbrush even though the price was about 40 times greater than that for conventional toothbrushes.[11]

A company should also review its past experience and, where possible, that of its competitors with similar products. Of course, the availability of this alternative depends on the records maintained—and too often they are inadequate or nonexistent. Whenever a new experiment in price reduction is undertaken, it would be desirable to compile a complete story of its impact on demand, the reactions of dealers and customers, and the promptness with which competitors meet the price reduction. Such a record will prove valuable in connection with future experiments of a similar nature.

The Role of Costs

In the period following World War II there developed a widespread belief that a company sets prices by determining its unit costs to which it adds a liberal profit margin. This belief was encouraged by the standards used in connection with wartime price fixing and in renegotiation of government contracts and by the periodic statements of company officials that prices had to be raised because of higher costs. The price increases in the latter case really were obtainable because of the general inflation prevailing.

In many instances the cost explanation appears to be a publicly acceptable rationale for price increases. The fact that rising incomes and demand make it possible to pass on higher costs to the customer commonly is ignored in public explanations of price rises. But clearly it is a power factor. Very rarely will a company indicate that it expects consumer acceptance of the higher price. An exception was Seymour J. Phillips, President of Phillips-Van Heusen Corporation, who announced a price increase for shirts in an advertisement in April 1960 and frankly

[11] *Printers' Ink* (July 20, 1962), pp. 44–45.

stated: "The consumer is well conditioned to price increases in all categories of merchandise, and we strongly predict that he will accept the new $4.50 price." [12]

While sellers would like to recover all costs plus an adequate profit on each product, there is no assurance that they can do so. Other factors, such as the level of demand, competition, and excess capacity, may make it impossible to recover all costs.

Economists generally point out that in the long run price and cost tend to converge under conditions of competition. This is sometimes erroneously interpreted to mean that costs determine price. Actually, the economist is describing tendencies in the economy and the manner in which cost-price relationships operate to allocate resources rather than the way in which prices are set in industry. Thus, when costs and prices are out of line, forces are set into motion to bring them together. If costs are above prices, profits disappear, marginal producers may be forced out of the industry, and marginal facilities may be abandoned.

In this connection, *Business Week* reported that for electrical appliances the following changes had developed:

> . . . The Crosley-Bendix division of Avco Manufacturing Company is halting its sales of room air conditioners, chest freezers, water heaters, and garbage disposal units. Motor Products Corporation closed down its Deep-Freeze division—a brand that gave a generic name to the type of appliance—after operating at a loss for 2½ years. . . . In the last two booming years, the ranks of makers of home freezers were dropped from 52 to 32.
>
> But the sharpest cutbacks have come in room air conditioners and TV sets. Two years ago, the Air Conditioning and Refrigeration Institute took a survey at the peak of the manufacturing craze, counted approximately 100 companies selling air conditioners. At the last check, three months ago, the number was down to 50, and there has probably been some drop since. . . .
>
> Among TV brands, the slaughter has been even rougher. At the peak a few years back, almost 175 "makers" had their brands on TV receivers. Today about 50 are still selling sets. [13]

Conversely, if profits are very attractive and entry is free, new producers may be induced to enter the industry. At the same time, existing producers may expand their capacity. The result is an increase in supply and the establishment of new cost-price relationships. The large increase

[12] *Daily News Record* (April 4, 1960).
[13] *Business Week* (October 8, 1955), p. 43.

in the number of electronics companies in the 1950's and 1960's illustrates these tendencies. Costs and prices must be out of line and profit opportunities must appear to be attractive to set these corrective actions into operation.

A consideration of costs as *one* factor in pricing is a markedly different situation from setting prices on the basis of costs. This is recognized in other countries as well as in the United States. A study of Danish pricing, for example, pointed out: "A much more common feeling . . . is that the calculated product cost must be regarded as advisory and only as an indication of the price which ought to be set. The calculated product cost, therefore, must be considered as point of reference for further deliberations." [14]

The danger of basing prices on costs has been described by Robert C. Gunness, a Vice-President of Standard Oil of Indiana, who reported that until the early 1930's that company set its price by adding to the refinery price transportation to the community in which gasoline was sold. "This charmingly simple state of affairs failed to last." The company then shifted to the price at Tulsa plus transportation to destination. However, ". . . by the fall of 1949 we had completely abandoned the Tulsa-plus formula" as a result of competitive pressures.[15]

A special situation involving costs is found in connection with technological improvements. It is not unusual for companies to announce that prices have been held down or reduced because of advances in technology. Eastman Kodak, for example, has explained that its improvement program enabled it "to keep down selling prices in a period of generally rising costs." [16]

In many such instances it must be recognized that only by reducing prices can the company expand its sales. Although the public emphasis may be given to savings in costs, certainly one objective of a price reduction is to broaden markets. Otherwise the company could increase its profits per unit by retaining the old prices.

Price often determines costs rather than the reverse. This is evident in connection with products, such as apparel, that are sold at customary price lines. The price charged determines the costs that may be incurred. Under these conditions, declining cost often make it possible to offer better quality at the same price, and rising costs lead to a deterioration of quality.

[14] B. Fog, *Industrial Pricing Policies*, North-Holland Publishing Company, Amsterdam, 1960, p. 61. This is an excellent review of the factors affecting pricing in practice.
[15] Robert C. Gunness, "Gasoline Prices and Pricing Policy," a lecture delivered at the University of Chicago, School of Business (January 28, 1959).
[16] Eastman Kodak, *Annual Report*, 1956, p. 14.

Problems of Cost Determination

How are "costs" determined? What is included in "costs"? Are past, present, or future costs included? How is the break-even point determined? What time period is covered? What is done if your competitor has a higher or lower price? Are cost records available in a form useful for pricing? Questions such as the foregoing point up some of the difficulties encountered in attempting to set prices on the basis of costs.

There are many other problems. For example, a report of a Federal Trade Commission Committee pointed out: "Cost accounting is not and can never become an exact science because of the inherent element of judgment. Despite the prescription of uniform and detailed cost accounting procedures, two equally competent cost accountants may obtain different results from the same data." [17] Which set of costs will be used when "equally competent" accountants report different results?

Moreover, the cost data available often are not significant for purposes of pricing. A National Association of Cost Accountants study concluded: "The concepts of cost which are most appropriate for pricing purposes differ in many respects from the concepts of cost used for cost control and financial reporting purposes." [18]

Many costs are joint costs and can only be allocated on an arbitrary basis. If there is a strong demand and a higher price for one product sold by a firm, a larger share of such joint costs may be loaded on that item than on one for which demand is low. In some industries it is impossible to know the exact cost. Boyd MacNaughton, of the Hawaiian Pineapple Company, has commented on the role of joint costs in the production of pineapples as follows:

> We have to admit that any division of fruit cost between various products must be based upon opinion and is without foundation in fact. . . . To illustrate, we cannot grow No. 2½ fruit without producing a quantity of No. 2 and vice versa. Then how can it be said that some definite part of plantation cost is attributable to one size fruit and another certain part tributable to the other? [19]

Multiproduct companies must face this problem of cost allocation all the time. It has been reported that

[17] "Advisory Committee on Cost Justification Report to the Federal Trade Commission," February 1956, reproduced in Herbert F. Taggart, *Cost Justification*, Bureau of Business Research, University of Michigan, Ann Arbor, 1959, p. 560.

[18] *NACA Bulletin* (August 1953), p. 1673.

[19] Boyd MacNaughton, "Product Costs for Pricing Purposes," National Association of Cost Accountants, *Research Series No. 24* (August 1953), p. 1696.

The pricing problem of a firm like Merck that makes and sells thousands of products is not the simple one of setting a price on a single product or even that of setting prices on a series of single products, each in a hermetically isolated environment of market and cost forces, but of pricing a line of products so as to achieve satisfactory distribution of all of them and a profitable relation between the total cash inflow and outflow resulting from all of them. The resulting mosaic represents a situation in which some products are priced at very little above cost or even below total costs, while others must carry offsetting prices which bear little relation to costs. Pricing a line forces pricing at the market with little consideration given to costs.[20]

Cost plays even a less important role in connection with new products than with older ones. Until the market is tested and some idea is obtained as to volume, it usually is impossible to determine unit costs with any accuracy. There is no experience with costs. And the volume achieved will depend on the philosophy of pricing, as is noted later.

In light of the preceding considerations, it seems evident that the role of costs in pricing has been considerably exaggerated. Certainly, costs cannot be ignored in pricing. But neither can many other factors. While cost-price relationships may be important, it does not follow that cost determines price. On the contrary, under many circumstances the flow is in the opposite direction. The price that can be obtained under prevailing conditions of demand and the pressures of competition often determine the costs that a company may profitably incur.

As R. S. Alexander has so succinctly observed: "The idea of setting prices on a cost-plus basis is a beguiling one to logicians and observers with little knowledge of practical pricing problems. Unfortunately, the consumer knows little about the manufacturer's cost and cares less." [21]

Rate of Return Analysis

Rate of return analysis involves a special use of cost as a guide to operating policy and price determination. This approach is used mainly by some large companies which seek to determine the advisability of investment in a particular facility as compared with alternative investment opportunities. The test is the rate of return that can be earned on

[20] Memorandum from R. S. Alexander to Merck & Company included in "Hearings on Administered Prices," *op. cit.*, Part 15, p. 8688.
[21] *Ibid.*

the investment required for a given productive capacity.[22] The procedure may be summarized as follows:

1. Determine the physical investment in tools and structure required to produce the product after making provision for ordinary "down-time" and the peak market demand. Estimate the dollar investment required.
2. Determine the average utilization over a rather long period of time (standard volume) and express this total as a percentage (often about 80%) of theoretical maximum capacity.
3. Estimate the annual overhead cost for the indicated capacity and allocate it over the standard volume to obtain an estimated average unit fixed cost.
4. Estimate average variable unit costs at standard volume.
5. Determine the additional investment in working capital required.
6. Determine the minimum rate of return required to justify the investment; this will vary with the risks involved in the particular investment. Convert this total to a per unit basis at standard volume.
7. The first approximation to the unit selling price is established by adding up the items listed above. This price is then compared to the price being charged by competitors.

If the analysis discloses that the competitive price is lower than that required to achieve the desired rate of return, management will then have to decide whether (1) to proceed with the investment at the lower indicated rate of return, or (2) to redesign the product in order to reduce costs and thus obtain the desired profit margin, or (3) to abandon the project. Ordinarily, it is the second alternative which must be adopted for products the company already is selling.

When volume exceeds standard volume at the estimated costs, the rate of return earned on investment will exceed the average anticipated rate. When volume falls short of standard volume, the return will be less than the anticipated rate. If actual volume equals standard volume, average profits over a period of years will tend to approximate the target. A leading exponent of this method of rate of return and operation analysis has been General Motors Corporation.[23]

[22] The desired rate of return may vary widely. One study showed a range of after-tax profits goals ranging from 8 to 20 per cent on investment. Kaplan et al., *op. cit.*, *passim.*
[23] The earliest public explanation of this policy appeared in 1924. See Donaldson Brown, "Pricing in Relation to Financial Control," *Management and Administration*

General Electric has used this approach to decide whether to expand its facilities for products it is already producing. Under its seven-twenty formula, the decision to expand facilities "should be undertaken only where it is estimated that such investments have prospects of earning a return of at least 7% net of sales after taxes or 20% return after taxes on the money invested in that particular expansion." However, as Ralph Cordiner, former Chairman of General Electric, noted: "It is recognized that in the intensively competitive climate in which we operate, it is the customers, and not the General Electric Company, who determine the return on sales or on investment we can achieve." [24]

Rate of return analysis is a valuable tool to determine whether a particular level of prices will yield a satisfactory return on the investment required to produce designated products. This means that the price obtainable is tested by such an analysis, not that the price is established by adding together standard costs and some desired profit margin.

As Ernest Breech, formerly of the Ford Motor Company, has pointed out, standard prices provide a "useful guide to judgment, but the actual price set may be lower. The final prices are, of course, determined by the competitive situation. . . . We find that the standard price offers a good measuring stick for financial purposes but we know that the real test of our pricing—and of all our policies—comes finally in the market place." [25]

Excess Capacity and Prices

At times, various supply factors have assumed significance in pricing. For example, excess capacity became an increasingly important consideration in pricing starting late in the 1950's. Excess capacity may reflect one of several developments, as these illustrations from that period indicate—a temporary decline in demand (e.g., steel), expansion in response to competitive pressures (e.g., airlines), a permanent decline in demand (e.g., coal), or an excessive increase in capacity because the market has been overestimated (e.g., refrigerators).

Surplus capacity has plagued many industries including aluminum, steel, electrical equipment, and glass. The existence of such excess capacity influences pricing decisions. For example, Pittsburgh Plate Glass

(February, March, and April 1924), pp. 195–98, 283–286, and 417–22. This material is digested in Jules Backman, *Price Practices and Price Policies*, Ronald Press, New York, 1953, pp. 359–365.
[24] From a Press Conference early in 1957.
[25] Ernest R. Breech, "The American Method of Pricing," an address before the American Marketing Association (June 11, 1947), pp. 19–20.

announced that plate glass prices had to be reduced in 1962 because of the overcapacity that characterized the industry.[26]

Overhead costs continue when a plant operates below capacity. However, at low levels of operation, overhead costs must be spread among fewer units, thereby raising unit costs. Thus there is a strong incentive to accept new orders which make some contribution for overhead charges even though they do not yield a profit.

Under some circumstances price cutting becomes so severe that too much business may be accepted at prices involving substantial losses. A company must decide to what extent it will lower its prices and the maximum volume that will be sold at these low prices. Beyond that point it should forego orders.

Geographic Pricing

Goods often must be transported a great distance and hence transportation charges may be a significant element in the determination of some prices. Two broad approaches to geographic pricing may be distinguished, f.o.b. (free on board) pricing and delivered pricing. Under *f.o.b pricing* the producer sells to all customers at the same price at his plant. The price quoted includes the expense of placing the goods on the transportation vehicle at the producer's plant. The customer takes delivery at that point and pays the cost of transportation himself. Although the selling company receives the same price from all buyers under this system, the final cost to the buyer varies, depending on the cost of transportation.

Delivered pricing systems include postage stamp pricing, zone pricing, freight equalization, and basing point pricing. The price quoted includes transportation to the plant of the customer. Thus the customer buys a combination of transportation service and the product. The seller usually receives varying net mill prices, while all customers in a given locality pay the same price regardless of the producer from whom they buy or the location of the seller's plants from which the product is shipped.

Under *postage stamp pricing,* a company sells its product at the same price for delivery any place in the country. Many drug products, cosmetics, and candy bars are sold in this way.

Under *zone pricing,* the market is divided into zones with a single delivered price for each zone. The number of zones is determined by the relative importance of transportation costs. Where such costs are

[26] For experience in the chemical industry, see "Competition in the Chemical Industry," *op. cit.*, pp. 32–33, 86–87.

relatively high the zones tend to be smaller. This type of pricing has been used for some electrical appliances, business furniture, and paints.

Under *freight equalization,* the customer pays the lower transportation charge at which he could obtain delivery from a competing seller. If the seller charged an f.o.b. uniform price to all customers, he would not be able to compete for distant customers because the customer must pay the full freight to his plant. Accordingly, the seller absorbs the difference in freight costs. In this manner he is able to seek business in more distant markets but must accept a lower mill net than he obtains on nearby sales. The steel industry has followed this type of pricing since it abandoned multiple basing point pricing in 1948.

Under the *single basing point system,* the price of a product at any destination point is the cost in the basing point city plus the cost of all rail freight from that city to the destination regardless of the location of the plant from which it is shipped.

Under the *Pittsburgh plus* system used by the steel industry until 1924, for example, the price to any customer was the cost in Pittsburgh plus the freight cost from Pittsburgh to that destination. This price was quoted regardless of the location of the plant from which the steel was shipped. For maple flooring this system was known as Cadillac plus, for cast iron pipe as Birmingham-plus, and for corn syrup and malt as Chicago-plus.[27]

Under the *multiple basing point system,* several basing points are designated. Usually any plant which produces more than can be sold in its general vicinity will be designated as a basing point. The price to any destination is the lowest combination of base price plus all rail freight. In the Cement Case,[28] the Supreme Court held that "concerted maintenance of the basing point delivered price system is an unfair method of competition prohibited by the Federal Trade Commission Act. . . ."

Legal Factors

Price administrators must keep in mind a number of federal and state laws as well as precedents established by court decisions.[29] Any collusion with competitors in setting prices is a *per se* violation of the Sherman Act. Charging different prices for the same product to com-

[27] Clair Wilcox, *Public Policies Toward Business,* Richard D. Irwin, Homewood, Ill., 1960, p. 268.
[28] *Federal Trade Commission v. Cement Institute, et al.,* 333 U.S. 683–729 (1948).
[29] For a comprehensive evaluation see *Report of the Attorney General's National Committee to Study the Antitrust Laws,* U.S. Government Printing Office, Washington, D.C. (March 31, 1955).

parable buyers involves price discrimination under the Robinson-Patman Act.[30]

Court decisions may make today's legal pricing illegal tomorrow. This is what happened in connection with basing-point pricing in the 1940's.[31]

Prices charged for raw materials and for fabricated products by an integrated company must be kept in such a relationship that independent fabricators cannot be squeezed. Thus, in a court decision Alcoa was enjoined "from selling aluminum ingot for the fabrication of aluminum sheet or aluminum alloy sheet at higher than fair prices, if the fabricator of such sheets is thereby prevented from fabricating and selling (those products) at a reasonable profit, provided that such fabricator is efficient, well-equipped and otherwise able to fabricate and sell such sheet on a fully competitive basis." Alcoa also was enjoined from selling aluminum sheet and aluminum alloy sheet "at prices below its selling prices for aluminum ingot plus the cost of manufacturing and selling such sheet." [32]

United Shoe Machinery Company had to price its machines for sale after the court declared it could no longer confine its activity to leasing.[33] International Business Machines agreed to follow a similar policy.

The so-called fair-trade laws affect the retail pricing of many products, including drugs and appliances. Since 1959 a number of state laws have been invalidated, thus reducing the effectiveness of fair-trade pricing in many areas. In 1960 the Supreme Court limited certain types of enforcement of fair-trade pricing.[34]

The price-fixing conspiracy disclosed in the electrical machinery industry in 1960 came as a shock to corporate officials throughout our economy. It undoubtedly resulted in a review of practices by many companies. The adverse effect on public confidence, the jail sentences imposed on guilty officials, and the costly financial penalties experienced

---

[30] The most comprehensive review of the Robinson-Patman Act is found in Corwin D. Edwards, *The Price Discrimination Law*, The Brookings Institution, Washington, D. C. (1959). For a discussion of the impact of this law on the pricing policies of A & P, see M. A. Adelman, *A & P: A Study in Price-Cost Behavior and Public Policy*, Harvard University Press, Cambridge, 1959.

[31] See *Corn Products Refining Company v. Federal Trade Commission*, 324 U.S. 726 (1945), *Federal Trade Commission v. Cement Institute, et. al.* 333 U.S. 683 (1948) and *Federal Trade Commission v. A. E. Staley Manuacturing*, 324 U.S. 746 (1945).

[32] *U.S. v. Aluminum Co. of America et al.*, U.S. District Court, Southern District of New York, Judgment on Mandate against Aluminum Co. of America et al., Equity 85–73 (April 23, 1946), p. 18.

[33] For a discussion of this case, see Carl Kaysen, *United States v. United Shoe Machinery Corporation*, Harvard University Press, Cambridge, 1956.

[34] *U.S. v. Parke, Davis and Company*, February 29, 1960. See also "The Fair Trade Question," *Studies in Business Economics*, Number Forty-eight, National Industrial Conference Board, New York, 1955.

by the companies involved demonstrated that conspiratorial price-fixing could be very damaging to an industry. The rule is very simple. When in doubt consult your antitrust lawyer and lean over backward to avoid any discussions of prices with your competitors.[35]

Political Pressures

Political pressure has affected pricing by the larger companies in some industries. In this connection Roger Blough, Chairman of the Board of the United States Steel Corporation, told the Kefauver committee that in setting steel prices in 1957: "We took into account the publicly stated desire of not only the President of the United States but of many other people in this country, to act as conservatively as all of us possibly could in this type of situation."[36] In the Spring of 1962 pressure by President Kennedy and other officials played a major role in the rescinding of announced higher steel prices by United States Steel and other leading producers. On the other hand, the President took no action when selective steel price increases were announced in the Spring of 1963.

The significance of political pressures has been increasing. If the proposals made by some groups are followed, prenotification[37] of price increases would have to be given by large companies and then the proposed increases would be subject to public hearings. Under such programs, the importance of political factors would increase significantly.

Public Relations

That companies feel compelled to issue explanations as to why they increase or decrease prices is one of the most interesting recent developments in connection with pricing. Actually, a company is free to set a

[35] For a discussion of the pricing of electrical machinery and appliances see Jules Backman, *The Economics of the Electrical Machinery Industry*, New York University Press, New York, 1962, Chap. V. Thomas M. Kerr, Jr., Chief Counsel, Antitrust Section, Westinghouse Electric Corporation in a speech has stated: "We tell our people there are many legitimate meetings that then turn illegitimate, all of a sudden. You are in a hotel room and you are there for a proper purpose, and then somebody says, 'Well, let's do it this way.' We tell them there has never been a hotel room, and there has never been a room, where there was not a pitcher of water, or perhaps something a little harder to get off a suit, and we suggest that when the improper conduct begins the Westinghouse man is to leave, but in order to create an evidentiary circumstance, he is to leave and spill the water on somebody there." (Thomas M. Kerr, Jr., "The Westinghouse Experience," in *The Climate of Antitrust*, National Industrial Conference Board, New York, March 7, 1963.)
[36] "Hearings on Administered Prices," *op. cit.*, Part 2, p. 298.
[37] "Hearings on Administered Prices," *op. cit.*, Part 11, Washington, D.C., 1959.

price at any level or to make any change in either direction so long as it operates within the framework of the laws described earlier. If the price established is too high, no explanation will overcome the unwillingness of consumers to pay those prices.

One reason for this development is that the corporate image has been a matter of increasing concern to many large companies. One aspect of that image is the reaction of customers to changes in prices. In this connection, one study of big business pricing concluded:

> The management of large corporations explained that they often avoided taking all the traffic would bear because from the standpoint of continuing market response it was wiser not to profiteer. The steel and oil companies, and General Motors, Alcoa, and Goodyear, among others, forsook short-term profits that they could easily have obtained immediately after the Second World War by allowing prices to rise to match the demand.[38]

This factor undoubtedly affects the public explanations offered when price increases are announced. In many instances in the post-World War II years higher costs were considered to be an acceptable reason for higher prices, and hence this factor was emphasized wherever possible. However, when the general inflationary pressures subsided after 1957, many companies found that they could not obtain higher prices despite rising costs and narrowing profit margins. The experience illustrated the public relations aspect of cost explanations of price rises.

The Role of Judgment

Pricing is an art, not a science. The "feel" of the market by the price maker is far more significant than his adeptness with a calculating machine. This is why simple formulas for pricing represent a yearning rather than reality. The various factors affecting prices cannot be fed into a computing machine to determine the "right" price. Basically, it is the judgment of the price maker which is the catalytic agent that fuses these various factors into a final decision concerning price.

Theodore Yntema, Vice-President of Ford Motor Company, has summarized the problem of pricing as follows: "I have sat in the middle of this pricing process and I tell you it is very hard to describe. It is almost as hard to describe as the process by which a man chooses a wife. It is very difficult to explain what goes on in the minds of men." [39] This is a

[38] Kaplan et al., *op. cit.*, p. 269.
[39] "Hearings on Administered Prices," *op. cit.*, Part 6, pp. 2682–2683.

very interesting statement because Dr. Yntema became an official of Ford after many years of service as an academic economist.

At every stage of the pricing process, decisions must be made between alternative interpretations of the pertinent factors, most of which cannot be reduced to figures. They reflect subjective valuations by the price executive. To reach an informed judgment the price maker should have available various types of information, including a complete record of the past price history for the product, the trend of its sales over time, the experience with special deals, and the price lists and advertising of competitors.

The record also should include salesmen's reports on reactions of customers to price cutting and special deals by competitors as well as the company's sales during such periods, special sales campaigns by competitors, reactions of competitors to price moves in the past, the timing of competitors' price changes and the factors that seem to initiate them, and the changing share of the market. Much of this information is never recorded although it may come to the attention of the price maker at some time. But our memories are notoriously bad. If the price maker's judgment is to be *informed*, he must have such information available on a continuing basis.

PRICING NEW PRODUCTS

New products fall into two categories: (1) those which are substitutable for existing products and (2) those which are completely new. For products in the first category a company usually has market guides as to what the price should be. In some instances, the prices of substitute products may provide one benchmark. The various miracle fibers, for example, had to compete directly with natural fibers, the prices of which limited the freedom in setting prices for the new fibers. Similarly, Alcoa introduced aluminum building sheet "at prices competitive with galvanized steel and kindred major building materials." [40]

For a completely new product, such as television sets, no convenient price benchmarks are available. For such products, the philosophy of pricing may be the primary determinant of the initial offering price. Two alternative approaches to pricing new products have been characterized as skimming prices and penetration prices.

A *penetration price* policy uses low price to develop a mass market quickly. If this approach is successful in achieving large volume, it will

[40] *News Releases* (October 5, 1959).

result in low unit costs. Such a low price also will tend to reduce unit profits and hence to discourage would-be competitors from entering the field. In many instances, the pricing officials start with the price that will be low enough to achieve these objectives and then they determine the costs that can be incurred for profitable operations. It is probable that penetration pricing will be most effective for consumers' goods. Detergents and some appliances provide good illustrations.

Under a *skimming price policy* high prices are charged initially to those who are willing and able to pay the highest prices; later the price is reduced. Interesting illustrations are the pricing of ball-point pens and television sets in the early post-World War II years. This approach results in lower volume initially and thus will be accompanied by high unit costs. It will often be used where a product is distinctive and/or entry by competitors is blocked by patents.

Skimming sometimes is considered to be a safe method of pricing where customer acceptability is uncertain and cost reductions are difficult to predict. It also is a desirable method of pricing for products with an inelastic demand. Skimming is designed to finance high development costs or to provide for their recovery more promptly where product obsolescence may be rapid.

Du Pont's philosophy in pricing new products has been summarized as follows:

> . . . a product like nylon, when first introduced, has no established market. It offers properties duplicated nowhere else. However, the manufacturer cannot be arbitrary in setting a price. If he quotes too high a figure, he will drive away potential customers, and restrict the product's future growth. If he quotes too low a figure, he will have no chance to recover his costs and in years to come make a profit. Thus the market and the costs set the introductory price. When and if the market expands, and manufacturing can be made more efficient by virtue of increased volume and improved process equipment, the introductory price can be adjusted downward.[41]

The prices of a number of Du Pont products have been reduced in accordance with this policy. For example, the price of fluoro-alcohols was reduced from a development price of $30 to $40 per pound in 1958 to $10 a year later. The price of lysine amino acid was reduced from $12 a pound to $6 a pound in a similar period. Cellophane was sold at $2.65

[41] *The Story of Competition in the American Market*, E. I. Du Pont de Nemours and Company, 1959, pp. 28–29.

a pound when introduced in 1924 and after 21 price reductions was selling at 40 cents a pound in 1939.[42]

The judgment of corporate executives is of crucial importance in pricing new products. If the price is set too high, the result will be a lower volume of sales. If the price is set too low, volume may be greater, but profits may be too low or nonexistent if the production problems have not been fully solved. Market surveys including test prices in carefully selected markets can provide valuable information for new products.

RETAIL PRICING

Retail pricing is influenced by the various factors discussed earlier. However, there are some special aspects of retail pricing that should be noted.[43] To the retailer, the *gross margin* (the difference between the sales price and the invoice cost as a percentage of the sales price) is more important than the price he charges. The combination of products he offers for sale often will be significantly influenced by the average gross margin sought on total volume.

The margin usually varies widely among the products sold. The primary determinant of the margin for specific goods is the *turnover*.[44] For products which are sold in very large volume (and usually are subject to frequent purchase), the margin tends to be low; it is usually high for products with low turnover. The difference between margins on sugar, bread, and milk, on the one hand, and those for caviar, on the other, are illustrative. The same principle applies as between different types of establishments. Thus grocery stores with their high rate of turnover may operate on margins below 20 per cent, while furniture stores require in excess of 40 per cent.

The amount of service offered also affects the gross margin required

[42] E. I. Du Pont de Nemours and Company, *Product Information Service* (June 26, 1959); *Nutrition News Service* (April 15, 1959); *Press Release* (October 23, 1957).
[43] Two excellent articles describing retail pricing are Oswald Knauth, "Considerations in the Setting of Retail Prices," *The Journal of Marketing*, (July 1949), pp. 1–12 and Q. Forrest Walker, "Some Principles of Department Store Pricing," *The Journal of Marketing* (January 1950), pp. 529–537. See also Stanley C. Hollander, *Explorations in Retailing*, Michigan State University, East Lansing, 1959.
[44] Turnover describes the relationship between sales volume and investment. The larger the size of sales volume in relationship to investment, the smaller the profit margin on sales required to yield a given return on investment. For example, a store with a turnover of five times requires only a 2 per cent profit on sales to earn 10 per cent on its investment, while a store with a turnover of two times requires a profit margin of 5 per cent to obtain the 10 per cent return on investment.

to operate profitably. The discount house with a minimum of service and a very high rate of turnover has been able to operate profitably with a gross margin less than half as large as that of the department store with its emphasis on service, including delivery, credit, more sales personnel, etc. Thus the difference in price between these types of stores reflects to a large degree the difference in service offered and the favorable effect of a high rate of turnover. Similarly, the higher price often charged by the neighborhood store reflects the advantages to the customer of convenience and greater personal attention.

As a result of differentiation of products and proliferation of brand names, nonprice factors are more important than price for many products. Customer loyalty is built up by past performance and extensive advertising. Each manufacturer seeks to pre-empt a share of the market in which he can be protected in whole or in part against the countermoves of other producers. These factors are reflected in the retail prices.

Retail pricing has evolved from a situation where the customer haggled over price to the *one price policy* now in effect in most stores. Such retail establishments as Lord & Taylor, R. H. Macy, and A. T. Stewart pioneered in the adoption of one-price policy in this country. Under such a policy, a store offers the same price to all consumers and will not bargain (haggle) with them.

Merchandise sold at retail often is quoted as *customary, psychological, or odd prices* such as 49 cents and 98 cents. Some consumers have grown so accustomed to these odd prices that it is feared problems might develop if the prices were rounded out to even amounts. As a practical matter, however, the addition of sales taxes for many localities has made these customary prices not too meaningful.

Price lining is the establishment of a designated price at which the product will be sold. The manufacturer then seeks to produce continuously over a long period of time items that can be sold at that price. The product becomes associated in the customer's mind with a designated unchanging price, often a customary price. This type of pricing is characteristic of various apparel lines, such as ladies' coats, suits, and dresses, men's shirts and hats, and some electrical appliances. The price line is maintained and changes are made in size, quality, or style when there are major changes in costs. The changes in the size of the "five cent" chocolate bar since 1940 is a familiar illustration. The price is considered to be unchangeable, but all other aspects of the product can be changed. This is a clear-cut illustration of the price determining the cost that profitably can be incurred.

Markdowns are an important part of retail pricing, particularly in the larger stores. Markdowns refer to reductions in a retail price and fall into three categories: (1) to correct a price that was mistakenly set too high and has proved unacceptable to customers, (2) to dispose of odd sizes toward the end of a season (e.g., dresses, shoes), and (3) as part of a planned merchandising policy (e.g., the announcement of a sale of an important type of product such as chinaware at one-third to one-half of an original price which may be set above the market level to give the appearance of a large slash).

The term *loss leader* is widely used to describe reductions in prices that are designed to induce a greater flow of traffic into a store. There is no agreement on a definition of loss leaders. The term has been used to describe situations varying from prices set below invoice costs to prices which fail to recover invoice costs plus all allocated costs plus a "fair" profit. Legislators have justified the enactment of "fair trade" laws and "loss limitation" laws [45] in part as a defense against the practice of using loss leaders. It is sometimes contended that the retailer must overcharge on other products to offset the "losses" incurred on loss leaders. While this may sometimes occur, such an interpretation ignores the main role of loss leaders, namely, to build up store traffic. It is by increasing the volume of other merchandise sold at the competitive level that the retailer profitably uses loss leaders. In other words, it is a form of advertising, and any costs involved can be recouped from the added volume of sales, not by overcharges on other products.

Bait pricing is a technique that is used in some retail stores. A very low price may be advertised for a product, but the concern then seeks to discourage a prospective purchaser from buying that product. Sales personnel emphasize the disadvantages of the low quality item used as a bait and endeavor to have customers shift to the purchase of better quality and more expensive commodities. The use of this technique on a wide scale will result in complaints to Better Business Bureaus and to the local authorities who then seek to end the practice.

Prestige pricing provides a contrast. Consumers usually believe there is a direct relationship between quality and price. By featuring several high quality expensive items, a store may seek to create an image that it is a high quality store. Sometimes a manufacturer features the fact that a higher retail price is charged for its product and associates that

---

[45] Under "*fair trade*" laws manufacturers may fix the retail prices of trademarked, branded, or otherwise identifiable products. In many states a manufacturer may set a price for the entire state by an agreement with a single retailer (the nonsigners clause). Under the "*loss limitation*" laws a price floor is established on the basis of costs as defined in the state law. The latter laws apply mainly to grocery products.

higher price with superior quality, taste, or satisfaction (e.g., the advertising of Chock full o' Nuts coffee and Bayer aspirin).

CONCLUSIONS AND SUGGESTIONS FOR FURTHER RESEARCH

It is only since World War II that information has become available concerning actual pricing policies and practices. Much of this information is scattered and hence not readily obtainable. When the information is comprehensive and detailed, it soon becomes out of date because no provision is made for updating or for a continuous flow of information. The reason for the paucity of materials is clear. This is a sensitive area to many companies. Publication of detailed information concerning pricing procedures could readily lead to charges of collusive pricing, for it might be interpreted as a form of communication to competitors. Discussion with competitors about pricing is a *per se* violation of the antitrust laws, and hence industrywide statements concerning pricing policy are ruled out. For the same reason, trade associations usually shun the publication of material designed to explain price policies or price procedures.

Nevertheless, it is possible to obtain a considerable amount of information concerning pricing in a particular industry from an examination of the trade press, price catalogues issued by individual companies, annual reports of companies, speeches by company officials, and occasionally from the press releases announcing changes in prices. Certainly anyone interested in pricing in a specific industry should start by mobilizing these "bits and pieces." In many instances a valuable picture of an industry's general pricing practices can be obtained in this way. Wherever possible, it is desirable to attempt to check published statements about a specific company's pricing with that company—unfortunately full cooperation will not always be forthcoming.

An understanding of proper pricing may be obtained despite the paucity of information noted above. Pricing is influenced to a significant extent by the economic characteristics of the product. A full understanding of these characteristics provides the indispensable background to pricing the products involved. There is considerable need for studies of pricing to increase our understanding in this area. The following questions are suggestive:

1. What factors induce a company to change its price? To what degree must they be present before action takes place? Do the same factors trigger price increases and price decreases?

2. What has been the relationship between changes in price and changes in sales? Do special sales have more favorable effects than more permanent price cuts? Do price changes or nonprice factors (quality, style, advertising, brand names) have a greater impact on sales?

3. How significant are price differentials in steering the flow of orders between different qualities or different sizes of the same product?

4. What has been the past pattern of price behavior for the product? Is there a tendency to shade list prices before the quoted price is reduced?

5. What types of discounts are granted and how have they been changed in the past? When a change is desired, is there a greater reliance on changes in discounts or on changes in list prices?

6. Has the emphasis been given to price competition or to nonprice competition? What types of nonprice competition have been emphasized? What form does price competition take—announced cuts in list price, shading of prices for special deals, new discount arrangements, combination deals?

7. What factors are considered in pricing a new consumer good? A new producer good? Does the company follow a consistent policy of high prices initially (skimming) or low prices (penetration)?

8. Which corporate executives participate in pricing decisions? How often are these decisions reviewed?

9. How does a concern react when a competitor offers a special price to obtain a big order?

10. How important is intracompany pricing? What policy is followed in setting prices for such internal sales?

BIBLIOGRAPHY

Administered Prices, Hearings before the Subcommittee on Antitrust and Monopoly of the Senate Committee on the Judiciary, 28 volumes, U.S. Government Printing Office, 1957–1963, for pricing of steel, automobiles, electrical equipment, bread, and drugs.

Administered Prices: A Compendium on Public Policy, Subcommittee on Antitrust and Monopoly of the Senate Committee on the Judiciary, 88th Congress, 1st Session, U.S. Government Printing Office, 1963.

American Management Association, *Pricing: The Critical Decision*, New York, 1961.

Backman, Jules, *Price Practices and Price Policies*, Ronald Press, New York, 1953.

————*Pricing: Policies and Practices*, National Industrial Conference Board, New York, 1961.

———— *Chemical Prices, Productivity, Wages, and Profits*, Manufacturing Chemists' Assn., Washington, D.C., 1964, Chs. 1 and 2.

Dean, Joel, *Managerial Economics*, Prentice-Hall, New York, 1951, Chs. 7–9.

Edwards, Corwin, *The Price Discrimination Law*, The Brookings Institution, Washington, D.C., 1959.

Haynes, Warren W., *Pricing Decisions in Small Business,* University of Kentucky Press, Lexington, 1962.

Karger, Theodore and Thompson, G. Clark, "Pricing Policies and Practices," *The Business Record,* National Industrial Conference Board, New York, September 1957.

Kaplan, A. D. H., Dirlam, Joel B., and Lanzillotti, Robert F., *Pricing in Big Business,* The Brookings Institution, Washington, D.C., 1958.

Nourse, Edwin G., *Price Making in a Democracy,* The Brookings Institution, Washington, D.C., 1944.

Oxenfeldt, Alfred R., *Pricing For Marketing Executives,* Wadsworth Publishing Co., San Francisco, 1961.

United States Steel Corporation, *Steel vs. Inflation,* New York, 1957.

11

Trading Areas

JAC GOLDSTUCKER

INTRODUCTION

A firm's location is a significant ingredient for generating sales. The American business executive is seldom, if ever, satisfied with his firm's present sales volume. A strong feeling exists within the business community "that permanent injury is being done to a business that permits its total sales volume to decline sharply (even though all of its rivals are experiencing the same decline) and that it is desirable to expand sales even at the sacrifice of profits . . ." [1] This statement suggests that there are more than material returns involved in many executive decisions. Perhaps more important is the egotistic satisfactions which accrue to the executive from his identification with a large and powerful enterprise.[2]

The impetus for growth and power is present within the executive. However, he must develop a strategy to translate this drive into action. Merchandising, in its broadest meaning, is the strategic weapon on which executives can rely to increase a firm's sales. Astute buying, forceful and well-timed promotion and provisions for service are among the factors which comprise the firm's strategy for growth and power.

The merchandising strategy influences customers to patronize one firm rather than another. In many cases (such as retail stores) the pressure is to persuade the customer to travel from his base to a given store location. In other circumstances, a firm sends salesmen to seek out

[1] A. R. Oxenfeldt, *Industrial Pricing and Market Practices*, Prentice-Hall, Englewood Cliffs, New Jersey, 1951, pp. 178–179.
[2] The entire subject of size, growth, and prestige as management incentives is explored in W. G. Scott, *Human Relations in Management*, Richard D. Irwin, Homewood, Ill., 1962, Ch. 17.

potential patrons. The salesmen hope to find a receptive audience already favorably conditioned by the firm's strategy.

Growth stimulates growth. Therefore, as a firm increases in size, it tends to seek sales over larger and larger geographic expanses. It is apparent that beyond some point geographic distances become so great that buyers and sellers lose contact. It is then that vendors—manufacturers, wholesalers, and retailers—attempt to narrow the breach. Firms which operate branch plants, branch warehouses, and multiple stores use the approach of multiple unit operation toward that end. They recognize that customers will endure only limited inconveniences in seeking a vendor, particularly when alternatives are available. Therefore the executive must in the long run locate his branches so that they are convenient to the customers. However, this decision also involves cost considerations.

Size, growth, and power are no doubt valued for reasons not fully explained by material gain. Nevertheless, material gain, in the form of profit, assures that resources will be available to perpetuate and expand the enterprise. Therefore, location decisions are inextricably enmeshed with costs. The costs involve physical effort by the seller in supplying the consumer and physical effort and inconvenience on the part of the consumer to secure the products. These costs are generally expressed as utility or satisfaction from the point of view of the consumer and profit from the businessman's point of view. *Thus, a "natural" trading area might be defined as an area in which the costs of contact between buyers and sellers are minimal.* Where contact costs are minimal, the satisfactions of both consumers and businessmen must be optimal.

For decades trading area analysts have tried to define, in general terms, the greatest geographic area over which buyers and sellers can maintain contact while still optimizing their respective satisfactions and profit. This goal requires that analysts identify variables affecting consumer satisfaction and businessman's profit. Then, it is necessary to develop yardsticks in order to measure optimum profit and optimum satisfaction. For only through such measures can the appropriate intensive and extensive limits of a trading area be set.

The task is difficult as it presents a two-faced problem. One of the problems is that thus far no one has discovered all the variable components of consumer utility or satisfaction. In addition, while some variables are known, means of measuring and weighting them are unavailable. The second problem concerns businessmen's profits. This problem is also one of identifying and measuring variables comprising costs of contacting the consumer. Accountants find that marketing or distribution cost components—advertising, personal selling, packaging—

are difficult to measure.[3] Therefore, with respect to quantifying consumer utility and marketing costs, the difficulty involved in developing yardsticks to measure trading areas has not yet been overcome.

This chapter is devoted to a survey of the available knowledge concerning the dimensions of retail, wholesale, manufacturing and extractive trading areas. The purpose is to focus attention on what we know about trading areas, what gaps exist in our knowledge, and the direction which further inquiry might take to fill in these gaps. This in turn should advance understanding of trading areas and hence contribute to their more efficient coverage with benefits accruing both to business and to consumers.

LOCATION OF ECONOMIC ACTIVITY

The location and development of economic activity have long been of interest to geographers and sociologists, who developed a general principle which is the basis for trading area concepts. They pointed to the natural tendency toward the centralization of human activities and institutions. The result is that the "central place" dominates the activities of the surrounding population.[4]

The establishment and growth of towns and central places, between the lower Rhine and the Seine in the Middle Ages, were the result of the relationship between defense and trade.[5] Merchants did not realize enough business in one place to sustain themselves. Hence, they moved from place to place. As they traveled, they needed resting places and storage facilities for their stock of goods. This was particularly important during winter months. The greatest safety was under the protection of an abbey or fortress; traders attached themselves to such a complex, not unlike a present-day suburb. Artisans attached themselves to the community to provide the traders with wares to sell. Tavernkeepers joined the group to supply food and drink. Groups of boatmakers, longshoremen, and others who provided transport vehicles and facilities also gathered together. Eventually the economic power of the trading complex grew and attracted larger and larger populations. Soon this economic power exceeded that of the abbey and fortress so that their positions became subservient to the needs of the larger community.

A combination of religion, refuge, and a rich consumer fostered the

[3] C. T. Horngren, *Cost Accountancy*, Prentice-Hall, Englewood Cliffs, New Jersey, 1962, p. 517.
[4] W. Christaller, *Die Centralen Orte in Suddeutschland*, Erlangen, 1933.
[5] This discussion is based on H. Heaton, *Economic History of Europe*, Harper, New York, 1948.

development of towns. In order to grow, however, a town must possess economic or geographic advantage. If the town had a strategic defense position, a dominant location with respect to trade routes, and agricultural or mineral resources, its growth and effectiveness could be favorably predicted almost with certainty. The town's economic importance was dependent upon its location and its site.

Location was important in terms of collecting, sorting, and dispersing the products of the area. This was true of both mining and agricultural areas. At the seaside centralized pockets developed to catch, process, and ship fish. In textile areas there was also need for centralization to weave, dye, finish, and sell the textiles. The wider the trade movements, the greater the need for central places to serve as resting places, storage places, and points for transshipment.

The factors just mentioned fostered the location of a town in a certain district but did not determine the actual site of the town within that district. Deciding the site was a function of its suitability for defense and of its command over roads and waterways. Towns developed where trade routes crossed, where natural transshipment points existed, or on the highest point that ships could reach on navigable streams.

This centralization of people into central places resulted in considerable industrial development. Areas which had surplus ore, for example, did more than simply accommodate local demand. Incentive for greater returns encouraged metal fabricators to expand output and to supply deficient areas. Monasteries, taking advantage of natural resources, produced surplus wines, leather goods, and other commodities and engaged in trade of these surpluses. Industry and trade were established and grew.

Heaton's observations about the location, growth, and development of medieval towns and industry partially explain the growth of certain American cities, such as Chicago, Salt Lake City, and San Francisco. Many of these major cities started as defense outposts located on or near navigable waterways or at cross country transit routes which offered the least formidable barriers to access.

The preceding is a brief synthesis of the determinants of location and development of towns, industry, and trade. More formal interest in location theory, however, has prevailed since the early nineteenth century.[6] A major, modern definitive work in the field was written by August Losch, *The Economics of Location*.[7] Hoover and Isard also made

[6] A. Muller, *Die Elemente der Staatskunst*, 3 Berlin 1809; J. H. von Thunen, *Der Isoliente Staat in Befiehung auf Landwirtschaft und Nationalokonomie* (Hamburg, 1826), and A. Weber, *Ueber den Standort der Industrien*, Part I, Reine Theorie des Standorts, Tubingen, 1909.

[7] A. Losch, *The Economics of Location*, Yale University Press, New Haven, Conn., 1954.

important contributions.[8] Losch's study involved the theory of the location of agriculture, industry, and individual firms.[9] He also discussed "reasons for town settlement" and characteristics and influences of economic regions.[10]

An economic region is defined as follows: (1) one center of economic control, (2) greater internal homogeneity than would be the case if it merged with contiguous areas, (3) a characteristic group of import products, and (4) a characteristic group of export products.[11] Located within each economic region are cities, towns, and villages. As the population has become increasingly urbanized, the resulting agglomerations have been the bases for the Standard Metropolitan Areas concept used by the Bureau of the Census.[12] These metropolitan areas frequently provide an environment for centers of economic control.

The total economic activity within one region is made up of a wide variety of firms and industries which are most likely located within the region's metropolitan areas. These retail, wholesale, and manufacturing firms view the geographic expanse as a trading area. The extent of a firm's trading area depends on a variety of things which will be discussed later. Nevertheless, there is an idea that a given firm (and a given community as well) has a "natural" trading area which it *should* serve. This area is not necessarily consistent with its *actual* trading area.

Given the proper set of assumptions, one can safely theorize about the most likely shape of trading areas. A good beginning is to consider Marshall's definition of a "market":

> Thus the more nearly perfect a market is, the stronger is the tendency for the same price to be paid for the same thing at the same time in all parts of the market: but, of course, if the market is large, allowance must be made for the expense of delivering the goods to different purchasers; each of whom must be supposed to pay, in addition to the market price, a special charge on account of delivery.[13]

Marshall focuses attention on price and geographic outreach in a perfectly competitive market. He implies that the geographic area of a

[8] E. M. Hoover, *The Location of Economic Activity*, 1st ed., McGraw-Hill, New York, 1948, and W. Isard, *Location and Space Economy*, Wiley, 1956.
[9] Losch, *op. cit.*, Chs. 2, 4, and 5.
[10] Losch, *op. cit.*, Part A.
[11] See R. L. Vaile, E. T. Grether, and R. Cox, *Marketing in the American Economy*, Ronald Press, New York, 1952, pp. 488 ff.
[12] Bureau of the Budget, Executive Office of the President, *Standard Metropolitan Areas*, July 28, 1950.
[13] A. Marshall, *Principles of Economics*, 8th ed., 1956 reprint, Macmillan, London, pp. 270–271.

market depends on the price of the goods plus the cost of transporting them. The higher the price (including the price of the transportation), the smaller will be the area of demand and the wider the area of supply. Secondly, by focusing attention on the geographic expanse of the trading area, it is practical to apply this type of definition to many marketing problems. For example, in the marketing of a homogeneous product like cement, geography is a prime consideration.[14]

If firms operated in a perfect market, they would tend toward equal size and the market for each firm would be a circle.[15] Until all space was occupied, new firms would find it profitable to enter. With all space finally occupied, the trading area of each firm would be hexagonal.[16] These hexagons, absorbing all space, would take on the appearance of a honeycomb as illustrated in Figure 11.1.[17]

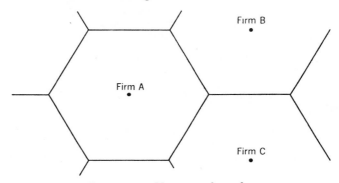

Figure 11.1 Honeycomb markets.

These assumptions of symmetry obviously do not apply in the real world. Firms are not the same. Their offerings differ. In the real world, the determinants of the dimensions of trading areas are believed to be (1) the extent of product differentiation and the relative effectiveness

[14] G. J. Stigler, *The Theory of Price*, revised ed., Macmillan, New York, 1952, pp. 55–56.

[15] Market boundaries are also discussed by F. A. Fetter, "The Economic Law of Market Areas," *Quarterly Journal of Economics*, Vol. XXXVIII (May 1924), pp. 520–530; also A. Losch, *op. cit.*, pp. 105–108.

[16] The theory of hexagonal trading areas assumes that the firms in the industry are symmetrical with respect to buyers as well as to each other. See A. Losch, *op. cit.*, Ch. 10 and E. Ullman, "A Theory for the Location of Cities," *American Journal of Sociology*, Vol. XLVI (May 1941), pp. 853–864.

[17] S. Valavanis, "Losch on Location," *American Economic Review*, Vol. XLV (September 1955), p. 640, and E. S. Mills and M. R. Lav, "A Model of Market Areas with Free Entry," *The Journal of Political Economy*, Vol. LXXII (June, 1964), pp. 278–288.

of brand promotion, (2) the range of choice in administered pricing made possible by product differentiation, oligopoly, and other influences, (3) the ratio of fixed to total costs, (4) the economies of scale of production at each center, (5) the burden of transfer costs in total delivered prices to customers, and (6) the availability of adequate markets within a radius of economical outreach.[18]

These factors can be applied to explain the pattern of trading area coverage by manufacturers, wholesalers, and retailers. They influence decisions with respect to branch merchandising, chain store location and multiregion establishments by manufacturers, distributors, and retailers. They explain why some types of products are sold over limited geographical expanses while others are sold over vast areas. They explain why some firms in the same industry are local and others are regional.

These brief comments on some of the theories of location provide sufficient background for an examination of the available trading area knowledge. Products are made either to be consumed directly or are made to facilitate the production of goods used to produce consumer goods. Therefore, it seems logical to begin with a discussion of retail trading areas. The discussion then moves to considerations of wholesale, manufacturing, and extractor trading areas.

RETAIL TRADING AREAS [19]

The retailer who understands (knows) certain characteristics of his trading area is in a position to make more accurate business decisions with respect to sales forecasting, financing, and budgeting activities. Merchandising and promotion policies are more likely to reflect the tastes and preferences of consumers. Indeed, such knowledge aids in determining when and where to open new branches as well as their most appropriate nature and characteristics. Finally, familiarity with the many facets of the trading area is of benefit to the entire community. Merchants can organize cooperative activities directed at known rather than unknown or fancied objectives, the result being progress and development within the community.

---

[18] R. S. Vaile, E. T. Grether, and R. Cox, op. cit., pp. 525–526.
[19] Several basic texts in marketing and in retailing discuss retail trading areas. See W. R. Davidson and P. L. Brown, Retailing Management, 2nd ed., Ronald Press, New York, 1960, Chs. 3 and 4; D. J. Duncan and C. F. Phillips, Retailing, Principles and Methods, 6th ed., Richard D. Irwin, Homewood, Ill., 1963, Ch. 4; E. A. Duddy and D. A. Revzan, Marketing, An Institutional Approach, 2nd ed., McGraw-Hill, New York, 1953, Ch. 23; and R. S. Vaile, E. T. Grether, and R. Cox, op. cit., Ch. 27.

Factors Influencing Retail Trading Areas [20]

Product

The class of product influences retail trading areas. By definition, there are fewer substitutes for specialty goods than there are for convenience and shopping goods, and the demand is more limited and diffused. As a result, trading areas for specialty goods are typically more extensive than they are for convenience and shopping goods. Hence within a community the trading area for retail firms handling one class of goods differs from that of firms selling other classes.[21]

If one defines product to include not only the merchandise item itself but also the brand name, the service, prestige, and location of the store, then even among stores of the same general class there is variation in trading areas. A specialty store such as Saks Fifth Avenue, because of its great prestige, serves a larger trading area than would likely be served by a store which carries identical merchandise but which fails to achieve a comparable reputation.

Variations within a Store

Variations within a given store also influence the store's trading area. For example, a department store which stocks convenience, shopping, and specialty goods might find that its trading area varies for each class of good. Furthermore, the extent of the trading area for each class is influenced by the others. A store noted for its specialty goods offerings may have a greater trading area for its convenience and shopping goods than is typical. Customers coming from afar to buy the specialty goods are likely to buy other types of goods as well.

Comparative Prices

A retailer can expand his selling area by reducing price on nationally recognized brands of merchandise if rivals do not retaliate. Thus one finds that large retailers, buying large quantities of merchandise at a discount, can sell at lower prices and over greater distances than can their smaller competitors.

Product prices altered by government action change the retail trading area. For example, a city sales tax increases the price of goods. In a community such as New York City there is a great deal of inter-

[20] The list of factors and the discussion are from R. S. Vaile, E. T. Grether, and R. Cox, *op. cit.*, pp. 557–567, where they are discussed in greater detail.
[21] See R. Cassady, Jr. and H. Ostlund, *The Retail Distribution Structure of the Small City*, The University of Minnesota Press, Minneapolis, 1935.

territorial travel (commuting between the city and New Jersey or Connecticut). Commuters can delay the purchase of many items until they arrive in the low cost territory.[22]

There is also another similar type factor affecting price and trade territories. Resale price maintenance can diffuse trade. If a customer must pay the same price no matter where he made the purchase, he will tend to buy at the nearest store. The lack of resale price maintenance in Missouri had a definite effect on sales of appliances in East St. Louis, Alton, and Woodriver, Illinois. It was only a 15-minute drive to St. Louis from these communities. The saving resulting from lower Missouri prices was worth the effort involved in going from the Illinois communities to Missouri. Some states provide for "transition" areas which allow a little relief for those border retailers who are affected. This is further proof of the effect of such laws on retail trading areas.

The Automobile

The automobile has had both a centralizing and decentralizing effect on the extent of retail trading areas. It has enabled people, urban and rural, to reach the central business district with greater facility. This extended the outreach of larger centers at the expense of the small country villages. Thus, the automobile along with improved highways contributed to the centralization of trading areas.

The increased number of automobiles in use has generated traffic congestion in central areas. This has encouraged consumers to seek more accessible areas in which to shop. Suburban shopping centers with branches of major central city retailers and containing ample parking have developed to meet these needs. The result is decentralization within a retailing trading area. This decentralization process might be viewed as a source for new small trading areas.[23]

Growth of Metropolitan Areas

The increase in population plus the movement from rural to urban areas have resulted in the marked growth of cities and their suburbs. In most cases, while both cities and suburbs have grown, suburban in-

---

[22] See "City Told Taxes Drive Out Trade," *New York Times*, Vol. 602, No. 38 (May 17, 1963), p. 1 and p. 22 and "A 5% Sales Tax Rate Looms for Pennsylvania," in Tax Report of *Wall Street Journal*, Vol. 53, No. 154 (May 22, 1963), p. 1.
[23] See W. K. Bowden and Ralph Cassady, Jr., "Decentralization of Retail Trade in the Metropolitan Market Area," *Journal of Marketing*, Vol. V, No. 3 (January 1941), pp. 270–275; and Ralph Cassady, Jr. and W. K. Bowden, "Shifting Retail Trade Within the Los Angeles Metropolitan Market," *Journal of Marketing*, Vol. VIII, No. 4 (April 1944), pp. 398–399.

creases have been at a faster rate. This has given further impetus to decentralization of retail trading areas.[24]

Flow of Goods and of Traffic

The flexibility and growth of transportation facilities have enabled downtown stores to deliver goods over wide areas from decentralized warehouses. Furthermore, traffic flow analysis has facilitated the location and relocation of stores and additional units of chain stores and of branches.

Geography

The geographic location of a retail center influences the extent of its market. For example, the mountains to the west of Denver limit the city's trading area in that direction. The same barriers limit Salt Lake City's area to the east. Chicago and Milwaukee are limited on the east by Lake Michigan.

Miscellaneous Factors

There are additional factors which influence consumer purchasing habits. Outstanding merchandising institutions such as Neiman-Marcus of Dallas exert a greater than average influence on trading areas. The extent of group action also influences outreach. For example, Chicago's State Street Council engages in continuous concerted action to attract customers from the city and suburbs into the Loop shopping area. Cities with convention facilities, artistic and sports activities, and other such attractions are able to draw large transient groups, many of whom buy merchandise while in the center. Finally, Weigand makes the point that the tendency for individuals "to live in one area, work in a second, worship in a third, and recreate in a fourth means that the consumer may shop in any one or more of these areas; or he may confuse the situation by shopping in yet a different one."[25] The point is that different areas have diverse "pulls" on a family. complicating retail trading area analysis.

While it is generally believed that these variables influence the extent of the retail trading area, tools to measure their influence are not avail-

---

[24] See R. Cox, "Impact of Changes in the Size and Structure of Cities," in *Explorations in Retailing*, Stanley C. Hollander (ed.), Bureau of Business and Economic Research, College of Business and Public Service, Michigan State University, East Lansing, 1961, pp. 15–22.

[25] R. E. Weigand, "Exclusive Dealerships—A Different View," *Journal of Retailing*, Vol. XXXVIII, No. 1 (Spring 1962), p. 17.

able. Furthermore, the list probably is not entirely exhaustive. The uncertainty is reflected in such statements as "not too much is known about the whole subject of retail trading areas." [26] The lack of knowledge may be related to the fact that there is a lack of agreement among marketing people as to the precise meaning of the term. The absence of a universally accepted definition hinders formulation of a standard research methodology and of principles universally applicable to trading area analysis.

Some who use the term "retail trading area" do not define it at all. Others define it, but the definitions differ. Each reflects the particular frame of reference or point of view of the user. A review of only a few of the varying concepts will serve to emphasize the point.

One definition is formulated in terms of the commodities being sold. "(A trading area) is a district whose boundaries are usually determined by the economical selling range for a commodity or group of commodities sold by a middleman or a group of middlemen located in the district." [27]

Another concept is of a store trading area. "Markets usually contain stores of different types and sizes. Each store has its own trading area." [28] "Store trading areas are the joint product of many simultaneous interacting factors so numerous that they defy generalization." [29] Defined in terms of an individual retail establishment, a trading area is "that geographic area from which the particular station draws the majority of its business." [30]

Definitions also are framed in terms of a retail trading area of a community. For example, Larson and Poteat state "Trading areas may be defined as those areas in which a seller may reasonably expect to vend a profitable volume of his goods or services. From the viewpoint of the buyer, a trading area is that region inside which he may reasonably expect to find goods and services at competitive and prevailing prices. There are, of course, many refinements to these definitions." [31] Fine defines a community retail trading area as "the area surrounding the

[26] E. A. Duddy and D. A. Revzan, *op. cit.*, p. 401.
[27] National Association of Marketing Teachers, "Definition of Marketing Terms," *National Marketing Review* (Fall 1935), p. 166.
[28] W. Applebaum and S. B. Cohen, "Store Trading Areas in a Changing Market," *Journal of Retailing*, Vol. XXXVI, No. 3 (Fall 1961), p. 14.
[29] *Ibid.*, p. 16.
[30] W. S. Penn, Jr., "Measurement of Service Station Trading Areas," API Publication No. 1546, *Case Histories in Petroleum Marketing*, American Petroleum Institute, New York.
[31] G. E. Larson and M. N. Poteat, "Selling the United States Market," *Domestic Commerce Series, No. 29 (New Series)*, U.S. Department of Commerce, Government Printing Office, Washington, D.C., 1951, p. 13.

community from which it secures approximately 90 per cent of its sales of a representative group of commodities." [32]

It is well recognized that definitions and research methodology with respect to retail trading areas vary widely. Nevertheless, many studies of particular trading areas have been undertaken over the past years by Chambers of Commerce, university research bureaus, private firms, and governmental agencies. [33] These are in the nature of applied research. They are usually concerned with providing insights or solutions to business problems related to trading area analysis. In addition, many other studies attest to the earnest desire to develop definitions and methodology with universal applicability. As a result, several methods have been devised to define and delimit retail trading areas.

Methods Used to Measure Retail Trading Areas [34]

One method is based on an audit of *automobile license numbers*. By identifying the residences of the owners of cars (from state motor-vehicle license records) parked at a store, a shopping center, or the central business district of a community, one could determine from where the particular retail complex draws its customers. These points, plotted on a map, define the particular retail trading area. Of course, the total number of automobiles owned in the area should be determined as a basis for comparison. Furthermore, the sample of the license check should be made on an average day, in order to avoid abnormal influences such as special sales or the Christmas season. [35]

Another method is based on *circulation of newspapers* from competing

[32] I. V. Fine, "Retail Trade Area Analysis," *Wisconsin Commerce Papers*, Vol. I, No. 6, University of Wisconsin, Bureau of Business Research and Service, Madison (January 1954), pp. 10–12. The use of 90% "tends to hold overlap of trading areas between competing centers to a minimum. . . ."

[33] A few such studies are *Retail and Wholesale Trading Areas of Minneapolis and St. Paul*, revised 1951, prepared by the Economic Research Department, Minneapolis Chamber of Commerce; "How to Make a Local Area Trade Survey," Domestic Distribution Department, U.S. Chamber of Commerce, Washington, D.C. (June 1940); *Water for the Future*, Vol. I, "Resources of the Texas Gulf Basin," Bureau of Business Research, The University of Texas, Austin, Texas, 1959. This study consists of several volumes. Volume I indicate that "To facilitate analysis the survey area was divided into subareas called 'trading areas'." (p. 2); F. G. Coolsen and W. S. Myers, *Kentucky Retail Market Areas and Trading Centers*, Bureau of Business Research, University of Kentucky, Frankfort, Kentucky, 1953. G. E. Larson and M. N. Poteat, *op. cit.*, and W. S. Penn, Jr., *op. cit.*

[34] From E. A. Duddy and D. A. Revzan, *op. cit.*, Ch. 23.

[35] F. M. Jones used this method in "A Survey of a Retail Trading Area," *Bureau of Business Research Bulletin 44*, College of Commerce and Business Administration, University of Illinois, Urbana, 1932.

centers. The assumption is that the newspapers draw consumers into the trading center. There is a positive correlation between the sale of shopping goods and newspaper circulation.[36] However, it is not quite clear whether readership leads to buying or whether buying leads to readership.[37] Furthermore, other communication media are directed at influencing retail customers. In considering such factors, it is therefore commonly held that newspaper circulation and retail trade are influenced by the same or similar factors.[38]

A widely used method of defining retail trading area limits is to determine where customers make their purchases. This can be done indirectly by examining the *customers' addresses*.[39] Addresses of credit and cash customers of important stores in competing centers are collected and plotted on a map. The method is used primarily to check shopping goods sales for a limited time period. A direct method of determining where consumers buy is to contact them either by *personal interview* or *mailed questionnaire*.[40]

Batcher used bank checks as a basis for defining the extent of a trading area.[41] Checks used to pay retail accounts are noted as to addresses of the writers as they are given to the retailer and cleared through local banks. These points are mapped and become the basis for determining retail trading areas.

Nelson suggests a method of retail trading area analysis to determine approximate store or shopping center location. This is referred to as the *microanalysis technique*.[42] It requires that the analyst "think deliberately and specifically about small areas that he can more easily understand."[43] Trading areas are first divided into small areas. The

[36] A. S. Donnahoe, "Can Advertising Markets Be Defined Or Measured As Geographical Areas?," *Journal of Marketing*, Vol. XVIII, No. 2 (October 1953), p. 121.
[37] V. W. Bennett, "Consumer Buying Habits in a Small Town Located Between Two Large Cities," *Journal of Marketing*, Vol. VIII, No. 4 (April 1944), p. 414.
[38] This has been noted by E. V. W. Read in "Analysis of Retail Trading Relationships of Elgin, Illinois, A Satellite City," *Journal of Business*, Vol. IX, No. 1, University of Chicago, 1938, pp. 46–47; and W. J. Reilly, *The Law of Retail Gravitation*, 1st ed., University of Texas, Austin, 1931.
[39] W. J. Reilly plotted retail trading areas from charge accounts of department and specialty stores as a basis against which he could compare other methods in checking the operation of his "law." See W. J. Reilly, "Methods for the Study of Retail Relationships," *Bureau of Business Research Monograph No. 4*, University of Texas, Austin (November 22, 1929).
[40] This method is used by V. W. Bennett, *op. cit.*
[41] A. S. Batcher, *A Method of Delineating Retail Trading Zones*, School of Business and Public Administration, University of Arizona, Tucson, 1939.
[42] R. L. Nelson, *The Selection of Retail Locations*, F. W. Dodge Corporation, New York, 1958, p. 148.
[43] *Ibid.*, p. 153.

amount of business available from each one is determined. Customers in the areas are interviewed to see where they live, what their income is, and what their buying patterns are with respect both to where they buy and how much. Nelson indicates that the microanalysis technique has the following advantages: [44]

1. The analyst thinks in units small enough for human comprehension.
2. The detailed study uncovers unusual situations.
3. In this kind of research a multiplicity of judgments does not result in errors that are cumulative.
4. In the process of detailed study, a great deal of information can be uncovered about the trading area and the people in it which will be useful in the design of the store and its promotional activities.

This method is applied in detail in subsequent chapters of Nelson's book. However, the analysis is based on assumed data. Hence, this writer has no basis on which to judge the technique one way or the other. It is primarily a survey technique and in that respect is not unorthodox. The method, however, is an indication of the continuing search for tools to analyze retail trading areas more accurately and more consistently.

Pfanner discusses a statistical method for determining the power which a city has for attracting retail trade. He makes the assumption that a state is a self-contained trading area. Then, by multiple correlation analysis and by using income-tax returns and automobile registrations as independent variables, he estimates from census data the per capita sales of furniture, jewelry, women's apparel, and automobile accessories in 90 cities and by counties for the state of Ohio. "The difference between the estimated sales figure (as reported in the Census of Retail Trade) for that city is the estimate of the amount of trade in a particular commodity group that the city draws from outside its boundaries. This figure, expressed as a percentage of actual sales of a city, is the drawing power of that city." The study also reveals variations among product areas and among cities.[45]

Huff has proposed a method for estimating the "trade potential of prospective shopping developments." [46] He developed a model and de-

---

[44] *Ibid.*, pp. 153–154.

[45] J. A. Pfanner, "A Statistical Study of the Drawing Power of Cities for Retail Trade," *Studies in Business Administration*, Vol. X, No. 3, University of Chicago, 1940, p. 14.

[46] This and the quotation that follows are from D. L. Huff, "A Probabilistic Analysis of Consumer Spatial Behavior," *Emerging Concepts of Marketing*, W. S. Decker (ed.), American Marketing Association, Chicago, 1963, pp. 443–461; also, D. L. Huff, "Defining and Estimating a Trading Area," *Journal of Marketing*, Vol. XXVIII (July 1964), pp. 34–38.

duced mathematical conclusions from it. Next, he used the empirical data gathered from a suburban community in the Los Angeles Metropolitan Area. When he compared the expected consumer behavior with the empirically determined behavior, he found a high positive correlation. This led Huff to conclude that on the basis of his pilot study the model can be used successfully "to estimate demand for agglomeration of retail firms."

Reilly's Law

By far the most widely and consistently used, tested, and discussed technique for measuring retail trading areas is W. J. Reilly's law of retail gravitation. Reilly attempted to formulate a principle which would explain how boundaries of trading areas are determined. The principle can be expressed as a mathematical formula to facilitate the delineation of a center's retail trading area with respect to a competing center in the same geographic area. The law was formulated to apply principally to fashion and shopping goods. It states that "two cities attract retail trade from any intermediate city or town in the vicinity of the breaking point, approximately in direct proportion to the populations of the two cities and in inverse proportion to the square of the distances of these two cities to the intermediate town." [47] The formula which expressed this relationship is as follows:

$$\frac{B_a}{B_b} = \left(\frac{P_a}{P_b}\right) \left(\frac{D_b}{D_a}\right)^2$$

where B_a is the proportion of the trade from the intermediate city attracted by City A

B_b is the proportion attracted by City B

P_a is the population of City A

P_b is the population of City B

D_a is the distance from the intermediate town to City A

D_b is the distance from the intermediate town to City B

Reilly recognized that about a dozen factors influence retail trade. However, he believed population and distance to be reliable indices of the behavior of other factors. Reilly then applied his "law." To test the formula he conducted field studies of pairs of trading centers. The result was sufficient to prove to Reilly that his law worked—that customers between the two cities generally gravitate to the larger city.[48]

[47] W. J. Reilly, *The Law of Retail Gravitation*, 1st ed., The University of Texas, Austin, 1931.

[48] From W. J. Reilly, "Methods for the Study of Retail Relationships," *op. cit.*

This "law" has been the basis for many studies. Some of them apply the formula to determine the retail trading area for a particular community.[49] Others are directed at testing its validity and reliability or at improving the law itself.

Converse made major contributions when he undertook research to verify the Reilly formula.[50] He used Urbana-Champaign and five other competing primary centers as a basis for his research. Thirteen other towns located between Urbana-Champaign and the five primary centers were studied. Converse, using Reilly's formula, predicted the division of trade between Urbana-Champaign and each of the five primary centers. Then, through field research, he surveyed families to determine where they made their shopping goods purchases. He concluded that "on the whole, it (Reilly's law) works rather accurately." [51]

In a later study, Converse tested the law. He again found that the law was substantially accurate. Nevertheless, he cautioned against its indiscriminate use, stressing that his empirical studies included primary trading centers which were substantially larger than the intermediate towns. He suggested that perhaps if the size of the primary and intermediate towns had been more nearly comparable, Reilly's "law" might be less accurate.[52] Douglas, in the reference cited, also found that "Reilly's law of retail gravitation provides a remarkably accurate delineation of the Charlotte retail trading area as judged by the other methods." [53]

Converse developed his "breaking point formula" also to measure the flow of shopping goods trade. It is as follows:

$$\text{Breaking point—miles from } B = \frac{\text{Miles between } A \text{ and } B}{1 + \sqrt{\dfrac{\text{Population of } A}{\text{Population of } B}}}$$

[49] E. Douglas, "Measuring the General Retail Trading Area—A Case Study," *Journal of Marketing*, Vol. XIII, No. 4 (April 1949) and Vol. XIV, No. 1 (July 1949). This study applied four other methods in addition to Reilly's "law" to define the trading area of Charlotte, North Carolina.

[50] P. D. Converse, *A Study of Retail Trade Areas in East Central Illinois*, University of Illinois Press, Urbana, 1943.

[51] *Ibid.*, pp. 44–48.

[52] P. D. Converse, *Retail Trade Areas in Illinois*, University of Illinois, Urbana, 1946.

[53] E. Douglas, *op. cit.*, Vol. XIV, No. 1 (July 1949), p. 60; and V. W. Bennett's study, *op. cit.* The method has received similar confirmation in H. G. Canoyer, "Selecting A Store Location," *Economic Series No. 56*, Department of Commerce, Washington, 1946, p. 9.

The author suggests that Reilly's formula aids in determining how trade between two trading centers should be divided. The "breaking point" formula, on the other hand, can be used to determine a town's normal trading area without performing any field work.[54]

Converse also developed the "new law of retail gravitation," which states that "a trading center and a town in or near its trade area divide the trade of the town approximately in direct proportion to the populations of the two towns and inversely as the squares of the distance factors, using 4 as the distance factor of the home town." [55] The formula is:

$$\frac{B_a}{B_b} = \left(\frac{P_a}{H_b}\right)\left(\frac{4}{d}\right)^2$$

where B_a is the proportion of trade going to the outside town
    B_b is the proportion of trade retained by the home town
    P_a is the population of the outside town
    H_b is the population of the home town
    d is the distance to the outside town
    4 is the inertia factor [56]

Converse suggested that the "new law" has several uses. "It can be applied to satellite towns or other towns inside the trade area of a larger town. It gives an appropriate measure of how the trade is divided without making a survey. Surveys can be made to check actual results against predicted or 'average' results." [57]

R. B. Reynolds tested the Converse formula. He used data of trade movement in Iowa for the years 1935 and 1949 which had been gathered by two Iowa state agencies. As a result of the test, Reynolds suggested that the formula "did not hold in Iowa for the year 1935 unless our sample was remarkably aberrant." [58] This comment was challenged by Converse on the basis that the survey on which the Reynolds study was based may not have been entirely accurate and that Reynolds included products such as groceries and lumber which the formula was not intended to measure. Reynolds subsequently defended his position.[59]

The report of another test of Reilly's law was published by A. F. Jung.

[54] P. D. Converse, "New Laws of Retail Gravitation," *Journal of Marketing*, Vol. XIV, No. 3 (October 1949), pp. 379–380.
[55] *Ibid.*, p. 382.
(October 1953), pp. 170–171, and 172–174.
[56] *Ibid.* The method of testing this formula is discussed in the article, pp. 380–382.
[57] *Ibid.*
[58] R. B. Reynolds, "A Test of the Law of Retail Gravitation," *Journal of Marketing*, Vol. XVII, No. 3 (January 1953), p. 275.
[59] P. D. Converse, "Comment on Movement of Retail Trade in Iowa," and R. B. Reynolds, "A Rejoinder," both in *Journal of Marketing*, Vol. XVIII, No. 2

He suggested that according to the law, citizens of Columbia, Missouri, should have given St. Louis a substantial part of their patronage. Instead they showed little preference between St. Louis and Kansas City.[60] He stated that "the conduct of the residents of Columbia cannot be explained adequately in the light of Reilly's Law of Retail Gravitation. Probably the law does not hold for distances as great as those encountered in this study. Where the size of each city exceeds several hundred thousand people, perhaps it makes little difference to the consumer which city is patronized."

Finally, Schwartz synthesized the empirical studies of the Reilly and Converse laws and concluded that "available information does not offer evidence for a rejection of the laws." However, he questioned "whether the formulas can yet be regarded as marketing *laws*." [61]

The purpose of this rather comprehensive survey of Reilly's and Converse's "laws" and of the literature pertaining to them has been to emphasize the contribution of these two men to retail trading area analysis. The "laws" have certain acknowledged limitations: the primary criticisms are that they are not precise; they should not be called "laws"; and that they apply primarily to shopping and to style or specialty goods rather than to convenience goods. The formula considers distance and population as proxy variables in influencing the division of retail trade between two primary centers. It has already been noted that other factors exert influences causing deviations from "normal" as postulated by Reilly. Distance alone should not be the measure. In this modern day, distance and time are usually related. The important factor may be the time which is required to travel a distance. Specifically, where population depends on public transportation, retailers tend to locate in areas serviced by the public facilities. Customers then will be attracted from large areas, and the extent will depend in part on accessibility. Reilly recognized these possibilities and others as well. However, he concluded that "other factors are either so closely related to, or so directly dependent upon these two primary factors that the effects of the dependent factors tend to balance out when cities are compared on the basis of population and distance." However, this writer is of the opinion that these assumptions cannot be accepted as reducing the need to identify, test, and measure other variables which influence the extent of retail trading areas.

Although it has limitations, Reilly's law can be very useful. It need not

[60] A. F. Jung, "Is Reilly's Law of Retail Gravitation Always True?," *Journal of Marketing*, Vol. XXIV, No. 2 (October 1959), p. 63. The study refers to the relative influence of Kansas City and St. Louis on retail patronage of consumers from Columbia, Missouri.

[61] G. Schwartz, "Laws of Retail Gravitation: An Appraisal," *University of Washington Business Review*, Vol. XXII, No. 1 (October 1962), p. 69.

be perfect to facilitate analysis. In fact, the tools furnished by Reilly and Converse probably are most helpful when other evidence is not available or when the expense of compiling the other evidence is too great. The formula can be applied by shopping and fashion goods retailers to locate the breaking points between their town and other competing retail trade centers. Then, by combining the method with others such as automobile license checks and consumer questionnaires, each serves as a means of checking the others. Merchants are then in a position to determine whether or not they are serving the most appropriate trading area.

Retail Trading Areas—A Synthesis

This review of the literature points up the fact that as yet no principles have been developed which can be universally applied in the analysis of trading areas. Retail trading areas are a particularly complex aspect of spatial economics. That is due to the multiplicity of variables involved— the large number and varied types of retail stores, the classes and variety of goods handled, the location and accessibility of the community, and perhaps others. Furthermore, the human behavior variable is still difficult to measure and predict, advances made by the sociologists and psychologists notwithstanding. The mores of a population, the community's policy with respect to growth and development, the inertia of the shoppers plays a part in retail trading area determination. Each one of these—and there are undoubtedly many others—is a component of this human behavior variable.

Man, more than perhaps any other living organism, is able to adjust quickly to environmental changes. The direction which the adjustment may take is usually predictable only with a very wide range and in a short time interval. Hence, given the present level of knowledge with respect to human behavior, developing theories which give both precise and consistent results, is much more difficult in the social sciences than in the physical sciences where variables, once identified, are more readily controllable. Such factors must explain at least partially the shortcomings of such theories as Reilly's "law."

Principles are derived from theories which have proven to yield valid and reliable predictions after many testings. Because of the complex interaction among many variables, not all of which have been identified, rarely are sharp boundaries among firms and among centers found. Overlapping trading areas are more common than not. The width and depth of merchandise vary among firms and centers. Furthermore, while conditions may appear to be the same between two trade centers, the trading area of one could be quite different from that of the other. Hence, outreach or overlap cannot be predicted except in general terms.

This no doubt explains why definitions and methodology with respect to trading area analysis vary—why they are designed to fit the particular rather than the general case.

This synthesis suggests areas where further research might be profitably pursued to develop the theories, principles, and yardsticks needed to augment our understanding of retail trading areas. These suggested areas for additional research are discussed in detail in the final section of the chapter.

WHOLESALE TRADING AREAS [62]

When urban areas become large enough to support many retail outlets, wholesale establishments arise to supply them. Thus, one finds wholesale centers, large and small, throughout the entire United States. Wholesale activities are essentially of two kinds: (1) those that assemble the products of primary producers and disperse the products to the market, and (2) those concerned with collecting, sorting, and dispersing finished goods. The market for wholesalers engaged in these latter activities consists of retail and industrial users who are frequently located over a large geographic area. However, firms at each location are faced with a problem of the distances over which they can economically operate. Costs, competition, and prices influence their outreach.

Although there are many wholesale centers, about 44 per cent of the wholesale sales volume is concentrated in the ten largest of the present 212 Standard Metropolitan Areas.[63] With few exceptions (notably the heavily populated East and California), each economic region has a wholesale center which is dominant in that region.

The Bureau of Census divides the United States into nine regions or geographic areas which approximate the "natural" economic regions as described on page 285. Within each region are several Standard Metropolitan Areas, and each has its own wholesale trade. There are four characteristics common to a wholesale center: "(1) a large population whose consumption needs must be met, (2) a great deal of manufacturing and processing, (3) a wealth of agencies for transporting, warehousing, financing, and trading, and (4) enterprises and facilities for handling and reshipping goods into domestic and foreign commerce." [64]

[62] A basic text in wholesaling is T. N. Beckman, N. H. Engle, and R. D. Buzzell, *Wholesaling*, 3rd ed., Ronald Press, 1959. Also see *Journal of Marketing*, Vol. XIV, No. 2 (September 1949). The entire issue is devoted to various aspects of wholesaling.

[63] Derived from the *Census of Business, Wholesale Trade*, 1958.

[64] Vaile, Grether, and Cox, *op. cit.*, p. 537.

Factors Influencing Wholesale Trading Areas [65]

If wholesalers handling the same kind of goods operated in a perfect market, the territory which each served would in the long run be hexagonal just as would be the case with retail trade territories (see page 286). The wholesale market is, however, imperfect; in fact, one can make a logical case that it is an oligopoly.[66] In other than the very largest wholesale centers, the number of wholesale firms is small.[67]

Wholesalers, operating in an imperfect market and selling differentiated products, employ various marketing strategies to influence their market shares. Depending on the degree of success of these strategies, market areas vary among firms in the industry and among product lines within the firm. Through research and observation, certain factors which are thought to influence wholesale trading areas have been noted. Some of these are the class of goods, the kind of firm, relative prices among firms, transportation costs, selling costs, geography, and the characteristics of a firm's management.

Product and Firm Differences

Trading areas for wholesalers are partly a function of the classes of products they sell. Lewis found that even within one city, wholesalers handling the same line of products have vastly different territories.[68] This is partially a reflection of the marketing functions or services extended to customers. Wholesalers who offer wide varieties of services, such as credit, delivery, and promotional aids, can expect to sell over greater areas than do competing firms which sell the same lines but offer more limited groups of service.

Territorial coverage of firms marketing products which are staple and relatively undifferentiated is usually localized. When a wholesaler of this type of goods is located in a large city, his area of coverage may be no

---

[65] This discussion is taken in part from Vaile, Grether, and Cox, *op. cit.*, pp. 540–548.

[66] "In its simplest form oligopoly is found in an industry in which the competing firms (producing either close or perfect substitute outputs) are several, but few enough and large enough so that each controls enough of the total industry output that a moderate extension of its output will reduce the sales of rivals by a noticeable amount." J. S. Bain, *Pricing, Distribution, and Employment*, revised ed., Holt, New York, 1953, p. 70.

[67] Derived from the *Census of Business, Wholesale Trade, and Retail Trade,* 1958. There are more than six times as many retail outlets in the United States as there are wholesale firms.

[68] E. H. Lewis, *Marketing Patterns of Philadelphia Wholesalers*, published by the author, Philadelphia, 1948.

more than a single section of that city. These city wholesalers are not likely to operate in small secondary centers. As a result, small wholesalers are able to operate from secondary centers and service them with little competition from large city wholesalers.[69] Several factors account for the profitability of this type of operation within a narrow area. Physical handling, selling, and delivery are often economical. Short-distance deliveries and prompt service to customers provide the small local wholesaler with an advantage over his large city competitors in supplying the secondary center.

Specialty wholesalers generally have larger trading areas than do staple wholesalers, although both are usually concentrated in a few metropolitan areas.[70] Geographic concentration of sources of supply provides both width and depth of assortment, which is of great importance to retail buyers in selecting merchandise for their stores. This wide assortment, along with other types of differentiation, enables a given firm to extend its outreach relative to other competitive firms, the extent depending on relative differentiation among firms. While specialty goods are normally sold over wider areas than are staples, a general-line wholesaler with a wide assortment may extend his trading area far beyond that of his specialty goods rivals located in the same center.

Where there are two equally attractive shopping goods wholesale centers, the advantage may go to the one with the stronger specialty goods offerings. Retail buyers seeking wide and varied assortments both in price and quality take advantage of the available shopping goods which are offered at the wholesale center. The specialty goods are also a major attracting force. While individual shopping goods firms may vary in both extensive and intensive coverage, the aggregation of firms selling both specialty and shopping goods strengthens the market position for all of the wholesalers in the center.

Price

Price exerts an important influence on market outreach. It is generally accepted that those who buy for business use are more objective and unemotional in making their purchases than are household consumers. They are fairly expert and are concerned with the price of the products which they must buy. Since wholesalers deal with businesses, institutions, and governmental agencies, it is reasonable to assume that a given vendor is able to sell farther from his home location when his price is lower than that of his local competition and that of competition located in other

[69] *Ibid.*
[70] *Atlas of Wholesale Dry Goods Trading Areas,* Department of Commerce, Washington, D.C., 1941.

centers. If products were homogeneous and transfer costs were proportional to distance, lower prices at one wholesale center would enable firms located there to press farther out toward competing centers. But staple and nationally branded products being relatively homogeneous, the prices and terms are usually uniform between competing wholesale centers. Hence each wholesale center is somewhat insulated from the competition of other nearby centers, and one finds that markets for staples are fairly narrow.

A price advantage also can be gained when a firm is able to lower costs through economies of scale. When a wholesaler who is located within a wholesale center is able to realize such economies, he may be able to price his offerings below those of his competitors. He then successfully can extend his geographic outreach. Of course, the saving resulting from these economies must be greater than the added cost of transporting the goods over wider areas. If this is not possible, there would be little or no economic advantage in expanding the market area.

Many wholesalers have integrated their operations with the hope that resulting economies of scale will enable the enterprise to follow price policies which will broaden its market outreach. On the other hand, since firms of different size survive, it may be assumed that size is not the sole determinant of survival. Since there is little quantitative evidence of the effects of economies of scale in wholesaling, any conclusions in this area must depend on the assumptions which are made.[71]

Transportation Costs

Transportation costs are usually an important consideration in determining the boundaries of wholesale trading areas, since variations in freight rates are associated with price differences. The landed cost of goods to the wholesaler affects the prices he must charge for his merchandise. Hence, the freight rate structure influences the extent of a trading area because of its bearing on selling price.[72]

Transportation costs also influence the shape of a trading area. The major source of supplies of most types of products is in the eastern part of the United States. As a result, the wholesale trading area of any center is wider toward the west than toward the east. Expressed differently, this means that any given wholesaler generally sells farther to his west than to his east. This is related to the backhaul cost in selling east of the center.[73]

---

[71] Stigler, op. cit., p. 144 and p. 223.
[72] E. M. Hoover, op. cit.
[73] E. M. Hoover, op. cit., pp. 51–53, especially the map on page 52 derived from the Atlas of Wholesale Dry Goods Trading Areas, op. cit.

One study indicates that "in the distribution of merchandise on which shipping costs are high, the area from which most of the wholesalers sales volume is drawn is elliptical in shape." [74] Petersen compares this to Fetter's discussion of the market boundaries being hyperbolic curves. He concludes that

> . . . where a market is surrounded by competing markets, as is Denver or St. Louis, the hyperbolic curve spoken of by Professor Fetter tends to be bent inward toward the extremities to form an ellipse. This 'bending' is due to the impacts of impinging markets upon the area within the curved lines at distances from the focus.
>
> With few exceptions, every wholesale market area of considerable size in the eastern half of the United States and Canada, is essentially elliptical in shape with its longest diameter extending east and west. If each market center is taken as the focus, it will be seen that the market area surrounding it is shallow to the east and deep to the west. The only exceptions to the rule occur on the Pacific coast and in the intermountain region. In the former, because the large market centers are situated directly on the coast line, the market areas must extend toward the east. In the Rocky Mountain Region, the ellipse of the market areas of Denver and Salt Lake City are longest to the north and south. This characteristic is due to the distribution of population. . . . But the phenomenon of the location of the principal trading center nearer the eastern edge of the ellipse still prevails in each area. [75]

Transportation costs are associated not only with freight rate structures but also with the quantity of merchandise purchased. Less-than-carload (LCL) rates are higher, and often substantially so, than carload (CL) rate. So when a gap between the two is narrow, the local jobber is better able to service his locality; he can compete successfully with large wholesalers both in his locality and from other wholesale centers. [76]

The expansion of motor trucking over the past decades has introduced greater flexibility into transport service. The rates of motor trucks are usually as low or lower than the LCL rates of the railroads. Many localities, formerly isolated because of lack of rail facilities, are now served by highways and can therefore be serviced easily and economically by trucks.

[74] Reported interview of T. Hart Anderson, Jr., President, Anderson, Davis and Hyde, "Wholesale Areas Found Elliptical," *New York Times* (October 27, 1929).
[75] E. A. Petersen, *A Market Analysis of the Denver Wholesale Trade Territory*, University of Colorado Press, Boulder, 1936, p. 40.
[76] E. A. Petersen, *op. cit.*

This service has tended to enable large wholesalers to extend their trading areas. At the same time, local jobbers are able to operate profitably.[77]

Selling Costs

Another factor influencing trading areas is the cost of soliciting business by personal salesmen. Other things being equal, selling costs will increase rapidly on a percentage basis as the enterprise reaches farther out. Expenses incurred when a firm elects to keep a salesman on the road and time spent traveling rather than selling will affect outreach. These costs increase as population density decreases. It should be noted, however, that the selling function can be performed in many different ways. Some of these methods are less expensive than others. For example, in areas where potential customers are sparse, mail-order catalog selling is a substitute for personal selling. Manufacturers' representatives may be substituted for the company sales force. Where personal selling must be used, the frequency of sales calls may be reduced in those areas which do not justify more intensive selling.

Geography

A region's physical characteristics affect the extent of wholesale trading areas. The geographic location of major wholesale centers in the United States has one of two general characteristics. Some are located on or near waterways, rivers, or oceans and function in both foreign and domestic commerce. Others are located in the interior but are transportation junction points. Most major wholesale centers have one or both of these characteristics. This is true of New York, Chicago, Denver, Minneapolis, Salt Lake City, and many others. Furthermore, Hartsough observes that

> The conditions—the necessities of people—which have made and limited trade centers as they exist today, confine them to local territory about five hundred miles in extent, as instance the following: classing Philadelphia, Baltimore, and Boston with New York, we have New York to Buffalo and Pittsburgh; Pittsburgh and Buffalo to Chicago; Chicago to Kansas City, Omaha, St. Paul and Minneapolis; Kansas City and Omaha to Denver; Denver to Ogden; Ogden to Helena; each equidistant about five hundred miles. The single exception is St. Paul and Minneapolis to Helena.[78]

[77] For a discussion of transport costs as they affect trading areas, see D. P. Locklin, *Economics of Transportation*, 5th ed., Richard D. Irwin, Homewood, Ill., 1960, Ch. 4.
[78] Mildred L. Hartsough, *Twin Cities as a Metropolitan Market*, University of Minnesota Press, Minneapolis, 1925, footnote 18, page 13.

Geography has contributed to these patterns. Apparently a firm's attempt to expand beyond boundaries set by natural geographic barriers meets severe resistance.[79]

Methods Used to Measure Wholesale Trading Areas

In spite of manufacturers' and distributors' interest in wholesale trading areas, there are relatively few published studies in this field. Those available are in the nature of atlases of trading areas for particular goods (see footnotes 69 and 70) or deal with specific wholesale markets. These latter studies are concerned, primarily, with the geographic extent of the trading area of wholesale firms located within a particular community or region.[80]

In most of the studies cited, interest centers on the extent of a wholesale trading area. The method used to delimit the territories is primarily that of mapping the location of each wholesaler's customers. By interviewing the wholesaler, checking his records (such as sales invoices or call reports), and contacting his customers, the researcher determines the trading area. Then by summing the customers of the entire agglomeration of wholesalers in a given center, the magnitude of the wholesale trading area is determined. If the trading area for a particular product is desired, only wholesalers selling that product line are considered.[81]

E. H. Lewis noted both the dearth and limitations of wholesale trading area research. He observed that "Very few attempts have been made to show the variations in the density of market coverage. The writer has felt that studies of a more precise type . . . which deal with both extensive and intensive phases of market coverage are needed." [82]

To achieve his end, Lewis analyzed the markets of Philadelphia wholesalers of drugs, groceries, dry goods, confectionery, and tobacco. He secured sales data by customer location from selected full-service and

[79] See J. L. Goldstucker, "A Study of Wholesale Trading Areas," *Journal of Marketing*, Vol. XXVI, No. 7 (April 1962), pp. 22–25.

[80] A number of such studies are "Major Trade Areas In Eleven Western States," *University of Denver Business Review*, Vol. VII, No. 4, The University of Denver (April 1931); E. A. Petersen, *op. cit.*; C. D. Harris, *Salt Lake City, A Regional Capital*, University of Chicago Press, 1940; E. G. Rasmussen, "Hardware Trading Centers and Trading Territories in Nine Southeastern States," *Journal of Marketing*, Vol. VIII, No. 2 (October 1943); R. D. Tousley and R. F. Lanzillotti, "The Spokane Wholesale Market," *Economic and Business Studies*, Bulletin No. 18, The State College of Washington, Pullman, 1951; and E. H. Lewis, *Wholesaling in the Twin Cities*, University of Minnesota Press, Minneapolis, 1952.

[81] For example, see R. D. Tousley and R. F. Lanzillotti, *op. cit.*, for a map of the wholesale trading area of Spokane, p. 809; in the same volume are more than a dozen wholesale trade area maps by product.

[82] E. H. Lewis, "Wholesale Market Patterns," *Journal of Marketing*, Vol. XII, No. 3 (January 1948), p. 317.

limited function wholesalers. The data were from company sales records. He then developed a marketing pattern scheme:

> A market pattern can be shown in several ways but the type illustrated (see Figure 11.2) was found to be particularly useful. Sales of the wholesalers interviewed were tabulated by counties. The counties were then ranked according to the sales made in them and split into three groups as indicated by Figure 11.2.
>
> In most cases dollar sales were used to construct the market patterns. However, some patterns were developed from the ratios of wholesale sales to retail sales of groups. . . . The ratio type of market pattern has the merit of indicating the relationship between actual sales and the potential market, and it reveals areas in which wholesalers located in other cities are offering strong competition.[83]

By applying the market pattern method, Lewis was able to measure both the sales density and the extent of trading areas of the Philadelphia wholesalers. The end product is the map illustrated in Figure 11.2. This map shows both intensive and extensive trading area coverage of six Philadelphia dry goods houses. Furthermore, the method revealed variation, extensive and intensive, in market coverage by commodity lines and by size and type of wholesale establishment.

D. J. Bowersox has developed a mathematical technique to determine the optimum location of a food distribution center. He states that "The basic goal in selecting a distribution center location is to achieve one-day delivery to each supermarket at the lowest possible distribution cost. Therefore, the optimum location solution is one which determines that geographic point from which all supermarkets can be replenished at least cost. The critical costs stem from local delivery to supermarkets." [84]

Bowersox discusses a variety of mathematical and nonmathematical techniques to determine optimum location. He develops three models based on three geographic market patterns which are representative of normal spatial relationships between retail outlets served from a single

[83] *Ibid.*, p. 318.
[84] D. J. Bowersox, "Food Distribution Center Location: Technique and Procedure," *Marketing and Transportation Paper No. 12*, Bureau of Business and Economic Research, Graduate School of Business Administration, Michigan State University, East Lansing, 1962. The food distribution center may be either an independent food wholesaler or a warehouse of a retail food chain. Also see "Evaluating Delivery Operations of Wholesale Food Distributors," *Marketing Research Report No. 502*, United States Department of Agriculture, Washington, D.C. (October 1961), and R. M. Hiel, "Techniques of Measuring Market Potential for Wholesalers," *Bureau of Business Management Bulletin No. 820*, College of Commerce and Business Administration, University of Illinois, Urbana (March 1962).

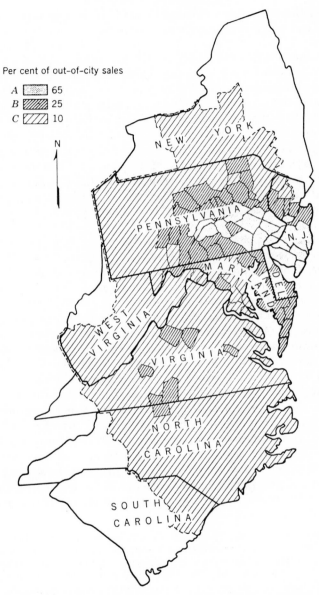

Per cent of out-of-city sales

A [   ] 65
B [////] 25
C [////] 10

N

*Figure 11.2   Market pattern of six dry goods houses. Source:
E. H. Lewis, "Wholesale Market Patterns," Journal of
Marketing, national quarterly publication of the American
Marketing Association, Volume XII (January 1948), p. 319.*

distribution center. Model A (his standard) is a spatially concentrated group of retail stores; Model B is a group of retail outlets spatially dispersed but proportionally distributed over the area; and Model C is spatially dispersed but nonproportionally distributed. As a standard for evaluating alternative locations he compares distribution costs based on a transportation cost model.

Simulation of these three models provides a framework for location testing. Model A is not tested because of the unique nature of its market area. Retail food chains having supermarkets spatially concentrated are commonly found in large metropolitan areas. In such concentrated areas, the distribution center location is dictated by a unique set of requirements dissimilar to those in the other models. The small geographic area under construction will, at any given time, have only a limited number of location sites available for construction. Therefore, under these circumstances, the most efficient procedure is to determine the sites having the necessary characteristics and then to select the one which provides the least-cost location. The reason for constructing Model A in the current research is to demonstrate the contrast between Model A and Models B and C.

"The fundamental purpose of simulating retail market patterns is to achieve a method for generalizing the research findings beyond the limitations of a case-study approach. In the experiment, operating information from two retail food chains is used. These operating statistics are referred to as primary data. They represent supermarket locations and annual tonnage shipped to each. One chain under study has the physical characteristics simulated in Model B and the other represents a case of non-proportional distribution simulated in Model C. By contrasting the various mathematical and non-mathematical location solutions for each model, understanding of the impact of geographic market area upon distribution center location is gained.[85]

Summary Comments Concerning Wholesale Trading Areas

A survey of wholesaling literature leads one to a basic conclusion. Little has been done to develop research techniques and tools with which to analyze and measure wholesale trading areas. Although it is generally recognized that the wholesaling industry arises primarily to meet the needs of retail trade, it is also clear that retailing and wholesaling trading areas are not coextensive.

[85] *Ibid.*, p. 21.

What a firm's wholesale trading area should be in order for it to be covered efficiently cannot be determined without appropriate yardsticks. Indeed, what the territory actually is depends primarily on a highly subjective evaluation of what executives *feel* that their particular territory should be. The evaluation is frequently based on incomplete knowledge of the marginal cost and marginal revenue relations at the periphery of the firm's trading area.

Fundamentally, there are no empirically tested yardsticks to measure wholesaling trading areas. Lewis's method has had little follow-up. Bowersox's is too new to evaluate. Perhaps the lack of research and methodology means that enough information is available to fit the present needs of wholesalers and other marketing people. This writer doubts that such is the case.

PRIMARY PRODUCERS' TRADING AREAS [86]

The theoretical trading area determination under the assumption of pure competition can be applied to primary products, both agricultural and extractive, with a minimum of alteration. Obviously, however, no markets are purely competitive. Still, primary products have at least some of the characteristics of such a market structure: (1) the products tend to be relatively homogeneous, at least within grades; (2) the products are usually supplied by many small, independent producers; (3) the relatively low specific value of the products mean that transportation costs weigh heavily on final market price thus influencing trading area outreach; and (4) supply and demand conditions exert a relatively strong pressure on determining market price.[87]

The importance of transportation costs explains why agricultural products tend to be produced, processed, and consumed locally. The exception is when production is highly concentrated and the demand is diffused, such as for sea foods, citrus fruits, redwood lumber, and some types of ore.

Factors Determining Trading Areas for Primary Products

Freight Rate Structures

If markets were perfectly competitive and transportation costs varied proportionately and directly with distance, the extent of the trading area

[86] Much of this section is based on R. S. Vaile, E. T. Grether, and R. Cox, *op. cit.*, Ch. 25.

[87] Where price supports exist, this statement is true only if the support price is below equilibrium price.

for producers of primary products would depend on transportation costs and demand elasticity. However, freight rate structures reflect a wide variety of built-in discriminations. Interstate truck lines are faced with size and weight limits and tax loads which limit the scope of the truck operations and, therefore, the extent of trading areas.[88]

Discrimination in favor of particular products or markets, freight equalization rates, and in-transit privileges make a trading area different from what it might otherwise be. Trading areas are influenced by the freight rates for a particular commodity in a particular market. Hence in order to define trading areas for primary products it is necessary to consider the general configuration of freight rates for the given commodity and also the specific point-to-point rates.[89]

Quality

Variations in the quality of primary and extractive products affect trading areas. Differences in quality of wheat, even though of the same grade, differences in quality of southern soft woods and western hard woods contribute to the extent of trading areas. These quality differences affect price and market flows.

Areas of Surplus and Deficit Production

A section in the *Year Book of Agriculture,* 1954, includes maps of surplus production areas by commodity.[90] Examination of these maps reveals principal directions of the flows which the commodities take from production to consumption areas. The shape of the trading area depends on the relative size of the surplus and deficit areas which in turn affects market price. For example, a major surplus area producing in large quantities at low cost may penetrate greater distances than areas with only minor surpluses and higher cost.

Interstate Trade Barriers

Interstate barriers are also frictions which distort trading areas. Some states ban or restrict out-of-state agricultural products. The intent is to reduce competition and enable local producers to sell for higher prices even though a variety of seemingly valid arguments are made to support

[88] "Highway Transportation Barriers in 20 States," *Marketing Research Report No. 157,* United States Department of Agriculture, Washington, D.C. (March 1957), p. 36; and "Effects of State and Local Regulations in Interstate Movement of Agricultural Products by Highway," *Marketing Research Report No. 496,* United States Department of Agriculture, Washington, D.C. (July 1961).
[89] R. S. Vaile, E. T. Grether, R. Cox, *op. cit.,* pp. 519–522.
[90] "An Atlas," *Year Book of Agriculture,* United States Department of Agriculture, Washington, D.C., 1954, pp. 402–490.

such restrictive behavior. For example, oleomargarine taxes in dairy-producing states serve this purpose. Consequently, the trading areas for such products are distorted.

The factors discussed are among the more important ones in influencing the trading areas for primary producers, agricultural and extractive. Each class of primary products is relatively homogeneous and in most cases is produced by many firms. The buyers are usually well informed with respect to product quality, availability, and prevailing price. Hence, in general terms, the theory of perfectly competitive models is useful in defining trading area limits for such products as these. Using the model as a basis for analysis, one is able to identify many of the so-called market frictions, thereby explaining the actual shape of the trading areas as opposed to its theoretical shape.

MANUFACTURERS' TRADING AREAS

Manufacturers typically are able to sell their products over a wider area than are retailers, wholesalers, or producers of primary products. Several factors make this possible:

1. Opportunity for successful product differentiation.
2. Pricing alternatives.
3. Opportunity for integration and economies of scale.
4. Ratio of transfer costs to total value of the product.
5. Ratio of fixed to total costs.
6. Dispersion of consumers in the market.
7. Management's desire and opportunity for expansion and control.

Opportunity for Successful Product Differentiation

Chamberlain points out that

> A general class of products is differentiated if any significant basis exists for distinguishing the goods (or services) of one seller from those of another. Such a basis may be real or fancied so long as it is of any importance whatever to buyers and leads to a preference for one variety of the product over another.[91]

Successful differentiation reduces the number of substitutes for a product. Hence manufacturers with highly differentiated products, real

---

[91] E. H. Chamberlain, *The Theory of Monopolistic Competition*, 8th ed., Harvard University Press, Cambridge, Mass., 1962, p. 56.

or imagined, are more likely to extend their trading areas. On the other hand, successful differentiation results in overlapping trading areas. If the products were homogeneous among manufacturers, the market of each would resemble a hexagon. Each producer would sell in his own area. With differentiation, several manufacturers sell in the same area. The share of the market which each obtains depends on how effectively each differentiates his product.

Transfer Costs, Prices, and Economies of Scale

These three factors are important determinants of trading area coverage. If transfer costs are great relative to the price of the product, market outreach is limited. Transfer costs are a part of total costs. The price of the product must be high enough to defray all costs. As manufacturers attempt to extend their trading areas, transfer costs increase more than proportionately to other costs. A higher price will compensate for the added costs. However, ability to increase price depends on competitive conditions, structure of transportation rates, and elasticity of demand. If the product is highly differentiated and therefore demand is inelastic, then manufacturers are able to shift the burden of transfer costs to the consumers. If the burden of transfer costs becomes too great, each producer will have an advantage in selling customers located only in the vicinity of his plant. The distant producer must then limit his trading area radius, absorb freight costs, or open branch operations. Each of these alternatives presents problems. However, space limitation prevents a discussion of them.

Economies of scale also affect market outreach. If economies result in lower at-the-plant costs, the product can bear a proportionately heavier transfer cost for any given price. Thus, the product can be marketed at a distance further than would be possible in the absence of economies of scale. If fixed costs are a relatively great proportion of total costs, then the impetus to expand output and extend trading areas is also great. Essentially, it is the spreading of large fixed costs over greater output which yields economies of scale. This relationship of fixed to total costs stimulates the search for distant markets.[92]

Dispersion of Customers

Selling costs influence both the size of a trading area and the manner in which it will be covered. Selling effort will be less costly when customers are highly concentrated because the time spent reaching the

[92] Basing-point pricing was an instrument devised to increase the market outreach of high fixed-cost producers.

customers is negligible. On the other hand, selling costs tend to increase when customers are widely dispersed. Salesmen must spend time traveling to reach these buyers. As a result, less time is available to devote to selling.

The relationship between dispersion of customers and selling costs requires that each seller make his own appraisal of market possibilities away from his home base. In the final analysis, the extent of a firm's trading area is governed by the ratio of costs to revenue at the periphery of the territory. The territory will be served as long as additional revenues exceed or equal the cost of selling in the territory. When revenues no longer sustain personal selling costs at the margin, such things as catalogs and price lists are substituted for salesmen. At such time as these nonpersonal selling methods do not bring in sufficient revenue to defray their cost, it is likely that they will be discontinued and along with them the territory which they are intended to reach.

Concentrated Manufacturing with Widespread Demand

It should be noted briefly that when customers for a product are widely dispersed and when manufacturing facilities of an industry are highly concentrated, manufacturers' trading areas tend to be large. For example, demand for photographic equipment is spread throughout the entire United States. Yet manufacture of the goods is highly concentrated.

We have suggested that the trading area which a manufacturer is able to serve depends on a number of variables, such as degree and success of product differentiation, pricing policies, burden of transfer costs, economies of scale, demand elasticity, and others. These factors are not mutually exclusive in exerting influence on the extent of a trading area. However, since we are unable to weight these variables, we are unable to determine what influence each has or what influence various combinations exert on manufacturers' trading area coverage.

CONCLUSIONS AND SUGGESTIONS FOR FURTHER RESEARCH

This chapter has been devoted to a survey of the available information pertaining to the analysis of trading areas of retailers, wholesalers, manufacturers, and primary producers. Techniques and theories for determining actual and potential trade territories have been examined. Synthesizing past and present research, the available information leads one to conclude that trading area analysis is as yet an art—not a science. In selecting locations, in selling and servicing territories, in comparing actual with potential sales, executives rely primarily on their experience and judgment, seeking corroboration from their associates. There is much to be done if the goal is to develop and practice a *science* of trading area analysis and that, indeed, appears to be the goal. The work of Reilly and Converse, the attempts by others to test and improve the pioneering methods of these two men, and current efforts to develop mathematical models with universal predictive properties indicate continuing interest in discovering a scientific method of dealing with trading area problems.

Business managers are continually selecting sites, building stores and plants, defining their trading areas, and making provisions to serve them These activities initially must have been based primarily on improvisations. However, the accumulated experience from such actions, along with some aid from the theoreticians, has developed within management a more sophisticated judgment. Nevertheless the decisions are being made, and without universal principles, theories, or models.

This survey of trading area research and literature suggests some topics into which further investigation offers promise of fruitful results. One such topic is that of consumer behavior with respect to purchasing decisions. While much has been learned in recent years about the consumer, there is still a void in our knowledge. I have defined a "natural" trading area as one where the cost of contact between sellers and buyers is minimal. Buyers' costs involve the physical effort, inconvenience, and actual dollar outlay incurred in securing goods. The buyer will buy a good so long as the utility or satisfaction resulting from possessing that good is greater than the cost of obtaining it. For such concepts as buyer cost and utility to be of use in helping to set limits to trading areas, one must be able to identify the components of both cost and utility. That being done, the need is then to measure each, weigh it in relation to the other variable components, and, finally, to determine the degree and direction of variability of each in relation to the others.

Another topic for further investigation has to do with motives and motivation of business executives. The lack of dependable yardsticks for trading area analysis is due partially to the fallacy of some of the assumptions on which the research in the field rests. Location theory, Reilly's law, and other concepts which have been examined are all concerned with profit maximizing behavior. If, as many behavioral scientists point out, business executives act to maximize a wide variety of nonmaterial gains, then trading area theory is perhaps seeking answers to the wrong questions. This suggests the need to augment our understanding of factors which move business executives to value power, size, and growth. These motivations may more fully explain policies with respect to trading area coverage than do the assumptions related to profit maximization and economic incentive.

One must recognize, however, that it is through profits that the so-called nonmaterial satisfaction can be realized. Size, growth, and power often are long-run consequences of a profitable operation. Therefore, those activities which contribute to profit help maximize nonmaterial gains. As a consequence, factors which are economic in nature should also be examined. This suggests yet another area in which continued research might make an important contribution to trading area analysis, and that is factors affecting costs. Accounting has developed adequate understanding of direct production costs. Available techniques provide a rather rigorous basis for their allocation. On the other hand, the allocation of indirect and joint costs is still a cause of some concern. As a result, continuing attention is being devoted to improving indirect and joint costing methods.

Distribution costs should be of greater concern than production costs to marketing people and their accountants. Although some attention has been devoted to the study of distribution costs and to developing means whereby they can be analyzed and allocated, progress in the area lags far behind the need for understanding. As pointed out previously, this is a reflection of the difficulty associated with costing nonproduction activities. For example, the purpose of newspaper advertising by a retail store is to generate sales. An advertisement is run which appears to yield few immediate results. However, the cumulative effect of that and other advertisements plus other promotional activities may in the long run generate a sales volume far greater than the sum of that resulting from each advertisement taken singly. Yet management has no way of knowing what long-run sales would have been had the advertisement not been run. Therefore, the cost of that particular advertisement cannot be allocated on a per sale basis with an adequate degree of objectivity. The same reasoning is applicable in assessing the effects of personal selling, delivery, and various other service functions sustained as a part of a firm's marketing activities.

Without adequate tools to measure the costs of these marketing activities, a firm suffers a disadvantage in attempting to assess the costs associated with serving a particular trading area. Thus, what "natural" trading area a firm can most efficiently serve is indeterminate. Hence, accelerated research in distribution cost analysis is inevitable if trading area analysis is to become less subjective and more scientific.

This overview suggests that the enrichment of trading area analysis is hampered by a dearth of empirically validated theories and principles necessary in order to advance understanding in the field. The barriers are the problems involved in identifying, measuring, and weighting the variables which determine the dimensions of trading areas. These barriers must be surmounted before real progress is made. Until then, determining the "natural" trading area of a firm or a community will continue to be an art, not a science.

BIBLIOGRAPHY

Anderson, T. Hart, "Wholesale Areas Found Elliptical," *New York Times* (October 27, 1929).

Applebaum, W. and S. B. Cohen, "Store Trading Areas in a Changing Market," *Journal of Retailing*, Vol. XXXVI, No. 3 (Fall 1961).

"An Atlas," *Year Book of Agriculture*, United States Department of Agriculture, Washington, D.C., 1954.

Atlas of Wholesale Dry Goods Trading Areas, Department of Commerce, Washington, D.C., 1941.

Bain, J. S., *Pricing, Distribution, and Employment*, Holt, New York, 1953.

Batcher, A. S., *A Method of Delineating Retail Trading Zones*, School of Business and Public Administration, University of Arizona, Tucson, 1939.

Beckman, T. N., N. H. Engle, and R. D. Buzzell, *Wholesaling*, Ronald Press, 1959.

Bennett, V. W., "Consumer Buying Habits in a Small Town Located Between Two Large Cities," *Journal of Marketing*, Vol. VIII, No. 4 (April 1944).

Bowden, W. K. and R. J. Cassady, Jr., "Decentralization of Retail Trade in the Metropolitan Market Area," *Journal of Marketing*, Vol. V, No. 3 (January 1941).

Bowersox, D. J., "Food Distribution Center Location: Technique and Procedure," *Marketing and Transportation Paper No. 12*, Bureau of Business and Economic Research, Graduate School of Business Administration, Michigan State University, East Lansing, Michigan, 1962.

Canoyer, H. G., "Selecting a Store Location," *Economic Series No. 56*, Department of Commerce, Washington, D.C., 1946.

Cassady, R. J., Jr. and W. K. Bowden, "Shifting Retail Trade Within the Los Angeles Metropolitan Market," *Journal of Marketing*, Vol. VIII, No. 4 (April 1944).

Cassady, R. J., Jr. and H. S. Ostlund, *The Retail Distribution Structure of the Small City*, University of Minnesota Press, Minneapolis, 1935.

Census of Business, Wholesale Trade, and Retail Trade, 1958.

Chamberlain, E. H., *The Theory of Monopolistic Competition*, 8th ed., Harvard University Press, Cambridge, Mass., 1962.

Christaller, W., *Die Centralen Orte in Suddeutschland*, Erlangen, 1933.

"City Told Taxes Drive Out Trade," *New York Times*, Vol. 602, No. 38 (May 17, 1963).

Converse, P. D., "Comment on Movement of Retail Trade in Iowa," *Journal of Marketing*, Vol. XVIII, No. 2 (October 1953).

———, "New Laws of Retail Gravitation," *Journal of Marketing*, Vol. XIV, No. 3 (October 1949).

———, *Retail Trade Areas in Illinois*, University of Illinois Press, Urbana, 1946.

———, *A Study of Retail Trade Areas in East Central Illinois*, University of Illinois Press, Urbana, 1943.

Coolsen, F. G. and W. S. Myers, *Kentucky Retail Market Areas and Trading Centers*, Bureau of Business Research, University of Kentucky, Frankfort, 1953.

Cox, R., "Impact of Changes in the Size and Structure of Cities," *Explorations in Retailing*, Stanley C. Hollander (ed.), Bureau of Business and Economic Research, College of Business and Public Service, Michigan State University, East Lansing, 1961.

Davidson, W. R. and P. L. Brown, *Retailing Management*, 2nd ed., Ronald Press, New York, 1960.

"Definition of Marketing Terms," *National Marketing Review*, National Association of Marketing Teachers (Fall 1935).

Donnahoe, A. S., "Can Advertising Markets Be Defined or Measured as Geographical Areas?," *Journal of Marketing*, Vol. XVIII, No. 2 (October 1953).

Douglas, E., "Measuring the General Retail Trading Area—A Case Study," *Journal of Marketing*, Vol. XIII (April 1949) and Vol. XIV (July 1949).

Duddy, E. A. and D. A. Revzan, *Marketing, An Institutional Approach*, McGraw-Hill, New York, 1953.

Duncan, D. J. and C. F. Phillips, *Retailing, Principles and Methods*, 6th ed., Richard D. Irwin, Homewood, Ill., 1963.

"Effects of State and Local Regulations in Interstate Movement of Agricultural Products by Highway," *Marketing Research Report No. 496*, United States Department of Agriculture, Washington, D.C. (July 1961).

"Evaluating Delivery Operations of Wholesale Food Distributors," *Marketing Research Report No. 502*, United States Department of Agriculture, Washington, D.C. (October 1961).

Fetter, F. A., "The Economic Law of Market Areas," *Quarterly Journal of Economics*, Vol. XXXVIII (May 1924).

Fine, I. V., "Retail Trade Area Analysis," *Wisconsin Commerce Papers*, Vol. I, No. 6, University of Wisconsin, Bureau of Business Research and Service, Madison (January 1954).

"A Five Percent Sales Tax Rate Looms for Pennsylvania," Tax Report of the *Wall Street Journal*, Vol. 53, No. 154 (May 22, 1963).

Goldstucker, J. L., "A Study of Wholesale Trading Areas," *Journal of Marketing*, Vol. XXVI, No. 2 (April 1962).

Harris, C. D., *Salt Lake City, A Regional Capital*, University of Chicago Press, 1940.

Hartsough, M. L., *Twin Cities as a Metropolitan Market*, University of Minnesota Press, Minneapolis, 1925.

Heaton, H., *Economic History of Europe*, Harper, New York, 1948.

Hiel, R. M., "Techniques of Measuring Market Potential for Wholesalers," *Bureau of Business Management Bulletin No. 820*, College of Commerce and Business Administration, University of Illinois, Urbana, 1962.

"Highway Transportation Barriers in Twenty States," *Marketing Research Report No. 157*, United States Department of Agriculture, Washington, D.C. (March 1962).

Hoover, E. M., *The Location of Economic Activity*, McGraw-Hill, New York, 1948.

Horngren, C., *Cost Accountancy*, Prentice-Hall, Englewood Cliffs, N.J., 1962.

"How to Make a Local Area Trade Survey," *Domestic Distribution Department*, United States Chamber of Commerce, Washington, D.C. (June 1940).

Huff, D. L., "A Probabilistic Analysis of Consumer Spatial Behavior," *Emerging Concepts of Marketing*, W. S. Decker (ed.), American Marketing Association, Chicago, 1963.

————, "Defining and Estimating a Trading Area," *Journal of Marketing*, Vol. XXVIII (July 1964).

Isard, W., *Location and Space Economy*, Wiley, New York, 1956.

Jones, F. M., "A Survey of a Retail Trading Area," *Bureau of Business Research Bulletin No. 44*, College of Commerce and Business Administration, University of Illinois, Urbana, 1932.

Jung, A. F., "Is Reilly's Law of Retail Gravitation Always True?," *Journal of Marketing*, Vol. XXIV, No. 2 (October 1959).

Larson, G. E. and M. N. Poteat, "Selling the United States Market," *Domestic Commerce Series No. 29 (New Series)*, United States Department of Commerce, Government Printing Office, Washington, D.C., 1961.

Lewis, E. H., *Marketing Patterns of Philadelphia Wholesalers*, published by the author, Philadelphia, 1948.

————, "Wholesale Market Patterns," *Journal of Marketing*, Vol. XII, No. 3 (January 1948).

————, *Wholesaling in the Twin Cities*, University of Minnesota Press, Minneapolis, 1952.

Locklin, D. P., *Economics of Transportation*, 5th ed., Richard D. Irwin, Homewood, Ill., 1960.

Losch, A., *Economics of Location*, Yale University Press, New Haven, Conn., 1954.

"Major Trade Areas in Eleven Western States," *University of Denver Business Review*, Vol. VII, No. 4, The University of Denver (April 1931).

Marshall, A., *Principles of Economics*, 8th ed., 1956 reprint, Macmillan and Company, Ltd., London, 1956.

Mills, E. S. and M. R. Lav, "A Model of Market Areas with Free Entry," *The Journal of Political Economy*, Vol. LXXII (June 1964).

Muller, A., *Die Elemente der Staatskunst*, 3 Berlin 1809.

Nelson, R. L., *The Selection of Retail Locations*, F. W. Dodge Corporation, New York, 1958.

Oxenfeldt, A. R., *Industrial Pricing and Market Practices*, Prentice-Hall, New York, 1951.

Penn, W. S., Jr., "Measurement of Service Station Trading Areas," API Publication No. 1546, *Case Histories in Petroleum Marketing*, American Petroleum Institute, New York.

Petersen, E. A., *A Market Analysis of the Denver Wholesale Trade Territory*, University of Colorado Press, Boulder, 1936.

Pfanner, J. A., "A Statistical Study of the Drawing Power of Cities for Retail Trade," *Studies in Business Administration*, Vol. No. 3, University of Chicago, 1940.

Read, E. V. W., "Analysis of Retail Trading Relationships of Elgin, Illinois, A Satellite City," *Journal of Business*, Vol. IX, No. 1, University of Chicago, 1938.

Reilly, W. J., *The Law of Retail Gravitation*, 1st ed., University of Texas, Austin, 1931.

————, "Methods for the Study of Retail Relationships," *Bureau of Business Research Monograph No. 4*, University of Texas, Austin (November 22, 1929).

Retail and Wholesale Trading Areas of Minneapolis and St. Paul, Economic Research Department, Minneapolis Chamber of Commerce, 1951.

Reynolds, R. B., "A Rejoinder to P. D. Converse's 'Comment on Movement of Retail Trade in Iowa'," *Journal of Marketing*, Vol. XVIII, No. 2 (October 1953).

————, "A Test of the Law of Retail Gravitation," *Journal of Marketing*, Vol. XVII, No. 3 (January 1953).

Rasmussen, E. G., "Hardware Trading Centers and Trading Territories in Nine Southeastern States," *Journal of Marketing*, Vol. VIII, No. 2 (October 1943).

Schwartz, G., "Laws of Retail Gravitation: An Appraisal," *University of Washington Business Review*, Vol. XXII, No. 1 (October 1962).

Scott, W. G., *Human Relations in Management*, Richard D. Irwin, Homewood, Ill., 1962.

Standard Metropolitan Areas, Bureau of the Budget, Executive Office of the President, Washington, D.C. (July 28, 1950).

Stigler, G. J., *The Theory of Price*, revised ed., Macmillan, New York, 1952.

Tousley, R. D. and R. F. Lanzillotti, "The Spokane Wholesale Market," *Economic and Business Studies*, Bulletin No. 18, The State College of Washington, Bureau of Economic and Business Research, Pullman, Wash. (November 1951).

Ullman, E., "A Theory for the Location of Cities," *American Journal of Sociology*, Vol. XLVI (May 1941).

Vaile, R. L., E. S. Grether, and R. Cox, *Marketing in the American Economy*, Ronald Press, New York, 1952.

Valavanis, S., "Losch on Location," *American Economic Review*, Vol. XLV, No. 4 (September 1955), pp. 637–644.

Von Thunen, J. H., *Der Isolierte Staat in Befiehung auf Landwirtschaft und Nationalokonomie*, Hamburg, 1826.

Weber, A., *Ueber den Standort der Industrien*, Part I, Reine Theorie des Standorts, Tubingen, 1909.

Weigand, R. E., "Exclusive Dealerships—A Different View," *Journal of Retailing*, Vol. XXXVIII, No. 1 (Spring 1962).

12

Marketing Channels:
Analytical Systems and Approaches

BERT C. MC AMMON, JR. AND ROBERT W. LITTLE

INTRODUCTION

Distribution intermediaries are encountered in all, even the most primitive, societies.[1] Depending on the culture in which they operate, such intermediaries may be tribal chieftains, "mammy" traders, cooperative enterprises, or profit seeking entities. Consequently, they vary widely in terms of their goals, operating methods, social roles, and scales of operation. All intermediaries have one characteristic in common, however; they are part of an institutional mechanism that moves goods from points of production to points of use. Very little is known about this mechanism. Relatively few scholars have analyzed the structure of distribution either empirically or theoretically, and most of the studies that have been undertaken tend to be descriptive rather than analytical in nature.

The institutional mechanism for dispersing goods in a free economy is the marketing channel, and, like other vertical networks, it has been studied sparingly. Several hypotheses can be advanced to explain this scholarly neglect.

1. Marketing scholars, as well as those in related disciplines, are primarily interested in the theory of the firm. In some analyses the firm is at least implicitly assumed to operate in a quasi-vacuum, and little or no attention is paid to its environment or to its relationships with other

---

[1] For excellent discussions of primitive trade networks, see Karl Polanyi, *The Great Transformation*, Beacon Press, Boston, 1957, and Karl Polanyi, Conrad M. Arensberg, and Harry W. Pearson (eds.), *Trade and Market in the Early Empires*, The Free Press, Glencoe, Ill., 1957.

enterprises. Thus the primary system of which the firm is a member—its marketing channel—receives scant attention.

2. Marketing channels have been neglected as a separate area of inquiry because their complexity discourages investigators. Channels, in a very real sense, are among the most complicated phenomena encountered in an advanced economy. They are elaborate economic, political, and social systems that usually involve many decision makers and often extend over a wide geographical area. A sophisticated understanding of these phenomena requires an eclectic approach—an integration of concepts from a variety of disciplines, including sociology, economics, political science, cultural anthropology, regional science, marketing and social psychology. For this reason, if for no other, the nature of marketing channels has not been explored satisfactorily, either from an empirical or theoretical point of view.

3. The neglect of marketing channels as a separate area of inquiry is partially attributable to recent trends in marketing thought. Early scholars in the field of marketing were institutionalists or functionalists and were, therefore, interested in exploring vertical interfirm alignments. Since the early 1950's, however, most marketing scholars have adopted what is usually called a managerial point of view, and this preoccupation with the firm's internal operations has resulted in less emphasis being placed on channel systems *per se*. The managerial analyst, to the extent he is concerned with channels, is interested in the techniques that can be used by a particular enterprise to exploit its channel "opportunities".[2]

Thus the literature dealing with marketing channels as organized behavior systems is relatively sparse, and it is presumptuous to talk about definitive scientific findings in this area. Fortunately, numerous authors have investigated *selected* aspects of channel behavior, and the literature contains a coherent body of concepts, theories, and hypotheses that partially explain the nature of interfirm alignments. These contributions will be examined in the following paragraphs to the extent that they provide a viable basis for additional research or for effective channel programing. More specifically, the functional approach to marketing and selected definitional issues will be discussed in the first section of this chapter. Marketing channels as organized behavior systems will be examined next, followed by an analysis of selected determinants of channel behavior. The topic of channel management and recent contributions in the field of physical distribution will be covered in the fourth and fifth sec-

[2] See, for example, Julian H. Handler, *How to Sell the Supermarkets*, Fairchild Publications, New York, 1959, and E. B. Weiss, *Selling to and through the New Department Store*, Printers' Ink Publishing Company, New York, 1948.

tions of this chapter; the final section will contain suggestions for additional channel research.

THE CHANNEL AS A UNIT OF STUDY

Functionalist Contributions

Early writers envisioned the marketing process as consisting of identifiable, discrete and indispensable functions. Shaw was the first to develop a list of marketing functions,[3] and his conceptualization was subsequently accepted by Weld[4] and Cherington[5] with only modest changes. All three authors contend that certain activities must be performed to consummate market transactions. Furthermore, they argue that analysis of these activities should be separated from a discussion of the agencies performing them. Cherington, in particular, stresses the need for analyzing the functions separately from their actual performance. He believes that the functional approach, in order to have analytical significance, must be used to examine the problems involved in performing specific activities and that secondary attention should be placed on the ways in which agencies currently perform them. In short, he views the agency structure as a temporary or transient mechanism for performing necessary tasks.[6]

Other scholars subsequently developed slightly modified functional lists, but each worked within the framework established by Shaw, Weld, and Cherington. In 1950, however, McGarry developed a new classification approach to marketing functions,[7] and Vaile, Grether, and Cox also developed a differentiated list of functions in 1952.[8] Using the term "flow" rather than "function" to indicate that marketing is a continuous process, Vaile, Grether, and Cox define a channel of distribution as "the combination and sequence of agencies through which one or more of these marketing flows moves" and they emphasize that not only is each

[3] Arch Wilkinson Shaw, *Some Problems in Market Distribution*, Harvard University Press, Cambridge, Mass., 1915, pp. 4–28.

[4] L. D. H. Weld, "Marketing Functions and Mercantile Organization," *American Economic Review* (June 1917), pp. 306–318.

[5] Paul T. Cherington, *Elements of Marketing*, Macmillan, New York, 1920, p. 44.

[6] *Ibid.*, pp. 56–59.

[7] Edmund D. McGarry, "Some Functions of Marketing Reconsidered," *Theory in Marketing*, Reavis Cox and Wroe Alderson (eds.), Richard D. Irwin, Homewood, Ill., 1950, pp. 269–273.

[8] Roland S. Vaile, E. T. Grether, and Reavis Cox, *Marketing in the American Economy*, Ronald Press, New York, 1952, p. 113.

flow an integral part of the marketing process, but it is also a "series of movements from one agency to another." [9]

McGarry, and Vaile, Grether, and Cox, as well as their predecessors, developed functional lists that are macrooriented. They view the marketing process from the vantage point of the social scientist rather than from the point of view of the operating executive. Staudt broke with this tradition by developing a list of marketing management functions in 1958.[10] Staudt asserts that marketing executives supervise a complex of functions that are common to all types of firms; each manager is therefore confronted by similar conceptual problems that must be solved if the firm is to survive.

The marketing channel is obviously the economic instrumentality that performs the functions identified by Shaw, Weld, Cherington, McGarry, and others. The firm within the channel, on the other hand, is the instrumentality that engages in the activities described by Staudt. Consequently, an awareness of the functions to be performed by either the channel or the firm constitutes a logical point of origin for subsequent analysis of channel behavior.

Some Definitional Issues

The term *marketing channel* may be defined in a variety of ways, depending on the purpose of the analysis or the preference of the author. Most writers, when identifying a specific channel, accept the following definitional constraints:

1. In the case of a manufacturer selling to wholesale middlemen, the channel is defined to include the manufacturer, a specific *type* of wholesale middleman, the customers of this intermediary, and the ultimate buyers (assuming they do not buy from the wholesale organization in question). Thus, a vertical alignment that includes a toy manufacturer, drug wholesalers, the latters' variegated trade customers, and consumers would be described as a *single* marketing channel. In similar fashion, a vertical alignment consisting of a manufacturer, industrial distributors, and the latters' customers (industrial, institutional and governmental users) would also be regarded as a *single* channel. Consequently, the *type* of decision maker in the channel is specified with precision only at the first level of distribution. After this point, the resellers or ultimate buyers lose their typological identities.

2. In the case of a manufacturer marketing directly to retailers, the

[9] *Ibid.*, p. 121.
[10] Thomas A. Staudt, "The Managerial Functions of Marketing," *Managerial Marketing: Perspectives and Viewpoints*, William Lazer and Eugene J. Kelley (eds.), Richard D. Irwin, Homewood, Ill., 1958, pp. 385–393.

channel consists of the manufacturing enterprise and a particular *type* of retail establishment. Thus, a vertical alignment involving a toy manufacturer, discount department stores, and consumers would be considered to be a *single* marketing channel. Again, the *type* of firm in the channel is specified only at the first level of distribution, but since this is the only intervening level between the manufacturer and the ultimate buyer, less institutional detail is sacrificed than in the preceding illustration.

3. In the case of an industrial goods firm marketing directly to users, the channel consists of the manufacturing enterprise and specific *types* of users. Manufacturers selling simultaneously to institutional, governmental, and industrial users would be regarded as using *three* marketing channels. Once more, the type of customer involved is identified only at the first level of distribution, but since this is the final stage of distribution little detail is lost.

These approaches have several distinguishing characteristics. All are manufacturer oriented, since they reflect the limitations of the manufacturer's accounting data. More specifically, most manufacturers, on the basis of their internal records, know very little about the composition of the market below the first stage of distribution, and the channel definitions just cited reflect this ignorance by omitting the characteristics of buyers below the first reseller level—an omission that oversimplifies the nature of interfirm alignments. A specific type of wholesaler, for example, might simultaneously serve 10 or 15 different types of retailers and the foregoing definitions have nothing to say about this complexity. Consequently, the definitions fail to provide a basis for measuring shifts in intertype power below the first reseller level.

It is also implicitly assumed in these definitions that reseller groups, classified by type, are homogeneous—an assumption that is manifestly untrue in many, if not all, lines of trade. A specific group of wholesalers, for example, will vary widely in terms of their methods of operation, product assortments, scales of operation, and services offered. The heterogeneity of firms within a given category has already lead to at least two attempts to develop new classification systems. Revzan, in 1961, reclassified wholesale establishments to produce greater homogeneity within each category,[11] and Entenberg, in 1960, undertook the same task in the retailing sector.[12] Additional efforts to develop new classification systems, or improve existing ones, should lead to further gains.

[11] David A. Revzan, *Wholesaling in Marketing Organization,* Wiley, New York, 1961, pp. 27–30.
[12] Robert D. Entenberg, "Suggested Changes in Census Classifications of Retail Trade," *Journal of Marketing* (January 1960), pp. 39–43.

More significantly, marketing channels, as conventionally defined, include only firms or individuals who participate directly in the buying and selling process. The presence of facilitating agencies and the functions they perform are excluded by definition. A marketing channel should include *all* firms and individuals that perform one or more of the functions required to market the goods in question. Buying and selling are only two of the activities needed to move goods from points of production to points of use; merchandise must also be transported, stored, (re)packaged, and financed. In addition, prospective buyers must be notified that the merchandise is available and their desire to purchase it must be stimulated. Firms undertaking these "facilitating" functions are as necessary as the buyers and sellers. Consequently, facilitating agencies (financial institutions, common carriers, public warehouses, advertising agencies, factors, advertising media and other providers of business services) should be included when describing the marketing channel for a specific product. Such inclusion is necessary because

1. It provides a more comprehensive basis for explaining the marketing process and for examining the institutional network that transmits goods from producers to users.

2. It provides a more adequate basis for isolating and analyzing the total cost of marketing, since it reveals all of the potential sources of cost improvement.

3. It emphasizes the fact that the marketing process consists of a variety of supporting activities, as well as buying and selling.

4. It emphasizes the fact that facilitating agencies are partial substitutes for middlemen. The public warehouse, for example, is a partial substitute for a wholesaler, and a factor performs most of the functions normally handled by a manufacturer's credit department. The awareness of this partial substitutability is useful to analysts interested in designing new channel networks or in improving existing ones, and thus the presence of facilitating agencies in a given system should be acknowledged.

5. It provides a basis for examining the *nature* of interfirm alignments. The presence (or absence) of facilitating agencies in a channel affects the bargaining positions of other firms. Consequently, the role played by these intermediaries must be acknowledged when analyzing discount structures, contract provisions, and bargaining tactics in a given industry.

Conventional definitions of marketing channels, in addition to excluding facilitating agencies, also exclude "influentials." Research undertaken among farmers, physicians, consumers, and purchasing agents indicates that buying decisions are heavily influenced by the opinions of informed individuals within the affected group.[13] Because this is a structural characteristic of the marketing process, the channel should be defined to include influentials as well as original sellers, facilitating agencies, middlemen, and ultimate buyers.

An operational definition of a marketing channel should also provide a basis for identifying functional relationships between firms. Breyer initially,[14] Revzan,[15] Vaile, Grether, and Cox later,[16] developed notational systems that indicate the extent to which specific types of firms perform a given function. The resulting schematics are not completely satisfactory, but they are more useful than the elliptic channel diagrams contained in most of the literature. A new approach to charting channel relationships is required. The notational systems developed in sociometry and in matrix algebra may be useful in this regard.

In summary, conventional analysis and description of marketing channels oversimplifies reality and obscures the nature and complexity of interfirm alignments. A verbal or visual representation of a marketing channel should indicate the *types* of decision makers involved at each stage in the product flow. Facilitating agencies and influentials should definitely be included in this representation, and the functional relationships between all participants should be identified. Finally, all channel members should be classified so that each identified group is sufficiently homogeneous to permit generalization about its behavior. Irrespective of the definition used, a marketing channel is an important economic entity that deserves serious attention by marketing scholars.

THE SYSTEMS APPROACH TO MARKETING CHANNELS

Alderson, Mallen, Ridgeway, and others argue that a marketing channel is an operating system with an identifiable and distinctive pattern of behavior. This approach is illustrated in the following quotations from Ridgeway.

> The economic process, beginning with the acquisition of resources and running through manufacturing to the ultimate con-

---

[13] For excellent discussions of the diffusion process, see *Group Influence in Marketing and Public Relations* and *The Adoption of New Products: Process and Influence*, The Foundation for Research on Human Behavior, Ann Arbor, Mich., 1956 and 1959, respectively.

[14] Ralph F. Breyer, *Quantitative Systematic Analysis and Control: Study No. 1, Channel and Channel Group Costing*, Wharton School of Finance and Commerce, University of Pennsylvania, Philadelphia, 1949.

[15] Revzan, *op. cit.*, pp. 112–115.

[16] Vaile, Grether, and Cox, *op. cit.*, pp. 121–133.

sumption of products, is a continuous process, but in many industries the economic flow is the result of the work of a number of organizations, each with an independent identity and separate legal status. The manufacturer has crucial relationships with both suppliers and distributors. Despite the independent identity of these three classes of organizations, their activities must form one extended system—a fact usually ignored in administrative and organizational theory.

Together the manufacturer with his suppliers and/or dealers comprise a system in which the manufacturer may be designated as the primary organization and the dealers and suppliers designated as secondary organizations. This system is in competition with similar systems in the economy, and in order for the system to operate effectively as an integrated whole there must be some administration of the system as a whole, not merely administration of the separate organizations within that system.

Decisions are to be made by both the primary and secondary organizations and it is desirable that these decisions be consistent or mutually supporting. There must be programing and it is desirable that the programs mesh. There must be two-way communication between primary and secondary organizations and among the secondary organizations. Standards of performance must be established and enforced through a manipulation of the available rewards and penalties; and rewards and penalties must be created where they do not exist. And finally, there must be reappraisal of the decisions of primary and secondary organizations to provide for coordinated change and growth.[17]

Alderson, in a similar vein, notes that:

The functionalist approach to marketing theory begins with the study of organized behavior systems. Marketing functions are discharged by behavior systems or by individuals acting within systems. The type of system of interest here is classed as an ecological system because of the peculiar nature of the bond among the components. They are sufficiently integrated to permit the system to operate as a whole, but the bond is loose enough to allow for the replacement or addition of components.[18]

[17] Valentine F. Ridgeway, "Administration of Manufacturer–Dealer Systems," *Administrative Science Quarterly* (March 1957), pp. 464–467.
[18] Wroe Alderson, *Marketing Behavior and Executive Action*, Richard D. Irwin, Homewood, Ill., 1957, p. 32.

In short, the individual firm and its executives are parts of a larger and more complex system than has been traditionally assumed by many writers.

The channel, in more specific terms, is an operating system with the following formal characteristics.

1. The channel consists of interrelated components that are structured to produce predetermined results. These components may include two or more of the following: original sellers, agent middlemen, merchant middlemen, facilitating agencies, and influentials within the communication network, and ultimate buyers.

2. Members of the channel strive to achieve mutually acceptable objectives. The goals of individual participants are often incompatible but, through a process of bargaining and accommodation, divergent aspirations are reconciled and the need for cooperation is recognized. In cohesive channels the firms think of themselves as being highly interdependent and in some instances they achieve what Durkheim has called "organic solidarity." In other cases the relationships between firms are loosely structured and fluid. Even in these situations, however, there is interaction and interdependency because transactions must be consummated. Perceived mutuality of interest, however slight, is a basic characteristic of marketing channels.

3. Activities performed by channel members are undertaken sequentially and thus it is logical to think of such activities as "marketing flows." Inventory, for example, moves from producers to users through a series of intermediaries and information flows through the same or a similar network.

4. A marketing channel is an open system in the sense that participation in it is voluntary. Firms enter a channel freely, subject to institutional and market constraints, and withdraw with comparable ease. A firm participates in a particular channel alignment because such affiliation is presumed to be in the best interests of the enterprise. As other institutional possibilities develop, alignments sometimes change swiftly and the initial channel may lapse into a state of decline.

5. A single enterprise usually "administers" the channel. It initiates, coordinates, and controls most or all of the activities undertaken. Davidson and McCarthy use the term "channel captain" to identify this leadership role, which Fisk describes as follows:

> [Marketing channels are usually] . . . under the control of a single firm in the sense that a single enterprise directs the allocation of resources for all agencies in the channel without interfering with

the objectives of independent agencies which participate in the channel flows. Manufacturers, farm marketing cooperatives, wholesale cooperatives, retail chain and buying cooperatives are illustrations of integrated organizations that direct the activities of other channel agencies by their choices among goals. These controllers or decision makers do not set goals for other firms in the constituent marketing channels, but they do decide what kind of agencies shall be combined to form the distribution network for systems they organize. In this sense their executives control by optimizing, sub-optimizing, maximizing, and minimizing, the work input combinations of micromarketing systems.[19]

6. The behavior of channel members, particularly in a well established channel, is "regulated" by a code that specifies types of acceptable competitive behavior. The occupational code consists of informally established group norms, and a subtle but clear array of sanctions is used in most channels to control the behavior of participants.

Viewing the channel as an organized behavior system has several intrinsic advantages. First, this approach recognizes the fact that a channel is a purposive and rational assemblage of firms rather than a random collection of enterprises. Second, the systems concept emphasizes the existence of cooperative, as well as antagonistic, behavior within the channel. Third, the channel is perceived as a unique social organism that reflects the hopes, goals, and aspirations of its participants. Fourth, the marketing channel, from a systems point of view, is recognized as a basic "unit of competition"—a concept that broadens the study of economic rivalry. Systems theorists point out, for example, that a firm can fail not only because of its own imperfections but also because it is a member of the wrong system.[20] Fifth, the notion that a channel is an operating system provides a basis for identifying dysfunctions that are system generated. Forrester, as an illustration, has isolated a variety of situations in which facilities are wastefully utilized because of buying practices and decision rules followed in the channel. The resulting uneconomic allocation of resources is a property of the system *per se*, which

[19] George Fisk, "The General Systems Approach to the Study of Marketing," *The Social Responsibilities of Marketing*, William D. Stevens (ed.), American Marketing Association, Chicago (December 1961), p. 210.
[20] Several writers have extended the systems concept to shopping centers. See Alderson, *op. cit.*, pp. 336–337 and Paul E. Smith, and Eugene J. Kelley, "Competing Retail Systems: The Shopping Center and the Central Business District," *Journal of Retailing* (Spring 1960), pp. 11–17.

could not be discovered if the operations of individual firms were analyzed separately rather than collectively.[21]

Verbal Descriptions of Channel Systems

Several writers have attempted to verbally describe interaction patterns among channel members. The "marketing flows" concept promulgated by Vaile, Grether, and Cox [22] and the elaborate notational systems developed by these authors and by Breyer [23] and Revzan [24] are perhaps the best known of these attempts. Revzan's notational system is particularly interesting because it provides a basis for symbolically indicating the types of intermediaries participating in the channel as well as the extent to which each participates in specified functional flows. Furthermore, his system provides a basis for identifying the span of ownership and the locus of power in the channel. An analyst, using Revzan's system, can systematically plot interaction patterns in the channel. He can also isolate situations that may involve excessive costs and needless duplication of functions. The Vaile, Grether, and Cox approach, although less elaborate, leads to a similar understanding of the system's characteristics.

The flow concept popularized in the industrial goods field is similar to the approaches just discussed.[25] This concept emphasizes the need for greater coordination of marketing efforts. Specifically, the proponents of the flow concept contend that distribution is a continuous and related sequence of activities involving manufacturers, industrial distributors, and ultimate users. Total distribution costs can be reduced when all parties in the system integrate their activities more closely. Proponents of this concept have focused their attention on coordinating functions performed by all channel members, such as inventory management, information gathering and dissemination, "combining activities," and transfer of ownership. Flow analysts, for example, stress the presence of inventory "float" in the marketing channel. Manufacturers carry stocks of finished goods to supply industrial distributors, who carry inventory to supply their customers, who maintain inventory to satisfy short-run production requirements. Concern about the size of this inventory float

[21] Jay W. Forrester, "Industrial Dynamics: A Major Breakthrough for Decision Makers," *Harvard Business Review* (July–August 1958), p. 38.
[22] Vaile, Grether, and Cox, *op. cit.*, pp. 121–133.
[23] Breyer, *op. cit.*, pp. 12–48.
[24] Revzan, *op. cit.*, pp. 112–115.
[25] For an excellent discussion of the flow concept, see "Innovation in the Age of Distribution," *Industrial Distribution* (May 1963), pp. 96–102.

has led to several steps to reduce it. Procurement innovations, such as stockless purchasing, contract buying, and blanket ordering, are being used to reduce inventories at the user level, and economic order quantity programing has been adopted by an increasing number of industrial distributors to minimize their inventory holdings.

Ownership and information flows are also important in industrial goods marketing. During recent years, there has been a pronounced effort to simplify these flows by developing integrated data processing systems, that is, suppliers, industrial distributors, and users are now beginning to use compatible data processing techniques to simplify the ordering process. Finally, flow analysts emphasize the need for seeking out new combinational possibilities to reduce waste and duplication in the system. New combinations of services, products and availabilities are being used to effect a better meshing of supply and demand. The acceptance of the flow concept in industrial goods marketing represents an application of earlier work done by marketing scholars; as more rigorous analytical techniques are developed, further progress in effecting channel economies can be expected.

Verbal descriptions of channel systems are effective devices for detecting and emphasizing the complexity of interfirm alignments. They also provide a basis for isolating grossly inefficient linkages, but they lack the analytical rigor and the preciseness of recently developed simulation models.

Mathematical Simulation of Marketing Channels

Forrester began to simulate company systems on computers during the middle 1950's.[26] The term "company system" includes the firm's relationships with suppliers and intermediaries as well as its internal operations. Consequently, Forrester simulates a major part of the firm's marketing channel. He justifies this approach by arguing that "manufacturing, finance, distribution, organization, advertising, and research have too often been viewed as separate skills and not as part of a unified system." [27] Predictably, he deplores this tendency and states that "the task of management is to interrelate the flows of information, materials, manpower, money, and capital equipment so as to achieve a higher standard of living, stability of employment, profit to the owners, and rewards appropriate to the success of the managers." [28] Forrester's models are programed to depict interrelationships between these five

---

[26] Forrester, *op. cit.*, pp. 37–67.
[27] Forrester, *op. cit.*, p. 37
[28] Forrester, *op. cit.*, p. 38.

flows. The development of this type of model requires data on the number and types of firms in the channel, on the delays in decisions and actions that are characteristic of the channel, and on the participants' ordering and inventory policies. Given these and other required inputs in appropriate mathematical form, the programer can simulate the behavior of a channel over time.

Balderston and Hoggatt have developed a simulation model that describes channel behavior in the lumber industry.[29] This model is designed "to show how limits on market information, decentralization of market decisions and institutional alignments affect and are affected by economic forces,"[30] and it contains six types of variables:

1. Economic forces (price, quantity, cost, and demand data).
2. Commodity flows (designed to reflect distribution patterns in the lumber trade).
3. Accounting and cash flow data (including an accounting structure for each firm in the channel and an appropriate mathematical treatment of cash flow patterns).
4. Decision rule data (for each type of firm in the channel).
5. Information flows (between firms).
6. Institutional forces and norms of behavior (these are represented explicitly in the model).

The Balderston and Hoggatt model, like Forrester's, simulates interaction patterns that are often too complicated to reduce to analytical solution. Consequently, the concept of a system in equilibrium and the notion of achieving an optimal solution are ideas that have to be discarded in many cases. Simulation models, however, provide a basis for determining the extent to which specified alternatives yield improved results, and thus they have considerable managerial significance.

Amstutz and Tallman have also attempted to simulate the behavior of a marketing channel, and their model is apparently quite similar to those just discussed.[31] In fact, all channel simulation models have several common characteristics.

1. They are programed on digital computers and are designed to

---

[29] Frederick E. Balderston, and A. C. Hoggatt, "Simulation Models: Analytical Variety and the Problem of Model Reduction," *Symposium on Simulation Models: Methodology and Applications to the Behavioral Sciences*, South-Western Publishing Company, Cincinnati, Ohio, 1963, pp. 182–191.

[30] *Ibid.*, p. 183.

[31] Arnold Amstutz and Gerald B. Tallman, "Dynamic Simulation Applied to Marketing," *Marketing Keys to Profits in the 1960's*, Wenzil K. Dolva (ed.), American Marketing Association, Chicago, 1959, pp. 78–95.

depict comprehensively the operating characteristics of a system. This results in complex interaction patterns; the Balderston and Hoggatt model, for example, can accommodate 30 supplier firms, 15 wholesalers, and 60 retailers. Despite the fact that the number of firms is limited, over 16,000 variables must be "tracked" during each time interval.[32]

2. All simulation models are dynamic rather than static.

3. If the decision maker accepts the assumptions included in the model, the probable consequences of alternative courses of action can be predicted.

4. Simulation models provide a basis for isolating system generated fluctuations. These are described by Forrester in the following terms:

> As a system the company has certain characteristics which are completely independent of individual functions or departments, just as an electronic computer has certain characteristics as a system of parts. For instance, there is what the engineer might call "amplification," caused by inventory accumulation, filling of supply pipelines, and inept extrapolation of trends. There are delays in decisions, shipping, communications, and accounting. These all combine to cause production fluctuations, construction of excess plant capacity, creation of company-generated sales cycles, and detrimental advertising policies.[33]

Although channel simulation models are still in the experimental stage, they represent a logical mathematical extension of the systems concept in marketing and thus they complement the work of earlier theorists.

Necessary Modifications of the Systems Concept

The contention that marketing channels are organized behavior systems should not obscure the fact that they often consist of independent and idiosyncratic intermediaries. Alderson and McVey both emphasize this potential source of channel disharmony in their analyses. Alderson, for example, argues that a channel is a group of firms that "constitute a loose coalition engaged in exploiting joint opportunity in the market;" McVey's position may be stated as follows:

> The middleman is not a hired link in a chain forged by a manu-

---

[32] F. E. Balderston, "Analytical Models Versus Computer Simulation—A Comparison, with Illustrations from the Lumber Trade," *Marketing Concepts in Changing Times*, Richard M. Hill (ed.), American Marketing Association, Chicago, 1960, p. 148.

[33] Forrester, *op. cit.*, p. 38.

facturer, but rather an independent market, the focus of a large group of customers for whom he buys. Subsequent to some market analysis of his own, he selects products and suppliers, thereby setting at least one link in the channel.

After some experimentation, he settles upon a method of operation, performing those functions he deems inescapable in the light of his own objectives, forming policies for himself wherever he has freedom to do so.

. . . his choices are in many instances tentative proposals. He is subject to much influence from competitors, from aggressive suppliers, from inadequate finances and faulty information, as well as from habit. Nonetheless, many of his choices are independent.

As he grows and builds a following, he may find that his prestige in his market is greater than that of the suppliers whose goods he sells. In some instances his local strength is so great that a manufacturer is virtually unable to tap that market, except through him. In such a case the manufacturer can have no channel policy with respect to that market.[34]

Alderson and McVey also view the channel as a derivative operating system and this point needs emphasis. Firms in the channel are not principally concerned with the channel's growth or even its survival; instead, they are preoccupied with internal operations and their own rate of growth. Thus the channel is not an institution that inspires strong entrepreneurial loyalties or that serves as a source of inspiration.

Integrated action up and down a channel is a rare luxury in marketing. Why? It may be that the "channel of distribution" is a concept that is principally academic in usage and unfamiliar to many firms selling to and through these channels.

Instead of a channel, a businessman is likely to concern himself merely with suppliers and customers. His dealings are not with all of the links in the channel but only with those immediately adjacent to him, from which he buys and to which he sells. He may little know nor care what becomes of his products after they leave the hands of some merchant middleman who has paid him for them and released him to return to problems involving his special functions. A manufacturer may not even consider himself as standing at the head of a channel, but only as occupying a link in a channel that begins with his suppliers.[35]

[34] Phillip McVey, "Are Channels of Distribution What the Textbooks say?," *Journal of Marketing* (January 1960), p. 65.
[35] *Ibid.*, p. 62.

Finally, it should be observed that channels may be highly unstable systems, that is, the configuration of the firms involved in the channel may change dramatically from one time period to another. These observations lead to the inevitable conclusion that a channel can benefit from purposive direction and executive leadership. The literature on channel management reflects this point of view, and its usefulness as a separate area of inquiry is self-evident. A review of this important area follows later in the chapter.

DETERMINANTS OF CHANNEL BEHAVIOR

Marketing channels are complex economic, political and social entities, and the analyst must incorporate all these factors into his channel model. The following paragraphs deal with some of the principal determinants of channel behavior. The economic rationale of marketing channels is analyzed initially, followed by a brief discussion of political, psychological, and sociological factors that affect channel performance. Existing legislation also influences interfirm alignments to some extent, but this area will not be explored because of its specialized and complex nature.

Economic Theory and Marketing Channels

Economists have analyzed marketing channels from several perspectives. Balderston and Bucklin have attempted to develop channel decision rules for the firm, and Stigler, Coase, Heflebower, and Hirshman have constructed analytical models for explaining and predicting channel evolution. The resulting theory is admittedly elliptic in that it focuses on a limited number of relationships while ignoring others, but it still represents a useful point of departure for subsequent analysis.

Stigler, in his analysis of vertical disintegration, postulates that a manufacturing enterprise simultaneously performs several activities, each of which has a distinctively shaped cost curve.[36] Some activities may be subject to increasing returns rather quickly, others may have moderately declining cost curves over an extended range of output, and a third group may have pronounced U-shaped cost functions. Furthermore, team or project-oriented tasks may have corkscrew-shaped cost curves. The firm's average cost curve is the sum of the cost curves associated with performing a given set of activities. The firm will strive to produce at the level of

[36] George J. Stigler, "The Division of Labor is Limited by the Extent of the Market," *Journal of Political Economy* (June 1951), pp. 185–193.

output at which marginal cost equals marginal revenue, which occurs at or to the left of the lowest point on the average cost curve. However, all economies inherent in performing specific activities will not be exhausted at this production level. Even though the firm is producing at a level which enables it to achieve relatively low per unit costs, it could still perform some activities more economically than at present if output were increased. Put another way, even though the firm is operating at an optimum position, savings could still be effected if certain activities were performed at a higher level of output than others. A firm in a competitive industry will delegate increasing returns activities to enterprises specializing in these activities. Specialized enterprises (middlemen, subsidiary producers, and facilitating agencies) offer external economies to their customers. These savings are achieved in one or more of the following situations:

1. Specialized enterprises, by aggregating client requirements, can perform a designated activity in a given location at its optimum scale and by so doing can achieve lower per unit costs than could be achieved by any of the client firms.
2. Specialized companies, by aggregating client requirements, can utilize existing, though nonoptimum facilities in a given location more intensively than can the client firms, which results in lower per unit costs for the system as a whole.
3. Specialist companies, by aggregating client requirements, can fully utilize an existing, but nonoptimum "plant" in a specific location, which results in the lowest per unit costs that can be achieved for the activity given current physical facilities.

The firm, by delegating selected activities, is able to lower average and marginal costs, and thus it improves its competitive position. This line of argument when applied to marketing indicates that middlemen and facilitating agencies are sources of external economies for manufacturers, since they can perform the delegated functions at a lower cost per unit than their clients.

The analysis developed by Stigler also specifies the point at which manufacturers will reabsorb hitherto delegated activities. As output expands, or as technology changes, client firms reach a point at which they can perform the delegated activities at an optimum scale. When this point is reached, such activities tend to be reabsorbed and the channel becomes more completely integrated. Small manufacturers, for example, rely heavily on agent middlemen to represent them in the field. As these firms expand, they frequently dispense with agents and begin to rely on their own field selling forces. The same pattern of vertical disintegration followed by vertical integration is characteristic of other marketing functions, such as storage, transportation, and financing. The process of reintegration is not necessarily frictionless. Both middlemen and facilitating agencies attempt to avoid being "integrated out" of the channel by changing their method of operation so that their service conforms more closely to client requirements. Manufacturer's agents in the electronics field have retained their principals by carrying inventory, and building supply wholesalers have been able to retain the patronage of large developers by offering goods on a cash and carry basis.

Stigler's cost-oriented model, with its emphasis on external economies, provides a basis for explaining existing interfirm alignments and for predicting the extent to which costs or technology have to change in order to justify the discontinuance of present institutional relationships. Coase's explanation of institutional change [37] is similar to Stigler's in that both rely on cost data to explain entrepreneurial decisions. Coase, in examining the nature of the firm, contends that an enterprise will perform activities if it can do so at an internal cost that is lower than prevailing market prices.[38] If the cost curve conected with the activity is such that the firm's internal costs are greater than prevailing market prices, then the enterprise will use outside suppliers for the function in question. Coase, therefore, envisions the managerial process as involving a continuous series of "make or buy" decisions. The firm, in this context, is constantly examining its internal cost structure to determine whether it should perform the activity in question or delegate it. The existence of a channel network indicates a priori that the firms involved are using the services of the other participants because the latter can perform one or more activities at a lower cost per unit than the former. Coase's analysis, like Stigler's, accepts external economies as the most serviceable basis for explaining interfirm alignments.

Bucklin uses a similar conceptual approach to analyze vertical relationships.[39] His analysis begins with an identification of the functions performed within a marketing channel, and he uses four criteria to isolate these relevant functions:

1. The activities included in each function must be so related as to

[37] R. H. Coase, "The Nature of the Firm," *Economica*, New Series (November 1937), pp. 386–405.

[38] Coase also considers managerial and competitive factors in his analysis, but his explanation is essentially cost-oriented. For an interesting summary and application of Coase's approach, see Walter Taplin, *Advertising, A New Approach*, Little, Brown Company, Boston, 1960, pp. 203–204.

[39] Louis P. Bucklin, "The Economic Structure of Channels of Distribution," *Marketing: A Maturing Discipline*, Martin T. Bell (ed.), American Marketing Association, Chicago, 1960, pp. 379–385.

make it necessary for some firm to organize and direct the performance of all or none of the activities.

2. The activities included in each function must have sufficient scope to allow the firm to specialize in them to the exclusion of all others.
3. The activities included in each function should incur substantial cost.
4. Each activity undertaken in the marketing channel must be placed in one, and only one, functional category.

On the basis of these criteria Bucklin isolates the following functions:

1. Transit(T)—all activities required to move goods between two points.
2. Inventory (I)—all activities required to move goods in and out of storage, sort and store them.
3. Search (S)—all activities required to communicate offers to buy and sell and transfer title.
4. Persuasion (P)—all activities incurred to influence the beliefs of a buyer or seller.
5. Production (Pr)—all activities necessary to create a good with any desired set of specifications.

By using this set of functions, Bucklin is able to diagram the structure of most existing channels. The familiar manufacturer, wholesaler, retailer, consumer channel, for example, may be symbolically diagramed as follows:

$$(PrITSP) \rightarrow (SITSP) \rightarrow (SISP) \leftarrow (STI).$$

The manufacturer, wholesaler, retailer, and consumer are designated, respectively, by the bracketed symbols (PrITSP), (SITSP), (SISP), and (STI), indicating that the manuacturer performs all five marketing functions; the wholesaler performs four but must search twice to contact both manufacturers and retailers; the retailer performs three but must also search twice to maintain liaison with wholesalers and consumers; and the consumer performs three marketing functions when dealing with retailers.

Bucklin's analysis from this point parallels Stigler's in that he emphasizes the need for developing average cost curves for each function. Furthermore, he hypothesizes that the cost curves, in most cases, will behave in the familiar fashion, that is, average costs will initially decline to some minimal point and then increase due to managerial inefficiencies at higher operating levels. Total cost curves for channel members performing multiple functions may be derived by aggregating the costs associated with each function. Consequently, Bucklin's analysis provides a conceptual basis for determining cost-volume relationships in existing channels. It also provides a basis for redesigning channels to accommodate demand patterns better and to take full advantage of potential economies. Bucklin uses the term "normative channel" to describe this latter alignment. More specifically, it is "the channel that would exist if all institutions in the extant channel and all potential entrants were fully adapted to current economic conditions. In such a channel there would be no tendency for new firms to enter, old ones to exit or to shift functions among themselves." [40] In short, Bucklin's normative channel is in a state of equilibrium in that all potential economies have been exhausted and consumer demand is satisfied to the extent that technology, factor costs, and geography permit.

Bucklin's analysis differs from Stigler's in two important respects. First, he focuses more specifically on the marketing implications of functional cost analysis than does Stigler, and second, he is more explicit in his treatment of demand analysis as a basis for explaining the firm's behavior. Stigler's analysis focuses principally on the institutional changes produced by an expansion of demand given an undefined degree of competition. Bucklin, on the other hand, analyzes patterns of interfirm alignments that may emerge in six different, and progressively more complex, environments: perfect competition, pure competition, monopolistic competition caused by spatial differentiation, monopolistic competition caused by product differentiation, and oligopoly. In summary, he provides a basis for determining the optimum channel given demand, cost, and competitive data. The analyst, using Bucklin's approach, can therefore ascertain the extent to which the extant channel deviates from the normative channel.

The foregoing analyses suggest that marketing functions will be shifted from one level of the channel to another depending on the economies that can be realized. These economies are a function of technology and demand. A shift in demand, for example, may result in a sufficiently large increase in output to justify recombinations of activities in a channel. Alternatively, an improvement in technology may result in the development of a new type of marketing institution or a recombination of existing enterprises. In this context, marketing intermediaries (merchant middlemen, agent middlemen, and facilitating agencies) are sources of external economies for client firms, and they will be used by client firms to the extent that cost considerations warrant. The analyses are, therefore, manufacturer oriented. There is no reason, however, why these conceptual schemes can not be used to explain the intermediary's channel decisions, too. A retail firm considering the possibility of using the

[40] *Ibid.*, p. 382.

services of a resident buying office or evaluating the possibility of joining a nonprofit shipping association or contemplating the purchase of a production facility can use the above frames of reference in the same manner as does a manufacturer, because each alternative cited represents an opportunity for the retailer to achieve systemic economies.

The explanation of channel alignments on the basis of external economies is a recurring theme throughout the literature of marketing, too. The following quotations from Vaile, Grether, and Cox reflect this particular orientation:

> The optimum scale of operation differs at successive stages of marketing and processing . . . only by accident will successive processes achieve minimum cost with the same rates of output . . . at each stage in the marketing process, units [firms] must change their scale upward or downward to minimize costs . . . whenever a change of scale offers an economic advantage, pressure appears for the development of a new type of distributing agency.[41]

Economic analysis of channel alignments can be carried much further, but the operational significance of this approach is limited because it ignores the sociological aspects of channel behavior; it also assumes that cost curves can be derived for each function given different levels of output and different scales. The sociological aspects of marketing channels will be discussed in a following section. Before moving to this analysis, however, a few comments about the measurement of functional costs are necessary.

The analysis of cost curves typically assumes (1) that the "product" is homogeneous at each successive level of output, (2) that the nature of the output can be defined rigorously, (3) that plant capacity can be measured precisely, and (4) that most of the costs incurred by the firm are "production" rather than "selling" costs.[42] These conditions rarely hold in real life, and thus relatively few empirical studies of cost behavior have been undertaken. Gort, as an illustration, remarks that "no direct measures of economies of scale exist at present for any broad list of industries," [43] and Bain in his analysis of industrial organization is often forced to rely on impressionistic observations when dealing with econ-

---

[41] Vaile, Grether, and Cox, *op. cit.*, pp. 134–137.
[42] For a more complete discussion of these issues, see Edna Douglas, "Size of Firm and the Structure of Costs in Retailing," *Journal of Business* (April 1962), pp. 158–190, and Richard Holton, "Scale, Specialization and Costs in Retailing," *Marketing: A Maturing Discipline*, Martin T. Bell (ed.), American Marketing Association, Chicago, 1960, pp. 459–466.
[43] Michael Gort, *Stability and Change in Market Shares*, University of Chicago, 1963, p. 18.

omies of scale phenomena.[44] The absence of definitive empirical work on cost curves is particularly noticeable in the fields of retailing and whole-saling. The pioneering work done by Dean and subsequent studies under-taken by Douglas, Bass, and Bellamy, among others, constitute the extant literature, and all these studies are concerned with cost relation-ships at the firm level rather than at the functional level.[45] Thus they fail to provide a basis for determining either the scale or the level at which specific functions should be performed within the channel. In addi-tion, they fail to resolve the problem of how to reconcile the require-ments of analytical simplicity with the complex reality involved. Re-tailers, for example, market a "product" that is extremely difficult to define; they also market a "different product" at successive sales levels, incur selling rather than production costs in the main, and have no defin-able upper limit on capacity.[46] Hence it is extremely difficult, if not impos-sible, to discuss economies of scale in retailing, particularly at the functional level.[47] This argument applies with equal validity to most wholesale establishments and facilitating agencies.

Clearly, the difficulties connected with measuring cost curves for specific activities inhibit the application of economic theory to channel problems. The economist, however, has developed an important frame of reference for explaining and predicting the nature of interfirm align-ments, and sophisticated cost studies have been undertaken with respect to some functions, such as transportation and warehousing.

Political Aspects of Channel Behavior

The preceding analysis suggests that interfirm alignments are deter-mined primarily by cost-revenue considerations. Stigler, Coase, Bucklin, and others who work within the context of formal economic theory postu-late that channel linkages are forged by rational, profit-maximizing entrepreneurs who are uninfluenced by social, political, and psychological considerations. Thus formal economic theory, when applied to the prob-lem of interfirm alignments, yields a meaningful, but largely mechanistic,

[44] Joe S. Bain, "Advantages of the Large Firm: Production, Distribution, and Sales Promotion," *The Journal of Marketing* (April 1956), pp. 336–346.
[45] For a comprehensive bibliography of relevant studies, see Douglas, *op. cit.*, pp. 189–190.
[46] For some interesting approaches to the problem of defining capacity in retailing, see Bob R. Holdren, *The Structure of a Retail Market and the Market Behavior of Retail Units*, Prentice-Hall, Englewood Cliffs, N. J., 1960, pp. 27–66.
[47] For an effective treatment of this problem, see Richard H. Holton, "On the Measurement of Excess Capacity in Retailing," *The Review of Economic Studies*, No. 63, pp. 43–48.

explanation of channel behavior. A channel is a political, social, and economic complex, and the alignments that prevail reflect all these influences. A channel is a political system in at least three senses. First, some or all of its participants may achieve a high degree of group solidarity so that they bargain with other social systems on a collective as well as an individual basis. The legislative machinations described by Palamountain in *The Politics of Distribution* [48] and the recent "dealer revolt" in the automobile industry are illustrations of channel members exercising this type of political power.

Second, the marketing channel is a political system because the participants strive to control the behavior of other members. Rationalized enterprises have extremely high fixed costs. As a result, they are unusually vulnerable to sales fluctuations and must maintain volume at a high level to realize an adequate rate of return on investment. A firm operating under these conditions attempts to dominate its environment. It strives to create a loyal customer following through aggressive promotional effort, and it attempts to manipulate the behavior of other channel members so that their support is maintained.[49] Numerous authors have analyzed this struggle for channel control. Grether, noting that "the prime issue in the conflict within channels of distribution is where dominance will rest," [50] has provocatively explored the conditions under which resellers are likely to engage in cooperative efforts to strengthen their channel position.[51] Revzan has also analyzed the managerial struggle for channel control, and he contends it is one of the principal variables that must be included in any analysis of channel behavior.[52] Balderston, in his statement of the critical issues confronting the channel analyst, asserts that an understanding of power alignments is necessary to the development of a theory of marketing channels.[53]

Wholesalers dominated their channels during the nineteenth century. With the development of mass markets in the twentieth century, manufacturers achieved salient power positions in most lines of trade. This

[48] Joseph Cornwall Palamountain, Jr., *The Politics of Distribution*, Harvard University Press, Cambridge, Mass., 1955.

[49] For a theoretical discussion of this phenomenon see Roderick Seidenberg, *Posthistoric Man: An Inquiry*, Beacon Press, Boston, 1950, p. 8.

[50] R. S. Vaile, "Changing Distribution Channels," (Report of round table discussion), *American Economic Association Papers and Proceedings* (March 1939), p. 105.

[51] E. T. Grether, "Solidarity in the Distribution Trades," *Law and Contemporary Problems* (June 1937), pp. 376–391.

[52] Revzan, *op. cit.*, pp. 143–150.

[53] Frederick E. Balderston, "Theories of Marketing Structure and Channels," *Proceedings: Conference of Marketing Teachers from Far Western States*, University of California, Berkeley (September 1958), pp. 134–145.

pattern prevailed rather uniformly until the late 1940's when retailers, either individually or collectively, obtained control in several instances.[54] Today a mixed pattern prevails; in numerous lines of trade the eventual outcome of the struggle for power is problematic. In any case, most marketing channels are characterized by a continuous struggle for economic power, and this long-run source of conflict must be acknowledged in any definitive discussion of channel behavior.

Third, a channel is a power entity because the participants constantly bargain for favorable terms of trade—a process that involves strategy, bluff, subterfuge, and other political devices. Hence, conflict, as well as cooperation, is characteristic of most interfirm alignments. A detailed description of buyer-seller negotiation is beyond the scope of this paper, but Heflebower,[55] Machlup and Taber,[56] and Koo,[57] among others, have dealt systematically with selected aspects of this conflict relationship. Furthermore, the literature on countervailing power represents an extended inquiry into the nature of vertical rivalry between firms. Most of the literature on bargaining theory, however, is either descriptive or highly theoretical. In the latter instance, it possesses the same limitations as economic theory because it fails to explain why "uneconomic" alignments not only persist but expand over time. Entrepreneurial behavior must therefore be analyzed from a sociological and psychological point of view to explain vertical coalitions fully.

Entrepreneurial Frames of Reference as Determinants of Channel Behavior

Research undertaken at all levels of the distribution system indicates that the firm's behavior and decisions are strongly conditioned by the entrepreneur's value hierarchy. With respect to marketing institutions, large resellers tend to be growth oriented, and their decisions are based on economic criteria. Most large resellers evaluate alternative interfirm alignments on the basis of "profitability" analysis, and their behavior is reasonably consistent with that postulated in the economist's model.

[54] For an historical analysis of the struggle for channel control, see David R. Craig, and Werner K. Gabler, "The Competitive Struggle for Market Control," *The Annals of the American Academy of Political and Social Science* (May 1940), pp. 84–107.
[55] Richard B. Heflebower, "Mass Distribution: A Phase of Bilateral Oligopoly or of Competition?," *Adaptive Behavior in Marketing*, American Marketing Association, Chicago, 1957, pp. 139–152.
[56] Fritz Machlup and Martha Taber, "Bilateral Monopoly, Successive Monopoly and Vertical Integration," *Economica* (May 1960), pp. 101–120.
[57] A. Y. C. Koo, "A Theoretical Note on the Dealer-Manufacturer Relationship in the Automobile Industry," *Quarterly Journal of Economics* (May 1959), pp. 316–325.

The smaller reseller's frame of reference and set of expectations are different, however. Wittreich, on the basis of his research, concludes that small retailers (and probably small wholesalers as well) have relatively static expectations.[58] They are interested in reaching and maintaining a given scale of operation and are relatively uninterested in opportunities for growth beyond this point. Small resellers tend to view their demand curve as being relatively fixed and are inclined to resist change because it presumably cannot improve their position and could conceivably disrupt an acceptable *status quo*. Kriesberg, after analyzing the behavior of retail furriers, reaches essentially the same conclusions.[59] The small furriers studied by Kriesberg tended to value stability more highly than growth, and their participation in the channel was motivated by a desire for "personal security." In short, they were relatively unconcerned about achieving other business objectives that are usually assumed to guide entrepreneurial decision making. Vidich and Bensman, in their study of life in a small town, conclude that small retailers are reluctant to reinvest earnings in their businesses.[60] Instead they manifest a strong preference for withdrawing funds from their operations and investing them in real estate, securities, and other assets that are presumed to represent relatively low-risk opportunities. Apparently small resellers value stability and security more highly than growth, and thus they enter the channel with sets of goals and expectations that are dramatically different from those of larger firms. This difference in entrepreneurial image or point of view partially explains the conflict inherent in many channel alignments. The large, growth-oriented manufacturing firm is often forced to market its line through enterprises that are interested in maintaining the *status quo*. Acrimony and frustration for both parties should not be a surprising consequence.

The large manufacturer's point of view also differs from the small reseller's in other important respects. For example, the manufacturer tends to have a national or regional market orientation, whereas small resellers are predictably interested in local market conditions.[61] Manufacturing executives tend to use the vocabulary of professional management, whereas the small reseller clings to a set of terms that is personal rather than professional. In addition, the large manufacturing enterprise has a programmatic orientation toward decision making in that the firm

[58] Warren J. Wittreich, "Misunderstanding the Retailer," *Harvard Business Review* (May–June 1962), pp. 147–155.

[59] Louis Kriesberg, "The Retail Furrier: Concepts of Security and Success," *American Journal of Sociology* (March 1952), pp. 478–485.

[60] Arthur J. Vidich and Joseph Bensman, *Small Town in Mass Society*, Doubleday, Garden City, New York, 1960, pp. 73 and 91–93.

[61] Many of the conclusions in the remainder of this section are based on Wittreich, *op. cit.*, pp. 147–155.

depends on research and planning to guide its actions. Resellers, both large and small, tend to prefer an adaptive approach to decision making. They try to avoid long-run commitments and strive to remain flexible to reduce research and planning costs. Stated more formally, the large manufacturer attempts to reduce uncertainty through planning and research; the reseller, on the other hand, tends to accept uncertainty as being inevitable and strives to remain adaptable so that the firm can adjust quickly to its changing environment. Neither approach to decision making is inherently better than the other, but they are different, and this disparity is a communications barrier and a source of conflict within the channel.

Another intrinsic difference between manufacturers and resellers is that the latter tend to be "brand and item indifferent," since they handle numerous competing products. Most resellers evaluate their operation by analyzing the performance of total merchandise categories. They are relatively unconcerned about the comparative performance of specific brands except in the case where a brand is obviously producing unsatisfactory results. Manufacturers, on the other hand, are preoccupied with the performance of their brands and are secondarily interested in the product category. Again, this difference in perspective is probably another source of conflict within the channel.

In summary, the goals and orientations of manufacturers and resellers often differ, and this is particularly true when large manufacturing enterprises deal with small resellers. Such differences tend to aggravate the inherent conflict between buyers and sellers, and the adjustments made by each take into consideration psychological, as well as economic, factors.

Status Aspiration as a Determinant of Channel Behavior

An entrepreneur's status in society is partially attributable to the economic role he performs. Thus firms participating in a channel do so for status, as well as economic, reasons. Vidich and Bensman found that small retailers believe they have suffered a decline in status during the past three decades; [62] hence they tend to resist any institutional change that would further depress their relative position in the community even though such a change might produce economic benefits. This observation at least suggests why voluntary and cooperative groups have not been more successful. Retailers participating in these programs sacrifice some of their autonomy, the loss of which may be perceived as a loss of status. Wroe Alderson, in another context, hypothesizes that a system

---

[62] Vidich and Bensman, *op. cit.*, pp. 73 and 91–93.

will survive as long as it fulfills the status expectations of participants.[63] Since the small retailer's status is a function of "being in business for himself," the desire to maintain independence may partially explain his rejection of contractual integration as well as the persistence of "uneconomic" institutions and channels. Clearly, the interfirm linkages that prevail in the marketplace reflect status as well as economic aspirations.

Occupational Group Influences and Channel Behavior

Neither the firm nor its employees operate in a vacuum. All participants in the marketing process are members of one or more groups. These group memberships, according to the findings of recent studies in sociology, significantly influence the individual's behavior. Katona,[64] Alderson,[65] and Phillips,[66] among others, argue convincingly that the role of group influences is so pervasive that marketing must be viewed as a form of group behavior in order to arrive at definitive conclusions.

Sociologists have used several criteria to classify the types of groups to which individuals "belong." The professional participants in one seminar, as an illustration, agreed that the following classification is useful for analytical purposes:

1. *Membership* groups are those to which the individual actually belongs. These can be groups in which frequent association is the rule, or groups in which actual membership is held, but in which personal contacts between members are transient and infrequent.

2. *Categorical* groups are those to which a person *automatically* belongs by virtue of age, sex, education, marital status, or other characteristics. This type of group membership involves the concept of an individual's role in society. An individual belonging to a categorical group continually asks himself whether a proposed course of action is congruent with the role, or combination of roles, he is expected to play by society.

3. *Anticipatory* groups are those the individual desires to join. An individual who aspires to membership in a particular group may

[63] Wroe Alderson, "Survival and Adjustment in Organized Behavior Systems," *Theory in Marketing*, Reavis Cox, and Wroe Alderson (eds.), Richard D. Irwin, Homewood, Ill., 1950, p. 80.

[64] G. Katona, "Changing Assumptions in the Theory of Business Behavior," *Industrial Relations Research Association Proceedings* (December 1952), pp. 58–62.

[65] Wroe Alderson, "The Analytical Framework for Marketing," *Proceedings: Conference of Marketing Teachers from Far Western States*, University of California, Berkeley (September 1958), pp. 15–28.

[66] Almarin Phillips, *Market Structure Organization and Performance*, Harvard University Press, Cambridge, Mass., 1962.

be more likely to refer to its standards than to the standards of the group to which he actually belongs, but would like to leave. This type of group obviously involves the concept of upward mobility. Thus, it provides a basis for explaining a wide variety of economic decisions made in a society that places a high value on achievement.

4. *Dissociative* groups are those the individual is attempting to escape. In some cases the individual is actually a member of this type of group, but he attempts to avoid all behavior associated with it. In other instances the individual does not belong to the group, and predictably he avoids any pattern of behavior that would lead others to believe he is a member.[67]

The group(s) to which an individual belongs can be classified on the basis of functional criteria, too. Some groups, for example, are social in nature, whereas others are religious or political. Furthermore, there are occupational groups to which individuals belong. Membership in this type of group significantly affects reseller behavior. Kriesberg, for instance, has analyzed the behavior of steel warehouse distributors in terms of their occupational loyalties.[68] The substance of his analysis is briefly summarized in the following paragraph.

There is a dominant marketing channel for most lines of merchandise. This channel, as compared with other institutional alignments, has the greatest prestige and often handles the bulk of the industry's output. Behavior within the channel is regulated by an informal occupational code that "controls" pricing policies, sales promotion practices, and other related activities. The code, in essence, is a statement of group norms. Deviations from the code's prescriptions are punished in a variety of ways, ranging from colleague ostracism to economic sanctions. In this context, marketing institutions can be classified in terms of their relationship to the dominant marketing channel and in terms of their adherence to group norms. *Insiders* are members of the dominant channel. They have continuous access to preferred sources of supply, and possess relatively high status in the trade as a by-product of channel membership. The insiders, as a group, prescribe the contents of the occupational code and enforce it. As individuals they recognize the interdependency of firms in the system, and they want the respect of their colleagues. In short, the insider has made an emotional and financial commitment to the dominant channel and is interested in perpetuating it. *Strivers* are firms located outside the dominant channel who want to become a part

[67] *Group Influence in Marketing and Public Relations*, Foundation for Research on Human Behavior, Ann Arbor, Mich., 1956, pp. 1-2.
[68] Louis Kriesberg, "Occupational Controls Among Steel Distributors," *American Journal of Sociology* (November 1955), pp. 203-212.

of the system. These firms have discontinuous access to preferred resources. During periods of short supply, they may be "short ordered" or not shipped at all. The striver, since he wants to become a member of the system, is responsive to the occupational code and will not engage in deviate behavior under normal economic conditions. Thus he utilizes the same marketing practices as the insider. *Complementors* are not part of the dominant channel, nor do they desire to obtain membership. They perform functions not normally performed by other channel members, or they serve customers not usually solicited, or they stock qualities of merchandise not carried by the dominant channel. Complementors are marginally affiliated with the dominant channel and want to see it survive. Their expectations are of a long-run nature and they respect prevailing group norms. *Transients* also occupy a position outside the dominant channel but do not seek membership in it. Many transients are mobile entrepreneurs who move from one line of trade to another; other transients are firms that consider themselves to be members of other channels. Transients, by definition, have short-run expectations and other controlling interests; therefore the occupational code in the dominant channel is not an effective constraint on their behavior.

Classification of firms into these four categories helps to explain some of the competitive patterns that have emerged in the ready-to-wear field, the toy industry, and the TBA market. Transient firms in these merchandise lines have disrupted the *status quo* by engaging in deviate competitive activities, such as loss leader selling, "in and out" merchandising, and "bait" advertising.

None of the four types of firms just described is likely to introduce major marketing innovations. Insiders and strivers are primarily interested in maintaining existing institutional arrangements. Complementors also have a vested interest in the *status quo,* and transients are not sufficiently dependent on the product line to develop an entirely new method of distribution. If the foregoing analysis is valid, it suggests that a firm completely outside the system will introduce basic innovations, and historically this has usually been the case. Logically, then, a fifth category, *outside innovators,* is necessary to explain major institutional realignments.

Kriesberg's study suggests that group norms are a significant determinant of entrepreneurial behavior. These pressures condition behavior within the enterprise, too. French, in his analysis of retail furniture salesmen, found that the most productive salesmen consistently violated group norms.[69] Predictably these individuals were the "most rejected

[69] Cecil L. French, "Correlates of Success in Retail Selling," *American Journal of Sociology* (September 1960), pp. 128–134.

and rejecting members of their group." That is, they violated group norms because they did not identify with their associates nor did other members of the group accept them. If this is so, an aggressive retail selling organization could be one in which group norms support management's desire to achieve high productivity or one in which social isolates disregard the occupational code.

While occupational group influences affect interfirm relationships and partially determine the enterprise's performance capabilities, other sociological and psychological variables may have comparable significance. Krugman, after analyzing the behavior of insurance salesmen, found that the most productive field personnel are those who are least concerned about intruding on the privacy of prospective customers.[70] Furthermore, he found that there is a closer correlation between this personal characteristic and productivity than between other characteristics and sales success. Consequently, it appears that psychological predispositions of personnel can markedly affect the capability of an organization. Tucker, to cite another illustration, believes that the concept of "social distance" helps to explain the success of one salesman versus another.[71] Tucker contends that customers are much more inclined to buy from salesmen of their own social class than they are to buy from salesmen above or below it. If he is correct, social class considerations are likely to influence the operations of reseller organizations. Finally, Dunnette and Kirchner argue that the psychological profiles of industrial and retail salesmen are quite different.[72] Many of the psychological differences discovered by these investigators are not surprising. Others, however, are more subtle and an organization could conceivably fail to exploit its market potential because too many of the personnel employed have inappropriate psychological profiles, even though they are otherwise qualified and apparently well trained for the jobs they hold.

Horizontal Communication Networks in Marketing Channels

The sociologists cited above are primarily interested in analyzing the *extent* to which group pressures influence individual decisions. Others are interested in the same phenomenon, but they are principally in-

[70] Herbert E. Krugman, "Salesmen in Conflict: A Challenge to Marketing," *Journal of Marketing* (July 1958), pp. 59–61.

[71] W. T. Tucker, *The Social Context of Economic Behavior*, Holt, Rinehart and Winston, New York, 1964, pp. 70–71.

[72] M. D. Dunnette, and W. K. Kirchner, "Psychological Test Differences Between Industrial Salesmen and Retail Salesmen," *Journal of Applied Psychology*, 1960, pp. 121–125.

terested in analyzing and describing the *processes* by which pressures are transmitted within the group. Thus the literature on the "diffusion process" complements the research of Kriesberg, French and others, since it represents a different approach to the same set of problems.

Horizontal communication networks exist within most social systems. These are usually informal, "word of mouth," networks that supplement formal communication channels. Although the networks themselves are not tightly programed, they usually contain one or more opinion leaders who serve as focal communication points and as sources of influence. Recent research indicates that these horizontal communication networks often play a vital role in disseminating marketing information. Their significance is particularly important in the marketing of new products or in the dissemination of new ideas.

A new product or a new idea is, by definition, unproven. Prospective users or acceptors do not know with certainty what benefits, if any, will be derived from the innovation. A decision maker, who is unsure of his own judgement, often turns to his group for guidance. More specifically, he tends to rely heavily on the recommendations of opinion leaders within the group and their suggestions often determine the rate at which a new product or practice is accepted. The individual decision maker therefore relies on group approval and consensual validation to support decisions that involve a high degree of uncertainty. Most of the diffusion process studies undertaken to date deal with the dispersion of new products and new practices among ultimate buyers, including farmers, physicians, purchasing agents and consumers.[73] Unfortunately, little research of this nature has been undertaken among resellers. Since ultimate buyers are an integral part of the marketing structure, however, the existing literature is relevant for the channel analyst.

Rural sociologists have been particularly interested in the diffusion process. Beal and Rogers, two of the pioneers in this field, classify the participants in the diffusion process as follows: (1) innovators (the developers, or initial acceptors of a new idea), (2) early adopters, (3) majority adopters, and (4) laggards. They also contend that there are indirect participants in the process who occupy important positions in the communication network but do not actually make decisions. The indirect participants are identified as communicators, influentials, and skeptics.[74] Each of these participants in the communication network has

[73] See Herbert F. Lionberger, *Adoption of New Ideas and Practices*, The Iowa State University Press, Ames, 1960, pp. 119–159.
[74] E. M. Rogers, and G. M. Beal, *Reference Group Influence in the Adoption of Agricultural Technology*, The Iowa State University Press, Ames, 1958, p. 33.

a distinctive socio-economic profile and a differentiated mode of behavior. Researchers, by analyzing interaction patterns among farmers, can predict the rate at which a new idea, product, or practice will be accepted within the group.[75] These findings have obvious marketing implications. The farmer is an indispensable participant in the marketing channel for agricultural goods, and he relies on the informal communication network within his community to guide buying decisions. A manufacturer's failure to secure group approval for a new product or new practice may slow down the rate at which these innovations are accepted. In extreme cases, the new idea or practice may be rejected (or adopted on only a token basis) if consensual validation is not obtained.[76]

Horizontal interpersonal networks are important conveyors of information and attitudes among physicians and consumers, too. Research indicates that these networks are rather similar to those encountered in agricultural communities, with each individual performing an identifiable function. The role of opinion leaders in consumer networks is particularly interesting. These individuals normally possess important differentiating characteristics. They use formal communication channels much more extensively than the passive members of their group. They also tend to have highly specialized interests and acquire recognized expertise in a limited number of choice areas. The fashion leader, for example, is usually not the same individual as the homemaking influential. Furthermore, opinion leaders within a particular social and economic stratum appear to have little or no influence outside it. Thus there is a "layering" of influence within the community because of social class differences.[77]

Research undertaken by Coleman, Katz, and Menzel among physicians has produced similar findings.[78] Influentials within the medical community actively seek to maintain professional relationships with their colleagues, and thus they tend to be highly integrated members of their group. Because of their constant interaction with others, they are regarded as important sources of information and their advice is particularly sought when the use of a new drug is being considered. The physician, under these circumstances, has little empirical data and no direct experience to guide his decision. The results of the proposed treatment are therefore regarded as being highly problematic. Consequently, he tends to rely on the advice received from opinion leaders to guide his

---

[75] S. C. Dodd, "Diffusion is Predictable: Testing Probability Models for Laws of Interaction," *American Sociological Review* (August 1955), pp. 392–401.
[76] Robert C. Brooks, Jr., "Word-of-Mouth Advertising in Selling New Products," *Journal of Marketing* (October 1957), p. 156.
[77] *Ibid.*, pp. 157–158.
[78] James Coleman, Elihu Katz, and Herbert Menzel, "The Diffusion of an Innovation among Physicians," *Sociometry* (December 1957), pp. 253–270.

choice. Communication and influence within the group move out from a central nucleus until the new drug gains widespread acceptance. At this point, the importance of the communication network declines, and the members of the group subsequently rely on formal channels for additional data.[79]

The horizontal networks mentioned above are informal in nature. Formal interpersonal networks also convey information in a marketing channel, particularly in the case of industrial goods. Patterns of influence in industrial plants have been studied intensively during recent years. The findings indicate that a preponderance of buying decisions are the result of complex executive interaction. University Research Associates, for example, surveyed a group of executives in the electronics industry, including purchasing agents, administrative managers, engineering executives, research managers, and basic researchers.[80] All respondents participated actively in the buying process. The functions they performed reflected not only their particular areas of specialization but also the extent to which their departments were affected by the purchase in question. As many as 40 per cent of the respondents were consulted on some purchases, and at least 13 per cent participated in all buying decisions.[81] Consequently, it is naive to talk about the industrial buyer as a single individual. The buying process in most industrial firms reflects the composite judgment of many executives. Firms marketing to these organizations must maintain contact with all members of the formal communication network, and the designer of a channel system must include these networks in his analysis of channel behavior.

Quite obviously buying decisions cannot be entirely explained in terms of horizontal communication networks. Consumer behavior, for example, is the result of numerous interacting factors. Martineau contends that social class membership is an important determinant of store choices; [82] Stone argues that the housewife's "self-image" significantly influences her patronage decisions; [83] and Granbois believes that the family's decision-making process is an important variable in a variety of situations.[84] The buying behavior of physicians, farmers, and industrial

[79] Ibid., p. 266.
[80] How the Electronics Industry Buys, Hayden Publishing Company, New York, 1963.
[81] Ibid., pp. 11–23.
[82] P. Martineau, "The Personality of the Retail Store," Harvard Business Review (January–February 1958), pp. 47–55.
[83] G. P. Stone, "City Shoppers and Urban Identification: Observations on the Social Psychology of City Life," American Journal of Sociology (July 1954), pp. 36–45.
[84] Donald H. Granbois, "The Role of Communication in the Family Decision-Making Process," Toward Scientific Marketing, Stephen A. Greyser (ed.), American Marketing Association, Chicago, 1963, pp. 44–57.

users is equally complex. The communication network, in this context, is one of the mechanisms that conveys relevant information to decision makers and, since it is a part of the channel structure, its presence and importance must be recognized by the channel theorist.

CHANNEL MANAGEMENT AS A SEPARATE AREA OF INQUIRY

The producer serves as channel captain in most lines of trade. Consequently, the literature on channel management is manufacturer rather than reseller oriented. Furthermore, the manufacturer is viewed as making three basic channel decisions. The firm

1. selects the marketing channel(s) to be employed.
2. chooses the intermediaries to be used and develops appropriate distribution policies regarding them.
3. devises information and control mechanisms to insure that planned and actual performance coincide.

Most of the literature pertaining to these decision-making areas consists of *ad hoc* statements and plausible but unsupported generalizations. In spite of this, the existing frames of reference are useful, since they provide a reasonably satisfactory basis for making intelligent channel decisions. Furthermore, some writers have devised new techniques for dealing with the problems involved. Artle and Berglund, for example, have developed a rigorous mathematical approach for dealing with the channel selection problem which involves the use of algebraic models and indifference formulas to determine the conditions under which a manufacturer should sell directly to retailers rather than through wholesalers.[85] The Artle and Berglund models consider most of the variables that influence field selling costs. In addition, they are marginal cost models and thus are sensitive enough to show the "profit consequences" of selected alternatives. Unfortunately, the authors focus only on field selling costs, ignoring all other expenses incurred in the distribution process; they also assume a known, constant rate of sales, irrespective of the marketing mix used. Although incomplete, the Artle and Berglund models do provide a rigorous frame of reference for selecting a marketing channel. In addition, they can be adapted to include other variables. Consequently, researchers interested in substituting rigorous analysis for

[85] Roland Artle, and S. Berglund, "A Note on Manufacturers' Choice of Distribution Channel," *Management Science* (July 1959), pp. 460–471.

ad hoc generalizations in the field of channel management have a useful point of origin for their work.

Berg, Mallen, and Ridgeway have effectively applied administrative theory to channel problems. Berg's comments illustrate the position taken by all three men:

> Any manufacturing enterprise can be viewed as an input-output system consisting of three parts: (1) the internal organization of the firm, (2) the company environment, and (3) various kinds of external organizations serving to link the internal organization with its economic milieu for the interorganizational transmission and processing of inputs and outputs.
>
> Connections with suppliers, networks of financial intermediaries, and trade channels are examples of external organizations. Although they may not appear on company charts or in manuals, these should be regarded as logical extensions to the internal organization of the firm. Internal and external organizations are similar in that both deal with economic functions performed by interdependent human agents requiring motivation and coordination through communication. Both involve continuous personal relationships, routinized tasks, and stable expectations of reciprocal performance.
>
> Failure to pay due respect to the systemic nature of the enterprise and to the fundamental similarities between internal and external organizations has resulted in schizoid thinking in management and marketing. Management theorists have been preoccupied with problems of *internal organization* and have failed to show how the firm is connected to its environment via externally organized linkages and an unnatural cleavage between internal and external aspects of structure has developed in the management literature.[86]

Berg proceeds from this point to argue that the process of designing a channel network involves five steps. First, executives should develop an over-all channel strategy that is realistic in terms of the firm's environmental and internal constraints—a step that usually involves a comprehensive marketing audit of the company's operation. Second, the firm's channel requirements should be specified in conspicuous detail, that is, the enterprise should determine what has to happen in the channel for the firm to achieve its goals. Third, the identified marketing tasks should be grouped into economic work units. This involves an appraisal of the

[86] Thomas L. Berg, "Designing the Distribution System," *The Social Responsibilities of Marketing*, William D. Stevens (ed.), American Marketing Association, Chicago, 1962, p. 482.

economies that can be achieved through alternative modes of specialization. Fourth, the manufacturer should allocate the specified tasks to appropriate middlemen. Fifth, the firm should devise appropriate structural relationships for the channel, that is, the firm should develop realistic inducement and control mechanisms so that the channel will function efficiently throughout its programed existence.[87]

Mallen and Ridgeway have developed similar approaches, but neither writer is as programmatic as Berg. Ridgeway, for example, stresses the political and sociological aspects of channel control [88] and Mallen is principally concerned with questions involving managerial "styles." [89] Other authors have also contributed importantly to the literature on channel management. Duncan has developed a systematic approach to the problem of selecting marketing channels,[90] and Howard, by focusing on the three variables of coverage, cost and promotion, has neatly summarized the significant factors in the channel choice process.[91] Finally, Jones has developed an excellent summary of conventional approaches to channel problems.[92]

Marketing Theory and Channel Management

Marketing theorists through the years have contributed importantly to a conceptual understanding of the channel management process. For the most part, their ideas have been widely accepted in the literature and to repeat them here is unnecessary. Several concepts are unusually pertinent, however, and each deserves some emphasis.

The concept that marketing is essentially a "matching" process is a logical point of origin for channel decision making. Producers and users are geographically separated in a modern economy. Furthermore, individual buyers usually demand different quantities of merchandise than can be supplied by individual producers, and prospective users of a specific product are often geographically dispersed. Thus demand tends to be heterogeneous within a given region, and some requirements can be satisfied only by "importing" goods from distant areas. The basic purpose of marketing, in this context, is to "match" supply and demand

[87] *Ibid.*, pp. 485–489.
[88] Ridgeway, *op. cit.*, pp. 464–483.
[89] Bruce Mallen, "A Theory of Retailer–Supplier Conflict, Control, and Cooperation," *Journal of Retailing* (Summer 1963), pp. 24–32.
[90] Delbert J. Duncan, "Selecting a Channel of Distribution," *Marketing Channels for Manufactured Products*, Richard M. Clewett (ed.), Richard D. Irwin, Homewood, Ill., 1954, pp. 367–403.
[91] John A. Howard, *Marketing Management: Analysis and Planning*, Richard D. Irwin, Homewood, Ill., 1957, p. 183.
[92] Fred Jones, "Marketing Channels," *Marketing Handbook*, Paul Nystrom (ed.), Ronald Press, New York, 1949.

so that producers can obtain economies of scale and users can purchase in whatever quantities and from whatever assortments they choose. The marketing structure is the institutional device used to disperse goods in accordance with demand and to process goods in economic quantities at particular points in the product flow. Consequently, marketing may be viewed as a process in which a wide variety of enterprises handle different quantities and assortments of goods to satisfy demand while achieving systemic economies.

Clark and Clark, in an early treatment of this topic, argue that marketing consists of three basic processes—concentration, equalization, and dispersion. They contend that economic goods, particularly those sold in their natural state, must be initially assembled into quantities that can be marketed economically. The goods, having been "concentrated" at particular points, are subsequently moved to central markets. Supply and demand is balanced or "equalized" at this stage in the marketing process. Resellers tend to be the most active buyers in central markets, and they perform the "dispersion" function by routing goods to distant trading areas.[93] The concept of concentration, equalization and dispersion can be used to explain channel alignments in which central markets or redistribution activities are important. The usefulness of this concept in the case of more direct channels is questionable.

Vaile, Grether, and Cox also deal with the "matching" process in their discussion of collecting, sorting, and dispersing. The term "collecting" refers to the initial assembly process in which large lots of a single good or an assortment of varied goods are put together to achieve processing economies. Some of these collections of goods are transmitted directly to subsequent channel members, but others are "sorted"—a process that involves selecting particular items from available collections either to satisfy demand or to effect further economies as the goods move from assembly points to areas of high consumption. "Dispersing" is the final step, and it involves the allocation of goods to final users.[94] Alderson deals with the same set of relationships in his discussion of sorting out, accumulation, allocation, and assorting.[95]

Alderson, and Vaile, Grether, and Cox contend that their concepts can be used to establish better interfirm alignments. Admittedly their ideas provide a basis for analyzing physical distribution networks. The usefulness of these concepts to explain promotional or financial "flows" is problematic, however, since the latter often traverse different "routes" than the goods themselves.

[93] Fred E. Clark, and Carrie P. Clark, *Principles of Marketing*, 3rd ed., Macmillan, New York, 1942, pp. 4–7.
[94] Vaile, Grether, and Cox, *op. cit.*, pp. 134–150.
[95] Alderson, *op. cit.*, pp. 195–228.

The literature on intermediaries as a source of transactional efficiency represents another important contribution of marketing theorists. The exchange process can be effected on a direct basis, with each producer exchanging his surplus for the surpluses of others, or on an indirect basis, with intermediaries handling all transactions. If each producer in a primitive economy exchanges his surplus for the surpluses of others, the total market contacts needed to complete this process are $n(n-1)/2$ with n representing the number of producers. The use of an intermediary to collect and disperse goods reduces the number of market contacts to n. Thus the inclusion of an intermediary in the network reduces the number of transactions required to complete the exchange cycle, making more time available for the creation of economic goods. Both Alderson and Banks elaborate significantly on this theme. Alderson has developed an index of sorting balance that shows the extent to which wholesalers reduce the number of contacts between manufacturers and retailers.[96] Banks refines Alderson's ratio, which is a relatively gross measure of efficiency, by breaking it down into three subratios—the index of transactional efficiency, the index of bulk breaking, and the index of assembly.[97] Banks' ratios, like Alderson's, indicate the extent to which wholesalers reduce transaction expenses in the channel. These ratios involve relatively simple algebraic equations, but they lend precision to the idea that intermediaries exist because they effect economies in the exchange process. Balderston, for example, has used the transactional efficiency concept to develop a theory of channel communication.[98] Thus the ideas promulgated by Alderson and Banks represent a logical point of origin for anyone interested in analyzing the rationale of channel alignments. Furthermore, they provide a basis for measuring the efficiency of a channel and a means for comparing the relative productivity of different alignments.

Aspinwall is also managerially oriented. He emphasizes the need for a systems approach to marketing problems, and he hypothesizes that five product characteristics determine the promotional and channel requirements for consumer goods. These characteristics are:

1. Replacement rate—the rate at which a good is purchased and consumed by users.

[96] Wroe Alderson, "Scope and Place of Wholesaling in the United States," *Journal of Marketing* (September 1949), pp. 145–155.

[97] Seymour Banks, "Comments on Alderson's Index of Sorting Balance," *Journal of Marketing* (January 1951), pp. 331–335.

[98] F. E. Balderston, "Communication Networks in Intermediate Markets," *Management Science* (January 1958), pp. 154–171.

2. Gross margin—the difference between billed cost delivered and final selling price.
3. Adjustment activity—the services applied to goods in order to meet the exact needs of the consumer.
4. Time of consumption—the time during which the good gives up the utility desired.
5. Searching time—the measure of average time and distance that separates the customer from the store carrying the good in question.

All products can be described in terms of these attributes, and they can be measured and arrayed on a scale ranging from the highest to the lowest value for each attribute. For example, the replacement rates for all consumer products can be determined, and these data can be arrayed on a continuous scale indicating which products are replaced with low, medium, and high frequency. In like manner a product's gross margin, its adjustment requirements, its economic life, and the extent to which consumers have to search for it can be measured. Aspinwall concludes his analysis by hypothesizing that long marketing channels and "broadcast" promotion are required for products with high replacement rates and low gross margins, adjustment requirements, consumption times, and searching times. A product at the opposite end of the scale should be marketed through short channels and be supported by direct (selective) promotion.[99] Aspinwall's theory is useful because it illustrates the interrelationship between the characteristics of a product and its probable channel requirements. In addition, it provides a basis for isolating situations in which channel alignments may be uneconomic.

Control and Efficiency Concepts in Channel Management

The problems associated with measuring marketing efficiency constitute another important part of the literature on channel management. Some authors are concerned with macroanalysis, while others have developed analytical approaches that can be used by individual firms. Barger, Cox, Stewart, Dewhurst, Field, Lough, and Gainsbrugh, among others, have estimated the magnitude of total marketing costs in the United States economy.[100] Unfortunately, they define the term "marketing costs" differently, and thus their data are not comparable. The re-

---

[99] Leo V. Aspinwall, *Four Marketing Theories,* Bureau of Business Research, University of Colorado, Boulder, 1961.
[100] For a brief summary of these studies, see Paul D. Converse, Harvey W. Huegy, and Robert V. Mitchell, *Elements of Marketing,* Prentice-Hall, Englewood Cliffs, N.J., 1958, pp. 742–745.

sulting estimates, however, do provide a basis for determining the cost incurred to maintain the total marketing structure. Buzzell, in a more recent study, analyzes the costs incurred by industrial distributors. He uses the value added concept in his analysis and develops productivity ratios that can be used to compare the performance of different types of wholesale middlemen.[101]

The aggregative studies cited above constitute a useful point of departure for the channel analyst. The analysis of operating efficiency in a channel, however, requires different analytical techniques and more refined measurements of productivity than those used by macrotheorists. Writers who are concerned with the measurement of channel efficiency have usually followed one of three approaches. The first group has developed check lists or marketing audit forms that can be used by manufacturers to evaluate the performance of designated channels. The second group of writers has concentrated on developing appropriate measurements of efficiency and the final group has been principally concerned with applying accepted distribution cost accounting techniques to channel problems.

The marketing audit approach to decision making was popularized during the early 1950's and since then numerous audit forms have been developed.[102] Some of these are quite sophisticated, but many are simply refined check lists. Revzan,[103] Clewett,[104] Christian,[105] and Smith,[106] among others, have developed channel forms that can be used to "audit" the performance of a company's distribution network.

The work of Cox and Goodman is an outstanding example of research undertaken to develop specialized measurements of channel efficiency. In their pioneering study, "Marketing of Housebuilding Materials," (*Journal of Marketing,* July, 1956), they use the following criteria to appraise the efficiency of product channels:

1. The number of geographic places where materials are extracted,

---

[101] Robert D. Buzzell, *Value Added by Industrial Distributors,* Bureau of Business Research, The Ohio State University, Columbus, 1959.
[102] For discussions of the marketing audit concept, see, *Analyzing and Improving Marketing Performance (Management Report No. 32),* American Management Association, New York, 1959.
[103] Revzan, *op. cit.,* pp. 151–155.
[104] Richard M. Clewett, *Checking Your Marketing Channels,* Small Business Administration, Washington, D.C., January, 1961.
[105] Richard C. Christian, "Industrial Marketing: Three Step Method to Better Distribution Channel Analysis," *Journal of Marketing* (October 1958), pp. 191–192.
[106] Charles W. Smith, "Are You Paying Too Much for Distribution?," *Dun's Review and Modern Industry* (January 1958), p. 42.

processed or handled. (A "geographic place" is defined as an identifiable city or town, although in a few cases it was necessary to use a metropolitan area, a county, or a region surrounding some city or town.)

2. The number of times materials are loaded, moved, and unloaded, during their progress from the places where they were extracted to the building site.

3. The number of ton-miles of transportation involved in moving the materials from place of extraction to the building site.

4. The number of days taken to extract each of the principal materials, process it, and move it onto the building site. (The authors include the time normally spent by goods in the operating inventories of extractors, processors and distributors, as well as the time required to transport the goods.)

5. The dollar-days of investment accumulated in the materials as they move from first extraction to final assembly at the site. (A dollar-day is the owning of one dollar's worth of material for one day.)

6. The number of owning and nonowning business entities that participate in extracting, processing and handling of the materials.

7. The number of transactions arranged in moving the materials from place of extraction to the building site. (The term "transaction" includes both transfers of title and intrafirm transfers.)

Cox and Goodman use these measurements to evaluate channel performance and to estimate the extent to which savings could be effected if selected flows were altered.

Writers in the field of distribution cost accounting are also interested in quantitatively measuring the performance of specific marketing channels. Breyer, in his pioneering work during the 1940's, developed a set of techniques that can be used to classify and assemble functional expenses at both the firm and channel level. Breyer is particularly interested in the phenomenon of "nexus" costs which he defines as the cost incurred to perform complementary functions in the channel. A good example of a "nexus" cost is the total cost incurred by wholesalers and retailers to maintain contact with each other. In brief, Breyer's techniques can be used not only to determine the expenses incurred to perform specific functions in the channel, but also to isolate cost-volume relationships and to prepare channel operating budgets. Finally, the data derived from Breyer's system provide a basis for estimating the savings that could be effected if alternative channel alignments were used.[107] Though conceptually sound, Breyer's approach is complicated, and the

[107] Breyer, *op. cit.*, pp. 269–278.

simpler cost accounting methods advocated by Sevin,[108] Longman and Shiff,[109] and Heckart and Miner [110] have enjoyed greater usage. Mossman,[111] Barnet,[112] Culliton,[113] and others have also contributed to the literature by developing new techniques for classifying and analyzing channel expenses.

PHYSICAL DISTRIBUTION MANAGEMENT AND RELATED LINES OF INQUIRY

Marketing channels perform the task of physically moving goods from points of production to points of ultimate use. Consequently, channel theorists must incorporate an understanding of marketing logistics into their analyses. Physical distribution specialists, management scientists, and locational theorists have made important contributions to the literature on channel management during recent years. Physical distribution specialists advocate a systems approach to distribution management, and thus their work complements the research undertaken by systems theorists in other fields. Management scientists are principally interested in developing mathematical models and analytical techniques that can be used to solve recurring physical distribution problems, and locational theorists are interested in developing optimal positioning patterns for physical facilities in channel networks.

Three Important Distribution Concepts

Distribution specialists point out that direct materials, direct labor, and physical distribution costs are the three most important expense

[108] C. H. Sevin, *Distribution Cost Analysis* (Economic Series, #50) and *How Manufacturers Reduce Their Distribution Costs* (Economic Series #72), U.S. Department of Commerce, Washington, D.C., 1946 and 1948, respectively.
[109] D. R. Longman, and M. Schiff, *Practical Distribution Cost Analysis*, Richard D. Irwin, Homewood, Ill., 1955.
[110] T. B. Heckert, and R. B. Miner, *Distribution Cost Accounting*, Ronald Press, New York, 1953.
[111] Frank H. Mossman, *Differential Distribution Cost and Revenue Analysis: A New Approach*, Marketing and Transportation Paper No. 10, Bureau of Business and Economic Research, Graduate School of Business Administration, Michigan State University, East Lansing, 1962.
[112] Edward M. Barnet, *Innovate or Perish*, Graduate School of Business, Columbia University, New York, 1954.
[113] J. W. Culliton, *The Management of Marketing Costs*, Graduate School of Business Administration, Harvard University, Boston, 1958.

categories for the typical manufacturing firm.[114] Furthermore, they argue that physical distribution costs can be reduced significantly through better planning and coordination. Widespread recognition of these facts has led to the development of the *physical distribution concept*. The proponents of this concept contend that a company's distribution network should be managed as an integrated system. They also argue that all physical distribution activities—planning and control of finished goods inventory, warehousing, materials handling, data processing, traffic, and packing—should be under the jurisdiction of a single executive at the vice-presidential level. An executive, given this broad span of authority, can maintain continuous control over all physical distribution activities and thus is in a position to minimize total movement costs. The idea of economic trade-offs is inherent in this concept. Higher field warehousing costs, for example, are acceptable if these cost increases can be more than offset by transportation savings achieved through shipping in carload quantities.

The *materials management concept* is closely related to the physical distribution concept. Goubean defines materials management as

> that aspect of industrial management concerned with the activities involved in the acquisition and use of all materials employed in the production of the finished product. These activities may include production and inventory control, purchasing, traffic, materials handling and receiving.[115]

The materials manager attempts to minimize the costs incurred to perform such activities, and thus his frame of reference is similar to the physical distribution executive's. The former is interested in designing an optimum materials handling system within the plant, while the latter is interested in minimizing distribution costs in the company's marketing channel. *Rhochrematics* is a broader concept still, since it encompasses activities included in both the physical distribution and materials management functions. More specifically, the proponents of rhochrematics are interested in minimizing the cost of materials movement throughout the enterprise's operating system.[116]

[114] *Management of the Physical Distribution Function* (Management Report Number 49), American Management Association, New York, 1960.
[115] Quoted in Stanley H. Brewer, *Rhocrematics: A Scientific Approach to the Management of Material Flows*, Bureau of Business Research, College of Business Administration, University of Washington, Seattle, Wash., 1960, p. 2.
[116] *Ibid.*, p. 4.

Selected Management Science Contributions

Management scientists, as indicated above, are interested in developing mathematical models and rigorous analytical techniques that can be used to guide executive decision making. Most of their work is concerned with physical distribution problems, and much of it is useful to the channel analyst. Some relevant models and techniques are briefly noted in the following paragraphs.

Standard Transportation Models

The standard transportation model involves the use of linear programming techniques to determine the most economical method for transferring known quantities of a single commodity from several specified origins to a number of specified destinations. Each location in the model serves as either a shipping or receiving point, that is, direct shipments from any source to any destination are assumed to be more economical than transshipments through other sources or destinations. Furthermore, no source is permitted to supply quantities of the commodity in excess of its stated capacity and no destination receives less of the commodity than its stated requirements. Thus the standard transportation model is a reasonably uncomplicated linear programming application that yields a least cost distribution schedule for a complex of interconnected shipping and receiving points; as such, it provides a basis for economically routing shipments through the channel network.[117]

Transshipment Models

These models are variations of the standard transportation model. They differ in that they provide a basis for determining least cost distribution schedules under conditions that permit *any* location within the network to either ship or receive. The transshipment models, therefore, allow for the inclusion of "mixing" or redistribution points in the network and, as a consequence, they more accurately reflect the complicated distribution patterns encountered in most marketing channels.[118]

Multi-Echelon Inventory Models

Management scientists have developed a variety of techniques for controlling inventory at a single location in the production-distribution

[117] For a brief discussion of the standard transportation model, see Richard E. Quandt, "Models of Transportation and Optimal Network Construction," *Journal of Regional Science*, 1960, pp. 27–45.
[118] Charles H. Kriebel, "Warehousing with Transshipment Under Seasonal Demand," *Journal of Regional Science*, 1961, pp. 57–69.

system. The resulting theory, though useful to the decision maker within the firm, has little to say about approaches that can be used to determine optimal inventory positions for the marketing channel as a whole. Fortunately, there are some exceptions to this generalization. Clark and Scarf, for example, have analyzed the economics of inventory planning and control in multi-echelon systems in which certain locations within the system serve as stocking points and others serve as demand points. The stocking points perform the function of (re)supplying demand points; thus a wholesaler-retailer alignment is one example of a multi-echelon system. Clark and Scarf's model yields an optimal solution given rather restrictive assumptions about demand, ordering costs, transportation costs, and inventory decision rules followed by the firms in the system.[119] Hanssmann has also developed a multi-echelon inventory model that enables the decision maker to determine where inventory should be carried in the system and how much inventory should be stocked at the selected locations in order to minimize total costs.[120] Continued research in this area could lead to the development of systemic decision rules with respect to the inventory planning and control function in marketing channels.

Redistribution Models

These models are similar to multi-echelon inventory models since they deal with inventory holdings at successive levels in the distribution process. In many distribution systems, deliveries are made to receiving points according to a predetermined schedule; but demands made on each point cannot be predicted with certainty and therefore inventories have to be redistributed in the system to prevent "stock outs" before the next scheduled delivery. Decision makers, using redistribution models, can predict whether a given receiving point in the system will have excess or deficit inventories for the period in question, and they can determine the most economical method for redistributing inventories from points of excess supply to points of excess demand. The applicability of redistribution models to channel problems is fairly self-evident.[121] Warehouse distributors in the automotive parts and accessories field, for example, continuously shuffle inventories from one location to another and a

[119] Andrew Clark, and Herbert Scarf, "Optimal Policies for a Multi Echelon Inventory Problem," *Management Science* (July 1960), pp. 475–490.
[120] Fred Hanssmann, "Optimal Inventory Location and Control in Production and Distribution Networks," *Operations Research* (July–August 1959), pp. 483–498.
[121] For a brief discussion of redistribution models, see S. G. Allen, "A Redistribution Model with Set-Up Charges," *Management Science* (October 1961), pp. 99–108.

comparable pattern prevails in other fields whenever wholesalers and/or sales branches have reciprocal "buying out" agreements. Redistribution models, in these situations, provide a conceptual basis for determining the most economic procedure for reallocating merchandise within the system.

Integrated Simulation Models

Shycon and Maffei have successfully simulated an entire distribution network by fusing relevant transshipment, warehousing, and multi-echelon inventory models,[122] and Meier and Newell are currently engaged in comparable research at the University of Washington. The latter model is particularly interesting because it simulates a complicated distribution network involving multiple products, branches, and plants. Furthermore, the Meier and Newell model is one of the first to utilize SIMSCRIPT—a computer language that substantially reduces the data processing time required to simulate complex interaction patterns. The lines of inquiry noted here are unusually promising because the mathematical techniques now available are sophisticated enough to permit the development of an optimal solution to a channel's physical distribution problems. Consequently, the channel captain now has the conceptual tools required to maximize his system's competitive advantage.

The Contributions of Locational Theorists

Regional scientists are concerned with aggregate product flows, transportation networks, and related topics, whereas other theorists, like Hoover [123] and Greenhut,[124] are interested in plant and warehouse location decisions. The resulting body of literature is only marginally useful to the analyst interested in designing channel systems. Central place theorists, however, are interested in a variety of topics that directly relate to the study of marketing channels. More specifically, they have developed several important techniques for analyzing the size and overlap of trading areas. They have also developed concepts that can be used to determine the minimum market needed to support a specified type of facility. Finally, and perhaps most significantly, central place theorists are interested in analyzing the spatial structure of business firms, or complexes of business firms, in one or more geographical areas.[125] This

[122] Harvey N. Shycon, and Richard B. Maffei, "Simulation-Tool for Better Distribution," *Harvard Business Review* (November–December 1960), pp. 66–75.
[123] Edgar M. Hoover, *The Location of Economic Activity*, McGraw-Hill, New York, 1948.
[124] M. L. Greenhut, "The Size and Shape of the Market Area of a Firm," *Southern Economic Journal* (July 1952), pp. 37–50.
[125] B. J. L. Berry, and W. L. Garrison, "Recent Developments in Central Place Theory," *Regional Science Association, Proceedings*, 1958, pp. 107–120.

line of inquiry is obviously relevant to the channel designer, since he is interested in selecting the optimum "path" for his product line within a given institutional network. Predictably, the central place theorist relies on geographical considerations to explain decision making, while explicitly or implicitly ignoring other determinants of behavior. The Baumol and Ide consumer behavior model is an excellent illustration of a theoretical construct that embodies important central place concepts. In their model, the consumer's decision to patronize a given shopping center is explained in terms of the number of items offered for sale in the center and the "costs" incurred to reach and use the center.[126] Huff's topological preference models also provide a basis for exploring the relationship between consumers in a given geographical area and the stores they patronize.[127] In brief, central place theorists are interested in locational interrelationships between channel participants, and some of their work provides a conceptual basis for designing optimally positioned networks.

NEW DIRECTIONS FOR RESEARCH

Many of the ideas discussed in this chapter are speculations, deductions, and conceptualizations based on limited empirical evidence. Consequently, it is difficult to appraise their validity and many would be considered to be "unscientific," particularly if they are evaluated within the empirical context of science discussed at the beginning of the book. The reader is therefore justified in asking why such ideas were included in this chapter. Some of the ideas were included because they represent the findings of rigorously conducted, though inconclusive, research; other ideas were included because existing concepts and hypotheses, though inadequately tested, often provide a basis for subsequent investigation. Admittedly, many would argue that empirical research should be undertaken before exploratory hypotheses are developed. The individuals in this group contend that their approach is more reliable than that used by the "theory first" advocates. They also believe that their approach circumvents a frequently encountered situation in which theorists never proceed beyond their intuitions. The purpose of these concluding remarks, however, is not to defend or to denigrate the past, but to suggest directions for future research.

[126] William J. Baumol, and E. A. Ide, "Variety in Retailing," *Management Science* (October 1956), pp. 93–101.
[127] David L. Huff, "A Typographical Model of Consumer Space Preferences," *Papers and Proceedings of the Regional Science Association*, 1960, pp. 159–173, and "Ecological Characteristics of Consumer Behavior," *Papers and Proceedings of the Regional Science Association*, 1961, pp. 19–28.

A theory of channel behavior based on empirical data would be singularly useful to marketing researchers. Scholars interested in developing such a theory would probably have to use an eclectic approach, borrowing and integrating knowledge from sociology, cultural anthropology, social psychology, political science, management science, and economics, as well as marketing. At a less ambitious level, but of equal importance, is the need for additional taxonomic work in marketing. The criteria currently used to classify channel phenomena are not precise enough to support rigorous analysis; therefore, extensions of Entenberg's and Revzan's classification efforts would be useful. The development of a comprehensive notational system to describe interaction patterns is also required. Ultimately, such a notational system could provide a basis for simulating the behavior of complete channel systems. Of course, more emphasis on systems analysis should be encouraged. The simulations developed by Forrester, Balderston, Hoggatt, Shycon, and Maffei are important contributions, but their ultimate value cannot be tested until the model's predictions are compared with actual responses and behavior. In summary, rigorous research is required to provide empirical knowledge about channel behavior. Such knowledge could eventually be incorporated into a science of marketing channels, and the resulting concepts, theories, and laws could be used for both descriptive and predictive purposes.

BIBLIOGRAPHY

BOOKS

Alderson, Wroe, *Marketing Behavior and Executive Action*, Richard D. Irwin, Homewood, Ill., 1957.

Bakken, Henry H., *Theory of Markets and Marketing*, Mimir Publishers, Madison, Wisc., 1953.

Bartels, Robert (ed.), *Comparative Marketing: Wholesaling in Fifteen Countries*, Richard D. Irwin, Homewood, Ill., 1963.

————, *The Development of Marketing Thought*, Richard D. Irwin, Homewood, Ill., 1962.

Breyer, Ralph F., *Commodity Marketing*, McGraw-Hill, New York, 1931.

————, *The Marketing Institution*, McGraw-Hill, New York, 1934.

Burns, Arthur R., *The Decline of Competition*, McGraw-Hill, New York, 1936.

Cassady, Ralph, Jr., *Competition and Price Making in Food Retailing*, Ronald Press, New York, 1962.

Chamberlain, Neil W., *A General Theory of Economic Process*, Harper, New York, 1955.

————, *The Firm: Micro-Economic Planning and Action*, McGraw-Hill, New York, 1962.

Chandler, Alfred D., Jr., *Strategy and Structure*, MIT Press, Cambridge, Mass., 1962.

Clark, Fred E. and Carrie P. Clark, *Principles of Marketing*, 3rd ed., Macmillan, New York, 1942.

Clewett, Richard M. (ed.), *Marketing Channels for Manufactured Products*, Richard D. Irwin, Homewood, Ill., 1954.

Cole, Robert H., Lloyd M. De Boer, Richard D. Millican and Nugent Wedding, *Manufacturer and Distributor Brands*, Bureau of Economic and Business Research, University of Illinois, Urbana, 1955.

Commons, John R., *Institutional Economics*, Macmillan, New York, 1934.

Converse, Paul D., Harvey W. Huegy and Robert V. Mitchell, *Elements of Marketing*, Prentice-Hall, Englewood Cliffs, N.J., 1958.

Coolsen, Frank G., *Marketing Thought in the United States in the Late Nineteenth Century*, The Texas Technical Press, Lubbock, Texas, 1960.

Copeland, Melvin T., *Principles of Merchandising*, McGraw-Hill, New York, 1929.

Corey, Raymond, *The Development of Markets for New Materials*, Bureau of Research, Harvard University, Graduate School of Business Administration, Cambridge, Mass., 1956.

Cox, Reavis and Wroe Alderson (eds.), *Theory in Marketing*, Richard D. Irwin, Chicago, 1950.

Cyert, Richard M. and James G. March, *A Behavioral Theory of the Firm*, Prentice-Hall, Englewood Cliffs, N.J., 1963.

Dahl, Robert A., Mason Haire, and Paul F. Lazarsfeld, *Social Science Research on Business: Product and Potential*, Columbia University Press, New York, 1959.

Davison, Charles N., *The Marketing of Automotive Parts*, University of Michigan, Ann Arbor, 1954.

Day, Clive, *A History of Commerce*, Longmans, Green and Company, New York, 1938.

Diamond, William M., *Distribution Channels for Industrial Goods*, Ohio State University, Bureau of Business Research, Columbus, 1964.

Duddy, Edward A. and David A. Revzan, *Marketing: An Institutional Approach*, McGraw-Hill, New York, 1953.

Durkheim, Emile, *The Division of Labor in Society*, The Free Press, Glencoe, N.Y., 1963.

Etzioni, Amitai, *Complex Organizations—A Sociological Reader*, Holt, Rinehart and Winston, New York, 1961.

Hagen, Everett E., *On the Theory of Social Change*, The Dorsey Press, Homewood, Ill., 1962.

Haire, Mason (ed.), *Modern Organization Theory*, Wiley, New York, 1959.

Hall, Margaret, *Distributive Trading*, Hutchinson's University Library, London, 1944.

Hall, Margaret, John Knapp, and Christopher Winsten, *Distribution in Great Britain and North America*, Oxford University Press, Oxford, Eng., 1962.

Handler, Julian H., *How to Sell the Supermarkets*, Fairchild Publications, New York, 1959.

Heckert, T. B. and R. B. Miner, *Distribution Cost Accounting*, Ronald Press, New York, 1953.

Henell, Olof, *Some Science in Personal Selling*, Esselte Reklam AB, Stockholm, 1961.

Holdren, Bob R., *The Structure of a Retail Market and the Market Behavior of Retail Units*, Prentice-Hall, Englewood Cliffs, N.J., 1960.

Hollander, Stanley, *Explorations in Retailing*, Bureau of Business and Economic Research, Michigan State University, East Lansing, Mich., 1959.

Hoover, Edgar M., *The Location of Economic Activity*, McGraw-Hill, New York, 1948.

Hoselitz, Berthold F., *Sociological Aspects of Economic Growth*, Research Center in Economic Development and Cultural Change, University of Chicago, Chicago, 1960.

Hotchkiss, George Burton, *Milestones of Marketing*, Macmillan, New York, 1938.

Howard, John A., *Marketing Management: Analysis and Planning*, revised ed., Richard D. Irwin, Homewood, Ill., 1963.

————, *Marketing: Executive and Buyer Behavior*, Columbia University Press, New York, 1963.

Hungate, Robert P., *Interbusiness Financing: Economic Implications for Small Business*, U.S. Government Printing Office, Washington, D.C., 1962.

Isard, Walter, *Location and Space Economy*, Technology Press of MIT and Wiley, New York, 1956.

Jeffereys, James B., *The Distribution of Consumer Goods*, University Press, Cambridge, England, 1950.

————, *Retail Trading in Britain*, University Press, Cambridge, England, 1954.

Johnson, Richard A., Fremont E. Kast, and James E. Rosenzweig, *The Theory and Management of Systems*, McGraw-Hill, New York, 1963.

Killough, Hugh B., *The Economics of Marketing*, Harper, New York, 1933.

Lewis, Edwin H., *Marketing Electrical Apparatus and Supplies*, McGraw-Hill, New York, 1961.

Lionberger, Herbert F., *Adoption of New Ideas and Practices*, The Iowa State University Press, Ames, Iowa, 1960.

Longman, D. R. and M. Schiff, *Practical Distribution Cost Analysis*, Richard D. Irwin, Homewood, Ill., 1955.

Losch, August, *The Economics of Location*, Yale University Press, New Haven, 1954.

McClelland, David C., *The Achieving Society*, Van Nostrand, Princeton, N.J., 1961.

McGuire, Joseph W. (ed.), *Interdisciplinary Studies in Business Behavior*, Southwestern Publishing Company, Cincinnati, Ohio, 1962.

Magee, J. F., *Production Planning and Inventory Control*, McGraw-Hill, New York, 1958.

March, James G. and Herbert A. Simon, *Organizations*, Wiley, New York, 1958.

Mead, Margaret (ed.), *Cultural Patterns and Technical Change*, UNESCO, Paris, 1953.

Mitchell, Robert V. (ed.), *Changing Structure and Strategy in Marketing*, Bureau of Economic and Business Research, University of Illinois, Urbana, Ill., 1958.

Nurkse, Ragnar, *Patterns of Trade and Development*, Basil Blackwell, Oxford, 1959.

Nystrom, Paul (ed.), *Marketing Handbook*, Ronald Press, New York, 1949.

Palamountain, Joseph Cornwall, Jr., *The Politics of Distribution*, Harvard University Press, Cambridge, Mass., 1955.

Pashigian, Bedros Peter, *The Distribution of Automobiles, An Economic Analysis of the Franchise System*, Prentice-Hall, Englewood Cliffs, N.J., 1961.

Penrose, Edith Tipton, *The Theory of the Growth of the Firm*, Wiley, New York, 1959.

Phillips, Almarin, *Market Structure Organization and Performance*, Harvard University Press, Cambridge, Mass., 1962.

Polanyi, Karl, *The Great Transformation*, Beacon Press, Boston, 1957.
Polanyi, Karl, Conrad M. Arensberg, and Harry W. Pearson (eds.), *Trade and Market in the Early Empires*, The Free Press, Glencoe, N.Y., 1957.
Revzan, David A., *Wholesaling in Marketing Organization*, Wiley, New York, 1961.
Robinson, E. A. G., *The Structure of Competitive Industry*, University of Chicago Press, 1958.
Rogers, E. M. and G. M. Beal, *Reference Group Influence in the Adoption of Agricultural Technology*, Iowa State University, Ames, Iowa, 1958.
Rubenstein, Albert H. and Chadwick J. Haberstron, *Some Theories of Organization*, The Dorsey Press, Homewood, Ill., 1960.
Schwartz, George, *Development of Marketing Theory*, South-Western Publishing Co., Cincinnati, Ohio, 1963.
Shaw, Arch Wilkinson, *Some Problems in Market Distribution*, Harvard University Press, Cambridge, Mass., 1915.
Shuchman, Abe, *Scientific Decision Making in Business*, Holt, Rinehart and Winston, New York, 1963.
Simon, Herbert A., *Administrative Behavior*, Macmillan, New York, 1960.
Smelser, Neil J., *The Sociology of Economic Life*, Prentice-Hall, Englewood Cliffs, N.J., 1963.
Smith, Henry, *Retail Distribution*, Oxford University Press, London, 1937.
Smykay, Edward W., Donald J. Bowersox, and Frank H. Mossman, *Physical Distribution Management*, Macmillan, New York, 1961.
Stacey, Nicholas A. H. and Aubrey Wilson, *The Changing Pattern of Distribution*, Business Publications Limited, London, 1958.
Tucker, W. T., *The Social Context of Economic Behavior*, Holt, Rinehart and Winston, New York, 1964.
Ullman, Edward L., *American Commodity Flow*, University of Washington Press, Seattle, 1957.
Vaile, Roland S., E. T. Grether, and Reavis Cox, *Marketing in the American Economy*, Ronald Press, New York, 1952.
Vidich, Arthur J. and Joseph Bensman, *Small Town in Mass Society*, Doubleday, New York, 1960.
Warshaw, Martin R., *Effective Selling Through Wholesalers*, Bureau of Business Research, School of Business Administration, The University of Michigan, Ann Arbor, 1961.
Wedding, Nugent, *Vertical Integration in Marketing*, Bureau of Economic and Business Research, University of Illinois, Urbana, 1952.
Weiss, E. B., *The Vanishing Salesman*, McGraw-Hill, New York, 1962.
————, *Mass Marketing to the '400' Mass Retailers*, Printers' Ink Publishing Company, New York, 1950.
————, *Selling to and through the New Department Store*, Printers' Ink Publishing Company, New York, 1948.
Whitin, T. M., *Theory of Inventory Management*, Princeton University Press, Princeton, 1953.
Zober, Martin, *Marketing Management*, Wiley, New York, 1964.

PERIODICALS: AUTHORS KNOWN

Abbott, J. C., "The Role of Marketing in the Development of Backward Agricultural Economies," *Journal of Farm Economics* (May 1962), pp. 349–362.
Abrahamsen, Martin A., "Vertical Integration," *Cartel* (January 1959), pp. 9–15.

Adams, R. W. and J. T. Wheeler, "External Economies and the Falling Supply Curve," *Review of Economic Studies,* No. 1, 1952, pp. 24–39.

Alchian, A. A., "Biological Analogies in the Theory of the Firm: Comment" (followed by S. Enke's further comment and E. T. Penrose's rejoinder) *American Economic Review* (September 1953), pp. 600–609.

Alderson, Wroe, "A Formula for Measuring Productivity in Distribution," *Journal of Marketing* (April 1948), pp. 442–448.

Allen, S. G., "A Redistribution Model with Set-Up Charges," *Management Science* October 1961), pp. 99–108.

————, "Computation for the Redistribution Model with Set-Up Charge," *Management Science* (July 1962), pp. 482–489.

Alt, R. M., "Competition Among Types of Retailers in Selling the Same Commodity," *Journal of Marketing* (October 1959), pp. 441–447.

Alton, A. J., "The Influence of Manufacturers' Price Policies Upon Price Determination by Wholesalers," *Miami Business Review* (October 1957), pp. 1–4.

Anshen, Melvin, "Management Science in Marketing: Status and Prospects," *Management Science* (April 1956), pp. 222–231.

Applebaum, William, "Studying Customer Behavior in Retail Stores," *Journal of Marketing* (October 1951), pp. 172–178.

———— and S. B. Cohen, "Trading Area Networks and Problems of Store Saturation," *Journal of Retailing* (Winter 1961–62), pp. 32–43, 55.

Argyris, C., "Leadership Pattern in the Plant," *Harvard Business Review* (January–February, 1954), pp. 63–75.

Arndt, H. W., "External Economies in Economic Growth," *Economic Record* (November 1955), pp. 192–214.

Artle, Roland and S. Berglund, "A Note on Manufacturers' Choice of Distribution Channel," *Management Science* (July 1959), pp. 460–471.

Aspinwall, Leo V., "Parallel Systems of Promotion and Distribution," *Cost and Profit Outlook* (October 1956).

Atkinson, J. W. and B. F. Hoselitz, "Entrepreneurship and Personality," *Explorations in Entrepreneurial History* (April 1958), pp. 107–112.

Backman, J., "Why Wages are Lower in Retailing," *Southern Economic Journal* (January 1957), pp. 295–305.

Bain, Joe S., "Advantages of the Large Firm: Production, Distribution, and Sales Promotion," *The Journal of Marketing* (April 1956), pp. 336–346.

Balderston, F. E., "Communication Networks in Intermediate Markets," *Management Science* (January 1958), pp. 154–171.

————, "Models of Multiple Branch Organization," *California Management Review* (Spring 1962), pp. 40–57.

————, "Scale of Output and Internal Organization of the Firm," *Quarterly Journal of Economics* (February 1955), pp. 45–70.

Banks, S., "Comments on Alderson's Index of Sorting Balance," *Journal of Marketing* (January 1951), pp. 331–335.

Barnet, Edward M., "Showdown in the Market Place," *Harvard Business Review* (July–August, 1956), pp. 85–95.

Bauer, P. T., "Concentration in Tropical Trade: Some Aspects and Implications of Oligopoly," *Economica. New Series* (November 1953), pp. 302–321.

Baumol, William J. and E. A. Ide, "Variety in Retailing," *Management Science* (October 1956), pp. 93–101.

Baumol, William J. and Charles H. Sevin, "Market Costs and Mathematical Programming," *Harvard Business Review* (September–October 1957), pp. 52–60.

Baumol, William J. and Philip Wolfe, "A Warehouse Location Problem," *Operations Research* (March–April 1958), pp. 252–263.

Beckley, D. K., "Identifying Problems of Human Relations in Retailing," *Journal of Marketing* (July 1955), pp. 51–53.

Beckman, M. and R. Muth, "An Inventory Policy for a Case of Lagged Delivery," *Management Science* (January 1956), pp. 145–155.

Beckman, Martin, "An Inventory Model for Arbitrary Interval and Quantity Distributions of Demand," *Management Science* (October 1961), pp. 35–57.

———— and T. Marschak, "An Activity Analysis Approach to Location Theory," *Kyklos*, 1955, pp. 125–141.

Bellman, Richard, "On the Theory of Dynamic Programming—A Warehousing Problem," *Management Science* (April 1956), pp. 272–274.

————, I. Glicksburg and O. Gross, "On the Optimal Inventory Equation," *Management Science* (October 1955), pp. 83–104.

Berman, Edward B., "A Regional Production and Transportation Model," *Management Science* (April 1959), pp. 319–326.

Bliss, Perry, "Schumpeter, the 'Big' Disturbance and Retailing," *Social Forces* (October 1960), pp. 72–76.

————, "Supply Considerations and Shopper Convenience," *Journal of Marketing* (July 1960), pp. 43–45.

Boulding, Kenneth E., "Organizing Growth," *Challenge* (December 1959), pp. 31–36.

Bowman, Edward H., "Scale of Operations: An Empirical Study," *Operations Research* (May–June 1958), pp. 320–28.

Brooks, R. C., Jr. "'Word-of-Mouth' Advertising in Selling New Products," *Journal of Marketing* (October 1957), pp. 154–161.

Brown, R. J., "The Domino Game of Distribution," *Industrial Marketing* (February 1956), p. 64.

Bucklin, Louis P., "Retail Strategy and the Classification of Consumer Goods," *Journal of Marketing* (January 1963), pp. 51–56.

Buzzell, Robert B. and Charles C. Slater, "Decision Theory and Marketing Management," *Journal of Marketing* (July 1962), pp. 7–16.

Cairns, James P., "Suppliers, Retailers, and Shelf Space," *Journal of Marketing* (July 1962), pp. 34–36.

Caplow, Theodore and John J. Raymond, "Factors Influencing the Selection of Pharmaceutical Products," *Journal of Marketing* (July 1954), pp. 18–23.

Cassady, R., Jr., "The Integrated Marketing Institution and Public Welfare," *Journal of Marketing* (January 1942), pp. 252–266.

————, "The New York Department Store Price War of 1951: A Microeconomic Analysis," *Journal of Marketing* (July 1957), pp. 3–11.

Chalkey, L., Jr., "The Flow of Sales through Retail Drug Stores: a Factual Study," *Harvard Business Review* (July 1934), pp. 427–436.

Chappel, E. D. and G. Donald, Jr., "An Evaluation of Department Store Sales-People by the Interaction Chronograph" (A study of the Gilchrist Company in Boston), *Journal of Marketing* (October 1947), pp. 173–185.

Charnes, A. and W. W. Cooper, "The Stepping Stone Method of Explaining Linear Programming Calculations in Transportation Problems," *Management Science* (October 1954), pp. 49–69.

Cherington, Paul T. and Harrison A. Roddick, "Strategies and Policies in Marketing," *The Annals of the American Academy of Political and Social Science* (May 1940), pp. 79–83.

Christian, Richard C., "Industrial Marketing: Three Step Method to Better Distribution Channel Analysis," *Journal of Marketing* (October 1958), pp. 191–192.

Clark, Andrew and Herbert Scarf, "Optimal Policies for a Multi-Echelon Inventory Problem," *Management Science* (July 1960), pp. 475–490.

Cohen, Kalman J., "Simulation of the Firm," *American Economic Review* (May 1960), pp. 534–540.

Collins, A. L., "Warehouse Distribution of Steel," *Journal of Marketing* (September 1949), pp. 358–361.

Collins, N. R. and J. A. Jamison, "Mass Merchandising and the Agricultural Producer," *Journal of Marketing* (April 1958), pp. 357–366.

Collins, N. R. and R. H. Holton, "Programming Changes in Marketing in Planned Economic Development, *Kyklos* (January 1963), pp. 123–137.

Converse, Paul D., "Twenty-Five Years of Wholesaling: A Revolution in Food Wholesaling," *Journal of Marketing* (July 1957), pp. 40–53.

Copeland, Melvin T., "Relation of Consumers' Buying Habits to Marketing Methods," *Harvard Business Review* (April 1923), pp. 282–289.

Cooper, W., "A Proposal for Extending the Theory of the Firm," *Quarterly Journal of Economics*, 1951, pp. 87–109.

Cox, Reavis, "Consumer Convenience and the Retail Structure of Cities," *Journal of Marketing* (April 1959), pp. 355–362.

Cox, R. and C. S. Goodman, "Marketing of Housebuilding Materials," *Journal of Marketing* (July 1956), pp. 36–61.

Craig, David R. and Warner K. Gabler, "The Competitive Struggle for Market Control," *The Annals of the American Academy of Political and Social Science* (May 1940), pp. 84–107.

Crowther, John F., "Rationale for Quantity Discounts," *Harvard Business Review* (March–April 1964), pp. 121–127.

Cyert, R. H. Simon and D. Trow, "Observations of a Business Decision," *Journal of Business*, 1956, pp. 237–248.

Cyert, R., E. Fiegenbaum, and J. March, "Models in a Behavioral Theory of the Firm," *Behavioral Science* (April 1959), pp. 81–95.

Cyert, R. and J. March, "Organizational Structure and Pricing Behavior in an Oligopolistic Market," *Quarterly Journal of Economics*, 1956, pp. 237–248.

Dale, Ernest, "The Changing Channels of Distribution: Lower Costs, New Freedom for Consumers," *Printers' Ink* (July 11, 1958), pp. 21–27.

Dantzig, George B., "On the Shortest Route Through a Network," *Management Science* (January 1960), pp. 187–190.

Darling, S. L., "The Lumber Wholesaler," *Journal of Marketing* (September 1949), pp. 349–354.

Das, N., "The Ecology of Economic Power," *Indian Journal of Economics* (July 1958), pp. 71–75.

Davies, J. H., "Entrepreneurial Behavior and Market Environment," *Review of Economic Studies* (February 1958), p. 131.

Douglas, Edna, "Size of Firm and the Structure of Costs in Retailing," *Journal of Business* (April 1962), pp. 158–190.

Dodd, S. C., "Diffusion is Predictable: Testing Probability Models for Laws of Interaction," *American Sociological Review* (August 1955), pp. 392–401.

Dreyfus, Stuart, "An Analytic Solution to the Warehouse Problem," *Management Science* (October 1957), pp. 99–104.

Dunnette, M. D. and W. K. Kirchner, "Psychological Test Differences Between

Industrial Salesmen and Retail Salesmen," *Journal of Applied Psychology,* 1960, pp. 121–125.

Eastman, Willard, "A Note on the Multi-Commodity Warehouse Problem," *Management Science* (April 1959), pp. 327–331.

Edwards, C. D., "The Struggle for the Control of Distribution," *Journal of Marketing* (January 1937), pp. 212–17.

—————, "Vertical Integration and the Monopoly Problem," *Journal of Marketing* (April 1953), pp. 404–410.

Entenberg, Robert D., "Suggested Changes in Census Classifications of Retail Trade," *Journal of Marketing* (January 1960), pp. 39–43.

Etzioni, A., "Industrial Sociology: the Study of Economic Organizations," *Social Research* (October 1958), pp. 303–24.

Evans, Keith J., "When and How Should You Sell Through Distributors," *Industrial Marketing* (March 1959), pp. 41–44.

Evely, R. W., "Distribution Methods and Costs in the U.S.A.," *Review of Economic Studies,* 1946, pp. 16–33.

Ezekiel, H., "The Supply Curve of a Buyer Seller," *Indian Economic Journal* (October 1957), pp. 156–61.

Falk, D. R., "Central Buying By Department-Store Mergers," *Harvard Business Review* (April 1930), pp. 265–73.

Farrell, M. J., "An Application of Activity Analysis to the Theory of the Firm," (followed by D. G. Champernowne's note), *Econometrica* (July 1954), pp. 291–309.

Ferndon, Edwin W., Jr., "Easter Island Exchange Systems," *Southern Journal of Anthropology,* 1958, pp. 136–151.

Fisk, George, "A Conceptual Model for Studying Customer Image," *Journal of Retailing* (Winter 1961–62), pp. 1–8.

Forrester, Jay W., "Advertising: A Problem in Industrial Dynamics," *Harvard Business Review* (March–April 1959), pp. 100–110.

—————, "Industrial Dynamics: A Major Breakthrough for Decision Makers," *Harvard Business Review* (July–August, 1958), pp. 37–67.

French, Cecil L., "Correlates of Success in Retail Selling," *American Journal of Sociology* (September 1960), pp. 128–134.

Fullbrook, Earl S., "The Functional Concept in Marketing," *The Journal of Marketing* (January 1940), pp. 229–237.

Geisler, Murray A., "A Study of Inventory Theory," *Management Science* (April 1963), pp. 490–497.

—————, "Logistics Research and Management Science," *Management Science* (July 1960), pp. 444–454.

Gillespie, S. C. and K. W. Rothschild, "Migration and the Distributive Trades," *Review of Economic Studies,* 1946, pp. 81–83.

Girdner, William, "Integrated Marketing Institutions," *The Annals of The American Academy of Political and Social Science* (May 1940), pp. 55–61.

Greenhut, M. L., "The Size and Shape of the Market Area of a Firm," *Southern Economic Journal* (July 1952), pp. 37–50.

Grether, E. T., "Solidarity in the Distribution Trades," *Law and Contemporary Problems* (June 1937), pp. 376–391.

Gruen, Walter, "Preference for New Products and its Relationship To Different Measures of Conformity," *Journal of Applied Psychology* (December 1960), pp. 361–364.

Guetzkow, Harold and Herbert A. Simon, "The Impact of Certain Communication Nets Upon Organization and Performance in Task-Oriented Groups," *Management Science* (April–July, 1955), pp. 233–250.

Hall, William P., "Franchising — New Scope for an Old Technique," *Harvard Business Review* (January–February, 1964), pp. 60–72.

Haney, Lewis H., "Intergration in Marketing," *American Economic Review* (September 1920), pp. 528–545.

Hart, L. C., "Essentials of Successful Marketing: A Case History in Manufacturer-Distributor Collaboration," *Journal of Marketing* (October 1948), pp. 195 ff.

Heflebower, R. B., "Economics of Size," *Journal of Business* (October 1951), pp. 253–68.

Heim, Peggy, "Merchandise Management Accounting: A Retailing Experiment in Marginal Calculation," *Quarterly Journal of Economics* (November 1963).

Helmberger, Peter and Sidney Hoos, "Cooperative Enterprise and Organization Theory," *Journal of Farm Economics* (May 1962), pp. 275–290.

Hill, W. Clayton, "Reorganizing Distribution for Higher Profits," *Industrial Marketing* (February 1963), pp. 77–84.

Hill, W. C. and J. D. Scott, "Competition Between Different Types of Retail Outlets in Selling the Same Commodity," *Harvard Business Review* (July 1933), pp. 519–27.

Hirsch, W. Z., "Toward a Definition of Integration," *Southern Economic Journal* (October 1950), pp. 159–65.

Hollander, Stanley C., "The American Retailer—Subservient to the Public?" *Journal of Retailing* (Fall 1958), pp. 143–53. ff.

————, "The Wheel of Retailing," *Journal of Marketing* (July 1960), pp. 37–42.

Holton, Richard H., "On the Measurement of Excess Capacity in Retailing," *The Review of Economic Studies*, 1956–57, pp. 43–48.

————, "Marketing Structure and Economic Development," *Quarterly Journal of Economics* (August 1953), pp. 344–61.

————, "Price Discrimination at Retail: The Supermarket Case," *Journal of Industrial Economics* (October 1957), pp. 13–32.

Howard, M. C., "Interfirm Relations in Oil Products Markets," *Journal of Marketing* (April 1956), pp. 356–366.

Isard, Walter and Eugene W. Schooler, "Industrial Complex Analysis, Agglomeration Economics and Regional Development," *Journal of Regional Science* (Spring 1959), pp. 19–34.

Jack, A. B., "The Channels of Distribution for an Innovation: The Sewing Machine Industry in America, 1860-65," *Explorations in Entrepreneurial History* (February 1957), pp. 113–141.

Jarman, Hugh G., "Materials Handling Missing Link," *Distribution Age* (September 1956), pp. 58–60.

Jonassen, Christen T., "Contributions of Sociology to Marketing," *Journal of Marketing* (October 1959), pp. 29–35.

Karlin, Samuel, "Dynamic Inventory Policy with Varying Stochastic Demands," *Management Science* (April 1960), pp. 231–258.

Katz, Elihu, "The Social Itinerary of Technical Change: Two Studies on the Diffusion of Innovation," *Human Organization* (Summer 1961), pp. 70–82.

————, "The Two-Step Flow of Communication: An Up-to-Date Report on an Hypothesis," *Public Opinion Quarterly* (Spring 1957), pp. 61–78.

Kelley, William, "Specification Buying by the Large-Scale Retailer," *Journal of Marketing* (January 1954), pp. 255–65.

Kessler, Friedrich, Newton D. Brenner and Richard H. Stern, "Automobile Dealer Franchises: Vertical Integration by Contract," *The Yale Law Journal*, 1959, pp. 1–129.

Kohls, R. L., "Decision Making in Integrated Production and Marketing Systems," *Journal of Farm Economics* (December 1958), pp. 1801–1811.

Koo, A. Y. C., "A Theoretical Note on the Dealer-Manufacturer Relationship in the Automobile Industry, *Quarterly Journal of Economics* (May 1959), pp. 316–25.

Kreisberg, Louis, "Occupational Controls Among Steel Distributors," *American Journal of Sociology* (November 1955), pp. 203–212.

————, "The Retail Furrier: Concepts of Security and Success," *American Journal of Sociology* (March 1952), pp. 478–85.

Kriebel, Charles H., "Warehousing with Transshipment Under Seasonal Demand," *Journal of Regional Science*, 1961, pp. 57–69.

Krugman, H. E., "Salesmen in Conflict: A Challenge to Marketing," *Journal of Marketing* (July 1958), pp. 59–61.

Lazer, William and Eugene J. Kelley, "The Retailing Mix: Planning and Management," *Journal of Retailing* (Spring 1961).

Lewis, E. H., "Comeback of the Wholesaler," *Harvard Business Review* (November–December, 1955), pp. 115–25.

Lewis, H. T., "Industrial Procurement and Marketing," *Harvard Business Review* (September 1950), pp. 49–58.

Levy, Seymour and Gordon Donhowe, "Exploration of a Biological Model of Industrial Organization, *The Journal of Business* (October 1962), pp. 335–42.

Lieberman, Irving J., "A Mathematical Model for Integrated Business Systems," *Management Science* (July 1958), p. 327–336.

Livesey, C. A., "The Steel Warehouse Distributor," *Harvard Business Review* (Spring 1947), p. 397.

McClelland, W. G., "Pricing for Profit in Retailing," *Journal of Industrial Economics* (July 1959), pp. 159–174.

McClelland, W. S., "The Least-Cost Level of Stocks and the Rate of Interest," *Journal of Industrial Economics* (March 1960), pp. 151–171.

McFarland, S. W., "The Marketing Position of Industrial Distributors," *Journal of Marketing* (April 1953), pp. 394–403.

McGarry, Edmund D., "The Contactual Function in Marketing," *Journal of Business* (April 1951), pp. 96–113.

————, "The Propaganda Function in Marketing," *Journal of Marketing* (October 1958), pp. 131–139.

————, "Some Viewpoints in Marketing," *Journal of Marketing* (July 1953), p. 36.

McVey, Phillip, "Are Channels of Distribution What the Textbooks Say?" *Journal Of Marketing* (January 1960), pp. 61–65.

Machlup, Fritz and Martha Taber, "Bilateral Monopoly, Successive Monopoly and Vertical Integration," *Economica* (May 1960), pp. 101–120.

Mack, R. P. and V. Zarnowitz, "Cause and Consequence of Changes in Retailer's Buying," *American Economic Review* (March 1958), pp. 18–49.

Magee, John F., "Guides to Inventory Policy: Functions and Lot Size," *Harvard Business Review* (January–February, 1956), pp. 49–60.

————, "Guides to Inventory Policy: Problems of Uncertainty," *Harvard Business Review* (March–April, 1956), pp. 103–116.

————, "Guides to Inventory Policy: Anticipating Future Needs," *Harvard Business Review* (May–June, 1956), pp. 57–70.

————, "The Logistics of Distribution," *Harvard Business Review* (July–August, 1960), pp. 89–101.

Mainer, Robert and Charles C. Slater, "Markets in Motion," *Harvard Business Review* (March–April, 1964), pp. 75–82.

Mallen, Bruce, "A Theory of Retailer-Supplier Conflict, Control and Cooperation," *Journal of Retailing* (Summer 1963), pp. 24–32.

Mandell, Melvin, "Should the Warehouse Be Automated?" *Dun's Review and Modern Industry* (October 1961).

Martineau, P., "The Personality of the Retail Store," *Harvard Business Review* (January–February, 1958), pp. 47–55.

Matuszewski, T. I., "Trader's Behavior: An Alternate Explanation," *Review of Economic Studies* (February 1958), pp. 126–130.

Mehta, M. M., "Inter-relationship Between Size, Location and Integration," *Indian Economic Journal* (April 1955), pp. 311–321.

Meij, J. L., "A Note on the Concept of Stocks," *Journal of Industrial Economics*, 1956–57, pp. 137–152.

Menzel, H. and E. Katz, "Social Relations and Innovation in the Medical Profession: The Epidemiology of a New Drug," *Public Opinion Quarterly* (Winter 1955–56), pp. 337–352.

Meyer, John R., "Regional Economics: A Survey," *The American Economic Review* (December 1962), pp. 19–54.

Miller, Stanley, "How to Get the Most Out of Value Analysis," *Harvard Business Review* (January–February, 1955), pp. 123–132.

Mintz, Sidney W., "The Jamaican Internal Marketing Pattern: Some Notes and Hypotheses," *Social and Economic Studies* (March 1955), pp. 95–103.

Mintz, Sidney W., "The Role of the Middleman in the Internal Distribution System of a Caribbean Peasant Economy," *Human Organizations* (Summer 1956), pp. 18–23.

Morrell, J. G., "Furniture for the Masses," *Journal of Industrial Economics* (November 1956), 24–29.

Moore, F. T., "Economies of Scale: Some Statistical Evidence," *Quarterly Journal of Economics* (May 1959), pp. 232–245.

Moore, Wilbert E., "Labor Attitudes Toward Industrialization in Underdeveloped Countries," *American Economic Review* (May 1955), pp. 156–165.

Naddor, Eliezer, and Sidney Saltzman, "Optional Re-Order Periods for an Inventory System with Variable Costs of Ordering," *Operations Research* (September–October, 1958), pp. 676–685.

Nicosia, F. M., "Marketing and Alderson's Functionalism," *The Journal of Business* (October 1962), pp. 403–413.

Orden, Alex, "The Transshipment Problem," *Management Science* (April 1956), pp. 276–285.

Parker, Donald D., "Improved Efficiency and Reduced Cost in Marketing," *Journal of Marketing* (April 1962), pp. 15–21.

Parker, H. R., "The Propensity to Conserve," *Metroeconomica* (August 1953), pp. 87–89.

Parr, C. M., "Why the Middleman?" *Journal of Business* (January 1944), pp. 23–36.

Payne, P. L., "The Role of the Salesman and the Commission Agent in the Early

Years of the British Rubber Mechanicals Industry," *Explorations in Entrepreneurial History* (April 1955), pp. 205–214.

Penrose, E. T., "Biological Analogies in the Theory of the Firm," *American Economic Review* (December 1952), pp. 804–819.

————, "Research on the Business Firm, Limits to the Growth and Size of Firms," *American Economic Review* (May 1955), pp. 531–543.

Preston, Lee E., "Markups, Leaders and Discrimination in Retail Pricing," *Journal of Farm Economics* (May 1962), pp. 291–306.

————, and R. Hertford, "The Anatomy of Retail Price Competition," *California Management Review* (Spring 1962), pp. 13–30.

Quandt, Richard E., "Models of Transportation and Optimal Network Construction," *Journal of Regional Science*, 1960, pp. 27–45.

Ray, Ewell P., "Alternative Ways of Coordinating Production and Marketing," *Journal of Farm Economics* (December 1958), pp. 1790–1797.

Reese, Bud, "Physical Distribution: the Neglected Marketing Function," *Industrial Marketing* (October 1961), pp. 102–106.

Ridgeway, Valentine F., "Administration of Manufacturer-Dealer Systems," *Administrative Science Quarterly* (March 1957), pp. 464–477.

Robinson, Newton Y., "The Acceleration Principle: Department Stores' Inventories 1920–1956," *American Economic Review* (June 1959), pp. 348–358.

Rose, A., "The Potential Contribution of Sociological Theory and Research to Economics," *American Journal of Economics and Sociology*, 1952, pp. 23–33.

Schwartzman, D., "The Methodology of the Theory of Returns to Scale," *Oxford Economic Papers* (February 1958), pp. 98–105.

Schweitzer, A., "A Critique of Countervailing Power," *Social Research* (October 1954), pp. 353–385.

Seagraves, J. A. and C. E. Bishop, "Impacts of Vertical Integration on Output Price and Industry Strutcure," *Journal of Farm Economics* (December 1958), pp. 1814–1824.

Seaver, Stanley K., "Discussion: Impacts of Vertical Integration on Output Price and Industry Structure," *Journal of Farm Economics* (December 1958), pp. 1824–1827.

Scitovsky, T., "Economies of Scale, Competition and European Integration," *American Economic Review* (March 1956), pp. 71–91.

Semlow, Walter J., "How Many Salesmen Do You Need?" *Harvard Business Review* (May–June, 1959), pp. 126–132.

Shaul, J. R. H., "Distributive Trades of Southern Rhodesia," *South African Journal of Economics* (June 1953), pp. 186–193.

Shaw, A. W., "Some Problems in Market Distribution," *Quarterly Journal of Economics* (August 1912), pp. 703–765.

Sheppard, E. J., "Marketing Integration in Early Ohio," *Journal of Marketing* (October 1954), p. 166–168.

Shibutani, Tamotsu, "Reference Groups as Perspectives," *American Journal of Sociology* (May 1955), pp. 562–69.

Shubik, M., "A Game Theorist Looks at the Antitrust Laws and the Automobile Industry," *Stanford Law Review*, 1956, pp. 594–630.

Shycon, Harvey N. and Richard B. Maffei, "Simulation-Tool for Better Distribution," *Harvard Business Review* (November–December, 1960), pp. 66–75.

Siddall, William R., "Wholesale-Retail Trade Ratios as Indices of Urban Centrality," *Economic Geography* (April 1961), pp. 124–132.

Silberman, Charles E., "The Revolutionists of Retailing," *Fortune* (April 1962), pp. 99–102, 254, 256, 258, 260, 265.

Silbert, T. H., "Financing and Factoring Accounts Receivable," *Harvard Business Review* (January–February, 1952), pp. 39–54.

Simon, S., "Theories of Decision-Making in Economics and Behavioral Science," *American Economic Review* (June 1959), p. 253.

Smith, Charles W., "Are You Paying Too Much for Distribution?" *Dun's Review and Modern Industry* (January 1958), p. 42.

Smith, Paul E. and Eugene J. Kelley, "Competing Retail Systems: The Shopping Center and the Central Business District," *Journal of Retailing* (Spring 1960), pp. 11–18.

Smith, Wendell R., "Product Differentiation and Market Segmentation as Alternative Marketing Strategies," *Journal of Marketing* (July 1956), pp. 3–8.

Smithies, A., "The Theory of Value Applied to Retail Selling," *Review of Economic Studies* (June 1939), pp. 215–221.

Solo, Robert A., "Intra-Enterprise Conspiracy and the Theory of the Firm," *Journal of Business* (April 1961), pp. 153–166.

Stevens, Thomas L., "Here Comes Vertical Marketing," *Industrial Marketing* (September 1963), pp. 123–127.

Stickney, Richard, "Deploying Multi-Line Salesmen," *Harvard Business Review* (March–April, 1960), pp. 110–112.

Stigler, George J., "The Division of Labor is Limited by the Extent of the Market," *Journal of Political Economy* (June 1951), pp. 185–193.

Stocking, G. W. and W. F. Mueller, "Business Reciprocity and the Size of Firms," *Journal of Business* (April 1957), pp. 73–95.

Stone, G. P., "City Shoppers and Urban Identification: Observations on the Social Psychology of City Life," *American Journal of Sociology* (July 1954), pp. 36–45.

Strassmann, W. P., "Creative Destruction and Partial Obsolescence in American Economic Development," *Journal of Economic History* (September 1959), pp. 335–349.

Todd, F. Beaman and Irving Scharf, "Profitable Inventory Levels," *Harvard Business Review* (September–October, 1953), pp. 101–108.

Trifon, R., "Guides for Speculation About the Vertical Integration of Agriculture with Allied Industries," *Journal of Farm Economics* (November 1959), pp. 734–746.

Vanderblue, Homer B., "The Functional Approach to the Study of Marketing," *Journal of Political Economy* (October 1921), pp. 676.

Warshaw, Martin R., "Pricing to Gain Wholesalers' Selling Support," *Journal of Marketing* (July 1962), pp. 50–54.

Weiss, E. B., "The Shrinking Headquarters Target," *Sales Management* (July 1962), pp. 44–48.

Weiss, Robert S. and Eugene Jacobson, "A Method for the Analysis of the Structure of Complex Organizations," *American Sociological Review* (December 1955), pp. 661–668.

Weld, L. D. H., "Marketing Agencies Between Manufacturer and Jobber," *American Journal of Economics* (August 1917), pp. 571–99.

————, "Marketing Functions and Mercantile Organization," *American Economic Review*, (June 1917), pp. 306–18.

Whitney, S. N., "Errors in the Concept of Countervailing Power," *Journal of Business* (October 1953), pp. 238–253.

Wilkening, Eugene A., "Roles of Communicating Agents in Technological Change in Agriculture," *Social Forces* (May 1956), pp. 361–367.

Williamson, Oliver E., "Selling Expenses as a Barrier to Entry," *Quarterly Journal of Economics* (February 1963), pp. 112–128.

Wispe, L. G., "A Sociometric Analysis of Conflicting Role-Expectancies," *American Journal of Sociology* (September 1955), pp. 134–137.

Wittreich, Warren J., "Misunderstanding the Retailer," *Harvard Business Review* (May–June, 1962), pp. 147–155.

Wolfe, H. D., "Dispersion of Consumer Purchases Among Competing Retail Outlets (in Ohio)," *Journal of Business* (April 1942), pp. 160–165.

PERIODICALS: AUTHORS UNKNOWN

"Branch Distribution Trend Gains," *Business Week* (September 10, 1960), p. 65.

"Distribution Studies: How They Can Build Sales and Lower Marketing Costs," *Printers' Ink* (January 16, 1959), pp. 49–50.

"Furniture for the Masses: A Comment," *Journal of Industrial Economics,* (March 1957), pp. 153–154.

"Gauging Costs of Distribution," *Business Week* (December 30, 1955), p. 166.

"Innovation in the Age of Distribution," *Industrial Distribution* (May 1963), pp. 96–102.

"Integrating Your Transportation: New Trends in Managing Transportation," *Dun's Review and Modern Marketing* (June 1959), pp. 102, 105–6, 108, 110, 112, 114, 116, 118–20, 122.

"New Theory on How to Make Geography Work for You," *Business Week* (April 3, 1954), pp. 62–64.

OTHER RELEVANT PUBLISHED MATERIALS

Adelman, M. A., "The 'Product' and 'Price' in Distribution," *Papers and Proceedings of the 69th Annual Meeting of the American Economic Association* (May 1957), pp. 266–273.

The Adoption of New Products: Process and Influence, The Foundation for Research on Human Behavior, Ann Arbor, Michigan, 1959.

Amstutz, Arnold and Gerald B. Tallman, "Dynamic Simulation Applied to Marketing," *Marketing Keys to Profits in the 1960's,* American Marketing Association, Chicago, 1960, pp. 78–95.

Analyzing and Improving Marketing Performance, (Management Report No. 32), American Management Association, New York, 1959.

Aspinwall, Leo V., "The Depot Theory of Distribution," *Managerial Marketing: Perspectives and Viewpoints,* Richard D. Irwin, Homewood, Ill., 1962, pp. 652–659.

————, *Four Marketing Theories,* Bureau of Business Research, University of Colorado, Boulder, Colorado, 1961.

Balderston, Frederick E. and Austin C. Hoggatt, *Simulation of Market Processes,* University of California, Institute of Business and Economic Research, Berkeley, Calif., 1962.

————, "Theories of Marketing Structure and Channels," *Proceedings: Conference of Marketing Teachers from Far Western States,* Berkeley, Calif., University of California, September, 1958, pp. 134–145.

————, "Analytic Models Versus Computer Simulation—A Comparison with Illustrations from the Lumber Trade," *Marketing Concepts in Changing Times,* American Marketing Association, Chicago, 1960, pp. 139–151.

————, and A. C. Hoggatt, "Simulation Models: Analytical Variety and the Problem of Model Reduction," *Symposiaum on Simulation Models: Methodology and Applications to the Behavioral Sciences*, 1963, Southwestern, Cincinnati, pp. 182–191.

Barnet, Edward M., *Innovate or Perish*, Graduate School of Business, Columbia University, New York, 1954.

Berg, Thomas L., "Designing the Distribution System," *The Social Responsibilities of Marketing*, American Marketing Association, Chicago, 1962, pp. 481–490.

Berry, B. J. L. and W. L. Garrison, "Recent Developments in Central Place Theory," *Regional Science Association Proceedings*, 1958, pp. 107–120.

Brewer, Stanley H., *"Rhocrematics," A Scientific Approach to the Management of Material Flows*, Bureau of Business Research, College of Business Administration, University of Washington, Seattle, Washington, 1960.

Breyer, Ralph F., *Quantitative Systematic Analysis and Control: Study No. 1, Channel and Channel Group Costing*, Wharton School of Finance and Commerce, University of Pennsylvania, Philadelphia, 1949.

Brink, Edward L., "Analog Computers in the Simulation of Marketing Systems," *Marketing and the Computer*, Prentice-Hall, Englewood Cliffs, N.J., 1963, pp. 248–259.

Bucklin, Louis P., "The Economic Structure of Channels of Distribution," *Marketing: A Maturing Discipline*, American Marketing Association, Chicago, 1960, pp. 379–385.

Buzzell, Robert D., *Value Added by Industrial Distributors*, Bureau of Business Research, The Ohio State University, Columbus, Ohio, 1959.

Cassady, Ralph, Jr., *The Changing Competitive Structure in the Wholesale Grocery Trade*, University of California, Berkeley and Los Angeles, 1949.

Clewett, Richard M., "Checking Your Marketing Channels," *Management Aids for Small Manufacturers*, Small Business Administration, Washington, D.C. (January 1961).

Coase, R. H., "The Nature of the Firm," *Readings in Price Theory*, Richard D. Irwin, Homewood, Ill., 1962, pp. 331–351.

Cox, Reavis, "Changes in the City as an Institution of Marketing," *Marketing Adjustment to the Environment*, American Marketing Association, Chicago, 1962.

Culliton, J. W., *The Management of Marketing Costs*, Bureau of Research, Harvard University, Graduate School of Business Administration, Cambridge, Mass., 1948.

Cyert, Richard M., James G. March and Charles G. Moore, "A Specific Price and Output Model," *Working Paper No. 30, Behavioral Theory of the Firm Project*, Carnegie Institute of Technology, Pittsburgh, 1961.

DeLoach, D. B., "Competition for Channel Control in the Food Industry," *Proceedings: Conference of Marketing Teachers from Far Western States*, University of California, Berkeley, Calif. (September 1958), pp. 119–128.

Economic Inquiry into Food Marketing, Part I: Concentration and Integration in Retailing, Staff Report to the Federal Trade Commission, United States Government Printing Office, Washington, D. C., 1960.

Economic Inquiry into Food Marketing, Part II: The Frozen Fruit, Juice and Vegetable Industry, Staff Report to the Federal Trade Commission, United States Government Printing Office, Washington, D.C., 1962.

Fisk, George, "The General Systems Approach to the Study of Marketing,"

The Social Responsibilities of Marketing, American Marketing Association, Chicago (December 1961), pp. 207–211.

Galbraith, J. K., "Countervailing Power," *American Economic Association Papers and Proceedings* (May 1954), pp. 1–6.

Gort, Michael, "Stability and Change in Market Shares," *Small Business Management Research Reports*, University of Chicago, Chicago, 1963.

Granbois, Donald H., "The Role of Communication in the Family Decision-Making Process," *Toward Scientific Marketing*, American Marketing Association, Chicago (December 1963), pp. 44–57.

Group Influence in Marketing and Public Relations, Foundation for Research on Human Behavior, Ann Arbor, Mich., 1956.

Hancock, Robert S. and Edwin H. Lewis, *The Franchise System of Distribution*, University of Minnesota, Minneapolis, Minn., 1963.

Heflebower, R. B., "Mass Distribution: A Phase of Bilateral Oligopoly or of Competition," *American Economic Association Papers and Proceedings* (December 1956), pp. 274–85.

————, "Toward a Theory of Industrial Markets and Prices," *American Economic Association Papers and Proceedings* (May 1954), pp. 121–139.

Hertz, David Bendel, "Information Flows and the Coordination of Business Functions," *Marketing and the Computer*, Prentice-Hall, Englewood Cliffs, N. J., 1963, pp. 80–95.

Holton, Richard, *The Supply and Demand Strutcure of Food Retailing Services: A Case Study*, Harvard Studies in Marketing Farm Products, Number 10-H, Harvard University, Cambridge, Mass., 1954.

————, "Scale, Specialization and Costs in Retailing," *Marketing: A Maturing Discipline*, American Marketing Association, Chicago (December 1960), pp. 459–66.

Huff, David L., "A Topographical Model of Consumer Space Preferences," *Papers and Proceedings of the Regional Science Association*, 1960, pp. 159–173.

————, "Ecological Characteristics of Consumer Behavior," *Papers and Proceedings of the Regional Science Association*, 1961, pp. 19–28.

Jones, Fred, *Middlemen in the Domestic Trade of the United States 1800–1860*, Illinois Studies in the Social Sciences, University of Illinois, Urbana, Ill., 1937.

Katona, G., "Changing Assumptions in the Theory of Business Behavior," *Industrial Relations Research Association Proceedings* (December 1952), pp. 58–62.

Koch, Robert A., and Milton M. Snodgrass, "Linear Programming Applied to Location and Product Flow Determination in the Tomato Processing Industry," *Papers and Proceedings—The Regional Science Association*, 1959, pp. 151–162.

Lee, Wayne, "Space Management in Retail Stores and Implications to Agriculture," *Marketing Keys to Profits in the 1960's*, American Marketing Association, Chicago, 1960, pp. 523–533.

Longman, Donald R., "Recent Developments in Distribution Cost Analysis," *Proceedings: Conference of Marketing Teachers from Far Western States*, University of California, Berkeley, Calif. (September 1958), pp. 60–74.

Magee, John F., "The Computer and the Physical Distribution Network," *Marketing and the Computer*, Prentice-Hall, Englewood Cliffs, N.J., 1963, pp. 60–79.

————, "Quantitative Analysis of Physical Distribution Systems," *The Social Responsibilities of Marketing*, American Marketing Association, Chicago, 1961, pp. 498–512.

Management of the Physical Distribution Function, American Management Association, New York, 1960.

Marketing and Distribution: Report of the Joint Commission of Agricultural Inquiry, 67th Congress, First Session, H. R. Report No. 48, Government Printing Office, Washington, D.C., 1922.

McCammon, Jr., Bert C., "Alternative Explanations of Institutional Change and Channel Evolution," *Toward Scientific Marketing*, American Marketing Association, Chicago (December 1963), pp. 477–490.

McKinsey-General Foods Study: The Economics of Food Distributors, General Foods Corp., White Plains, New York (October 1963).

McNair, Malcolm P., "Significant Trends and Developments in the Postwar Period," *Competitive Distribution in a Free High-Level Economy and Its Implications for the University*, University of Pittsburgh Press, Pittsburgh, 1958.

Messerole, W. H., "Warehouses and Computers," *Marketing and the Computer*, Prentice-Hall, Englewood Cliffs, N.J., 1963, pp. 50–58.

Miller, J. P., "Competition and Countervailing Power: Their Roles in the American Economy," *American Economic Association Papers and Proceedings* (May 1954), pp. 15–25.

Mossman, Frank H., *Differential Distribution Cost and Revenue Analysis: A New Approach*, Marketing and Transportation Paper No. 10, Bureau of Business and Economic Research, Graduate School of Business Administration, Michigan State University, East Lansing, Mich., 1962.

National Distribution Patterns and Problems of Pacific Northwest Manufacturers, Bureau of Business Research, College of Business Administration, University of Washington, Seattle, Wash., December, 1957.

Opportunities to Improve Relations Between Chains and Manufacturers, National Association of Food Chains, Washington, D.C. (October 1962).

Report of the Federal Trade Commission on Distribution Methods and Costs (Vols. 1–10), U.S. Government Printing Office, Washington, D.C., 1944.

Revzan, David A., "Some Selected Trends in Wholesaling," *Proceedings: Conference of Marketing Teachers from Far Western States*, University of California, Berkeley, Calif. (September 1958), pp. 99–118.

Sevin, C. H., *Distribution Cost Analysis* (Economic Series, #50), U.S. Department of Commerce, Washington, D.C., 1946.

————, *How Manufacturers Reduce Their Distribution Costs* (Economic Series #72), U.S. Department of Commerce, Washington, D.C., 1948.

Snyder, Richard E., "Physical Distribution Costs," *Distribution Age* (January 1963).

Stekler, N. O., *Profitability and Size of Firm*, University of California, Berkeley, Calif. (August 1963).

Tiebout, C. M., "Location Theory, Empirical Evidence and Economic Evolution," *Regional Science Association Proceedings*, 1957, pp. 74–86.

Vaile, R. S., "Changing Distribution Channels" (Report of round table discussion), *American Economic Association Papers and Proceedings* (March 1939), pp. 104–108.

Warntz, W., "Geography of Prices and Spatial Interaction (with discussion)," *Regional Science Association Proceedings*, 1957, pp. 118–136.

Weiss, E. B., *The Coming Era of Giant Leased-Department Chains*, Doyle, Dane, Bernbach, New York, 1961.

————, *Death of the Independent Retailer*, Doyle, Dane, Bernbach, New York, 1963.

Weld, L. D. H., "Market Distribution," *American Economic Association Papers and Proceedings* (March 1915), pp. 125–139.

Weymar, F. Helmut, "Industrial Dynamics: Interaction Between the Firm and Its Market," *Marketing and the Computer*, Prentice-Hall, Englewood Cliffs, N.J., 1963, pp. 260–276.

Whitin, Thomas M., "Managerial Economics and the Theory of the Firm," *American Economic Association Papers and Proceedings* (May 1960), pp. 549–555.

Whitney, S. N., "Vertical Disintegration in the Motion Picture Industry," *American Economic Association Papers and Proceedings* (May 1955), pp. 491–498.

Wingate, John W., "Contemporary Trends in Retailing," *Proceedings: Conference of Marketing Teachers from Far Western States*, University of California, Berkeley, California (September 1958), pp. 78–95.

Worthy, J. C., "Some Aspects of Organization Structure in Relation to Pressures on Company Decision-Making," *Industrial Relations Research Association Proceedings* (December 1952), pp. 66–79.

13

The Concept of the Marketing Mix

NEIL H. BORDEN

I have always found it interesting to observe how an apt or colorful term may catch on, gain wide usage, and help to further understanding of a concept that has already been expressed in less appealing and communicative terms. Such has been true of the phrase "Marketing Mix," which I began to use in my teaching and writing some fifteen years ago. In a relatively short time it has come to have wide usage. This note tells of the evolution of the marketing mix concept.

The phrase was suggested to me by a paragraph in a research bulletin on the Management of Marketing Costs written by my associate, James Culliton [1] in 1948. In this study of manufacturers' marketing costs he described the business executive as a

"decider," an "artist"—a "mixer of ingredients," who sometimes follows a recipe prepared by others, sometimes prepares his own recipe as he goes along, sometimes adapts a recipe to the ingredients immediately available, and sometimes experiments with or invents ingredients no one else has tried.

I liked his idea of calling a marketing executive a "mixer of ingredients," one who is constantly engaged in fashioning creatively a mix of marketing procedures and policies in his efforts to produce a profitable enterprise.

For many years previous to Culliton's cost study the wide variations in the procedures and policies employed by managements of manufacturing firms in their marketing programs and the correspondingly wide variation in the costs of these marketing functions, which Culliton aptly ascribed to the varied "mixing of ingredients," had become increasingly

[1] James W. Culliton, *The Management of Marketing Costs*, Division of Research, Graduate School of Business Administration, Harvard University, 1948.

evident as we had gathered marketing cases at the Harvard Business School. The marked differences in the patterns or formulas of the marketing programs not only were evident through facts disclosed in case histories but also were reflected clearly in the figures of a cost study of food manufacturers made by the Harvard Bureau of Business Research in 1929.[2] The primary objective of this study was to determine common figures of expenses for various marketing functions among food manufacturing companies, similar to the common cost figures which had been determined in previous years for various kinds of retail and wholesale businesses. In this manufacturer's study we were unable, however, with the data gathered to determine common expense figures that had much significance as standards by which to guide management, such as had been possible in the studies of retail and wholesale trades, where the methods of operation tended toward uniformity. Instead, among food manufacturers the ratios of sales devoted to the various functions of marketing, such as advertising, personal selling, and packaging, were found to be widely divergent, no matter how we grouped our respondents. Each respondent gave data that tended to uniqueness.

Culliton's study of Marketing Costs in 1947–48 was a second effort to find out, among other objectives, whether a bigger sample and a more careful classification of companies would produce evidence of operating uniformities that would give helpful common expense figures. But the result was the same as in our early study; there was wide diversity in cost ratios among any classifications of firms which were set up; no common figures were found that had much value. This was true whether companies were grouped according to similarity in product lines, amount of sales, territorial extent of operations, or other bases of classification.

Relatively early in my study of advertising, it had become evident that understanding of advertising usage by manufacturers in any case had to come from an analysis of advertising's place as one element in the total marketing program of the firm. I came to realize that it is essential always to ask: What over-all marketing strategy has been or might be employed to bring about a profitable operation in light of the circumstances faced by the management? What combination of marketing procedures and policies has been or might be adopted to bring about desired behavior of trade and consumers at costs that will permit a profit? Specifically how can advertising, personal selling, pricing, packaging, channels, warehousing, and the other elements of a marketing program be manipulated and fitted together in a way that will give a profitable operation?

[2] *Marketing Expenses of Grocery Manufacturers for 1929*, Bulletin No. 79, Bureau of Business Research, Graduate School of Business Administration, Harvard University, 1930.

In short, I saw that every advertising management case called for a consideration of the strategy to be adopted for the total marketing program with advertising recognized as only one element whose form and extent depended on its careful adjustment to the other parts of the program.

The soundness of this point of view was supported by case histories throughout my volume on *The Economic Effects of Advertising,* which was published in 1942. In the chapters devoted to the utilization of advertising by business, I had pointed out the innumerable combinations of marketing methods and policies that might be adopted by a manager in arriving at a marketing plan. For instance, in the area of branding, he might elect to adopt an individualized brand or a family brand. Or he might decide to sell his product unbranded or under private brands. Any decision in the area of brand policy in turn has immediate implications that bear on his selection of channels of distribution, sales force methods, packaging, promotional procedure, and advertising. Throughout the volume, the case materials cited show that the way in which any marketing function is designed and the burden placed on the function, is determined largely by the over-all marketing strategy adopted by managements to meet the market conditions under which they operate. The forces met by different firms vary widely. Accordingly, the programs fashioned differ widely.

Regarding advertising, which was the function under focus in the Economic Effects volume, I said at one point: [3]

> In all the above illustrative situations it should be recognized that advertising is not an operating method to be considered as something apart, as something whose profit value is to be judged alone. An able management does not ask, "Shall we use or not use advertising?" without consideration of the product and of other management procedures to be employed. Rather, the question is always one of finding a management formula giving advertising its due place in the combination of manufacturing methods, product form, pricing, promotion and selling methods and distribution methods. As previously pointed out different formulae, i.e., different combinations of methods, may be profitably employed by competing manufacturers.

From the above it can be seen why Culliton's description of a marketing manager as a "mixer of ingredients" immediately appealed to me as an apt and easily understandable phrase, far better than my previous

[3] Neil H. Borden, *The Economic Effects of Advertising,* Richard D. Irwin, Chicago, 1942, Chs. IV and V.

references to the marketing man as an empiricist seeking in any situation to devise a profitable "pattern" or "formula" of marketing operations from among the many procedures and policies that were open to him. If he was a "mixer of ingredients," what he designed was a "marketing mix."

It was logical to proceed from a realization of the existence of a variety of "marketing mixes" to the development of a concept that would comprehend not only this variety but also the market forces that cause managements to produce a variety of mixes. It is the problems raised by these forces that lead marketing managers to exercise their wits in devising mixes or programs which they hope will give a profitable business operation.

To portray this broadened concept in a visual presentation requires merely:

1. a list of the important elements or ingredients that make up marketing programs.
2. a list of the forces that bear on the marketing operation of a firm and to which the marketing manager must adjust in his search for a mix or program that can be successful.

THE LIST OF ELEMENTS

The list of elements of the marketing mix in such a visual presentation can be long or short, depending on how far one wishes to go in his classification and subclassification of the marketing procedures and policies with which marketing managements deal when devising marketing programs. The list of elements which I have employed in my teaching and consulting work covers the principal areas of marketing activities which call for management decisions as revealed by case histories. I realize others might build a different list. Mine is as follows:

Elements of the Marketing Mix of Manufacturers

1. *Product planning.* Policies and procedures relating to
    (a) product lines to be offered—qualities, design, etc.
    (b) the markets to sell—whom, where, when and in what quantity.
    (c) new product policy—research and development program.
2. *Pricing.* Policies and procedures relating to
    (a) the level of prices to adopt.
    (b) the specific prices to adopt (odd-even, etc.).

    (c) price policy—one price or varying price, price maintenance, use of list prices, etc.

    (d) the margins to adopt—for company; for the trade.

3. *Branding.* Policies and procedures relating to

    (a) selection of trade marks.

    (b) brand policy—individualized or family brand.

    (c) sale under private brand or unbranded.

4. *Channels of Distribution.* Policies and procedures relating to

    (a) the channels to use between plant and consumer.

    (b) the degree of selectivity among wholesalers and retailers.

    (c) efforts to gain cooperation of the trade.

5. *Personal Selling.* Policies and procedures relating to

    (a) the burden to be placed on personal selling and the methods to be employed in (i) the manufacturer's organization, (ii) the wholesale segment of the trade, (iii) the retail segment of the trade.

6. *Advertising.* Policies and procedures relating to

    (a) the amount to spend—i.e., the burden to be placed on advertising.

    (b) the copy platform to adopt (i) product image desired, (ii) corporate image desired.

    (c) the mix of advertising—to the trade; through the trade—to consumers.

7. *Promotions.* Policies and procedures relating to

    (a) the burden to place on special selling plans or devices directed at or through the trade.

    (b) the form of these devices for consumer promotions, for trade promotions.

8. *Packaging.* Policies and procedures relating to

    (a) formulation of package and label.

9. *Display.* Policies and procedures relating to

    (a) the burden to be put on display to help effect sales.

    (b) the methods to adopt to secure display.

10. *Servicing.* Policies and procedures relating to

    (a) providing service needed.

11. *Physical Handling.* Policies and procedures relating to

    (a) warehousing.

    (b) transportation.

    (c) inventories.

12. *Fact Finding and Analysis.* Policies and procedures relating to

    (a) the securing, analysis, and use of facts in marketing operations.

The List of Behavioral Forces

If one were to make a list of all the forces which managements weigh at one time or another when formulating their marketing mixes, it would be very long indeed, for the behavior of individuals and of groups in all spheres of life have a bearing, first, on what goods and services are produced and consumed and, secondly, on the procedures that may be employed in bringing about exchange of these goods and services. However, the important forces which bear on marketers, all arising from the behavior of individuals or groups, may readily be listed under four heads, namely, the behavior of (1) consumers, (2) the trade, (3) competitors, and (4) government.

The outline below contains these four behavioral forces with notations of some of the important behavioral determinants within each force. These must be studied and understood by the marketer if his marketing mix is to be successful. The great quest of marketing management is to understand the behavior of humans in response to the stimuli to which they are subjected. The skillful marketer is he who is a perceptive and practical psychologist and sociologist, who has keen insight into individual and group behavior, who can foresee changes in behavior that develop in a dynamic world, who has creative ability for building well-knit programs because he has the capacity to visualize the probable response of consumers, trade, and competitors to his moves. His skill in forecasting response to his marketing moves should be supplemented by a further skill in devising and using tests and measurements to check consumer or trade response to his program or parts thereof, for no marketer has so much prescience that he can proceed without empirical check.

Below, then, is the suggested outline of forces which govern the mixing of marketing elements. This list and the list of the elements taken together provide a visual presentation of the concept of the marketing mix.

MARKET FORCES BEARING ON THE MARKETING MIX OF MANUFACTURERS

1. *Consumers' Buying Behavior:* as determined by
   (a) their motivation in purchasing.
   (b) their buying habits.
   (c) their living habits.

(d) their environment (present and future as revealed by trends, for environment influences consumers' attitudes toward products and their use of them).

(e) their number (i.e., how many).

(f) their buying power.

2. *The Trade's Behavior.* Wholesalers' and retailers' behavior, as influenced by

(a) their motivations.

(b) their structure, practices, and attitudes.

(c) trends in structure and procedures that portend change.

3. *Competitors' Position and Behavior:* as influenced by

(a) industry structure and the firm's relation thereto (i) size and strength of competitors, (ii) number of competitors and degree of industry concentration, and (iii) indirect competition—i.e., competition from other products.

(b) relation of supply to demand—oversupply or undersupply.

(c) product choices offered consumers by the industry: (i) in quality, (ii) in price, and (iii) in service.

(d) degree to which competitors compete on price versus nonprice bases.

(e) competitors' motivations and attitudes—their likely response to the actions of other firms.

(f) trends technological and social, portending change in supply and demand.

4. *Governmental Behavior—Controls over Marketing.*

(a) regulations over products.

(b) regulations over pricing.

(c) regulations over competitive practices.

(d) regulations over advertising and promotional methods.

APPRAISAL OF FIRM RESOURCES WHEN DEVISING A MARKETING MIX

When building a marketing program to fit the needs of his firm, the marketing manager has to weigh the behavioral forces and then juggle marketing elements in his mix with a keen eye on the resources with which he has to work. His firm is but one small organism in a large universe of complex forces. His firm is only a part of an industry that is competing with many other industries. What does the firm have in terms of money, product line, organization, and reputation with which to work?

The manager must devise a mix of procedures that fit these resources. If his firm is small, he must judge the response of consumers, trade, and competition in light of his position and resources and the influence that he can exert in the market. He must look for special opportunities in product or method of operation. The small firm cannot employ the procedures of the big firm. Although he may sell the same kind of product as the big firm, his marketing strategy is likely to differ widely in many respects from that of the large firm. Innumerable instances of this fact might be cited. For example, in the industrial goods field, small firms often seek to build sales on a limited and highly specialized line, whereas industry leaders seek patronage for full lines. Small firms often elect to go in for regional sales rather than attempt the national distribution practised by larger companies. Again, the company of limited resources often elects to limit its production and sales to products whose potential is too small to attract the competition of big fellows. Still again, companies with small resources in the cosmetic field not infrequently have set up introductory marketing programs employing aggressive personal selling and a "push" strategy with distribution limited to leading department stores. Their small advertising funds at the start have been directed through these selected retail outlets with the offering of the products and their story told over the signatures of the stores. The strategy has been to borrow kudos for their products from the leading store's reputations and to gain a gradual radiation of distribution to smaller stores in all types of channels, such as often comes from the trade's follow-the-leader behavior. Only after resources have grown from mounting sales has a dense retail distribution been aggressively sought and a shift made to place the selling burden more and more on company-signed advertising.

This strategy was employed for *Toni* products and *Stoppette* deodorant in their early marketing stages when the resources of their producers were limited.[4] In contrast, cosmetic manufacturers with large resources have generally followed a "pull" strategy for the introduction of new products, relying on heavy campaigns of advertising in a rapid succession of area introductions to induce a hoped-for, complete retail coverage from the start.[5] These introductory campaigns have been undertaken only after careful programs of product development and test marketing have given assurance that product and selling plans had high promise of success.

Many additional instances of the varying strategy employed by small

[4] See the case of Jules Montenier Inc., N. H. Borden and M. V. Marshall, *Advertising Management, Text and Cases*, Richard D. Irwin, Homewood, Ill., 1959, p. 498.
[5] *Ibid.*, see Case of Bristol Meyers Co., p. 519.

versus large enterprises might be cited. But those given serve to illustrate the point that managements must fashion their mixes to fit their resources. Their objectives must be realistic.

LONG-TERM VERSUS SHORT-TERM ASPECTS OF THE MARKETING MIX

The marketing mix of a firm in large part is the product of the evolution that comes from day to day marketing. At any time the mix represents the program that a management has evolved to meet the problems with which it is constantly faced in an ever-changing, ever-challenging market. There are continuous tactical maneuvers: the new product introduced by a competitor, an aggressive promotion, or a price change by him must be considered and met; the failure of the trade to provide adequate market coverage or display must be remedied; a faltering salesforce must be reorganized and stimulated; a decline in sales share must be diagnosed and remedied; an advertising approach that has lost effectiveness must be replaced; a general business decline must be countered. All such problems call for a management's maintaining effective channels of information relative to its own operations and to the day-to-day behavior of consumers, competitors and the trade. Thus we may observe that short-range forces play a large part in the fashioning of the mix to be used at any time and in determining the allocation of expenditures among the various functional accounts of the operating statement.

But the over-all strategy employed in a marketing mix is the product of longer range plans and procedures dictated in part by past empiricism and in part, if the management is a good one, by management foresight as to what needs to be done to keep the firm successful in a changing world. As the world has become more and more dynamic, blessed is that corporation which has managers who have foresight, who can study trends of all kinds—natural, economic, social, and technological—and, guided by these, devise long-range plans that give promise of keeping their corporations afloat and successful in the turbulent sea of market change. Accordingly, when we think of the marketing mix, we need to give particular heed today to the devising of a mix based on long-range planning that promises to fit the world of five or ten or more years hence. Provision for effective long-range planning in corporate organization and procedure has become more and more recognized as the earmark of good management. This viewpoint has come because the world has become increasingly subject to rapid change.

To cite an instance of the foregoing, among American marketing organizations which have shown foresight in adjusting their marketing mix to meet social and economic change, I look on Sears Roebuck and Company as providing an outstanding example. After building an unusually successful mail-order business to meet the needs of a rural America, Sears management foresaw the need to depart from its marketing pattern as a mail-order company catering primarily to farmers. The trend from a rural to an urban United States was going on apace. The automobile and good roads promised to make town and city stores increasingly available to those who continued to be farmers. Relatively early came Sears' launching of a chain of stores across the land, each easily accessible by highways to both farmers and city residents and with adequate parking space for customers. In time there followed the remarkable telephone and mail-order plan directed at urban residents to make buying easy for Americans when congested city streets and highways made shopping increasingly distasteful. Similarly, in the areas of planning products which would meet the desires of consumers in a fast changing world, of shaping its servicing to meet the needs of a wide variety of mechanical products, of pricing procedures to meet the challenging competition that came with the advent of discount retailers, the Sears organization has shown a foresight, adaptability, and creative ability worthy of emulation. The amazing growth and profitability of the company attest the foresight and skill of its management. Its history shows the wisdom of careful attention to market forces and their impending change in devising marketing mixes that may assure growth.

THE USE OF THE MARKETING MIX CONCEPT

Like many concepts, the marketing mix concept seems relatively simple, once it has been expressed. I know that before the ideas involved were ever tagged with the nomenclature of "concept," the ideas were widely understood among marketers as a result of the growing knowledge about marketing and marketing procedures that came during the preceding half century. But I have found for myself that once the ideas were reduced to a formal statement with an accompanying visual presentation, the concept of the mix has proved for me a helpful device in teaching, in business problem solving, and generally as an aid to thinking about marketing. First of all, it is helpful in giving an answer to the question often raised as to "what is marketing?" The chart which shows the elements of the mix and the forces that bear on the mix help to bring understanding of what marketing is. It helps to explain why in our dynamic world, the thinking of management in all its functional areas must be oriented to the market.

In recent years I have kept an abbreviated chart showing the elements and the forces of the marketing mix in front of my classes at all times. In case discussion it has proved a handy device by which to raise queries as to whether the student has recognized the implications of any recommendation he might have made in the areas of the several elements of the mix. Or referring to the forces we can question whether all the pertinent market forces have been given due consideration. Continual reference to the mix chart leads me to feel that the students' understanding of what marketing is is strengthened. The constant presence and use of the chart leave a deeper understanding that marketing is the devising of programs that meet successfully the forces of the market.

In problem solving, the marketing mix chart is a constant reminder of

1. the fact that a problem seemingly lying in one segment of the mix must be deliberated with constant thought regarding the effect of any change in that sector on the other areas of marketing operations. The necessity of integration in marketing thinking is ever present.
2. the need of careful study of the market forces as they might bear on problems in hand.

In short, the mix chart provides an ever-ready check list as to areas into which to guide thinking when considering marketing questions or dealing with marketing problems.

MARKETING—SCIENCE OR ART?

The quest for a "science of marketing" is hard upon us. If science is in part a systematic formulation and arrangement of facts in a way to help understanding, then the concept of the marketing mix may possibly be considered a small contribution in the search for a science of marketing. If we think of a marketing science as involving the observation and classification of facts and the establishment of verifiable laws that can be used by the marketer as a guide to action, with assurance that predicted results will ensue, then we cannot be said to have gone far toward establishing a science. The concept of the mix lays out the areas in which facts should be assembled, these to serve as a guide to management judgment in building marketing mixes. In the last few decades American marketers have made substantial progress in adopting the scientific method in assembling facts. They have sharpened the tools of fact finding, both those arising within the business and those external to it. Aided by these facts and by the skills developed through careful observation and experience, marketers are better fitted to practice the art of designing marketing mixes than would be the case had not the techniques of gathering facts been advanced as they have been in recent decades. Moreover, marketers have made progress in the use of the scientific method in designing tests whereby the results from mixes or parts of mixes can be measured. Thereby marketers have been learning how to subject the hypotheses of their mix artists to empirical check.

With continued improvement in the search for and the recording of facts pertinent to marketing, with further application of the controlled experiment and with an extension and careful recording of case histories, we may hope for a gradual formulation of clearly defined and helpful marketing laws. Until then, and even then, marketing and the building of marketing mixes will largely lie in the realm of art.

14

Comparative Marketing
and Economic Development

STANLEY J. SHAPIRO

Practitioners as well as teachers of American marketing are displaying an ever-increasing interest in how goods and services are distributed in other countries. The leadership taken by the American Marketing Association in establishing an International Marketing Federation and the recent publication by an AMA sub-committee of a bibliography on domestic marketing systems abroad are concrete indications of this interest.[1] Also significant is the publication during 1963 of a study of comparative wholesaling and of an international advertising handbook.[2]

Two factors appear to explain this interest in what might be called either "Domestic Marketing Abroad" or "Comparative Marketing Systems." First, the relative importance of international business has increased steadily as firms realized that foreign markets can be more profitable than domestic ones. The perils as well as the profit potential of international business are frequently publicized. Consequently, a decision to initiate or to expand foreign operations is often preceded by a detailed examination of the structural and environmental factors which will affect the marketing of the firm's products. The domestic marketing structure abroad is only one of the important factors reviewed by potential exporters and American firms considering the establishment of

[1] Donald F. Mulvihill (ed.), *Bibliography on Domestic Marketing Systems Abroad*, Kent State University, Bureau of Economic and Business Research, Printer Series No. 2, Kent, Ohio, 1962.
[2] S. Watson Dunn (ed.), *International Advertising Handbook*, McGraw-Hill, New York, 1963. Robert Bartels (ed.), *Comparative Marketing: Wholesaling in Fifteen Countries*, Richard D. Irwin, Homewood, Ill., 1963.

foreign subsidiaries. The would-be international operator is primarily concerned with tariffs, the effects of common markets, currency restrictions, changes in trade regulations, and the dangers of expropriation. Managerial issues, such as the degree of control to be exercised by the parent corporation and the relative merits of licensing and branch plant construction, are also considered.[3]

Teachers of marketing, economic historians, and, to a surprisingly limited extent, specialists in economic development constitute the second major group interested in domestic marketing abroad. For the most part, this group has restricted itself to describing marketing systems in various countries and to explaining the factors which contributed to the development of the system being examined. Some attempts to compare and to contrast the nature of marketing practices and the role of marketing agencies in different countries have also been made. Only a few researchers have considered the related questions of marketing efficiency and marketing reform. An examination of these efforts—to describe and to explain, to compare and to contrast, to evaluate and to reform—points up a number of problem areas of considerable theoretical and practical importance. In the remainder of this chapter, certain controversial topics on which economists and students of marketing have implicitly or explicitly disagreed among themselves are explored. Also, attention is called to important, heretofore neglected, issues in comparative marketing and economic development. More specifically, the limitations and inconsistencies of the available literature as it deals with the following topics are explored:

1. the appropriate frame of reference for the comparison of national marketing systems.
2. the applicability in other countries of American marketing techniques.
3. the possible existence of stages of marketing development.
4. the role of the market economy and of market structure in economic development.
5. the desirability of stimulating consumer wants in underdeveloped countries.
6. the wisdom of efforts to reform the marketing systems of underdeveloped countries.
7. the contribution that marketing can make to economic development.

These issues must be resolved before the study of comparative market-

[3] These and other important issues are considered at length in Roland L. Kramer, *International Marketing*, South-Western Publishing Company, Cincinnati, 1959.

ing systems can make the greatest possible contribution to the economic development of emerging nations and the substantive content of marketing science.

ISSUE 1. WHAT FRAME OF REFERENCE SHOULD BE USED IN THE COMPARISON OF NATIONAL MARKETING SYSTEMS?

Examination of the published literature reveals a complete lack of uniformity in the available descriptions of domestic marketing abroad.[4] A variety of approaches is employed, and each article emphasizes those aspects of marketing operations and structure with which the observer of the foreign scene has become most familiar. Although such diversity in the literature is understandable and perhaps even inevitable, it severely complicates the task of comparing and contrasting domestic marketing systems. Clearly, a more uniform approach to the study of comparative marketing is needed and must inevitably be adopted.

The existing literature on domestic marketing abroad and the approaches to comparative marketing analysis which have been advocated or employed can be assigned to one of four categories.

Marketing in X—A Study of Depth

In the author's opinion, Robert Bartels of The Ohio State University has prepared the only detailed outline for use in comparative marketing analysis.[5] A study of marketing in any given country built around the Bartels framework would be informative in its own right. Widespread use of this approach would greatly facilitate efforts to make meaningful comparisons among nations. Bartels stresses the impact on marketing of social, political, economic, and geographic factors. He builds his analysis of marketing around functions which are influenced by environmental considerations but which must be performed in any marketing system. More specifically, Bartels proposes that any study of comparative marketing contain the following elements.

1. An introductory statement dealing with such topics as the role that marketing plays in a particular society, the present stage of marketing development, and the nation's principal marketing problems.

2. A description of pertinent aspects of factors such as the nation's size, location, physical features, natural resources, racial stock, sovereign identity, and age, with some bearing on the marketing analysis to follow.

3. A description of the society in sufficient detail for marketing to be interpreted in subsequent sections as a social phenomenon. The distinc-

[4] Mulvihill, *op. cit.*
[5] Bartels, *op. cit.*, pp. 299–308.

tive features of such major social institutions as the family, the church, the school, and the government should be investigated. The role of the military and of leisure-connected considerations must also be examined in order to determine the factors which shape the needs and wants of the society.

4. A discussion which provides information on such topics as the following: the role of barter and credit, the degree of self-sufficiency of the economy, the principal forms of production and the relative importance of marketing services, the state of technology, the pattern and availability of employment, the distribution of wealth and income, the scale of business operations, the balances of trade and of payments, and the national industrialization programs in effect.

5. A report on the economic and demographic characteristics of the market and the barriers which exist to the successful completion of the transactions required to supply the material wants of consumers. These barriers would be classified as functional, informational, spatial, temporal, or financial. The tasks each type of separation imposes on the marketing structure would be indicated.

6. A discussion of how marketing operates as a social process to meet socially created wants. Emphasis would be placed on the following: the methods by which existing barriers are overcome and market transactions successfully completed, the manner in which the work of distribution is divided among the various marketing agencies, and the role of marketing agencies as social institutions in the performance of essential marketing tasks.

7. The relative importance of preplanning, the market mechanism, countervailing power, voluntary restraints, government regulation, social ethics and consumer resistance as elements which control marketing in the country under study.

The approach outlined above would produce reports on domestic marketing abroad far superior to any that presently exist. Unfortunately, however, widespread use of the Bartels outline or of any equally comprehensive plan cannot be expected in the immediate future. Studies of comparative marketing made on such a scale would be expensive undertakings, requiring the services of highly trained, interdisciplinary research teams. Another complicating factor is the absence throughout the world of the most basic types of marketing and economic data—material essential to the type of study Bartels advocates. The difficulty of determining how conflicting value systems influence the marketing structure of socially and culturally diverse countries must not be underestimated. In many parts of the world, the boundaries of what are now independent nations were determined primarily by the shifting political fortunes of

European colonial powers. As a recent study of Belgium indicates, even long-established small nations contain socially and culturally diverse elements. Such differences can have important marketing ramifications.[6]

In the introductory marketing texts used in the United States, very little attention is paid to prevailing social institutions and value systems. These topics may be excluded due to a belief that students are aware of the values which dominate our society and the manner in which the prevailing system of values influences and is influenced by social institutions. This assumption is questionable. In any case, the plethora of existing introductory marketing texts does not obviate the need for a special study of marketing in the United States along lines that will facilitate international analysis. Although such a study would be an ambitious undertaking, comparable examinations of less developed but less homogeneous societies would be equally difficult to conduct.

Comparative Studies of Limited Scope

Since immediate acceptance of the Bartels outlines is not expected, emphasis must be placed on a more limited and feasible method of comparative study. Bartels' role as editor of a publication on comparative wholesaling is evidence that he recognizes the merit of less ambitious studies.[7] Also noteworthy in this connection is the publication of the *International Advertising Handbook* in 1963. The handbook provides information on advertising practices and institutions in all the major national and regional markets of the world.[8] These two publications on limited aspects of comparative marketing are major contributions to the available literature. They are not, however, the only comparative studies of some relevance. Reports on European marketing productivity and comparisons of American and English retailing structures have also been made.[9] Also worthy of mention are two recent studies of European retailing.[10]

Rather than concentrating on areas such as advertising or wholesaling,

[6] Albert B. Stridsberg, "Launching Your Product in Belgium," *Journal of Marketing*, Vol. XXVI, No. 1 (January 1962), pp. 12–18.

[7] Bartels, *op. cit.*

[8] Dunn, *op. cit.*

[9] James B. Jefferys, Simon Hausberger, and Goran Lindblad, *Productivity in the Distributive Trade in Europe*, Organization for European Economic Cooperation, Paris, 1954; Margaret Hall, John Knapp, and Christopher Winsten, *Distribution in Great Britain and North America; A Study in Structure and Productivity*, Oxford University Press, London, 1961.

[10] James Jefferys and Derek Knee, *Retailing in Europe, Present Structure and Future Trends*, The Macmillan Company, London, 1963. Robert T. Davis, *The Changing Pattern of Europe's Grocery Trade*, Graduate School of Business, Stanford, Calif., n.d.

researchers who wish to make comparative studies might emphasize the manner in which certain functions common to all marketing systems are performed. A decade ago, McGarry proposed a definition of marketing and a set of marketing functions which would be equally applicable (1) to an economy of free enterprise, (2) to an economy based on purely communistic principles, where ownership is held by the state, and (3) to a purely cooperative economy where ownership and operation of production facilities are in the hands of consumers.[11] A study of comparative marketing systems could be built around the manner in which McGarry's contactual, merchandising, pricing, propaganda, physical distribution, and termination functions are performed in various countries.[12] Bartels advocates a somewhat similar approach when he suggests that attention be focused on how the functional, informational, spatial, temporal, and financial barriers to the completion of transactions are overcome.[13]

For reasons previously mentioned, comparative studies of the scope required to determine the validity of an international set of marketing functions may not prove practical. It should be possible, however, to compare the manner in which a single marketing concept is applied in different countries. Reavis Cox employed such an approach in a study made in the summer and fall of 1963. Cox has been a leading advocate of the use of the flow concept in marketing. He views the marketing channel as the combination and sequence of agencies through which one or more of the marketing flows move.[14] In the last decade, the flow concept has been employed as an analytical as well as a conceptual tool.[15] Its most recent use was as a vehicle for comparing marketing channel relationships in European countries.[16] The marketing channel was also emphasized by Ernest Enright in a study of Turkish marketing. Enright, of the International Marketing Institute, studied several lines of trade and placed special emphasis on which agencies in the marketing channel exercised leadership in performing necessary marketing functions.[17]

One might question whether comparative studies of advertising, whole-

---

[11] Edmund D. McGarry, "Some Functions of Marketing Reconsidered," Reavis Cox and Wroe Alderson (eds.), *Theory in Marketing—Selected Essays*, Richard D. Irwin, Chicago, Ill., 1950, pp. 266–267.

[12] *Ibid.*

[13] See paragraphs 5 and 6 of the outline of the Bartels approach found in the preceding subsection.

[14] Roland S. Vaile, E. T. Grether, and Reavis Cox, *Marketing in the American Economy*, Ronald Press, New York, 1952, p. 121.

[15] Reavis Cox and Charles S. Goodman, "Marketing of Housebuilding Materials," *Journal of Marketing*, Vol. XXI, No. 3 (July 1956), pp. 36–61.

[16] Dr. Cox's study was only in the planning stage at the time this article was written.

[17] The Enright report has not yet been published.

saling, or channel relationships can be made independently of the social structure and marketing system of which they are a part. This issue loses significance provided that limited aspects of marketing are studied in relative rather than complete isolation. In a comparative study of wholesaling, for example, unique social and economic conditions which influence the nation's marketing system and wholesaling practices could be given consideration. Comparative studies of selected aspects of national marketing systems appear justified provided that major external factors are not neglected in this approach.[18]

A more significant weakness of such studies is the possible absence of strict comparability. The quality and comprehensiveness of marketing data differ among nations, and standardized definitions are not generally employed. Consequently, the accuracy and comparability of some of the figures cited in comparative studies are questionable. Also, the nature of the material being considered may prevent meaningful international analysis. Difficulties inherent in comparisons of national income, for example, are too numerous and too well known to be detailed here.[19] Finally, the task of developing a standard format which will facilitate comparative analysis without undue neglect of conditions unique to a single nation can be a difficult one.

Journal Articles on Domestic Marketing Abroad

The bulk of literature on domestic marketing abroad consists of relatively brief accounts highlighting certain aspects of a single foreign marketing system.[20] Such articles have been authored by American marketing professors who have traveled and taught abroad, marketing practitioners serving on United States foreign aid teams, and American executives presently or previously employed in foreign countries. Occasionally foreign graduate students and visiting foreign executives have described marketing in the country of which they are citizens. All this material provides some information on domestic marketing but is of limited value. As was pointed out earlier, its major weakness is wide diversity in the approaches taken and in the different aspects of market-

[18] An effort being made by George Fisk of the University of Pennsylvania to employ formal systems concepts to American marketing is worthy of mention because of its possible relevance to comparative marketing analysis. Such an approach would eliminate the danger of any important aspects of national marketing systems being overlooked.

[19] Milton Gilbert and Irving B. Kravis, *An International Comparison of National Products and the Purchasing Power of Currencies*, The Organization for European Economic Cooperation, Paris, n.d.

[20] Mulvihill, *op. cit.*

ing which are discussed. Absence of a common framework makes meaningful analysis impossible.

Another shortcoming of such articles is the limited attention given to environmental factors. Why the marketing system operates in the manner described is a subject too often neglected or sketchily treated. The discussion of Oriental philosophy and metaphysics found in Hirsch's report on the North Indian sugar industry is one illustration of what can and should be done.[21] The absence of similar treatments in journal articles of domestic marketing abroad reduces the interest and the value of the material presented. It is not enough to learn that in most countries product quality is poor and product assortment limited, retail margins high and retail volume low, and general stores the dominant form of retailing everywhere but in the largest cities. The similarities among such marketing systems may not be due to the existence of a homogeneous set of underlying conditions.[22]

A number of articles have been written on various aspects of marketing in the Soviet Union. The work of Goldman and Phelps is especially noteworthy.[23] That some academicians and businessmen should be particularly interested in Soviet marketing is understandable. The U.S.S.R. is a cold-war rival, the world's second greatest economic power and a nation where the free market plays only a limited role in guiding the distributive system.

Is "marketing" an appropriate term to describe the process by which resources are allocated, demand stimulated, and goods are moved from production to consumption in a centrally planned economy? It has been argued that no marketing takes place without a change in ownership.[24] The prevailing opinion, however, is that restricting the term "marketing" to capitalistic economies would only further complicate the already formidable semantic problems of our discipline. If marketing were to be

[21] Leon V. Hirsch, *Marketing in an Underdeveloped Economy: The North Indian Sugar Industry*, Prentice-Hall, Englewood Cliffs, N.J., 1961.

[22] In commenting on a first draft of this paper, Ernest Enright of the International Marketing Institute informed the author that a recent article providing a general description of marketing in Afghanistan might in his opinion just as accurately have been entitled Marketing in Pakistan, Egypt, or India. See Hakima Hamid, "Marketing and Business Practices in Afghanistan," *The Middle East Journal*, Vol. XIV (Winter 1960), pp. 87–93.

[23] Marshall J. Goldman, "Marketing—A Lesson for Marx," *Harvard Business Review*, Vol. XXXVIII (January–February 1960), pp. 79–86; "Retailing in the Soviet Union," *Journal of Marketing*, Vol. XXV (July 1961), pp. 7–14; *Soviet Marketing: Distribution in a Controlled Economy*, The Free Press of Glencoe, New York, 1963; Maynard Phelps, "Soviet Marketing—Stronger Than We Think," *Harvard Business Review*, Vol. XXXIX (July–August 1961), pp. 69–80.

[24] Vaile, Grether, and Cox, *op. cit.*, p. 151.

considered solely as an appendage of a more (or less) free enterprise economy, a means of identifying and an appropriate term for describing the collectivist equivalent of marketing would have to be developed. Also, the broader phenomenon of which capitalistic "marketing" and its socialist counterpart are subclasses would have to be identified. An all encompassing use of the term "marketing" is generally advocated, therefore, even though the difficulties of identifying the essence or essential features of the term when so defined are recognized.

In a somewhat naive type of trade press marketing literature, the authors, and presumably their audience, resemble little Orphan Annie in that they "feel good all over" whenever the U.S.S.R. introduces Western marketing tcehniques. These commercial patriots notwithstanding, the adoption by the Soviet Union of procedures long employed in American marketing does not in itself demonstrate the inherent superiority of capitalism over communism. Such action is significant, however, because it indicates that in some cases the burden of physical distribution is a more potent determinant of marketing practices than the form of economic organization. Many aspects of marketing organization may be influenced primarily by the volume of goods and services the system must deliver. After having made an intensive study of marketing in the U.S.S.R., Goldman concluded that increasing similarities in structure between Western and Soviet marketing systems are to be expected for this reason.

> The marketing system is remarkably similar to that of the United States. Types of retail outlet . . . administrative and wholesaling structures . . . pricing methods . . . financial planning . . . and delegation of trust—all these features of the marketing system resemble the capitalist pattern very closely. And the resemblance grows as the Soviet economy becomes more prosperous and Soviet planners more sophisticated.
>
> In fact . . . the whole development of Soviet marketing reveals little real difference in basic marketing functions as we know them, despite state control and Marxist doctrine. Retailing and wholesaling seem to be indispensable at any stage of economic development. As the economy expands, the standard of living improves, and a discretionary buyer's market develops. To avoid gluts and excess inventories, the planners must resort to other familiar marketing practices—flexible pricing policies, advertising, product differentiation, even installment credit.[25]

[25] This quotation is from the book jacket of *Soviet Marketing:* . . . Goldman has authorized its use as representative of his views on this subject.

Domestic Marketing Abroad and the American Past

Similarities are often cited between the marketing system of the United States of some fifty or seventy-five years ago and conditions presently existing in other countries. Drawing on his earlier study of nineteenth century marketing thought, Coolsen devoted much of a recent article to pointing out certain of these similarities.[26] The American past is also used as a point of reference in discussing nations where general stores are presently predominant or wholesalers exercise control over most marketing channels. Two issues related to the use of such an approach are worthy of comment. First, one must consider the predictive implications of these comparisons. American marketing has changed steadily over the last seventy-five years. Whether and to what extent the marketing systems of foreign countries develop along similar lines remains to be seen. In any case, presently existing marketing systems are sure to change at a faster pace. This increased rate of change is attributable to efforts to speed economic development by adoption of the most advanced production and marketing techniques.[27]

It is in this context that the next question to be considered becomes relevant. Can an examination of the history of American marketing contribute to the economic development of other nations? This issue was explored at a recent conference on the implications of marketing history.[28] The role of marketing in economic development is discussed at great length in a subsequent section. It is sufficient here to note that the group exploring this issue concluded that the American experience could not make its maximum contribution to economic development without considerable research into the history of American marketing. It is presently impossible, for example, to answer the following questions: What has been the role of marketing attitudes and techniques in stimulating economic development in relatively advanced countries? Where has the locus of marketing initiative resided and what have been the effects on economic development of this initiative over time? Have marketing attitudes and techniques been dependent or independent variables

---

[26] Frank G. Coolsen, "Marketing and Economic Development," in William S. Decker (ed.), *Emerging Concepts in Marketing: Proceedings of the December 1962 Winter Conference*, American Marketing Association, Chicago, 1963, pp. 26–37.

[27] *Ibid.*, p. 26.

[28] Kenneth H. Myers, Jr., and Orange A. Smalley, "Marketing History and Economic Development," *The Business History Review*, Vol. XXXIII, (Autumn 1959), pp. 387–401.

in economic development? [29] Unfortunately, financial support for a center of marketing studies charged with the responsibility for studying these and related issues has not been forthcoming.

ISSUE 2. ARE AMERICAN MARKETING TECHNIQUES AND ATTITUDES UNIVERSALLY APPLICABLE?

The possible contributions of American marketing history to the development of domestic marketing abroad have just been considered. The extent to which contemporary American marketing practices can be applied outside of the United States is a related problem. Innumerable articles have been written as to whether or not American innovations in marketing techniques and marketing institutions will be accepted in Europe. The same argument takes many different forms. Is translation all that is required to make American advertising suitable for foreign markets? Will use of the "twisted kidney" and the "aching colon" offend the sensibility of Europeans? Is the supermarket so alien to the prevailing social pattern of France that this form of retailing cannot succeed?

This dispute appears to have produced more heat than light. One can cite many cases where the direct importation of American techniques has had disastrous results. In contrast, many examples are available of when and how the same policy has been successful.[30] One source of confusion may be the failure of those studying the issue to distinguish between two factors. An unqualified transfer of American marketing practices without due allowance for similarities and differences in the foreign environment may be poor business practice. For example, European consumers may be offended and react adversely to selling approaches which would be accepted and successful in the United States. Nevertheless, the American view of marketing as a demand-creating force which expands the range of human wants and then strives to satisfy these wants may be exportable.

Harper Boyd has argued that the application of the marketing concept is of greater value to a country with a developing economy than to a mature industrialized nation.[31] His opinion was based on a study of the

---

[29] *Ibid.*, pp. 389–390.

[30] For an interesting summary statement, see Arthur C. Nielson, Jr., "Do's and Don'ts in Selling Abroad," *Journal of Marketing*, Vol. XXIII, No. 2 (April 1959), pp. 405–411.

[31] Harper W. Boyd, Jr., Abdel Aziz El Sherbini, and Ahmed Fouad Sherif, "Egypt's Need for Marketing Management," *Business Horizons*, Vol. IV (Spring 1961), p. 84.

Egyptian economy which revealed the following conditions: marketing is presently viewed with disdain; firms sell in protected markets with little local competition; there is no concept of demand creation through the manipulation of the various elements of the marketing mix; little attention is paid to the wants and needs of consumers; and advertising is regarded with hostility. Boyd and his associates concluded that the marketing concept must be adopted if Egypt's efforts at rapid industrialization are to succeed.[32] The article cited implies that changing the Egyptian attitude toward marketing will be a necessary but not an easy task. How this concept, first introduced to describe a desirable business orientation in an affluent society, could be implemented in an underdeveloped economy is not indicated. In any case, marketing techniques first perfected in the United States may prove to have international relevance if they are applied in each country with due regard for prevailing social structures and value systems.

Two additional factors complicate the dispute as to the universality of American marketing practices. First, those who doubt that American techniques will work in other parts of the world too often neglect the dynamic aspects of marketing. The marketing system can influence customs and mores as well as be influenced by them. The supermarkets recently opened in France may not adopt all the operating practices of their American counterparts. But while the new supermarkets are influenced by prevailing French practices, they are likely to alter significantly the existing pattern of consumer-retailer relationships.[33] On the other hand, the introduction of many American practices and institutions may become feasible only when (1) per capita income, or at least, the income of a numerically large social class, reaches a certain level, (2) local industry learns how to produce goods of consistent quality, and (3) the environment is conducive to cultural innovation.[34] The possible relevance of the marketing concept and of techniques for creating demand is not a real issue in those parts of the world where per capita income is pitifully low and innovations that would significantly modify the social order are not well received.

---

[32] *Ibid.*, pp. 80–84.

[33] Watson Dunn, "French Retailing and the Common Market," *Journal of Marketing*, Vol. XXVI, No. 1 (January 1962), pp. 19–22. In commenting on an earlier draft of this paper, Stanley Hollander pointed out that the marketing system of underdeveloped economies could be viewed as a bit of anthropological data designed to help in the understanding of other phenomena within the same country. See Alice Dewey, *Peasant Marketing in Java*, The Free Press of Glencoe, New York, 1962, especially pp. 27–50.

[34] The importance of consistency in product quality was called to the author's attention by Ernest Enright.

ISSUE 3. CAN NATIONS BE ASSIGNED TO STAGES OF MARKETING DEVELOPMENT?

The possible relationship of American marketing techniques to the level of national income points up another issue of importance. Are there clearly discernible levels of marketing development to which each of the nations of the world can be assigned? If so, what form does this classification take and what should be the basis for placing a national marketing system in one or another of the existing categories?

One approach to the problem of classifying national marketing systems would be to utilize some pre-existing formulation of levels of economic growth. The best known discussion of stages in economic development has some obvious marketing implications. W. W. Rostow maintains that "it is possible to identify all societies in their economic dimensions as lying within one of five categories: the traditional society, the pre-conditions for take-off, the take-off, the drive to maturity, and the age of high mass consumption." [35] A judgment as to the validity of the preceding statement is beyond the scope of this paper. As Rostow indicated, it is difficult for any classification to be "correct" in the absolute sense of that term. The classes must be broad enough to encompass uniquely national as well as more uniform elements, and they must facilitate the study of a substantial range of interests. [36] Nevertheless, the implications for marketing of Rostow's as well as of competing general formulations should be examined.

A primarily marketing-oriented classification of nations, rather than one dependent on the condition of the economy as a whole, may be in order. An attempt to categorize nations in terms of their marketing development was made by Ernest Dichter. Using the size and importance of the middle class as a measure of achievement and concentrating specifically on the society's attitude toward automobiles, Dichter employed the following general classifications: contented countries, affluent countries, countries in transition, revolutionary countries, primitive countries, and the new class society. [37] Although Dichter's approach may be of some value, conceptual and operational limitations of his classification need not be elaborated on at this time.

[35] W. W. Rostow, *The Stages of Economic Growth: A Non-Communist Manifesto*, The University Press, Cambridge, England, 1960, p. 4.
[36] *Ibid.*, pp. 1–2.
[37] Ernest Dichter, "The World Customer," *Harvard Business Review*, Vol. XXXX (July–August 1962), pp. 118–121.

An attempt to point up similarities in the marketing patterns within a given class of countries was made as early as 1948. Solomon generalized about marketing practices in the belt of densely populated underdeveloped economies stretching from southeastern Europe through the Middle East to India and China. Careful study of the marketing of personal services, perishable produce, agricultural staples, manufactured consumer goods, and capital goods reveals, Solomon argued, that marketing practices and structures are essentially the same throughout this extensive and in many ways diverse area.[38] Also significant is Solomon's insistence that a different set of marketing patterns exists in *underpopulated*, underdeveloped areas.[39] If this is true, the existing level of national income would not be in itself an adequate basis for classification in terms of marketing development.

Goldman argues that there are essentially two stages in the development of the marketing system of most societies. In the first stage, retailing and wholesaling are the characteristic marketing agencies, the population is largely agricultural and the standard of living quite low.[40] In commenting on the Russian experience, Goldman maintains that the marketing innovations made during this first period were intended primarily to increase the efficiency of the middleman and to reduce the costs of distribution.[41] The secondary stage of marketing, in contrast, is characterized by a fundamental change in supply and demand relations. "Instead of long queues and perennial shortages, nationwide buyer's markets develop. Furthermore, a large number of consumers begin to have surplus or discretionary income." [42] To deal with the problems of this secondary stage, the Soviet Union has had to adopt such traditionally capitalistic marketing techniques as price reductions, advertising, product differentiations, and installment credit.[43] This fact leads Goldman to conclude that the similarities between Soviet and Western marketing systems in this secondary stage are far more significant than the differences.[44]

The validity of any device used for ranking or classification depends

---

[38] Morton R. Solomon, "The Structure of the Market in Underdeveloped Economies," *Quarterly Journal of Economics*, Vol. LXII (August 1948), pp. 519–537. (This article was reprinted in adapted form in Lyle W. Shannon (ed.), *Underdeveloped Areas: A Book of Readings and Research*, Harper, New York, 1957, pp. 131–140.

[39] *Ibid.*, p. 519.

[40] Goldman, *Soviet Marketing: Distribution* . . . . *op. cit.*, pp. 188–189.

[41] *Ibid.*, pp. 190–191.

[42] *Ibid.*, p. 191.

[43] *Ibid.*, pp. 191–198.

[44] *Supra*, p. 406.

in large part on its suitability for the purpose at hand. The assignment of nations to levels of marketing development would most likely be motivated by and precede action taken to speed the process of economic growth in less favored countries.

ISSUE 4. WHAT IS THE ROLE OF THE MARKET ECONOMY AND OF MARKET STRUCTURE IN ECONOMIC DEVELOPMENT?

One of the central economic debates of twentieth century life concerns the policies of government that will make the greatest contribution to economic development. Some argue that government ought to restrict itself to facilitating private efforts. Others maintain that the magnitude of the task of overcoming almost universal poverty makes dependence on the vagaries of a free market unwise and impossible.[45] To view the alternatives as capitalism or socialism unduly simplifies matters. More accurately phrased, the dispute concerns the relative importance, under a given set of circumstances, of the price system and central planning.[46] Many facets of this complex and emotionally charged issue are beyond the scope of this chapter. Only a few aspects of the problem of the most immediate interest to students of marketing will be discussed.

The controversy over the role of government is generally one of degree and extent. No dispute exists, for example, over the fact that the government must invest heavily in social capital and perform a host of facilitating functions. Development economists, convinced of the advantages of a free market, admit that government must be active in many spheres.[47] They may, however, couple this reluctant concession with a plea that such activities widen rather than narrow existing areas of individual freedom of choice.[48] This standard for evaluating government actions, the effect on the alternatives open to the populace, was

[45] For a provocative and somewhat atypical discussion of the alleged deficiencies both of market institutions and market-oriented economic theory, particularly with respect to the process of economic development, see William C. Frederick, "The Market as a Factor in Economic Growth," *The Southwestern Social Science Quarterly*, Vol. XXXXI (June 1960), pp. 63–71. The market system is condemned for having retained ceremonial and nonproductive elements resulting in an uneconomic use of resources that underdeveloped nations cannot afford. Received economic theory is criticized by Frederick for failing to provide a theoretical explanation of these elements.

[46] Charles P. Kindleberger, *Economic Development*, McGraw-Hill, New York, 1958, pp. 131–148.

[47] *Ibid.*, pp. 16, 137–140.

[48] Peter T. Bauer and Basil S. Yamey, *The Economics of Underdeveloped Countries*, The University of Chicago Press, Chicago, 1957, pp. 152–155.

established by economists who believe that the governments of under-developed countries all too often unduly restrict the economic activities of their citizens. This standard might nevertheless be used as a neutral measure to help determine the impact of government on the marketing system. Emphasis on how the interpretation of government policy affects individual freedom of choice would in many cases be more significant than measures of government ownership or control of resources and facilities.

It must also be realized that in discussions of economic development, emphasis is not always placed on the market for goods and services. Indeed, specialists in this area appear more concerned with the existence or absence of a free market for economic factors. Apparently factor markets can be rigidly controlled by the forces of tradition or by government action at a time when the market for merchandise is subjected to only minor external restraints. Polanyi has argued convincingly that the development in the nineteenth century of world-wide commodity markets was accompanied by an ever-increasing number of restrictions on the market for land, labor, and capital.[49] Extensive literature exists on how conditions in factor markets affect economic development. Areas of controversy appear to outnumber those of agreement. Fortunately, marketing students need deal only tangentially with factor markets while emphasizing the distribution of consumer and capital goods—a process which must go on whatever the role of the state in economic life.

Also to be considered are the effects of various types of market structures—in the price theory sense of that term—on economic development. In the manufacturing industries of underdeveloped countries, a relatively high degree of concentration is likely to exist. The factors contributing to this condition may include any or all of the following: limited markets, significant economies of scale, large initial capital requirements—a particularly important barrier in underdeveloped countries—and government policies.[50] The effects of heavy concentration in manufacturing on the nature and speed of economic development remain to be determined. Whether political or economic action should be taken to reduce the degree of concentration is a still more complex problem that must be resolved on an industry-by-industry, nation-by-nation basis.[51]

As far as the retailing and wholesaling of food are concerned, examina-

[49] Karl Polanyi, *The Great Transformation*, Beacon Press, Boston, 1957, pp. 76–77.
[50] Willard F. Mueller, "Some Market Structure Considerations in Economic Development," *Journal of Farm Economics*, Vol. XLI, No. 2 (May 1959), pp. 420–421; Alfred Thorne, "Monopoly–Oligopoly–Economic Development: The Underdeveloped Americas and the Caribbean." *Cartel*, Vol. X (April 1960), pp. 58–65.
[51] Hugh L. Cook, "Observations on Market Structures and National Economic Development in the Philippines," *Journal of Farm Economics*, Vol. XLI, No. 3 (August 1959), pp. 517–518; Thorne, *op. cit.*, pp. 59, 64.

tion of a number of studies has convinced Mueller that the market structure is best characterized as being monopolistically competitive. A relatively large number of wholesalers and retailers sell slightly differentiated products. Transportation and communication facilities are poor, and information as to prices in surrounding areas is often unavailable. Since capital requirements are low, only limited skill necessary, and alternate forms of employment often nonexistent, marketing intermediaries are confronted by a steady stream of new competitors. Such conditions usually lead to pitifully low rates of turnover, which keep middlemen from making excess profits or even a living wage. At the same time, marketing margins are larger than if no differentiation existed.[52] Whether and to what extent such a condition calls for remedial action is a controversial issue discussed in a subsequent section.

The limited amount of available evidence indicates that the export and import markets of underdeveloped countries are also highly concentrated.[53] P. T. Bauer's study of West African trade is the most frequently cited source of statistics on this subject, and Bauer's conclusion that oligopoly is to be expected in both the import and the export markets of underdeveloped countries is generally accepted.[54] Bauer examined the nature of the restrictions on entry into the import and export trades of what was formerly British West Africa. He discussed at considerable length the harmful effects associated with the existence of oligopolistic conditions in that territory.[55] His *laissez faire* bias leads Bauer to dismiss the possibility that the concentration of market power in a limited number of organizations would facilitate efforts to improve the marketing system. One of his conclusions, interestingly enough, is that arbitrary political and administrative measures had been as much or even more of a barrier to the survival and growth of would-be competitors than natural scarcities and collusive marketing agreements.[56] Thorne shares Bauer's view as to the prevalence and ill-effects of oligopoly in importing and exporting as well as the role that government frequently contributes to its existence.[57]

The existence of marketing boards with exclusive control over the sale of regulated products is a notable feature of agricultural marketing

[52] Mueller, *op. cit.*, pp. 416–417.
[53] *Ibid.*, p. 421; Thorne, *op. cit.*, pp. 59–60, 63–64.
[54] P. T. Bauer, "Concentration in Tropical Trade: Some Aspects and Implications of Oligopoly," *Economica*, Vol. XX, No. 4 (November 1953), pp. 302–321.
[55] P. T. Bauer, *West African Trade: A Study of Competition, Oligopoly and Monopoly in a Changing Economy*, The University Press, Cambridge, England, 1954, pp. 47–259.
[56] *Ibid.*, p. 86.
[57] Thorne, *op. cit.*, pp. 62–64.

throughout the British Commonwealth.[58] Such boards are often established to supervise the assembling and sale of the export commodities on which many underdeveloped countries are economically dependent. Objectives of the board may include stabilizing prices, improving the quality and reputation of the product, strengthening the bargaining power in international trade of the country's numerous small producers, and regulating trade in the national interest. All efforts to evaluate the social and economic effects of state-sanctioned selling monopolies are complicated by uncertainty as to the conditions which would have prevailed under any other marketing system. Evaluation becomes even more difficult when the exclusive selling agency also has the power to control total production, assign individual quotas, determine the location and operating procedures of assembly markets, establish grade differentials and set the prices producers will receive for their commodities. Bauer bitterly attacked the price policies and operating procedures of the West African Marketing Boards.[59] Thorne is not quite so positive in his condemnation of the export boards operating in South and Central America. He recognized the possible bargaining power of such boards but believes their existence leads to greater inequality in income distribution.[60] The conditions, if any, under which state-sanctioned or state-operated marketing monopolies and income inequality facilitate rather than hinder economic development remain to be determined.

ISSUE 5. SHOULD CONSUMER WANTS BE STIMULATED IN UNDERDEVELOPED COUNTRIES?

One of the tasks of marketing, it has been argued, is to make consumption dynamic.[61] The Russian experience, however, indicates that economic development can be facilitated by central planning which reduces the freedom of choice of individual consumers and limits the percentage of total resources allocated to satisfying consumer wants. Should, then, restrictions be placed on the efforts of marketing agencies in underdeveloped countries to increase consumer wants by stimulating demand? If so, how can such a conclusion be reconciled with the state-

[58] For an examination of the activities of one such board operating in a developed economy, see Stanley J. Shapiro, "The Survival Concept and the Nonprofit Behavior System," Reavis Cox, Wroe Alderson, and Stanley J. Shapiro (eds.), *Theory in Marketing: Second Series*, Richard D. Irwin, Homewood, Ill., 1964, pp. 109–124.
[59] Bauer, *West African Trade: . . .* , *op. cit.*, pp. 263–343.
[60] Thorne, *op. cit.*, p. 60.
[61] Vaile, Grether, and Cox, *op. cit.*, p. 24.

ment made by Boyd and his colleagues that introduction of the marketing concept in a developing economy would be beneficial? [62]

High-level consumption in underdeveloped countries is considered undesirable by some authorities primarily because of its allegedly adverse impact on the rate of capital formation. Discussion of the so-called "International Demonstration Effect" is relevant at this point. Professor Nurske has argued that the efforts of poor countries to amass capital are handicapped by the desire of their citizens to enjoy the same level of goods and services obtainable in richer nations. Whenever possible, the less favored populations will use additional income to increase personal consumption expenditures rather than to augment the supply of savings available for investment.[63] This phenomenon has been labeled the "International Demonstration Effect" because the items purchased have been popularized throughout the world by motion pictures, radio, the printed word, and the activities of dispersed communities of foreigners.[64] (In one respect, the term is ill-chosen, for it obscures the fact that the increased personal income might be used to purchase necessities rather than luxuries.) [65]

Some students of economic development question the existence of the "International Demonstration Effect" and its allegedly adverse impact on the rate of capital formation. Why do internal discrepancies in wealth, which are often quite marked within underdeveloped countries, not have the same harmful effects as international differences? [66] Could not the accumulation of capital assets carry with it as much prestige as the purchase and use of consumption items? [67] Might not the desire for a higher and more varied level of consumption goods lead to an increased emphasis on production for the market, a necessary prerequisite of economic growth? [68]

> Indeed, in the private sector the prospect of a higher level of consumption is more likely to promote than to hinder capital formation and economic development generally. Contact with the more advanced economies not only stimulates new wants and new activities to satisfy these but also often helps to provide the wherewithal

[62] Boyd, Sherbini, and Sherif, op. cit., p. 84.
[63] Ragnar Nurske, *Problems of Capital Formation in Underdeveloped Countries* fifth ed., Oxford University Press, New York, 1952, pp. 61–75.
[64] Bauer and Yamey, op. cit., p. 138.
[65] The author again is indebted to Dr. Enright for this observation.
[66] Bauer and Yamey, op. cit., p. 138.
[67] *Ibid.*, p. 138.
[68] *Ibid.*, pp. 139–140.

to satisfy them; familiar instances include the introduction of new crops, the transmission of improved techniques, and the opening up of new markets.[69]

Smithies shares the sentiments just expressed and argues that development planners should place greater emphasis on stimulating individuals to make additional efforts and exercise greater ingenuity.[70] If the spur of increased consumer demand caused labor to become more efficient, the forced accumulation of capital would be unnecessary.[71] Smithies discusses at some length the conditions under which the output of capital and consumer goods could increase simultaneously. He concludes that policies of extreme austerity should be relaxed in economic development programs and individuals encouraged to acquire rising expectations.[72]

Attention has so far been focused on the desirability of changes in the aggregate level of consumer demand. The suitability of a single consumer product for sale in an underdeveloped market also deserves some comment. Robinson has argued that two factors should be weighed in deciding whether production and promotion of any nonessential consumer product by a foreign corporation is in the national interest. The relevant considerations are the resources used in its production and the extent to which an unsatisfied popular demand already exists. A product manufactured locally with readily available materials and utilizing otherwise unemployed labor is more desirable than one which requires that consumer demand be created.[73]

ISSUE 6. HOW JUSTIFIABLE ARE EFFORTS TO REFORM MARKETING SYSTEMS OF UNDERDEVELOPED COUNTRIES?

Support exists for the argument that in underdeveloped countries the wholesalers and retailers of consumer goods and the initial assemblers of primary products operate under conditions of profitless monopolistic competition.[74] Some authorities maintain that the high costs of market-

[69] Ibid., p. 141.
[70] A. Smithies, "Rising Expectations and Economic Development," The Economic Journal, Vol. LXXI (June 1961), p. 255.
[71] Ibid., p. 256.
[72] Ibid., pp. 260–271.
[73] Richard D. Robinson, "The Challenge of the Underdeveloped National Market," Journal of Marketing, Vol. XXV, No. 4 (October 1961), pp. 23–25.
[74] Mueller, op. cit., pp. 416–418.

ing, the low profits of middlemen, and the limited scale of operations make a simplification of marketing channels and a reduction in the number of intermediaries imperative.

Many factors have contributed to the agitation for major marketing reforms. The ethics, the business practices, and the economic contribution of middlemen are invariably criticized by agricultural producers. Most of the population in underdeveloped countries engage in some type of farming and share the universal hostility toward market intermediaries. The belief also persists that instead of trade being mutually beneficial, one man's gain must be at another's expense. Other relevant attitudes include the hostility toward alien groups prominent in trade—a characteristic of emerging nationalism—and a deep-seated bureaucratic abhorrence of "messy" (complicated and complex) channels of distribution.[75]

Bias and prejudice notwithstanding, one can argue on economic grounds for changes in the number, activities, and scale of operation of marketing intermediaries. The position that such changes would greatly reduce the costs of distribution in underdeveloped areas is taken throughout the Galbraith and Holton study of marketing in Puerto Rico.[76] These authors first examined the structure and the costs associated with food distribution and reviewed prevailing managerial practices and attitudes. They then developed model food distribution systems which pointed up, by comparison, the shortcomings of the existing marketing structure. The models were designed to be as realistic as possible and assumed no change in national income, consumer tastes, the level of technology, or the network of transportation facilities. Each of the proposed wholesale or retail enterprises was expected to be no more efficient than similar establishments then operating in Puerto Rico. More than one marketing system was designed, due to the different combination of services that could be offered and the possible variations in wholesaler-retailer relations. Depending on the assumptions adopted, it was argued that the total food bill of the island could be reduced on the order of 16 to 19 per cent.[77]

In addition to designing model distribution systems for food and nonfood items, Galbraith and Holton made a number of specific suggestions for improving marketing efficiency in Puerto Rico.[78] In a similar fashion,

[75] Bauer, *West African Trade:* . . . , *op. cit.*, pp. 39–90, 145–155.

[76] John K. Galbraith and Richard H. Holton, *Marketing Efficiency in Puerto Rico,* Harvard University Press, Cambridge, Mass., 1955.

[77] *Ibid.*, pp. 5–124. For a briefer discussion of the then existing marketing structure of Puerto Rico, see Richard H. Holton, "Marketing Structure and Economic Development," *Quarterly Journal of Economics,* Vol. LXVII (August 1953), pp. 344–361.

[78] Galbraith and Holton, *op. cit.*, pp. 177–198.

Boyd took the position that certain changes in the activities of marketing intermediaries would contribute to the economic development of Egypt. Existing distribution channels would be shortened by the adoption of the policies he recommended. Boyd, however, did not state that vertical integration would in itself contribute to greater efficiency.[79] Generalizing on a broader scale, Mueller maintained that marketing costs in all underdeveloped countries would fall sharply, and the ill-effects of monopolistic competition would be partially alleviated by the introduction of grading systems, the use of standard weights and measures, and the broader dissemination of price information.[80]

The desirability of rationalizing distribution channels and reducing the number of market intermediaries is not, however, universally accepted. A number of disadvantages and misconceptions associated with such action have been pointed up by critics of the policy. Of considerable significance is the customary absence of alternate employment opportunities for displaced market intermediaries. Galbraith and Holton never squarely face this issue although they acknowledge its existence. The marketing system in most underdeveloped countries is described as a form of unemployment relief for those who would otherwise be idle. Galbraith and Holton insist that it is an inefficient and regressive type of relief, unfairly taxing those least able to pay. Nevertheless, a pious wish that marketing reforms be accompanied by careful and compassionate consideration of those displaced is not enough.[81] Are efforts to reduce the number of people employed in trade in order as long as alternate sources of employment are unavailable? It has been argued that such action is not justified.[82]

Economic as well as moral arguments have been raised against efforts to "reform" the marketing system. Bauer and Yamey's defense of the existing marketing structure in one underdeveloped area was based on the following arguments: (1) critics were confusing technical with economic efficiency and urging innovations of value only in already developed countries; (2) primary producers and ultimate consumers are skillful bargainers and thus not exploited by marketing intermediaries;

[79] Harper W. Boyd, Jr., Abdel Aziz el Sherbini, and Ahmed Fouad Sherif, "Channels of Distribution for Consumer Goods in Egypt," *Journal of Marketing*, Vol. XXV, No. 4 (October 1961), pp. 29–33.

[80] Mueller, *op cit.*, p. 424.

[81] Galbraith and Holton, *op. cit.*, pp. 1–4.

[82] Sidney W. Mintz, "The Role of the Middleman in the Internal Distribution System of a Caribbean Peasant Economy," in S. George Walters, Max D. Snider, and Morris L. Sweet (eds.), *Readings in Marketing*, South-Western Publishing Company, Cincinnati, 1962, p. 797. The Mintz article originally appeared in *Human Organization*, Vol. XV (Summer 1956), pp. 18–23.

(3) the activities of traders contribute to the development of a market economy and the formation of capital; and (4) complex marketing arrangements are quite rational when due allowance is made for the scarcity of capital and the abundance of labor.[83] These authors are not alone in arguing along such lines. An observer of Caribbean marketing has reached similar conclusions.

> Given the low level of the total economy, the internal marketing arrangements in such areas can not be called inefficient insofar as they do not absorb larger quantities of scarce resources than are needed for the performance of the services required by the customers. The multiplicity of traders is an aspect of the generally low level of such economies. It seems doubtful that the forcible elimination of these traders would be economically advisable. Given the scarcity of capital for economic development, use of available capital to eliminate higglers might adversely affect other existing economic arrangements.[84]

The desirability of eliminating middlemen and shortening channels thus remains a subject of debate. The consequences of efforts to rationalize distribution systems may depend on local conditions and thus differ markedly from nation to nation. Research along the lines advocated by Hollander in a discussion of retailing and its environment might reveal the conditions under which marketing reform would be feasible and desirable.[85]

ISSUE 7. WHAT ROLE CAN MARKETING PLAY IN ECONOMIC DEVELOPMENT?

Capital formation, the characteristics and growth rate of the population, and the availability of trade have each been presented as the decisive ingredient in economic development.[86] Examination of the pertinent literature, however, reveals an almost complete neglect of market-

---

[83] P. T. Bauer and B. S. Yamey, "The Economics of Marketing Reform," *Journal of Political Economy*, Vol. LXII (June 1954), pp. 210–235.

[84] Mintz, *op. cit.*, p. 795.

[85] Stanley C. Hollander, "Retailing: Cause or Effect?," William S. Decker (ed.), *Emergeing Concepts in Marketing: Proceedings of the December, 1962, Winter Conference*, American Marketing Association, Chicago, 1963, pp. 220–230.

[86] Kindleberger, *op. cit.*, pp. 10–12.

ing problems and institutions.[87] Most of the authorities in the field fail to believe either that changes in marketing practice can facilitate economic development or, conversely, that inefficient marketing practices can hinder the process. Marketing is considered a passive element which will adapt to whatever changes are made in the more important aspects of the economy. This position is understandable if not excusable in that economists have traditionally failed to consider the complexities of selling and distributing goods in a world of imperfect information. Conditions have not changed in the decade since 1953 when Holton cited this traditional bias and other factors as underlying the widespread lack of interest in marketing.[88]

The importance of marketing has been recognized by a few specialists in economic development. Kindleberger, for example, pointed out that a commercial revolution has preceded an industrial revolution in most of the presently developed countries of the world.[89] He also stressed the need for better roads and improved transportation facilities in order that the size of markets might be expanded—a development which Adam Smith recognized as essential if the benefits of the specialization of labor were to be enjoyed.[90] The work of Galbraith and Holton, as well as that of Bauer and Yamey in the marketing area has previously been discussed. The writings of these men and their emphasis on marketing, however, are not typical of the mainstream of economic development literature.

The secondary significance attached to marketing is demonstrated in the hiring policies of the succession of foreign aid agencies established by the United States government. Emphasis has been placed on the recruitment of financial experts and specialists in agricultural and industrial production with marketing being considered a problem of only limited importance.[91] All too frequently, such policies have resulted in the production of commodities for which there is neither an existing nor potential demand. Also, inadequate emphasis is placed on cultural differences and problems of exchange and physical distribution.

Students of marketing have also neglected to explore the possible

[87] Arthur Hazlewood, *The Economics of "Underdeveloped" Areas: An Annotated Reading List of Books, Articles, and Official Publications*, 2nd enlarged ed.; Oxford University Press, London, 1959. Of the 1027 items listed in this bibliography, only 29 are classified under "Commerce and Marketing."

[88] Holton, *op. cit.*, pp. 344–349.

[89] Kindleberger, *op. cit.*, pp. 103–105.

[90] *Ibid.*, pp. 92–93, 95–99.

[91] Woodruff J. Emlen, "Let's Export Marketing Know-How," *Harvard Business Review*, Vol. XXXVI (November–December 1958), pp. 71–72.

contribution of the marketing system to economic development. The work of the relatively few marketing specialists who have concerned themselves with this issue has previously been mentioned and can be briefly summarized. Robinson's attempt at determining the suitability of a foreign-owned corporation offering a given product for sale in an underdeveloped country, Coolsen's comparison of the American past and conditions presently existing in emerging nations, and Hollander's study of the interrelationships between retailing and the environment in which it takes place were noteworthy efforts.[92] Various implications of Harper Boyd's argument that application of the marketing concept can contribute to the economic development of emerging nations was examined in two of the preceding sections.[93] Also reviewed was the urging of an interdisciplinary panel that the history of American marketing be studied in search of obtaining information which would facilitate economic development.[94] The same panel recognized the need to investigate a problem central to this final issue: whether improvements in the pattern of marketing attitudes and techniques existing in underdeveloped countries would make a greater contribution to raising the standard of living than continued emphasis on improvement in methods of production.[95]

The most forthright assertion that marketing can contribute meaningfully to economic development was made by Peter Drucker.

> My thesis is very briefly as follows. Marketing occupies a critical role in respect to the development of (underdeveloped) "growth" areas. Indeed, marketing is the most important "multiplier" of such development. It is in itself in every one of these areas the least developed, the most backward part of the economic system. Its development, above all others, makes possible economic integration and the fullest utilization of whatever assets and productive capacity an economy already possesses. It mobilizes latent economic energy. It contributes to the greatest needs: that for the rapid development of entrepreneurs and managers, and at the same time, it may be the easiest area of managerial work to get going . . . (since) it is the most systematized and, therefore, the most learnable and the most teachable of all areas of business management and entrepreneurship.[96]

[92] Supra, p. 407 and p. 420, respectively.
[93] Supra, pp. 408–409.
[94] Myers and Smalley, op. cit., pp. 395–399.
[95] Ibid., pp. 389–393.
[96] Peter Drucker, "Marketing and Economic Development," Journal of Marketing, Vol. XXII, No. 1 (January 1958), p. 253.

One might dispute Drucker's claim that marketing is the easiest of the business disciplines to teach. His view of marketing as an appendage of a free market economy rather than as a function which must be performed, whatever the prevailing mode of economic organization, could also be challenged. Nevertheless, his comments concerning the importance of marketing in developing entrepreneurs and the existing state of distribution in underdeveloped countries appear quite valid.[97] His statement of marketing's importance to economic development in a free economy has been seconded by Hans Thorelli, a political scientist by training. "No vehicle is more powerful than contemporary marketing philosophy in changing attitudes in a manner conducive to improving standards of living in a democratic society."[98]

Because of their professional commitment to the discipline, the readers of this chapter are likely to share Drucker's belief that marketing can contribute meaningfully to economic development. Unfortunately, however, the manner in which that contribution can be maximized has not been thoroughly investigated.

The most frequently cited demonstration of marketing's potential concerns the impact of Sears Roebuck on the economic development of several Latin American countries. Admittedly, Sears has revolutionized retailing in those areas in which it operates and helped to establish hundreds of firms which supply the products sold in the company's retail outlets.[99] As Hollander has argued, however, a society may have to achieve a certain level of development before the type of merchandising associated with a Sears Roebuck can succeed.[100] Although it can be argued that all underdeveloped countries would benefit from the introduction of such techniques, the means of reaching a level at which a Sears operation can prosper as a business venture while favorably affecting the economic structure of the nation remains to be determined.

We do not presently know if anything in the history of marketing in more developed countries will be of value and assistance to emerging nations. The conditions under which American marketing techniques will prove applicable in other parts of the world remain to be determined. Even if American marketing innovations are found to be universally effective, the desirability of stimulating consumer demand in underde-

[97] *Ibid.*, pp. 255–259.
[98] Hans B. Thorelli, "Political Science and Marketing," in Reavis Cox, Wroe Alderson, and Stanley J. Shapiro (eds.), *Theory in Marketing: Second Series*, Richard D. Irwin, Homewood, Ill., 1964.
[99] Drucker, *op. cit.*, p. 257; Richardson Wood and Virginia Keyser, *United States Business Performance Abroad; The Case Study of Sears, Roebuck de Mexico S. A.*, National Planning Association, Washington, 1953.
[100] Hollander, *op. cit.*, p. 228.

veloped countries can be questioned. The effect of such action on the rate of capital formation in particular and on economic development in general is still a subject of controversy. Finally, proposals to reform marketing systems have been challenged on economic as well as on ethical grounds.

To the best of the present author's knowledge, there exists only one detailed discussion of how the potential benefits of exporting marketing knowledge might be realized.[101] Emlin shares Drucker's view that marketing is a teachable discipline which by its ability to develop entrepreneurs and managers can make a significant contribution to economic development. He also recognizes the importance of the marketing concept being adopted and Western business practices introduced in a manner consistent with the existing cultural framework. The large and experienced class of merchants and traders in underdeveloped countries would be a source of potential entrepreneurs if this group learned that marketing should be oriented to meeting the desires and needs of consumers.[102] Emlin urged that experts in modern marketing techniques stay for long periods in underdeveloped countries in order to become aware of all pertinent cultural considerations. These men could use their talents to spark a program of case method education for those with limited training and of market place discussion groups for merchants and traders with no understanding of the managerial task.[103] The policies Emlin recommends would make marketing a much more productive element in the underdeveloped economy. Nevertheless, the important issues discussed in previous sections of this paper would remain unresolved.

TOWARD THE SOLUTION OF UNRESOLVED ISSUES

The preceding sections have pointed up existing areas of ignorance and controversy as to the following issues:

1. the appropriate frame of reference for the comparison of national marketing systems.
2. the applicability in other countries of American marketing techniques.
3. the possible existence of stages of marketing development.
4. the role of the market economy and of market structure in economic development.

[101] Emlin, *op. cit.*, pp. 70–76.
[102] *Ibid.*, pp. 71–73.
[103] *Ibid.*, pp. 72–75. The International Marketing Institute, located at the Harvard Business School, has conducted a number of programs for foreign executives in which the case method is the primary tool of instruction.

5. the desirability of stimulating consumer wants in underdeveloped countries.
6. the wisdom of efforts to reform the marketing systems of under-developed countries.
7. the contribution that marketing can make to economic development.

An article in a volume on science in marketing should contain some indication of the empirical research that would resolve these problems. Unfortunately, the author is not presently able to spell out in detail a series of studies and projects that would clarify all the areas of uncertainty previously discussed. Research efforts in any of the social sciences are complicated by the impossibility of experimentation in the rigid fashion characteristic of the natural sciences. The problems of the researcher become still more complex when one's major interest is comparative studies of entire nations rather than individuals or segments of a single population.

Once adequate attention is focused on the problem, fairly rapid progress should be made in developing the appropriate framework for the description and analysis of comparative marketing systems. An outline similar at least in some respects to that advocated by Bartels must be perfected and generally employed.[104] Otherwise, the welter of articles being published on domestic marketing abroad will continue to be of only limited usefulness. A standardized reporting format has been employed successfully by cultural anthropologists studying hundreds of tribal and national groups. The agreed-upon framework facilitates comparisons and contrasts while allowing due attention to be paid the unique features of any given group.[105] Similar standardization in the description of marketing systems is a necessary prerequisite to meaningful comparative analysis.

Additional research into the possibility of assigning nations to various stages of marketing development is clearly in order. Almost all efforts previously made along these lines have been by-products of studies primarily designed for other purposes.[106] Among the topics deserving attention is the possible existence of a "life cycle" or developmental pattern for marketing systems. If such a cycle or pattern can be identified, the independent variables that determine the level or stage to which

---

[104] *Supra,* pp. 400–401.
[105] Stanley Hollander mentioned to the author the usefulness of the uniform classification method used in the Human Relations Area Files. See the preface to Murdock et al., *Outline of Cultural Materials,* 4th revised ed., Human Relations Area Files, New Haven, 1961.
[106] *Supra,* pp. 410–412.

a given system belongs at any time and the speed at which the system matures must be discovered. The reasons that underlie any variations in the life cycle of the marketing system of different nations must also be investigated.[107] The process of cross-cultural transfer, as it applies to marketing systems and the environmental factors influencing such systems, is also worthy of especially close attention.[108]

Designing a program of meaningful empirical research becomes especially complex when one considers the various aspects of the relationship of marketing to economic development. This problem is central to the last four of the seven unresolved issues just discussed. The position taken, however, as to the desirability of stimulating consumer demand, of introducing marketing reforms and innovations, and of allowing market forces to direct resource allocation is influenced in large part by value judgments made by the observer. Given the conditions existing in today's world, it is hard to propose meaningful research which would allow fact to supersede opinion on these points. Plans for economic development are being formulated in nations determined to overcome poverty and deprivation. Those in charge cannot be expected to make a systematic effort to solve the various questions raised earlier as to the prospective contribution of marketing to this process. All that can be hoped for is a long overdue awareness that marketing must be considered in the design and implementation of development planning. Once increased attention is paid to marketing practices and innovations, the results associated with different policies can be measured. The unique features of each nation notwithstanding, careful observation might provide the basis for meaningful hypotheses concerning the role of marketing in economic development.

Economists from many nations have contributed to the existing body of economic theory. A concern with marketing theory, however, appears to be a uniquely American phenomenon. The degree of marketing development reached in the United States and the existence of problems of high level consumption are most likely the reasons why marketing theory and marketing science are almost exclusively an American interest. As the other contributions to this volume indicate, the development of a science which explains the complexities of marketing in the American economy will not be an easy task. Nevertheless, the relevance

[107] The existence of a life cycle for marketing systems is a possibility called to the attention of the author by George Schwartz, the editor of this volume.
[108] In their review of an earlier draft, both Stanley Hollander and Watson Dunn mentioned the importance of cross-cultural transfer. For an introduction into the literature on this subject, see Jacobson, Kumala, and Gullahorn, "Cross-cultural Contributions to Attitude Research," *Public Opinion Quarterly*, Vol. XXI (Summer 1960), pp. 205–223.

of any true science cannot be limited to the territory of a single country or the operations of a given economic order. A center for marketing studies which would investigate the possible contributions of marketing history and marketing change to economic development has been advocated for some time.[109] Although the existence of a separate research entity devoting itself to these issues would be desirable, it is not essential. What appears imperative, however, is a coordinated research program which will facilitate comparative marketing analysis and, to the extent possible, indicate the conditions under which marketing can contribute to economic development. Until considerable progress is made in these areas, the state of marketing knowledge as it relates to economic development can hardly be termed "marketing science."

[109] Myers and Smalley, *op. cit.*, pp. 398–401; Coolsen, *op. cit.*, pp. 36–37.

BIBLIOGRAPHY

BOOKS

Bartels, Robert (ed.), *Comparative Marketing: Wholesaling in Fifteen Countries*, Richard D. Irwin, Homewood, Ill., 1963.

Bauer, Peter T., *West African Trade: A Study of Competition, Oligopoly and Monopoly in a Changing Economy*, The University Press, Cambridge, England, 1954.

————, and Basil S. Yamey, *The Economics of Underdeveloped Countries*, The University of Chicago Press, Chicago, 1957.

Davis, Robert T., *The Changing Pattern of Europe's Grocery Trade*, Graduate School of Business, Stamford, Calif., n. d.

Dewey, Alice, *Peasant Marketing in Java*, The Free Press of Glencoe, New York, 1962.

Dunn, S. Watson (ed.), *International Advertising Handbook*, McGraw-Hill, New York, 1963.

Galbraith, John K., and Richard H. Holton, *Marketing Efficiency in Puerto Rico*, Harvard University Press, Cambridge, Mass., 1955.

Gilbert, Milton and Irving B. Kravis, *An International Comparison of National Products and the Purchasing Power of Currencies*, The Organization for European Economic Cooperation, Paris, France, n. d.

Goldman, Marshall J., *Soviet Marketing: Distribution in a Controlled Economy*, The Free Press of Glencoe, New York, 1963.

Hall, Margaret, John Knapp, and Christopher Winsten, *Distribution in Great Britain and North America: A Study in Structure and Productivity*, Oxford University Press, London, England.

Hazlewood, Arthur, *The Economics of "Underdeveloped" Areas: An Annotated Reading List of Books, Articles, and Official Publications*, 2nd enlarged ed., Oxford University Press, London, England.

Hirsch, Leon V., *Marketing in an Underdeveloped Economy: The North Indian Sugar Industry*, Prentice-Hall, Englewood Cliffs, N. J., 1961.

Jefferys, James B., Simon Hausberger, and Goran Lindblad, *Productivity in the*

Distributive Trade in Europe, The Organization for European Economic Co-operation, Paris, France, 1954.

————, and Derek Knee, *Retailing in Europe, Present Structure and Future Trends,* The Macmillan Company, London, England, 1963.

Kindleberger, Charles P., *Economic Development,* McGraw-Hill, New York, 1958.

Kramer, Roland L., *International Marketing,* South-Western Publishing Company, Cincinnati, Ohio, 1959.

Mulvihill, Donald F. (ed.), *Bibliography on Domestic Marketing Systems Abroad,* Kent State University, Bureau of Economic and Business Research, Printed Series No. 2, Kent, Ohio, 1962.

Murdock et al., *Outline of Cultural Materials,* 4th revised ed., Human Relations Area Files, New Haven, Conn., 1961.

Nurske, Ragnar, *Problems of Capital Formation in Underdeveloped Countries,* Oxford University Press, New York, 1952.

Polanyi, Karl, *The Great Transformation,* Beacon Press, Boston, Mass., 1957.

Rostow, W. W., *The Stages of Economic Growth: A Non-Communist Manifesto,* The University Press, Cambridge, England, 1960.

Vaile, Roland S., E. T. Grether, and Reavis Cox, *Marketing in the American Economy,* Ronald Press, New York, 1952.

Wood, Richardson, and Virginia Keyser, *United States Business Performance Abroad: The Case Study of Sears, Roebuck de Mexico S. A.,* National Planning Association, Washington, D.C., 1953.

ARTICLES

Bauer, Peter T., "Concentration in Tropical Trade: Some Aspects and Implications of Oligopoly," *Economica,* Vol. XX (November 1953).

————, and Basil S. Yamey, "The Economics of Marketing Reform," *Journal of Political Economy,* Vol. LXII (June 1954).

Boyd, Harper W., Jr., Abdel Aziz Sherbini, and Ahmed Fouad Sherif, "Channels of Distribution for Consumer Goods in Egypt," *Journal of Marketing,* Vol. XXV (October 1961).

————, "Egypt's Need for Marketing Management," *Business Horizons,* Vol. IV (Spring 1961).

Cook, Hugh L., "Observations on Market Structures and National Economic Development in the Philippines," *Journal of Farm Economics,* Vol. XLI (August 1959).

Cox, Reavis and Charles S. Goodman, "Marketing of Housebuilding Materials," *Journal of Marketing,* Vol. XXI (July 1956).

Coolsen, Frank G., "Marketing and Economic Development," in William S. Decker, (ed.), *Emerging Concepts in Marketing: Proceedings of the December, 1962, Winter Conference,* American Marketing Association, Chicago, 1963.

Dichter, Ernest, "The World Customer," *Harvard Business Review,* Vol. XXXX, (July–August 1962).

Drucker, Peter, "Marketing and Economic Development," *Journal of Marketing,* Vol. XXXII (January 1958).

Dunn, S. Watson, "French Retailing and the Common Market," *Journal of Marketing,* Vol. XXVI (January 1962).

Frederick, William C., "The Market as a Factor in Economic Growth," *The Southwestern Social Science Quarterly,* Vol. XXXXI (June 1960).

Emlen, Woodruff J., "Let's Export Marketing Know-How," *Harvard Business Review*, Vol. XXVI (November–December 1958).

Goldman, Marshall J., "Marketing—A Lesson for Marx," *Harvard Business Review*, Vol. XXXVIII (January–February 1960).

——, "Retailing in the Soviet Union," *Journal of Marketing*, Vol. XXIV (April 1960).

——, "The Marketing Structure of the Soviet Union," *Journal of Marketing*, Vol. XXV (July 1961).

Hamid, Hakima, "Marketing and Business Practices in Afghanistan," *The Middle East Journal*, Vol XIV (Winter 1960).

Hollander, Stanley C., "Retailing: Cause or Effect?" in William S. Decker (ed.), *Emerging Concepts in Marketing: Proceedings of the December, 1962, Winter Conference*, American Marketing Association, Chicago, 1963.

Holton, Richard H., "Marketing Structure and Economic Development," *Quarterly Journal of Economics*, Vol. LXVII (August 1953).

Jacobson, E., H. Kumata, and J. F. Gullahorn, "Cross Cultural Contributions to Attitude Research," *Public Opinion Quarterly*, Vol. XXIV (Summer 1960)

Mintz, Sidney W., "The Role of the Middleman in the Internal Distribution System of a Caribbean Peasant Economy," in S. George Walters, Max D. Snyder, and Morris L. Sweet (eds.), *Readings in Marketing*, South-Western Publishing Company, Cincinnati, Ohio, 1962. Originally in *Human Organization*, Vol. XV (Summer 1956).

McGarry, Edmund D., "Some Functions of Marketing Reconsidered," in Reavis Cox and Wroe Alderson, (eds.), *Theory in Marketing—Selected Essays*, Richard D. Irwin, Chicago, 1950.

Mueller, William F., "Some Market Structure Considerations in Economic Development," *Journal of Farm Economics*, Vol. XLI (May 1959).

Myers, Kenneth H., Jr. and Orange A. Smalley, "Marketing History and Economic Development," *The Business History Review*, Vol. XXXIII (Autumn 1959).

Nielson, Arthur C., Jr., "Do's and Don'ts in Selling Abroad," *Journal of Marketing*, Vol. XXIII (April 1959).

Phelps, Maynard, "Soviet Marketing—Stronger Than We Think," *Harvard Business Review*, Vol. XXXIX (July–August 1961).

Robinson, Richard D., "The Challenge of the Underdeveloped National Market," *Journal of Marketing*, Vol. XXV (October 1961).

Shapiro, Stanley J., "The Survival Concept and the Non-Profit Behavior System," in Reavis Cox, Wroe Alderson, and Stanley J. Shapiro (eds.), *Theory in Marketing:* Second Series, Richard D. Irwin, Homewood, Ill., 1964.

Smithies, Arthur, "Rising Expectations and Economic Development," *The Economic Journal*, Vol. LXXI (June 1961).

Solomon, Morton R., "The Structure of the Market in Underdeveloped Economies," *Quarterly Journal of Economics*, Vol. LXII (August 1948).

Stridsberg, Albert B., "Launching Your Product in Belgium," *Journal of Marketing*, Vol. XXVI (January 1962).

Thorelli, Hans B., "Political Science and Marketing," in Reavis Cox, Wroe Alderson, and Stanley J. Shapiro (eds.), *Theory in Marketing: Second Series*, Richard D. Irwin, Homewood, Ill., 1964.

Thorne, Alfred, "Monopoly-Oligopoly-Economic Development: The Underdeveloped Americas and the Caribbean," *Cartel*, Vol. X (April 1960).

15

Operations Research and

Marketing Science

WILLIAM LAZER

THE OPERATIONS RESEARCH PERSPECTIVE

Many disciplines and fields of study are contributing to the development of marketing science. The interdisciplinary approach has been suggested as a very fruitful avenue for the development of marketing knowledge and theory. The value of incorporating findings from the behavioral sciences and quantitative methods has been stressed.[1] Operations research which utilizes quantitative methods has a decided contribution to make to marketing science.

Operations research approaches vary from other marketing approaches in at least two respects. First of all, operations researchers use different tools for problem solving. They make frequent recourse to mathematical and statistical tools. Mathematical models are part of the normal problem-solving kit of the operations researcher. Marketing executives expect operations researchers to demonstrate a degree of skill in applying quantitative techniques not required of other management people. The application of mathematical models to marketing problems should advance the development of marketing science in the following ways: [2]

> 1. The models are useful in theory construction. When quantitative models are formulated and data from the real world are mapped into them, a theory about the data results.

[1] William Lazer and Eugene J. Kelley, "Interdisciplinary Contributions to Marketing Management," *Marketing and Transportation Paper No. 5*, Bureau of Business and Economic Research, Michigan State University.
[2] For a detailed discussion of models in marketing, see William Lazer, "The Role of Models in Marketing," *Journal of Marketing*, Vol. 26, No. 2 (April 1962).

2. Simulation, or experimentation, on the models can generate further theories and hypotheses about marketing and provide valuable insights for marketing science.

3. Models have provided the most successful predicting system so far produced, the predicting systems used in science.[3]

4. Quantitative models help portray marketing situations in simplified forms so they can be analyzed. They help explain relationships and reactions which are critical in developing marketing science.

5. Quantitative models tend to be objective rather than intuitive, and they can often pursue analyses not feasible through other techniques.

The second major difference in operations research approaches is one of perspective. Operations researchers adopt a systems perspective. In trying to solve marketing problems they view marketing not in terms of a group of functions that must be performed, or in terms of manufacturing, wholesaling, and retailing institutions, but as a total system of business action. The impact of systems thinking, advanced by the operations researcher, is being felt in marketing.

The most widely hailed marketing development in the postwar period is the acceptance of the marketing philosophy of business operation as was discussed by King in an earlier chapter. This viewpoint, however, is merely the outward manifestation of a more fundamental and significant development that has occurred. Marketing executives have adopted a new perspective of marketing operations. They are embracing the systems viewpoint of marketing action.[4] The systems approach is fundamental to the marketing concept, to the role of models in marketing, and to the application of computers.

Under the systems concept, marketing institutions and operation are viewed as complex, large-scale, dynamic action systems. A marketing system is comprised of a group of marketing elements and operations which are interrelated and connected and can be delineated conceptually or physically. The characteristic which differentiates a system from a jumble of parts and pieces is that they form a coherent group. Systems thinking, therefore, is based on the integration and coordination of marketing activity. A marketing organization is seen not merely as a number of separate departmental units, processes, and activities; it is a system of action.

The systems approach in marketing turns on the central theme that marketing reality occurs in systems. A business, or part of it, can be

[3] Irwin D. J. Bross, *Design for Decisions*, Macmillan, New York, 1953, p. 169.
[4] For a detailed discussion of systems concept, see William Lazer and Eugene J. Kelley, *Managerial Marketing: Perspectives and Viewpoints*, revised ed., Richard D. Irwin, Homewood, Ill., 1962.

represented by some suitable system. The system may culminate in a simulation model, a flow diagram, a physical replica, or a chart. Marketing managers have the major responsibility of recognizing the relationships among the elements of the system, comprehending their potential combinations, and coordinating and integrating business factors so that goals are achieved effectively. This implies that the master model for marketing activity is the systems model.

The marketing management concept, which is a signal breakthrough in the management thinking, by its very nature implies a systems approach to the management of marketing effort. It requires a recognition of the interrelations and interconnections between marketing and other business elements. It involves the integration of all the components of the marketing program into a coordinated marketing mix. It demands the establishment of a communications network and linkages between the various functionaries and activities necessary for the accomplishment of marketing missions. It is concerned with the flows of information and resources through a firm to the marketplace. Even the implementation of the marketing concept requires the grouping of marketing activities and the designation of a top-level executive to integrate both authority and responsibility.

OPERATIONS RESEARCH APPROACHES

Operations research is suggested by such terms as waiting-line theory, simulation, linear programming, dynamic programming, game theory, Markov processes, and decision theory. This analytical technique emphasizes the use of mathematical tools. Yet, operations research groups are not comprised solely of mathematicians. They include engineers, logicians, physicists, accountants, biologists, and statisticians as well as various types of business executives.

Operations research in one sense is broader in scope than any functional discipline. It cuts across functional lines and is applicable to all types of organizations, institutions, and activities, private and governmental, concerned with allocating scarce resources among alternative means to try to achieve objectives effectively. It stresses the similarities and analogies of quantitative approaches from widely diverse fields. It is not just a group of mathematical techniques. OR is eclectic in nature. It utilizes all branches of scientific endeavor to solve problems.

Operations research as applied to marketing science then is concerned with techniques and methodology for solving operating marketing problems. It is not merely concerned with knowledge for the sake of knowledge. It does not have an organized body of knowledge in the sense that cultural anthropology, social psychology, or political science does. The characteristic that links operations researchers in many fields is problem-solving techniques. Operations research then spans a wide and diverse subject matter, is concerned with a multitude of operational problems, and emphasizes problem solving rather than knowledge.

OR emphasizes individual and specialized applications of techniques. Analytical methods are developed for solving the marketing problems of individual organizations. The operations researcher is more concerned with attaining specific solutions to problems than he is in developing more generalized models. For although it is often possible to change a problem to fit some general solution method, in practice, when this is done, the actual solution may have very little meaning. It is the ability to generate solutions to real problems that is important rather than success in molding problems so that answers, however unrealistic, are obtained through available tools.

For the evolution of marketing science, it might be more useful to develop generalized models. The difficulties encountered, however, are enormous. Although there are similarities between marketing organizations, the problems confronting them are often exceedingly different. Marketing organizations differ in size, resources, objectives, complexity, scope, and limitations. This tends to preclude a high degree of generalization of models, and demands that operations researchers be adaptive, flexible, and creative so that specific techniques for specialized situations can be employed.

Operations researchers are concerned with investigating goal-directed or purposeful operating systems. OR studies systems of action rather than individuals. For example, researchers are interested in purposeful marketing systems in which specific objectives are pursued and in which choices from among alternative courses of action are present.

Operations researchers study patterns of marketing activities. However, they do not seem to study interactions of people. Operations researchers seem most interested in those properties of a marketing system that would not change if the people involved were replaced by others. This strips away many essential aspects of marketing operations and could lead to a concentration on some of the less significant factors.

One of the most important characteristics of operations research methods is its practical aim. It is not just a descriptive, theoretical activity. OR is concerned with the practical operation and management of an organization. It deals with practical decisions and programs of action. Costs, profits, losses, competitors' actions, and the impact of changing strategies, all are of concern to the operations researcher. While operations researchers use theory, and adapt abstract models and tools from various sciences, they must provide practical information and specific answers to problem situations. Their recommendations must face the demanding tests of the marketplace.

Operations researchers often work in teams. In dealing with new problems and technologies team effort has proven to be productive. The OR team is often composed of people who have diverse backgrounds, interests, and skills. The team brings together men from various disciplines, such as mathematics, statistics, logic, physics, engineering, biology, and philosophy, with a breadth of experience who focus attention on the same problem.

Although OR utilizes the synthesis of various disciplines in studying systems and operations, this does not mean that OR will take over other disciplines. For example, research findings from systems engineering, communications theory, and computer technology, are used by OR to solve marketing problems. The individual identities of each have and will continue to have an independent usefulness. At the same time, marketing science is benefiting from the higher order integration of sciences and technologies. Through such collaboration, broader approaches to marketing problems are being taken than would otherwise be the case.

Marketing problems, because of their complexity, often cannot be solved effectively by the tools, concepts, and findings of a specific discipline. "The aspects of the system which can be manipulated so as to improve its performance are likely to come from many different disciplines." [5] As the disciplines involved in the study of marketing increase their research power, the problem of selecting the most appropriate ones to improve organizational performance will become increasingly difficult to solve. It will require an integrated examination of marketing organizations as systems.

Operations research techniques have increased the effectiveness of the decision-making process in marketing. They hold great promise for achieving more effective allocation of marketing resources and a better matching of resources and opportunities. Marketing is developing as a more scientific discipline. The factors in the marketing program and their impact are becoming measurable. Operations research methodology is assisting marketing in its progression as a scientific discipline. The sophisticated and rigorous tools of operations analysis are resulting in more adequate and pertinent data, the ability to multiply experimentation in marketing, and the development of measurements not previously available.

[5] Russell L. Ackoff, "The Meaning, Scope, and Methods of Operations Research," *Progress in Operations Research*, Vol. I, Wiley, New York, 1962.

OPERATIONS RESEARCH AS A SCIENCE

Is operations research a science? Although many operations researchers may proclaim that it is, this may not be the case. For instance, Lathrop suggests that "Perhaps it is best described as the application of scientists from various disciplines to the solution of operating problems. The opportunity to be called a science and to do scientific research on top management problems must be earned and not demanded. The question facing the operations researcher is how to earn it." [6]

In the same vein, Stafford Beer in the *Operational Research Quarterly* (Vol. 9, 1958) states that OR as subject matter is not a science. Operations research emerges rather as a group of scientific methods appropriate to the analysis of activity. These methods *per se,* however, do not form a science. Rather, they refer to the attack of modern science on probability type problems which arise in the management, and the control of men, machines, materials, and money in their natural environment.

At present it appears that OR is not an applied discipline. Operations research might even be thought of as the application of scientists to new problems—problems which may be unrelated to the content of their original training and experience. OR may be considered as a stage in the development of an applied subject-matter field rather than the actual discipline itself. It reflects approaches or methods. Like most effective methods, OR is scientific. As such, it can further and extend the scientific approach to the study and management of marketing activity.

OPERATIONS RESEARCH DEFINED

There is no wide consensus on the definition of operations research. We may gain some perspective of its scope and boundaries, however, by considering a few of the definitions appearing in the literature. This will permit the delineation of some of OR's distinguishing major characteristics and methods of problem solving.

Among the many definitions offered of OR are (1) "a scientific method of providing executives with the quantitative basis for making decisions with regard to operations under their control." [7] (2) "the application of scientific method of industrial problems leading to recommendations that

[6] John Lathrop, "A Letter to Ellis Johnson," *Operations Research,* (July–August 1960), p. 576.
[7] W. G. Ireson and E. L. Grant (eds.), *Handbook of Industrial Engineering and Management,* Prentice-Hall, Englewood Cliffs, N. J., 1955, p. 1015.

in turn lead to action." [8] (3) "the convergence of a research region, concerned with the preparation of management decisions at various levels and in various contexts, and the application of a method of approach which is rigorously scientific, a method which used quite an arsenal of techniques and often employs speedy and powerful calculating tools. Therefore, operations research is above all dependent on an attitude of mind in regard to the problems put by management." [9] (4) "the exacting and critical application of the scientific method by scientists and subject specialists to the study of basic laws governing a given operation. Its purpose is to give administrators a basis for predicting quantitatively the most effective results of an operation under a given set of variable conditions and thereby narrow the area of choices of action in making final decisions." [10]

A careful scrutiny of the foregoing definitions, and others appearing in the literature, will reveal the following major characteristics of OR:

1. Scientists from a variety of fields and scientific methods are used to solve operating problems.
2. Quantitative techniques are emphasized.
3. Optimal solutions to problems, rather than mere description, are emphasized.
4. A systems or total perspective is adopted in problem solving.

Operations research then is research intended to help solve practical, immediate problems in the fields of marketing, and other business administration areas, as well as in governmental and military administration. As for its place in marketing, operations research serves as an adjunct to, not a substitute for, marketing research, distribution cost accounting, sales forecasting, and physical distribution. Operations research draws on information from these subjects, calls on the services of varied company specialists, and cuts across lines of functional authority in sublimating the objectives of subgroups to the over-all objective of the company. It is not designed to reduce the responsibilities of marketing management but rather to add new scope and dimensions to the marketing tasks and to help marketing managers deal more effectively with the crucial decisions they must make.

OR is oriented toward the similarities and analogies of quantitative problems from widely different fields. It is concerned with the application

[8] *Managements' Operations Research Digest*, Vol. 1, No. 11 (October 1955), back cover.
[9] Philip M. Morse and George E. Kimball, *Methods of Operations Research*, Wiley, New York, 1951, p. 1.
[10] T. C. Schelling, *The Review of Economics and Statistics*, Vol. XL (August 1958), p. 221.

of models and theories to problem solving. Some of the OR approaches may even be suggested by the problems that marketing managers tackle, such as measuring advertising impact, determining the number of check-out counters to have in supermarkets, establishing inventory controls, and developing better sales forecasts.

Operations research as applied to marketing, therefore, should be viewed from two perspectives: (1) It is an attitude of mind toward the relation between a business and its marketing environment, and (2) it is a body of methods for the solution of marketing problems which arise in that relationship.[11] The former may result in increased understanding of the marketing environment and its resulting impact on company operations. This may be one of the most important contributions of OR methods to marketing science.

COMMENTS ON CURRENT STATUS OF OR IN MARKETING

The use of OR tools and techniques in marketing stems from three desires of marketing executives: (1) to obtain more pertinent, up-to-date, and adequate information for decision-making purposes, (2) to control marketing resources and operations more effectively, and (3) to develop more adequate and rational marketing objectives, policies, strategies, and programs. OR does not obsolete but tends to complement conventional marketing management. OR is directed toward "providing executive departments with the quantitative basis for decisions regarding the operations under their control."[12] By so doing, it should improve the effectiveness of marketing managers.

Despite these significant aims, the application of operations research methods in solving marketing problems, to date, has been quite limited. Marketing practitioners and academicians, nevertheless, are beginning to accept some of the newer approaches of OR. The development of skills in operations research and interest in applying the techniques has been slower in marketing than it has been in other areas, such as production, engineering, and the military sciences. Only recently have modern mathematical tools been applied to develop better marketing practice and theory.

A good proportion of the research that has been undertaken in marketing has been verbal rather than quantitative. Much of it reports evalua-

[11] See "The Teaching of Operational Research," *Operational Research Quarterly*, Vol. IX, 1958, p. 267.

[12] Philip M. Morse and George E. Kimball, *Methods of Operations Research*, Wiley, New York, 1951, p. 1.

tions made on a relative basis of good or poor marketing practice. Some of it is definitional in nature, drawing functional distinctions among marketing institutions and activities. These research efforts have indeed made valuable contributions to science in marketing. They have led to improved marketing insights. However, they have also neglected the quantitative emphasis. In fact, marketing scholars themselves have often resisted analytical generalizations. They seem to do so by taking refuge in statements about the difficulties of analyzing marketing factors quantitatively.

It is true that to some extent the problems in the fields of marketing appear to be mathematically intractable. They tend to lie somewhere between problems in the applied areas of engineering on the one hand, which lend themselves to a quantitative approach, and those of the behavioral science, such as economics, sociology, social psychology, on the other hand, which often do not.

The problems faced in marketing are exceedingly complex, and many of the important factors surrounding marketing decisions are not quantifiable. Some factors, although quantifiable conceptually, elude actual measurement. Other factors are so inextricably intertwined that the operations researchers' models and analytical techniques are ineffective in sorting them out and evaluating their impact and significance. Marketing is a difficult discipline for operations research convergence. Despite such limitations, marketing managers should not adopt a defensive posture and ignore the benefits of operations research.

In trying to understand why OR has not caught on in marketing at a more rapid rate, one should remember the tastes and training of people in executive positions in marketing. Most are unskilled in mathematical and statistical methods. They are "people-oriented" rather than "technique and analytically oriented." They have tended to follow the lore of the trade, to use rules of thumb, and often to apply various generalizations. Moreover, many have been extremely successful.

Rationally, there ought not to be any distrust of mathematical tools and techniques on the part of marketing academicians and administrators. The fact remains, however, that business administrators are sometimes prone to look with a certain amount of disfavor, and even distrust, on anything that is not familiar and anything that is couched in abstract, mathematical, or statistical terms.

Only recently have people with quantitative training, aptitudes, and interests delved into the fruitful and significant areas of marketing. This trend has been encouraged by the establishment of formal marketing research departments, the availability of computers, and the use of external marketing research and management science services by companies.

Marketing presents a more difficult challenge to operations researchers than many other business areas do. Operations researchers face exceptional difficulties when they try to handle marketing factors and interpret market conditions. Part of the reason for this is that marketing operations introduce the human element, especially in terms of consumer attitudes, opinions, motives, and behavior, and the reactions of wholesalers, retailers, and manufacturers, and their employees as decision makers.

In developing marketing models, the operations researcher must deal with conditions of great uncertainty. Marketing factors that are not as concrete as those of certain production and inventory problems must be handled. Moreover, the specific facts necessary for generating solutions are often unknown. As a result, the operations researcher is forced to rely on complex mathematical techniques and manipulations, especially probability theory.

The fact that marketing executives do not understand OR and the associated mathematical techniques seems to result in two opposing executive reactions. On the other hand, there seems to be a tendency among marketing managers who are not trained in quantitative techniques, and who are immersed in operating problems, to treat operations researchers with a "halo effect." Individuals who can manipulate symbols, use computers, refer to the proper mystic and mathematical concepts, and arrive at solutions are accorded status. And yet, there is also a suspicion of, and negative reaction to, operations researchers and mathematical tools. This often leads to an outright rejection of the idea that marketing factors and activities can be quantified.

To improve marketing management and enhance marketing science, the role of computers, quantitative techniques, models, and operations researchers in the marketing decision process must be viewed in a positive light. All marketing organizations are confronted with a problem of making optimal use of scarce resources in a manner that maximizes profits and/or minimizes costs. The operations researcher can often approach such problems through mathematical programming by stating in algebraic terms the function to be minimized or maximized, the alternatives that may be used in achieving this objective function, the constraints which are imposed by various factors, and manipulating the equations or inequalities to achieve the best solution. It is the realistic appraisal of the value of such methods to marketing that is one of the challenges now facing marketing academicians and practitioners.

OPERATIONS RESEARCH IN MARKETING:
A CRITICAL ASSESSMENT

Operations researchers do not operate in an environmental vacuum. They function in a marketing setting. Although marketing parameters have the greatest impact on significant business decisions, they are often skirted and ignored. Operations researchers in their investigations tend to assume away marketing factors. They appear to place a heavy emphasis on problems outside the marketing area while neglecting more significant marketing considerations.

In reality, operations researchers have a great stake in the development of marketing thought and knowledge. They must concern themselves with the primacy of marketing factors in enterprise decisions. They must recognize the extended influence of marketing forces. They must realize that the development of a richer body of scientific knowledge pertaining to management is inextricably intertwined with a better understanding of marketing factors.

The virtues of operations research have been extolled in many articles readily available to the reader. It might be profitable to explore the limitations of operations research in marketing. A review of marketing-related articles appearing in operations research and management science journals suggests several criticisms of operations research approaches to marketing. The following material presents a critical assessment of operations research treatments of marketing problems.

Much of the progress made in the extension of management science has been attributed to the use of models. Models are truly useful tools of analysis. Some of the more sophisticated mathematical models have received widespread acclaim for their accomplishments. Yet, when evaluated against the spectrum of significant marketing problems, the accomplishments of models, and particularly mathematical models, have been sparse indeed. The value of mathematical models in solving marketing problems, perhaps with the exception of linear programming, is quite limited. In fact, it is the promise of *potential applications* in marketing, rather than *actual application,* to which operations researchers refer fondly.

Operations research models are not ends in themselves. They are the means to an end. In marketing they are the means to better marketing decisions. Yet, in model building, operations researchers seem to get lost in heroic mathematical abstractions. They appear to develop a preference for rigor over realism, for manipulative potentiality over practicality, and for mathematical sophistication over immediate problem-solving capability in marketing. Marketing models, like other kinds of models, seem to result in "the unlimited postulation of irrelevant truths," [13] or what has been termed mathematicians' aphasia.[14]

Operations researchers tend to obliterate marketing factors. In their models, critical marketing factors are usually assumed away. For instance, demand is assumed; consumer behavior is taken as given; promotional effects are treated as knowns, competitive strategies and reactions are assumed; marketing share and sales potential are treated as known quantities. Given such assumptions, answers to important business problems are then found.

There exists at least one obvious flaw in this procedure. Despite the intellectual and rigorous exercise pursued, the major aspects of the problem, the factors that usually impose the most serious management constraints, those factors that are most significant are whisked away. As a result, to a large extent, solutions reached are relatively impotent. The models developed often contain less reality within the model than actually exist outside the model.[15] What is often obtained by operations research procedures are neat mathematical formulations that need not pertain to marketing reality, that are ineffective as decision tools but that furnish impressive looking manuscripts for esoteric journals.

Operations research often provides fragmented solutions. In applying models and mathematical techniques, operations researchers often attack small segments of marketing problems. This approach seems to make good analytical sense. It can, however, result in rather poor operational results.

For instance, in dealing with transportation, warehousing, or inventory control problems, solutions are often obtained which reduce costs in one of these decision areas. Many of the solutions reached, however, place a burden on other business cost centers, such as personal selling and advertising, and can increase total costs.

Operations research studies neglect human factors. The very crux of marketing activities centers on humans and human behavior. Customers and consumers are focal points of marketing and, in essence, manage-

[13] H. Theil, *Economic Forecasts and Policy*, Amsterdam, North Holland, 1958, p. 4.

[14] See Herbert A. Simon, *The New Science of Management Decision*, Harper, New York, 1960, p. 18.

[15] A good example of this is the development of an advertising model which first appeared in a leading management journal and has since been reprinted in, and referred to in, marketing books. The model seems to be acclaimed by management scientists as the type of progress being made in the application of mathematical models to marketing. However, it is referred to by the company executives as being useless in solving their problems and as a waste of research funds.

ment action. Yet, the marketing models developed by management scientists do not portray this. They do not account for human behavior. They seem to consider human beings as "black boxes" with input-output characteristics. Most operations research models are developed, analyzed, and interpreted as though the interaction of people is of little consequence.

Operations researchers seem to tackle the least crucial problems. The types of marketing problems that have been handled reflect an unbalanced problem-solving emphasis. In marketing, quantitative techniques and models have been applied successfully to physical distribution and inventory-type problems. Although they are worthy problem areas, they are not the most crucial problems in marketing management today. Perhaps they are the easiest to handle mathematically. However, they may also be the easiest problems to handle by conventional and less exacting techniques.

There also seems to be a tendency for management scientists to ignore and sometimes even degrade other types of marketing problems that are more significant than those that have been handled. The problems surrounding personal selling and salesmanship, for instance, are often viewed with a jaundiced eye as to their academic respectability. Problems related to mass production, on the other hand, seem to be entirely respectable. Yet, the former are very significant to the welfare of individual firms and our economy. These problems cannot be skipped over lightly or ignored in the management of business systems.

Operations research models often fail to portray a proper perspective of marketing productivity. Marketing expenditures seem to be viewed as costs, expenses, and often as wastes. In reality, marketing activities are among the most productive management activities—they may even be more productive than the activities related to physical shaping, forming, and creating a product. Marketing tasks, including advertising, selling, sales promotion, and marketing research, should be perceived and treated as business investments. Surely they are as significant investments as expenditures on capital equipment, plant, warehouses, and furniture. Ownership of market position is as important to a company, and perhaps even more so, than ownership of productive capacity.

In reality, operations researchers do not understand our marketing system too well. They have failed to mark the pivotal role of marketing in management. In the future, operations researchers will recognize that they are challenged with understanding marketing not only to help our competitive economy function more effectively but also to help less mature economies achieve greater progress and to develop management science.

OR AND MARKETING SCIENCE: LACK OF COMMUNICATION

The field of operations research is a highly technical one. "Management opinion, or judgment about OR applications or techniques, can generally be accorded lay standing only. This does not mean, however, that management must assume a subordinate role to the practitioner in dealing with his problems." [16] It does mean that marketing managers should become acquainted with these newer techniques and apprised of OR achievements. Marketing executives must recognize the evolution that is occurring in the methodology for problem solving. Complex marketing problems do require the use, on a broad base, of more powerful decision tools than is currently the case. Marketing executives must strive to achieve better understanding of the newer techniques.

Communication between operations researchers and marketing academicians and executives, or for that matter with executives in other functional areas of management, is clearly lacking. Marketing personnel in general do not know what is happening in the operations research field that is, or should be, of interest to them. They are not familiar with the available tools that can be of assistance in solving marketing problems.

Most people in marketing cannot read the specialized journals and volumes containing operations research material. This in turn tends to generate a defensive attitude and some skepticism of operations research. While operations researchers share common problems with top management, interestingly enough there has not yet been a common operating terminology developed and a satisfactory level of communication achieved.

Operations researchers, rather than striving for good communications, often help to create communication barriers. They adhere to the language and approaches which are useful for their purposes but are usually foreign and meaningless to others. In reality, they should avoid trying to overwhelm or impress management with the language developed for, and understood by, members of the OR fraternity only. Operations researchers should stress clearer communications with management.

Realistically, for adequate communications to take place between marketing personnel and operations researchers, each must understand some of the dimensions of the other's job. Only under these conditions can OR make its greatest contribution to marketing science. The opera-

---

[16] W. W. Cooper, "Operations Research and Economics," *The Review of Economics and Statistics*, Vol. XL (August 1958), p. 196.

tions researcher should be attuned to the fact that marketing problems requiring solutions first come to the attention of marketing management. If marketing management fails to perceive the problems, or fails to recognize the possibility that OR may be helpful in seeking a solution and is not willing to allocate the necessary budget, much of the effectiveness of OR is lost.

Lathrop adopts the view that the burden of communication is on the OR man, that the researcher must give "his answer to the impatient and fretting decision maker in the decision maker's own language in a form he can use at once." The burden and total responsibility, however, do not lie solely with OR personnel. Those in marketing must re-educate themselves to understand OR methods and techniques. Meaningful communication is one of the challenges confronting both the operations researcher in dealing with marketing and the marketing manager in dealing with effective problem solving.

Marketing scientists in the future will not have to become operations researchers or skilled mathematicians. They will not have to understand the many nuances and intricacies of the newer quantitative techniques. They will, however, have to attain a better grasp of what the new quantitative tools are, the types of problems for which operations researchers can furnish assistance, and the potentialities and limitations of operations research techniques.

An extensive body of operations research literature currently exists for the mathematically sophisticated person and for operations research technicians. Relatively little material is available to the professional manager who lacks a technical background. Yet, problem solving in marketing and marketing science cannot be advanced solely by operations researchers communicating among themselves. The institution of a two-way communication channel is necessary to ensure that operations researchers will have the required working laboratory and that the potential benefits from applying operations research to marketing will accrue.

It is essential that operations researchers communicate among themselves in a technical manner in order to advance the field of operations research. It is also necessary that they establish rapport with marketing scientists. They must understand marketing problems, see that operations research approaches and contributions to marketing are recognized. The veil of symbolism and mysticism that surrounds the application of mathematical models and techniques in marketing, and the semantic barriers raised by the technical nature of operations research materials, must be erased if operations research ideas and findings are to be presented to a broader marketing science audience.

There does not seem to be the free interchange of ideas in the area of operations research that exists in many other management areas where specialized staff personnel and consultants play an important role. One reason for this is that management executives do not feel competent or qualified to comprehend and assess operations research approaches and applications. A way must be found to communicate successful applications and potential application of OR to marketing, to erase some of the ignorance and suspicion of OR applications on the part of marketing personnel, and to open the way for greater professionalization of marketing and the development of marketing science.

16

Stochastic Models

of Brand Switching

JOHN U. FARLEY AND ALFRED A. KUEHN

Consumer brand choice has for a number of years interested both market researchers and marketing management. Knowledge and measurement of the marketing influences leading the consumer to be loyal to a brand or to switch to another brand are recognized as the keys to understanding marketing processes. With the recent advent of mathematical model building and the availability of electronic computers, some headway has been made in the attempt to make explicit and to test various theories of brand shifting. This chapter examines some of these theories, pointing out the insights they provide, and their strengths and weaknesses in application. The empirical evidence available for testing the alternative models will be reviewed. Finally, we shall discuss potentially promising directions for future research along these lines.

THE EVOLUTION OF BRAND SWITCHING ANALYSIS

Consumers make choices in their purchase of brands of a product as a result of many influences—habit, in response to merchandising cues, or with explicit consideration of alternatives. A prime goal in the development of marketing theory is to understand better the process which underlies such behavior and to cast it in a framework suitable for evaluation of market factors and the prediction of their influence on sales.

Early work on the study of brand choice behavior focused upon evidence of consumer loyalty to individual brands of a product. For example, George Brown[1] examined sequences of consumer purchases

[1] G. H. Brown, "Brand Loyalty—Fact or Fiction," *Advertising Age*, June 9, 1952, June 30, 1952, August 11, 1952, October 6, 1952, December 1, 1952, and January 26, 1953.

for what seemed to be patterns of brand choice—perfect loyalty, divided but stable loyalty, and so forth. Comparisons were made among brands and, in some cases, across product classes to demonstrate differences in consumer purchasing behavior. However, a major difficulty was encountered in the study—the development of clear, concise and meaningful classifications of behavior. Although Brown defined the classification of patterns in great detail, his classifications were ambiguous, and subsequent efforts by other researchers have frequently been unable to duplicate his results.

Cunningham, aware of the difficulty in defining patterns of behavior, followed up Brown's research by classifying consumers with respect to the share of purchases a household would make of a specific brand or set of brands.[2] He reported various aggregates of this statistic for seven product classes and stressed especially each family's loyalty to its most frequently purchased brand. While the cross-sectional "share of purchases" statistic avoided the definitional problems in Brown's research and permitted a stable comparison of behavior over the various product classes, it offered little insight into the dynamics of consumer behavior. The consumer who alternated his purchases between two brands ("divided but stable loyalty") was classified with the consumer who split his purchases between two brands by buying one brand during the first half of the time period studied and the other brand during the latter half of the study.

The need to develop an understanding of the dynamics of consumer brand choice led to the examination of the frequency of occurrences of various configurations in short purchase sequences. Kuehn[3] studied 2, 3, 4, and 5 purchase sequences for several products, and others have focused their attention on consumer buying behavior in terms of two-purchase sequences.[4] These studies led to the examination of consumer brand choice as stochastic or probabilistic processes. The two-purchase sequence analysis underlies the widely-discussed first-order purchase-to-purchase Markov brand shifting analysis, which is taken up in the next section. The study of longer purchase sequences has led to the brand shifting "learning model" also described later in this chapter.

[2] R. M. Cunningham, "Brand Loyalty—What, Where, How Much?" *Harvard Business Review* (January–February 1956).

[3] A. Kuehn, "Consumer Brand Choice—A Learning Process?", in R. E. Frank et al., *Quantitative Techniques in Marketing Analysis*, Richard D. Irwin, Homewood, Ill., 1962.

[4] F. Harary and B. Lipstein, "The Dynamics of Brand Loyalty: A Marketing Approach," *Operations Research* (January–February 1962); and R. B. Maffei, "Brand Preferences and Simple Markov Processes," *Operations Research* (March–April 1960).

Purchase-to-Purchase Brand Shifting

Difficulties in classifying consumers by examining long purchase records and cross-sectional summary measures indicated a need for a theory of brand shifting sufficiently realistic and responsive to changes in market conditions to provide a useful framework for analysis. The simplest and most natural starting point towards such a theory is the examination of two-purchase sequences. For descriptive convenience, data collected from consumers are frequently summarized in a table showing the number of occurrences of various pairs of purchases for a large number of consumers or families. Table 16.1 illustrates how the sequential purchase records of three families with the following buying histories might be aggregated and presented.

Family 1 AAAAAABACAAA
       2 CBBBBBBBBA
       3 CCCCCCCBCAA

Table 16.1   Occurrences in Pairs of Purchases in Purchase Sequences of Three Families

		Brand purchased on occasion n		
		A	B	C
	A	8	1	1
Brand purchased on occasion $n-1$	B	2	7	1
	C	2	2	6

An examination of such an array might disclose some interesting patterns. For example, if the relative frequencies shown in Table 16.1 were to hold for a large number of consumers, it would appear that buyers tend to repurchase A more frequently than the other two brands and that C has the lowest level of repeat purchases. The relative sizes of the off-diagonal entries might also provide insights as to the degree of competitive interaction among pairs of brands. Other measures of consumers' buying behavior could also be tabulated in similar arrays or matrices. For example, we might record the average volumes purchased on each occasion, the average prices paid, or the percentage of purchases made on deals. Such tabulations can be used to determine the extent to which larger volumes are bought on repeat purchases, the extent to which repeat purchases are made at higher average prices, and the relative rates of purchase of deal merchandise by repeat and shifting customers.

The data in Table 16.1 can also be used to develop estimates of purchase-to-purchase transition probabilities—an analytic step which has caused wide discussion in the literature.[5] If each element in the array is divided by the sum of the elements in the row in which it occurs, the result is a table or matrix which describes the likelihood of a consumer's purchasing any given brand on the next purchase given information about the brand bought on the immediately preceding purchase. For example, estimates of transition probabilities from Table 16.1 are shown in Table 16.2.

Table 16.2 Matrix of Transition Probabilities

| | | Brand purchased on occasion n | | |
		A	B	C
Brand purchased on occasion $n-1$	A	0.8	0.1	0.1
	B	0.2	0.7	0.1
	C	0.2	0.2	0.6

Since the entries in the matrix are probabilities, they are necessarily equal to or greater than 0. Also, since the states are exhaustive, the probabilities in each row sum to 1. In the example in Table 16.2 the events (purchases of particular brands) also represent the states of the process. Frequently, however, the event will not provide complete information about the state. For example, in a second-order purchase-to-purchase Markov process we define the states of the process as sequences of two purchases, but the event continues to be a single subsequent purchase. Similarly, in the learning model to be described later we define the states as probability vectors representing the probability of a consumer buying each brand on the next trial. The event is again a single purchase which modifies the consumer's probability vector and thereby alters the state in which the consumer is at any given time.

Powerful mathematical techniques [6] for the analytical treatment of transition matrices, subject to certain assumptions, have led to the development of a number of closely related brand switching models. Such models are needed because data such as are summarized in Table 16.1 do not in and of themselves have much meaning. A frame of reference or theory or model is needed to interpret data and to study their relevance to specific marketing problems.

[5] J. D. Herniter and F. Magee, "Customer Behavior as a Markov Process," *Operations Research* (January–February 1961); and Maffei, *loc. cit.*
[6] J. G. Kemeny and J. L. Snell, *Finite Markov Chains*, Van Nostrand, Princeton, N. J., 1960.

In one sense, the step from the transition matrix described above to the development of a stochastic (probabilistic) model of brand switching is quite small. (The problem of developing realistic models of consumer brand switching useful in guiding marketing managers is, however, another matter.) A stochastic model is a model or theory which attempts to depict in probabilistic terms the likelihood of a process passing from one state of nature to another. That is, given that the process under examination has a certain history at time t (for instance, a consumer purchased Brand A on purchase occasion $n-1$), a stochastic model will attempt to set forth the probabilities of the process being in any particular state in subsequent periods (i.e., the probabilities of the consumer purchasing any given brand on the next purchase occasion). Stochastic models are constructed on the premise that, while it may be impossible to predict deterministically the outcome of any given trial, it is frequently possible to predict with reasonable success the probabilities with which the various outcomes might occur.

BRAND PREFERENCES AND SIMPLE MARKOV PROCESSES

The first-order purchase-to-purchase Markov process was the first application of a stochastic model to describe brand switching. This model assumes that each purchase is affected in a stochastic sense only by the preceding purchase and is statistically independent of prior purchases. Thus, a transition matrix such as was presented in Table 16.2 might be used to describe consumer switching from one brand to another. If (and only if) the probabilities shown in the matrix were constant and if the consumer's brand purchase probabilities depended only upon the most recent purchase, a variety of interesting results would follow.[7] For example, it would be possible to calculate market shares in any succeeding period given market shares in the present period, and it would also be easy to calculate long-run market shares by solving a set of simultaneous linear equations. (In the case of the example in Table 16.2, the long-run share of market for A is 0.5, for B 0.2, and for C 0.3; these shares are independent of initial market shares.) Moreover, the rate of approach to these equilibrium shares could be studied as could the time path followed.

This straightforward descriptive work was followed up with more sophisticated descriptions of how the world might come to be Markovian and how the marketing manager might behave in such an environment.[8] One approach suggested was to say that a certain expenditure (say on promotion) secures a certain transition matrix which is stably

[7] Maffei, *loc. cit.*.
[8] Herniter and Magee, *loc. cit.*

associated with that expenditure. Given knowledge of the transition probabilities which might be purchased at a series of costs, it is possible mathematically to derive optimal expenditure strategies to achieve certain goals such as maximum profits. Recognizing that some buyers are not in the market in each period, and that these might be considered as transferring to and from a state outside a market (null state), estimates of total quantities of the product sold and number of people in a market at a given time period could be derived. In this vein, one could also examine whether it would be profitable to try to bring buyers in from the outside or whether it would be more profitable to attempt to attract brand-switching customers.

What's Wrong with the Simple Markov Formulations?

The considerable intuitive descriptive appeal of couching brand switching analysis in terms of simple Markov processes caused a flurry of activity among the mathematically inclined. However, a number of problems with the Markov formulation soon became evident and led to work along more complicated lines.

1. The basic Markov assumption that the likelihood of purchase on trial t depends only on the immediately preceding purchase is inconsistent with available evidence. The basis for criticism also has intuitive appeal—if the last purchase influences this purchase, is it not reasonable that the second-last purchase also influences this purchase, even though its influence might be somewhat less? One way that a number of authors have suggested to circumvent this problem is to abandon the simple Markov chain formulations in favor of so-called higher order chains. Here the states are defined as a series of purchases, rather than as single purchases. For instance, a second-order chain has pairs of purchases for the last event and the next event. The transition matrix for a second-order chain in a two brand market is shown in Table 16.3.

Table 16.3 Matrix of Second-Order Transition Probabilities

		Purchases at trials n and $n+1$			
		AA	AB	BA	BB
	AA	0.8	0.2	0.0	0.0
Purchases at trials	AB	0.0	0.0	0.1	0.9
$n-1$ and n	BA	0.6	0.4	0.0	0.0
	BB	0.0	0.0	0.3	0.7

The second letter in the row headings coincides with the first in the column headings, so naturally some combinations are impossible. For instance, movement from state AB to AB is impossible because the second purchase of the first and the first purchase of the second, both of which are the purchase at time n, do not match. Even higher order chains can be developed in this manner, but this is also not without difficulties. The matrices quickly become difficult to manage because of their size. (The number of states is N^n where N is the number of brands and n the order of the chain. A six-brand, third-order model has 216 states. Many real markets have more than a dozen major brands.) Even though there are a large number of superfluous zero entries, the requirements for data to estimate the nonzero transition probabilities are very large, and even second-order analyses have proved to be operationally infeasible. Yet the first-order Markov purchase-to-purchase formulation clearly overstates the rates of long-term market share movement by a substantial amount.

By extending the analysis to purchase sequences of 6, Kuehn [9] found a pattern of influence on any given purchase where, on the average for a group of consumers, the previous purchases in the sequence tended to have an exponentially declining influence on a given purchase. This led to the development and use of the stochastic learning model described later in this chapter. This model permits the use of multiple brands in the short term without overstating long-term brand shifting.

2. A second problem stemming from the simple Markov formulation, if the Markov properties are taken at all seriously, is the assumption that the probabilities in the transition matrix are stable over time. All the long-run implications drawn from Markov analysis depend on this assumption. Yet if this assumption were to hold, marketing would be sterile. Marketing variables would have no influence on sales, and shares of market would soon be stable. Recognition of this problem has attracted attention away from simplified mathematical assumptions and focused it upon empirical considerations and influence processes of marketing activities. Work in these areas will also be discussed in a later section.

The Learning Model

If the simple Markov process is not an adequate description of the brand-shifting phenomenon, and if second- and third-order processes are unwieldy and even then solve only part of the problems, where might a solution be found? The problem was to find a manageable model which would incorporate the effects of a string of past purchases

[9] Kuehn, "Consumer Brand Choice—A Learning Process?," *loc. cit.*.

on subsequent brand choice behavior. On the basis of Kuehn's [10] empirical results, it appeared reasonable that the probability of subsequent purchases of a given brand increases as a result of purchases of that brand and decreases when other brands are chosen. A model with these characteristics was developed. It is a generalized form of the learning models developed independently by Estes [11] and by Bush and Mosteller [12] and can be used to predict the *probability* that a buyer will repeat the purchase of a given brand, given that he has either purchased or not purchased that brand on a series of previous trials.

The mechanism underlying the model is shown in Figure 16.1. Two functions or "operators" determine the new probability level for a

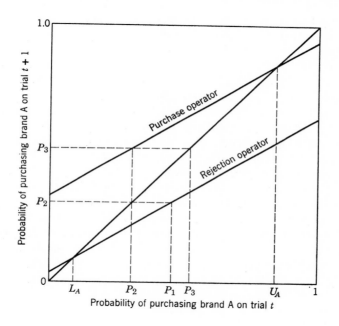

Figure 16.1   A brand switching "learning" model.

brand after each purchase. The rejection operator takes effect if a buyer has failed to purchase the brand on a given trial; the purchase

[10] *Ibid.*

[11] W. K. Estes, "Individual Behavior in Uncertain Situations: An Interpretation in Terms of Statistical Association Theory," in R. M. Thrall, C. H. Coombs, and R. L. Davis (eds.), *Decision Processes*, Wiley, New York, 1954.

[12] R. R. Bush and F. Mosteller, *Stochastic Models for Learning*, Wiley, New York, 1955.

operator comes into play if the consumer has purchased the brand in question. The probability of purchase of brand A on a given trial is read from the horizontal axis. If he fails to buy A on that trial, the probability of his buying the brand on the next trial is read from the intersection of a vertical line from the initial probability (P_1) with the rejection operator—in this case resulting in P_2. The 45° line is used to project P_2 back on the horizontal axis for the following trial. Notice that the probability of purchasing A has decreased as a result of the consumer's failing to purchase it on the last trial. Suppose on the second trial that the buyer purchases brand A. The probability of purchasing A on the third trial is then read from the intersection of the vertical line through P_2 with the purchase operator, resulting in P_3. P_3, projected back onto the horizontal axis, is clearly larger than P_2, although it may or may not be larger than P_1, depending on the slopes of the operators and their intercepts. It is clear that, as long as the rejection operator intersects the left axis above 0, the probability of purchasing brand A never becomes 0, but rather approaches L_A. Similarly, since the purchase operator intersects the right axis below 1, the probability of purchase of brand A never becomes 1. In the learning context this is called incomplete extinction and incomplete learning. It implies that the consumer never develops such strong brand loyalties that he is absolutely and permanently wedded to a given brand. Furthermore, it never becomes certain the consumer will not buy a particular brand.

While means are available to estimate the four parameters of the model (the intercept and slope of each of the operators), it has also been convenient to recast the learning model into a Markov model equivalent in an expected value sense to the learning model. This will be discussed later in connection with a complex mathematical model of brand switching which attempts to simulate the influences of market variables upon the equivalent transition probability matrix.

Data and Aggregation

The discussion so far has dealt with the purchase sequence as if the data were always reliable and as if there were some obvious way of defining a "trial" so that it is comparable over families. Such is not the case. Both the basic data and the aggregation of consumer purchase records into a common framework pose a variety of problems. Some of these problems are now reasonably well understood but others still frequently go unrecognized.

Two types of data have been used in obtaining records of sequences of consumer purchases:

1. Data reported by members of continuous consumer panels. While there are a number of recognized biases and defects with these data [13] consumer panels have provided a wealth of information that has proved useful in developing and testing models of brand choice.

2. Data reported in surveys which attempt to reconstruct historical sequences of brand choice on the basis of questions about the last purchase or the purchase before that. This procedure frequently tends to overestimate the market shares of leading brands and, because of high error in brand recall among families with low repeat purchase probabilities, may provide misleading information on trends in brand-switching behavior.[14] Reporting and response errors of various types may also cause relatively severe problems in the off-diagonal cells of the transition matrices produced from panel data, since errors tend to be concentrated in these brand-switching cells. The smaller sample size in these cells, relative to repeat purchases, tends to accentuate the problem. A closely related problem of panel data is the apparent tendency for the size of many of these errors to vary over product classes.[15]

Certain definitional and operational problems of data aggregation arise since individuals buy products with differing frequencies and since the data from a large number of families must be summarized to provide sufficient sample sizes for meaningful analyses. If every member of the sample bought the product at the same time, or even once and only once in a period like a month, direct tabulation of the data into transition matrices in the manner described earlier would be acceptable. Furthermore, these estimates would have a number of attractive statistical properties if the data were actually generated by a Markov process.[16] However, such straightforward methods are not applicable, because in fact most products are bought too irregularly to permit such a simple treatment in the framework of a Markov "trial." Two solutions to this problem have been tried, and each faces similar problems: (1) The sequence reported by each household might be treated as if it were a series of trials even though the time periods between purchases vary. (2) A trial may be defined as occurring in a fixed time period but using a constructed state called a null state. If a household purchases

[13] H. W. Boyd and R. L. Westfall, *An Evaluation of Continuous Consumer Panels as a Source of Marketing Information*, American Marketing Association, Chicago, 1960.

[14] S. Banks, "The Relationship between Preference and Purchase of Brands," *Journal of Marketing* (October 1950).

[15] S. Sudman, "On the Accuracy of Recording of Consumer Panels," *Journal of Marketing Research*, Vol. 1 (May and August, 1964).

[16] P. Billingsly, "Statistical Methods in Markov Chains," *Annals of Mathematical Statistics*, 1961.

in a given period (trial) but not in the next, it is said to have gone into the null state. If it does not purchase in a period and then later enters the market, it has made the transition from the null state to the brand purchased. While this approach would appear to solve the definitional problem, it is an undesirable approach in that it tends to discard much information available about the past purchasing behavior of all but the frequent buyers. It also does not solve the problem of multiple purchases by a consumer in a single time period.

Enormous differences among families in purchase rates of a product class, apparent from a glance at panel data, accentuate the above aggregation problems. It would be easy enough to estimate transition probabilities in the straightforward ways discussed earlier (with the light buyers being simply counted less frequently or ending up in the null state very often), but this procedure is dangerous. There is some evidence that infrequent buyers tend to behave differently from frequent buyers. For example, Kuehn [17] has reported that, in the learning model context, rejection and purchase operators are functions of the elapsed time between purchases. For heavy buyers, the slopes of the operators are quite high and the intercepts very close to 0 and 1 respectively (Figure 16.2). For light buyers, the operators tend to be flat and, in the

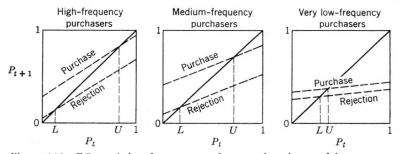

Figure 16.2   Effect of time between purchases on learning model operators.

limit, the probability of a buyer's purchasing a given brand tends to that brand's market share. These differences would, in aggregation, tend to give erroneous estimates of the parameters of the learning process if the estimates were not made time-dependent.

Because of the difficulties in estimating the parameters of the learning model discussed in the previous section and the limitations of the first-order purchase-to-purchase Markov model as a description of consumer brand switching, an intermediate type of analysis has been developed. This approach, now in wider use among United States firms than either the Markov or learning models, has the advantage of com-

[17] Kuehn, "Consumer Brand Choice—A Learning Process?," *loc. cit.*

putational simplicity and also approximates with reasonable accuracy some of the results available through use of the learning model. The state of the consumer is represented by the mix of brands actually purchased (share of purchases) in a given time period much as the learning model depicts the state as the probabilities of the consumer purchasing various brands at a point in time. The changes that are observed from period to period are then transformed into entries in a matrix which might be treated as transition probability equivalents. The mechanics of the brand-mix model, its relationship to the learning model, and applications that have been made with it are presented in a pair of articles by Rohloff [18] and Kuehn. [19]

This blend of the Markov and learning models recognizes that most consumers buy several brands of most products. Consequently it does not overstate long-term market share movements to the extent observed in the Markov purchase-to-purchase matrix. Also, the problems posed by infrequent buyers and the "null state" previously discussed are reduced. The brand-mix model is an intermediate step which offers a better package of cost and results than is now available by other means.

EVALUATION OF EFFECTS OF MARKETING VARIABLES IN STOCHASTIC FRAMEWORKS

The discussion so far has centered on the use of stochastic models as descriptions of the processes generating purchase sequences. Naturally, it is desirable to tie brand choice analyses, in frameworks such as the Markov models, to important marketing variables. Two such attempts are discussed here: (1) least squares estimation of the influence of a limited set of variables on consumer brand switching and (2) complex mathematical modeling of the entire system. The former concentrates on developing a statistically manageable formulation of the problem and the latter on realistic modeling. Each illustrates the many problems standing in the way of reaching the ultimate goal of tying consumer behavior to marketing activities.

Least Squares Estimates of Transition Probabilities

Lester Telser has done two studies using least squares to estimate the effects of important marketing variables on transition probabilities of a first-order Markov process. The first study considered brand-to-

---

[18] A. C. Rohloff, "New Ways to Analyze Brand-to-Brand Competition," published in S. Greyser (ed.), *Towards Scientific Marketing*, American Marketing Association, Chicago, 1963.
[19] A. Kuehn, "Effectiveness of Consumer Deals," *ibid*.

brand transition probabilities as a function of lagged market share and relative prices for a number of products as reported by a consumer panel.[20] The second study used aggregate sales and advertising data to estimate the effectiveness of cigarette advertising on market shares of brands [21] and included estimates of the effect of relative advertising on brand-to-brand transition probabilities. The research is not aimed directly at estimating the transition probabilities, although such estimates prove to be of interest in themselves. In the first case, the author is interested in price elasticities and in the second case he estimates the marginal effectiveness of advertising as a capital expenditure. The basic model of brand switching in both studies is:

$$\text{Market share } (i,t) = a_i \text{ Market share } (i,t-1) +$$
$$b_i \left[1 - \text{Market share } (i,t-1) \right]$$

where the term (i,t) indicates the brand and time period, a_i is the conditional probability of purchasing brand i given purchases of brand i in period $t-1$, and b_i is the conditional probability of purchasing i given purchases of other brands in period $t-1$. This equation is a simple Markov process which might be used to describe the influence of a wide variety of market variables by making the coefficients functions of these variables. For simplicity, however, Telser argues that the major marketing influence is price in the case of such products as orange juice and margarine, and that the major influence for cigarettes is advertising. (He shows that cigarette prices of major brands were almost always equal during the period he studied.) The models are developed very much in the tradition of formal economic analysis and provide considerable enrichment of this theory. Besides extending econometric model building, these papers outline procedures for treating the extreme estimation difficulties caused by collinearity of lagged market shares and also consider the special problems created by the unity constraint on the sum of the elements of a row in the transition matrix.

The estimates of transition probabilities are of special interest in that they imply elasticities with respect to price and advertising, and elasticities in turn imply information about competitive states of industries. One such conclusion in the study of margarine and orange juice is that the markets are quite price competitive. In the case of cigarettes,

[20] L. G. Telser, "The Demand for Branded Goods as Estimated from Consumer Panel Data," *Review of Economics and Statistics* (August 1962).
[21] L. G. Telser, "Advertising and Cigarettes," *The Journal of Political Economy* (October 1962); Telser, "Least Squares Estimates of Transition Probabilities," published in Don Patinkin (ed.), *Measurement in Economics*, Stanford University Press, Stanford, Cal., 1963.

the estimates again tend to support Telser's contention that advertising is a key variable. The estimates also indicate rates of decay of the fund of good will built up by advertising.

These analyses illustrate the empirical difficulties of tying marketing variables to sales. Estimating the price variable involves problems of substituting average prices for actual prices paid, and of assuming that observed prices paid provide information on prices of foregone brands. For cigarettes, we know only dollar expenditure on advertising and nothing of copy quality and product characteristics considered so vital by the industry. Furthermore, despite the fact that a convincing argument can be made in each case that the major marketing variable has been identified, it is clear that other variables may be important. But measurement and estimation problems, difficult in the case of single variables, are much larger in the case of multiple causation. Telser's effort to construct a product quality index in the cigarette case illustrates many of these problems.

A Modified Markov Model of Brand Shifting

Kuehn has developed a stochastic brand choice model which attempts to relate a variety of marketing variables directly to consumer brand shifting.[22] In this formulation, the first-order Markov matrix of transition probabilities is interpreted as the resultant of two sets of parameters—a retention factor, r_i, and a merchandising factor, a_i, for each brand. The transition matrix has the following form:

Brand purchased at time t

		A	B	C
Brand purchased at time $t-1$	A	$r_A+(1-r_A)a_A$	$(1-r_A)a_B$	$(1-r_A)a_C$
	B	$(1-r_B)a_A$	$r_B+(1-r_B)a_B$	$(1-r_B)a_C$
	C	$(1-r_C)a_A$	$(1-r_C)a_B$	$r_C+(1-r_C)a_C$

Each element on the diagonal is composed of a fraction of purchases retained by the brand through habit (r_i) and a portion of last period's purchases not automatically retained by the brand as a result of habit but rather reattracted by the brand's own merchandising activity $[(1-r_i)a_i]$. Each off-diagonal element represents a loss of purchases by brand i to brand j and is made up of the portion of sales not held by brand i which is attracted by brand j's *merchandising* $[(1-r_i)a_j]$. Logic requires the r_i's to be between 0 and 1, and that the a_i's be posi-

[22] A. Kuehn, "A Model for Budgeting Advertising" in F. M. Bass, et al., *Mathematical Models and Methods in Marketing*, Richard D. Irwin, Homewood, Ill., 1961.

tive and sum to 1. It has also been shown that the learning model discussed earlier and this first-order Markov formulation are equivalent in an expected value sense.

The Markov model yields a difference equation for brand i's sales:

$$S_{i,t} = r_i S_{i,t-1} + I_{t-1}(1 - \overline{r_t}) Z_{i,T}$$

where $S_{i,t}$ is brand i's sales at time t

r_i the repeat probability of purchase of brand i

I_t industry sales volume in period t

$\overline{r_t}$ average repeat rate of all brands weighted by sales

$Z_{i,T}$ fraction of potential brand shifters attracted in time t as a result of merchandising in time T.

The formulation is similar to Telser's basic equation, but the model is then developed in a much more complex form which is beyond complete presentation here. However, the Z_i function, which takes the following form, is of particular interest and illustrates the fundamental nature of the model:

$$Z_i = b_p \frac{P_i}{\Sigma P_i} + b_d \frac{D_i}{\Sigma D_i} + b_a \frac{A_i}{\Sigma A_i} + b_{pd} \frac{(PD)_i}{\Sigma(PD)_i}$$
$$+ b_{pa} \frac{(PA)_i}{\Sigma(PA)_i} + b_{da} \frac{(DA)_i}{\Sigma(DA)_i} + b_{pda} \frac{(PDA)_i}{\Sigma(PDA)_i}$$

where　　　P_i is the share of shifters attracted by brand i if price and product were the only merchandising variables; D_i and A_i are defined similarly for distribution and advertising respectively.

$(PD)_i$ the share of shifters attracted by i if the joint effect of price, product and distribution were the only variables. The other interactions are similarly defined.

The b's are weighting factors, ranging from 0 to 1, for the importance of each single variable or variable interaction indicated by the subscript. Limited experimental testing of this model suggested that this equation might be simplified by setting b_p, b_d, b_a, b_{pa}, and b_{da} equal to zero. This can be rationalized by arguing that the effect of distribution is not independent of the price, product and advertising variables, and that in any case, price and product and distribution must be part of the marketing mix.

However, a look at the equation for Z, even in a simplified form, suggests a variety of major empirical difficulties. If the simpler Telser formulation made extreme demands on types of data now available and on available statistical estimation techniques, this more complex model makes even more severe demands. Estimates of certain parameters have been made on a marginal basis by testing out various implications of the mathematical formulation under a variety of conditions, but full-scale simultaneous empirical estimation is currently impossible except through the use of computational search techniques which do not provide estimates of variances associated with parameter estimates.

Recent extensions of this approach which recognize the segmentation of markets in terms of product characteristics, advertising appeals, and distribution further complicate the model, which might now best be described as a simulation of the market. In the absence of established statistical procedures for the estimation of parameter variances in such complex models, it has been necessary to generate hypothetical data through simulation for use in evaluating computational search estimation procedures. As is the case in all model building, however, no meaningful statistical standards can be specified as to the validity of the model itself. The ultimate test of the model will be its value in providing meaningful guidance to marketing managers and in providing insight to students as to the nature of the marketing influence process.

DIRECTIONS FOR FUTURE RESEARCH

In view of the continued interest in the application of various stochastic models to marketing problems, the richness which has already been built into theories of certain aspects of human behavior, and the fact that stochastic theory is still in a state of development, it is reasonable to predict that a great deal of work will be done in the future in this area. A word of caution, however: as the models become more sophisticated and more descriptively appealing, they also become more analytically complex and pose ever-increasing statistical inference problems. At the moment, as the previous discussion indicated, stochastic theory available for model building has far outstripped statistical inference techniques. Furthermore, the data required to test these models are far in excess of those normally required for market research, and such data are not generally now available on a large scale. Development of such data is one of the important requirements for future extension of this work.

Some of the specific areas in which research would appear to show promise are outlined below:

1. *Improved measures of marketing influences.* In actual application, the problem is to relate any of these models of consumer brand shifting to market influences which tend to change over time. Research into measures of these marketing factors and studies of their influence are sorely needed to help provide meaningful inputs for the development

of improved marketing models. Examination of brand shifting data is of limited practical value until integrated with information about the various competitive factors underlying the market. For example, current market statistics provide little data on the influence of shelf space and point of purchase promotions on sales although these measures appear to interact strongly with the effectiveness of advertising.

2. *Time-continuous Markov chains.* One widely suggested direction for future research is the freeing of the analysis from problems of defining discrete "trials" in such a way as to require dividing already sparse data into smaller classes for complete analysis. The learning model represents one such approach. Another possible attack on this problem is to maintain the Markov transition framework but to consider the time between events as an additional stochastic variable governed by a probability distribution about which inferences may be made. These are the so-called time-continuous or semi-Markovian processes. Such a model might better cope with the problems imposed in a simple Markov framework by either no purchase or multiple purchases occurring in an arbitrary time period.

3. *Age-dependent Markov processes.* Age-dependent processes represent a second possibility in the development of richer Markov models. For example, various combinations of birth, death, and migration models might be used to study in a stochastic framework the appearance or entry of certain types of consumer influences, their development, and their ultimate disappearance. Recurrent events with age-dependent probabilities might use nonfinite Markov models to describe strings of consumer choices. The probabilities might be defined as functions of the important influences, which might work with ever-decreasing effect on consumers as the runs of purchases become longer. This approach is likely to pose even more difficulties than the methods attempted to date but might lead to a more realistic model.

4. *Improved inference techniques.* A third direction of needed research is the development of better inference techniques and statistical tests of series for Markov properties. Some of this work has already been cited, and some in other areas, such as Bayesian estimation techniques using multivariate Beta distribution as priors, is said to be underway.

5. *Extension of the brand mix concept.* It has frequently been assumed that various brands of a product are substitutes for one another, and that a break in an observed purchase sequence indicates a break in the consumer's loyalty to a brand. It has been noted, however, that for some products and for some households, this assumption is not correct. For example, the following sequence of cigarette purchases

ABABABABABABABABABABA

may indicate extreme loyalty of each of two members of a family, who smoke an equal amount, to two brands of cigarettes. Interpretation of such behavior would in practice be further complicated by stochastic elements, resulting in two or more complex stochastic processes being embedded together by the happenstance that panel data are reported by family rather than user. A number of product classes which exhibit such difficulties have been cited—toilet soap, cereal, toothpaste. Even frozen orange juice poses similar problems, not because of use of the product by different family members or for different end uses but rather because of the store-shifting behavior of consumers coupled with limited distribution. This problem might also arise in the modeling of sequential behavior in store choice, where a family may have a favorite supermarket, a favorite meat market, and so forth. Both the brand mix model and the learning model discussed earlier provide a start toward the solution of this problem.

6. *Specification problems.* It is clear that some households are extremely loyal while others tend to be much less loyal, even given comparable rates of purchase. Although such behavior is not inconsistent with the results obtained in simulation of consumer behavior with the learning model, it raises the possibility that some other variables—social, demographic, psychological—may be associated with certain types of brand choice behavior. Although this area has as yet failed to yield much in the way of promising results,[23] these relationships may be specific to certain product classes.

SUMMARY

Stochastic models have provided a framework in which theories of consumer brand choice have been built and, to some extent, tested. The history of development of this branch of marketing research shows steady progress from descriptive to highly analytical work. The ultimate goal, as in virtually all research associated with marketing, is to relate sales of a product to important merchandising variables such as price, advertising, and distribution.

Insight into the characteristics of the sequences in which consumers buy brands has been provided by stochastic models of the Markov and learning types. Some progress has been made in the direction of tying

[23] J. Farley, "Testing a Theory of Brand Loyalty," published in S. Greyser (ed.), *Towards Scientific Marketing*, American Marketing Association, Chicago, 1963.

these models to important marketing variables. It seems reasonable to predict that additional progress is to be expected in both research on brand choice and in applying similar techniques to other sequential consumer choice problems such as traffic flow in stores, store shifting, and even patterns of use of entire product categories.

17

Ethics and Science in Marketing

EUGENE J. KELLEY

The challenge, as I see it, is that we have to be as dynamic, imaginative, and research-minded in the ethical field as we have been in the scientific and materialistic fields. We must accept this new world as a new opportunity for being ethical. The case is far from hopeless.[1]

Research methodology and decisions in marketing are influenced by the interacting cultural approaches of the "manager," the "scientist," and the "humanist." These approaches are considered in this chapter as they relate to ethics and science in marketing and to the social functions of marketing. The purpose of this chapter is to raise some questions about the philosophical dimension of ethics as it relates to marketing. This is a relatively new area of marketing inquiry. The thoughts presented are designed to stimulate independent and intelligent thought about the ethical issues inherent in the practice of marketing.

In this chapter some marketing questions with ethical dimensions are identified and definitions are suggested. Two important statements, an article, and a book, useful in gaining understanding of the ethics and science integration problem in management are then discussed. The article cited concerns the field of management theory. The book serves to illuminate the question of diverse cultural approaches to marketing. Finally, the question of the ethical stages of a discipline is raised and the place of ethics in a discussion of the social functions of marketing is considered.

[1] James W. Culliton, "The Problem of Ethics in Business," in *Ethics in Business*, Robert Bartels (ed.), Bureau of Business Research, Columbus, Ohio, 1963, p. 9. A comprehensive forty-three page annotated bibliography on the general subject of ethics in business is included in this book.

SOME MARKETING ETHICS QUESTIONS

Some marketing questions with ethical dimensions include the following:

1. Are marketing scientists and individual contributors to marketing morally responsible for the marketing decisions to which they contribute their talents?

This is not a new issue in business. For instance, in marketing the question of moral responsibility has arisen to confront advertising executives. Are executives in advertising agencies "morally responsible for the advertising they create," and "are media executives morally responsible for the advertising contents their media carry?" [2] A common position of advertising people in the face of such questions traditionally has been that the advertising agency is a technical service group with the job of creating and placing advertisements. Responsibility belongs with the client according to this view. Whether an agency is or is not morally responsible for client's claims or is or is not acting simply as a technician is a question being discussed in advertising today.

2. As an example, does the marketing scientist concerned with developing media allocation models have any responsibility for the messages carried in those media? Or is he only concerned with the techniques involved, not with the messages sent to sell products of which he might not personally approve—cigarettes, liquor, or anything else?

3. Is a marketing scientist concerned with the ethics of persuading people to do something which might not be in their long-term interest? What are the responsibilities, ethically, of the motivation researcher and the manager who uses his findings? The ultimate objective of much research in marketing is to influence or manipulate purchase behavior through probing into the consciousness of individual consumers. The question of the use to which the work of marketing scientists and individual contributors to marketing is put is a difficult one. Scientists in other fields have faced it. One conclusion of interest is that

> It is inevitable that in the long run researchers as a group will have to be concerned with the applications of their work, in the same way that atomic scientists formed a federation so that as citizens they would have a voice in determining the utilization of what they had developed as technicians. [3]

[2] *New York Times* (February 16. 1964).
[3] Robert Ferber, Donlad F. Blankertz, and Sidney Hollander, Jr., *Marketing Research*, Ronald Press, New York, 1964, p. 602.

4. Is the marketing scientist concerned with the ethical problems involved in programs of planned product obsolescence? Many product programs can be seen as efforts to make a product obsolete before it is completely worn out. Many projects in which marketing science studies are undertaken are done with the direct objective of obsoleting present products even though a measure of utility remains.

5. Is the marketing scientist concerned with any aspect of marketing other than the efficient movement of goods on a profitable basis? Does a marketing scientist have responsibility for developing standards for measuring contributions other than efficiency—perhaps by contributing to the development of "ethical science"?

6. There is some evidence that profits are taking on a subsidiary role in many business problems. Questions of economic and social stability, public relations, and a fear of government intervention have proved strong influences on executive decisions in the past. These factors have modified the traditional view of the profit maximization objective to the extent that profit maximization rules provide limited guidance for business executives. Are there ethical implications of significance to marketing science in the development of the "corporate conscience" and the social responsibility view of business? There is a danger of becoming concerned for the sake of ethics alone. It has been suggested that an attitude of this kind can prove harmful and even undermine the enterprise system. Levitt has said, "In the end business has two responsibilities—to obey the canons of everyday face-to-face civility, (honesty, good faith and so on), and to seek material gain and to seize profit. Anything beyond this gets very complicated." [4]

Such questions can be answered on two levels. One is the level of facts. This is the area in which scientists deal or at least prefer to deal. Another is the ethical level. This level requires that standards for approval or disapproval be used.

Disagreements about the place of ethical issues in business sometimes reflect the fact that the conception and definition of ethics is often a highly personal matter. A set of definitions is offered here in the hope that it might facilitate discussion and further exploration of the questions raised in this chapter.

DEFINITIONS

Marketing

Marketing can be perceived as a field of management practice, as a

[4] Theodore Levitt "Dangers of Social Responsibility," *Harvard Business Review*, Vol. XXXVI, (September 1958), pp. 41–60.

social discipline, or as a developing science. As a field of business practice, marketing consists of the activities involved in the generation of markets and customers and in the development and distribution of customer-satisfying goods and services. As a socio-management activity, marketing includes all the tasks involved in the development and delivery of a flow of goods and services from production to consumption. As a social discipline, marketing is the study of the economic and social instrumentality through which a standard of living is delivered to consumers.

Marketing Science

Marketing science is the application of scientific method to marketing problems. One aspect of this science is the use of quantitative approaches to problem solving and decision making. The computer is one important tool of management science; more important is the scientific approach, which involves the use of reliable research methods to unearth valid marketing knowledge and the use of such knowledge in order to better attain marketing objectives. The task of the marketing scientist is to provide decision makers who have the responsibility of committing corporate resources with the scientific and technical input required to reduce or eliminate the areas of uncertainty in marketing problem solving.

Ethics

Ethics as used in this chapter refers to the philosophy of moral values or moral norms, that is, normative ethics. As used here, ethics does not belong to empirical science, but to a division of philosophy—the study and philosophy of human conduct with emphasis on the determination of right and wrong. By definition, it is concerned with good and evil, what is right and what is wrong, what should be, rather than what exists. As White stated, "The purpose of philosophical, or normative, ethics is to state norms for human action or judgments about moral values." [5]

Moral Values

Moral values refer to the degree of conformity to right conduct. This involves questions of the sense of good, the true and right. History is replete with examples of men being actuated by a sense of good, true

[5] Morton White, *The Age of Analysis*, The New American Library, New York, 1955, p. 217, in William Lazer and Eugene J. Kelley, *Managerial Marketing: Perspectives and Viewpoints*, Richard D. Irwin, Homewood, Ill., 1962, p. 50.

and right procedures to accomplish dubious or even satanic ends. Ethics refers to the rules of human behavior considered right and proper by a society at a specified time. Moral becomes a descriptive adjective denoting a study of standard ethical behavior.

Marketing Ethics

Marketing ethics is the area of marketing study and thought concerned with defining norms for judgments about the moral consequences of marketing actions. In practice, marketing ethics is concerned with standards of adequate behavior in terms of marketing policies and practices within legal and social constraints at a point in time. The concern of the theorist is with what is acceptable behavior in terms of right and wrong in a culture at a point in time so that decision making can be more successful.

Ethics are not linked to any narrow part of life. It can be argued that there are no "marketing ethics," that there may or may not be any "business ethics," and ethics are only a matter for individuals concerned with marketing or any other activity. Thus it is held there are no marketing ethics, medical ethics, or legal ethics, and ethics are considered as being concerned with all rational behavior. Accordingly, criticisms of marketing activity are really criticisms of the level of ethics of a business system or of a society. The criticism of marketing comes about, in this view, primarily because marketing is by nature more visible and conspicuous than other areas of business practice. The point of view of this chapter is that for analytical purposes it is at times useful to think of a level of ethics in business and marketing as it exists at a point in decision time and place.

Meta-Marketing

Meta-marketing (beyond marketing) as in metaphysics, metapsychology, or in other disciplines, is used to designate a new, although related, discipline which deals critically with marketing as a discipline. All concerned with marketing can contribute to what may be this promising direction. Marketing is a discipline offering multiple opportunities for speculations on the interrelationships of mental and physical processes to supplement the facts and empirical regularities of marketing science. Kane, in discussing the need for new approaches to planning methodology in national security planning, suggested the term "meta-planning" to seek to bring in the whole of experience and of the human personality to bear on planning.[6] The concern of meta-marketing is

[6] Francis X. Kane, "Security Is Too Important to be Left to Computers," *Fortune*, Vol. LXIX, No. 4 (April 1964), p. 147.

similar—to bring the whole of scientific, social, ethical, and managerial experience to bear on marketing.

The fact that disagreement exists about these terms reflects the fact that marketing is a field of study and a business activity with significant economic, social, and administrative dimensions. It is not surprising that an economist, mathematician, sociologist, or a manager would tend to define terms differently and that different approaches to definitions, and to research, produce different results. As Bartels said:

> . . . research findings are dependent not only upon the hypotheses, data, methodology, etc. which comprises scientific research practice, but also upon subjective factors such as the researcher's area and intensity of interest, economic opportunism, social affiliations, personality, background, concepts and the like.[7]

An example is that some scientists are reluctant to raise ethical questions which involve moral judgments because such considerations do not advance the body of the science with which they are concerned. However, the interdisciplinary approach to marketing is proving to be of sufficient value so that some students are willing to explore the possible contributions of hybrid disciplines such as marketing ethics. Marketing science itself is essentially a "multisexual" discipline, to use a term from Boulding,[8] and a natural area of convergence for the interdisciplinary approach to business administration.

One indication that marketing is a natural focal point of ethical problems and considerations in business is that much government regulation is designed to govern marketing activities. Presumably, some regulation developed because of the feeling that businessmen were failing to regulate themselves according to the proper ethical standards. There is a continuing dialogue between business and government on the question of regulation of business. The legal conflicts can be settled by legislation and the courts. The conflict discussed here between ethical concepts and marketing practice is philosophical. It exists because philosophers concerned with ethical issues are concerned with an ideal in which absolute ethical values and concepts are superimposed on the

[7] Robert Bartels, "A Methodological Framework for Comparative Marketing Study," in *Toward Scientific Marketing*, Stephen A. Greyser (ed.), Proceedings of the 1963 Winter Conference of the American Marketing Association, Chicago, 1964, p. 383.
[8] Kenneth E. Boulding, "General Systems Theory—The Skeleton of Science." *Management Science* (April 1956). See also the discussion in William Lazer and Eugene J. Kelley, *Interdisciplinary Contributions to Marketing Management*, Bureau of Business Research, E. Lansing, Michigan, 1959, pp. 1–31.

culture according to the highest moral values. But the standards of
ethical behavior in business which influence the areas in which management scientists operate are taken from the prevailing culture of the
time. The standards may be far from the philosophic ideal. So, by
definition, ethics is a subject which is not related primarily to business
practices but rather to the promise and potential of a higher climate.
Discussions of marketing issues with ethical dimensions can help to
develop an appreciation of the relations between existing business practices and ethical concepts and standards.

While marketing scientists can abstract ethical and moral decisions
from many problems, and students of marketing ethics can choose not
to communicate with management scientists, management must face
the task of integration. Management decision making inevitably involves the balancing of ethical and moral issues with scientific approaches. A manager rarely has to contend with a problem which is
exclusively a marketing science or a marketing ethics problem any
more than he has to contend with problems which are exclusively economic in nature. He deals routinely with complex, multidisciplinary
problems.

One academic viewpoint is that problems of ethics and morality in
business need not be discussed in any formal way in the business
schools. (This attitude may be one reason why there are relatively few
business ethics courses.) Those holding this view, who think ethical
questions should be discussed at all, feel that each teacher should
handle ethical problems of business in his own course, just as each
businessman should handle such problems in his own firm. Some marketing practitioners have also expressed doubt that fields called "Marketing Science" or "Marketing Theory" can be identified. Others accept
the existence of these fields but see them as unrelated. Probably most
readers of this chapter are willing to grant the existence of an area
called marketing science. Perhaps not so many would be as tolerant of
marketing ethics.

Managers are not usually concerned with whether they are "marketing scientists" or "ethical scientists." Their position is they are practicing executives attempting to manage the efforts of an organization to
accomplish corporate objectives. Even though staff advice inside the
business tends to come from men committed to one or another basic
position, the manager does not normally expect the marketing scientist
to integrate ethical considerations in the body of his science. Managers
have long accepted the notion of division of labor; managers are prepared to integrate where their specialized staff and professional personnel are unwilling or unable to integrate. However, managers are

usually pleased to find technicians who have the ability to do relational thinking. This ability is one measure of a person's ability to change roles from marketing scientist or social marketer to marketing management.

It may be that the survival of the enterprise system depends on the manager's ability to integrate the contributions of the scientist and of the ethical scientist or social philosopher. In a university the marketing teacher might well have to consider the extent to which he should attempt the integration of the sometimes polarized forces of quantifiable goals, and moral values.

The integrating task of management is no easier than the task of the social historian, political scientist, or economist who attempts to bridge cultures. One reason the integration problem for managers is complex, is that management theory and practice are in a transitional stage, and the manager is confronted with several diverse approaches to the problem of integrating ethics and science.

THE MANAGEMENT THEORY JUNGLE

One article which illustrates the difficulty of integrating diverse approaches to management described the field of management theory as "entangled by a jungle of approaches and approachers." [9] Koontz's classification of the major schools of management theory is of interest to those concerned with the problem of integrating "scientific" and "ethical" approaches to marketing. Koontz stated that most of the approaches to management theory can be classified as one of the following so-called schools:

1. *The Management Process School.* This approach "perceives management as a process of getting things done through and with people operating in organized groups."

2. *The Empirical School.* In this school are those who see management as a study of experience. "This approach, as often applied, assumes that by finding out what worked or did not work in individual circumstances the student or the practitioner will be able to do the same in comparable situations."

3. *The Human Behavior School.* This is the approach variously described as "human relations," "leadership," or "behavioral." It centers the study of management on interpersonal relations.

4. *The Social System School.* This is related to the human behavior school but includes people who perceive management as a social system or a system of cultural interrelationships.

[9] Harold Koontz, "The Management Theory Jungle," *Journal of the Academy of Management,* Vol. IV, No. 3 (December 1961), p. 174.

5. *The Decision Theory School.* This growing group "concentrates on rational approach to decision—the selection from among possible alternatives of a course of action or of an idea."

6. *The Mathematical School.* This school is typified by the operations researchers, "who have sometimes anointed themselves with the rather pretentious name of 'management scientists'." The orientation of theories in this group is to see management in terms of a system of mathematical models and processes.

Each of these approaches has proved valuable in understanding and solving marketing problems. But since any single approach has limits, the task of the practitioner is to recognize these limitations and extract the limit of contribution from a particular approach to business problem solving. The job of the marketing manager is in part, therefore, one requiring ability to utilize and manage the contributions of mathematicians, behavioral scientists, managers, and individual contributors to accomplish business objectives. The manager is not as interested in criticizing the answers or the methodology of the particular disciplines concerned as he is with utilizing the results.

THE TWO CULTURES AND THE SCIENTIFIC REVOLUTION

The problem of integrating science and ethics is one of broad social, rather than exclusively managerial, concern. The difficulty and the importance of integrating diverse approaches to human problems was illustrated in an important publication. In May 1959 C. P. Snow, British novelist and scientist, gave the Rede Lecture at Cambridge University.[10] For a time the lecture seemed to enjoy the fate of most such efforts, to be delivered and all but forgotten, perhaps to be remembered fondly only by the lecturer. But after a decent interval it became apparent that the 1959 Rede Lecture was destined for a different reception. As was customary, the lecture was published as a paper-covered pamphlet. (In the United States it was published as a hard-cover book.) At the end of the first year of publication, according to Snow, "Articles, references, letters, blame, praise, were floating in often from countries where I was otherwise unknown."[11] The discussion continued and the flood of literature stimulated by the lecture has continued to mount.

The lecture which produced this unusual reaction was titled, "The Two Cultures and the Scientific Revolution." Snow stated the case for

[10] C. P. Snow, *The Two Cultures and the Scientific Revolution,* Cambridge University Press, New York, 1959.
[11] C. P. Snow, *The Two Cultures: and a Second Look,* The New American Library of World Literature, New York, 1964, p. 54.

his view that, "The intellectual life of the whole of Western society is increasingly being split into two polar groups." At one pole Snow placed the literary intellectuals and at the other scientists, with the physical scientist selected as the most representative scientist. Snow saw a dangerous and widening split existing between these two polarized groups. The "gulf of mutual incomprehension," particularly among the young, according to Snow, was reflected in hostility and dislike. But above all, the result was lack of understanding. Snow went on to demonstrate that the literary and scientific communities had distorted images of each other and that their different attitudes were such that even on the level of emotions they had difficulty finding common ground. The discussion was further stimulated by Snow's views that the misunderstanding, insufficient communication between the two cultures, and resulting attitudes were such that the West would well lose its advantages in science and technology. The problem was seen as so important that the only way to survival was for science, tradition, and art to unite. (Perhaps it was this threat of forced marriage which added fuel to the controversy.) In a later statement Snow saw the rise of a "third culture" consisting of people who devote their energies to meeting the main problem, "the human effects of the scientific revolution." [12] The loss due to this polarization is more than intellectual. It also concerns our practical and creative lives.

Classifications have advantages when they stimulate thought and discussion and suggest courses of action. The "cultures" and "schools" identified are influencing the practice of marketing and are therefore worthy of study. Any system of classification in the social area has weaknesses. It is quite possible to disagree with Snow that there are "two cultures" and with Koontz that there are "six schools." Conceivably the classification might be extended to twenty-two cultures or two hundred twenty-two cultures, or from six to sixty-six schools. Perhaps there are as many "schools" of marketing as there are professors of marketing.

"THREE CULTURES" AND MARKETING

In this chapter it is suggested that three "cultures" are converging on marketing thought and practice and that members of each culture might be able to improve their contributions by greater understanding and tolerance of the needs and problems of representatives of the other

[12] *Ibid.*, p. 67.

cultures. Culture is used here in the anthropological sense of describing "a group of persons living in the same environment, linked by common habits, common assumptions, a common way of life." In this sense the three cultures, or subcultures if one prefers to speak of a huge scientific-technological-socio-business system, which surround the firm, are the following.

Traditional Managerial Approaches to Marketing

These are the approaches of the present-day operating manager. The managerial approach centers on the functions performed by marketing managers to achieve business goals. The traditional functions are planning, organization, and control applied to functional areas such as marketing or production, or to the entire firm. Some of the theoretical underpinnings of this approach were summarized by Koontz:

1. that managing is a process and can best be dissected intellectually by analyzing the functions of the manager.
2. that long experience with management in a variety of enterprise situations can be grounds for distillation of certain fundamental truths or generalizations—usually referred to as principles—which have a clarifying and predictive value in the understanding and improvement of managing.
3. that these fundamental truths can become focal points for useful research both to ascertain their validity and to improve their meaning and applicability in practice.
4. that such truths can furnish elements, at least until disproved, and certainly until sharpened, of a useful theory of management.
5. that managing is an art, but one like medicine or engineering, which can be improved by reliance on the light and understanding of principles.
6. that principles in management, like principles in the biological and physical sciences, are nonetheless true even if a prescribed treatment or design by a practitioner in a given case situation chooses to ignore a principle and the costs involved, or attempts to do something else to offset the costs incurred (this is, of course, not new in medicine, engineering, or any other art, for art is the creative task of compromising fundamentals to attain a desired result).
7. that, while the totality of culture and of the physical and biological universe has varying effects on the manager's environment and subjects, as indeed they do in every other field of science and art, the theory of management does not need to encompass the

field of all knowledge in order for it to serve as a scientific or theoretical foundation.[13]

Managerial approaches rely heavily on business experiences. The case method of instruction is an educational application of what Koontz refers to as the "empirical school." The basic literature of this field approach is drawn from management and business administration sources. The literature is built on the writings of Fayol, Taylor, and their followers in the scientific management movement. It has been extended by recent authors.

Scientific-Technological Approaches

These approaches are reflected in the decision-theory and mathematical schools. The approach of the decision-theory school may be

> . . . to deal with the decision itself, or to the persons or organizational group making the decision, or to an analysis of the decision process. Some limit themselves fairly much to the economic rationale of the decision, while others regard anything which happens in an enterprise the subject of their analysis, and still others expand decision theory to cover the psychological and sociological aspect and environment of decisions and decision makers.[14]

These approaches lead to efforts to analyze management problems and divisions as a logical process expressed in terms of mathematical relationships and computerized logic. The approaches rely heavily on models designed to simulate a situation in terms of given goals. Some chapters in this book are illustrative. The basic intellectual strength comes from mathematics, not from management literature.

Humanistic Approaches

These approaches have their roots in the social sciences and philosophy. They include the people-centered approach of psychologists and the social system approach which is sociological in orientation. In terms of planning, these approaches stress the desires and actions of individually unique creative humans, and of acts of intuition, volition, and purposeful will.

A difference between the humanist and scientific approaches was drawn in an article dealing with national security.

---

[13] Koontz, *Journal of the Academy of Management*, Vol. 4, p. 176.
[14] *Ibid.*, p. 180.

The realm of the planner is human events in the real world. The realm of the scientist, on the other hand, is what Max Planck, the originator of the quantum theory, calls "physical events." Both the planner and the scientist are concerned with forecasting future events in the real world, but the events are of two different types. Human actions, in the planner's world, are "purposeful," a word foreign to the physical sciences. Forecasting the future is not an end in itself. The planner seeks ways of translating acts of will, the choice of ends and goals, into practical courses of action. He seeks to do more than know what is going to happen; he seeks to *control* what will happen, to ensure that the future state of events will be the one he desires.[15]

Possibly some readers primarily interested in marketing can place people in one or another of the preceding classifications, or in all three of them. But aside from such harmless sport, it is to be noted that a good deal of the energy and time of members of one school, or discipline, or cult (depending on the emotional content of the situation) are given over to forms of struggle aimed at "denying the approaches of others." This is so even though, as Koontz points out, "Like the widely differing and often contentious denominations of the Christian religion, all have essentially the same goals and deal with essentially the same world." As Culliton remarked, reviewing his experiences during a Foundation seminar which concerned business and ethics, "as soon as economists started to put love in some business analysis they got into trouble. This illustrates that in a pluralistic society it is hard to get universal agreement concerning norms."[16]

Since marketing can be studied from these several viewpoints, it is not surprising to find a frequent lack of communication between those whose interests converge on the marketplace. Marketing writers viewing the field from one position frequently fail to take into account the needs of others who may consider the field from other viewpoints or who are faced with particular problems. This is a natural situation found in all fields of scholarship and specialization. Advances in knowledge for the most part seem to come from committed specialists working in depth on particular problems which challenge the individual researcher or research team. This is a condition which managers and students attempting to integrate a field must recognize.

Ethical decisions can be seen as the job of the manager, not the

[15] Kane, *Fortune*, Vol. LXIX, pp. 147, 231.
[16] Culliton, *Ethics in Business*, p. 6.

marketing scientist. This is not an unreasonable division of responsibility. The question remains whether marketing scientists and other individual contributors are or are not morally responsible for the marketing programs they help to create. Do such individuals have any specific concern with the common good? Or is it enough that they contribute to the long-run goal of profit maximization of the firm?

Scientists prefer to avoid expressing approval or disapproval of the results of their discoveries because, as Simon put it, "there is no place for ethical assertions in the body of a science." [17] The manager usually cannot take this position; he is concerned with applications. The ethical demands, just as the scientific demands, placed on managers are part of his environment and inevitably influence many business decisions. Managers are not concerned with advancing science as much as they are with the survival, growth, and profitability of a firm.

Management scientists and social marketers, over the long run, have to learn to communicate. A marketing scientist attempts to understand all he can about the environment in which the firm operates. And the student concerned with marketing as a social discipline recognizes that the character and nature of marketing are being changed, possibly fundamentally, by the marketing science developments described in this book. Presumably the contributions of scientists to the firm are ultimately measured by their contributions to management and corporate goals. So there is incentive to understand each other.

ETHICAL STAGES

Since ethics are concerned with standards of conduct and decision making at a point in time, it is useful to identify ethical stages. In an historical sense marketing has completed the *laissez faire* period where each businessman and firm operated with a minimum of restraint.[18] We may now be in a stage where ethics and legality are generally equated and operating under a kind of minimal operating ethic, in which

[17] Herbert A. Simon, *Administrative Behavior*, Macmillan, New York, 1957, p. 253. See also the discussion of Simon's views by Rocco Carzo, Jr., "Administrative Science and the Role of Value Judgments," *Journal of the Academy of Management*, Vol. III, No. 3 (December 1960), p. 178.

[18] Eugene J. Kelley, "Marketing and Moral Values in an Acquisitive Society," in *Marketing: A Maturing Discipline*, Martin L. Bell (ed.), Proceedings of the 1960 Winter Conference of the American Marketing Association, Chicago, pp. 195–203. The treatment of ethical stages in the present chapter is based on this earlier statement.

some rules have been established and others are understood. Much marketing activity seems to exist in this rather elastic, ethical, legally dominated framework. Occasional price-fixing scandals and large-scale frauds offer reminders that some individuals and firms are not willing to obey the law. But the law does offer one ethical code from which ethical decision-making problems in business can be made.

The next stage may be one in which ethical obligations will develop which will be well ahead of existing legal strictures. This third stage may have been suggested by Cabot when he identified a stage of Christian ethics, "a sample of which is the effort to satisfy real, deep, and permanent desires, and not merely obvious desires in others as well as ourselves." This might be called an ideal, the maximum ethic, perhaps the ultimate Christian ethic.[19]

We now seem to be at a point of revising approaches to the study of marketing. Is it possible we may be on the verge of moving from the stage of precision to generalization, from an essentially descriptive, institutionalized, functional approach to the study of the process of marketing from an administrative and social viewpoint, and from a minimum ethic to a maximum ethic? If we are, what are the implications for marketing science and management in such a critical transitional period? How will the managerial and the social functions of marketing change?

SOCIAL FUNCTIONS OF MARKETING

Ethical issues are necessarily involved in any discussion of the social functions of marketing. Business, and specifically marketing, includes many social institutions which are important influences on the value of society. Because marketing is so significant to society, the question of social goals and social responsibility inevitably must be faced. If business does not establish its own social goals and design programs to achieve those social goals, it is a certainty that society will fill the void. There inevitably are social functions of business in contemporary society. Eells and Walton have suggested four social functions.[20] These are functions which concern marketing management and which should be

---

[19] Richard C. Cabot, *Adventures on the Borderlands of Ethics*, Harper, New York, 1926, p. 89, in William Lazer and Eugene J. Kelley, *Managerial Marketing: Perspectives and Viewpoints*, Richard D. Irwin, Homewood, Ill., 1962, p. 54.
[20] Richard Eells and Clarence Walton, *Conceptual Foundations of Business*, Richard D. Irwin, Homewood, Ill., 1961, pp. 432–433.

considered by marketing scientists. Each function has marketing overtones; the functions can be perceived as the social functions of marketing.

Survival

This may be the basic and the ultimate goal of a business and the prime measure of marketing activity. Profits are both a prerequisite for survival and a test of survivability; service is the road to customer satisfactions and, therefore, to survival in a competitive economic climate. Social responsibility is probably a necessary condition of survival over the long run. Many marketing strategies can be designed to achieve the survival goal. At the ethical level questions about the strategies of growth, institutional survival, subsidies, and institutional and enterprise abandonment, are in part ethical questions.

Profit Making

A business is the only human organization whose existence depends on profit. As Eells and Walton point out, governments can tax, churches can call on members for support, and the family can survive without profits. But a business requires profits to justify its existence. Profit making is a basic goal of business and the profit concept underlies marketing. Profit goals are achieved in the marketplace, and the basic task of the marketing manager is to serve consumer needs profitably in a way which will be consistent with long-range survival goals.

There are many ethical aspects to questions about business goals, such as the following:

Growth of the firm, of a division, a product line or a product.
Short-term profit maximization.
Profit maximization over the long run.
Service to the country, society, and the common good.
Service to customers.
Enlargement of size of market.
Maintenance or increase in share of market.
Establishment of an image for the firm, division or product.
Diversification of corporate activity.
Achievement of industry leadership.
Development of reputation and stature of management.
Employee welfare and satisfactions.
Securing a balance between government and domestic business.
Securing a balance between domestic and foreign business.

Making the firm a satisfying one for employees and managers to work.

Maintaining employment at certain levels in particular plants.

Minimize risk of government antitrust enforcement activities.

The length of the list may suggest that goal setting is not a simple matter or that it can be undertaken on purely factual terms.

Service

Business has service functions to perform in addition to profit making. Timothy E. Shea, Vice President in Charge of Engineering of Western Electric Company, has said, "Business is a vehicle through which man serves society." Such a view of service and profits requires a balancing of functions by managers. Customer service is one of the keys to survival and profit. The serving of customer needs profitably is the basic concern of marketing executives. Service to customers and to society concepts rests on an ethical view of business practice.

Social Responsibility

Another social function of business is the obligation of a firm to meet its social responsibilities to its employees, the community, and the public, as well as to its owners and customers. Social responsibilities are those of corporate good citizenship in a society. Sometimes social and economic goals and the functions required to perform them may be in conflict. More often, in the long run, enlightened self-interest and the corporate sense of social responsibility coincide. When they do not, managers acting as both businessmen and citizens attempt to reconcile conflicts knowing that failure to do so may mean additional government regulation.

Business itself is a social instrumentality of society designed to facilitate the achievement of given ends. Marketing, or any business function, is a corporate activity designed to achieve given objectives. The genius of American business is that through the marketing system consumers are offered an infinite variety of goods and services from which they can choose those which will best enable free individuals to approach fulfilling their own view of the good life. Critics of marketing frequently neglect the point that the pursuit of the good life may be largely an individual matter and that restrictions on selling effort almost always result in restrictions on the buyers' freedom to choose and act.

A business manager is, of course, concerned with the social view of business problems just as he is concerned with the economic environment in which the firm operates. But the operating manager is primarily concerned with other problems, such as managing marketing activity in order to achieve particular corporate goals in a market society. As such, he tends to see social and economic areas not as ends in themselves but as environmental restraints on corporate activity or as areas of marketing opportunity. However, top management does have as one of its major challenges the job of answering the question whether a free market economy can provide social welfare with individual freedom as it meets the material need of free consumers. This is a difficult and complex question; the degree of success of business executives in answering it will, to a large extent, determine the future of the free enterprise system.

Business executives are aware that strategies to fulfill these social functions have varying levels of ethical acceptability. It is interesting to consider the relationship between the acceptability level and profit returns. Simon has suggested that ethical considerations can be introduced into computer programmed business games and that the higher the acceptability level, the less the profit return to the alternative.[21] There does not seem to be any computer business game which at present has built into it a set of strategies, opportunities, and tactics that would have varying degrees of moral acceptability as judged by our business society. It is possible to build into a game strategies or varying degrees of moral acceptability which would have payoffs attached corresponding to the payoffs they might produce in the real world. Simon suggests such acts as "gouging customers in an emergency, moving out of a small town precipitately, cutting off established dealers, and using unfair sources of information." Players in such a game could be told that they would be judged as both profit makers and as ethical businessmen. As Simon put it, they would not necessarily be told what calculus, if any, is used to make ethics and profits commensurable. The real world does not offer any such calculus as an accurate guide to ethical costs. Possibly players will be told that not only their scores but their particular ethical acts would be publicized to the other players in the game. An interesting line of experimentation is opened up by such suggestions.

On a pragmatic basis it is possible to relate the level of ethical expectations of a society to the negative control of government regulation of business. In a complex industrial society it is government which sets the legal boundaries and enforces the rules of business conduct. Their

[21] J. L. Simon, "How Do Beliefs Affect Business Performance?" (Unpublished manuscript, Urbana, Illinois, 1963, p. 36.) For a report on an empirical study of business ethics see Raymond C. Baumhart, "How Ethical Are Businessmen?" *Harvard Business Review*, Vol. XXXIX, (July–August 1961), p. 6.

rules do much to mold the environment of business and the climate in which marketing decisions are made. In marketing terms it can be said that the consumer is the controller of a firm's destiny. But on a broader scale, it is the government, representing public concensus, which exercises the ultimate control over business. In some societies the government is more important than the market as the dominating mechanism of society. A prime function of decision-makers then becomes the management of policies and conditions which will minimize public demands for regulation of business. But the ultimate case for ethical behavior does not rest on these grounds, although such might be an acceptable form of corporate rationalization of efforts to better ethical levels. Efforts to still or neutralize the voices of protest are not the reasons. Perhaps it is that the business of business is to serve society—and that this is difficult, if not impossible, unless the ethical norms of society are understood and fulfilled, and over the long run, perhaps exceeded.

INTEGRATING ETHICS AND SCIENCE IN MARKETING

The anticipation of tomorrow is one of the major concerns of managers, and a function of marketing scientists is to help marketing managers anticipate the future. Thus marketing scientists are concerned with the subject of changing moral values of society. All concerned with advancing science in marketing must understand the nature of the rising standards of ethical expectations of business on the part of the public. To ignore these would be as unwise as to ignore changing educational, income or other levels of consumer expectations or behavior. The integration of science and ethics can today be questioned on the grounds that it means a mix of rational scientific information (facts) with moral judgments. However, the trends of history seem to indicate the promise of a greater degree of integration between these two cultural approaches to the problems of meeting man's material needs. The hope is not inconsistent with scientific method.

One step toward science-ethics-management integration is to be aware of the problem of relating moral and ethical considerations to marketing practice. Another step is to ponder, study, and research the area of ethical and marketing science relationships. Perhaps what is called for is experimentation with new approaches which will enable us to overcome existing barriers to communication and understanding between cultural representatives. This is a hoped-for outcome of the meta-marketing approach as it might fuse marketing science and theory, management policy, and social philosophy to meet the challenges of the scientific revolution.

18

Marketing Science:

Past, Present, and Future Development

GEORGE SCHWARTZ

This book has focused on answering four questions:

1. What is the nature and what are the goals of marketing science?
2. What is the usefulness of a science of marketing?
3. What is the current state of knowledge about marketing?
4. What aspects of marketing might fruitfully be researched in order that knowledge about marketing not now available might be unearthed?

The objective of this cooperative effort has been to stimulate and facilitate the growth of a body of knowledge about marketing which will be useful to those in society who are concerned with this ubiquitous aspect of our lives.

At the beginning of this book, marketing science was portrayed as a body of empirically validated descriptive, predictive, and control knowledge. Such a body of knowledge would provide true information (1) about the activities and institutions which comprise marketing, (2) which would enable those concerned with marketing to predict the consequences of their actions or the behavior of variable marketing phenomena, and (3) which would enable those concerned with marketing to control the variation of marketing phenomena. It is desirable to devote resources to the development of a science of marketing because such a body of knowledge would enable businessmen, consumers, students of marketing, teachers of marketing, and government officials concerned with marketing better to attain their desirable goals.

This overview chapter on the development of marketing science is unable to discuss the development of marketing science in the past. No such discourse is now possible because no historical appraisal of efforts to develop a science of marketing has yet been made. The work that comes closest to doing this is that done by Bartels, whose chapter traces the development of marketing thought and writings from 1900 to to present. Bartels' extensive study of the marketing literature, however, does not attempt to sift out of this literature that which constitutes knowledge rather than erroneous speculation, intuition, or conceptualization.

Bartels' study of marketing literature leads him to divide the development of marketing thought into the following six segments:

1900–1910	Period of Discovery
1910–1920	Period of Conceptualization
1920–1930	The Period of Integration
1930–1940	The Period of Development
1940–1950	The Period of Reappraisal
1950–1960	The Period of Reconceptualization

In Bartels' opinion most contributions to marketing thought have stemmed from the need to solve particular marketing problems which prevailed at specific times during these six decades. He regards marketing thought as adequate and mature because "it serves the purposes for which it was developed." The principal purpose of this literature has been, according to Bartels, the development of marketing specialists.

THE STATE OF MARKETING KNOWLEDGE

The Marketing Concept

Any appraisal of the state of marketing knowledge might well begin with the marketing concept. This concept holds that a company's efforts are likely to be successful if it organizes and conducts the relevant activities of the enterprise so that the company operates with the objective of satisfying the needs and wants of the people and/or business establishments who constitute its actual and potential customers. Not only has this concept permeated the marketing literature extensively, but more and more companies have announced that they are adopting this concept as the philosophic basis of their operations.[1]

King's evaluation of the literature concerning the marketing concept reveals that the desirability of its acceptance and implementation by a business enterprise rests not so much on evidence that such action will

[1] In June of 1964 the American Marketing Association devoted its national conference to a discussion of the theme: "The Marketing Concept in Action."

enable a company better to attain specified goals but rather on plausibility. That is, it seems to make sense to believe that a company which organizes its activities so as to meet the needs and wants of its actual and potential customers is likely to be able to attain its goals. However, in the absence of evidence that this is the case, statements as to the desirability of the marketing concept remain in the area of belief rather than substantiated fact.

Consumer Behavior

It has not been possible to attempt a complete treatment of all the aspects of consumer behavior in this volume. The focus of the discussion by Pratt and Bilkey has been on the psychological and economic aspects of consumer behavior. Regrettably, no extensive discussion of the state of knowledge with respect to the sociological and anthropological aspects of consumer behavior was feasible in the preparation of this book.

Essentially, Pratt's chapter on the psychological aspects of consumer behavior maintains that in an affluent society the traditional economic explanations of consumer behavior are no longer accurate. Rather, the marketing analyst must look to other aspects of behavior if he is to understand the behavior of many consumers in a wealthy society such as that of the United States. He concludes that an explanation of consumer behavior in an affluent society requires an understanding of certain psychological concepts, including those of intervening variables, motivation, and learning.

While Pratt states his conclusion about the relevance of psychology to an understanding of consumer behavior with confidence, he also reveals that the state of knowledge about this behavioral component is not yet well developed. The whole subject, he writes, is in ferment with wide disagreement among psychologists, and between psychologists and economists. The picture he paints is that of an area of study beset with polemics rather than adequate empirical evidence.

Bilkey's evaluation of the state of knowledge with respect to consumer disbursements concludes that this knowledge "is at such a fragmentary state that *nobody* can construct a more-or-less comprehensive hypothesis regarding it and indicate the accuracy of the prediction that it yields." Research to date, he writes, has focused essentially on the analysis of aggregate consumption expenditures, and relatively little attention has been given to the question of consumer expenditure allocation between disbursement categories or between brands, subjects which are of obvious importance to marketers.

Product Development

Stewart's extensive review of the state of knowledge in the product development area leads him to conclude that the current situation leaves much to be desired. Practitioners use a wide variety of techniques aimed at successfully finding new products, estimating their probable success, and introducing such new products into the market, but the facts of marketing life point up the extent of ignorance about successful product development that prevails. A manifestation of this state of affairs is reflected in Stewart's statement that in the execution of new product plans, the chances of success are rather low and the cost of failure rather high.

Personal Selling

Although the salesman is probably the most researched person in the business world, Hauk deplores the state of knowledge with respect to personal selling. Past research, he writes, has been concerned largely with managing salesmen and with salesmanship, focusing largely on selecting, training, motivating, evaluating, and compensating salesmen.

In many respects, Hauk writes, personal selling has been substantially neglected by marketing scientists in the academic world. This neglect is reflected by the shortage of current, published research, a neglect which is magnified when research on personal selling is compared with the attention that is devoted to unearthing knowledge about advertising.

Pricing

Backman's review of the literature relating to pricing leads him to conclude that our knowledge of (1) the pricing practices of marketers, and (2) how to set prices in order to achieve specific objectives, is indeed small.

It is only since World War II, he writes, that some information has become available concerning actual pricing policies and practices. Much of this information is scattered and not readily available. And much of what is available soon becomes out of date because no provision is made for updating or for a continuous flow of information, Backman writes. He attributes the paucity of available knowledge about business pricing to the fact that this is a sensitive area to many companies.

Publication of detailed information concerning pricing procedures by a company, Backman points out, could result in a charge of collusive pricing under the anti-trust laws, since it might be interpreted as a form of communication to competitors. For the same reason, according to Backman, trade associations usually avoid the publication of information which explains price policies or price procedures.

Trading Areas

Goldstucker's chapter reviewed the available information pertaining to the analysis of trading areas of retailers, wholesalers, manufacturers, and primary producers. This review has produced the conclusion that trading area analysis is as yet only an art. Goldstucker writes that in selecting locations, in selling and servicing territories, and in comparing actual with potential sales obtained from a trading area, executives are forced, by the absence of knowledge, to rely primarily on their experience and judgment, seeking corroboration from their associates. Universal principles, theories, or models are not available as a more accurate substitute for executive experience and judgment.

Marketing Channels

The review of the literature on marketing channels by McCammon and Little leads them to conclude that very little is known about this mechanism. Relatively few scholars, they write, have studied the structure of distribution. Moreover, most of the studies that have been undertaken have not gone beyond description into the analysis of the behavior of channel components.

Of the published material on marketing channels that is available, a substantial part consists of speculations, assertions, arguments, deductions, and conceptualizations based on limited evidence. Because the latter is the case, McCammon and Little are unable to state to what extent the sparse available information on marketing channels constitutes knowledge which is in accord with the real marketing world.

Marketing Mix

Borden, who originated the term *marketing mix,* has found this concept to be a helpful device in teaching, in business problem solving, and generally as an aid to thinking about marketing. The collection of elements which comprise the marketing mix, he writes, serves as a check list as to areas into which to guide thinking when considering marketing questions or dealing with marketing problems.

However, Borden writes, if one thinks of a marketing science as involving the observation and classification of facts and the establishment of verifiable laws that can be used by the marketer as a guide to action with assurance that predicted results will ensue, then students of marketing cannot be said to have progressed far toward establishing a science of marketing. To Borden, the concept of the marketing mix lays out the areas in which facts need to be assembled, and these facts serve as a useful guide to management judgment in building marketing mixes.

Comparative Marketing and Economic Development

In his chapter on comparative marketing and economic development, Shapiro's discussion reflects the fact that in this aspect of marketing, knowledge is at best at a rudimentary stage. In fact, the entire chapter is devoted to a discussion of the ignorance and controversy that exist with respect to a number of major topics.

Operations Research and Marketing

In his chapter on operations research, Lazer writes that this kit of analytical tools, which utilize quantitative methods, has a decided contribution to make to marketing science. However, his evaluation of the contribution of operations research to marketing up to now causes him to conclude that this contribution has been "quite limited." Lazer writes:

> Much of the progress made in the extension of management science has been attributed to the use of models. Models are truly useful tools of analysis. Some of the more sophisticated mathematical models have received widespread acclaim for their accomplishments. Yet, when evaluated against the spectrum of significant marketing problems, the accomplishments of models, and particularly mathematical models, have been sparse indeed. The value of mathematical models in solving marketing problems, perhaps with the exception of linear programming, is quite limited. In fact, it is the promise of *potential application* in marketing, rather than *actual application* to which operations researchers refer fondly.
>
> Operations research models are not ends in themselves. They are the means to an end. In marketing they are the means to better marketing decisions. Yet, in model building operations researchers seem to get lost in heroic mathematical abstractions. They appear to develop a preference for rigor over realism, for manipulative potentiality over practicality, and for mathematical sophistication over immediate problem-solving capacity in marketing. Marketing models, like other kinds of models, seem to result in the "unlimited postulation of irrelevant truths," or what has been termed mathematicians' aphasia.

Stochastic Models of Brand Switching

Farley and Kuehn discuss the work that has been done with the aim of developing stochastic models that would enable (1) a company to predict its market share, and (2) provide guidance to marketing managers in the use of various marketing tools. While they write that such models have provided a framework in which theories of consumer brand choice have been built, and, to some extent, tested, their discussion points up the various deficiencies and problems that exist in the use of such formulations as the Markov, learning, and brand-mix models.

In their over-all evaluation of the current state of the development of stochastic models of brand switching, Farley and Kuehn point out that:

1. stochastic theory is still developing;
2. as the models become more sophisticated and more descriptively appealing, they also become more analytically complex and pose ever-increasing statistical inference problems;
3. stochastic theory available for model building has far outstripped statistical inference techniques;
4. the data required to test stochastic brand switching models are far in excess of that normally required from market research, and that such data are not generally available on a large scale.

STATE OF MARKETING KNOWLEDGE: SUMMARY

While this cooperative review of the state of marketing knowledge is incomplete in that it has not treated every aspect of marketing, for example, advertising, enough has been revealed to permit a conclusion that marketing has not yet become a science within the concept of science presented at the beginning of this book.

From the review of the marketing concept to the evaluation of the contribution of operations research to marketing, large areas of ignorance have time and time again been revealed by the cooperating authors. Despite this ignorance, businessmen conduct their affairs, attain many of their objectives, and the marketing system serves our society in a manner which many consider to be more than satisfactory.

But the marketing scientist is somewhat of a do-gooder. He is of the opinion that more knowledge about marketing will enable those concerned with marketing better to attain their legitimate goals. He believes that decisions and actions based on empirically validated knowledge will be more accurate than decisions and actions based on speculation, intuition, or the dogmatic assertions of some self-styled expert.

The marketing scientist states that it is worth devoting resources to unearthing realistic and useful knowledge about marketing because such knowledge will enable

1. businessmen to make fewer mistakes and better attain their legitimate goals.
2. teachers and students of marketing to spend their time and effort teaching and learning material which is likely to be useful to future businessmen.
3. consumers to understand the contribution that marketers make to their welfare and dis-welfare.
4. government administrators better to regulate marketing in the public interest.

It is to the unearthing of useful and realistic knowledge about marketing that the remainder of this chapter is devoted.

FUTURE DEVELOPMENT OF MARKETING SCIENCE: SOME RESEARCH SUGGESTIONS

The Marketing Concept

To determine whether the marketing concept will do what it is said to do for business enterprises, King suggests studies to determine (1) whether individual firms have undertaken programs of marketing concept implementation, (2) the degree to which they have succeeded in doing so, where attempted, and (3) whether implementation, where it has occurred, has, in fact, enabled the company to achieve specified goals. He recommends that the development of a scale or measure of implementation should prove helpful in obtaining answers to the latter questions.

Consumer Behavior

To make knowledge about consumer behavior more adequate and useful to marketers, Pratt suggests the following:

1. Because some of the currently available knowledge about consumer behavior is not being used by marketers, Pratt recommends that an effort be made to improve communication among social scientists, and between the latter and marketing practitioners. Effort in this direction is needed because economists do not understand psychologists, and these social scientists frequently do not understand the sociologist or the anthropologist. Yet information studied by all of these is pertinent to the marketer's understanding of consumer behavior.

2. By way of research projects which would yield new substantive information and research techniques, Pratt suggests the following: (a) Studies involving the application of social science concepts to specific marketing problems; and (b) Studies aimed at developing new techniques of empirical research for (i) the measurement of psychological variables, and (ii) the application of longitudinal analysis to the solution of marketing problems. Longitudinal analysis consists of obtaining information from the same sample at different points in time.

3. The development of realistic and useful models of consumer behavior.

Bilkey's suggestions for research which would unearth new useful knowledge about consumer behavior can be summarized as follows:

1. *Living Pattern Studies.* Bilkey is of the opinion that many insights can be obtained by analyzing living patterns on the basis of consumer interviews and then determining what goods or services would more perfectly complete these living patterns. This type of analysis, he writes, might enable researchers to anticipate many potential desires of which consumers themselves may be unaware.

2. *Buying Decision Games.* Bilkey suggests these games as a potentially useful device for ascertaining the effects of such factors as the following on buyer behavior: income uncertainty, changes in the distribution of income, price changes, and changes in fixed consumer commitments such as taxes.

3. Bilkey also suggests questionnaire studies which might reveal the following type of information: reasons for borrowing, place of borrowing, etc. His idea is that such studies would enable the marketing analyst to ascertain by income bracket whether various savings and credit institutions are complementary or competitive and whether such firms are adjusting their services to the desires of the various income groups.

Product Development

Stewart writes that it is useful to think of product development as a means of need fulfillment. Such thought, he states, shifts attention from the product itself to consumer needs. When product development is viewed in this manner, emphasis is placed on the importance of gaining a thorough understanding of consumer needs, how they arise, why they exist, and how they are satisfied.

Stewart strongly suggests research which would permit

1. a sophisticated means of describing the needs (or wants) of indi-

viduals (including the establishment of new units of measure) and techniques for measuring these needs.

2. a sophisticated means for describing the manner in which products (or services) fulfill the needs of individuals.

3. a sophisticated means of describing large collections of individual needs, that is, the needs of "the market," or segments thereof.

4. the development of strategies which will help guide management to act profitably in the fulfillment of market needs.

Personal Selling

To provide new useful knowledge in the area of personal selling Hauk suggests the following studies:

1. Because it has been asserted that personal selling as a marketing activity has been declining in magnitude and importance, Hauk recommends that it would be useful to conduct a study which sought to yield data reflecting on the truth or falsity of this assertion.

2. Hauk is of the opinion that emphasis should be placed on a broad approach to the study of personal selling. He recommends that personal selling should be studied from more than an occupational standpoint. Rather, personal selling should be studied as part of the marketing mix.

3. Hauk notes that persuasion, communication, and service characterize the important aspects of nearly any selling position. For this reason research in the personal selling area should emphasize the unearthing of knowledge which will enable the salesman more effectively to persuade, communicate, and provide service.

4. Hauk also suggests that research studies need to be undertaken with respect to the economic effects of personal selling. For example, (a) Does personal selling cause excess capacity? and (b) What is the relationship between personal selling and economic development?

5. In the area of sales management, Hauk suggests that research needs to be conducted to answer the question: How much should a company spend on salesmen in its marketing mix?

6. Another problem which requires study, according to Hauk, is what he terms the sales territory problem. This problem has at least three dimensions: (a) the problem of establishing territories for individual salesmen, (b) the problem of establishing territories for branch offices and other field sales facilities, and (c) the problem of establishing sales territories for the company as a whole.

7. Despite the fact that much has been written allegedly answering the question of salesman selection, Hauk opines that not much is known

about correct selection. This is another important problem in the personal selling area that needs to be investigated.

Pricing

Backman writes that there is a great need for studies of the pricing practices and policies of specific industries. Such studies, when taken together, would enlarge our understanding of the actual pricing behavior of businessmen.

He writes that it is possible to obtain a considerable amount of information concerning pricing in a particular industry from an examination of the trade press, price catalogues issued by individual companies, annual reports of companies, speeches by company officials, and occasionally from press releases announcing changes in price. He suggests a number of questions which might usefully be answered in any study of pricing in a particular industry:

1. What factors induce a company to change a price? To what degree must they be present before action is taken? Do the same factors trigger price increases and price decreases?

2. What has been the relationship between changes in price and changes in sales? Do special sales have more favorable effects than more permanent price cuts? Do price changes or nonprice factors, such as quality, style, advertising, and brand names, have a greater impact on sales?

3. How significant are price differentials in steering the flow of orders between different qualities or different sizes of the same product?

4. What has been the past pattern of price behavior for the product? Is there a tendency to shade list prices before the quoted price is reduced?

5. What types of discounts are granted and how have they been changed in the past? When a change is desired, is there greater reliance on changes in discounts or on changes in list prices?

6. Has the emphasis been given to price competition or to nonprice competition? What types of nonprice competition have been emphasized? What form does price competition take: announced cuts in list price, shading of prices for special deals, new discount arrangements, or combination deals?

7. What factors are considered in pricing a new consumer good? A new producer good? Does the company follow a consistent policy of high prices initially (skimming) or low prices (penetration)?

8. Which corporate executives participate in pricing decisions? How often are these decisions reviewed?

9. How does the company react when a competitor offers a special price to obtain a big order?

10. How important is intracompany pricing? What policy is followed in setting prices for such internal sales?

Trading Areas

To remove some of the gaps in the available knowledge about trading areas, Goldstucker suggests the following research projects:

1. Goldstucker has defined what he terms a "natural" trading area as one where the cost of contact between sellers and buyers is minimal. Buyers' costs, according to Goldstucker, involve the physical effort, inconvenience, and actual dollar outlay incurred in securing goods. He believes that a buyer will buy a good as long as the utility or satisfaction resulting from possessing that good is greater than the cost of obtaining it. For such concepts as buyer cost and utility to be of use in helping to set limits to trading areas, Goldstucker writes, there is a need for the marketing analyst to be able to identify and measure the components of both cost and utility. Goldstucker is of the opinion that it is worth doing research on this subject.

2. Another area worthy of investigation with respect to trading areas concerns the motives of business executives. The lack of dependable yardsticks for trading area analysis is due partially, Goldstucker writes, to the fallacy of some of the assumptions on which the research in the field rests. Much of the research with respect to trading area analysis has rested on the assumption of profit-maximizing behavior. If, as many behavioral scientists assert, business executives act to satisfy a wide variety of nonmaterial gains, then Goldstucker writes, trading area research is perhaps seeking answers to the wrong questions.

3. Goldstucker also suggests the need for more study of the costing of marketing activities. He writes that while some attention has been devoted to the study of distribution costs and to developing means whereby they can be analyzed and allocated, progress in the area lags far behind the need for understanding. According to Goldstucker, without adequate tools to measure the costs of marketing activities, a firm is unable to measure accurately the costs associated with serving a particular trading area. Such a measure is an important element in trading area analysis aimed at maximizing profits.

Marketing Channels

McCammon and Little indicate that much additional work needs to be done in studying marketing channels if the development of this component of marketing science is to advance.

Among the suggestions they make, they call for an improvement in the taxonomy of channel phenomena. This suggestion is made because the criteria currently used to classify channel phenomena are not precise enough to permit rigorous analysis.

McCammon and Little also suggest that the development of a comprehensive notational system for channel phenomena would be useful. Such a system could be used to describe and analyze interaction patterns among members of a marketing channel and to provide a basis for validly simulating complete channel systems.

Ultimately, when sufficient factual knowledge is available about marketing channels, McCammon and Little are hopeful that it will be possible to formulate a usefully predictive theory of channel behavior. In their opinion, scholars interested in developing such a theory would probably have to use an eclectic approach. That is, a theory of channel behavior would need to be based on integrated knowledge taken from sociology, cultural anthropology, social psychology, political science, and economics, as well as marketing.

Comparative Marketing and Economic Development

Shapiro's study of the literature pertaining to comparative marketing and economic development leads him to suggest the following research studies:

1. There is a need for the development and acceptance of a frame of reference which can be used in the comparison of national marketing systems. Shapiro makes this suggestion because his examination of the published literature revealed a complete lack of uniformity in the available descriptions of domestic marketing abroad. Each article that he examined emphasized those aspects of marketing operations and structure with which the researcher had become most familiar. This diversity, Shapiro writes, severely complicates the task of comparing and contrasting domestic marketing systems.

2. Differences of opinion exist as to the extent that contemporary American marketing practices can be applied outside the United States. Shapiro suggests the need for reliable evidence rather than polemics to answer this question.

3. Shapiro writes that it would be useful to determine whether nations can be assigned to stages of marketing development. He asks whether there are clearly discernible levels of marketing development to which each of the nations of the world can be assigned? If so, what form does this classification take and what should be the basis for placing a national marketing system in one or another of the existing categories?

4. In view of the importance of economic development in U.S. foreign

policy and in international affairs, Shapiro suggests research effort in the direction of determining the role of the market economy and of market structure in economic development. Knowledge yielded by such studies, he writes, are likely to be useful in assisting governments in making decisions which contribute to economic development.

5. Disagreement exists as to whether economic development should be promoted through the stimulation of consumer wants in underdeveloped countries. Shapiro suggests that research might fruitfully be undertaken to resolve this dispute.

6. Various suggestions have been made by students of underdeveloped nations for the reform of the marketing systems of these countries. The validity of these suggestions is largely unknown. Shapiro suggests that research needs to be undertaken to determine the validity of these suggestions.

7. Economists, when they write about economic development, usually refer to capital formation, the characteristics and growth rate of the population, and the availability of trade as decisive determinants of economic development. Shapiro's examination of the literature revealed an almost complete neglect of marketing problems and institutions in the literature of economic development. Since marketing is relevant to problems of economic development, Shapiro suggests that fruitful research might be undertaken with a view to learning the role that marketing can play in economic development.

Stochastic Models of Brand Switching

In order to facilitate the further development of realistic and useful stochastic models of brand shifting, Farley and Kuehn suggest a number of areas in which useful research might be conducted:

1. *Improved Measures of Marketing Influences.* Farley and Kuehn write that research which measures the effect of marketing factors and tools on sales is sorely needed to provide meaningful inputs for the development of improved marketing models. Examination of brand shifting data, they write, is of limited practical value until such data are integrated with information about various competitive factors operating in a market.

2. *Improvement of the Markov Approach.* One widely suggested direction for future research, cited by Farley and Kuehn, is the freeing of the Markov analysis from problems of defining discrete "trials" in such a way as to require dividing already sparse data into smaller classes for complete analysis. The learning model illustrates one such approach.

Farley and Kuehn also cite age dependent processes as representing a second possibility in the development of richer Markov models. They illustrate this possibility with the suggestion that various combinations of birth, death, and migration models might be used to study in a stochastic framework, the appearance or entry of certain types of consumer influences, their development, and their ultimate disappearance.

3. *Improved Inference Techniques.* A third direction of needed research, cited by Farley and Kuehn, is the development of better inference techniques and statistical tests of series for Markov properties.

4. *Extension of the Brand Mix Concept.* Farley and Kuehn are of the opinion that work in this area is likely to benefit from the appropriate incorporation of the brand mix concept into the future development of stochastic models of brand shifting. That is, empirical evidence reveals that purchase units such as the family may buy several brands of the same product in order to suit the individual preferences of different family members, and that a purchase unit may purchase from several food stores such as a favorite supermarket, a favorite meat market, etc. Where this is the case, Farley and Kuehn suggest that models ought to focus on a mix of brands rather than one brand.

5. *Specification Problems.* In seeking to understand why some households are extremely brand loyal while others are much less so, some stochastic model analysts have used the learning hypothesis as a possible explanation. Farley and Kuehn suggest that research into the relevance of other variables such as those in the sociological, psychological, and demographic areas, may yield valid explanations of degrees of brand loyalty with respect to certain product classes.

Marketing Science and Marketing Ethics

This book has been concerned with the development of a science of marketing and has devoted relatively little attention to the ethics of marketing practices. This has been in accordance with the specific objectives of the volume.

However, the ethics of marketing practice are relevant to marketing science, for it is hoped that the knowledge which the marketing scientist unearths will not be used to defraud or deceive, or in other socially objectionable conduct. Rather, it is hoped that those concerned with marketing will use such knowledge to attain their legitimate goals by contributing to the happiness of people. The marketer, no less than persons in other occupations, needs to be mindful of his social obligations as he seeks to attain personal and company objectives.

Author Index

Subject Index

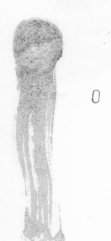

0

/3

00